Sweet & Maxwell's Statutes Series

EU Law
2003/04

AUSTRALIA
Law Book Co.
Sydney

CANADA and USA
Carswell
Toronto

HONG KONG
Sweet & Maxwell Asia

NEW ZEALAND
Brookers
Wellington

SINGAPORE and MALAYSIA
Sweet & Maxwell Asia
Singapore and Kuala Lumpur

Sweet & Maxwell's
Statutes Series

EU Law
2003/04

Edited by
GAVIN LOVE MA, LLB AND
NICHOLAS HEAD LLM
Senior Technical Editors
Sweet & Maxwell

Second Edition

LONDON
SWEET & MAXWELL
2003

First Edition 2002
Second Edition 2003

Published by Sweet & Maxwell Limited of
100 Avenue Road, Swiss Cottage, London NW3 3PF
www.sweetandmaxwell.co.uk
Typeset by Mendip Communications Ltd, Frome, Somerset
Printed in England by Ashford Color Printers

No natural forests were destroyed to make this product:
only farmed timber was used and replanted

A CIP catalogue record for this book is available from the British Library

ISBN 0421 847 808

PREFACE TO THE FIRST EDITION

This collection of EU legislative materials is aimed primarily at students reading European Union Law. While no collection would be complete without at least the full texts of the Treaty on European Union (otherwise, the "EU Treaty" or "Treaty of Maastricht") and the Treaty establishing the European Community (the "EC Treaty" or "Treaty of Rome"), we have selected "core" primary and secondary EU legislation that will be of most use to those studying institutional and substantive EU law. We have grouped the materials under the headings of

- Founding Treaties (including relevant Protocols)
- Institutions
- Free movement of goods
- Free movement of persons
- Competition policy
- Social policy (covering employee protection and equal treatment)
- Human rights.

We have not included any relevant provisions of the Treaty establishing the European Coal and Steel Community following its demise on 23 July 2002.

The texts that we have reproduced are, apart from the more recent amendments to the Court of Justice's Rules of Procedure, those in force as at the end of April 2003. Where measures have been amended, we have "consolidated" the texts so that readers can immediately see what text is in force without having to trail through the amending measures. Each amended provision is accompanied by the relevant legislative history.

The principal additions to this edition are the texts of the EU and EC Treaties consolidated for the amendments introduced by the Treaty of Nice since its entry into force earlier this year, including the new single Protocol on the Statute of the Court of Justice, and the text of Regulation 1/2003 establishing the revised and devolved EC competition law regime that comes into force just in time for students taking examinations on the subject in 2004! We have taken the opportunity to expand the range of competition materials in the book and to omit some of the less used materials in the sections on the Institutions and on mutual recognition of qualifications.

Many changes are in the offing for the European Union and the European Communities, with 10 new Member States scheduled to accede from 1 May 2004 and the "EU Constitution" being considered for adoption by an Intergovernmental Conference from September 2003. These changes are, happily, a matter for future editions of this book, but users are, in the meantime urged to keep abreast of these and other developments through our online service, *WestlawUK* (*www.westlaw.co.uk*).

For ease of use of the materials in this volume, all texts, where appropriate, reflect the renumbering of both the EU and EC Treaties by the

Treaty of Amsterdam by substituting the references to the current provisions of those Treaties for previous references. For example, in preambles to Directives based on former Article 100a of the EC Treaty, we have substituted a reference to "Article [95]". The notes accompanying each Article of the EU and EC Treaties indicate the former Article number and any other relevant legislative history.

For convenience, the Annex to the Treaty of Amsterdam (Chapter 3) sets out tables of equivalence of previous and current numbering of provisions of the EU and EC Treaties. When using this table, it should be remembered, however, that the "old provisions" referred to are those provisions *as amended by the Treaty of Amsterdam*. For example, what is currently Art. 141 of the EC Treaty — establishing the principle of equal pay for men and women — is identified in the table of equivalence as formerly being Art. 119. However, Art. 119 was itself amended by the Treaty of Amsterdam. Similarly, what is currently Art. 13 of the EC Treaty — the power to take "appropriate action against various forms of discrimination — is identified in the table of equivalence as formerly being Art. 6a. This provision was added by the Treaty of Amsterdam and did not exist before that Treaty entered into force.

Despite pressures of space, we considered it important to include the preambles to all measures as they are especially helpful in identifying the legal basis of measures, the legislative procedure followed, the wider context of the measures and the underlying reasons for introducing them. It is only in recent years that EU legislation has taken to numbering individual recitals to preambles; in order to assist the reading of preambles of measures enacted before this practice was adopted, we have numbered all recitals.

Using this volume

To find materials or provisions in this volume, you should use:

- the main contents list;
- the chronological lists of Treaties, Regulations, Directives and other measures; or
- the topic-based index.

Other features that we hope will help readers speedily identify relevant provisions are (1) headings in square brackets in bold type added to individual provisions, summarising their content and (2) added guide numbers in the margins. These marginal numbers comprise a prefix, corresponding to a Chapter number, and a sequential number (for example, 1–002 being the second number in Chapter 1). The index uses these marginal numbers to take you directly to the relevant provision, while the contents lists refer you to the first page numbers of measures.

Texts used in this volume

The texts used in this collection are based on official texts as published by the Office for Official Publications and as supplied to us by Ellis Publications acting under licence. While the greatest care has been taken in the preparation of these materials to ensure their accuracy, especially where they have been consolidated, we would stress that they are "unofficial" texts. Only texts published in the paper version of the *Official Journal of the European Union* can be regarded as official. We are hopeful, however, that readers will find this volume a little more convenient than searching a law library for the relevant issues of the *Official Journal.*

All Sweet and Maxwell editorial interpolations — additional, amended or deleted texts, current references to the EU or EU Treaties in pre-Treaty of Amsterdam measures, and Article headings — are set out within square brackets.

If you wish to check if any of the measures in this volume have been (further) amended since the end of April 2003, an easy way to do so is to make use of *WestlawUK* – the most comprehensive, authoritative online legal information service available to students, academics and practitioners (*www.westlaw.co.uk*). The Celex reference number that we have provided at the head of every Regulation or Directive reproduced in this volume can assist in the search for the relevant measures.

We wish to express our thanks to our colleagues at Ellis Publications and Craig Butcher, our house editor at Sweet and Maxwell, for their enormous contributions to the preparation of this volume.

We would welcome any comments from readers on how useful they have found this collection of materials and any suggestions as to what may usefully be added to or omitted from future editions.

Gavin Love
Nicholas Head
Buckingham and Bicester
St Swithin's Day 2003

TABLE OF ABBREVIATIONS

ACP	African, Caribbean and Pacific Countries
Art.	Article
CEEP	European Centre of Enterprises with Public Participation
CFSP	Common Foreign and Security Policy
COR	Committee of the Regions
COREPER	Committee of Permanent Representatives
EAEC	European Atomic Energy Community
E.C.	European Community/European Community Treaty
ECB	European Central Bank
ECR	European Court Reports
ECJ	Court of Justice of the Euopean Communities
ECSC	European Coal and Steel Community (expired July 23, 2002)
ECU	European Currency Unit
EEA	European Economic Area
EEC	(former) European Economic Community (now European Community)
EFTA	European Free Trade Association
EIB	European Investment Bank
EMI	European Monetary Institute (replaced by European Central Bank)
EMU	Economic and Monetary Union
ESC	Economic and Social Committee
ESCB	European System of Central Banks
ETUC	European Trade Union Confederation
E.U.	European Union
EUR	euro (single European currency)
Euratom	European Atomic Energy Community
JHA	Justice and Home Affairs
J.O.	*Journal Officiel* (French language edition of the *Official Journal of the European Communities*)
OCT	Overseas Countries and Territories
O.J. "L" Series	*Official Journal of the European Communities*, Legislation Series (cited by year, issue number and page)
O.J. "C" Series	*Official Journal of the European Communities*, Information Series (cited by year, issue number and page)
SE	*Societas Europaea* (European Public Limited Liability Company)
SEA	Single European Act
TEU	Treaty on European Union
UNICE	Union of industrial and Employer's Confederation of Europe
WEU	Western European Union

CONTENTS

PART I FOUNDING TREATIES

CHAPTER 1 – TREATY ON EUROPEAN UNION

CHAPTER 2 – TREATY ESTABLISHING THE EUROPEAN COMMUNITY

CHAPTER 6 – FREE MOVEMENT OF PERSONS

SECTION 1 – FREE MOVEMENT AND RIGHTS OF RESIDENCE

SECTION 2 – MUTUAL RECOGNITION OF QUALIFICATIONS

SECTION 3 – LAWYERS

SECTION 4 – POSTING OF WORKERS ABROAD

SECTION 5 – SOCIAL SECURITY FOR MIGRANT WORKERS

CHAPTER 7 – COMPETITION

CHRONOLOGICAL CONTENTS

Directives

PART I: FOUNDING TREATIES

CHAPTER 1

TREATY ON EUROPEAN UNION

(7 February 1992)

([2002] OJ C325/3)

[**Editorial note**—The text reproduced below is the consolidated version of the Treaty on European Union of 7 February 1992, as subsequently amended by the Treaty of Amsterdam with effect from 1 May 1999 and by the Treaty of Nice with effect from 1 February 2003 as published at [2002] OJ C325/3. The provisions of the Union Treaty were renumbered by virtue of the Treaty of Amsterdam, Art. 12(1) and Annex. References in those provisions to Articles, Titles and Sections of both the Union Treaty itself and the EC Treaty have been adapted accordingly (Treaty of Amsterdam, Art. 12(2)). Each Article of the Union Treaty set out below is accompanied by a note indicating its previous numbering. In other provisions such as Protocols and declarations, references to Articles, Titles and Sections of both the Union Treaty and the EC Treaty have been adapted to reflect the renumbering (Treaty of Amsterdam, Art. 12(3)).] **1–001**

His Majesty the King of the Belgians, Her Majesty the Queen of Denmark, the President of the Federal Republic of Germany, the President of the Hellenic Republic, His Majesty the King of Spain, the President of the French Republic, the President of Ireland, the President of the Italian Republic, His Royal Highness the Grand Duke of Luxembourg, Her Majesty the Queen of the Netherlands, the President of the Portuguese Republic, Her Majesty the Queen of the United Kingdom of Great Britain and Northern Ireland,

[1] Resolved to mark a new stage in the process of European integration undertaken with the establishment of the European Communities,

[2] Recalling the historic importance of the ending of the division of the European continent and the need to create firm bases for the construction of the future Europe,

[3] Confirming their attachment to the principles of liberty, democracy and respect for human rights and fundamental freedoms and of the rule of law,

[4] Confirming their attachment to fundamental social rights as defined in the European Social Charter signed at Turin on 18 October 1961 and in the 1989 Community Charter of the Fundamental Social Rights of Workers,[1]

[5] Desiring to deepen the solidarity between their peoples while respecting their history, their culture and their traditions,

[6] Desiring to enhance further the democratic and efficient functioning of the institutions so as to enable them better to carry out, within a single institutional framework, the tasks entrusted to them,

[7] Resolved to achieve the strengthening and the convergence of their economies and to establish an economic and monetary union including, in accordance with the provisions of this Treaty, a single and stable currency,

[8] Determined to promote economic and social progress for their peoples, taking into account the principle of sustainable development and within the context of the accomplishment of the internal market and of reinforced cohesion and environmental protection, and to implement policies ensuring that advances in economic integration are accompanied by parallel progress in other fields,[2]

[9] Resolved to establish a citizenship common to nationals of their countries,

[10] Resolved to implement a common foreign and security policy including the progressive framing of a common defence policy, which might lead to a common defence in accordance with the provisions of Article 17, thereby

---

[1] Recital inserted by Treaty of Amsterdam, Art. 1(1).

[2] Recital replaced by Treaty of Amsterdam, Art. 1(2).

reinforcing the European identity and its independence in order to promote peace, security and progress in Europe and in the world,[3]

[11] Resolved to facilitate the free movement of persons, while ensuring the safety and security of their peoples, by establishing an area of freedom, security and justice, in accordance with the provisions of this Treaty,[4]

[12] Resolved to continue the process of creating an ever closer union among the peoples of Europe, in which decisions are taken as closely as possible to the citizen in accordance with the principle of subsidiarity,

[13] In view of further steps to be taken in order to advance European integration,

Have decided to establish a European Union and to this end have designated as their Plenipotentiaries:

[Designation of plenipotentiaries omitted]

Who, having exchanged their full powers, found in good and due form, *Have agreed as follows.*

TITLE I—COMMON PROVISIONS

Article 1[5] [Establishment of the EU]

1–002 By this Treaty, the High Contracting Parties establish among themselves a European Union, hereinafter called "the Union".

This Treaty marks a new stage in the process of creating an ever closer union among the peoples of Europe, in which decisions are taken as openly as possible and as closely as possible to the citizen.[6]

The Union shall be founded on the European Communities, supplemented by the policies and forms of cooperation established by this Treaty. Its task shall be to organise, in a manner demonstrating consistency and solidarity, relations between the Member States and between their peoples.

Article 2[7] [Objectives of the EU]

1–003 The Union shall set itself the following objectives:

— to promote economic and social progress and a high level of employment and to achieve balanced and sustainable development, in particular through the creation of an area without internal frontiers, through the strengthening of economic and social cohesion and through the establishment of economic and monetary union, ultimately including a single currency in accordance with the provisions of this Treaty;

— to assert its identity on the international scene, in particular through the implementation of a common foreign and security policy including the progressive framing of a common defence policy, which might lead to a common defence, in accordance with the provisions of Article 17;

— to strengthen the protection of the rights and interests of the nationals of its Member States through the introduction of a citizenship of the Union;

— to maintain and develop the Union as an area of freedom, security and justice, in which the free movement of persons is assured in conjunction with appropriate measures with respect to external border controls, asylum, immigration and the prevention and combating of crime;

— to maintain in full the *acquis communautaire* and build on it with a view to considering to what extent the policies and forms of cooperation introduced by this Treaty may need to be revised with the aim of ensuring the effectiveness of the mechanisms and the institutions of the Community.

---

[3] Recital replaced by Treaty of Amsterdam, Art. 1(3).

[4] *ibid.*

[5] Formerly Art. A.

[6] Paragraph replaced by Treaty of Amsterdam, Art. 1(4).

[7] Formerly Art. B; replaced by Treaty of Amsterdam, Art. 1(5).

The objectives of the Union shall be achieved as provided in this Treaty and in accordance with the conditions and the timetable set out therein while respecting the principle of subsidiarity as defined in Article 5 of the Treaty establishing the European Community.[8]

Article 3[9] **[Consistency and continuity of EU activities]**

The Union shall be served by a single institutional framework which shall ensure the consistency and the continuity of the activities carried out in order to attain its objectives while respecting and building upon the *acquis communautaire*. **1–004**

The Union shall in particular ensure the consistency of its external activities as a whole in the context of its external relations, security, economic and development policies. The Council and the Commission shall be responsible for ensuring such consistency and shall cooperate to this end. They shall ensure the implementation of these policies, each in accordance with its respective powers.[10]

Article 4[11] **[Role of the European Council]**

The European Council shall provide the Union with the necessary impetus for its development and shall define the general political guidelines thereof. **1–005**

The European Council shall bring together the Heads of State or Government of the Member States and the President of the Commission. They shall be assisted by the Ministers for Foreign Affairs of the Member States and by a member of the Commission. The European Council shall meet at least twice a year, under the chairmanship of the Head of State or Government of the Member State which holds the Presidency of the Council.

The European Council shall submit to the European Parliament a report after each of its meetings and a yearly written report on the progress achieved by the Union.

Article 5[12] **[Institutions' exercise of powers under Union Treaty]**

The European Parliament, the Council, the Commission, the Court of Justice and the Court of Auditors shall exercise their powers under the conditions and for the purposes provided for, on the one hand, by the provisions of the Treaties establishing the European Communities and of the subsequent Treaties and Acts modifying and supplementing them and, on the other hand, by the other provisions of this Treaty. **1–006**

Article 6[13] **[Principles underlying the EU]**

1. The Union is founded on the principles of liberty, democracy, respect for human rights and fundamental freedoms, and the rule of law, principles which are common to the Member States. **1–007**

2. The Union shall respect fundamental rights, as guaranteed by the European Convention for the Protection of Human Rights and Fundamental Freedoms

[8] See Arts 11–28 for common foreign and security policy; Arts 29–42 for provisions on police and judicial cooperation; Arts 17–22 EC for citizenship of the Union; Arts 39–48 EC for free movement of persons; Arts 61–69 EC for visa, asylum and immigration policies; Arts 98–124 EC for economic and monetary policy; Arts 125–130 EC for EC employment policy; and Arts 155—162 EC for economic and social cohesion.

[9] Formerly Art. C.

[10] Paragraph replaced by Treaty of Amsterdam, Art. 1(6).

[11] Formerly Art. D.

[12] Formerly Art. E; substituted by Treaty of Amsterdam, Art. 1(7).

[13] Formerly Art. F. Paragraph 1 replaced, para. 3 inserted and para. 4 renumbered by Treaty of Amsterdam, Art. 1(8).

signed in Rome on 4 November 1950 and as they result from the constitutional traditions common to the Member States, as general principles of Community law.

3. The Union shall respect the national identities of its Member States.

4. The Union shall provide itself with the means necessary to attain its objectives and carry through its policies.[14]

Article 7[15] **[Serious and persistent breaches of EU principles]**

1–008 1. On a reasoned proposal by one third of the Member States, by the European Parliament or by the Commission, the Council, acting by a majority of four-fifths of its members after obtaining the assent of the European Parliament, may determine that there is a clear risk of a serious breach by a Member State of principles mentioned in Article 6(1), and address appropriate recommendations to that State. Before making such a determination, the Council shall hear the Member State in question and, acting in accordance with the same procedure, may call on independent persons to submit within a reasonable time limit a report on the situation in the Member State in question.

The Council shall regularly verify that the grounds on which such a determination was made continue to apply.

2. The Council, meeting in the composition of the Heads of State or Government and acting by unanimity on a proposal by one third of the Member States or by the Commission and after obtaining the assent of the European Parliament, may determine the existence of a serious and persistent breach by a Member State of principles mentioned in Article 6(1), after inviting the government of the Member State in question to submit its observations.

3. Where a determination under paragraph 2 has been made, the Council, acting by a qualified majority, may decide to suspend certain of the rights deriving from the application of this Treaty to the Member State in question, including the voting rights of the representative of the government of that Member State in the Council. In doing so, the Council shall take into account the possible consequences of such a suspension on the rights and obligations of natural and legal persons.

The obligations of the Member State in question under this Treaty shall in any case continue to be binding on that State.

4. The Council, acting by a qualified majority, may decide subsequently to vary or revoke measures taken under paragraph 3 in response to changes in the situation which led to their being imposed.

5. For the purposes of this Article, the Council shall act without taking into account the vote of the representative of the government of the Member State in question. Abstentions by members present in person or represented shall not prevent the adoption of decisions referred to in paragraph 2. A qualified majority shall be defined as the same proportion of the weighted votes of the members of the Council concerned as laid down in Article 205(2) of the Treaty establishing the European Community.

This paragraph shall also apply in the event of voting rights being suspended pursuant to paragraph 3.

6. For the purposes of paragraphs 1 and 2, the European Parliament shall act by a two-thirds majority of the votes cast, representing a majority of its Members.

---

[14] See further, Declaration (No. 1) on the abolition of the death penalty and Declaration (No. 11) on the status of churches and non-confessional organisations both annexed to the Final Act of the Treaty of Amsterdam, and the Nice Charter of fundamental rights of the EU ([2000] OJ C364/1).

[15] Article 7 replaced by Treaty of Nice, Art. 1(1). Formerly Art. F.1; inserted by Treaty of Amsterdam, Art. 1(9).

TITLE II—PROVISIONS AMENDING THE TREATY ESTABLISHING THE EUROPEAN ECONOMIC COMMUNITY WITH A VIEW TO ESTABLISHING THE EUROPEAN COMMUNITY

Article 8[16] **[Amendments to EC Treaty]**

The Treaty establishing the European Economic Community shall be amended in accordance with the provisions of this Article, in order to establish a European Community. **1–009**

[Amendments not reproduced here]

TITLE III—PROVISIONS AMENDING THE TREATY ESTABLISHING THE EUROPEAN COAL AND STEEL COMMUNITY

Article 9[17] **[Amendments to ECSC Treaty]**

[Amendments not reproduced]

TITLE IV—PROVISIONS AMENDING THE TREATY ESTABLISHING THE EUROPEAN ATOMIC ENERGY COMMUNITY

Article 10[18] **[Amendments to EAEC Treaty]**

[Amendments not reproduced]

TITLE V—PROVISIONS ON A COMMON FOREIGN AND SECURITY POLICY

Article 11[19] **[Objectives of CFSP]**

1. The Union shall define and implement a common foreign and security policy covering all areas of foreign and security policy, the objectives of which shall be: **1–010**

— to safeguard the common values, fundamental interests, independence and integrity of the Union in conformity with the principles of the United Nations Charter;
— to strengthen the security of the Union in all ways;
— to preserve peace and strengthen international security, in accordance with the principles of the United Nations Charter, as well as the principles of the Helsinki Final Act and the objectives of the Paris Charter, including those on external borders;
— to promote international cooperation;
— to develop and consolidate democracy and the rule of law, and respect for human rights and fundamental freedoms.

2. The Member States shall support the Union's external and security policy actively and unreservedly in a spirit of loyalty and mutual solidarity.

The Member States shall work together to enhance and develop their mutual political solidarity. They shall refrain from any action which is contrary to the interests of the Union or likely to impair its effectiveness as a cohesive force in international relations.

The Council shall ensure that these principles are complied with.

Article 12[20] **[Implementation of CFSP objectives]**

The Union shall pursue the objectives set out in Article 11 by: **1–011**

— defining the principles of and general guidelines for the common foreign and security policy;

[16] Formerly Art. G.
[17] Formerly Art. H.
[18] Formerly Art. I.
[19] Formerly Art. J.1; replaced by Treaty of Amsterdam, Art. 1(10).
[20] Formerly Art. J.2; replaced by Treaty of Amsterdam, Art. 1(10).

— deciding on common strategies;
— adopting joint actions;
— adopting common positions;
— strengthening systematic cooperation between member states in the conduct of policy.

Article 13[21] **[Roles of European Council and Council of EU]**

1–012 1. The European Council shall define the principles of, and general guidelines for, the common foreign and security policy, including for matters with defence implications.[22]

2. The European Council shall decide on common strategies to be implemented by the Union in areas where the Member States have important interests in common.

Common strategies shall set out their objectives, duration and the means to be made available by the Union and the Member States.

3. The Council shall take the decisions necessary for defining and implementing the common foreign and security policy on the basis of the general guidelines defined by the European Council.

The Council shall recommend common strategies to the European Council and shall implement them, in particular by adopting joint actions and common positions.

The Council shall ensure the unity, consistency and effectiveness of action by the Union.

Article 14[23] **[Joint actions]**

1–013 1. The Council shall adopt joint actions. Joint actions shall address specific situations where operational action by the Union is deemed to be required. They shall lay down their objectives, scope, the means to be made available to the Union, if necessary their duration, and the conditions for their implementation.

2. If there is a change in circumstances having a substantial effect on a question subject to joint action, the Council shall review the principles and objectives of that action and take the necessary decisions. As long as the Council has not acted, the joint action shall stand.

3. Joint actions shall commit the Member States in the positions they adopt and in the conduct of their activity.

4. The Council may request the Commission to submit to it any appropriate proposals relating to the common foreign and security policy to ensure the implementation of a joint action.

5. Whenever there is any plan to adopt a national position or take national action pursuant to a joint action, information shall be provided in time to allow, if necessary, for prior consultations within the Council. The obligation to provide prior information shall not apply to measures which are merely a national transposition of Council decisions.

6. In cases of imperative need arising from changes in the situation and failing a Council decision, Member States may take the necessary measures as a matter of urgency having regard to the general objectives of the joint action. The Member State concerned shall inform the Council immediately of any such measures.

7. Should there be any major difficulties in implementing a joint action, a Member State shall refer them to the Council which shall discuss them and seek

[21] Formerly Art. J.3; replaced by Treaty of Amsterdam, Art. 1(10).

[22] See Protocol (No. 5) on the position of Denmark, Art. 6, as regards actions having defence implications.

[23] Formerly Art. J.4; replaced by Treaty of Amsterdam, Art. 1(10).

appropriate solutions. Such solutions shall not run counter to the objectives of the joint action or impair its effectiveness.

Article 15[24] **[Common positions]**

The Council shall adopt common positions. Common positions shall define the approach of the Union to a particular matter of a geographical or thematic nature. Member States shall ensure that their national policies conform to the common positions. **1–014**

Article 16[25] **[Member State information and consultation]**

Member States shall inform and consult one another within the Council on any matter of foreign and security policy of general interest in order to ensure that the Union's influence is exerted as effectively as possible by means of concerted and convergent action. **1–015**

Article 17[26] **[Progressive development of common defence policy]**

1. The common foreign and security policy shall include all questions relating to the security of the Union, including the progressive framing of a common defence policy, which might lead to a common defence, should the European Council so decide. It shall in that case recommend to the Member States the adoption of such a decision in accordance with their respective constitutional requirements. **1–016**

The policy of the Union in accordance with this Article shall not prejudice the specific character of the security and defence policy of certain Member States and shall respect the obligations of certain Member States, which see their common defence realised in the North Atlantic Treaty Organisation (NATO), under the North Atlantic Treaty and be compatible with the common security and defence policy established within that framework.

The progressive framing of a common defence policy will be supported, as Member States consider appropriate, by cooperation between them in the field of armaments.

2. Questions referred to in this Article shall include humanitarian and rescue tasks, peacekeeping tasks and tasks of combat forces in crisis management, including peacemaking.

3. Decisions having defence implications dealt with under this Article shall be taken without prejudice to the policies and obligations referred to in paragraph 1, second subparagraph.

4. The provisions of this Article shall not prevent the development of closer cooperation between two or more Member States on a bilateral level, in the framework of the Western European Union (WEU) and NATO, provided such cooperation does not run counter to or impede that provided for in this Title.

5. With a view to furthering the objectives of this Article, the provisions of this Article will be reviewed in accordance with Article 48.[27]

---

[24] Formerly Art. J.5; replaced by Treaty of Amsterdam, Art. 1(10).

[25] Formerly Art. J.6; replaced by Treaty of Amsterdam, Art. 1(10).

[26] Article 17 replaced by Treaty of Nice, Art. 1(2). Formerly Art. J.7; replaced by Treaty of Amsterdam, Art. 1(10).

[27] See further Protocol (No. 1) on Art. 17 of the Treaty on European Union (EU and WEU to draw up arrangements for enhanced cooperation between them); Declaration (No. 2) on enhanced cooperation between the European Union and the Western European Union and Declaration (No. 3) relating to Western European Union both annexed to the Final Act of the Treaty of Amsterdam; Decision 1999/321/CFSP on practical arrangements for participation in tasks for which the EU avails itself of the WEU ([1999] OJ L123/14); and Decision 1999/404/CFSP on arrangements for enhanced cooperation with WEU ([1999] OJ L153/1). See also Protocol (No. 5) on the position of Denmark, Art. 6, as regards actions having defence implications.

Article 18[28] **[Central role of the EU Presidency in CFSP]**

1–017 1. The Presidency shall represent the Union in matters coming within the common foreign and security policy.

2. The Presidency shall be responsible for the implementation of decisions taken under this Title; in that capacity it shall in principle express the position of the Union in international organisations and international conferences.

3. The Presidency shall be assisted by the Secretary-General of the Council who shall exercise the function of High Representative for the common foreign and security policy.

4. The Commission shall be fully associated in the tasks referred to in paragraphs 1 and 2. The Presidency shall be assisted in those tasks if need be by the next Member State to hold the Presidency.

5. The Council may, whenever it deems it necessary, appoint a special representative with a mandate in relation to particular policy issues.[29]

Article 19[30] **[Member State obligations in international forums]**

1–018 1. Member States shall coordinate their action in international organisations and at international conferences. They shall uphold the common positions in such fora.

In international organisations and at international conferences where not all the Member States participate, those which do take part shall uphold the common positions.

2. Without prejudice to paragraph 1 and Article 14(3), Member States represented in international organisations or international conferences where not all the Member States participate shall keep the latter informed of any matter of common interest.

Member States which are also members of the United Nations Security Council will concert and keep the other Member States fully informed. Member States which are permanent members of the Security Council will, in the execution of their functions, ensure the defence of the positions and the interests of the Union, without prejudice to their responsibilities under the provisions of the United Nations Charter.[31]

Article 20[32] **[Diplomatic and consular missions; Commission Delegations]**

1–019 The diplomatic and consular missions of the Member States and the Commission Delegations in third countries and international conferences, and their representations to international organisations, shall co-operate in ensuring that the common positions and joint actions adopted by the Council are complied with and implemented.

They shall step up cooperation by exchanging information, carrying out joint assessments and contributing to the implementation of the provisions referred to in Article 20 of the Treaty establishing the European Community.[33]

Article 21[34] **[Role of European Parliament in CFSP]**

1–020 The Presidency shall consult the European Parliament on the main aspects and the basic choices of the common foreign and security policy and shall ensure that

[28] Formerly Art. J.8; replaced by Treaty of Amsterdam, Art. 1(10).
[29] See Art. 37 below on application of Art. 18 to police and judicial cooperation in criminal matters.
[30] Formerly Art. J.9; replaced by Treaty of Amsterdam, Art. 1(10).
[31] See Art. 37 below on application of Art. 19 to police and judicial cooperation in criminal matters.
[32] Formerly Art. J.10; replaced by Treaty of Amsterdam, Art. 1(10).
[33] See Art. 20 EC on access to diplomatic or consular protection by EU citizens.
[34] Formerly Art. J.11; replaced by Treaty of Amsterdam, Art. 1(10).

the views of the European Parliament are duly taken into consideration. The European Parliament shall be kept regularly informed by the Presidency and the Commission of the development of the Union's foreign and security policy.

The European Parliament may ask questions of the Council or make recommendations to it. It shall hold an annual debate on progress in implementing the common foreign and security policy.[35]

Article 22[36] [CFSP matters referred to the Council]

1. Any Member State or the Commission may refer to the Council any question relating to the common foreign and security policy and may submit proposals to the Council. **1–021**

2. In cases requiring a rapid decision, the Presidency, of its own motion, or at the request of the Commission or a Member State, shall convene an extraordinary Council meeting within forty-eight hours or, in an emergency, within a shorter period.

Article 23[37] [Procedures in Council for taking decisions under CFSP]

1. Decisions under this Title shall be taken by the Council acting unanimously. Abstentions by members present in person or represented shall not prevent the adoption of such decisions. **1–022**

When abstaining in a vote, any member of the Council may qualify its abstention by making a formal declaration under the present sub-paragraph. In that case, it shall not be obliged to apply the decision, but shall accept that the decision commits the Union. In a spirit of mutual solidarity, the Member State concerned shall refrain from any action likely to conflict with or impede Union action based on that decision and the other Member States shall respect its position. If the members of the Council qualifying their abstention in this way represent more than one third of the votes weighted in accordance with Article 205(2) of the Treaty establishing the European Community, the decision shall not be adopted.

2. By derogation from the provisions of paragraph 1, the Council shall act by qualified majority:

— when adopting joint actions, common positions or taking any other decision on the basis of a common strategy;
— when adopting any decision implementing a joint action or a common position;
— when appointing a special representative in accordance with Article 18(5).[38]

If a member of the Council declares that, for important and stated reasons of national policy, it intends to oppose the adoption of a decision to be taken by qualified majority, a vote shall not be taken. The Council may, acting by a qualified majority, request that the matter be referred to the European Council for decision by unanimity.

The votes of the members of the Council shall be weighted in accordance with Article 205(2) of the Treaty establishing the European Community. For their adoption, decisions shall require at least 62 votes in favour, cast by at least 10 members.

This paragraph shall not apply to decisions having military or defence implications.[39]

3. For procedural questions, the Council shall act by a majority of its members.

[35] Formerly Art. J.4; replaced by Treaty of Amsterdam, Art. 1(10).
[36] Formerly Art. J.12; replaced by Treaty of Amsterdam, Art. 1(10).
[37] Formerly Art. J.13; replaced by Treaty of Amsterdam, Art. 1(10).
[38] Third indent of Art. 23(2) added by Treaty of Nice, Art. 1(3).
[39] For prospective amendment to Art. 23(2), see Art. 3(1)(b) of the Protocol on enlargement of the EU, annexed to this Treaty by the Treaty of Nice.

Article 24[40] **[Procedure for concluding international agreements]**

1–023 When it is necessary to conclude an agreement with one or more States or international organisations in implementation of this Title, the Council may authorise the Presidency, assisted by the Commission as appropriate, to open negotiations to that effect. Such agreements shall be concluded by the Council on a recommendation from the Presidency.

2. The Council shall act unanimously when the agreement covers an issue for which unanimity is required for the adoption of internal decisions.

3. When the agreement is envisaged in order to implement a joint action or common position, the Council shall act by a qualified majority in accordance with Article 23(2).

4. The provisions of this Article shall also apply to matters falling under Title VI. When the agreement covers an issue for which a qualified majority is required for the adoption of internal decisions or measures, the Council shall act by a qualified majority in accordance with Article 34(3).

5. No agreement shall be binding on a Member State whose representative in the Council states that it has to comply with the requirements of its own constitutional procedure; the other members of the Council may agree that the agreement shall nevertheless apply provisionally.

6. Agreements concluded under the conditions set out by this Article shall be binding on the institutions of the Union.[41]

Article 25[42] **[Political and Security Committee]**

1–024 Without prejudice to Article 207 of the Treaty establishing the European Community, a Political and Security Committee shall monitor the international situation in the areas covered by the common foreign and security policy and contribute to the definition of policies by delivering opinions to the Council at the request of the Council or on its own initiative. It shall also monitor the implementation of agreed policies, without prejudice to the responsibility of the Presidency and the Commission.

Within the scope of this Title, this Committee shall exercise, under the responsibility of the Council, political control and strategic direction of crisis management operations.

The Council may authorise the Committee, for the purpose and for the duration of a crisis management operation, as determined by the Council, to take the relevant decisions concerning the political control and strategic direction of the operation, without prejudice to Article 47.[43]

Article 26[44] **[Role of Council Secretary-General under CFSP]**

1–025 The Secretary-General of the Council, High Representative for the common foreign and security policy, shall assist the Council in matters coming within the

[40] Formerly Art. J.14; replaced by Treaty of Amsterdam, Art. 1(10). Article 24 replaced by Treaty of Nice, Art. 1(4).

[41] See further Art. 38 below on application of Art. 24 to agreements to further police and judicial cooperation in criminal matters; and Declaration (No. 4) on Art. [24 and 38] of the Treaty on European Union annexed to the Final Act of the Treaty of Amsterdam.

[42] Formerly Art. J.15; replaced by Treaty of Amsterdam, Art. 1(10). Article 25 replaced by Treaty of Nice, Art. 1(5).

[43] See further, Declaration (No. 5) on Art. [25] of the Treaty on European Union annexed to the Final Act of the Treaty of Amsterdam.

[44] Formerly Art. J.16; replaced by Treaty of Amsterdam, Art. 1(10).

scope of the common foreign and security policy, in particular through contributing to the formulation, preparation and implementation of policy decisions, and, when appropriate and acting on behalf of the Council at the request of the Presidency, through conducting political dialogue with third parties.[45]

Article 27[46] **[Commission to be associated with work under CFSP]**

The Commission shall be fully associated with the work carried out in the common foreign and security policy field. **1–026**

Article 27a[47] **[Enhanced cooperation]**

1. Enhanced cooperation in any of the areas referred to in this Title shall be aimed at safeguarding the values and serving the interests of the Union as a whole by asserting its identity as a coherent force on the international scene. It shall respect: **1–027**
- principles, objectives, general guidelines and consistency of the common foreign and security policy and the decisions taken within the framework of that policy;
- the powers of the European Community, and
- consistency between all the Union's policies and its external activities.

2. Articles 11 to 27 and Articles 27b to 28 shall apply to the enhanced cooperation provided for in this Article, save as otherwise provided in Article 27c and Articles 43 to 45.

Article 27b[48] **[Scope of enhanced cooperation]**

Enhanced cooperation pursuant to this Title shall relate to implementation of a joint action or a common position. It shall not relate to matters having military or defence implications. **1–028**

Article 27c[49] **[Enhanced cooperation authorisation procedure]**

Member States which intend to establish enhanced cooperation between themselves under Article 27b shall address a request to the Council to that effect. **1–029**

The request shall be forwarded to the Commission and to the European Parliament for information. The Commission shall give its opinion particularly on whether the enhanced cooperation proposed is consistent with Union policies. Authorisation shall be granted by the Council, acting in accordance with the second and third subparagraphs of Article 23(2) and in compliance with Articles 43 to 45.

Article 27d[50] **[Transparency of enhanced cooperation]**

Without prejudice to the powers of the Presidency or of the Commission, the Secretary-General of the Council, High Representative for the common foreign **1–030**

[45] See Declaration (No. 6) on the establishment of a policy planning and early warning unit annexed to the Final Act of the Treaty of Amsterdam.
[46] Formerly Art. J.17; replaced by Treaty of Amsterdam, Art. 1(10).
[47] Article 27a inserted by Treaty of Nice, Art. 1(6).
[48] Article 27b inserted by Treaty of Nice, Art. 1(6).
[49] Article 27c inserted by Treaty of Nice, Art. 1(6).
[50] Article 27d inserted by Treaty of Nice, Art. 1(6).

and security policy, shall in particular ensure that the European Parliament and all members of the Council are kept fully informed of the implementation of enhanced cooperation in the field of the common foreign and security policy.

Article 27e[51] [Participation in enhanced cooperation]

1–031 Any Member State which wishes to participate in enhanced cooperation established in accordance with Article 27c shall notify its intention to the Council and inform the Commission. The Commission shall give an opinion to the Council within three months of the date of receipt of that notification. Within four months of the date of receipt of that notification, the Council shall take a decision on the request and on such specific arrangements as it may deem necessary. The decision shall be deemed to be taken unless the Council, acting by a qualified majority within the same period, decides to hold it in abeyance; in that case, the Council shall state the reasons for its decision and set a deadline for re-examining it.

For the purposes of this Article, the Council shall act by a qualified majority. The qualified majority shall be defined as the same proportion of the weighted votes and the same proportion of the number of the members of the Council concerned as those laid down in the third subparagraph of Article 23(2).

Article 28[52] [Application of EC institutional provisions]

1–032 1. Articles 189, 190, 196 to 199, 203, 204, 206 to 209, 213 to 219, 255 and 290 of the Treaty establishing the European Community shall apply to the provisions relating to the areas referred to in this Title.

2. Administrative expenditure which the provisions relating to the areas referred to in this Title entail for the institutions shall be charged to the budget of the European Communities.

3. Operational expenditure to which the implementation of those provisions gives rise shall also be charged to the budget of the European Communities, except for such expenditure arising from operations having military or defence implications and cases where the Council acting unanimously decides otherwise.

In cases where expenditure is not charged to the budget of the European Communities it shall be charged to the Member States in accordance with the gross national product scale, unless the Council acting unanimously decides otherwise. As for expenditure arising from operations having military or defence implications, Member States whose representatives in the Council have made a formal declaration under Article 23(1), second sub-paragraph, shall not be obliged to contribute to the financing thereof.

4. The budgetary procedure laid down in the Treaty establishing the European Community shall apply to the expenditure charged to the budget of the European Communities.[53]

TITLE VI—PROVISIONS ON POLICE AND JUDICIAL COOPERATION IN CRIMINAL MATTERS

Article 29[54] [Objective of safety within area of freedom, security and justice]

1–033 Without prejudice to the powers of the European Community, the Union's objective shall be to provide citizens with a high level of safety within an area of freedom, security and justice by developing common action among the Member

[51] Article 27e inserted by Treaty of Nice, Art. 1(6).
[52] Formerly Art. J.18; replaced by Treaty of Amsterdam, Art. 1(10).
[53] For budgetary procedure, see Arts 268—280 EC
[54] Formerly Art. K.1; replaced by Treaty of Amsterdam, Art. 1(11).

States in the fields of police and judicial cooperation in criminal matters and by preventing and combating racism and xenophobia.[55]

That objective shall be achieved by preventing and combating crime, organised or otherwise, in particular terrorism, trafficking in persons and offences against children, illicit drug trafficking and illicit arms trafficking, corruption and fraud, through:

— closer cooperation between police forces, customs authorities and other competent authorities in the Member States, both directly and through the European Police Office (Europol), in accordance with the provisions of Articles 30 and 32;
— closer cooperation between judicial and other competent authorities of the Member States, including cooperation through the European Judicial Cooperation Unit ("Eurojust"), in accordance with the provisions of Articles 31 and 32;[56]
— approximation, where necessary, of rules on criminal matters in the Member States, in accordance with the provisions of Article 31(e).[57]

Article 30[58] [Common action in field of police cooperation]

1. Common action in the field of police cooperation shall include: **1–034**

(a) operational cooperation between the competent authorities, including the police, customs and other specialised law enforcement services of the Member States in relation to the prevention, detection and investigation of criminal offences;
(b) the collection, storage, processing, analysis and exchange of relevant information, including information held by law enforcement services on reports on suspicious financial transactions, in particular through Europol, subject to appropriate provisions on the protection of personal data;
(c) cooperation and joint initiatives in training, the exchange of liaison officers, secondments, the use of equipment, and forensic research;
(d) the common evaluation of particular investigative techniques in relation to the detection of serious forms of organised crime.

2. The Council shall promote cooperation through Europol and shall in particular, within a period of five years after the date of entry into force of the Treaty of Amsterdam:

(a) enable Europol to facilitate and support the preparation, and to encourage the coordination and carrying out, of specific investigative actions by the competent authorities of the Member States, including operational actions of joint teams comprising representatives of Europol in a support capacity;
(b) adopt measures allowing Europol to ask the competent authorities of the Member States to conduct and coordinate their investigations in specific cases and to develop specific expertise which may be put at the disposal of Member States to assist them in investigating cases of organised crime;
(c) promote liaison arrangements between prosecuting/investigating officials specialising in the fight against organised crime in close cooperation with Europol;
(d) establish a research, documentation and statistical network on cross-border crime.[59]

---

[55] See Art. 42 for alternative action in this area under EC Treaty Title IV on visas, asylum and immigration and other policies related to free movement of persons.

[56] Second indent of second paragraph of Art. 29 replaced by Treaty of Nice, Art. 1(7).

[57] See Art. 40 for application of Art. 29 to enhanced Member State cooperation in the field of police and judicial cooperation in criminal matters.

[58] Formerly Art. K.2; replaced by Treaty of Amsterdam, Art. 1(11).

[59] See Art. 40 for application of Art. 30 to enhanced Member State cooperation in the field of police and judicial cooperation in criminal matters; see also Declaration (No. 7) on Art. [30] of the Treaty on European Union annexed to the the Final Act of Treaty of Amsterdam.

Article 31[60] **[Common action on judicial cooperation]**

1–035 1. Common action on judicial cooperation in criminal matters shall include:
(a) facilitating and accelerating cooperation between competent ministries and judicial or equivalent authorities of the Member States, including, where appropriate, cooperation through Eurojust, in relation to proceedings and the enforcement of decisions;
(b) facilitating extradition between Member States;
(c) ensuring compatibility in rules applicable in the Member States, as may be necessary to improve such cooperation;
(d) preventing conflicts of jurisdiction between Member States;
(e) progressively adopting measures establishing minimum rules relating to the constituent elements of criminal acts and to penalties in the fields of organised crime, terrorism and illicit drug trafficking.

2. The Council shall encourage cooperation through Eurojust by:
(a) enabling Eurojust to facilitate proper coordination between Member States' national prosecuting authorities;
(b) promoting support by Eurojust for criminal investigations in cases of serious cross-border crime, particularly in the case of organised crime, taking account, in particular, of analyses carried out by Europol;
(c) facilitating close cooperation between Eurojust and the European Judicial Network, particularly, in order to facilitate the execution of letters rogatory and the implementation of extradition requests.

Article 32[61] **[Operation of Member State authorities in other Member States]**

1–036 The Council shall lay down the conditions and limitations under which the competent authorities referred to in Articles 30 and 31 may operate in the territory of another Member State in liaison and in agreement with the authorities of that State.[62]

Article 33[63] **[Member States' reserved responsibilities in preserving law and order]**

1–037 This Title shall not affect the exercise of the responsibilities incumbent upon Member States with regard to the maintenance of law and order and the safeguarding of internal security.[64]

Article 34[65] **[Consultation and cooperation]**

1–038 1. In the areas referred to in this Title, Member States shall inform and consult one another within the Council with a view to coordinating their action. To that end, they shall establish collaboration between the relevant departments of their administrations.

2. The Council shall take measures and promote cooperation, using the appropriate form and procedures as set out in this Title, contributing to the pursuit of the objectives of the Union. To that end, acting unanimously on the initiative of any Member State or of the Commission, the Council may:

---

[60] Formerly Art. K.3; replaced by Treaty of Amsterdam, Art. 1(11). Article 31 replaced by Treaty of Nice, Art. 1(8). See Art. 40 for application of Art.31 to enhanced Member State cooperation in the field of police and judicial cooperation in criminal matters; see also Declaration (No. 8) on Art. [31(1)(e)] of the Treaty on European Union annexed to the Final Act of the Treaty of Amsterdam.
[61] Formerly Art. K.4; replaced by Treaty of Amsterdam, Art. 1(11).
[62] See Art. 40 for application of Art. 32 to enhanced Member State cooperation in the field of police and judicial cooperation in criminal matters.
[63] Formerly Art. K.5; replaced by Treaty of Amsterdam, Art. 1(11).
[64] See Art. 40 for application of Art. 33 to enhanced Member State cooperation in the field of police and judicial cooperation in criminal matters.
[65] Formerly Art. K.6; replaced by Treaty of Amsterdam, Art. 1(11).

(a) adopt common positions defining the approach of the Union to a particular matter;
(b) adopt framework decisions for the purpose of approximation of the laws and regulations of the Member States. Framework decisions shall be binding upon the Member States as to the result to be achieved but shall leave to the national authorities the choice of form and methods. They shall not entail direct effect;
(c) adopt decisions for any other purpose consistent with the objectives of this Title, excluding any approximation of the laws and regulations of the Member States. These decisions shall be binding and shall not entail direct effect; the Council, acting by a qualified majority, shall adopt measures necessary to implement those decisions at the level of the Union;
(d) establish conventions which it shall recommend to the Member States for adoption in accordance with their respective constitutional requirements. Member States shall begin the procedures applicable within a time limit to be set by the Council.

Unless they provide otherwise, conventions shall, once adopted by at least half of the Member States, enter into force for those Member States. Measures implementing conventions shall be adopted within the Council by a majority of two-thirds of the contracting parties.[66]

3. Where the Council is required to act by a qualified majority, the votes of its members shall be weighted as laid down in Article 205(2) of the Treaty establishing the European Community, and for their adoption acts of the Council shall require at least 62 votes in favour, cast by at least 10 members.[67]

4. For procedural questions, the Council shall act by a majority of its members.

Article 35[68] **[Jurisdiction of ECJ]**

1. The Court of Justice of the European Communities shall have jurisdiction, subject to the conditions laid down in this Article, to give preliminary rulings on the validity and interpretation of framework decisions and decisions, on the interpretation of conventions established under this Title and on the validity and interpretation of the measures implementing them. **1–039**

2. By a declaration made at the time of signature of the Treaty of Amsterdam or at any time thereafter, any Member State shall be able to accept the jurisdiction of the Court of Justice to give preliminary rulings as specified in paragraph 1.[69]

3. A Member State making a declaration pursuant to paragraph 2 shall specify that either:
(a) any court or tribunal of that State against whose decisions there is no judicial remedy under national law may request the Court of Justice to give a preliminary ruling on a question raised in a case pending before it and concerning the validity or interpretation of an act referred to in paragraph 1 if

[66] See Art. 35(6), (7) for judicial review of framework decisions and decisions and ECJ jurisdiction to interpret and rule on application of acts etc. adopted or established under Art. 34(2), and Art. 39 on role of European Parliament in adopting measures under Art. 34(2)(b), (c) and (d). See also Declaration (No. 9) on Article [34](2) of the Treaty on European Union annexed to the Final Act of the Treaty of Amsterdam (publication of measures in the *Official Journal*).

[67] For prospective replacement of Art. 34(3), see Art. 3(1)(c) of the Protocol on enlargement of the EU annexed to this Treaty by the Treaty of Nice. See Art. 40 for application of Art. 34 to enhanced Member State cooperation in the field of police and judicial cooperation in criminal matters.

[68] Formerly Art. K.7; replaced by Treaty of Amsterdam, Art. 1(11).

[69] See Declaration (No. 10) on Art. [35] of the Treaty on European Union annexed to the Final Act of the Treaty of Amsterdam.

that court or tribunal considers that a decision on the question is necessary to enable it to give judgment; or

(b) any court or tribunal of that State may request the Court of Justice to give a preliminary ruling on a question raised in a case pending before it and concerning the validity or interpretation of an act referred to in paragraph 1 if that court or tribunal considers that a decision on the question is necessary to enable it to give judgment.

4. Any Member State, whether or not it has made a declaration pursuant to paragraph 2, shall be entitled to submit statements of case or written observations to the Court in cases which arise under paragraph 1.

5. The Court of Justice shall have no jurisdiction to review the validity or proportionality of operations carried out by the police or other law enforcement services of a Member State or the exercise of the responsibilities incumbent upon Member States with regard to the maintenance of law and order and the safeguarding of internal security.

6. The Court of Justice shall have jurisdiction to review the legality of framework decisions and decisions in actions brought by a Member State or the Commission on grounds of lack of competence, infringement of an essential procedural requirement, infringement of this Treaty or of any rule of law relating to its application, or misuse of powers. The proceedings provided for in this paragraph shall be instituted within two months of the publication of the measure.

7. The Court of Justice shall have jurisdiction to rule on any dispute between Member States regarding the interpretation or the application of acts adopted under Article 34(2) whenever such dispute cannot be settled by the Council within six months of its being referred to the Council by one of its members. The Court shall also have jurisdiction to rule on any dispute between Member States and the Commission regarding the interpretation or the application of conventions established under Article 34(2)(d).[70]

Article 36[71] **[Coordinating Committee]**

1–040 1. A Coordinating Committee shall be set up consisting of senior officials. In addition to its coordinating role, it shall be the task of the committee to:

— give opinions for the attention of the Council, either at the Council's request or on its own initiative;

— contribute, without prejudice to Article 207 of the Treaty establishing the European Community, to the preparation of the Council's discussions in the areas referred to in Article 29.

2. The Commission shall be fully associated with the work in the areas referred to in this title.[72]

Article 37[73] **[Defending common positions in international forums]**

1–041 Within international organisations and at international conferences in which they take part, Member States shall defend the common positions adopted under the provisions of this Title.

Articles 18 and 19 shall apply as appropriate to matters falling under this title.[74]

---

[70] See Art. 40 for application of Art. 35 to enhanced Member State cooperation in the field of police and judicial cooperation in criminal matters.

[71] Formerly Art. K.8; replaced by Treaty of Amsterdam, Art. 1(11).

[72] See Art. 40 on application of Art. 36 to enhanced Member State cooperation in the field of police and judicial cooperation in criminal matters. EC Treaty, Art. 207 establishes COREPER and Council General Secretariat.

[73] Formerly Art. K.9; replaced by Treaty of Amsterdam, Art. 1(11).

[74] See Art. 40 on application of Art. 37 to enhanced Member State cooperation in the field of police and judicial cooperation in criminal matters.

Article 38[75] **[Agreements with third countries]**

Agreements referred to in Article 24 may cover matters falling under this Title.[76] **1–042**

Article 39[77] **[Role of European Parliament in police and judicial cooperation]**

1. The Council shall consult the European Parliament before adopting any measure referred to in Article 34(2)(b), (c) and (d). The European Parliament shall deliver its opinion within a time-limit which the Council may lay down, which shall not be less than three months. In the absence of an opinion within that time-limit, the Council may act. **1–043**

2. The Presidency and the Commission shall regularly inform the European Parliament of discussions in the areas covered by this Title.

3. The European Parliament may ask questions of the Council or make recommendations to it. Each year, it shall hold a debate on the progress made in the areas referred to in this title.[78]

Article 40[79] **[Enhanced Member State cooperation]**

1. Enhanced cooperation in any of the areas referred to in this Title shall have the aim of enabling the Union to develop more rapidly into an area of freedom, security and justice, while respecting the powers of the European Community and the objectives laid down in this Title. **1–044**

2. Articles 29 to 39 and Articles 40a to 41 shall apply to the enhanced cooperation provided for by this Article, save as otherwise provided in Article 40a and in Articles 43 to 45.

3. The provisions of the Treaty establishing the European Community concerning the powers of the Court of Justice and the exercise of those powers shall apply to this Article and to Articles 40a and 40b.

Article 40a[80] **[Enhanced cooperation authorisation procedure]**

1. Member States which intend to establish enhanced cooperation between themselves under Article 40 shall address a request to the Commission, which may submit a proposal to the Council to that effect. In the event of the Commission not submitting a proposal, it shall inform the Member States concerned of the reasons for not doing so. Those Member States may then submit an initiative to the Council designed to obtain authorisation for the enhanced cooperation concerned. **1–045**

2. The authorisation referred to in paragraph 1 shall be granted, in compliance with Articles 43 to 45, by the Council, acting by a qualified majority, on a proposal from the Commission or on the initiative of at least eight Member States, and after consulting the European Parliament. The votes of the members of the Council shall be weighted in accordance with Article 205(2) of the Treaty establishing the European Community.

[75] Formerly Art. K.10; replaced by Treaty of Amsterdam, Art. 1(11).

[76] See Art. 24 for procedure under CFSP for concluding agreements 80with third countries, Art. 40 on application of Art. 38 to enhanced Member State cooperation in the field of police and judicial cooperation in criminal matters and Declaration (No. 4) on Arts [24 and 38] of the Treaty on European Union annexed to the Final Act of the Treaty of Amsterdam.

[77] Formerly Art. K.11; replaced by Treaty of Amsterdam, Art. 1(11).

[78] See Art. 40 on application of Art. 39 to enhanced Member State cooperation in the field of police and judicial cooperation in criminal matters.

[79] Article 40 replaced by Arts 40, 40a and 40b by Treaty of Nice, Art. 1(9). Formerly Art. K.12; replaced by Treaty of Amsterdam, Art. 1(11).

[80] *ibid.*

A member of the Council may request that the matter be referred to the European Council. After that matter has been raised before the European Council, the Council may act in accordance with the first subparagraph of this paragraph.

Article 40b[81] **[Participation in enhanced cooperation]**

1–046 Any Member State which wishes to participate in enhanced cooperation established in accordance with Article 40a shall notify its intention to the Council and to the Commission, which shall give an opinion to the Council within three months of the date of receipt of that notification, possibly accompanied by a recommendation for such specific arrangements as it may deem necessary for that Member State to become a party to the cooperation in question. The Council shall take a decision on the request within four months of the date of receipt of that notification. The decision shall be deemed to be taken unless the Council, acting by a qualified majority within the same period, decides to hold it in abeyance; in that case, the Council shall state the reasons for its decision and set a deadline for re-examining it.

For the purposes of this Article, the Council shall act under the conditions set out in Article 44(1).

Article 41[82] **[Application of EC institutional provisions and EC budget]**

1–047 1. Articles 189, 190, 195, 196 to 199, 203, 204, 205(3), 206 to 209, 213 to 219, 255 and 290 of the Treaty establishing the European Community shall apply to the provisions relating to the areas referred to in this Title.

2. Administrative expenditure which the provisions relating to the areas referred to in this title entail for the institutions shall be charged to the budget of the European Communities.

3. Operational expenditure to which the implementation of those provisions gives rise shall also be charged to the budget of the European Communities, except where the Council acting unanimously decides otherwise. In cases where expenditure is not charged to the budget of the European Communities it shall be charged to the Member States in accordance with the gross national product scale, unless the Council acting unanimously decides otherwise.

4. The budgetary procedure laid down in the Treaty establishing the European Community shall apply to the expenditure charged to the budget of the European Communities.

Article 42[83] **[Application of EC rules on visas, etc.]**

1–048 The Council, acting unanimously on the initiative of the Commission or a Member State, and after consulting the European Parliament, may decide that action in areas referred to in Article 29 shall fall under Title IV of the Treaty establishing the European Community, and at the same time determine the relevant voting conditions relating to it. It shall recommend the Member States to adopt that decision in accordance with their respective constitutional requirements.

---

[81] *ibid.*

[82] Formerly Art. K.13; replaced by Treaty of Amsterdam, Art. 1(11).

[83] Formerly Art. K.14; replaced by Treaty of Amsterdam, Art. 1(11).

TITLE VII—PROVISIONS ON ENHANCED COOPERATION[84]

Article 43[85] [Limits on use of EU institutions for enhanced cooperation]

Member States which intend to establish enhanced cooperation between themselves may make use of the institutions, procedures and mechanisms laid down by this Treaty and by the Treaty establishing the European Community provided that the proposed cooperation: **1–049**

(a) is aimed at furthering the objectives of the Union and of the Community, at protecting and serving their interests and at reinforcing their process of integration;
(b) respects the said Treaties and the single institutional framework of the Union;
(c) respects the *acquis communautaire* and the measures adopted under the other provisions of the said Treaties;
(d) remains within the limits of the powers of the Union or of the Community and does not concern the areas which fall within the exclusive competence of the Community;
(e) does not undermine the internal market as defined in Article 14(2) of the Treaty establishing the European Community, or the economic and social cohesion established in accordance with Title XVII of that Treaty;
(f) does not constitute a barrier to or discrimination in trade between the Member States and does not distort competition between them;
(g) involves a minimum of eight Member States;
(h) respects the competences, rights and obligations of those Member States which do not participate therein;
(i) does not affect the provisions of the Protocol integrating the Schengen *acquis* into the framework of the European Union;
(j) is open to all the Member States, in accordance with Article 43b.

Article 43a[86] [Enhanced cooperation as last resort]

Enhanced cooperation may be undertaken only as a last resort, when it has been established within the Council that the objectives of such cooperation cannot be attained within a reasonable period by applying the relevant provisions of the Treaties. **1–050**

Article 43b[87] [Participants in enhanced cooperation]

When enhanced cooperation is being established, it shall be open to all Member States. It shall also be open to them at any time, in accordance with Articles 27e and 40b of this Treaty and with Article 11a of the Treaty establishing the European Community, subject to compliance with the basic decision and with the decisions taken within that framework. The Commission and the Member States participating in enhanced cooperation shall ensure that as many Member States as possible are encouraged to take part. **1–051**

---

[84] Title heading replaced by Treaty of Nice, Art. 1(10). Formerly Title VIa, inserted by Treaty of Amsterdam, Art. 1(12).
[85] Article 43 replaced by Treaty of Nice, Art. 1(11). Formerly Art. K.15; inserted by Treaty of Amsterdam, Art. 1(12).
[86] Article 43a inserted by Treaty of Nice, Art. 1(12).
[87] Article 43b inserted by Treaty of Nice, Art. 1(12).

Article 44[88] [Implementing enhanced cooperation]

1–052 1. For the purposes of the adoption of the acts and decisions necessary for the implementation of enhanced cooperation referred to in Article 43, the relevant institutional provisions of this Treaty and of the Treaty establishing the European Community shall apply. However, while all members of the Council shall be able to take part in the deliberations, only those representing Member States participating in enhanced cooperation shall take part in the adoption of decisions. The qualified majority shall be defined as the same proportion of the weighted votes and the same proportion of the number of the Council members concerned as laid down in Article 205(2) of the Treaty establishing the European Community, and in the second and third subparagraphs of Article 23(2) of this Treaty as regards enhanced cooperation established on the basis of Article 27c. Unanimity shall be constituted by only those Council members concerned.

Such acts and decisions shall not form part of the Union *acquis*.

2. Member States shall apply, as far as they are concerned, the acts and decisions adopted for the implementation of the enhanced cooperation in which they participate. Such acts and decisions shall be binding only on those Member States which participate in such cooperation and, as appropriate, shall be directly applicable only in those States. Member States which do not participate in such cooperation shall not impede the implementation thereof by the participating Member States.

Article 44a[89] [Costs of enhanced cooperation]

1–053 Expenditure resulting from implementation of enhanced cooperation, other than administrative costs entailed for the institutions, shall be borne by the participating Member States, unless all members of the Council, acting unanimously after consulting the European Parliament, decide otherwise.

Article 45[90] [Monitoring enhanced cooperation]

1–054 The Council and the Commission shall ensure the consistency of activities undertaken on the basis of this Title and the consistency of such activities with the policies of the Union and the Community, and shall cooperate to that end.

TITLE VIII—FINAL PROVISIONS[91]

Article 46[92] [Jurisdiction of ECJ]

1–055 The provisions of the Treaty establishing the European Community, the Treaty establishing the European Coal and Steel Community and the Treaty establishing the European Atomic Energy Community concerning the powers of the Court of Justice of the European Communities and the exercise of those powers shall apply only to the following provisions of this Treaty:

[88] Article 44 replaced by Art. 44 and 44a by Treaty of Nice, Art. 1(13). Formerly Art. K.16; inserted by Treaty of Amsterdam, Art. 1(12).

[89] Article 44 replaced by Art. 44 and 44a by Treaty of Nice, Art. 1(13).

[90] Article 45 replaced by Treaty of Nice, Art. 1(14). Formerly Art. K.17; inserted by Treaty of Amsterdam, Art. 1(12).

[91] Formerly Title VII.

[92] Article 46 replaced by Treaty of Nice, Art. 1(15). Formerly Art. L; replaced by Treaty of Amsterdam, Art. 1(13).

(a) provisions amending the Treaty establishing the European Economic Community with a view to establishing the European Community, the Treaty establishing the European Coal and Steel Community and the Treaty establishing the European Atomic Energy Community;
(b) provisions of Title VI, under the conditions provided for by Article 35;
(c) provisions of Title VII, under the conditions provided for by Articles 11 and 11a of the Treaty establishing the European Community and Article 40 of this Treaty;
(d) Article 6(2) with regard to action of the institutions, insofar as the Court has jurisdiction under the Treaties establishing the European Communities and under this Treaty;
(e) The purely procedural stipulations in Article 7, with the Court acting at the request of the Member State concerned within one month from the date of the determination by the Council provided for in that Article;
(f) Articles 46 to 53.

Article 47[93] [Interrelationship of Union and EC Treaties]

Subject to the provisions amending the Treaty establishing the European Economic Community with a view to establishing the European Community, the Treaty establishing the European Coal and Steel Community and the Treaty establishing the European Atomic Energy Community, and to these final provisions, nothing in this Treaty shall affect the Treaties establishing the European Communities or the subsequent Treaties and acts modifying or supplementing them. **1–056**

Article 48[94] [Amendments to the Treaties]

The government of any Member State or the Commission may submit to the Council proposals for the amendment of the Treaties on which the Union is founded. **1–057**

If the Council, after consulting the European Parliament and, where appropriate, the Commission, delivers an opinion in favour of calling a conference of representatives of the governments of the Member States, the conference shall be convened by the President of the Council for the purpose of determining by common accord the amendments to be made to those Treaties. The European Central Bank shall also be consulted in the case of institutional changes in the monetary area.

The amendments shall enter into force after being ratified by all the Member States in accordance with their respective constitutional requirements.

Article 49[95] [Accessions to the EU]

Any European State which respects the principles set out in Article 6(1) may apply to become a member of the Union. It shall address its application to the Council, which shall act unanimously after consulting the Commission and after receiving the assent of the European Parliament, which shall act by an absolute majority of its component members. **1–058**

The conditions of admission and the adjustments to the Treaties on which the Union is founded which such admission entails shall be the subject of an agreement between the Member States and the applicant State. This agreement shall be submitted for ratification by all the contracting States in accordance with their respective constitutional requirements.

---

[93] Formerly Art. M.

[94] Formerly Art. N; former Art. N(2) deleted and remaining paragraph unnumbered by virtue of Treaty of Amsterdam, Art. 1(14).

[95] Formerly Art. O; former Art. O, first paragraph replaced by Treaty of Amsterdam, Art. 1(15).

Article 50[96] **[Repeals]**

1–059 1. Articles 2 to 7 and 10 to 19 of the Treaty establishing a Single Council and a Single Commission of the European Communities, signed in Brussels on 8 April 1965, are hereby repealed.

2. Article 2, Article 3(2) and Title III of the Single European Act signed in Luxembourg on 17 February 1986 and in The Hague on 28 February 1986 are hereby repealed.

Article 51[97] **[Duration of the Treaty]**

1–060 This Treaty is concluded for an unlimited period.

Article 52[98] **[Ratification]**

1–061 1. This Treaty shall be ratified by the High Contracting Parties in accordance with their respective constitutional requirements. The instruments of ratification shall be deposited with the Government of the Italian Republic.

2. This Treaty shall enter into force on 1 January 1993, provided that all the instruments of ratification have been deposited, or, failing that, on the first day of the month following the deposit of the instrument of ratification by the last signatory state to take this step.

Article 53[99] **[Authentic versions]**

1–062 This Treaty, drawn up in a single original in the Danish, Dutch, English, French, German, Greek, Irish, Italian, Portuguese and Spanish languages, the texts in each of these languages being equally authentic, shall be deposited in the archives of the government of the Italian Republic, which will transmit a certified copy to each of the governments of the other signatory States.

Pursuant to the Accession Treaty of 1994, the Finnish and Swedish versions of this treaty shall also be authentic.

SELECTED PROTOCOLS

Protocol Annexed to the Treaty on European Union

PROTOCOL (NO. 1) ON ARTICLE [17] OF THE TREATY ON EUROPEAN UNION (1997)

The High Contracting Parties,

1–063 [1] Bearing in mind the need to implement fully the provisions of Article [17](1), second sub-paragraph, and (3) of the Treaty on European Union,

[2] Bearing in mind that the policy of the Union in accordance with Article 17 shall not prejudice the specific character of the security and defence policy of certain Member States and shall respect the obligations of certain Member States, which see their common defence realised in NATO, under the North Atlantic Treaty and be compatible with the common security and defence policy established within that framework,

Have agreed upon the following provision, which is annexed to the Treaty on European Union,

The European Union shall draw up, together with the Western European Union, arrangements for enhanced cooperation between them, within a year from the entry into force of the Treaty of Amsterdam.

[96] Formerly Art. P.

[97] Formerly Art. Q.

[98] Formerly Art. R.

[99] Formerly Art. S; second paragraph added by Treaty of Amsterdam, Art. 1(16).

PROTOCOLS ANNEXED TO THE TREATY ON EUROPEAN UNION AND THE TREATY ESTABLISHING THE EUROPEAN COMMUNITY

PROTOCOL (NO. 2) INTEGRATING THE SCHENGEN *ACQUIS* INTO THE FRAMEWORK OF THE EUROPEAN UNION (1997)

The High Contracting Parties,

[1] Noting that the Agreements on the gradual abolition of checks at common borders signed by some Member States of the European Union in Schengen on 14 June 1985 and on 19 June 1990 as well as related agreements and the rules adopted on the basis of these agreements, are aimed at enhancing European integration and, in particular, at enabling the European Union to develop more rapidly into an area of freedom, security and justice, **1–064**

[2] Desiring to incorporate the abovementioned agreements and rules into the framework of the European Union,

[3] Confirming that the provisions of the Schengen *acquis* are applicable only if and as far as they are compatible with the European Union and Community law,

[4] Taking into account the special position of Denmark,

[5] Taking into account the fact that Ireland and the United Kingdom of Great Britain and Northern Ireland are not parties to and have not signed the abovementioned agreements; that provision should, however, be made to allow those Member States to accept some or all of the provisions thereof,

[6] Recognising that, as a consequence, it is necessary to make use of the provisions of the Treaty on European Union and of the Treaty establishing the European Community concerning closer cooperation between some Member States and that those provisions should only be used as a last resort,

[7] Taking into account the need to maintain a special relationship with the Republic of Iceland and the Kingdom of Norway, both states having confirmed their intention to become bound by the provisions mentioned above, on the basis of the Agreement signed in Luxembourg on 19 December 1996,

Have agreed upon the following provisions, which shall be annexed to the Treaty on European Union and to the Treaty establishing the European Community.

Article 1 [Cooperation between contracting parties]

The Kingdom of Belgium, the Kingdom of Denmark, the Federal Republic of Germany, the Hellenic Republic, the Kingdom of Spain, the French Republic, the Italian Republic, the Grand Duchy of Luxembourg, the Kingdom of the Netherlands, the Republic of Austria, the Portuguese Republic, the Republic of Finland and the Kingdom of Sweden, signatories to the Schengen agreements, are authorised to establish closer cooperation among themselves within the scope of those agreements and related provisions, as they are listed in the Annex to this Protocol, hereinafter referred to as the "Schengen *acquis*". This cooperation shall be conducted within the institutional and legal framework of the European Union and with respect for the relevant provisions of the Treaty on European Union and of the Treaty establishing the European Community. **1–065**

Article 2 [Application of the Schengen *acquis*]

1. From the date of entry into force of the Treaty of Amsterdam,[1] the Schengen *acquis*, including the decisions of the Executive Committee established by the **1–066**

[1] Entry into force of Treaty of Amsterdam: 1 May 1999. See Declaration (No. 44) on Article 2 of the Protocol integrating the Schengen *acquis* into the framework of the European Union annexed to the Final Act of the Treaty of Amsterdam.

Schengen agreements which have been adopted before this date, shall immediately apply to the 13 Member States referred to in Article 1, without prejudice to the provisions of paragraph 2 of this Article. From the same date, the Council will substitute itself for the said Executive Committee.

The Council, acting by the unanimity of its members referred to in Article 1, shall take any measure necessary for the implementation of this paragraph. The Council, acting unanimously, shall determine, in conformity with the relevant provisions of the Treaties, the legal basis for each of the provisions or decisions which constitute the Schengen *acquis*.

With regard to such provisions and decisions and in accordance with that determination, the Court of Justice of the European Communities shall exercise the powers conferred upon it by the relevant applicable provisions of the Treaties. In any event, the Court of Justice shall have no jurisdiction on measures or decisions relating to the maintenance of law and order and the safeguarding of internal security.

As long as the measures referred to above have not been taken and without prejudice to Article 5(2), the provisions or decisions which constitute the Schengen *acquis* shall be regarded as acts based on Title VI of the Treaty on European Union.

2. The provisions of paragraph 1 shall apply to the Member States which have signed accession Protocols to the Schengen agreements, from the dates decided by the Council, acting with the unanimity of its members mentioned in Article 1, unless the conditions for the accession of any of those States to the Schengen acquis are met before the date of the entry into force of the Treaty of Amsterdam.

Article 3 [Position of Denmark]

1–067 Following the determination referred to in Article 2(1), second sub-paragraph, Denmark shall maintain the same rights and obligations in relation to the other signatories to the Schengen agreements, as before the said determination with regard to those parts of the Schengen *acquis* that are determined to have a legal basis in Title [IV] of the Treaty establishing the European Community.

With regard to those parts of the Schengen *acquis* that are determined to have legal base in Title [VI] of the Treaty on European Union, Denmark shall continue to have the same rights and obligations as the other signatories to the Schengen agreements.

Article 4 [Position of UK and Ireland]

1–068 Ireland and the United Kingdom of Great Britain and Northern Ireland, which are not bound by the Schengen *acquis*, may at any time request to take part in some or all of the provisions of this *acquis*.

The Council shall decide on the request with the unanimity of its members referred to in Article 1 and of the representative of the government of the State concerned.[2]

Article 5 [Development of *acquis*]

1–069 1. Proposals and initiatives to build upon the Schengen *acquis* shall be subject to the relevant provisions of the Treaties.

In this context, where either Ireland or the United Kingdom or both have not notified the President of the Council in writing within a reasonable period that they wish to take part, the authorisation referred to in Article [11] of the Treaty establishing the European Community or Article [40] of the Treaty on European Union shall be deemed to have been granted to the Member States referred to in

[2] See Declaration (No. 45) on Article 4 of the Protocol integrating the Schengen *acquis* into the framework of the European Union annexed to the Final Act of the Treaty of Amsterdam.

Article 1 and to Ireland or the United Kingdom where either of them wishes to take part in the areas of cooperation in question.

2. The relevant provisions of the Treaties referred to in the first sub-paragraph of paragraph 1 shall apply even if the Council has not adopted the measures referred to in Article 2(1), second sub-paragraph.[3]

Article 6 [Association of Iceland and Norway]

The Republic of Iceland and the Kingdom of Norway shall be associated with the implementation of the Schengen *acquis* and its further development on the basis of the Agreement signed in Luxembourg on 19 December 1996. Appropriate procedures shall be agreed to that effect in an agreement to be concluded with those states by the Council, acting by the unanimity of its members mentioned in Article 1. Such agreement shall include provisions on the contribution of Iceland and Norway to any financial consequences resulting from the implementation of this protocol. **1–070**

A separate agreement shall be concluded with Iceland and Norway by the Council, acting unanimously, for the establishment of rights and obligations between Ireland and the United Kingdom of Great Britain and Northern Ireland on the one hand, and Iceland and Norway on the other, in domains of the Schengen *acquis* which apply to these States.[4]

Article 7 [Schengen secretariat]

The Council shall, acting by a qualified majority, adopt the detailed arrangements for the integration of the Schengen Secretariat into the General Secretariat of the Council. **1–071**

Article 8 [Accession of new EU Member States]

For the purposes of the negotiations for the admission of new Member States into the European Union, the Schengen *acquis* and further measures taken by the institutions within its scope shall be regarded as an *acquis* which must be accepted in full by all States candidates for admission. **1–072**

ANNEX—SCHENGEN ACQUIS

1. The Agreement, signed in Schengen on 14 June 1985 between the governments of the states of the Benelux Economic Union, the Federal Republic of Germany and the French Republic on the gradual abolition of checks at their common borders. **1–073**

2. The Convention, signed in Schengen on 19 June 19 1990 between the Kingdom of Belgium, the Federal Republic of Germany, the French Republic, the Grand Duchy of Luxembourg and the Kingdom of the Netherlands, implementing the Agreement on the gradual abolition of checks at their common borders, signed in Schengen on 14 June 1985 with related Final Act and common declarations.

3. The Accession Protocols and Agreements to the 1985 Agreement and the 1990 Implementation Convention with Italy (signed in Paris on 27 November 1990), Spain and Portugal (signed in Bonn on 25 June 1991), Greece (signed in Madrid on 6 November 1992), Austria (signed in Brussels on 28 April 1995) and Denmark, Finland and Sweden (signed in Luxembourg on 19 December 1996), with related Final Acts and declarations.

[3] See Declaration (No. 46) on Article 5 of the Protocol integrating the Schengen *acquis* into the framework of the European Union annexed to the Final Act of the Treaty of Amsterdam.

[4] See Declaration (No. 47) on Article 6 of the Protocol integrating the Schengen *acquis* into the framework of the European Union annexed to the Final Act of the Treaty of Amsterdam.

4. Decisions and declarations adopted by the Executive Committee established by the 1990 Implementation Convention, as well as acts adopted for the implementation of the Convention by the organs upon which the Executive Committee has conferred decision making powers.

PROTOCOL (NO. 3) ON THE APPLICATION OF CERTAIN ASPECTS OF ARTICLE [14] OF THE TREATY ESTABLISHING THE EUROPEAN COMMUNITY TO THE UNITED KINGDOM AND TO IRELAND (1997)

The High Contracting Parties,

1–074 [1] Desiring to settle certain questions relating to the United Kingdom and Ireland,

[2] Having regard to the existence for many years of special travel arrangements between the United Kingdom and Ireland,

Have agreed upon the following provisions, which shall be annexed to the Treaty establishing the European Community and to the Treaty on European Union.

Article 1 [Preservation of UK border controls]

1–075 The United Kingdom shall be entitled, notwithstanding Article [14] of the Treaty establishing the European Community, any other provision of that Treaty or of the Treaty on European Union, any measure adopted under those Treaties, or any international agreement concluded by the Community or by the Community and its Member States with one or more third States, to exercise at its frontiers with other Member States such controls on persons seeking to enter the United Kingdom as it may consider necessary for the purpose:

(a) of verifying the right to enter the United Kingdom of citizens of States which are contracting parties to the Agreement on the European Economic Area and of their dependants exercising rights conferred by Community law, as well as citizens of other States on whom such rights have been conferred by an agreement by which the United Kingdom is bound; and

(b) of determining whether or not to grant other persons permission to enter the United Kingdom.

Nothing in Article [14] of the Treaty establishing the European Community or in any other provision of that Treaty or of the Treaty on European Union or in any measure adopted under them shall prejudice the right of the United Kingdom to adopt or exercise any such controls. References to the United Kingdom in this Article shall include territories for whose external relations the United Kingdom is responsible.

Article 2 [UK–Irish common travel area]

1–076 The United Kingdom and Ireland may continue to make arrangements between themselves relating to the movement of persons between their territories ("the Common Travel Area"), while fully respecting the rights of persons referred to in Article 1, first paragraph, point (a) of this Protocol. Accordingly, as long as they maintain such arrangements, the provisions of Article 1 of this Protocol shall apply to Ireland under the same terms and conditions as for the United Kingdom. Nothing in Article [14] of the Treaty establishing the European Community, in any other provision of that Treaty or of the Treaty on European Union or in any measure adopted under them, shall affect any such arrangements.

Article 3 [Entry into the rest of the EU from UK or Ireland]

1–077 The other Member States shall be entitled to exercise at their frontiers or at any point of entry into their territory such controls on persons seeking to enter their territory from the United Kingdom or any territories whose external relations are under its responsibility for the same purposes stated in Article 1 of this Protocol, or from Ireland as long as the provisions of Article 1 of this Protocol apply to Ireland.

Nothing in Article [14] of the Treaty establishing the European Community or in any other provision of that Treaty or of the Treaty on European Union or in any measure adopted under them shall prejudice the right of the other Member States to adopt or exercise any such controls.

PROTOCOL (NO. 4) ON THE POSITION OF THE UNITED KINGDOM AND IRELAND (1997)

The High Contracting Parties,

[1] Desiring to settle certain questions relating to the United Kingdom and Ireland, **1–078**

[2] Having regard to the Protocol on the application of certain aspects of Article [14] of the Treaty establishing the European Community to the United Kingdom and to Ireland,

Have agreed upon the following provisions which shall be annexed to the Treaty establishing the European Community and to the Treaty on European Union.

Article 1 [UK and Irish position on visa, asylum etc. policies]

Subject to Article 3, the United Kingdom and Ireland shall not take part in the adoption by the Council of proposed measures pursuant to Title IV of the Treaty establishing the European Community. By way of derogation from Article [205(2)] of the Treaty establishing the European Community, a qualified majority shall be defined as the same proportion of the weighted votes of the members of the Council concerned as laid down in the said Article [205(2)]. The unanimity of the members of the Council, with the exception of the representatives of the governments of the United Kingdom and Ireland, shall be necessary for decisions of the Council which must be adopted unanimously. **1–079**

Article 2 [Exclusion of UK and Ireland from measures]

In consequence of Article 1 and subject to Articles 3, 4 and 6, none of the provisions of Title IV of the Treaty establishing the European Community, no measure adopted pursuant to that Title, no provision of any international agreement concluded by the Community pursuant to that Title, and no decision of the Court of Justice interpreting any such provision or measure shall be binding upon or applicable in the United Kingdom or Ireland; and no such provision, measure or decision shall in any way affect the competences, rights and obligations of those States; and no such provision, measure or decision shall in any way affect the *acquis communautaire* nor form part of Community law as they apply to the United Kingdom or Ireland. **1–080**

Article 3 [Procedure for UK or Irish participation in measures]

1. The United Kingdom or Ireland may notify the President of the Council in writing, within three months after a proposal or initiative has been presented to the Council pursuant to Title IV of the Treaty establishing the European Community, that it wishes to take part in the adoption and application of any such proposed measure, whereupon that State shall be entitled to do so. By way of derogation from Article [205(2)] of the Treaty establishing the European Community, a qualified majority shall be defined as the same proportion of the weighted votes of the members of the Council concerned as laid down in the said Article [205(2)]. **1–081**

The unanimity of the members of the Council, with the exception of a member which has not made such a notification, shall be necessary for decisions of the Council which must be adopted unanimously. A measure adopted under this paragraph shall be binding upon all Member States which took part in its adoption.

2. If after a reasonable period of time a measure referred to in paragraph 1 cannot be adopted with the United Kingdom or Ireland taking part, the Council may adopt such measure in accordance with Article 1 without the participation of the United Kingdom or Ireland. In that case Article 2 applies.

Article 4 [Participation in measures once adopted]

1–082 The United Kingdom or Ireland may at any time after the adoption of a measure by the Council pursuant to Title [IV] of the Treaty establishing the European Community notify its intention to the Council and to the Commission that it wishes to accept that measure. In that case, the procedure provided for in Article [11(3)] of the Treaty establishing the European Community shall apply *mutatis mutandis*.

Article 5 [Financial implications of measures]

1–083 A Member State which is not bound by a measure adopted pursuant to Title [IV] of the Treaty establishing the European Community shall bear no financial consequences of that measure other than administrative costs entailed for the institutions.

Article 6 [Application of the EC Treaty]

1–084 Where, in cases referred to in this Protocol, the United Kingdom or Ireland is bound by a measure adopted by the Council pursuant to Title [IV] of the Treaty establishing the European Community, the relevant provisions of that Treaty, including Article [68],[5] shall apply to that State in relation to that measure.

Article 7 [Relationship to Schengen acquis]

1–085 Articles 3 and 4 shall be without prejudice to the Protocol integrating the Schengen *acquis* into the framework of the European Union.

Article 8 [Procedure for Ireland to disapply Protocol]

Ireland may notify the President of the Council in writing that it no longer wishes to be covered by the terms of this Protocol. In that case, the normal Treaty provisions will apply to Ireland.

PROTOCOL (NO. 5) ON THE POSITION OF DENMARK (1997)

The High Contracting Parties,

1–086 [1] Recalling the Decision of the Heads of State or Government, meeting within the European Council at Edinburgh on 12 December 1992 concerning certain problems raised by Denmark on the Treaty on European Union,

[2] Having noted the position of Denmark with regard to Citizenship, Economic and Monetary Union, Defence Policy and Justice and Home Affairs as laid down in the Edinburgh Decision,

[5] Art. 68 EC establishes the jurisdiction of the ECJ to hand down preliminary rulings on measures adopted under the EC visas, asylum, immigration and other policies related to free movement of persons.

[3] Bearing in mind Article 3 of the Protocol integrating the Schengen *acquis* into the framework of the European Union,

Have agreed upon the following provisions, which shall be annexed to the Treaty establishing the European Community and to the Treaty on European Union.

PART I

Article 1 [Position of Denmark on visa, asylum, etc. policy]

Denmark shall not take part in the adoption by the Council of proposed measures pursuant to Title [IV] of the Treaty establishing the European Community. By way of derogation from Article [205(2)] of the Treaty establishing the European Community, a qualified majority shall be defined as the same proportion of the weighted votes of the members of the Council concerned as laid down in the said Article [205(2)]. The unanimity of the members of the Council, with the exception of the representative of the Government of Denmark, shall be necessary for the decisions of the Council which must be adopted unanimously. **1–087**

Article 2 [Denmark excluded from application of measures]

None of the provisions of Title [IV] of the Treaty establishing the European Community, no measure adopted pursuant to that Title, no provision of any international agreement concluded by the Community pursuant to that Title, and no decision of the Court of Justice interpreting any such provision or measure shall be binding upon or applicable in Denmark; and no such provision, measure or decision shall in any way affect the competences, rights and obligations of Denmark; and no such provision, measure or decision shall in any way affect the *acquis communautaire* nor form part of Community law as they apply to Denmark. **1–088**

Article 3 [Financial implications of measures]

Denmark shall bear no financial consequences of measures referred to in Article 1, other than administrative costs entailed for the institutions. **1–089**

Article 4 [Third country nationals to possess visa; common format]

Articles 1, 2 and 3 shall not apply to measures determining the third countries whose nationals must be in possession of a visa when crossing the external borders of the Member States, or measures relating to a uniform format for visas. **1–090**

Article 5 [Procedures for implementing measures developing Schengen *acquis*]

1. Denmark shall decide within a period of six months after the Council has decided on a proposal or initiative to build upon the Schengen *acquis* under the provisions of Title [IV] of the Treaty establishing the European Community, whether it will implement this decision in its national law. If it decides to do so, this decision will create an obligation under international law between Denmark and the other Member States referred to in Article 1 of the Protocol integrating the Schengen *acquis* into the framework of the European Union as well as Ireland or the United Kingdom if those Member States take part in the areas of cooperation in question. **1–091**

2. If Denmark decides not to implement a decision of the Council as referred to in paragraph 1, the Member States referred to in Article 1 of the Protocol integrating the Schengen *acquis* into the framework of the European Union will consider appropriate measures to be taken.

Part II

Article 6 **[Denmark outside CFSP actions involving defence]**

1–092 With regard to measures adopted by the Council in the field of Articles [13(1)] and [17] of the Treaty on European Union, Denmark does not participate in the elaboration and the implementation of decisions and actions of the Union which have defence implications, but will not prevent the development of closer cooperation between Member States in this area. Therefore, Denmark shall not participate in their adoption. Denmark shall not be obliged to contribute to the financing of operational expenditure arising from such measures.

Part III

Article 7 **[Future position of Denmark]**

1–093 At any time Denmark may, in accordance with its constitutional requirements, inform the other member states that it no longer wishes to avail itself of all or part of this protocol. In that event, Denmark will apply in full all relevant measures then in force taken within the framework of the European Union.

Protocols Annexed to the Treaty on European Union and the Treaties Establishing the European Community, the European Coal and Steel Community and the European Atomic Energy Community

PROTOCOL (NO. 6) ANNEXED TO THE TREATY ON EUROPEAN UNION AND TO THE TREATIES ESTABLISHING THE EUROPEAN COMMUNITIES (1992)

1–094 *The High Contracting Parties,*
Have agreed upon the following provision, which shall be annexed to the Treaty on European Union and to the treaties establishing the European Communities:

Nothing in the Treaty on European Union, or in the Treaties establishing the European Communities, or in the Treaties or acts modifying or supplementing those treaties, shall affect the application in Ireland of Article 40.3.3 of the Constitution of Ireland.[6]

PROTOCOL (NO. 8) ON THE LOCATION OF THE SEATS OF THE INSTITUTIONS AND OF CERTAIN BODIES AND DEPARTMENTS OF THE EUROPEAN COMMUNITIES AND OF EUROPOL (1997)

The Representatives of the Governments of the Member States,

1–095 [1] Having regard to Article [289] of the Treaty establishing the European Community, Article 77 of the Treaty establishing the European Coal and Steel Community and Article 189 of the Treaty establishing the European Atomic Energy Community,

[2] Having regard to the Treaty on European Union,

[3] Recalling and confirming the Decision of 8 April 1965 and without prejudice to the decisions concerning the seat of future institutions, bodies and departments,

[6] Subsequent to the signature of the Union Treaty, the High Contracting Parties agreed a declaration giving the following legal interpretation to the above Protocol: "that it was and is their intention that the protocol shall not limit freedom to travel between member states or, in accordance with conditions which may be laid down, in conformity with Community law, by Irish legislation, to obtain or make available in Ireland information relating to services lawfully available in member states". At the same time the high contracting parties solemnly declared: "that, in the event of a future constitutional amendment in Ireland which concerns the subject matter of Article 40.3.3 of the Constitution of Ireland and which does not conflict with the intention of the High Contracting Parties hereinbefore expressed, they will, following the entry into force of the Treaty on European Union, be favourably disposed to amending the said Protocol so as to extend its application to such constitutional amendment if Ireland so requests".

Have agreed upon the following provisions, which shall be annexed to the Treaty on European Union and the Treaties establishing the European Communities.

Sole Article

(a) The European Parliament shall have its seat in Strasbourg where the 12 periods of monthly plenary sessions, including the budget session, shall be held. The periods of additional plenary sessions shall be held in Brussels. The committees of the European Parliament shall meet in Brussels. The General Secretariat of the European Parliament and its departments shall remain in Luxembourg. **1–096**
(b) The Council shall have its seat in Brussels. During the months of April, June and October, the Council shall hold its meetings in Luxembourg.
(c) The Commission shall have its seat in Brussels. The departments listed in Articles 7, 8 and 9 of the Decision of 8 April 1965 shall be established in Luxembourg.
(d) The Court of Justice and the Court of First Instance shall have their seats in Luxembourg.
(e) The Court of Auditors shall have its seat in Luxembourg.
(f) The Economic and Social Committee shall have its seat in Brussels.
(g) The Committee of the Regions shall have its seat in Brussels.
(h) The European Investment Bank shall have its seat in Luxembourg.
(i) The European Monetary Institute and the European Central Bank shall have their seat in Frankfurt.
(j) The European Police Office (Europol) shall have its seat in The Hague.

PROTOCOL (NO. 9) ON THE ROLE OF NATIONAL PARLIAMENTS IN THE EUROPEAN UNION (1997)

The High Contracting Parties,

[1] Recalling that scrutiny by individual national parliaments of their own government in relation to the activities of the Union is a matter for the particular constitutional organisation and practice of each Member State, **1–097**

[2] Desiring, however, to encourage greater involvement of national parliaments in the activities of the European Union and to enhance their ability to express their views on matters which may be of particular interest to them,

Have agreed upon the following provisions, which shall be annexed to the Treaty on European Union and the treaties establishing the European Communities.

I. INFORMATION FOR NATIONAL PARLIAMENTS OF MEMBER STATES

1. All Commission consultation documents (green and white papers and communications) shall be promptly forwarded to national parliaments of the Member States.

2. Commission proposals for legislation as defined by the Council in accordance with Article [207(3)] of the Treaty establishing the European Community, shall be made available in good time so that the government of each Member State may ensure that its own national parliament receives them as appropriate.

3. A six-week period shall elapse between a legislative proposal or a proposal for a measure to be adopted under Title [VI] of the Treaty on European Union being made available in all languages to the European Parliament and the Council by the Commission and the date when it is placed on a Council agenda for decision either for the adoption of an act or for adoption of a common position pursuant to Article [251] or [252] of the Treaty establishing the European Community, subject

to exceptions on grounds of urgency, the reasons for which shall be stated in the act or common position.

II. THE CONFERENCE OF EUROPEAN AFFAIRS COMMITTEES

4. The Conference of European Affairs Committees, hereinafter referred to as COSAC, established in Paris on 16–17 November 1989 may make any contribution it deems appropriate for the attention of the institutions of the European Union, in particular on the basis of draft legal texts which representatives of governments of the Member States may decide by common accord to forward to it, in view of the nature of their subject-matter.

5. COSAC may examine any legislative proposal or initiative in relation to the establishment of an area of freedom, security and justice which might have a direct bearing on the rights and freedoms of individuals. The European Parliament, the Council and the Commission shall be informed of any contribution made by COSAC under this point.

6. COSAC may address to the European Parliament, the Council and the Commission any contribution which it deems appropriate on the legislative activities of the Union, notably in relation to the application of the principle of subsidiarity, the area of freedom, security and justice as well as questions regarding fundamental rights.

7. Contributions made by COSAC shall in no way bind national parliaments or prejudge their position.

Protocol Annexed by the Treaty of Nice to the Treaty on European Union and to the Treaties Establishing the European Communities

PROTOCOL ON THE ENLARGEMENT OF THE EUROPEAN UNION

(Not reproduced here—for full text see Treaty establishing the European Community)

Protocol Annexed by the Treaty of Nice to the Treaty on European Union, to the Treaty Establishing the European Community and to the Treaty Establishing the European Atomic Energy Community

PROTOCOL ON THE STATUTE OF THE COURT OF JUSTICE

(Not reproduced here—for full text see Treaty establishing the European Community)

CHAPTER 2

TREATY ESTABLISHING THE EUROPEAN COMMUNITY

(25 March 1957)

([2002] OJ C325/33)

[**Editorial note**—The text reproduced below is the published consolidated version of the Treaty of Rome of 25 March 1957, as subsequently amended, *inter alia*, by the Single European Act ("SEA") (with effect from 1 July 1987), the Treaty on European Union ("Union Treaty") (with effect from 1 November 1993), the Treaty of Amsterdam (with effect from 1 May 1999), the Treaty of Nice (with effect from 1 February 2003) and the Acts of Accession of Denmark, Ireland and the UK (with effect from 1 January 1973), Greece (with effect from 1 January 1981), Spain and Portugal (with effect from 1 January 1986) and Austria, Finland and Sweden (with effect from 1 January 1995).

The Treaty establishing the European Economic Community was amended by the Union Treaty in order to establish the European Community, so that, *inter alia*, the term "European Economic Community" was replaced throughout by the term "European Community" (Union Treaty, Art. 8).

The provisions of the EC Treaty were renumbered by virtue of the Treaty of Amsterdam, Art. 12(1) and Annex. References in those provisions to Articles, Titles and Sections of both the Union Treaty and the EC Treaty itself have been adapted accordingly (Treaty of Amsterdam, Art. 12(2)). Each Article of the EC Treaty set out below is accompanied by an editorial note indicating the previous numbering of the provision, if different, and its history. In other provisions such as Protocols and Declarations, references to Articles, Titles and Sections of both the Union Treaty and the EC Treaty have been adapted to reflect the renumbering (Treaty of Amsterdam, Art. 12(3)).]

His Majesty the King of the Belgians, the President of the Federal Republic of Germany, the President of the French Republic, the President of the Italian Republic, Her Royal Highness the Grand Duchess of Luxembourg, Her Majesty the Queen of the Netherlands, **2–001**

[1] Determined to lay the foundations of an ever closer union among the peoples of Europe,

[2] Resolved to ensure the economic and social progress of their countries by common action to eliminate the barriers which divide Europe,

[3] Affirming as the essential objective of their efforts the constant improvement of the living and working conditions of their peoples,

[4] Recognising that the removal of existing obstacles calls for concerted action in order to guarantee steady expansion, balanced trade and fair competition,

[5] Anxious to strengthen the unity of their economies and to ensure their harmonious development by reducing the differences existing between the various regions and the backwardness of the less favoured regions,

[6] Desiring to contribute, by means of a common commercial policy, to the progressive abolition of restrictions on international trade,

[7] Intending to confirm the solidarity which binds Europe and the overseas countries and desiring to ensure the development of their prosperity, in accordance with the principles of the Charter of the United Nations,

[8] Resolved by thus pooling their resources to preserve and strengthen peace and liberty, and calling upon the other peoples of Europe who share their ideal to join in their efforts,

[9] Determined to promote the development of the highest possible level of knowledge for their peoples through a wide access to education and through its continuous updating,[1]

Have decided to create a European Community and to this end have designated as their plenipotentiaries:

[Designation of plenipotentiaries omitted]

---

[1] Ninth recital inserted by Treaty of Amsterdam, Art. 2(1).

Who, having exchanged their full powers, found in good and due form, *have agreed as follows*:

Part One—Principles

Article 1 [Establishment of the EC]

2–002 By this Treaty, the High Contracting Parties establish among themselves a European Community.

Article 2[2] [Tasks of the EC]

2–003 The Community shall have as its task, by establishing a common market and an economic and monetary union and by implementing common policies or activities referred to in Articles 3 and 4, to promote throughout the Community a harmonious, balanced and sustainable development of economic activities, a high level of employment and of social protection, equality between men and women, sustainable and non-inflationary growth, a high degree of competitiveness and convergence of economic performance, a high level of protection and improvement of the quality of the environment, the raising of the standard of living and quality of life, and economic and social cohesion and solidarity among Member States.

Article 3 [Activities of the EC]

2–004 1. For the purposes set out in Article 2, the activities of the Community shall include, as provided in this Treaty and in accordance with the timetable set out therein:

(a) the prohibition, as between Member States, of customs duties and quantitative restrictions on the import and export of goods, and of all other measures having equivalent effect;
(b) a common commercial policy;
(c) an internal market characterised by the abolition, as between Member States, of obstacles to the free movement of goods, persons, services and capital;
(c) measures concerning the entry and movement of persons as provided for in Title IV;
(d) a common policy in the sphere of agriculture and fisheries;
(e) a common policy in the sphere of transport;
(f) a system ensuring that competition in the internal market is not distorted;
(g) the approximation of the laws of Member States to the extent required for the functioning of the common market;
(h) the promotion of co-ordination between employment policies of the Member States with a view to enhancing their effectiveness by developing a coordinated strategy for employment;
(i) a policy in the social sphere comprising a European Social Fund;
(j) the strengthening of economic and social cohesion;
(k) a policy in the sphere of the environment;
(l) the strengthening of the competitiveness of Community industry;
(m) the promotion of research and technological development;
(n) encouragement for the establishment and development of trans-European networks;
(o) a contribution to the attainment of a high level of health protection;
(p) a contribution to education and training of quality and to the flowering of the cultures of the Member States;
(q) a policy in the sphere of development cooperation;
(r) the association of the overseas countries and territories in order to increase trade and promote jointly economic and social development;

---

[2] Article 2 replaced by Treaty of Amsterdam, Art. 2(2).

(s) a contribution to the strengthening of consumer protection;
(t) measures in the spheres of energy, civil protection and tourism.[3]

2. In all the activities referred to in this Article, the Community shall aim to eliminate inequalities, and to promote equality, between men and women.[4]

Article 4[5] **[EC economic policy]**

1. For the purposes set out in Article 2, the activities of the Member States and the Community shall include, as provided in this Treaty and in accordance with the timetable set out therein, the adoption of an economic policy which is based on the close co-ordination of Member States' economic policies, on the internal market and on the definition of common objectives, and conducted in accordance with the principle of an open market economy with free competition. **2–005**

2. Concurrently with the foregoing, and as provided in this Treaty and in accordance with the timetable and the procedures set out therein, these activities shall include the irrevocable fixing of exchange rates leading to the introduction of a single currency, the ECU,[6] and the definition and conduct of a single monetary policy and exchange-rate policy the primary objective of both of which shall be to maintain price stability and, without prejudice to this objective, to support the general economic policies in the Community, in accordance with the principle of an open market economy with free competition.[7]

3. These activities of the Member States and the Community shall entail compliance with the following guiding principles: stable prices, sound public finances and monetary conditions and a sustainable balance of payments.

Article 5[8] **[Subsidiarity and proportionality]**

The Community shall act within the limits of the powers conferred upon it by this Treaty and of the objectives assigned to it therein. **2–006**

In areas which do not fall within its exclusive competence, the Community shall take action, in accordance with the principle of subsidiarity, only if and insofar as the objectives of the proposed action cannot be sufficiently achieved by the Member States and can therefore, by reason of the scale or effects of the proposed action, be better achieved by the Community. Any action by the Community shall not go beyond what is necessary to achieve the objectives of this Treaty.[9]

Article 6[10] **[Integration of environmental protection into EC policies]**

Environmental protection requirements must be integrated into the definition and implementation of the Community policies and activities referred to in Article 3, in particular with a view to promoting sustainable development.[11] **2–007**

---

[3] Article 3, as replaced by Art. 8(B)(3) TEU, renumbered as Art. 3(1) by Treaty of Amsterdam, Art. 2(3)(a); Art. 3(1)(a) amended by Treaty of Amsterdam, Art. 6(I)(1); and Art. 3(1)(d) replaced, Art. 3(1)(i) added, Art. 3(1)(j)–(u) renumbered by Treaty of Amsterdam, Art. 2(3)(b)–(d).

[4] Article 3(2) added by Treaty of Amsterdam, Art. 2(3)(e).

[5] Formerly Art. 3a, originally inserted by Art. 8(4) TEU.

[6] References to the ECU in all legal instruments replaced by references to the euro from 1 January 1999 (Regulation 1103/97, OJ 1997 L162/1).

[7] Art. 4(2) does not apply to the UK (see Protocol (No. 25) on certain provisions relating to the UK, Art. 5).

[8] Formerly Art. 3b, originally inserted by Art. 8(5) TEU.

[9] See Protocol (No. 30) on the application of the principles of subsidiarity and proportionality (1997).

[10] Formerly Art. 3c, inserted by Treaty of Amsterdam, Art. 2(4).

[11] See Declaration (No. 12) on environmental impact assessments annexed to the Final Act of the Treaty of Amsterdam.

Article 7[12] **[EC Institutions]**

2–008 1. The tasks entrusted to the Community shall be carried out by the following institutions:
— a EUROPEAN PARLIAMENT,
— a COUNCIL,[13]
— a COMMISSION,
— a COURT OF JUSTICE,
— a COURT OF AUDITORS.

Each institution shall act within the limits of the powers conferred upon it by this Treaty.

2. The Council and the Commission shall be assisted by an Economic and Social Committee and a Committee of the Regions acting in an advisory capacity.

Article 8[14] **[Establishment of ESCB]**

2–009 A European System of Central Banks (hereinafter referred to as "ESCB") and a European Central Bank (hereinafter referred to as "ECB") shall be established in accordance with the procedures laid down in this Treaty; they shall act within the limits of the powers conferred upon them by this Treaty and by the Statute of the ESCB and of the ECB (hereinafter referred to as "Statute of the ESCB") annexed thereto.[15]

Article 9[16] **[Establishment of EIB]**

2–010 A European Investment Bank is hereby established, which shall act within the limits of the powers conferred upon it by this Treaty and the Statute annexed thereto.[17]

Article 10[18] **[Member States' obligations of sincere cooperation]**

2–011 Member States shall take all appropriate measures, whether general or particular, to ensure fulfilment of the obligations arising out of this Treaty or resulting from action taken by the institutions of the Community. They shall facilitate the achievement of the Community's tasks. They shall abstain from any measure which could jeopardise the attainment of the objectives of this Treaty.

Article 11[19] **[Enhanced cooperation]**

2–012 1. Member States which intend to establish enhanced cooperation between themselves in one of the areas referred to in this Treaty shall address a request to the Commission, which may submit a proposal to the Council to that effect. In the event of the Commission not submitting a proposal, it shall inform the Member States concerned of the reasons for not doing so.

2. Authorisation to establish enhanced cooperation as referred to in paragraph 1 shall be granted, in compliance with Articles 43 to 45 of the Treaty on European Union, by the Council, acting by a qualified majority on a proposal from the Commission and after consulting the European Parliament. When enhanced

[12] Formerly Art. 4, replaced by Art. 8(6) TEU.
[13] Council restyled as "Council of the European Union" by Council Decision 93/951 (OJ 1993 L281/18).
[14] Formerly Art. 4a, inserted by Art. 8(7) TEU.
[15] See Protocol (No. 18) on the Statute of the ECSB and of the ECB (1992).
[16] Formerly Art. 4b, inserted by Art. 8(8) TEU.
[17] Protocol (No. 10) on the Statute of the EIB (1957) (not reproduced in this volume).
[18] Formerly Art. 5.
[19] Article 11 replaced by Arts 11 and 11a by virtue of Treaty of Nice, Art. 2(1). Formerly Art. 5a, inserted by Treaty of Amsterdam, Art. 2(5).

cooperation relates to an area covered by the procedure referred to in Article 251 of this Treaty, the assent of the European Parliament shall be required.

A member of the Council may request that the matter be referred to the European Council. After that matter has been raised before the European Council, the Council may act in accordance with the first subparagraph of this paragraph.

3. The acts and decisions necessary for the implementation of enhanced cooperation activities shall be subject to all the relevant provisions of this Treaty, save as otherwise provided in this Article and in Articles 43 to 45 of the Treaty on European Union.

Article 11a[20] **[Enhanced cooperation authorisation procedure]**

Any Member State which wishes to participate in enhanced cooperation established in accordance with Article 11 shall notify its intention to the Council and to the Commission, which shall give an opinion to the Council within three months of the date of receipt of that notification. Within four months of the date of receipt of that notification, the Commission shall take a decision on it, and on such specific arrangements as it may deem necessary. **2–013**

Article 12[21] **[Discrimination based on nationality prohibited]**

Within the scope of application of this Treaty, and without prejudice to any special provisions contained therein, any discrimination on grounds of nationality shall be prohibited. **2–014**

The Council, acting in accordance with the procedure referred to in Article 251, may adopt rules designed to prohibit such discrimination.[22]

Article 13[23] **[Power to deal with other forms of discrimination]**

1. Without prejudice to the other provisions of this Treaty and within the limits of the powers conferred by it upon the Community, the Council, acting unanimously on a proposal from the Commission and after consulting the European Parliament, may take appropriate action to combat discrimination based on sex, racial or ethnic origin, religion or belief, disability, age or sexual orientation. **2–015**

2. By way of derogation from paragraph 1, when the Council adopts Community incentive measures, excluding any harmonisation of the laws and regulations of the Member States, to support action taken by the Member States in order to contribute to the achievement of the objectives referred to in paragraph 1, it shall act in accordance with the procedure referred to in Article 251.

Article 14[24] **[Establishment of internal market]**

1. The Community shall adopt measures with the aim of progressively establishing the internal market over a period expiring on 31 December 1992, in accordance with the provisions of this Article and of Articles 15, 26, 47(2), 49, 80, 93 and 95 and without prejudice to the other provisions of this Treaty. **2–016**

---

[20] Article 11 replaced by Arts 11 and 11a by virtue of Treaty of Nice, Art. 2(1).

[21] Formerly Art. 6; previously renumbered as Art. 6 EC by Art. 8(8) TEU, previously being Art. 7 EEC. See Art. 86 below for application to public undertakings.

[22] Former Art. 6, second paragraph, replaced by Treaty of Amsterdam, Art. 2(6); previously replaced by Art. 8(8) TEU.

[23] Article 13 renumbered as Art. 13(1) and Art. 13(2) added by Treaty of Nice, Art. 2(2). Formerly Art. 6a, inserted by Treaty of Amsterdam, Art. 2(7).

[24] Formerly Art. 7a; former Art. 7a(1) and (2) numbered and Art. 7a(3) added by Treaty of Amsterdam, Art. 6(I)(3)(a) and (c) respectively. References to repealed provisions of EC Treaty deleted by Treaty of Amsterdam, Art. 6(I)(3)(b). Former Art. 7a EC was renumbered by Art. 8(9) TEU, previously being Art. 8a EEC. Original Art. 8a inserted by Art. 13 SEA. See further Protocol (No. 3) on the application of certain aspects of Article [14] to the UK and Ireland.

2. The internal market shall comprise an area without internal frontiers in which the free movement of goods, persons, services and capital is ensured in accordance with the provisions of this Treaty.

3. The Council, acting by a qualified majority on a proposal from the Commission, shall determine the guidelines and conditions necessary to ensure balanced progress in all the sectors concerned.

Article 15[25] **[Differential progress towards internal market]**

2–017 When drawing up its proposals with a view to achieving the objectives set out in Article 14, the Commission shall take into account the extent of the effort that certain economies showing differences in development will have to sustain during the period of establishment of the internal market and it may propose appropriate provisions.

If these provisions take the form of derogations, they must be of a temporary nature and must cause the least possible disturbance to the functioning of the common market.

Article 16[26] **[Position of services of general economic interest]**

2–018 Without prejudice to Articles 73, 86 and 87, and given the place occupied by services of general economic interest in the shared values of the Union as well as their role in promoting social and territorial cohesion, the Community and the Member States, each within their respective powers, and within the scope of application of this Treaty, shall take care that such services operate on the basis of principles and conditions which enable them to fulfil their missions.[27]

Part Two—Citizenship of the Union

Article 17[28] **[EU citizenship established]**

2–019 1. Citizenship of the Union is hereby established. Every person holding the nationality of a Member State[29] shall be a citizen of the Union. Citizenship of the Union shall complement and not replace national citizenship.

2. Citizens of the Union shall enjoy the rights conferred by this Treaty and shall be subject to the duties imposed thereby.

Article 18[30] **[Right of free movement and residence]**

2–020 1. Every citizen of the Union shall have the right to move and reside freely within the territory of the Member States, subject to the limitations and conditions laid down in this Treaty and by the measures adopted to give it effect.[31]

---

[25] Formerly Art. 7c; previously Art. 8c EEC, renumbered by Art. 8(9) TEU. Original Art. 8c inserted by Art. 15 SEA.

[26] Formerly Art. 7d, originally inserted by Treaty of Amsterdam, Art. 2(8).

[27] See Declaration (No. 13) on Article [16] of the Treaty establishing the European Community annexed to the Final Act of the Treaty of Amsterdam.

[28] Formerly Art. 8. Former Art. 8(1) amended by Treaty of Amsterdam, Art. 2(9). Former Art. 8 originally inserted by Art. 8(C) TEU.

[29] See Declaration (No. 2) on nationality of a Member State annexed to the Final Act of the Treaty on European Union: "The Conference declares that, wherever in the Treaty establishing the European Community reference is made to nationals of the Member States, the question whether an individual possesses the nationality of a Member State shall be settled solely by reference to the national law of the Member State concerned. Member States may declare, for information, who are to be considered their nationals for Community purposes by way of declaration lodged with the Presidency and may amend any such declaration when necessary."

[30] Article 18 replaced by Treaty of Nice, Art. 2(3). Formerly Art. 8a. Former Art. 8a(2) replaced by Treaty of Amsterdam, Art. 2(10). Former Art. 8A originally inserted by Art. 8(C) TEU.

[31] Act of Accession of Austria, Finland and Sweden, Art. 70, 87 and 114 ([1994] O.J. C241) imposes limitation on acquisition of secondary residences.

2. If action by the Community should prove necessary to attain this objective and this Treaty has not provided the necessary powers, the Council may adopt provisions with a view to facilitating the exercise of the rights referred to in paragraph 1. The Council shall act in accordance with the procedure referred to in Article 251.

3. Paragraph 2 shall not apply to provisions on passports, identity cards, residence permits or any other such document or to provisions on social security or social protection.

Article 19[32] **[Electoral rights]**

1. Every citizen of the Union residing in a Member State of which he is not a national shall have the right to vote and to stand as a candidate at municipal elections in the Member State in which he resides, under the same conditions as nationals of that State. This right shall be exercised subject to detailed arrangements adopted by the Council, acting unanimously on a proposal from the Commission and after consulting the European Parliament; these arrangements may provide for derogations where warranted by problems specific to a Member State. **2–021**

2. Without prejudice to Article 190(4) and to the provisions adopted for its implementation, every citizen of the Union residing in a Member State of which he is not a national shall have the right to vote and to stand as a candidate in elections to the European Parliament in the Member State in which he resides, under the same conditions as nationals of that State. This right shall be exercised subject to detailed arrangements adopted by the Council, acting unanimously on a proposal from the Commission and after consulting the European Parliament; these arrangements may provide for derogations where warranted by problems specific to a Member State.

Article 20[33] **[Access to diplomatic or consular protection]**

Every citizen of the Union shall, in the territory of a third country in which the Member State of which he is a national is not represented, be entitled to protection by the diplomatic or consular authorities of any Member State, on the same conditions as the nationals of that State. Member States shall establish the necessary rules among themselves and start the international negotiations required to secure this protection. **2–022**

Article 21[34] **[Access to EC institutions and ombudsman]**

Every citizen of the Union shall have the right to petition the European Parliament in accordance with Article 194. **2–023**

Every citizen of the Union may apply to the Ombudsman established in accordance with Article 195.

[32] Formerly Art. 8b. Amended by Treaty of Amsterdam, Art. 6(I)(5)(a) and (b) to delete references to transition period. In former Art. 8b(2), reference to former Art. 138(4) (now Art. 190(4)) substituted by Treaty of Amsterdam, Art. 6(I)(5)(b). Former Art. 8b originally inserted by Art. 8(C) TEU.

[33] Formerly Art. 8c; reference to transition period deleted by Treaty of Amsterdam, Art. 6(I)(6). Former Art. 8c originally inserted by Art. 8(C) TEU.

[34] Formerly Art. 8d; third paragraph added by Treaty of Amsterdam, Art. 2(11). Former Art. 8d originally inserted by Art. 8(C) TEU.

Every citizen of the Union may write to any of the institutions or bodies referred to in this Article or in Article 7 in one of the languages mentioned in Article 314 and have an answer in the same language.

Article 22[35] **[Evolution of citizenship]**

2–024 The Commission shall report to the European Parliament, to the Council and to the Economic and Social Committee every three years on the application of the provisions of this Part. This report shall take account of the development of the Union.

On this basis, and, without prejudice to the other provisions of this Treaty, the Council, acting unanimously on a proposal from the Commission and after consulting the European Parliament, may adopt provisions to strengthen or to add to the rights laid down in this Part, which it shall recommend to the Member States for adoption in accordance with their respective constitutional requirements.

PART THREE—COMMUNITY POLICIES

TITLE I—FREE MOVEMENT OF GOODS

Article 23[36] **[Customs union]**

2–025 1. The Community shall be based upon a customs union which shall cover all trade in goods and which shall involve the prohibition between Member States of customs duties on imports and exports and of all charges having equivalent effect, and the adoption of a common customs tariff in their relations with third countries.

2. The provisions of Article 25 and of Chapter 2 of this Title shall apply to products originating in Member States and to products coming from third countries which are in free circulation in Member States.

Article 24[37] **[Free circulation of third country goods]**

2–026 Products coming from a third country shall be considered to be in free circulation in a Member State if the import formalities have been complied with and any customs duties or charges having equivalent effect which are payable have been levied in that Member State, and if they have not benefited from a total or partial drawback of such duties or charges.

CHAPTER 1—THE CUSTOMS UNION

Article 25[38] **[Intra-EC customs duties or equivalent charges prohibited]**

2–027 Customs duties on imports and exports and charges having equivalent effect shall be prohibited between Member States. This prohibition shall also apply to customs duties of a fiscal nature.[39]

Article 26[40] **[Fixing Common Customs Tariff]**

2–028 Common Customs Tariff duties shall be fixed by the Council acting by a qualified majority on a proposal from the Commission.

---

[35] Formerly Art. 8e; reference to transition period in first paragraph deleted by Treaty of Amsterdam, Art. 6(I)(7). Former Art. 8e originally inserted by Art. 8(C) TEU.

[36] Formerly Art. 9; references to provisions of the EC Treaty in Art. 23(2) adjusted by Treaty of Amsterdam, Art. 6(I)(8).

[37] Formerly Art. 10; former Art. 10(2) deleted by Treaty of Amsterdam, Art. 6(I)(9).

[38] Formerly Art. 12; former Art. 12 replaced by Treaty of Amsterdam, Art. 6(I)(12).

[39] See also prohibition of discriminatory or protective internal taxation of goods (Art. 90).

[40] Formerly Art. 28; former Art. 28 replaced by Treaty of Amsterdam, Art. 6(I)(16). Former Art. 28 previously replaced by Art. 16(1) SEA.

Article 27[41] **[Principles governing development of Customs Union]**

In carrying out the tasks entrusted to it under this Chapter the Commission shall be guided by: **2–029**

(a) the need to promote trade between Member States and third countries;

(b) developments in conditions of competition within the Community insofar as they lead to an improvement in the competitive capacity of undertakings;[42]

(c) the requirements of the Community as regards the supply of raw materials and semi-finished goods; in this connection the Commission shall take care to avoid distorting conditions of competition between Member States in respect of finished goods;

(d) the need to avoid serious disturbances in the economies of Member States and to ensure rational development of production and an expansion of consumption within the Community.

CHAPTER 2—PROHIBITION OF QUANTITIVE RESTRICTIONS BETWEEN MEMBER STATES

Article 28[43] **[Restrictions on intra-EC imports prohibited]**

Quantitative restrictions on imports and all measures having equivalent effect shall be prohibited between Member States. **2–030**

Article 29[44] **[Restrictions on intra-EC exports prohibited]**

Quantitative restrictions on exports, and all measures having equivalent effect, shall be prohibited between Member States. **2–031**

Article 30[45] **[Justifiable prohibitions or restrictions]**

The provisions of Articles 28 and 29 shall not preclude prohibitions or restrictions on imports, exports or goods in transit justified on grounds of public morality, public policy or public security; the protection of health and life of humans, animals or plants; the protection of national treasures possessing artistic, historic or archaeological value; or the protection of industrial and commercial property.[46] Such prohibitions or restrictions shall not, however, constitute a means of arbitrary discrimination or a disguised restriction on trade between Member States. **2–032**

Article 31[47] **[Position of Member State commercial monopolies]**

1. Member States shall adjust any State monopolies of a commercial character so as to ensure that no discrimination regarding the conditions under which goods are procured and marketed exists between nationals of Member States. **2–033**

The provisions of this Article shall apply to any body through which a Member State, in law or in fact, either directly or indirectly supervises, determines or

[41] Formerly Art. 29. Introductory wording of former Art. 29 adjusted by Treaty of Amsterdam, Art. 6(I)(17) to reflect revised structure of EC Treaty.

[42] See Arts. 81 *et seq.* for competition policy.

[43] Formerly Art. 30; wording of former Art. 30 adjusted by Treaty of Amsterdam, Art. 6(I)(19) to reflect repeal of former Arts 31–33 and 35 (original transitional provisions).

[44] Formerly Art. 34. Former Art. 34(2) deleted by Treaty of Amsterdam, Art. 6(I)(21).

[45] Formerly Art. 36. Introductory wording of former Art. 36 adjusted by Treaty of Amsterdam, Art. 6(I)(23) to reflect repeal of former Art. 31–33 (original transitional provisions).

[46] Member State rules governing property ownership not to be prejudiced by EC Treaty (Art. 295).

[47] Formerly Art. 37. Wording of former Art. 37(1) amended by Treaty of Amsterdam, Art. 6(I)(24)(a) to reflect removal of references to original transitional period and provisions. In former Art. 37(2), the word "prohibition" replaced by Treaty of Amsterdam, Art. 6(I)(24)(b). Former Art. 37(3), (5) and (6) deleted and para. (4) renumbered as para. (3) by Treaty of Amsterdam, Art. 6(I)(24)(c). Previous wording of renumbered para. (3) after the final word of the paragraph ("concerned") deleted by Treaty of Amsterdam, Art. 6(I)(24)(d).

appreciably influences imports or exports between Member States. These provisions shall likewise apply to monopolies delegated by the State to others.

2. Member States shall refrain from introducing any new measure which is contrary to the principles laid down in paragraph 1 or which restricts the scope of the Articles dealing with the prohibition of customs duties and quantitative restrictions between Member States.

3. If a state monopoly of a commercial character has rules which are designed to make it easier to dispose of agricultural products or obtain for them the best return, steps should be taken in applying the rules contained in this article to ensure equivalent safeguards for the employment and standard of living of the producers concerned.

TITLE II—AGRICULTURE

Article 32[48] [Common market for agriculture and fisheries]

2–034 1. The common market shall extend to agriculture and trade in agricultural products. "Agricultural products" means the products of the soil, of stockfarming and of fisheries and products of first-stage processing directly related to these products.

2. Save as otherwise provided in Articles 33 to 38, the rules laid down for the establishment of the common market shall apply to agricultural products.

3. The products subject to the provisions of Articles 33 to 38 are listed in Annex I to this Treaty.

4. The operation and development of the common market for agricultural products must be accompanied by the establishment of a common agricultural policy.

Article 33[49] [Objectives of the CAP]

2–035 1. The objectives of the common agricultural policy shall be:
(a) to increase agricultural productivity by promoting technical progress and by ensuring the rational development of agricultural production and the optimum utilisation of the factors of production, in particular labour;
(b) thus to ensure a fair standard of living for the agricultural community, in particular by increasing the individual earnings of persons engaged in agriculture;
(c) to stabilise markets;
(d) to assure the availability of supplies;
(e) to ensure that supplies reach consumers at reasonable prices.

2. In working out the common agricultural policy and the special methods for its application, account shall be taken of:
(a) the particular nature of agricultural activity, which results from the social structure of agriculture and from structural and natural disparities between the various agricultural regions;

[48] Formerly Art. 38. In former Art. 38(3) reference to Annex II replaced by reference to Annex I and second sentence (transitional provision) deleted by Treaty of Amsterdam, Art. 6(I)(25)(a). In former Art. 38(4), the words "among the Member States" at the end of the paragraph deleted by Treaty of Amsterdam, Art. 6(I)(25)(b).

[49] Formerly Art. 39.

(b) the need to effect the appropriate adjustments by degrees;
(c) the fact that in the Member States agriculture constitutes a sector closely linked with the economy as a whole.

Article 34[50] [Common organisation of agricultural markets]

1. In order to attain the objectives set out in Article 33, a common organisation of agricultural markets shall be established. **2–036**
This organisation shall take one of the following forms, depending on the product concerned:
(a) common rules on competition;
(b) compulsory co-ordination of the various national market organisations;
(c) a European market organisation.

2. The common organisation established in accordance with paragraph 1 may include all measures required to attain the objectives set out in Article 33, in particular regulation of prices, aids for the production and marketing of the various products, storage and carryover arrangements and common machinery for stabilising imports or exports.

The common organisation shall be limited to pursuit of the objectives set out in Article 33 and shall exclude any discrimination between producers or consumers within the Community.

Any common price policy shall be based on common criteria and uniform methods of calculation.

3. In order to enable the common organisation referred to in paragraph 1 to attain its objectives, one or more agricultural guidance and guarantee funds may be set up.

Article 35[51] [Additional measures within CAP]

To enable the objectives set out in Article 33 to be attained, provision may be made within the framework of the common agricultural policy for measures such as: **2–037**
(a) an effective co-ordination of efforts in the spheres of vocational training, of research and of the dissemination of agricultural knowledge; this may include joint financing of projects or institutions;
(b) joint measures to promote consumption of certain products.

Article 36[52] [Application of EC competition rules to agriculture]

The provisions of the Chapter relating to rules on competition shall apply to production of and trade in agricultural products only to the extent determined by the Council within the framework of Article 37(2) and (3) and in accordance with the procedure laid down therein, account being taken of the objectives set out in Article 33.[53] **2–038**

---

[50] Formerly Art. 40. Former Art. 40(1) deleted, Art. 40(2), (3) and (4) renumbered accordingly and references in former art. 40(2) and (3) to para. 2 replaced by references to para. 1 by Treaty of Amsterdam, Art. 6(I)(26).

[51] Formerly Art. 41.

[52] Formerly Art. 42.

[53] See Regulation 26/62 (O.J. 1959–1962, Eng. Spec. Ed., p.129) for application of certain rules of competition to production of and trade in agricultural products.

The Council may, in particular, authorise the granting of aid:
(a) for the protection of enterprises handicapped by structural or natural conditions;
(b) within the framework of economic development programmes.

Article 37[54] **[Establishment of CAP]**

2–039 1. In order to evolve the broad lines of a common agricultural policy, the Commission shall, immediately this Treaty enters into force, convene a conference of the Member States with a view to making a comparison of their agricultural policies, in particular by producing a statement of their resources and needs.

2. Having taken into account the work of the conference provided for in paragraph 1, after consulting the Economic and Social Committee and within two years of the entry into force of this Treaty, the Commission shall submit proposals for working out and implementing the common agricultural policy, including the replacement of the national organisations by one of the forms of common organisation provided for in Article 34(1), and for implementing the measures specified in this title.

These proposals shall take account of the interdependence of the agricultural matters mentioned in this Title.

The Council shall, on a proposal from the Commission and after consulting the European Parliament, acting by a qualified majority, make regulations, issue directives, or take decisions, without prejudice to any recommendations it may also make.

3. The Council may, acting by a qualified majority and in accordance with paragraph 2, replace the national market organisations by the common organisation provided for in Article 34(1) if:
(a) the common organisation offers Member States which are opposed to this measure and which have an organisation of their own for the production in question equivalent safeguards for the employment and standard of living of the producers concerned, account being taken of the adjustments that will be possible and the specialisation that will be needed with the passage of time;
(b) such an organisation ensures conditions for trade within the Community similar to those existing in a national market.

4. If a common organisation for certain raw materials is established before a common organisation exists for the corresponding processed products, such raw materials as are used for processed products intended for export to third countries may be imported from outside the Community.

Article 38[55] **[Countervailing charges]**

2–040 Where in a Member State a product is subject to a national market organisation or to internal rules having equivalent effect which affect the competitive position of similar production in another Member State, a countervailing charge shall be applied by Member States to imports of this product coming from the Member State where such organisation or rules exist, unless that State applies a countervailing charge on export.

[54] Formerly Art. 43. In former Art. 43(2), third sub-paragraph, reference to acting by qualified majority substituted by Treaty of Amsterdam, Art. 6(I)(27)(a). In former Art. 43(2) and (3), references to former Art. 40(1) substituted for former Art. 40(2) by Treaty of Amsterdam, Art. 6(I)(27)(b).
[55] Formerly Art. 46.

The Commission shall fix the amount of these charges at the level required to redress the balance; it may also authorise other measures, the conditions and details of which it shall determine.

TITLE III—FREE MOVEMENT OF PERSONS, SERVICES AND CAPITAL

CHAPTER 1—WORKERS

Article 39[56] [Free movement of workers]

1. Freedom of movement for workers shall be secured within the Community. **2–041**

2. Such freedom of movement shall entail the abolition of any discrimination based on nationality between workers of the Member States as regards employment, remuneration and other conditions of work and employment.

3. It shall entail the right, subject to limitations justified on grounds of public policy, public security or public health:
(a) to accept offers of employment actually made;
(b) to move freely within the territory of Member States for this purpose;
(c) to stay in a Member State for the purpose of employment in accordance with the provisions governing the employment of nationals of that State laid down by law, regulation or administrative action;
(d) to remain in the territory of a Member State after having been employed in that State, subject to conditions which shall be embodied in implementing regulations to be drawn up by the Commission.

4. The provisions of this Article shall not apply to employment in the public service.

Article 40[57] [Measures to achieve free movement]

The Council shall, acting in accordance with the procedure referred to in Article 251 and after consulting the Economic and Social Committee, issue directives or make regulations setting out the measures required to bring about freedom of movement for workers, as defined in Article 39, in particular: **2–042**
(a) by ensuring close cooperation between national employment services;
(b) by abolishing those administrative procedures and practices and those qualifying periods in respect of eligibility for available employment, whether resulting from national legislation or from agreements previously concluded between Member States, the maintenance of which would form an obstacle to liberalisation of the movement of workers;
(c) by abolishing all such qualifying periods and other restrictions provided for either under national legislation or under agreements previously concluded between Member States as imposed on workers of other Member States conditions regarding the free choice of employment other than those imposed on workers of the State concerned;
(d) by setting up appropriate machinery to bring offers of employment into touch with applications for employment and to facilitate the achievement of a balance between supply and demand in the employment market in such a way

[56] Formerly Art. 48. Reference in former Art. 48(1) to original transitional period deleted by Treaty of Amsterdam, Art. 6(I)(29).
[57] Formerly Art. 49. Transitional phrases in first sentence of former Art. 49 deleted by Treaty of Amsterdam, Art. 6(I)(30)(a). First sentence previously replaced by Art. 8(10) TEU and prior to that amended by virtue of Art. 6(3) SEA. In former Art. 49(b) and (c), the words "systematically and progressively" deleted by Treaty of Amsterdam, Art. 6(I)(30)(b).

as to avoid serious threats to the standard of living and level of employment in the various regions and industries.

Article 41[58] [Exchange of young workers]

2–043 Member States shall, within the framework of a joint programme, encourage the exchange of young workers.

Article 42[59] [Social security for workers and dependants]

2–044 The Council shall, acting in accordance with the procedure referred to in Article 251, adopt such measures in the field of social security as are necessary to provide freedom of movement for workers; to this end, it shall make arrangements to secure for migrant workers and their dependants:

(a) aggregation, for the purpose of acquiring and retaining the right to benefit and of calculating the amount of benefit, of all periods taken into account under the laws of the several countries;

(b) payment of benefits to persons resident in the territories of Member States.

The Council shall act unanimously throughout the procedure referred to in Article 251.

CHAPTER 2—RIGHT OF ESTABLISHMENT

Article 43[60] [Restrictions on setting up/conducting business in other Member States prohibited]

2–045 Within the framework of the provisions set out below, restrictions on the freedom of establishment of nationals of a Member State in the territory of another Member State shall be prohibited. Such prohibition shall also apply to restrictions on the setting-up of agencies, branches or subsidiaries by nationals of any Member State established in the territory of any Member State.

Freedom of establishment shall include the right to take up and pursue activities as self-employed persons and to set up and manage undertakings, in particular companies or firms within the meaning of the second paragraph of Article 48, under the conditions laid down for its own nationals by the law of the country where such establishment is effected, subject to the provisions of the chapter relating to capital.

Article 44[61] [Means of securing freedom of establishment]

2–046 1. In order to attain freedom of establishment as regards a particular activity, the Council, acting in accordance with the procedure referred to in Article 251 and after consulting the Economic and Social Committee, shall act by means of directives.

---

[58] Formerly Art. 50.

[59] Formerly Art. 51; replaced by Treaty of Amsterdam, Art. 2(12).

[60] Formerly Art. 52; former transitional phraseology in first and second sentences replaced by Treaty of Amsterdam, Art. 6(I)(31).

[61] Formerly Art. 54. Former Art. 54(1) deleted and para. (2) and (3) renumbered accordingly by Treaty of Amsterdam, Art. 6(I)(33)(a). In renumbered para. (1), transitional wording replaced by "attain" by Treaty of Amsterdam, Art. 6(I)(33)(b). As Art. 54(2), replaced by Art. 8(11) TEU. Former Art. 54(2), previously amended by Art. 6(4) SEA.

2. The Council and the Commission shall carry out the duties devolving upon them under the preceding provisions, in particular:

(a) by according, as a general rule, priority treatment to activities where freedom of establishment makes a particularly valuable contribution to the development of production and trade;

(b) by ensuring close cooperation between the competent authorities in the Member States in order to ascertain the particular situation within the Community of the various activities concerned;

(c) by abolishing those administrative procedures and practices, whether resulting from national legislation or from agreements previously concluded between Member States, the maintenance of which would form an obstacle to freedom of establishment;

(d) by ensuring that workers of one Member State employed in the territory of another Member State may remain in that territory for the purpose of taking up activities therein as self-employed persons, where they satisfy the conditions which they would be required to satisfy if they were entering that State at the time when they intended to take up such activities;

(e) by enabling a national of one Member State to acquire and use land and buildings situated in the territory of another Member State, in so far as this does not conflict with the principles laid down in Article 33(2);

(f) by effecting the progressive abolition of restrictions on freedom of establishment in every branch of activity under consideration, both as regards the conditions for setting up agencies, branches or subsidiaries in the territory of a Member State and as regards the subsidiaries in the territory of a Member State and as regards the conditions governing the entry of personnel belonging to the main establishment into managerial or supervisory posts in such agencies, branches or subsidiaries;

(g) by co-ordinating to the necessary extent the safeguards which, for the protection of the interests of members and others, are required by Member States of companies or firms within the meaning of the second paragraph of Article 48 with a view to making such safeguards equivalent throughout the Community;

(h) by satisfying themselves that the conditions of establishment are not distorted by aids granted by Member States.

Article 45[62] [Exercise of official authority]

The provisions of this Chapter shall not apply, so far as any given Member State is concerned, to activities which in that State are connected, even occasionally, with the exercise of official authority. **2–047**

The Council may, acting by a qualified majority on a proposal from the Commission, rule that the provisions of this Chapter shall not apply to certain activities.

Article 46[63] [Permissible restrictions on freedom of establishment]

1. The provisions of this Chapter and measures taken in pursuance thereof shall not prejudice the applicability of provisions laid down by law, regulation or administrative action providing for special treatment for foreign nationals on grounds of public policy, public security or public health. **2–048**

2. The Council shall, acting in accordance with the procedure referred to in Article 251, issue directives for the co-ordination of the abovementioned provisions.

[62] Formerly Art. 55.

[63] Formerly Art. 56. Former Art. 56(2) replaced by Treaty of Amsterdam, Art. 2(13); previously replaced by Art. 8(12) TEU and before that, Art. 56(2), second sentence replaced by Art. 6(5) SEA.

Article 47[64] [Mutual recognition of qualifications]

2–049 1. In order to make it easier for persons to take up and pursue activities as self-employed persons, the Council shall, acting in accordance with the procedure referred to in Article 251, issue directives for the mutual recognition of diplomas, certificates and other evidence of formal qualifications.

2. For the same purpose, the Council shall, acting in accordance with the procedure referred to in Article 251, issue directives for the co-ordination of the provisions laid down by law, regulation or administrative action in Member States concerning the taking-up and pursuit of activities as self-employed persons. The Council, acting unanimously throughout the procedure referred to in Article 251, shall decide on directives the implementation of which involves in at least one Member State amendment of the existing principles laid down by law governing the professions with respect to training and conditions of access for natural persons. In other cases the Council shall act by qualified majority.

3. In the case of the medical and allied and pharmaceutical professions, the progressive abolition of restrictions shall be dependent upon co-ordination of the conditions for their exercise in the various Member States.

Article 48[65] [Freedom of establishment for EC companies or firms]

2–050 Companies or firms formed in accordance with the law of a Member State and having their registered office, central administration or principal place of business within the Community shall, for the purposes of this Chapter, be treated in the same way as natural persons who are nationals of Member States.

"Companies or firms" means companies or firms constituted under civil or commercial law, including co-operative societies, and other legal persons governed by public or private law, save for those which are non-profit-making.[66]

CHAPTER 3—SERVICES

Article 49[67] [Freedom to provide cross-border services]

2–051 Within the framework of the provisions set out below, restrictions on freedom to provide services within the Community shall be prohibited in respect of nationals of Member States who are established in a State of the Community other than that of the person for whom the services are intended.

The Council may, acting by a qualified majority on a proposal from the Commission, extend the provisions of the Chapter to nationals of a third country who provide services and who are established within the Community.[68]

Article 50[69] [Services defined]

2–052 Services shall be considered to be "services" within the meaning of this Treaty where they are normally provided for remuneration, insofar as they are not governed by the provisions relating to freedom of movement for goods, capital and persons.

"Services" shall in particular include:

---

[64] Formerly Art. 57. Former art. 57(2) replaced by Treaty of Amsterdam, Art. 2(14). Former Art. 57 previously replaced by Art. 8(13) TEU. Former Art. 57(1) previously amended by Art. 6(6) SEA, and former Art. 57(2), first and second sentences, previously replaced by Art. 16(2) and 6(7) SEA respectively.

[65] Formerly Art. 58.

[66] For right to equal participation in company capital, see Art. 294.

[67] Formerly Art. 59. In former Art. 59, first paragraph, transitional wording replaced by "prohibited" by Treaty of Amsterdam, Art. 6(I)(34).

[68] Reference to qualified majority voting by the Council originally substituted by Art. 16(3) SEA.

[69] Formerly Art. 60.

(a) activities of an industrial character,
(b) activities of a commercial character,
(c) activities of craftsmen,
(d) activities of the professions.

Without prejudice to the provisions of the Chapter relating to the right of establishment, the person providing a service may, in order to do so, temporarily pursue his activity in the State where the service is provided, under the same conditions as are imposed by that State on its own nationals.

Article 51[70] **[Transport, banking and insurance services]**

1. Freedom to provide services in the field of transport shall be governed by the provisions of the Title relating to transport. **2–053**

2. The liberalisation of banking and insurance services connected with movements of capital shall be effected in step with the liberalisation of movement of capital.

Article 52[71] **[Means of securing freedom to provide cross-border services]**

1. In order to achieve the liberalisation of a specific service, the Council shall, on a proposal from the Commission and after consulting the Economic and Social Committee and the European Parliament, issue directives acting by a qualified majority. **2–054**

2. As regards the directives referred to in paragraph 1, priority shall as a general rule be given to those services which directly affect production costs or the liberalisation of which helps to promote trade in goods.

Article 53[72] **[Further liberalisation of cross-border services]**

The Member States declare their readiness to undertake the liberalisation of services beyond the extent required by the directives issued pursuant to Article 52(1), if their general economic situation and the situation of the economic sector concerned so permit. **2–055**

To this end, the Commission shall make recommendations to the Member States concerned.

Article 54[73] **[Existing restrictions on provision of services]**

As long as restrictions on freedom to provide services have not been abolished, each Member State shall apply such restrictions without distinction on grounds of nationality or residence to all persons providing services within the meaning of the first paragraph of Article 49. **2–056**

Article 55[74] **[Application of principles on establishment]**

The provisions of Articles 45 to 48 shall apply to the matters covered by this Chapter. **2–057**

[70] Formerly Art. 61. Former Art. 61(2) amended by Treaty of Amsterdam, Art. 6(I)(35) (deletion of "progressive").

[71] Formerly Art. 63. Former Art. 63(1) deleted and para. (2) and (3) renumbered accordingly by Treaty of Amsterdam, Art. 6(I)(37)(a). In renumbered para. (1), the word "achieve" replaced transitional wording and the words "by a qualified majority" replaced reference to transitional voting procedures, by virtue of Treaty of Amsterdam, Art. 6(I)(37)(b). In renumbered para. (2), introductory words replaced by Treaty of Amsterdam, Art. 6(I)(37)(c).

[72] Formerly Art. 64. In former Art. 64, first paragraph, reference to Art. 63(1) substituted by Treaty of Amsterdam, Art. 6(I)(38).

[73] Formerly Art. 65.

[74] Formerly Art. 66.

CHAPTER 4—CAPITAL AND PAYMENTS

Article 56[75] [Restrictions on movement of capital prohibited]

2–058 1. Within the framework of the provisions set out in this Chapter, all restrictions on the movement of capital between Member States and between Member States and third countries shall be prohibited.

2. Within the framework of the provisions set out in this Chapter, all restrictions on payments between Member States and between Member States and third countries shall be prohibited.

Article 57[76] [Capital movement to or from third countries]

2–059 1. The provisions of Article 56 shall be without prejudice to the application to third countries of any restrictions which exist on 31 December 1993 under national or Community law adopted in respect of the movement of capital to or from third countries involving direct investment—including in real estate—establishment, the provision of financial services or the admission of securities to capital markets.

2. Whilst endeavouring to achieve the objective of free movement of capital between Member States and third countries to the greatest extent possible and without prejudice to the other Chapters of this Treaty, the Council may, acting by a qualified majority on a proposal from the Commission, adopt measures on the movement of capital to or from third countries involving direct investment—including investment in real estate—establishment, the provision of financial services or the admission of securities to capital markets. Unanimity shall be required for measures under this paragraph which constitute a step back in Community law as regards the liberalisation of the movement of capital to or from third countries.

Article 58[77] [Right of Member States to apply tax laws]

2–060 1. The provisions of Article 56 shall be without prejudice to the right of Member States:

(a) to apply the relevant provisions of their tax law which distinguish between taxpayers who are not in the same situation with regard to their place of residence or with regard to the place where their capital is invested;

(b) to take all requisite measures to prevent infringements of national law and regulations, in particular in the field of taxation and the prudential supervision of financial institutions, or to lay down procedures for the declaration of capital movements for purposes of administrative or statistical information, or to take measures which are justified on grounds of public policy or public security.

2. The provisions of this Chapter shall be without prejudice to the applicability of restrictions on the right of establishment which are compatible with this Treaty.

3. The measures and procedures referred to in paragraphs 1 and 2 shall not constitute a means of arbitrary discrimination or a disguised restriction on the free movement of capital and payments as defined in Article 56.

Article 59[78] [Temporary safeguard measures *vis-à-vis* third countries]

2–061 Where, in exceptional circumstances, movements of capital to or from third countries cause, or threaten to cause, serious difficulties for the operation of economic and monetary union, the Council, acting by a qualified majority on a

[75] Formerly Art. 73b. Former Art. 73b inserted by Art. 8(15) TEU.
[76] Formerly Art. 73c. Former Art. 73c inserted by Art. 8(15) TEU.
[77] Formerly Art. 73d. Former Art. 73d inserted by Art. 8(15) TEU.
[78] Formerly Art. 73f. Former Art. 73f inserted by Art. 8(15) TEU.

proposal from the Commission and after consulting the ECB, may take safeguard measures with regard to third countries for a period not exceeding six months if such measures are strictly necessary.

Article 60[79] [Urgent measures resulting from CFSP]

1. If, in the cases envisaged in Article 301, action by the Community is deemed necessary, the Council may, in accordance with the procedure provided for in Article 301, take the necessary urgent measures on the movement of capital and on payments as regards the third countries concerned. **2–062**

2. Without prejudice to Article 297 and as long as the Council has not taken measures pursuant to paragraph 1, a Member State may, for serious political reasons and on grounds of urgency, take unilateral measures against a third country with regard to capital movements and payments. The Commission and the other Member States shall be informed of such measures by the date of their entry into force at the latest.

The Council may, acting by a qualified majority on a proposal from the Commission, decide that the Member State concerned shall amend or abolish such measures. The President of the Council shall inform the European Parliament of any such decision taken by the Council.

TITLE IV—VISAS, ASYLUM, IMMIGRATION AND OTHER POLICIES RELATED TO FREE MOVEMENT OF PERSONS

Article 61[80] [Common area of freedom, security and justice]

In order to establish progressively an area of freedom, security and justice, the Council shall adopt: **2–063**

(a) within a period of five years after the entry into force of the Treaty of Amsterdam, measures aimed at ensuring the free movement of persons in accordance with Article 14, in conjunction with directly related flanking measures with respect to external border controls, asylum and immigration, in accordance with the provisions of Article 62(2) and (3) and Article 63(1)(a) and (2)(a), and measures to prevent and combat crime in accordance with the provisions of Article 31(e) of the Treaty on European Union;

(b) other measures in the fields of asylum, immigration and safeguarding the rights of nationals of third countries, in accordance with the provisions of Article 63;

(c) measures in the field of judicial cooperation in civil matters as provided for in Article 65;

(d) appropriate measures to encourage and strengthen administrative cooperation, as provided for in Article 66;

(e) measures in the field of police and judicial cooperation in criminal matters aimed at a high level of security by preventing and combating crime within the Union in accordance with the provisions of the Treaty on European Union.

Article 62[81] [Freedom to travel]

The Council, acting in accordance with the procedure referred to in Article 67, shall, within a period of five years after the entry into force of the Treaty of Amsterdam, adopt: **2–064**

[79] Formerly Art. 73g. Former Art. 73g inserted by Art. 8(15) TEU.

[80] Formerly Art. 73i. Former Art. 73i inserted by Treaty of Amsterdam Art. 2(15).

[81] Formerly Art. 73j. Former Art. 73j inserted by Treaty of Amsterdam, Art. 2(15). See further in the context of free movement Protocol (No. 2) integrating the Schengen *acquis* into the framework of the EU (1997), the full text of which is reproduced in the Treaty on European Union, and Declaration (No. 15) on the preservation of the level of protection and security provided by the Schengen acquis annexed to the Final Act of the Treaty of Amsterdam.

(1) measures with a view to ensuring, in compliance with Article 14, the absence of any controls on persons, be they citizens of the Union or nationals of third countries, when crossing internal borders;
(2) measures on the crossing of the external borders of the Member States which shall establish:
 (a) standards and procedures to be followed by Member States in carrying out checks on persons at such borders,[82]
 (b) rules on visas for intended stays of no more than three months, including:
  (i) the list of third countries whose nationals must be in possession of visas when crossing the external borders and those whose nationals are exempt from that requirement;
  (ii) the procedures and conditions for issuing visas by Member States;
  (iii) a uniform format for visas;
  (iv) rules on a uniform visa;[83]
(3) measures setting out the conditions under which nationals of third countries shall have the freedom to travel within the territory of the Member States during a period of no more than three months.

Article 63[84] [Measures to be adopted by Council]

2–065 The Council, acting in accordance with the procedure referred to in Article 67, shall, within a period of five years after the entry into force of the Treaty of Amsterdam, adopt:
(1) measures on asylum, in accordance with the Geneva Convention of 28 July 1951 and the Protocol of 31 January 1967 relating to the status of refugees and other relevant treaties, within the following areas:
 (a) criteria and mechanisms for determining which Member State is responsible for considering an application for asylum submitted by a national of a third country in one of the Member States;
 (b) minimum standards on the reception of asylum seekers in Member States;
 (c) minimum standards with respect to the qualification of nationals of third countries as refugees;
 (d) minimum standards on procedures in Member States for granting or withdrawing refugee status;
(2) measures on refugees and displaced persons within the following areas:
 (a) minimum standards for giving temporary protection to displaced persons from third countries who cannot return to their country of origin and for persons who otherwise need international protection,
 (b) promoting a balance of effort between Member States in receiving and bearing the consequences of receiving refugees and displaced persons;
(3) measures on immigration policy within the following areas:
 (a) conditions of entry and residence, and standards on procedures for the issue by Member States of long term visas and residence permits, including those for the purpose of family reunion,[85]
 (b) illegal immigration and illegal residence, including repatriation of illegal residents;
(4) measures defining the rights and conditions under which nationals of third countries who are legally resident in a Member State may reside in other Member States.

[82] See Protocol (No. 31) on external relations of the Member States with regard to the crossing of external borders.
[83] See Declaration (No. 16) on Article [62(2)(b)] of the Treaty establishing the European Community annexed to the Final Act of the Treaty of Amsterdam.
[84] Formerly Art. 73k. Former Art. 73k inserted by Treaty of Amsterdam, Art. 2(15). See Declaration (No. 17) on Article [63] of the Treaty establishing the European Community annexed to the Final Act of the Treaty of Amsterdam.
[85] See Declaration (No. 18) on Article [63(3)(a)] of the Treaty establishing the European Community annexed to the Final Act of the Treaty of Amsterdam.

Measures adopted by the Council pursuant to points 3 and 4 shall not prevent any Member State from maintaining or introducing in the areas concerned national provisions which are compatible with this Treaty and with international agreements.

Measures to be adopted pursuant to points 2(b), 3(a) and 4 shall not be subject to the five-year period referred to above.

Article 64[86] **[Maintenance of law and order and internal security]**

1. This Title shall not affect the exercise of the responsibilities incumbent upon Member States with regard to the maintenance of law and order and the safeguarding of internal security.[87] **2–066**

2. In the event of one or more Member States being confronted with an emergency situation characterised by a sudden inflow of nationals of third countries and without prejudice to paragraph 1, the Council may, acting by qualified majority on a proposal from the Commission, adopt provisional measures of a duration not exceeding six months for the benefit of the member states concerned.

Article 65[88] **[Measures for judicial cooperation in civil matters]**

Measures in the field of judicial cooperation in civil matters having cross-border implications, to be taken in accordance with Article 67 and in so far as necessary for the proper functioning of the internal market, shall include: **2–067**

(a) improving and simplifying:
- the system for cross-border service of judicial and extrajudicial documents;
- cooperation in the taking of evidence;
- the recognition and enforcement of decisions in civil and commercial cases, including decisions in extrajudicial cases;

(b) promoting the compatibility of the rules applicable in the Member States concerning the conflict of laws and of jurisdiction;

(c) eliminating obstacles to the good functioning of civil proceedings, if necessary by promoting the compatibility of the rules on civil procedure applicable in the Member States.

Article 66[89] **[Member State cooperation]**

The Council, acting in accordance with the procedure referred to in Article 67, shall take measures to ensure cooperation between the relevant departments of the administrations of the Member States in the areas covered by this Title, as well as between those departments and the Commission. **2–068**

Article 67[90] **[Procedure for adopting measures]**

1. During a transitional period of five years following the entry into force of the Treaty of Amsterdam, the Council shall act unanimously on a proposal from the Commission or on the initiative of a Member State and after consulting the European Parliament. **2–069**

[86] Formerly Art. 73l. Former Art. 73l inserted by Treaty of Amsterdam, Art. 2(15).

[87] See Declaration (No. 19) on Article [64(1)] of the Treaty establishing the European Community annexed to the Final Act of the Treaty of Amsterdam.

[88] Formerly Art. 73m. Former Art. 73m inserted by Treaty of Amsterdam, Art. 2(15). See Declaration (No. 20) on Article [65] of the Treaty establishing the European Community annexed to the Final Act of the Treaty of Amsterdam.

[89] Formerly Art. 73n. Former Art. 73n inserted by Treaty of Amsterdam, Art. 2(15).

[90] Formerly Art. 73o. Former Art. 73o inserted by Treaty of Amsterdam, Art. 2(15). See Declaration (No. 21) on Article [67] of the Treaty establishing the European Community annexed to the Final Act of the Treaty of Amsterdam. See further, Protocol on Article 67 of the EC Treaty annexed to that Treaty.

2. After this period of five years:
— the Council shall act on proposals from the Commission; the Commission shall examine any request made by a Member State that it submit a proposal to the Council;
— the Council, acting unanimously after consulting the European Parliament, shall take a decision with a view to providing for all or parts of the areas covered by this title to be governed by the procedure referred to in Article 251 and adapting the provisions relating to the powers of the Court of Justice.

3. By derogation from paragraphs 1 and 2, measures referred to in Article 62(2)(b)(i) and (iii) shall, from the entry into force of the Treaty of Amsterdam, be adopted by the Council acting by a qualified majority on a proposal from the Commission and after consulting the European Parliament.

4. By derogation from paragraph 2, measures referred to in Article 62(2)(b)(ii) and (iv) shall, after a period of five years following the entry into force of the Treaty of Amsterdam, be adopted by the Council acting in accordance with the procedure referred to in Article 251.

5. By derogation from paragraph 1, the Council shall adopt, in accordance with the procedure referred to in Article 251:
— the measures provided for in Article 63(1) and (2)(a) provided that the Council has previously adopted, in accordance with paragraph 1 of this Article, Community legislation defining the common rules and basic principles governing these issues;
— the measures provided for in Article 65 with the exception of aspects relating to family law.[91]

Article 68[92] [Jurisdiction of ECJ to hand down preliminary rulings]

2–070 1. Article 234 shall apply to this Title under the following circumstances and conditions: where a question on the interpretation of this Title or on the validity or interpretation of acts of the institutions of the Community based on this Title is raised in a case pending before a court or a tribunal of a Member State against whose decisions there is no judicial remedy under national law, that court or tribunal shall, if it considers that a decision on the question is necessary to enable it to give judgment, request the Court of Justice to give a ruling thereon.

2. In any event, the Court of Justice shall not have jurisdiction to rule on any measure or decision taken pursuant to Article 62(1) relating to the maintenance of law and order and the safeguarding of internal security.

3. The Council, the Commission or a Member State may request the Court of Justice to give a ruling on a question of interpretation of this Title or of acts of the institutions of the Community based on this Title. The ruling given by the Court of Justice in response to such a request shall not apply to judgments of courts or tribunals of the Member States which have become *res judicata*.

Article 69[93] [Special positions of Denmark, Ireland and UK]

2–071 The application of this Title shall be subject to the provisions of the Protocol on the position of the United Kingdom and Ireland and to the Protocol on the

[91] Article 67(5) added by Treaty of Nice, Art. 2(4).
[92] Formerly Art. 73p. Former Art. 73p inserted by Treaty of Amsterdam, Art. 2(15).
[93] Formerly Art. 73q. Former Art. 73q inserted by Treaty of Amsterdam, Art. 2(15). Texts of Protocol (No. 3) on the application of certain aspects of Article 14 of the EC Treaty to the UK and Ireland (1997) (preservation of UK border controls), Protocol (No. 4) on the position of the UK and Ireland (1997) (UK and Irish position on visa, asylum, immigration and other policies) and Protocol (No. 5) on the position of Denmark (1997) (Danish position on visa, asylum, immigration and other policies) are set out in the Treaty on European Union above.

position of Denmark and without prejudice to the Protocol on the application of certain aspects of Article 14 of the Treaty establishing the European Community to the United Kingdom and to Ireland.

TITLE V—TRANSPORT

Article 70[94] **[Common transport policy]**

The objectives of this Treaty shall, in matters governed by this Title, be pursued by Member States within the framework of a common transport policy. **2–072**

Article 71[95] **[Implementation of transport policy]**

1. For the purpose of implementing Article 70, and taking into account the distinctive features of transport, the Council shall, acting in accordance with the procedure referred to in Article 251 and after consulting the Economic and Social Committee and the Committee of the Regions, lay down: **2–073**

(a) common rules applicable to international transport to or from the territory of a Member State or passing across the territory of one or more Member States;
(b) the conditions under which non-resident carriers may operate transport services within a Member State;
(c) measures to improve transport safety;
(d) any other appropriate provisions.

2. By way of derogation from the procedure provided for in paragraph 1, where the application of provisions concerning the principles of the regulatory system for transport would be liable to have a serious effect on the standard of living and on employment in certain areas and on the operation of transport facilities, they shall be laid down by the Council acting unanimously on a proposal from the Commission, after consulting the European Parliament and the Economic and Social Committee. In so doing, the Council shall take into account the need for adaptation to the economic development which will result from establishing the common market.

Article 72[96] **[Discrimination prohibited]**

Until the provisions referred to in Article 71(1) have been laid down, no Member State may, without the unanimous approval of the Council, make the various provisions governing the subject on 1 January 1958 or, for acceding States, the date of their accession less favourable in their direct or indirect effect on carriers of other Member States as compared with carriers who are nationals of that State. **2–074**

Article 73[97] **[Legitimate aid in transport sector]**

Aids shall be compatible with this Treaty if they meet the needs of co-ordination of transport or if they represent reimbursement for the discharge of certain obligations inherent in the concept of a public service. **2–075**

Article 74[98] **[Measures on transport rates and conditions]**

Any measures taken within the framework of this Treaty in respect of transport rates and conditions shall take account of the economic circumstances of carriers. **2–076**

---

[94] Formerly Art. 74.

[95] Formerly Art. 75. Former Art. 75(1), introductory section, replaced by Treaty of Amsterdam, Art. 2(16). Art. 75(2) deleted and Art. 75(3) renumbered accordingly by Treaty of Amsterdam, Art. 6(I)(40). Art. 75 previously replaced by Art. 8(15) TEU.

[96] Formerly Art. 76. In former Art. 76, the words "on January 1, 1958 or, for acceding States, the date of their accession" substituted by Treaty of Amsterdam, Art. 6(I)(41).

[97] Formerly Art. 77.

[98] Formerly Art. 78.

Article 75[99] [Discrimination based on origin/destination of transported goods]

2–077 1. In the case of transport within the Community, discrimination which takes the form of carriers charging different rates and imposing different conditions for the carriage of the same goods over the same transport links on grounds of the country of origin or of destination of the goods in question shall be abolished.

2. Paragraph 1 shall not prevent the Council from adopting other measures in pursuance of Article 71(1).

3. The Council shall, acting by a qualified majority on a proposal from the Commission and after consulting the Economic and Social Committee, lay down rules for implementing the provisions of paragraph 1. The Council may in particular lay down the provisions needed to enable the institutions of the Community to secure compliance with the rule laid down in paragraph 1 and to ensure that users benefit from it to the full.

4. The Commission shall, acting on its own initiative or on application by a Member State, investigate any cases of discrimination falling within paragraph 1 and, after consulting any Member State concerned, shall take the necessary decisions within the framework of the rules laid down in accordance with the provisions of paragraph 3.

Article 76[1] [No unauthorised transport subsidy or protection]

2–078 1. The imposition by a Member State, in respect of transport operations carried out within the Community, of rates and conditions involving any element of support or protection in the interest of one or more particular undertakings or industries shall be prohibited, unless authorised by the Commission.

2. The Commission shall, acting on its own initiative or on application by a Member State, examine the rates and conditions referred to in paragraph 1, taking account in particular of the requirements of an appropriate regional economic policy, the needs of underdeveloped areas and the problems of areas seriously affected by political circumstances on the one hand, and of the effects of such rates and conditions on competition between the different modes of transport on the other.

After consulting each Member State concerned, the Commission shall take the necessary decisions.

3. The prohibition provided for in paragraph 1 shall not apply to tariffs fixed to meet competition.

Article 77[2] [Charges in respect of frontier crossings]

2–079 Charges or dues in respect of the crossing of frontiers which are charged by a carrier in addition to the transport rates shall not exceed a reasonable level after taking the costs actually incurred thereby into account.

---

[99] Formerly Art. 79. In former Art. 79(1) and (3), references to transitional period deleted by Treaty of Amsterdam, Art. 6(I)(42).

[1] Formerly Art. 80. In former Art. 80(1), transitional wording deleted by Treaty of Amsterdam, Art. 6(I)(43).

[2] Formerly Art. 81.

Member States shall endeavour to reduce these costs progressively.
The Commission may make recommendations to Member States for the application of this Article.

Article 78[3] **[Disadvantages caused by former division of Germany]**

The provisions of this Title shall not form an obstacle to the application of measures taken in the Federal Republic of Germany to the extent that such measures are required in order to compensate for the economic disadvantages caused by the division of Germany to the economy of certain areas of the Federal Republic affected by that division. **2–080**

Article 79[4] **[Advisory Committee on transport matters]**

An Advisory Committee consisting of experts designated by the governments of Member States shall be attached to the Commission. The Commission, whenever it considers it desirable, shall consult the Committee on transport matters without prejudice to the powers of the Economic and Social Committee. **2–081**

Article 80[5] **[Scope of provisions on transport]**

1. The provisions of this Title shall apply to transport by rail, road and inland waterway. **2–082**

2. The Council may, acting by a qualified majority, decide whether, to what extent and by what procedure appropriate provisions may be laid down for sea and air transport.

The procedural provisions of Article 71 shall apply.

TITLE VI—COMMON RULES ON COMPETITION, TAXATION AND APPROXIMATION OF LAWS

CHAPTER 1—RULES ON COMPETITION[6]

SECTION 1—RULES APPLYING TO UNDERTAKINGS

Article 81[7] **[Prohibited anti-competitive agreements and practices]**

1. The following shall be prohibited as incompatible with the common market: all agreements between undertakings, decisions by associations of undertakings and concerted practices which may affect trade between Member States and which have as their object or effect the prevention, restriction or distortion of competition within the common market, and in particular those which: **2–083**
(a) directly or indirectly fix purchase or selling prices or any other trading conditions;
(b) limit or control production, markets, technical development, or investment;
(c) share markets or sources of supply;
(d) apply dissimilar conditions to equivalent transactions with other trading parties, thereby placing them at a competitive disadvantage;
(e) make the conclusion of contracts subject to acceptance by the other parties of supplementary obligations which, by their nature or according to commercial usage, have no connection with the subject of such contracts.

---

[3] Formerly Art. 82.

[4] Formerly Art. 83. In former Art. 83, reference to the transport section of the ESC replaced by a reference to the ESC by Treaty of Amsterdam, Art. 6(I)(44).

[5] Formerly Art. 84. In former Art. 84(2), reference to former Art. 75(1) and (2) changed to Art. 75 (now Art. 71) by Treaty of Amsterdam, Art. 6(I)(45). In former Art. 84(2), reference to qualified majority voting procedure inserted and second sub-paragraph added by Art. 16(5) and (6) SEA.

[6] For application of the competition rules to agriculture, see Art. 36.

[7] Formerly Art. 85. See Art. 86 for application of Art. 81 to public undertakings.

2. Any agreements or decisions prohibited pursuant to this Article shall be automatically void.
3. The provisions of paragraph 1 may, however, be declared inapplicable in the case of:
— any agreement or category of agreements between undertakings;
— any decision or category of decisions by associations of undertakings;
— any concerted practice or category of concerted practices;
which contributes to improving the production or distribution of goods or to promoting technical or economic progress, while allowing consumers a fair share of the resulting benefit, and which does not:
(a) impose on the undertakings concerned restrictions which are not indispensable to the attainment of these objectives;
(b) afford such undertakings the possibility of eliminating competition in respect of a substantial part of the products in question.

Article 82[8] [Abuse of dominant position]

2–084 Any abuse by one or more undertakings of a dominant position within the common market or in a substantial part of it shall be prohibited as incompatible with the common market in so far as it may affect trade between Member States. Such abuse may, in particular, consist in:
(a) directly or indirectly imposing unfair purchase or selling prices or other unfair trading conditions;
(b) limiting production, markets or technical development to the prejudice of consumers;
(c) applying dissimilar conditions to equivalent transactions with other trading parties, thereby placing them at a competitive disadvantage;
(d) making the conclusion of contracts subject to acceptance by the other parties of supplementary obligations which, by their nature or according to commercial usage, have no connection with the subject of such contracts.

Article 83[9] [Implementation of competition policy]

2–085 1. The appropriate regulations or directives to give effect to the principles set out in Articles 81 and 82 shall be laid down by the Council, acting by a qualified majority on a proposal from the Commission and after consulting the European Parliament.

2. The regulations or directives referred to in paragraph 1 shall be designed in particular:
(a) to ensure compliance with the prohibitions laid down in Article 81(1) and in Article 82 by making provision for fines and periodic penalty payments;
(b) to lay down detailed rules for the application of Article 81(3), taking into account the need to ensure effective supervision on the one hand, and to simplify administration to the greatest possible extent on the other;
(c) to define, if need be, in the various branches of the economy, the scope of the provisions of Articles 81 and 82;
(d) to define the respective functions of the Commission and of the Court of Justice in applying the provisions laid down in this paragraph;
(e) to determine the relationship between national laws and the provisions contained in this section or adopted pursuant to this Article.

[8] Formerly Art. 86. See Art. 86 below for application of Art. 82 to public undertakings. For merger control (control of concentrations creating or strengthening dominant positions significantly impeding intra-Community competition), see Reg. 4064/89 reproduced below.
[9] Formerly Art. 87. In former Art. 87(1), two sub-paragraphs merged and wording replaced to remove references to transitional procedures for adoption of competition rules by Treaty of Amsterdam, Art. 6(I)(46). See Reg. 17/62 (and its replacement, Reg. 1/2003) reproduced below for implementation of Art. 81 and 82.

Article 84[10] [Interim role of Member State authorities]

Until the entry into force of the provisions adopted in pursuance of Article 83, the authorities in Member States shall rule on the admissibility of agreements, decisions and concerted practices and on abuse of a dominant position in the common market in accordance with the law of their country and with the provisions of Article 81, in particular paragraph 3, and of Article 82. **2–086**

Article 85[11] [Commission role in enforcement of competition rules]

1. Without prejudice to Article 84, the Commission shall ensure the application of the principles laid down in Articles 81 and 82. On application by a Member State or on its own initiative, and in cooperation with the competent authorities in the Member States, who shall give it their assistance, the Commission shall investigate cases of suspected infringement of these principles. If it finds that there has been an infringement, it shall propose appropriate measures to bring it to an end. **2–087**

2. If the infringement is not brought to an end, the Commission shall record such infringement of the principles in a reasoned decision. The Commission may publish its decision and authorise Member States to take the measures, the conditions and details of which it shall determine, needed to remedy the situation.

Article 86[12] [Public undertakings]

1. In the case of public undertakings and undertakings to which Member States grant special or exclusive rights, Member States shall neither enact nor maintain in force any measure contrary to the rules contained in this Treaty, in particular to those rules provided for in Article 12 and Articles 81 to 89. **2–088**

2. Undertakings entrusted with the operation of services of general economic interest or having the character of a revenue-producing monopoly shall be subject to the rules contained in this Treaty, in particular to the rules on competition, in so far as the application of such rules does not obstruct the performance, in law or in fact, of the particular tasks assigned to them. The development of trade must not be affected to such an extent as would be contrary to the interests of the Community.

3. The Commission shall ensure the application of the provisions of this Article and shall, where necessary, address appropriate directives or decisions to Member States.

SECTION 2—AIDS GRANTED BY STATES

Article 87[13] [Position of state aid under the EC Treaty]

1. Save as otherwise provided in this Treaty, any aid granted by a Member State or through State resources in any form whatsoever which distorts or threatens to distort competition by favouring certain undertakings or the production of certain goods shall, in so far as it affects trade between Member States, be incompatible with the common market. **2–089**

2. The following shall be compatible with the common market:

(a) aid having a social character, granted to individual consumers, provided that such aid is granted without discrimination related to the origin of the products concerned;

---

[10] Formerly Art. 88.

[11] Formerly Art. 89. In former Art. 89(1), transitional wording deleted by Treaty of Amsterdam, Art. 6(I)(47). See Reg. 17/62 and 1/2003 below for procedure for enforcing Arts 81 and 82.

[12] Formerly Art. 90.

[13] Formerly Art. 92. In former Art. 92(3), second sentence in point (c) (reduction of aid for shipbuilding over transitional period) deleted by Treaty of Amsterdam, Art. 6(I)(51). Former Art. 93(2)(d) inserted and Art. 93(2)(e) relettered by Art. 8(D)(18) TEU.

(b) aid to make good the damage caused by natural disasters or exceptional occurrences;
(c) aid granted to the economy of certain areas of the Federal Republic of Germany affected by the division of Germany, in so far as such aid is required in order to compensate for the economic disadvantages caused by that division.

3. The following may be considered to be compatible with the common market:
(a) aid to promote the economic development of areas where the standard of living is abnormally low or where there is serious underemployment;
(b) aid to promote the execution of an important project of common European interest or to remedy a serious disturbance in the economy of a Member State;
(c) aid to facilitate the development of certain economic activities or of certain economic areas, where such aid does not adversely affect trading conditions to an extent contrary to the common interest;
(d) aid to promote culture and heritage conservation where such aid does not affect trading conditions and competition in the Community to an extent that is contrary to the common interest;
(e) such other categories of aid as may be specified by decision of the Council acting by a qualified majority on a proposal from the Commission.

Article 88[14] **[Procedure for reviewing Member State aid]**

2–090 1. The Commission shall, in cooperation with Member States, keep under constant review all systems of aid existing in those States. It shall propose to the latter any appropriate measures required by the progressive development or by the functioning of the common market.

2. If, after giving notice to the parties concerned to submit their comments, the Commission finds that aid granted by a State or through State resources is not compatible with the common market having regard to Article 87, or that such aid is being misused, it shall decide that the State concerned shall abolish or alter such aid within a period of time to be determined by the Commission.

If the State concerned does not comply with this decision within the prescribed time, the Commission or any other interested State may, in derogation from the provisions of Articles 226 and 227, refer the matter to the Court of Justice direct.

On application by a Member State, the Council may, acting unanimously, decide that aid which that State is granting or intends to grant shall be considered to be compatible with the common market, in derogation from the provisions of Article 87 or from the regulations provided for in Article 89, if such a decision is justified by exceptional circumstances. If, as regards the aid in question, the Commission has already initiated the procedure provided for in the first sub-paragraph of this paragraph, the fact that the State concerned has made its application to the Council shall have the effect of suspending that procedure until the Council has made its attitude known.

If, however, the Council has not made its attitude known within three months of the said application being made, the Commission shall give its decision on the case.

3. The Commission shall be informed, in sufficient time to enable it to submit its comments, of any plans to grant or alter aid. If it considers that any such plan is not compatible with the common market having regard to Article 87, it shall without delay initiate the procedure provided for in paragraph 2. The Member State

[14] Formerly Art. 93. See Reg. 659/1999 ([1999] OJ L83/1) for detailed rules for application of Art. 88.

concerned shall not put its proposed measures into effect until this procedure has resulted in a final decision.

Article 89[15] [Implementing regulations]

The Council, acting by a qualified majority on a proposal from the Commission and after consulting the European Parliament, may make any appropriate regulations for the application of Articles 87 and 88 and may in particular determine the conditions in which Article 88(3) shall apply and the categories of aid exempted from this procedure. **2–091**

CHAPTER 2—TAX PROVISIONS

Article 90[16] [Discriminatory or protective internal taxation prohibited]

No Member State shall impose, directly or indirectly, on the products of other Member States any internal taxation of any kind in excess of that imposed directly or indirectly on similar domestic products. **2–092**

Furthermore, no Member State shall impose on the products of other Member States any internal taxation of such a nature as to afford indirect protection to other products.

Article 91[17] [Limit on repayment of internal taxation on exported goods]

Where products are exported to the territory of any Member State, any repayment of internal taxation shall not exceed the internal taxation imposed on them whether directly or indirectly. **2–093**

Article 92[18] [Restrictions on equalisation charges or remissions]

In the case of charges other than turnover taxes, excise duties and other forms of indirect taxation, remissions and repayments in respect of exports to other Member States may not be granted and countervailing charges in respect of imports from Member States may not be imposed unless the measures contemplated have been previously approved for a limited period by the Council acting by a qualified majority on a proposal from the Commission. **2–094**

Article 93[19] [Harmonisation of indirect taxation]

The Council shall, acting unanimously on a proposal from the Commission and after consulting the European Parliament and the Economic and Social Committee, adopt provisions for the harmonisation of legislation concerning turnover taxes, excise duties and other forms of indirect taxation[20] to the extent that such harmonisation is necessary to ensure the establishment and the functioning of the internal market within the time-limit laid down in Article 14. **2–095**

CHAPTER 3—APPROXIMATION OF LAWS

Article 94[21] [Approximation of laws affecting functioning of common market]

The Council shall, acting unanimously on a proposal from the Commission and after consulting the European Parliament and the Economic and Social **2–096**

[15] Formerly Art. 94. Former Art. 94 previously replaced by Art. 8(19) TEU.

[16] Formerly Art. 95. Former Art. 95, third paragraph (transitional provision) deleted by Treaty of Amsterdam, Art. 6(I)(52). For prohibition of customs duties or equivalent charges on intra-Community imports, see Art. 25.

[17] Formerly Art. 96.

[18] Formerly Art. 98.

[19] Formerly Art. 99. Former Art. 99 replaced by Art. 8(20) TEU. Previously replaced by Art. 17 SEA.

[20] For harmonisation of direct taxes, see Art. 94 below.

[21] Formerly Art. 100. Former Art. 100 replaced by Art. 8(21) TEU.

Committee, issue directives for the approximation of such laws, regulations or administrative provisions of the Member States as directly affect the establishment or functioning of the common market.

Article 95[22] **[Procedure for measures completing the internal market]**

2–097 1. By way of derogation from Article 94 and save where otherwise provided in this Treaty, the following provisions shall apply for the achievement of the objectives set out in Article 14. The Council shall, acting in accordance with the procedure referred to in Article 251 and after consulting the Economic and Social Committee, adopt the measures for the approximation of the provisions laid down by law, regulation or administrative action in Member States which have as their object the establishment and functioning of the internal market.

2. Paragraph 1 shall not apply to fiscal provisions, to those relating to the free movement of persons nor to those relating to the rights and interests of employed persons.

3. The Commission, in its proposals envisaged in paragraph 1 concerning health, safety, environmental protection and consumer protection, will take as a base a high level of protection, taking account in particular of any new development based on scientific facts. Within their respective powers, the European Parliament and the Council will also seek to achieve this objective.

4. If, after the adoption by the Council or by the Commission of a harmonisation measure, a Member State deems it necessary to maintain national provisions on grounds of major needs referred to in Article 30, or relating to the protection of the environment or the working environment, it shall notify the Commission of these provisions as well as the grounds for maintaining them.

5. Moreover, without prejudice to paragraph 4, if, after the adoption by the Council or by the Commission of a harmonisation measure, a Member State deems it necessary to introduce national provisions based on new scientific evidence relating to the protection of the environment or the working environment on grounds of a problem specific to that Member State arising after the adoption of the harmonisation measure, it shall notify the Commission of the envisaged provisions as well as the grounds for introducing them.

6. The Commission shall, within six months of the notifications as referred to in paragraphs 4 and 5, approve or reject the national provisions involved after having verified whether or not they are a means of arbitrary discrimination or a disguised restriction on trade between Member States and whether or not they shall constitute an obstacle to the functioning of the internal market.

In the absence of a decision by the Commission within this period the national provisions referred to in paragraphs 4 and 5 shall be deemed to have been approved.

When justified by the complexity of the matter and in the absence of danger for human health, the Commission may notify the Member State concerned that the period referred to in this paragraph may be extended for a further period of up to six months.

7. When, pursuant to paragraph 6, a Member State is authorised to maintain or introduce national provisions derogating from a harmonisation measure, the

[22] Formerly Art. 100a. Former Art. 100a(3)–(10) replaced former para. (3)–(5) by virtue of Treaty of Amsterdam, Art. 2(17). Former Art. 100a previously replaced by Art. 8(22) TEU. Previous Art. 100a added by Art. 18 SEA. See Declaration (No. 22) regarding persons with a disability annexed to Final Act of Treaty of Amsterdam.

Commission shall immediately examine whether to propose an adaptation to that measure.

8. When a Member State raises a specific problem on public health in a field which has been the subject of prior harmonisation measures, it shall bring it to the attention of the Commission which shall immediately examine whether to propose appropriate measures to the Council.

9. By way of derogation from the procedure laid down in Articles 226 and 227, the Commission and any Member State may bring the matter directly before the Court of Justice if it considers that another Member State is making improper use of the powers provided for in this Article.

10. The harmonisation measures referred to above shall, in appropriate cases, include a safeguard clause authorising the Member States to take, for one or more of the non-economic reasons referred to in Article 30, provisional measures subject to a Community control procedure.

Article 96[23] **[Distortions of competition caused by differences in Member State laws]**

Where the Commission finds that a difference between the provisions laid down by law, regulation or administrative action in Member States is distorting the conditions of competition in the common market and that the resultant distortion needs to be eliminated, it shall consult the Member States concerned. **2–098**

If such consultation does not result in an agreement eliminating the distortion in question, the Council shall, on a proposal from the Commission, acting by a qualified majority, issue the necessary directives. The Commission and the Council may take any other appropriate measures provided for in this Treaty.

Article 97[24] **[Member States wishing to proceed with laws, etc. that could distort conditions of competition]**

1. Where there is a reason to fear that the adoption or amendment of a provision laid down by law, regulation or administrative action may cause distortion within the meaning of Article 96, a Member State desiring to proceed therewith shall consult the Commission. After consulting the Member States, the Commission shall recommend to the States concerned such measures as may be appropriate to avoid the distortion in question. **2–099**

2. If a State desiring to introduce or amend its own provisions does not comply with the recommendation addressed to it by the Commission, other Member States shall not be required, in pursuance of Article 96, to amend their own provisions in order to eliminate such distortion. If the Member State which has ignored the recommendation of the Commission causes distortion detrimental only to itself, the provisions of Article 96 shall not apply.

TITLE VII—ECONOMIC AND MONETARY POLICY

CHAPTER 1—ECONOMIC POLICY

Article 98[25] **[Conduct of Member State economic policies]**

Member States shall conduct their economic policies with a view to contributing to the achievement of the objectives of the Community, as defined in Article 2, and in **2–100**

[23] Formerly Art. 101. In former Art. 101, second paragraph, the words "acting by a qualified majority" substituted for transitional wording by Treaty of Amsterdam, Art. 6(I)(54).

[24] Formerly Art. 102.

[25] Formerly Art. 102a. Former Art. 102a replaced by Art. 8(25) TEU. Previous Art. 102a inserted by Art. 20(1) SEA.

the context of the broad guidelines referred to in Article 99(2).[26] The Member States and the Community shall act in accordance with the principle of an open market economy with free competition, favouring an efficient allocation of resources, and in compliance with the principles set out in Article 4.

Article 99[27] [Coordination of Member State economic policies]

2–101 1. Member States shall regard their economic policies as a matter of common concern and shall coordinate them within the Council, in accordance with the provisions of Article 98.

2. The Council shall, acting by a qualified majority on a recommendation from the Commission, formulate a draft for the broad guidelines of the economic policies of the Member States and of the Community, and shall report its findings to the European Council.

The European Council shall, acting on the basis of the report from the Council, discuss a conclusion on the broad guidelines of the economic policies of the Member States and of the Community.

On the basis of this conclusion, the Council shall, acting by a qualified majority, adopt a recommendation setting out these broad guidelines. The Council shall inform the European Parliament of its recommendation.

3. In order to ensure closer co-ordination of economic policies and sustained convergence of the economic performances of the Member States, the Council shall, on the basis of reports submitted by the Commission, monitor economic developments in each of the Member States and in the Community as well as the consistency of economic policies with the broad guidelines referred to in paragraph 2, and regularly carry out an overall assessment.

For the purpose of this multilateral surveillance, Member States shall forward information to the Commission about important measures taken by them in the field of their economic policy and such other information as they deem necessary.

4. Where it is established, under the procedure referred to in paragraph 3, that the economic policies of a Member State are not consistent with the broad guidelines referred to in paragraph 2 or that they risk jeopardising the proper functioning of economic and monetary union, the Council may, acting by a qualified majority on a recommendation from the Commission, make the necessary recommendations to the Member State concerned. The Council may, acting by a qualified majority on a proposal from the Commission, decide to make its recommendations public.

The President of the Council and the Commission shall report to the European Parliament on the results of multilateral surveillance. The President of the Council may be invited to appear before the competent committee of the European Parliament if the Council has made its recommendations public.

5. The Council, acting in accordance with the procedure referred to in Article 252, may adopt detailed rules for the multilateral surveillance procedure referred to in paragraphs 3 and 4 of this Article.

Article 100[28] [Reactive measures]

2–102 1. Without prejudice to any other procedures provided for in this Treaty, the Council, acting by a qualified majority on a proposal from the Commission, may decide upon the measures appropriate to the economic situation, in particular if severe difficulties arise in the supply of certain products.

---

[26] Member States to conduct economic policies in such a way as to strengthen economic and social cohesion (see Art. 159).

[27] Formerly Art. 103. Former Art. 103 replaced by Art. 8(25) TEU.

[28] Article 100 replaced by Treaty of Nice, Art. 2(5). Formerly Art. 103a. Former Art. 103a replaced by Art. 8(25) TEU.

2. Where a Member State is in difficulties or is seriously threatened with severe difficulties caused by natural disasters or exceptional occurrences beyond its control, the Council, acting by a qualified majority on a proposal from the Commission, may grant, under certain conditions, Community financial assistance to the Member State concerned. The President of the Council shall inform the European Parliament of the decision taken.

Article 101[29] **[Credit facilities with central banks prohibited]**

1. Overdraft facilities or any other type of credit facility with the ECB or with the central banks of the Member States (hereinafter referred to as "national central banks") in favour of Community institutions or bodies, central governments, regional, local or other public authorities, other bodies governed by public law, or public undertakings of Member States shall be prohibited, as shall the purchase directly from them by the ECB or national central banks of debt instruments. **2–103**

2. Paragraph 1 shall not apply to publicly owned credit institutions which, in the context of the supply of reserves by central banks, shall be given the same treatment by national central banks and the ECB as private credit institutions.

Article 102[30] **[Privileged access to financial institutions prohibited]**

1. Any measure, not based on prudential considerations, establishing privileged access by Community institutions or bodies, central governments, regional, local or other public authorities, other bodies governed by public law, or public undertakings of Member States to financial institutions, shall be prohibited.[31] **2–104**

2. The Council, acting in accordance with the procedure referred to in Article 252, shall, before 1 January 1994, specify definitions for the application of the prohibition referred to in paragraph 1.

Article 103[32] **[No EC liability for government/other public commitments]**

1. The Community shall not be liable for or assume the commitments of central governments, regional, local or other public authorities, other bodies governed by public law, or public undertakings of any Member State, without prejudice to mutual financial guarantees for the joint execution of a specific project. A Member State shall not be liable for or assume the commitments of central governments, regional, local or other public authorities, other bodies governed by public law, or public undertakings of another Member State, without prejudice to mutual financial guarantees for the joint execution of a specific project.[33] **2–105**

2. If necessary, the Council, acting in accordance with the procedure referred to in Article 252, may specify definitions for the application of the prohibition referred to in Article 101 and in this Article.

Article 104[34] **[Budgetary discipline]**

1. Member States shall avoid excessive government deficits. **2–106**

2. The Commission shall monitor the development of the budgetary situation and

[29] Formerly Art. 104. Former Art. 104 replaced by Art. 8(25) TEU. Provisions of Art. 101 applied from 1 January 1994 (see Art. 116).

[30] Formerly Art. 104a. Former Art. 104a replaced by Art. 8(25) TEU.

[31] Provisions of Art. 102(1) applied from 1 January 1994 (see Art. 116).

[32] Formerly Art. 104b. Former Art. 104b replaced by Art. 8(25) TEU.

[33] Provisions of Art. 103(1) applied from 1 January 1994 (see Art. 116).

[34] Formerly Art. 104c. Former Art. 104c replaced by Art. 8(25) TEU. Art. 104(2)–(8), (10), (12) and (13) applied from 1 January 1994, and Art. 104(1), (9), (11) and (14) applied from beginning of third stage of EMU (1 January 1999) (see Art. 116). Article 104(1), (9) and (11) do not apply to the UK (see Protocol (No. 25) on certain provisions relating to the UK, Art. 5).

of the stock of government debt in the Member States with a view to identifying gross errors. In particular it shall examine compliance with budgetary discipline on the basis of the following two criteria.

(a) whether the ratio of the planned or actual government deficit to gross domestic product exceeds a reference value, unless:
 — either the ratio has declined substantially and continuously and reached a level that comes close to the reference value;
 — or, alternatively, the excess over the reference value is only exceptional and temporary and the ratio remains close to the reference value;

(b) whether the ratio of government debt to gross domestic product exceeds a reference value, unless the ratio is sufficiently diminishing and approaching the reference value at a satisfactory pace.

The reference values are specified in the Protocol on the excessive deficit procedure annexed to this Treaty.[35]

3. If a Member State does not fulfil the requirements under one or both of these criteria, the Commission shall prepare a report. The report of the Commission shall also take into account whether the government deficit exceeds government investment expenditure and take into account all other relevant factors, including the medium-term economic and budgetary position of the Member State.

The Commission may also prepare a report if, notwithstanding the fulfilment of the requirements under the criteria, it is of the opinion that there is a risk of an excessive deficit in a Member State.

4. The Committee provided for in Article 114 shall formulate an opinion on the report of the Commission.

5. If the Commission considers that an excessive deficit in a Member State exists or may occur, the Commission shall address an opinion to the Council.

6. The Council shall, acting by a qualified majority on a recommendation from the Commission, and having considered any observations which the Member State concerned may wish to make, decide after an overall assessment whether an excessive deficit exists.

7. Where the existence of an excessive deficit is decided according to paragraph 6, the Council shall make recommendations to the Member State concerned with a view to bringing that situation to an end within a given period. Subject to the provisions of paragraph 8, these recommendations shall not be made public.

8. Where it establishes that there has been no effective action in response to its recommendations within the period laid down, the Council may make its recommendations public.

9. If a Member State persists in failing to put into practice the recommendations of the Council, the Council may decide to give notice to the Member State to take, within a specified time-limit, measures for the deficit reduction which is judged necessary by the Council in order to remedy the situation.

In such a case, the Council may request the Member State concerned to submit reports in accordance with a specific timetable in order to examine the adjustment efforts of that Member State.[36]

10. The rights to bring actions provided for in Articles 226 and 227 may not be exercised within the framework of paragraphs 1 to 9 of this Article.

11. As long as a Member State fails to comply with a decision taken in accordance with paragraph 9, the Council may decide to apply or, as the case may be, intensify one or more of the following measures:
 — to require the Member State concerned to publish additional information, to be specified by the Council, before issuing bonds and securities;

[35] Protocol (No. 20) on the excessive deficit procedure (1992).
[36] Article 104(9) and (11) do not apply to Member States with a derogation from EMU (see Art. 122).

— to invite the European Investment Bank to reconsider its lending policy towards the Member State concerned;
— to require the Member State concerned to make a non-interest-bearing deposit of an appropriate size with the Community until the excessive deficit has, in the view of the Council, been corrected;
— to impose fines of an appropriate size.

The President of the Council shall inform the European Parliament of the decisions taken.[37]

12. The Council shall abrogate some or all of its decisions referred to in paragraphs 6 to 9 and 11 to the extent that the excessive deficit in the Member State concerned has, in the view of the Council, been corrected. If the Council has previously made public recommendations, it shall, as soon as the decision under paragraph 8 has been abrogated, make a public statement that an excessive deficit in the Member State concerned no longer exists.

13. When taking the decisions referred to in paragraphs 7 to 9, 11 and 12, the Council shall act on a recommendation from the Commission by a majority of two-thirds of the votes of its members weighted in accordance with Article 205(2), excluding the votes of the representative of the Member State concerned.

14. Further provisions relating to the implementation of the procedure described in this Article are set out in the Protocol on the excessive deficit procedure annexed to this Treaty.[38]

The Council shall, acting unanimously on a proposal from the Commission and after consulting the European Parliament and the ECB, adopt the appropriate provisions which shall then replace the said Protocol.

Subject to the other provisions of this paragraph, the Council shall, before 1 January 1994, acting by a qualified majority on a proposal from the Commission and after consulting the European Parliament, lay down detailed rules and definitions for the application of the provisions of the said Protocol.

CHAPTER 2—MONETARY POLICY

Article 105[39] [Objectives and tasks of the ESCB]

1. The primary objective of the ESCB shall be to maintain price stability. Without **2–107**
prejudice to the objective of price stability, the ESCB shall support the general economic policies in the Community with a view to contributing to the achievement of the objectives of the Community as laid down in Article 2. The ESCB shall act in accordance with the principle of an open market economy with free competition, favouring an efficient allocation of resources, and in compliance with the principles set out in Article 4.

2. The basic tasks to be carried out through the ESCB shall be:
— to define and implement the monetary policy of the Community;
— to conduct foreign exchange operations consistent with the provisions of Article 111;
— to hold and manage the official foreign reserves of the Member States;
— to promote the smooth operation of payment systems.

3. The third indent of paragraph 2 shall be without prejudice to the holding and management by the governments of Member States of foreign-exchange working balances.

---

[37] *ibid.*

[38] Protocol (No. 20) on the excessive deficit procedure (1992).

[39] Formerly Art. 105. Former Art. 105 replaced by Art. 8(25) TEU. Article 105 took effect from the beginning of the third stage of EMU (1 January 1999) (see Art. 116). Article 105(1)–(3) and (5) do not apply to Member States with a derogation from EMU (see Art. 122); Art. 105(1)—(5) do not apply specifically to the UK (see Protocol (No. 25) on certain provisions relating to the UK, Art. 5).

4. The ECB shall be consulted:
— on any proposed Community act in its fields of competence;
— by national authorities regarding any draft legislative provision in its fields of competence, but within the limits and under the conditions set out by the Council in accordance with the procedure laid down in Article 107(6).

The ECB may submit opinions to the appropriate Community institutions or bodies or to national authorities on matters in its fields of competence.

5. The ESCB shall contribute to the smooth conduct of policies pursued by the competent authorities relating to the prudential supervision of credit institutions and the stability of the financial system.

6. The Council may, acting unanimously on a proposal from the Commission and after consulting the ECB and after receiving the assent of the European Parliament, confer upon the ECB specific tasks concerning policies relating to the prudential supervision of credit institutions and other financial institutions with the exception of insurance undertakings.

Article 106[40] **[Issue of banknotes and coins]**

2–108 1. The ECB shall have the exclusive right to authorise the issue of banknotes within the Community. The ECB and the national central banks may issue such notes. The banknotes issued by the ECB and the national central banks shall be the only such notes to have the status of legal tender within the Community.

2. Member States may issue coins subject to approval by the ECB of the volume of the issue. The Council may, acting in accordance with the procedure referred to in Article 252 and after consulting the ECB, adopt measures to harmonise the denominations and technical specifications of all coins intended for circulation to the extent necessary to permit their smooth circulation within the Community.

Article 107[41] **[Composition and rules of the ESCB]**

2–109 1. The ESCB shall be composed of the ECB and of the national central banks.

2. The ECB shall have legal personality.

3. The ESCB shall be governed by the decision-making bodies of the ECB which shall be the Governing Council and the Executive Board.

4. The Statute of the ESCB is laid down in a Protocol annexed to this Treaty.[42]

5. Articles 5.1, 5.2, 5.3, 17, 18, 19.1, 22, 23, 24, 26, 32.2, 32.3, 32.4, 32.6, 33.1(a) and 36 of the Statute of the ESCB may be amended by the Council, acting either by a qualified majority on a recommendation from the ECB and after consulting the Commission or unanimously on a proposal from the Commission and after consulting the ECB. In either case, the assent of the European Parliament shall be required.

6. The Council, acting by a qualified majority either on a proposal from the Commission and after consulting the European Parliament and the ECB or on a recommendation from the ECB and after consulting the European Parliament and the Commission, shall adopt the provisions referred to in Articles 4, 5.4, 19.2, 20, 28.1, 29.2, 30.4 and 34.3 of the Statute of the ESCB.

---

[40] Formerly Art. 105a. Former Art. 105a replaced by Art. 8(25) TEU. Article 106 took effect from beginning of third stage of EMU (1 January 1999) (see Art. 116) and does not apply to Member States with a derogation from EMU (see Art. 122). Article 106 does not apply specifically to the UK (see Protocol (No. 25) on certain provisions relating to the UK, Art. 5).

[41] Formerly Art. 106. Former Art. 106 replaced by Art. 8(25) TEU.

[42] Protocol (No. 18) on the Statute of the ESCB and of the ECB (1992).

Article 108[43] **[Independence of ECB and national central banks]**

When exercising the powers and carrying out the tasks and duties conferred upon them by this Treaty and the Statute of the ESCB, neither the ECB, nor a national central bank, nor any member of their decision-making bodies shall seek or take instructions from Community institutions or bodies, from any government of a Member State or from any other body. The Community institutions and bodies and the governments of the Member States undertake to respect this principle and not to seek to influence the members of the decision-making bodies of the ECB or of the national central banks in the performance of their tasks. **2–110**

Article 109[44] **[National laws to be compatible with EC Treaty]**

Each Member State shall ensure, at the latest at the date of the establishment of the ESCB, that its national legislation including the statutes of its national central bank is compatible with this Treaty and the Statute of the ESCB. **2–111**

Article 110[45] **[Rule-making powers of the ECB]**

1. In order to carry out the tasks entrusted to the ESCB, the ECB shall, in accordance with the provisions of this Treaty and under the conditions laid down in the Statute of the ESCB: **2–112**
— make regulations to the extent necessary to implement the tasks defined in Article 3.1, first indent, Articles 19.1, 22 and 25.2 of the Statute of the ESCB and in cases which shall be laid down in the acts of the Council referred to in Article 107(6);
— take decisions necessary for carrying out the tasks entrusted to the ESCB under this Treaty and the Statute of the ESCB;
— make recommendations and deliver opinions.

2. A regulation shall have general application. It shall be binding in its entirety and directly applicable in all Member States.

Recommendations and opinions shall have no binding force.

A decision shall be binding in its entirety upon those to whom it is addressed.

Articles 253 to 256 shall apply to regulations and decisions adopted by the ECB.

The ECB may decide to publish its decisions, recommendations and opinions.

3. Within the limits and under the conditions adopted by the Council under the procedure laid down in Article 107(6), the ECB shall be entitled to impose fines or periodic penalty payments on undertakings for failure to comply with obligations under its regulations and decisions.

Article 111[46] **[Exchange rate policy]**

1. By way of derogation from Article 300, the Council may, acting unanimously on a recommendation from the ECB or from the Commission, and after consulting the ECB in an endeavour to reach a consensus consistent with the objective of price stability, after consulting the European Parliament, in accordance with the **2–113**

[43] Formerly Art. 107. Former Art. 107 replaced by Art. 8(25) TEU. Article 108 took effect from beginning of third stage of EMU (1 January 1999) (see Art. 116). Article 108 does not apply to the UK (see Protocol (No. 25) on certain provisions relating to the UK, Art. 5).

[44] Formerly Art. 108. Former Art. 108 replaced by Art. 8(25) TEU. Article 109 does not apply to the UK (see Protocol (No. 25) on certain provisions relating to the UK, Art. 5).

[45] Formerly Art. 108a. Former Art. 108a replaced by Art. 8(25) TEU. Article 110 does not apply to Member States with a derogation from EMU (see Art. 122); specifically it does not apply to the UK (see Protocol (No. 25) on certain provisions relating to the UK, Art. 5).

[46] Formerly Art. 109. Former Art. 109 replaced by Art. 8(25) TEU. Provisions of Art. 111 took effect from beginning of third stage of EMU (1 January 1999) (see Art. 116(3)); Art. 111 does not apply to Member States with a derogation from EMU (see Art. 122); specifically it does not apply to the UK (see Protocol (No. 25) on certain provisions relating to the UK, Art. 5).

procedure in paragraph 3 for determining the arrangements, conclude formal agreements on an exchange rate system for the ECU in relation to non-Community currencies. The Council may, acting by a qualified majority on a recommendation from the ECB or from the Commission, and after consulting the ECB in an endeavour to reach a consensus consistent with the objective of price stability, adopt, adjust or abandon the central rates of the ECU within the exchange rate system. The President of the Council shall inform the European Parliament of the adoption, adjustment or abandonment of the ECU central rates.

2. In the absence of an exchange rate system in relation to one or more non-Community currencies as referred to in paragraph 1, the Council, acting by a qualified majority either on a recommendation from the Commission and after consulting the ECB or on a recommendation from the ECB, may formulate general orientations for exchange-rate policy in relation to these currencies. These general orientations shall be without prejudice to the primary objective of the ESCB to maintain price stability.

3. By way of derogation from Article 300, where agreements concerning monetary or foreign exchange regime matters need to be negotiated by the Community with one or more States or international organisations, the Council, acting by a qualified majority on a recommendation from the Commission and after consulting the ECB, shall decide the arrangements for the negotiation and for the conclusion of such agreements. These arrangements shall ensure that the Community expresses a single position. The Commission shall be fully associated with the negotiations.
Agreements concluded in accordance with this paragraph shall be binding on the institutions of the Community, on the ECB and on Member States.

4. Subject to paragraph 1, the Council, acting by a qualified majority on a proposal from the Commission and after consulting the ECB, shall decide on the position of the Community at international level as regards issues of particular relevance to economic and monetary union and on its representation, in compliance with the allocation of powers laid down in Articles 99 and 105.[47]

5. Without prejudice to Community competence and Community agreements as regards economic and monetary union, Member States may negotiate in international bodies and conclude international agreements.

CHAPTER 3—INSTITUTIONAL PROVISIONS

Article 112[48] [ECB Governing Council and Executive Board]

2–114 1. The Governing Council of the ECB shall comprise the members of the Executive Board of the ECB and the Governors of the national central banks.[49]

2.(a) The Executive Board shall comprise the President, the Vice-President and four other members.

(b) The President, the Vice-President and the other members of the Executive Board shall be appointed from among persons of recognised standing and professional experience in monetary or banking matters by common accord of the governments of the Member States at the level of Heads of State or Government, on a recommendation from the Council, after it has consulted the European Parliament and the Governing Council of the ECB.[50]

---

[47] Article 111(4) replaced by Treaty of Nice, Art. 2(6).

[48] Formerly Art. 109a. Former Art. 109a replaced by Art. 8(25) TEU. Provisions of Art. 112 took effect from beginning of third stage of EMU (1 January 1999) (see Art. 116(3)).

[49] Article 112(1) does not apply to the UK (see Protocol (No. 25) on certain provisions relating to the UK, Art. 5).

[50] Article 112(2)(b) does not apply to Member States with a derogation from EMU (see Art. 122); it does not apply to the UK by virtue of Protocol (No. 25) on certain provisions relating to the UK, Art. 5).

Their term of office shall be eight years and shall not be renewable.
Only nationals of Member States may be members of the Executive Board.

Article 113[51] **[ECB meetings and annual reports]**

1. The President of the Council and a member of the Commission may participate, without having the right to vote, in meetings of the Governing Council of the ECB. The President of the Council may submit a motion for deliberation to the Governing Council of the ECB. **2–115**

2. The President of the ECB shall be invited to participate in Council meetings when the Council is discussing matters relating to the objectives and tasks of the ESCB.

3. The ECB shall address an annual report on the activities of the ESCB and on the monetary policy of both the previous and current year to the European Parliament, the Council and the Commission, and also to the European Council. The President of the ECB shall present this report to the Council and to the European Parliament, which may hold a general debate on that basis.

The President of the ECB and the other members of the Executive Board may, at the request of the European Parliament or on their own initiative, be heard by the competent committees of the European Parliament.

Article 114[52] **[Economic and Financial Committee]**

1. In order to promote co-ordination of the policies of Member States to the full extent needed for the functioning of the internal market, a Monetary Committee with advisory status is hereby set up. **2–116**

It shall have the following tasks:

- to keep under review the monetary and financial situation of the Member States and of the Community and the general payments system of the Member States and to report regularly thereon to the Council and to the Commission;
- to deliver opinions at the request of the Council or of the Commission, or on its own initiative for submission to those institutions;
- without prejudice to Article 207, to contribute to the preparation of the work of the Council referred to in Articles 59, 60, 99(2), (3), (4) and (5), 100, 102, 103, 104, 116(2), 117(6), 119, 120, 121(2) and 122(1);
- to examine, at least once a year, the situation regarding the movement of capital and the freedom of payments, as they result from the application of this Treaty and of measures adopted by the Council; the examination shall cover all measures relating to capital movements and payments; the Committee shall report to the Commission and to the Council on the outcome of this examination.

The Member States and the Commission shall each appoint two members of the Monetary Committee.

2. At the start of the third stage, an Economic and Financial Committee shall be set up.

The Monetary Committee provided for in paragraph 1 shall be dissolved.

The Economic and Financial Committee shall have the following tasks:

[51] Formerly Art. 109b. Former Art. 109b replaced by Art. 8(25) TEU. Provisions of Art. 113 took effect from beginning of third stage of EMU (1 January 1999) (see Art. 116(3)).

[52] Formerly Art. 109c.

— to deliver opinions at the request of the Council or of the Commission, or on its own initiative for submission to those institutions;
— to keep under review the economic and financial situation of the Member States and of the Community and to report regularly thereon to the Council and to the Commission, in particular on financial relations with third countries and international institutions;
— without prejudice to Article 207, to contribute to the preparation of the work of the Council referred to in Articles 59, 60, 99(2), (3), (4) and (5), 100, 102, 103, 104, 105(6), 106(2), 107(5) and (6), 111, 119, 120(2) and (3), 122(2), 123(4) and (5), and to carry out other advisory and preparatory tasks assigned to it by the Council;
— to examine, at least once a year, the situation regarding the movement of capital and the freedom of payments, as they result from the application of this Treaty and of measures adopted by the Council; the examination shall cover all measures relating to capital movements and payments; the Committee shall report to the Commission and to the Council on the outcome of this examination.

The Member States, the Commission and the ECB shall each appoint no more than two members of the committee.

3. The Council shall, acting by a qualified majority on a proposal from the Commission and after consulting the ECB and the Committee referred to in this Article, lay down detailed provisions concerning the composition of the Economic and Financial Committee. The President of the Council shall inform the European Parliament of such a decision.

4. In addition to the tasks set out in paragraph 2, if and as long as there are Member States with a derogation as referred to in Articles 122 and 123, the Committee shall keep under review the monetary and financial situation and the general payments system of those Member States and report regularly thereon to the Council and to the Commission.

Article 115[53] **[Requests for Commission action]**

2–117 For matters within the scope of Articles 99(4), 104 with the exception of paragraph 14, 111, 121, 122 and 123(4) and (5), the Council or a Member State may request the Commission to make a recommendation or a proposal, as appropriate. The Commission shall examine this request and submit its conclusions to the Council without delay.

CHAPTER 4—TRANSITIONAL PROVISIONS

Article 116[54] **[Second stage of EMU]**

2–118 1. The second stage for achieving economic and monetary union shall begin on 1 January 1994.

2. Before that date:

(a) each Member State shall:
   — adopt, where necessary, appropriate measures to comply with the prohibitions laid down in Article 56 and in Articles 101 and 102(1);
   — adopt, if necessary, with a view to permitting the assessment provided for in sub-paragraph (b), multi-annual programmes intended to ensure the lasting convergence necessary for the achievement of economic and monetary union, in particular with regard to price stability and sound public finances;[55]

[53] Formerly Art. 109d. Former Art. 109d replaced by Art. 8(25) TEU.

[54] Formerly Art. 109e. Former Art. 109e replaced by Art. 8(25) TEU.

[55] In former Art. 109e(2)(a), first indent, the words ", without prejudice to Article 73e," deleted by Treaty of Amsterdam, Art. 6(I)(55).

(b) the Council shall, on the basis of a report from the Commission, assess the progress made with regard to economic and monetary convergence, in particular with regard to price stability and sound public finances, and the progress made with the implementation of Community law concerning the internal market.

3. The provisions of Articles 101, 102(1), 103(1) and 104 with the exception of paragraphs 1, 9, 11 and 14 shall apply from the beginning of the second stage.
The provisions of Articles 100(2), 104(1), (9) and (11), 105, 106, 108, 111, 112, 113 and 114(2) and (4) shall apply from the beginning of the third stage.

4. In the second stage, Member States shall endeavour to avoid excessive government deficits.

5. During the second stage, each Member State shall, as appropriate, start the process leading to the independence of its central bank, in accordance with Article 109.

Article 117[56] **[EMI]**

1. At the start of the second stage, a European Monetary Institute (hereinafter referred to as "EMI") shall be established and take up its duties; it shall have legal personality and be directed and managed by a Council, consisting of a President and the governors of the national central banks, one of whom shall be Vice-President. **2–119**
The President shall be appointed by common accord of the governments of the Member States at the level of Heads of State or Government, on a recommendation from the Council of the EMI, and after consulting the European Parliament and the Council. The President shall be selected from among persons of recognised standing and professional experience in monetary or banking matters. Only nationals of Member States may be President of the EMI. The Council of the EMI shall appoint the Vice-President.
The Statute of the EMI is laid down in a Protocol annexed to this Treaty.[57]

2. The EMI shall:
— strengthen cooperation between the national central banks;
— strengthen the co-ordination of the monetary policies of the Member States, with the aim of ensuring price stability;
— monitor the functioning of the European Monetary System;
— hold consultations concerning issues falling within the competence of the national central banks and affecting the stability of financial institutions and markets;
— take over the tasks of the European Monetary Co-operation Fund, which shall be dissolved; the modalities of dissolution are laid down in the Statute of the EMI;
— facilitate the use of the ECU and oversee its development, including the smooth functioning of the ECU clearing system.

3. For the preparation of the third stage, the EMI shall:

[56] Formerly Art. 109f. Former Art. 109f replaced by Art. 8(25) TEU.
[57] Protocol (No. 19) on the Statute of the EMI (1992) not reproduced in this work. In former Art. 109f(1), second sub-paragraph, the words "on a recommendation from the Council of the EMI" replaced the words "on a recommendation from, as the case may be, the Committee of Governors of central banks of the Member States (hereinafter referred to as "Committee of Governors") or the Council of the EMI" by virtue of Treaty of Amsterdam, Art. 6(I)(56)(a). Former Art. 109f(1), fourth sub-paragraph (dissolution of Committee of Governors at start of EMU stage 2) deleted by Treaty of Amsterdam, Art. 6(I)(56)(b).

— prepare the instruments and the procedures necessary for carrying out a single monetary policy in the third stage;
— promote the harmonisation, where necessary, of the rules and practices governing the collection, compilation and distribution of statistics in the areas within its field of competence;
— prepare the rules for operations to be undertaken by the national central banks within the framework of the ESCB;
— promote the efficiency of cross-border payments;
— supervise the technical preparation of ECU banknotes.

At the latest by 31 December 1996, the EMI shall specify the regulatory, organisational and logistical framework necessary for the ESCB to perform its tasks in the third stage. This framework shall be submitted for decision to the ECB at the date of its establishment.

4. The EMI, acting by a majority of two-thirds of the members of its Council, may:
— formulate opinions or recommendations on the overall orientation of monetary policy and exchange-rate policy as well as on related measures introduced in each Member State;
— submit opinions or recommendations to governments and to the Council on policies which might affect the internal or external monetary situation in the Community and, in particular, the functioning of the European Monetary System;
— make recommendations to the monetary authorities of the Member States concerning the conduct of their monetary policy.

5. The EMI, acting unanimously, may decide to publish its opinions and its recommendations.

6. The EMI shall be consulted by the Council regarding any proposed Community act within its field of competence.

Within the limits and under the conditions set out by the Council, acting by a qualified majority on a proposal from the Commission and after consulting the European Parliament and the EMI, the EMI shall be consulted by the authorities of the Member States on any draft legislative provision within its field of competence.

7. The Council may, acting unanimously on a proposal from the Commission and after consulting the European Parliament and the EMI, confer upon the EMI other tasks for the preparation of the third stage.

8. Where this Treaty provides for a consultative role for the ECB, references to the ECB shall be read as referring to the EMI before the establishment of the ECB.[58]

9. During the second stage, the term "ECB" used in Articles 230, 232, 233, 234, 237 and 288 shall be read as referring to the EMI.

Article 118[59] [Composition and value of the ECU/euro]

2–120 The currency composition of the ECU basket shall not be changed.

From the start of the third stage, the value of the ECU shall be irrevocably fixed in accordance with Article 123(4).

[58] Former Art. 109f(8), second sub-paragraph (pre-1994 references to EMI to be construed as references to Committee of Governors) deleted by Treaty of Amsterdam, Art. 6(I)(56)(c).

[59] Formerly Art. 109g. Former Art. 109g replaced by Art. 8(25) TEU. See also Reg. 1103/97 ([1997] OJ L162/1): references to the ECU in all legal instruments replaced by references to the euro from 1 January 1999; and Reg. 2866/98 ([1998] OJ L359/1): conversion rates between the euro and currencies of Member States adopting the euro.

Article 119[60] **[Member States with serious balance of payments problems]**

1. Where a Member State is in difficulties or is seriously threatened with difficulties as regards its balance of payments either as a result of an overall disequilibrium in its balance of payments, or as a result of the type of currency at its disposal, and where such difficulties are liable in particular to jeopardise the functioning of the common market or the progressive implementation of the common commercial policy, the Commission shall immediately investigate the position of the State in question and the action which, making use of all the means at its disposal, that State has taken or may take in accordance with the provisions of this Treaty. The Commission shall state what measures it recommends the State concerned to take. **2–121**

If the action taken by a Member State and the measures suggested by the Commission do not prove sufficient to overcome the difficulties which have arisen or which threaten, the Commission shall, after consulting the Committee referred to in Article 114, recommend to the Council the granting of mutual assistance and appropriate methods therefor.

The Commission shall keep the Council regularly informed of the situation and of how it is developing.

2. The Council, acting by a qualified majority, shall grant such mutual assistance, it shall adopt directives or decisions laying down the conditions and details of such assistance, which may take such forms as:

(a) a concerted approach to or within any other international organisations to which Member States may have recourse;
(b) measures needed to avoid deflection of trade where the State which is in difficulties maintains or reintroduces quantitative restrictions against third countries;
(c) the granting of limited credits by other Member States, subject to their agreement.

3. If the mutual assistance recommended by the Commission is not granted by the Council or if the mutual assistance granted and the measures taken are insufficient, the Commission shall authorise the State which is in difficulties to take protective measures, the conditions and details of which the Commission shall determine.

Such authorisation may be revoked and such conditions and details may be changed by the Council acting by a qualified majority.

4. Subject to Article 122(6), this Article shall cease to apply from the beginning of the third stage.

Article 120[61] **[Protective measures in cases of sudden balance of payments problems]**

1. Where a sudden crisis in the balance of payments occurs and a decision within the meaning of Article 119(2) is not immediately taken, the Member State concerned may, as a precaution, take the necessary protective measures. Such measures must cause the least possible disturbance in the functioning of the common market and must not be wider in scope than is strictly necessary to remedy the sudden difficulties which have arisen. **2–122**

2. The Commission and the other Member States shall be informed of such protective measures not later than when they enter into force. The Commission may recommend to the Council the granting of mutual assistance under Article 119.

[60] Formerly Art. 109h. Former Art. 109h replaced by Art. 8(25) TEU. Article 119 continues to apply to Member States with derogations from EMU (see Art. 122(6)).

[61] Formerly Art. 109i. Former Art. 109i replaced by Art. 8(25) TEU. Article 120 continues to apply to Member States with derogations from EMU (see Art. 122(6)).

3. After the Commission has delivered an opinion and the Committee referred to in Article 114 has been consulted, the Council may, acting by a qualified majority, decide that the State concerned shall amend, suspend or abolish the protective measures referred to above.

4. Subject to Article 122(6), this Article shall cease to apply from the beginning of the third stage.

Article 121[62] **[Progress towards EMU]**

2–123 1. The Commission and the EMI shall report to the Council on the progress made in the fulfilment by the Member States of their obligations regarding the achievement of economic and monetary union. These reports shall include an examination of the compatibility between each Member State's national legislation, including the statutes of its national central bank, and Articles 108 and 109 of this Treaty and the Statute of the ESCB. The reports shall also examine the achievement of a high degree of sustainable convergence by reference to the fulfilment by each Member State of the following criteria:

- the achievement of a high degree of price stability; this will be apparent from a rate of inflation which is close to that of, at most, the three best performing Member States in terms of price stability;
- the sustainability of the government financial position; this will be apparent from having achieved a government budgetary position without a deficit that is excessive as determined in accordance with Article 104(6);
- the observance of the normal fluctuation margins provided for by the exchange-rate mechanism of the European Monetary System, for at least two years, without devaluing against the currency of any other Member State;
- the durability of convergence achieved by the Member State and of its participation in the exchange rate mechanism of the European Monetary System being reflected in the long-term interest rate levels.

The four criteria mentioned in this paragraph and the relevant periods over which they are to be respected are developed further in a Protocol annexed to this Treaty.[63] The reports of the Commission and the EMI shall also take account of the development of the ECU, the results of the integration of markets, the situation and development of the balances of payments on current account and an examination of the development of unit labour costs and other price indices.

2. On the basis of these reports, the Council, acting by a qualified majority on a recommendation from the Commission, shall assess:

- for each Member State, whether it fulfils the necessary conditions for the adoption of a single currency;
- whether a majority of the Member States fulfil the necessary conditions for the adoption of a single currency,

and recommend its findings to the Council, meeting in the composition of the Heads of State or Government. The European Parliament shall be consulted and forward its opinion to the Council, meeting in the composition of the Heads of State or Government.

3. Taking due account of the reports referred to in paragraph 1 and the opinion of the European Parliament referred to in paragraph 2, the Council, meeting in the composition of the Heads of State or Government, shall, acting by a qualified majority, not later than 31 December 1996:

- decide, on the basis of the recommendations of the Council referred to in paragraph 2, whether a majority of the Member States fulfil the necessary conditions for the adoption of a single currency;

[62] Formerly Art. 109j. Former Art. 109j replaced by Art. 8(25) TEU.
[63] See Protocol (No. 21) on the convergence criteria referred to in Art. 121.

— decide whether it is appropriate for the Community to enter the third stage, and if so:
— set the date for the beginning of the third stage.

4. If by the end of 1997 the date for the beginning of the third stage has not been set, the third stage shall start on 1 January 1999. Before 1 July 1998, the Council, meeting in the composition of the Heads of State or Government, after a repetition of the procedure provided for in paragraphs 1 and 2, with the exception of the second indent of paragraph 2, taking into account the reports referred to in paragraph 1 and the opinion of the European Parliament, shall, acting by a qualified majority and on the basis of the recommendations of the Council referred to in paragraph 2, confirm which Member States fulfil the necessary conditions for the adoption of a single currency.

Article 122[64] **[Member States with a derogation]**

1. If the decision has been taken to set the date in accordance with Article 121(3), **2–124**
the Council shall, on the basis of its recommendations referred to in Article 121(2), acting by a qualified majority on a recommendation from the Commission, decide whether any, and if so which, Member States shall have a derogation as defined in paragraph 3 of this Article. Such Member States shall in this Treaty be referred to as "Member States with a derogation".

If the Council has confirmed which Member States fulfil the necessary conditions for the adoption of a single currency, in accordance with Article 121(4), those Member States which do not fulfil the conditions shall have a derogation as defined in paragraph 3 of this Article. Such Member States shall in this Treaty be referred to as "Member States with a derogation".

2. At least once every two years, or at the request of a Member State with a derogation, the Commission and the ECB shall report to the Council in accordance with the procedure laid down in article 121(1). After consulting the European Parliament and after discussion in the Council, meeting in the composition of the Heads of State or Government, the Council shall, acting by a qualified majority on a proposal from the Commission, decide which Member States with a derogation fulfil the necessary conditions on the basis of the criteria set out in Article 121(1), and abrogate the derogations of the Member States concerned.

3. A derogation referred to in paragraph 1 shall entail that the following Articles do not apply to the Member State concerned: Articles 104(9) and (11), 105(1), (2), (3) and (5), 106, 110, 111, and 112(2)(b). The exclusion of such a Member State and its national central bank from rights and obligations within the ESCB is laid down in Chapter IX of the Statute of the ESCB.

4. In Articles 105(1), (2) and (3), 106, 110, 111 and 112(2)(b), "Member States" shall be read as "Member States without a derogation".

5. The voting rights of Member States with a derogation shall be suspended for the Council decisions referred to in the Articles of this Treaty mentioned in paragraph 3. In that case, by way of derogation from Articles 205 and 250(1), a qualified majority shall be defined as two-thirds of the votes of the representatives of the Member States without a derogation weighted in accordance with article 205(2), and unanimity of those Member States shall be required for an act requiring unanimity.

[64] Formerly Art. 109k. Former Art. 109k replaced by Art. 8(25) TEU. For positions of UK and Denmark see relevant Protocols (Nos 25 and 26) below.

6. Articles 119 and 120 shall continue to apply to a Member State with a derogation.

Article 123[65] **[Establishment of ESCB and ECB; introduction of single currency]**

2–125 1. Immediately after the decision on the date for the beginning of the third stage has been taken in accordance with Article 121(3), or, as the case may be, immediately after 1 July 1998:

— the Council shall adopt the provisions referred to in Article 107(6);
— the governments of the Member States without a derogation shall appoint, in accordance with the procedure set out in Article 50 of the Statute of the ESCB, the President, the Vice-President and the other members of the Executive Board of the ECB. If there are Member States with a derogation, the number of members of the Executive Board may be smaller than provided for in article 11.1 of the Statute of the ESCB, but in no circumstances shall it be less than four.

As soon as the Executive Board is appointed, the ESCB and the ECB shall be established and shall prepare for their full operation as described in this Treaty and the Statute of the ESCB. The full exercise of their powers shall start from the first day of the third stage.

2. As soon as the ECB is established, it shall, if necessary, take over tasks of the EMI.[66] The EMI shall go into liquidation upon the establishment of the ECB; the modalities of liquidation are laid down in the Statute of the EMI.

3. If and as long as there are Member States with a derogation, and without prejudice to Article 107(3) of this Treaty, the General Council of the ECB referred to in Article 45 of the Statute of the ESCB shall be constituted as a third decision-making body of the ECB.

4. At the starting date of the third stage, the Council shall, acting with the unanimity of the Member States without a derogation, on a proposal from the Commission and after consulting the ECB, adopt the conversion rates at which their currencies shall be irrevocably fixed and at which irrevocably fixed rate the ECU shall be substituted for these currencies, and the ECU will become a currency in its own right. This measure shall by itself not modify the external value of the ECU. The Council, acting by a qualified majority of the said Member States, on a proposal from the Commission and after consulting the ECB, shall take the other measures necessary for the rapid introduction of the ECU as the single currency of those Member States. The second sentence of Article 122(5) shall apply.[67]

5. If it is decided, according to the procedure set out in Article 122(2), to abrogate a derogation, the Council shall, acting with the unanimity of the Member States without a derogation and the Member State concerned, on a proposal from the Commission and after consulting the ECB, adopt the rate at which the ECU shall be substituted for the currency of the Member State concerned, and take the other measures necessary for the introduction of the ECU as the single currency in the Member State concerned.[68]

---

[65] Formerly Art. 109l. Former Art. 109l replaced by Art. 8(25) TEU.
[66] See Protocol (No. 18) in the Statute of the ESCB and ECB, Art. 43.
[67] Article 123(4) replaced by Treaty of Nice, Art. 2(7). Article 123(4) does not apply to the UK (see Protocol (No. 25) on certain provisions relating to the UK, Art. 5). See Reg. 1103/97 ([1997] OJ L162/1): references to the ECU in all legal instruments replaced by references to the euro from 1 January 1999; and Reg. 2866/98 ([1998] OJ L359/1): conversion rates between the euro and currencies of Member States adopting the euro.
[68] Article 123(5) does not apply to the UK (see Protocol (No. 25) on certain provisions relating to the UK, Art. 5).

Article 124[69] **[Member State exchange rate policies]**

1. Until the beginning of the third stage, each Member State shall treat its exchange rate policy as a matter of common interest. In so doing, Member States shall take account of the experience acquired in cooperation within the framework of the European Monetary System (EMS) and in developing the ECU, and shall respect existing powers in this field. **2–126**

2. From the beginning of the third stage and for as long as a Member State has a derogation, paragraph 1 shall apply by analogy to the exchange rate policy of that Member State.

TITLE VIII—EMPLOYMENT

Article 125[70] **[Coordinated strategy for employment]**

Member States and the Community shall, in accordance with this Title, work towards developing a coordinated strategy for employment and particularly for promoting a skilled, trained and adaptable workforce and labour markets responsive to economic change with a view to achieving the objectives defined in Article 2 of the Treaty on European Union and in Article 2 of this Treaty. **2–127**

Article 126[71] **[Employment policies to be within guidelines on economic policies]**

1. Member States, through their employment policies, shall contribute to the achievement of the objectives referred to in Article 125 in a way consistent with the broad guidelines of the economic policies of the Member States and of the Community adopted pursuant to Article 99(2). **2–128**

2. Member States, having regard to national practices related to the responsibilities of management and labour, shall regard promoting employment as a matter of common concern and shall coordinate their action in this respect within the Council, in accordance with the provisions of Article 128.

Article 127[72] **[Objective of high levels of employment]**

1. The Community shall contribute to a high level of employment by encouraging cooperation between Member States and by supporting and, if necessary, complementing their action. In doing so, the competences of the Member States shall be respected. **2–129**

2. The objective of a high level of employment shall be taken into consideration in the formulation and implementation of Community policies and activities.

Article 128[73] **[Annual review of EC employment situation]**

1. The European Council shall each year consider the employment situation in the Community and adopt conclusions thereon, on the basis of a joint annual report by the Council and the Commission. **2–130**

2. On the basis of the conclusions of the European Council, the Council, acting by a qualified majority on a proposal from the Commission and after consulting the European Parliament, the Economic and Social Committee, the Committee of the Regions and the Employment Committee referred to in Article 130, shall each year draw up guidelines which the Member States shall take into account in their

[69] Formerly Art. 109m. Former Art. 109m replaced by Art. 8(25) TEU.
[70] Formerly Art. 109n. Former Art. 109n inserted by Treaty of Amsterdam, Art. 2(19).
[71] Formerly Art. 109o. Former Art. 109o inserted by Treaty of Amsterdam, Art. 2(19).
[72] Formerly Art. 109p. Former Art. 109p inserted by Treaty of Amsterdam, Art. 2(19).
[73] Formerly Art. 109q. Former Art. 109q inserted by Treaty of Amsterdam, Art. 2(19).

employment policies. These guidelines shall be consistent with the broad guidelines adopted pursuant to Article 99(2).

3. Each Member State shall provide the Council and the Commission with an annual report on the principal measures taken to implement its employment policy in the light of the guidelines for employment as referred to in paragraph 2.

4. The Council, on the basis of the reports referred to in paragraph 3 and having received the views of the Employment Committee, shall each year carry out an examination of the implementation of the employment policies of the Member States in the light of the guidelines for employment. The Council, acting by a qualified majority on a recommendation from the Commission, may, if it considers it appropriate in the light of that examination, make recommendations to Member States.

5. On the basis of the results of that examination, the Council and the Commission shall make a joint annual report to the European Council on the employment situation in the Community and on the implementation of the guidelines for employment.

Article 129[74] [Measures to encourage cooperation on employment]

2–131 The Council, acting in accordance with the procedure referred to in Article 251 and after consulting the Economic and Social Committee and the Committee of the Regions, may adopt incentive measures designed to encourage cooperation between Member States and to support their action in the field of employment through initiatives aimed at developing exchanges of information and best practices, providing comparative analysis and advice as well as promoting innovative approaches and evaluating experiences, in particular by recourse to pilot projects.

Those measures shall not include harmonisation of the laws and regulations of the Member States.

Article 130[75] [Employment Committee]

2–132 The Council, after consulting the European Parliament, shall establish an Employment Committee with advisory status to promote co-ordination between Member States on employment and labour market policies. The tasks of the Committee shall be:

— to monitor the employment situation and employment policies in the Member States and the Community;

— without prejudice to Article 207, to formulate opinions at the request of either the Council or the Commission or on its own initiative, and to contribute to the preparation of the Council proceedings referred to in Article 128.

In fulfilling its mandate, the Committee shall consult management and labour.

Each Member State and the Commission shall appoint two members of the Committee.[76]

[74] Formerly Art. 109r. Former Art. 109r inserted by Treaty of Amsterdam, Art. 2(19). See Declaration (No. 23) on incentive measures referred to in Article [129] of the Treaty establishing the European Community annexed to the Final Act of the Treaty of Amsterdam and Declaration (No. 24) on Article 129 of the Treaty establishing the European Community annexed to the Final Act of the Treaty of Amsterdam.

[75] Formerly Art. 109s. Former Art. 109s inserted by Treaty of Amsterdam, Art. 2(19).

[76] Formerly Art. 106. Former Art. 106 replaced by Art 8(25) TEU.

TITLE IX—COMMON COMMERCIAL POLICY

Article 131[77] [Wider international aims of EC customs union]

By establishing a customs union between themselves Member States aim to contribute, in the common interest, to the harmonious development of world trade, the progressive abolition of restrictions on international trade and the lowering of customs barriers. **2–133**

The common commercial policy shall take into account the favourable effect which the abolition of customs duties between Member States may have on the increase in the competitive strength of undertakings in those States.

Article 132[78] [Harmonisation of export aid systems]

1. Without prejudice to obligations undertaken by them within the framework of other international organisations, Member States shall progressively harmonise the systems whereby they grant aid for exports to third countries, to the extent necessary to ensure that competition between undertakings of the Community is not distorted. **2–134**

On a proposal from the Commission, the Council shall, acting by a qualified majority, issue any directives needed for this purpose.

2. The preceding provisions shall not apply to such a drawback of customs duties or charges having equivalent effect nor to such a repayment of indirect taxation including turnover taxes, excise duties and other indirect taxes as is allowed when goods are exported from a Member State to a third country, insofar as such a drawback or repayment does not exceed the amount imposed, directly or indirectly, on the products exported.

Article 133[79] [Implementation of the CCP]

1. The common commercial policy shall be based on uniform principles, particularly in regard to changes in tariff rates, the conclusion of tariff and trade agreements, the achievement of uniformity in measures of liberalisation, export policy and measures to protect trade such as those to be taken in the event of dumping or subsidies. **2–135**

2. The Commission shall submit proposals to the Council for implementing the common commercial policy.

3. Where agreements with one or more States or international organisations need to be negotiated, the Commission shall make recommendations to the Council, which shall authorise the Commission to open the necessary negotiations. The Council and the Commission shall be responsible for ensuring that the agreements negotiated are compatible with internal Community policies and rules.

The Commission shall conduct these negotiations in consultation with a special committee appointed by the Council to assist the Commission in this task and within the framework of such directives as the Council may issue to it. The Commission shall report regularly to the special committee on the progress of negotiations.

The relevant provisions of Article 300 shall apply.

4. In exercising the powers conferred upon it by this Article, the Council shall act by a qualified majority.

---

[77] Formerly Art. 110. See Arts 23–27 for EC customs union.

[78] Formerly Art. 112. In former Art. 112(1), first sub-paragraph, transitional wording deleted by Treaty of Amsterdam, Art. 6(I)(57)(a). In the second sub-paragraph, the words "acting by a qualified majority" replaced previous transitional wording by virtue of Treaty of Amsterdam, Art. 6(I)(57)(b).

[79] Article 133 replaced by Treaty of Nice, Art. 2(8). Formerly Art. 113. Former Art. 113(5) added by Treaty of Amsterdam, Art. 2(20). Former Art. 113 previously replaced by Art. 8(28) TEU.

5. Paragraphs 1 to 4 shall also apply to the negotiation and conclusion of agreements in the fields of trade in services and the commercial aspects of intellectual property, insofar as those agreements are not covered by the said paragraphs and without prejudice to paragraph 6.

By way of derogation from paragraph 4, the Council shall act unanimously when negotiating and concluding an agreement in one of the fields referred to in the first subparagraph, where that agreement includes provisions for which unanimity is required for the adoption of internal rules or where it relates to a field in which the Community has not yet exercised the powers conferred upon it by this Treaty by adopting internal rules.

The Council shall act unanimously with respect to the negotiation and conclusion of a horizontal agreement insofar as it also concerns the preceding subparagraph or the second subparagraph of paragraph 6.

This paragraph shall not affect the right of the Member States to maintain and conclude agreements with third countries or international organisations insofar as such agreements comply with Community law and other relevant international agreements.

6. An agreement may not be concluded by the Council if it includes provisions which would go beyond the Community's internal powers, in particular by leading to harmonisation of the laws or regulations of the Member States in an area for which this Treaty rules out such harmonisation.

In this regard, by way of derogation from the first subparagraph of paragraph 5, agreements relating to trade in cultural and audiovisual services, educational services, and social and human health services, shall fall within the shared competence of the Community and its Member States. Consequently, in addition to a Community decision taken in accordance with the relevant provisions of Article 300, the negotiation of such agreements shall require the common accord of the Member States. Agreements thus negotiated shall be concluded jointly by the Community and the Member States.

The negotiation and conclusion of international agreements in the field of transport shall continue to be governed by the provisions of Title V and Article 300.

7. Without prejudice to the first subparagraph of paragraph 6, the Council, acting unanimously on a proposal from the Commission and after consulting the European Parliament, may extend the application of paragraphs 1 to 4 to international negotiations and agreements on intellectual property insofar as they are not covered by paragraph 5.

Article 134[80] **[Protective measures]**

2–136 In order to ensure that the execution of measures of commercial policy taken in accordance with this Treaty by any Member State is not obstructed by deflection of trade, or where differences between such measures lead to economic difficulties in one or more Member States, the Commission shall recommend the methods for the requisite cooperation between Member States. Failing this, the Commission may authorise Member States to take the necessary protective measures, the conditions and details of which it shall determine.

In case of urgency, Member States shall request authorisation to take the necessary measures themselves from the Commission, which shall take a decision as soon as possible; the Member States concerned shall then notify the measures to the other Member States. The Commission may decide at any time that the Member States concerned shall amend or abolish the measures in question.

[80] Formerly Art. 115. Former Art. 115 replaced by Art. 8(30) TEU.

In the selection of such measures, priority shall be given to those which cause the least disturbance of the functioning of the common market.

TITLE X—CUSTOMS CO-OPERATION

Article 135[81] [Measures to strengthen intra-EC customs cooperation]

Within the scope of application of this Treaty, the Council, acting in accordance with the procedure referred to in Article 251, shall take measures in order to strengthen customs cooperation between Member States and between the latter and the Commission. These measures shall not concern the application of national criminal law or the national administration of justice. **2–137**

TITLE XI—SOCIAL POLICY, EDUCATION, VOCATIONAL TRAINING AND YOUTH

CHAPTER 1—SOCIAL PROVISIONS

Article 136[82] [Objectives of social policy]

The Community and the Member States, having in mind fundamental social rights such as those set out in the European Social Charter signed at Turin on 18 October 1961 and in the 1989 Community Charter of the Fundamental Social Rights of Workers, shall have as their objectives the promotion of employment, improved living and working conditions, so as to make possible their harmonisation while the improvement is being maintained, proper social protection, dialogue between management and labour, the development of human resources with a view to lasting high employment and the combating of exclusion. **2–138**

To this end the Community and the Member States shall implement measures which take account of the diverse forms of national practices, in particular in the field of contractual relations, and the need to maintain the competitiveness of the Community economy.

They believe that such a development will ensue not only from the functioning of the common market, which will favour the harmonisation of social systems, but also from the procedures provided for in this Treaty and from the approximation of provisions laid down by law, regulation or administrative action.

Article 137[83] [Role of EC in achieving social policy objectives]

1. With a view to achieving the objectives of Article 136, the Community shall support and complement the activities of the Member States in the following fields: **2–139**

(a) improvement in particular of the working environment to protect workers' health and safety;
(b) working conditions;
(c) social security and social protection of workers;
(d) protection of workers where their employment contract is terminated;
(e) the information and consultation of workers;
(f) representation and collective defence of the interests of workers and employers, including co-determination, subject to paragraph 5;

[81] Formerly Art. 116. Former Art. 116 inserted by Treaty of Amsterdam, Art. 2(21). Previous Art. 116 repealed by Art. 8(31) TEU.

[82] Formerly Art. 117. Former Art. 117 replaced by Treaty of Amsterdam, Art. 2(22). Article 136 incorporates the terms of Art. 1 of the Agreement on social policy attached to the Protocol on social policy repealed by Treaty of Amsterdam, Art. 2(58). The Protocol had been annexed to the EC Treaty by the Union Treaty.

[83] Article 137 replaced by Treaty of Nice, Art. 2(9). Formerly Art. 118. Former Art. 118 replaced by Treaty of Amsterdam, Art. 2(22). Article 137 incorporates the terms of Art. 2 of the Agreement on social policy attached to the Protocol on social policy repealed by Treaty of Amsterdam, Art. 2(58). The Protocol had been annexed to the EC Treaty by the Union Treaty. See also Declaration (No. 25) on Article [137] of the EC Treaty and Declaration (No. 26) on Article [137(2)] of the EC Treaty both annexed to the Final Act of the Treaty of Amsterdam.

(g) conditions of employment for third-country nationals legally residing in Community territory;
(h) the integration of persons excluded from the labour market, without prejudice to Article 150;
(i) equality between men and women with regard to labour market opportunities and treatment at work;
(j) the combating of social exclusion;
(k) the modernisation of social protection systems without prejudice to point (c).

2. To this end, the Council:
(a) may adopt measures designed to encourage cooperation between Member States through initiatives aimed at improving knowledge, developing exchanges of information and best practices, promoting innovative approaches and evaluating experiences, excluding any harmonisation of the laws and regulations of the Member States;
(b) may adopt, in the fields referred to in paragraph 1(a) to (i), by means of directives, minimum requirements for gradual implementation, having regard to the conditions and technical rules obtaining in each of the Member States. Such directives shall avoid imposing administrative, financial and legal constraints in a way which would hold back the creation and development of small and medium-sized undertakings.

The Council shall act in accordance with the procedure referred to in Article 251 after consulting the Economic and Social Committee and the Committee of the Regions, except in the fields referred to in paragraph 1(c), (d), (f) and (g) of this Article, where the Council shall act unanimously on a proposal from the Commission, after consulting the European Parliament and the said Committees. The Council, acting unanimously on a proposal from the Commission, after consulting the European Parliament, may decide to render the procedure referred to in Article 251 applicable to paragraph 1(d), (f) and (g) of this Article.

3. A Member State may entrust management and labour, at their joint request, with the implementation of directives adopted pursuant to paragraph 2.

In this case, it shall ensure that, no later than the date on which a directive must be transposed in accordance with Article 249, management and labour have introduced the necessary measures by agreement, the Member State concerned being required to take any necessary measure enabling it at any time to be in a position to guarantee the results imposed by that directive.

4. The provisions adopted pursuant to this Article:
— shall not affect the right of Member States to define the fundamental principles of their social security systems and must not significantly affect the financial equilibrium thereof;
— shall not prevent any Member State from maintaining or introducing more stringent protective measures compatible with this Treaty.

5. The provisions of this Article shall not apply to pay, the right of association, the right to strike or the right to impose lock-outs.

Article 138[84] [Management–labour dialogue]

2–140 1. The Commission shall have the task of promoting the consultation of management and labour at Community level and shall take any relevant measure to facilitate their dialogue by ensuring balanced support for the parties.

[84] Formerly Art. 118a. Former Art. 118a replaced by Treaty of Amsterdam, Art. 2(22). Previous Art. 118a(2), first sub-paragraph, replaced by Art. 8(33) TEU. Article 118a originally added to EEC Treaty by Art. 21 SEA. Article 138 incorporates the terms of Art. 3 of the Agreement on social policy attached to the Protocol on social policy repealed by Treaty of Amsterdam, Art. 2(58). The Protocol had been annexed to the EC Treaty by the Union Treaty.

2. To this end, before submitting proposals in the social policy field, the Commission shall consult management and labour on the possible direction of Community action.

3. If, after such consultation, the Commission considers Community action advisable, it shall consult management and labour on the content of the envisaged proposal. Management and labour shall forward to the Commission an opinion or, where appropriate, a recommendation.

4. On the occasion of such consultation, management and labour may inform the Commission of their wish to initiate the process provided for in Article 139. The duration of the procedure shall not exceed nine months, unless the management and labour concerned and the Commission decide jointly to extend it.

Article 139[85] [Implementation of management–labour dialogue]

1. Should management and labour so desire, the dialogue between them at Community level may lead to contractual relations, including agreements. **2–141**

2. Agreements concluded at Community level shall be implemented either in accordance with the procedures and practices specific to management and labour and the Member States or, in matters covered by Article 137, at the joint request of the signatory parties, by a Council decision on a proposal from the Commission.

The Council shall act by qualified majority, except where the agreement in question contains one or more provisions relating to one of the areas for which unanimity is required pursuant to Article 137(2). In that case, it shall act unanimously.[86]

Article 140[87] [Cooperation and coordination between Member States]

With a view to achieving the objectives of Article 136 and without prejudice to the other provisions of this Treaty, the Commission shall encourage cooperation between the Member States and facilitate the coordination of their action in all social policy fields under this Chapter, particularly in matters relating to: **2–142**

- employment;
- labour law and working conditions;
- basic and advanced vocational training;
- social security;
- prevention of occupational accidents and diseases;
- occupational hygiene;
- the right of association and collective bargaining between employers and workers.

To this end, the Commission shall act in close contact with Member States by making studies, delivering opinions and arranging consultations both on problems arising at national level and on those of concern to international organisations.

[85] Formerly Art. 118b. Former Art. 118b replaced by Treaty of Amsterdam, Art. 2(22). Previous Art. 118b added to EEC Treaty by Art. 22 SEA. Article 139 incorporates the terms of Art. 4 of the Agreement on social policy attached to the Protocol on social policy repealed by Treaty of Amsterdam, Art. 2(58). The protocol had been annexed to the EC Treaty by the Union Treaty.

[86] Article 139(2), second subparagraph replaced by Treaty of Nice, Art. 2(1). See Declaration (No. 27) on Article 139(2) of the EC Treaty annexed to the Final Act of the Treaty of Amsterdam.

[87] Formerly Art. 118c. Former Art. 118c added by Treaty of Amsterdam, Art. 2(22). Article 140 incorporates the terms of Art. 5 of the Agreement on social policy attached to the Protocol on social policy repealed by Treaty of Amsterdam, Art. 2(58). The Protocol had been annexed to the EC Treaty by the Union Treaty.

Before delivering the opinions provided for in this Article, the Commission shall consult the Economic and Social Committee.

Article 141[88] **[Equal pay for men and women]**

2–143 1. Each Member State shall ensure that the principle of equal pay for male and female workers for equal work or work of equal value is applied.

2. For the purpose of this Article, "pay" means the ordinary basic or minimum wage or salary and any other consideration, whether in cash or in kind, which the worker receives directly or indirectly, in respect of his employment, from his employer.[89]

Equal pay without discrimination based on sex means:

(a) that pay for the same work at piece rates shall be calculated on the basis of the same unit of measurement;

(b) that pay for work at time rates shall be the same for the same job.

3. The Council, acting in accordance with the procedure referred to in Article 251, and after consulting the Economic and Social Committee, shall adopt measures to ensure the application of the principle of equal opportunities and equal treatment of men and women in matters of employment and occupation, including the principle of equal pay for equal work or work of equal value.

4. With a view to ensuring full equality in practice between men and women in working life, the principle of equal treatment shall not prevent any Member State from maintaining or adopting measures providing for specific advantages in order to make it easier for the under-represented sex to pursue a vocational activity or to prevent or compensate for disadvantages in professional careers.[90]

Article 142[91] **[Paid holidays]**

2–144 Member States shall endeavour to maintain the existing equivalence between paid holiday schemes.

Article 143[92] **[Annual report on progress on social policy objectives]**

2–145 The Commission shall draw up a report each year on progress in achieving the objectives of Article 136, including the demographic situation in the Community. It shall forward the report to the European Parliament, the Council and the Economic and Social Committee.

The European Parliament may invite the Commission to draw up reports on particular problems concerning the social situation.

Article 144[93] **[Social Protection Committee]**

2–146 The Council, after consulting the European Parliament, shall establish a Social Protection Committee with advisory status to promote cooperation on social

---

[88] Formerly Art. 119. Former Art. 119 replaced by Treaty of Amsterdam, Art. 2(22). Article 141 incorporates the terms of Art. 6 of the Agreement on social policy attached to the Protocol on social policy repealed by Treaty of Amsterdam, Art. 2(58). The Protocol had been annexed to the EC Treaty by the Union Treaty.

[89] See further Protocol (No. 17) concerning Article [141] of the EC Treaty.

[90] See Declaration (No. 28) on Article [141(4)] of the EC Treaty annexed to the Final Act of the Treaty of Amsterdam.

[91] Formerly Art. 119a. Former Art. 119a replaced by Treaty of Amsterdam, Art. 2(22), previously having been Art. 120.

[92] Formerly Art. 120. Former Art. 120 replaced by Treaty of Amsterdam, Art. 2(22). Article 143 incorporates the terms of Art. 7 of the Agreement on social policy attached to the Protocol on social policy repealed by Treaty of Amsterdam, Art. 2(58). The Protocol had been annexed to the EC Treaty by the Union Treaty.

[93] Article 144 replaced by Treaty of Nice, Art. 2(11). Formerly Art. 121.

protection policies between Member States and with the Commission. The tasks of the Committee shall be:

— to monitor the social situation and the development of social protection policies in the Member States and the Community;
— to promote exchanges of information, experience and good practice between Member States and with the Commission;
— without prejudice to Article 207, to prepare reports, formulate opinions or undertake other work within its fields of competence, at the request of either the Council or the Commission or on its own initiative.

In fulfilling its mandate, the Committee shall establish appropriate contacts with management and labour.

Each Member State and the Commission shall appoint two members of the Committee.

Article 145[94] [Annual report to include chapter on social developments]

The Commission shall include a separate chapter on social developments within the Community in its annual report to the European Parliament. **2–147**

The European Parliament may invite the Commission to draw up reports on any particular problems concerning social conditions.

CHAPTER 2—THE EUROPEAN SOCIAL FUND

Article 146[95] [ESF established]

In order to improve employment opportunities for workers in the internal market and to contribute thereby to raising the standard of living, a European Social Fund is hereby established in accordance with the provisions set out below; it shall aim to render the employment of workers easier and to increase their geographical and occupational mobility within the Community, and to facilitate their adaptation to industrial changes and to changes in production systems, in particular through vocational training and retraining. **2–148**

Article 147[96] [Administration of ESF]

The Fund shall be administered by the Commission. **2–149**

The Commission shall be assisted in this task by a Committee presided over by a Member of the Commission and composed of representatives of governments, trade unions and employers' organisations.

Article 148[97] [Implementation of ESF]

The Council, acting in accordance with the procedure referred to in Article 251 and after consulting the Economic and Social Committee and the Committee of the Regions, shall adopt implementing decisions relating to the European Social Fund. **2–150**

CHAPTER 3—EDUCATION, VOCATIONAL TRAINING AND YOUTH

Article 149[98] [Development of quality education]

1. The Community shall contribute to the development of quality education by encouraging cooperation between Member States and, if necessary, by supporting **2–151**

---

[94] Formerly Art. 122.
[95] Formerly Art. 123. Former Art. 123 replaced by Art. 8(34) TEU.
[96] Formerly Art. 124.
[97] Formerly Art. 125. Former Art. 125 replaced by Treaty of Amsterdam, Art. 2(23). Former Art. 125 previously replaced by Art. 8(35) TEU.
[98] Formerly Art. 126. Former Art. 126 replaced by Art. 8(36) TEU.

and supplementing their action, while fully respecting the responsibility of the Member States for the content of teaching and the organisation of education systems and their cultural and linguistic diversity.

2. Community action shall be aimed at:
— developing the European dimension in education, particularly through the teaching and dissemination of the languages of the Member States;
— encouraging mobility of students and teachers, *inter alia* by encouraging the academic recognition of diplomas and periods of study;
— promoting cooperation between educational establishments;
— developing exchanges of information and experience on issues common to the education systems of the Member States;
— encouraging the development of youth exchanges and of exchanges of socio-educational instructors;
— encouraging the development of distance education.

3. The Community and the Member States shall foster cooperation with third countries and the competent international organisations in the field of education, in particular the Council of Europe.

4. In order to contribute to the achievement of the objectives referred to in this Article, the Council:
— acting in accordance with the procedure referred to in Article 251, after consulting the Economic and Social Committee and the Committee of the Regions, shall adopt incentive measures, excluding any harmonisation of the laws and regulations of the Member States;
— acting by a qualified majority on a proposal from the Commission, shall adopt recommendations.

Article 150[99] **[EC vocational training policy]**

2–152 1. The Community shall implement a vocational training policy which shall support and supplement the action of the Member States, while fully respecting the responsibility of the Member States for the content and organisation of vocational training.

2. Community action shall aim to:
— facilitate adaptation to industrial changes, in particular through vocational training and retraining;
— improve initial and continuing vocational training in order to facilitate vocational integration and reintegration into the labour market;
— facilitate access to vocational training and encourage mobility of instructors and trainees and particularly young people;
— stimulate cooperation on training between educational or training establishments and firms;
— develop exchanges of information and experience on issues common to the training systems of the Member States.

3. The Community and the Member States shall foster cooperation with third countries and the competent international organisations in the sphere of vocational training.

4. The Council, acting in accordance with the procedure referred to in Article 251 and after consulting the Economic and Social Committee and the Committee of

[99] Formerly Art. 127. Former Art. 127(4) replaced by Treaty of Amsterdam, Art. 2(24). Former Art. 127 replaced by Art. 8(36) TEU.

the Regions, shall adopt measures to contribute to the achievement of the objectives referred to in this Article, excluding any harmonisation of the laws and regulations of the Member States.

TITLE XII—CULTURE

Article 151[1] [Action to promote European culture]

1. The Community shall contribute to the flowering of the cultures of the Member States, while respecting their national and regional diversity and at the same time bringing the common cultural heritage to the fore. **2–153**

2. Action by the Community shall be aimed at encouraging cooperation between Member States and, if necessary, supporting and supplementing their action in the following areas:
— improvement of the knowledge and dissemination of the culture and history of the European peoples;
— conservation and safeguarding of cultural heritage of European significance;
— non-commercial cultural exchanges;
— artistic and literary creation, including in the audiovisual sector.

3. The Community and the Member States shall foster cooperation with third countries and the competent international organisations in the sphere of culture, in particular the Council of Europe.

4. The Community shall take cultural aspects into account in its action under other provisions of this Treaty, in particular in order to respect and to promote the diversity of its cultures.

5. In order to contribute to the achievement of the objectives referred to in this Article, the Council:
— acting in accordance with the procedure referred to in Article 251 and after consulting the Committee of the Regions, shall adopt incentive measures, excluding any harmonisation of the laws and regulations of the Member States. The Council shall act unanimously throughout the procedure referred to in Article 251;
— acting unanimously on a proposal from the Commission, shall adopt recommendations.

TITLE XIII—PUBLIC HEALTH

Article 152[2] [Action to protect public health]

1. A high level of human health protection shall be ensured in the definition and implementation of all Community policies and activities. **2–154**

Community action, which shall complement national policies, shall be directed towards improving public health, preventing human illness and diseases, and obviating sources of danger to human health. Such action shall cover the fight against the major health scourges, by promoting research into their causes, their transmission and their prevention, as well as health information and education.

The Community shall complement the Member States' action in reducing drugs-related health damage, including information and prevention.

2. The Community shall encourage cooperation between the Member States in the areas referred to in this article and, if necessary, lend support to their action.

Member States shall, in liaison with the Commission, coordinate among themselves their policies and programmes in the areas referred to in paragraph 1.

---

[1] Formerly Art. 128. Former Art. 128(4) replaced by Treaty of Amsterdam, Art. 2(25). Former Art. 128 inserted by Art. 8(37) TEU.

[2] Formerly Art. 129. Former Art. 129 replaced by Treaty of Amsterdam, Art. 2(26). Former Art. 129 previously replaced by Art. 8(38) TEU.

The Commission may, in close contact with the Member States, take any useful initiative to promote such coordination.

3. The Community and the Member States shall foster cooperation with third countries and the competent international organisations in the sphere of public health.

4. The Council, acting in accordance with the procedure referred to in Article 251 and after consulting the Economic and Social Committee and the Committee of the Regions, shall contribute to the achievement of the objectives referred to in this Article through adopting:
(a) measures setting high standards of quality and safety of organs and substances of human origin, blood and blood derivatives; these measures shall not prevent any Member State from maintaining or introducing more stringent protective measures;
(b) by way of derogation from Article 37, measures in the veterinary and phytosanitary fields which have as their direct objective the protection of public health;
(c) incentive measures designed to protect and improve human health, excluding any harmonisation of the laws and regulations of the Member States.

The Council, acting by a qualified majority on a proposal from the Commission, may also adopt recommendations for the purposes set out in this Article.

5. Community action in the field of public health shall fully respect the responsibilities of the Member States for the organisation and delivery of health services and medical care. In particular, measures referred to in paragraph 4(a) shall not affect national provisions on the donation or medical use of organs and blood.

TITLE XIV—CONSUMER PROTECTION

Article 153[3] [Action to protect consumers]

2–155 1. In order to promote the interests of consumers and to ensure a high level of consumer protection, the Community shall contribute to protecting the health, safety and economic interests of consumers, as well as to promoting their right to information, education and to organise themselves in order to safeguard their interests.

2. Consumer protection requirements shall be taken into account in defining and implementing other Community policies and activities.

3. The Community shall contribute to the attainment of the objectives referred to in paragraph 1 through:
(a) measures adopted pursuant to Article 95 in the context of the completion of the internal market;
(b) measures which support, supplement and monitor the policy pursued by the Member States.

4. The Council, acting in accordance with the procedure referred to in Article 251 and after consulting the Economic and Social Committee, shall adopt the measures referred to in paragraph 3(b).

5. Measures adopted pursuant to paragraph 4 shall not prevent any Member State from maintaining or introducing more stringent protective measures. Such

[3] Former Art. 129a. Former Art. 129a replaced by Treaty of Amsterdam, Art. 2(27). Former Art. 129a previously replaced by Art. 8(38) TEU.

measures must be compatible with this Treaty. The Commission shall be notified of them.

TITLE XV—TRANS-EUROPEAN NETWORKS

Article 154[4] **[Establishment and development of networks]**

1. To help achieve the objectives referred to in Articles 14 and 158 and to enable citizens of the Union, economic operators and regional and local communities to derive full benefit from the setting-up of an area without internal frontiers, the Community shall contribute to the establishment and development of trans-European networks in the areas of transport, telecommunications and energy infrastructures. **2–156**

2. Within the framework of a system of open and competitive markets, action by the Community shall aim at promoting the interconnection and interoperability of national networks as well as access to such networks. It shall take account in particular of the need to link island, landlocked and peripheral regions with the central regions of the Community.

Article 155[5] **[Action to support networks]**

1. In order to achieve the objectives referred to in Article 154, the Community: **2–157**
— shall establish a series of guidelines covering the objectives, priorities and broad lines of measures envisaged in the sphere of trans-European networks; these guidelines shall identify projects of common interest;
— shall implement any measures that may prove necessary to ensure the interoperability of the networks, in particular in the field of technical standardisation;
— may support projects of common interest supported by Member States, which are identified in the framework of the guidelines referred to in the first indent, particularly through feasibility studies, loan guarantees or interest rate subsidies; the Community may also contribute, through the Cohesion Fund set up pursuant to Article 161, to the financing of specific projects in Member States in the area of transport infrastructure.

The Community's activities shall take into account the potential economic viability of the projects.

2. Member States shall, in liaison with the Commission, coordinate among themselves the policies pursued at national level which may have a significant impact on the achievement of the objectives referred to in Article 154. The Commission may, in close cooperation with the Member State, take any useful initiative to promote such coordination.

3. The Community may decide to cooperate with third countries to promote projects of mutual interest and to ensure the interoperability of networks.

Article 156[6] **[Procedure for adopting EC measures]**

The guidelines and other measures referred to in Article 155(1) shall be adopted by the Council, acting in accordance with the procedure referred to in Article 251 and after consulting the Economic and Social Committee and the Committee of the Regions. **2–158**

---

[4] Former Art. 129b. Former Art. 129b replaced by Art. 8(38) TEU.

[5] Formerly Art. 129c. Former Art. 129c(1), third indent first part (up to and including the words "interest-rate subsidies;") replaced by Treaty of Amsterdam, Art. 2(28) and the words "Cohesion Fund set up" replaced for former wording by Treaty of Amsterdam, Art. 6(I)(58). Former Art. 129c originally replaced by Art. 8(38) TEU.

[6] Formerly Art. 129d. Article 129d, first paragraph replaced and third paragraph deleted by Treaty of Amsterdam, Art. 2(29). Article 129d originally replaced by Art. 8(38) TEU.

Guidelines and projects of common interest which relate to the territory of a Member State shall require the approval of the Member State concerned.

TITLE XVI—INDUSTRY

Article 157[7] [Action to promote competitiveness of EC industry]

2–159 1. The Community and the Member States shall ensure that the conditions necessary for the competitiveness of the Community's industry exist.

For that purpose, in accordance with a system of open and competitive markets, their action shall be aimed at:

— speeding up the adjustment of industry to structural changes;
— encouraging an environment favourable to initiative and to the development of undertakings throughout the Community, particularly small and medium-sized undertakings;
— encouraging an environment favourable to cooperation between undertakings;
— fostering better exploitation of the industrial potential of policies of innovation, research and technological development.

2. The Member States shall consult each other in liaison with the Commission and, where necessary, shall coordinate their action. The Commission may take any useful initiative to promote such co-ordination.

3. The Community shall contribute to the achievement of the objectives set out in paragraph 1 through the policies and activities it pursues under other provisions of this Treaty. The Council, acting in accordance with the procedure referred to in Article 251 and after consulting the Economic and Social Committee, may decide on specific measures in support of action taken in the Member States to achieve the objectives set out in paragraph 1.

This Title shall not provide a basis for the introduction by the Community of any measure which could lead to a distortion of competition or contains tax provisions or provisions relating to the rights and interests of employed persons.[8]

TITLE XVII—ECONOMIC AND SOCIAL COHESION

Article 158[9] [Economic and social cohesion to be strengthened]

2–160 In order to promote its overall harmonious development, the Community shall develop and pursue its actions leading to the strengthening of its economic and social cohesion.

In particular, the Community shall aim at reducing disparities between the levels of development of the various regions and the backwardness of the least favoured regions or islands, including rural areas.[10]

Article 159[11] [Attainment of economic and social cohesion]

2–161 Member States shall conduct their economic policies and shall coordinate them in such a way as, in addition, to attain the objectives set out in Article 158. The

[7] Formerly Art. 130. Former Art. 130 replaced by Art. 8(38) TEU.
[8] Article 157(3) replaced by Treaty of Nice, Art. 2(12)
[9] Formerly Art. 130a. Former Art. 130a, second paragraph replaced by Treaty of Amsterdam, Art. 2(30). Former Art. 130a previously replaced by Art. 8(38) TEU. Previous Art. 130a added by Art. 23 SEA.
[10] See Declaration (No. 30) on island regions annexed to the Final Act of the Treaty of Amsterdam.
[11] Formerly Art. 130b. Former Art. 130b replaced by Art. 8(38) TEU. Previous Art. 130b added by Art. 23 SEA.

formulation and implementation of the Community's policies and actions and the implementation of the internal market shall take into account the objectives set out in Article 158 and shall contribute to their achievement. The Community shall also support the achievement of these objectives by the action it takes through the Structural Funds (European Agricultural Guidance and Guarantee Fund, Guidance Section; European Social Fund; European Regional Development Fund), the European Investment Bank and the other existing financial instruments.

The Commission shall submit a report to the European Parliament, the Council, the Economic and Social Committee and the Committee of the Regions every three years on the progress made towards achieving economic and social cohesion and on the manner in which the various means provided for in this Article have contributed to it. This report shall, if necessary, be accompanied by appropriate proposals.

If specific actions prove necessary outside the Funds and without prejudice to the measures decided upon within the framework of the other Community policies, such actions may be adopted by the Council acting in accordance with the procedure referred to in Article 251 and after consulting the Economic and Social Committee and the Committee of the Regions.[12]

Article 160[13] **[Role of ERDF]**

The European Regional Development Fund is intended to help to redress the main regional imbalances in the Community through participation in the development and structural adjustment of regions whose development is lagging behind and in the conversion of declining industrial regions. **2–162**

Article 161[14] **[Tasks of Structural Funds and Cohesion Fund]**

Without prejudice to Article 162, the Council, acting unanimously on a proposal from the Commission and after obtaining the assent of the European Parliament and consulting the Economic and Social Committee and the Committee of the Regions, shall define the tasks, priority objectives and the organisation of the Structural Funds, which may involve grouping the funds. The Council, acting by the same procedure, shall also define the general rules applicable to them and the provisions necessary to ensure their effectiveness and the co-ordination of the funds with one another and with the other existing financial instruments. **2–163**

A Cohesion Fund set up by the Council in accordance with the same procedure[15] shall provide a financial contribution to projects in the fields of environment and trans-European networks in the area of transport infrastructure.

From 1 January 2007, the Council shall act by a qualified majority on a proposal from the Commission after obtaining the assent of the European Parliament and after consulting the Economic and Social Committee and the Committee of the Regions if, by that date, the multiannual financial perspective applicable from 1 January 2007 and the Interinstitutional Agreement relating thereto have been adopted. If such is not the case, the procedure laid down by this paragraph shall apply from the date of their adoption.[16]

---

[12] Article 159, third paragraph replaced by Treaty of Nice, Art. 2(13).

[13] Formerly Art. 130c. Former Art. 130c replaced by Art. 8(38) TEU. Previous Art. 130c added by Art. 23 SEA.

[14] Former Art. 130d. Former Art. 130d replaced by Art. 8(38) TEU. Previous Art. 130d added by Art. 23 SEA.

[15] The words "A Cohesion Fund ... the same procedure" replaced transitional wording by virtue of Treaty of Amsterdam, Art. 6(I)(59).

[16] Article 161, third paragraph added by Treaty of Nice, Art. 2(14).

Article 162[17] [ERDF implementing decisions]

2–164 Implementing decisions relating to the European Regional Development Fund shall be taken by the Council, acting in accordance with the procedure referred to in Article 251 and after consulting the Economic and Social Committee and the Committee of the Regions.

With regard to the European Agricultural Guidance and Guarantee Fund, Guidance Section, and the European Social Fund, Articles 37 and 148 respectively shall continue to apply.

TITLE XVIII—RESEARCH AND TECHNOLOGICAL DEVELOPMENT

Article 163[18] [Strengthening scientific and technological bases of industry]

2–165 1. The Community shall have the objective of strengthening the scientific and technological bases of Community industry and encouraging it to become more competitive at international level, while promoting all the research activities deemed necessary by virtue of other Chapters of this Treaty.

2. For this purpose the Community shall, throughout the Community, encourage undertakings, including small and medium-sized undertakings, research centres and universities in their research and technological development activities of high quality; it shall support their efforts to co-operate with one another, aiming, notably, at enabling undertakings to exploit the internal market potential to the full, in particular through the opening up of national public contracts, the definition of common standards and the removal of legal and fiscal obstacles to that cooperation.

3. All Community activities under this Treaty in the area of research and technological development, including demonstration projects, shall be decided on and implemented in accordance with the provisions of this Title.

Article 164[19] [EC activities]

2–166 In pursuing these objectives, the Community shall carry out the following activities, complementing the activities carried out in the Member States:

(a) implementation of research, technological development and demonstration programmes by promoting cooperation with and between undertakings, research centres and universities;
(b) promotion of cooperation in the field of Community research, technological development and demonstration with third countries and international organisations;
(c) dissemination and optimisation of the results of activities in Community research, technological development and demonstration;
(d) stimulation of the training and mobility of researchers in the Community.

Article 165[20] [EC–Member State coordination of activities]

2–167 1. The Community and the Member States shall coordinate their research and technological development activities so as to ensure that national policies and Community policy are mutually consistent.

2. In close cooperation with the Member State, the Commission may take any useful initiative to promote the coordination referred to in paragraph 1.

---

[17] Formerly Art. 130e. Former Art. 130e, first paragraph, replaced by Treaty of Amsterdam, Art. 2(31). Former Art. 130e replaced by Art. 8(38) TEU. Previous Art. 130e added by Art. 23 SEA.

[18] Formerly Art. 130f. Former Art. 130f replaced by Art. 8(38) TEU. Previous Art. 130f added by Art. 24 SEA.

[19] Formerly Art. 130g. Former Art. 130g replaced by Art. 8(38) TEU. Previous Art. 130g added by Art. 24 SEA.

[20] Formerly Art. 130h. Former Art. 130h replaced by Art. 8(38) TEU. Previous Art. 130h added by Art. 24 SEA.

Article 166[21] **[Multiannual framework programme]**

1. A multiannual framework programme, setting out all the activities of the Community, shall be adopted by the Council, acting in accordance with the procedure referred to in Article 251 after consulting the Economic and Social Committee. The framework programme shall: **2–168**
— establish the scientific and technological objectives to be achieved by the activities provided for in Article 164 and fix the relevant priorities;
— indicate the broad lines of such activities;
— fix the maximum overall amount and the detailed rules for Community financial participation in the framework programme and the respective shares in each of the activities provided for.

2. The framework programme shall be adapted or supplemented as the situation changes.

3. The framework programme shall be implemented through specific programmes developed within each activity. Each specific programme shall define the detailed rules for implementing it, fix its duration and provide for the means deemed necessary. The sum of the amounts deemed necessary, fixed in the specific programmes, may not exceed the overall maximum amount fixed for the framework programme and each activity.

4. The Council, acting by a qualified majority on a proposal from the Commission and after consulting the European Parliament and the Economic and Social Committee, shall adopt the specific programmes.

Article 167[22] **[Participation in and dissemination of research results]**

For the implementation of the multiannual framework programme the Council shall: **2–169**
— determine the rules for the participation of undertakings, research centres and universities;
— lay down the rules governing the dissemination of research results.

Article 168[23] **[Supplementary programmes]**

In implementing the multiannual framework programme, supplementary programmes may be decided on involving the participation of certain Member States only, which shall finance them subject to possible Community participation. **2–170**

The Council shall adopt the rules applicable to supplementary programmes, particularly as regards the dissemination of knowledge and access by other Member States.

Article 169[24] **[Participation in programmes undertaken by several Member States]**

In implementing the multiannual framework programme the Community may make provision, in agreement with the Member States concerned, for participation in research and development programmes undertaken by several Member States, including participation in the structures created for the execution of those programmes. **2–171**

[21] Formerly Art. 130i. Former Art. 130i(1), first sub-paragraph replaced by Treaty of Amsterdam, Art. 2(32). Former Art. 130i previously replaced by Art. 8(38) TEU. Previous Art. 130i added by Art. 24 SEA.

[22] Formerly Art. 130j. Former Art. 130j replaced by Art. 8(38) TEU. Previous Art. 130j added by Art. 24 SEA.

[23] Formerly Art. 130k. Former Art. 130k replaced by Art. 8(38) TEU. Previous Art. 130k added by Art. 24 SEA.

[24] Formerly Art. 130l. Former Art. 130l replaced by Art. 8(38) TEU. Previous Art. 130l added by Art. 24 SEA.

Article 170[25] **[Cooperation with third countries and organisations]**

2–172 In implementing the multiannual framework programme the Community may make provision for cooperation in Community research, technological development and demonstration with third countries or international organisations.

The detailed arrangements for such cooperation may be the subject of agreements between the Community and the third parties concerned, which shall be negotiated and concluded in accordance with Article 300.

Article 171[26] **[Structures for efficient execution of programmes]**

2–173 The Community may set up joint undertakings or any other structure necessary for the efficient execution of Community research, technological development and demonstration programmes.

Article 172[27] **[Procedures for adopting implementing provisions]**

2–174 The Council, acting by qualified majority on a proposal from the Commission and after consulting the European Parliament and the Economic and Social Committee, shall adopt the provisions referred to in Article 171.

The Council, acting in accordance with the procedure referred to in Article 251 and after consulting the Economic and Social Committee, shall adopt the provisions referred to in Articles 167, 168 and 169. Adoption of the supplementary programmes shall require the agreement of the Member States concerned.

Article 173[28] **[Annual report on R&TD activities and results]**

2–175 At the beginning of each year the Commission shall send a report to the European Parliament and the Council. The report shall include information on research and technological development activities and the dissemination of results during the previous year, and the work programme for the current year.

TITLE XIX—ENVIRONMENT

Article 174[29] **[Parameters of EC environmental policy]**

2–176 1. Community policy on the environment shall contribute to pursuit of the following objectives:
— preserving, protecting and improving the quality of the environment;
— protecting human health;
— prudent and rational utilisation of natural resources;
— promoting measures at international level to deal with regional or worldwide environmental problems.

2. Community policy on the environment shall aim at a high level of protection taking into account the diversity of situations in the various regions of the Community. It shall be based on the precautionary principle and on the principles that preventive action should be taken, that environmental damage should as a priority be rectified at source and that the polluter should pay.

In this context, harmonisation measures answering environmental protection requirements shall include, where appropriate, a safeguard clause allowing

[25] Formerly Art. 130m. Former Art. 130m replaced by Art. 8(38) TEU. Previous Art. 130m added by Art. 24 SEA.

[26] Formerly Art. 130n. Former Art. 130n replaced by Art. 8(38) TEU. Previous Art. 130n added by Art. 24 SEA.

[27] Formerly Art. 130o. Former Art. 130o replaced by Treaty of Amsterdam, Art. 2(33); previously replaced by Art. 8(38) TEU. Article 130o originally added by Art. 24 SEA.

[28] Formerly Art. 130p. Former Art. 130p replaced by Art. 8(38) TEU. Previous Art. 130p added by Art. 24 SEA.

[29] Formerly Art. 130r. Former Art. 130r(2) replaced by Treaty of Amsterdam, Art. 2(34). Former Art. 130r previously replaced by Art. 8(38) TEU. Previous Art. 130r added by Art. 25 SEA.

Member States to take provisional measures, for non-economic environmental reasons, subject to a Community inspection procedure.

3. In preparing its policy on the environment, the Community shall take account of:
— available scientific and technical data;
— environmental conditions in the various regions of the Community;
— the potential benefits and costs of action or lack of action;
— the economic and social development of the Community as a whole and the balanced development of its regions.

4. Within their respective spheres of competence, the Community and the Member States shall cooperate with third countries and with the competent international organisations. The arrangements for Community cooperation may be the subject of agreements between the Community and the third parties concerned, which shall be negotiated and concluded in accordance with Article 300.

The previous sub-paragraph shall be without prejudice to Member States' competence to negotiate in international bodies and to conclude international agreements.

Article 175[30] **[Implementation of environmental policy]**

1. The Council, acting in accordance with the procedure referred to in Article 251 and after consulting the Economic and Social Committee and the Committee of the Regions, shall decide what action is to be taken by the Community in order to achieve the objectives referred to in Article 174.[31] **2–177**

2. By way of derogation from the decision-making procedure provided for in paragraph 1 and without prejudice to Article 95, the Council, acting unanimously on a proposal from the Commission and after consulting the European Parliament, the Economic and Social Committee and the Committee of the Regions, shall adopt:
(a) provisions primarily of a fiscal nature;
(b) measures affecting:
  — town and country planning;
  — quantitative management of water resources or affecting, directly or indirectly, the availability of those resources;
  — land use, with the exception of waste management;
(c) measures significantly affecting a Member State's choice between different energy sources and the general structure of its energy supply.

The Council may, under the conditions laid down in the preceding sub-paragraph, define those matters referred to in this paragraph on which decisions are to be taken by a qualified majority.[32]

3. In other areas, general action programmes setting out priority objectives to be attained shall be adopted by the Council, acting in accordance with the procedure referred to in Article 251 and after consulting the Economic and Social Committee and the Committee of the Regions.[33]

---

[30] Former Art. 130s. Prior to Treaty of Amsterdam, former Art. 130s replaced by Art. 8(38) TEU. Previous Art. 130s added by Art. 25 SEA. See Declaration (No. 12) on environmental impact assessments annexed to the Final Act of the Treaty of Amsterdam.

[31] Former Art. 130s(1) replaced by Treaty of Amsterdam, Art. 2(35)(a).

[32] Article 175(2) replaced by Treaty of Nice, Art. 2(15). Former Art. 130s(2), introductory wording replaced by Treaty of Amsterdam, Art. 2(35)(b).

[33] Former Art. 130s(3), first sub-paragraph, replaced by Treaty of Amsterdam, Art. 2(35)(c).

The Council, acting under the terms of paragraph 1 or paragraph 2 according to the case, shall adopt the measures necessary for the implementation of these programmes.

4. Without prejudice to certain measures of a Community nature, the Member States shall finance and implement the environment policy.

5. Without prejudice to the principle that the polluter should pay, if a measure based on the provisions of paragraph 1 involves costs deemed disproportionate for the public authorities of a Member State, the Council shall, in the act adopting that measure, lay down appropriate provisions in the form of:
— temporary derogations, and/or
— financial support from the Cohesion Fund set up pursuant to Article 161.[34]

Article 176[35] [Member State protective measures]

2–178 The protective measures adopted pursuant to Article 175 shall not prevent any Member State from maintaining or introducing more stringent protective measures. Such measures must be compatible with this Treaty. They shall be notified to the Commission.

TITLE XX—DEVELOPMENT COOPERATION

Article 177[36] [Aims of EC development cooperation policy]

2–179 1. Community policy in the sphere of development cooperation, which shall be complementary to the policies pursued by the Member States, shall foster:
— the sustainable economic and social development of the developing countries, and more particularly the most disadvantaged among them;
— the smooth and gradual integration of the developing countries into the world economy;
— the campaign against poverty in the developing countries.

2. Community policy in this area shall contribute to the general objective of developing and consolidating democracy and the rule of law, and to that of respecting human rights and fundamental freedoms.

3. The Community and the Member States shall comply with the commitments and take account of the objectives they have approved in the context of the United Nations and other competent international organisations.

Article 178[37] [Taking account of development cooperation objectives]

2–180 The Community shall take account of the objectives referred to in Article 177 in the policies that it implements which are likely to affect developing countries.

Article 179[38] [Implementing measures]

2–181 1. Without prejudice to the other provisions of this Treaty, the Council, acting in accordance with the procedure referred to in Article 251, shall adopt the measures necessary to further the objectives referred to in Article 177. Such measures may take the form of multiannual programmes.

---

[34] In former Art. 130s(5), second indent, the words "Cohesion Fund set up pursuant to Article [161]" replaced transitional wording by virtue of Treaty of Amsterdam, Art. 6(I)(60).

[35] Formerly Art. 130t. Former Art. 130t replaced by Art. 8(38) TEU. Previous Art. 130t added by Art. 25 SEA.

[36] Formerly Art. 130u. Former Art. 130u replaced by Art. 8(38) TEU.

[37] Formerly Art. 130v. Former Art. 130v replaced by Art. 8(38) TEU.

[38] Formerly Art. 130w. Former Art. 130w(1) replaced by Treaty of Amsterdam, Art. 2(36). Former Art. 130w replaced by Art. 8(38) TEU.

2. The European Investment Bank shall contribute, under the terms laid down in its statute, to the implementation of the measures referred to in paragraph 1.

3. The provisions of this Article shall not affect cooperation with the African, Caribbean and Pacific countries in the framework of the ACP–EC Convention.[39]

Article 180[40] [Coordination of EC and Member State policies]

1. The Community and the Member States shall coordinate their policies on development cooperation and shall consult each other on their aid programmes, including in international organisations and during international conferences. They may undertake joint action. Member States shall contribute if necessary to the implementation of Community aid programmes. **2–182**

2. The Commission may take any useful initiative to promote the coordination referred to in paragraph 1.

Article 181[41] [Cooperation with third countries and organisations]

Within their respective spheres of competence, the Community and the Member States shall cooperate with third countries and with the competent international organisations. The arrangements for Community cooperation may be the subject of agreements between the Community and the third parties concerned, which shall be negotiated and concluded in accordance with Article 300. **2–183**

The previous paragraph shall be without prejudice to Member States' competence to negotiate in international bodies and to conclude international agreements.

TITLE XXI—ECONOMIC, FINANCIAL AND TECHNICAL COOPERATION WITH THIRD COUNTRIES[42]

Article 181a[43] [Cooperation measures]

1. Without prejudice to the other provisions of this Treaty, and in particular those of Title XX, the Community shall carry out, within its spheres of competence, economic, financial and technical cooperation measures with third countries. Such measures shall be complementary to those carried out by the Member States and consistent with the development policy of the Community. **2–184**

Community policy in this area shall contribute to the general objective of developing and consolidating democracy and the rule of law, and to the objective of respecting human rights and fundamental freedoms.

2. The Council, acting by a qualified majority on a proposal from the Commission and after consulting the European Parliament, shall adopt the measures necessary for the implementation of paragraph 1. The Council shall act unanimously for the

[39] Reference to ACP–EC Convention substituted for reference to ACP–EEC Convention by Treaty of Amsterdam, Art. 6(I)(61). See now Partnership Agreement between the ACP Group of States, of the one part, and the EC and its Member States of the other part signed at Cotonou on 23 June 2000 ([2000] OJ L317/3).

[40] Formerly Art. 130x. Former Art. 130x replaced by Art. 8(38) TEU.

[41] Formerly Art. 130y. Former Art. 130y replaced by Art. 8(38) TEU.

[42] Title XXI added by Treaty of Nice, Art. 2(16).

[43] Article 181a added by Treaty of Nice, Art. 2(16).

association agreements referred to in Article 310 and for the agreements to be concluded with the States which are candidates for accession to the Union.

3. Within their respective spheres of competence, the Community and the Member States shall cooperate with third countries and the competent international organisations. The arrangements for Community cooperation may be the subject of agreements between the Community and the third parties concerned, which shall be negotiated and concluded in accordance with Article 300.

The first subparagraph shall be without prejudice to the Member States' competence to negotiate in international bodies and to conclude international agreements.

Part Four—Association of the Overseas Countries and Territories[44]

Article 182[45] [Association of countries having special relations with Member States]

2–185 The Member States agree to associate with the Community the non-European countries and territories which have special relations with Denmark, France, the Netherlands and the United Kingdom. These countries and territories (hereinafter called the "countries and territories") are listed in Annex II to this Treaty.[46]

The purpose of association shall be to promote the economic and social development of the countries and territories and to establish close economic relations between them and the Community as a whole.

In accordance with the principles set out in the Preamble to this Treaty, association shall serve primarily to further the interests and prosperity of the inhabitants of these countries and territories in order to lead them to the economic, social and cultural development to which they aspire.

Article 183[47] [Aims of association]

2–186 Association shall have the following objectives.

(1) Member States shall apply to their trade with the countries and territories the same treatment as they accord each other pursuant to this Treaty.

(2) Each country or territory shall apply to its trade with Member States and with the other countries and territories the same treatment as that which it applies to the European state with which it has special relations.

(3) The Member States shall contribute to the investments required for the progressive development of these countries and territories.

(4) For investments financed by the Community, participation in tenders and supplies shall be open on equal terms to all natural and legal persons who are nationals of a Member State or of one of the countries and territories.

(5) In relations between Member States and the countries and territories the right of establishment of nationals and companies or firms shall be regulated in accordance with the provisions and procedures laid down in the Chapter relating to the right of establishment and on a non-discriminatory basis, subject to any special provisions laid down pursuant to Article 187.

---

[44] See Declaration (No. 36) on the overseas countries and territories (OCTs) annexed to the Final Act of the Treaty of Amsterdam.

[45] Formerly Art. 131.

[46] In former Art. 131, first paragraph, the words "Belgium" and "Italy" deleted and the reference to Annex IV replaced by a reference to Annex II by Treaty of Amsterdam, Art. 6(I)(62); Denmark and UK added to list of specified EC Member States respectively by virtue of Art. 2 of Treaty amending, with regard to Greenland, the Treaties establishing the European Communities (the Greenland Treaty), with effect from 1 January 1985 ([1985] OJ L29/1) and by virtue of Art. 24(1) of Act of Accession of Denmark, Ireland and the UK ([1972] OJ L73/1) (as adjusted by Decision of 1 January 1973, Art. 13 ([1973] OJ L2/1)), with effect from 1 January 1973.

[47] Formerly Art. 132.

Article 184[48] **[Customs duties]**

1. Customs duties on imports into the Member States of goods originating in the countries and territories shall be prohibited in conformity with the prohibition of customs duties between Member States in accordance with the provisions of this Treaty. **2–187**

2. Customs duties on imports into each country or territory from Member States or from the other countries or territories shall be prohibited in accordance with the provisions of Article 25.

3. The countries and territories may, however, levy customs duties which meet the needs of their development and industrialisation or produce revenue for their budgets.

The duties referred to in the preceding sub-paragraph may not exceed the level of those imposed on imports of products from the Member State with which each country or territory has special relations.

4. Paragraph 2 shall not apply to countries and territories which, by reason of the particular international obligations by which they are bound, already apply a non-discriminatory customs tariff.

5. The introduction of or any change in customs duties imposed on goods imported into the countries and territories shall not, either in law or in fact, give rise to any direct or indirect discrimination between imports from the various Member States.

Article 185[49] **[Measures to safeguard from deflections of trade]**

If the level of the duties applicable to goods from a third country on entry into a country or territory is liable, when the provisions of Article 184(1) have been applied, to cause deflections of trade to the detriment of any Member State, the latter may request the Commission to propose to the other Member States the measures needed to remedy the situation. **2–188**

Article 186[50] **[Reciprocal free movement of workers]**

Subject to the provisions relating to public health, public security or public policy, freedom of movement within Member States for workers from the countries and territories, and within the countries and territories for workers from Member States, shall be governed by agreements to be concluded subsequently with the unanimous approval of Member States. **2–189**

Article 187[51] **[Rules and procedure for association]**

The Council, acting unanimously, shall, on the basis of the experience acquired under the association of the countries and territories with the Community and of **2–190**

[48] Formerly Art. 133. In former Art. 133, transitional wording replaced with "prohibited" and "prohibition" in para. (1), "prohibited" in para. (2), "may not exceed" in para. (3) by Treaty of Amsterdam, Art. 6(I)(63)(a)–(c) and in para. (3), second sub-paragraph, former second sentence deleted by Treaty of Amsterdam, Art. 6(I)(63)(c) and transitional wording in para. (4) deleted by Art. 6(I)(63)(d).

[49] Formerly Art. 134.

[50] Formerly Art. 135.

[51] Formerly Art. 136. Former Art. 136 replaced by Treaty of Amsterdam, Art. 6(I)(64).

the principles set out in this Treaty, lay down provisions as regards the detailed rules and the procedure for the association of the countries and territories with the Community.

Article 188[52] **[Special position of Greenland]**

2–191 The provisions of Articles 182 to 187 shall apply to Greenland, subject to the specific provisions for Greenland set out in the Protocol on special arrangements for Greenland, annexed to this Treaty.

PART FIVE—INSTITUTIONS OF THE COMMUNITY

TITLE I—PROVISIONS GOVERNING THE INSTITUTIONS

CHAPTER 1—THE INSTITUTIONS

SECTION 1—THE EUROPEAN PARLIAMENT

Article 189[53] **[The European Parliament]**

2–192 The European Parliament, which shall consist of representatives of the peoples of the States brought together in the Community, shall exercise the powers conferred upon it by this Treaty.

The number of Members of the European Parliament shall not exceed 732.

Article 190[54] **[Election and composition of the European Parliament]**

2–193 1. The representatives in the European Parliament of the peoples of the States brought together in the Community shall be elected by direct universal suffrage.[55]

2. The number of representatives elected in each member state shall be as follows:

Belgium	25
Denmark	16
Germany	99
Greece	25
Spain	64
France	87
Ireland	15
Italy	87
Luxembourg	6
Netherlands	31
Austria	21
Portugal	25
Finland	16
Sweden	22
United Kingdom	87

[52] Formerly Art. 136a. Former Art. 136a added by Art. 3 of Treaty amending, with regard to Greenland, the Treaties establishing the European Communities (the Greenland Treaty), with effect from 1 January 1985 ([1985] OJ L29/1). See also Protocol (No. 15) on special arrangements for Greenland (1985).

[53] Article 189, second paragraph, replaced by Treaty of Nice, Art. 2(17). Formerly Art. 137. Former Art. 137, second paragraph added by Treaty of Amsterdam, Art. 2(37). Former Art. 137 previously replaced by Art. 8(39) TEU.

[54] Formerly Art. 138.

[55] In former Art. 138, text of Arts 1 and 2 of the Act concerning the election of representatives of the European Parliament by direct universal suffrage (annexed to Decision 76/787 ([1976] OJ L278/5)), as amended by Treaty of Amsterdam, Art. 5(1) (adding Art. 2, second paragraph) and by Decisions 95/1, Art. 5 ([1995] OJ L1/1) and 93/81 ([1993] OJ L33/15) (adjusting Member State representations in Art. 2), inserted as Art. 138(1) and (2) by Treaty of Amsterdam, Art. 6(I)(65)(a). Previous Art. 138(1) and (2) had lapsed in accordance with Art. 14 of the Act annexed to Decision 76/787. For prospective changes to representation upon enlargement of the EU, see Protocol on enlargement of the EU annexed to Treaty of Nice.

In the event of amendments to this paragraph, the number of representatives elected in each Member State must ensure appropriate representation of the peoples of the States brought together in the Community.[56]

3. Representatives shall be elected for a term of five years.[57]

4. The European Parliament shall draw up a proposal for elections by direct universal suffrage in accordance with a uniform procedure in all Member States or in accordance with principles common to all Member States.

The Council shall, acting unanimously after obtaining the assent of the European Parliament, which shall act by a majority of its component members, lay down the appropriate provisions, which it shall recommend to Member States for adoption in accordance with their respective constitutional requirements.[58]

5. The European Parliament, after seeking an opinion from the Commission and with the approval of the Council acting by a qualified majority, shall lay down the regulations and general conditions governing the performance of the duties of its Members. All rules or conditions relating to the taxation of Members or former Members shall require unanimity within the Council.[59]

Article 191[60] [Political parties]

Political parties at European level are important as a factor for integration within the Union. They contribute to forming a European awareness and to expressing the political will of the citizens of the Union. **2–194**

The Council, acting in accordance with the procedure referred to in Article 251, shall lay down the regulations governing political parties at European level and in particular the rules regarding their funding.

Article 192[61] [Legislative role of the European Parliament]

In so far as provided in this Treaty, the European Parliament shall participate in the process leading up to the adoption of Community acts by exercising its powers under the procedures laid down in Articles 251 and 252 and by giving its assent or delivering advisory opinions. **2–195**

The European Parliament may, acting by a majority of its Members, request the Commission to submit any appropriate proposal on matters on which it considers that a Community act is required for the purpose of implementing this Treaty.

Article 193[62] [Committees of Inquiry]

In the course of its duties, the European Parliament may, at the request of a quarter of its Members, set up a temporary Committee of Inquiry to investigate, without prejudice to the powers conferred by this Treaty on other institutions or bodies, alleged contraventions or maladministration in the implementation of Community law, except where the alleged facts are being examined before a court and while the case is still subject to legal proceedings. **2–196**

The temporary Committee of Inquiry shall cease to exist on the submission of its report.

---

[56] *ibid.*

[57] Text of Art. 3(1) of the Act concerning the election of representatives of the European Parliament by direct universal suffrage (annexed to Decision 76/787 ([1976] OJ L278/5)) inserted as Art. 138(3) by Treaty of Amsterdam, Art. 6(I)(65)(b).

[58] Former Art. 138(4) renumbered by Treaty of Amsterdam, Art. 6(I)(65)(c); first sub-paragraph replaced by Treaty of Amsterdam, Art. 2(38)(3). Previous Art. 138(3) replaced by Art. 8(40) TEU.

[59] Article 190(5) replaced by Treaty of Nice, Art. 2(18). Former Art. 138(5) renumbered by Treaty of Amsterdam, Art. 6(I)(65)(d); added by Treaty of Amsterdam, Art. 2(38)(4).

[60] Formerly Art. 138a; inserted by Art. 8(41) TEU. Article 191, second paragraph, added by Treaty of Nice, Art. 2(19).

[61] Formerly Art. 138b; inserted by Art. 8(41) TEU.

[62] Formerly Art. 138c; inserted by Art. 8(41) TEU.

The detailed provisions governing the exercise of the right of inquiry shall be determined by common accord of the European Parliament, the Council and the Commission.

Article 194[63] **[Right to petition Parliament]**

2–197 Any citizen of the Union, and any natural or legal person residing or having its registered office in a Member State, shall have the right to address, individually or in association with other citizens or persons, a petition to the European Parliament on a matter which comes within the Community's fields of activity and which affects him, her or it directly.

Article 195[64] **[The Ombudsman]**

2–198 1. The European Parliament shall appoint an Ombudsman empowered to receive complaints from any citizen of the Union or any natural or legal person residing or having its registered office in a Member State concerning instances of maladministration in the activities of the Community institutions or bodies, with the exception of the Court of Justice and the Court of First Instance acting in their judicial role.

In accordance with his duties, the Ombudsman shall conduct inquiries for which he finds grounds, either on his own initiative or on the basis of complaints submitted to him direct or through a Member of the European Parliament, except where the alleged facts are or have been the subject of legal proceedings. Where the Ombudsman establishes an instance of maladministration, he shall refer the matter to the institution concerned, which shall have a period of three months in which to inform him of its views. The Ombudsman shall then forward a report to the European Parliament and the institution concerned. The person lodging the complaint shall be informed of the outcome of such inquiries.

The Ombudsman shall submit an annual report to the European Parliament on the outcome of his inquiries.

2. The Ombudsman shall be appointed after each election of the European Parliament for the duration of its term of office. The Ombudsman shall be eligible for reappointment.

The Ombudsman may be dismissed by the Court of Justice at the request of the European Parliament if he no longer fulfils the conditions required for the performance of his duties or if he is guilty of serious misconduct.

3. The Ombudsman shall be completely independent in the performance of his duties. In the performance of those duties he shall neither seek nor take instructions from any body. The Ombudsman may not, during his term of office, engage in any other occupation, whether gainful or not.

4. The European Parliament shall, after seeking an opinion from the Commission and with the approval of the Council acting by a qualified majority, lay down the regulations and general conditions governing the performance of the Ombudsman's duties.

Article 196[65] **[Parliamentary sessions]**

2–199 The European Parliament shall hold an annual session. It shall meet, without requiring to be convened, on the second Tuesday in March.

---

[63] Formerly Art. 138d; inserted by Art. 8(41) TEU.

[64] Formerly Art. 138e; inserted by Art. 8(41) TEU.

[65] Formerly Art. 139. Former Art. 139, first paragraph, substituted by Treaty establishing a single Council and single Commission of the European Communities (Merger Treaty), Art. 27(1). Merger Treaty repealed by Treaty of Amsterdam, Art. 9(1). Powers conferred on European Parliament to be exercised in accordance with the EC and EAEC Treaties (Treaty of Amsterdam, Art. 9(2)). For continuity of legal effects, see Treaty of Amsterdam, Art. 10.

The European Parliament may meet in extraordinary session at the request of a majority of its Members or at the request of the Council or of the Commission.

Article 197[66] **[Election of officers; attendance by Commission and Council]**

The European Parliament shall elect its President and its officers from among its members. **2–200**

Members of the Commission may attend all meetings and shall, at their request, be heard on behalf of the Commission.

The Commission shall reply orally or in writing to questions put to it by the European Parliament or by its members.

The Council shall be heard by the European Parliament in accordance with the conditions laid down by the Council in its Rules of Procedure.

Article 198[67] **[Majority voting; quorum]**

Save as otherwise provided in this Treaty, the European Parliament shall act by an absolute majority of the votes cast. **2–201**

The Rules of Procedure shall determine the quorum.

Article 199[68] **[Rules of Procedure; publication of proceedings]**

The European Parliament shall adopt its Rules of Procedure, acting by a majority of its members. **2–202**

The proceedings of the European Parliament shall be published in the manner laid down in its Rules of Procedure.

Article 200[69] **[Debate on Commission annual general report]**

The European Parliament shall discuss in open session the annual general report submitted to it by the Commission. **2–203**

Article 201[70] **[Censure motions on Commission activities]**

If a motion of censure on the activities of the Commission is tabled before it, the European Parliament shall not vote thereon until at least three days after the motion has been tabled and only by open vote. If the motion of censure is carried by a two-thirds majority of the votes cast, representing a majority of the Members of the European Parliament, the Members of the Commission shall resign as a body. They shall continue to deal with current business until they are replaced in accordance with Article 214. In this case, the term of office of the Members of the Commission appointed to replace them shall expire on the date on which the term of office of the Members of the Commission obliged to resign as a body would have expired. **2–204**

SECTION 2—THE COUNCIL

Article 202[71] **[Functions of the Council]**

To ensure that the objectives set out in this Treaty are attained the Council shall, in accordance with the provisions of this Treaty: **2–205**

— ensure coordination of the general economic policies of the Member States;

[66] Formerly Art. 140.
[67] Formerly Art. 141.
[68] Formerly Art. 142.
[69] Formerly Art. 143.
[70] Formerly Art. 144. Former Art. 144, second paragraph, final sentence added by Art. 8(42) TEU.
[71] Formerly Art. 145; third indent added by Art. 10 SEA.

— have power to take decisions;
— confer on the Commission, in the acts which the Council adopts, powers for the implementation of the rules which the Council lays down. The Council may impose certain requirements in respect of the exercise of these powers. The Council may also reserve the right, in specific cases, to exercise directly implementing powers itself. The procedures referred to above must be consonant with principles and rules to be laid down in advance by the Council, acting unanimously on a proposal from the Commission and after obtaining the opinion of the European Parliament.[72]

Article 203[73] [Composition and presidency of the Council]

2–206 The Council shall consist of a representative of each Member State at ministerial level, authorised to commit the government of that Member State.

The office of President shall be held in turn by each Member State in the Council for a term of six months in the order decided by the Council acting unanimously.[74]

Article 204[75] [Meetings of the Council]

2–207 The Council shall meet when convened by its President on his own initiative or at the request of one of its members or of the Commission.

Article 205[76] [Majority voting procedures]

2–208 1. Save as otherwise provided in this Treaty, the Council shall act by a majority of its members.

2. Where the Council is required to act by a qualified majority, the votes of its members shall be weighted as follows:

Belgium	5
Denmark	3
Germany	10
Greece	5
Spain	8
France	10
Ireland	3
Italy	10
Luxembourg	2
Netherlands	5
Austria	4
Portugal	5
Finland	3
Sweden	4
United Kingdom	10

[72] See Council Decision 1999/348 laying down the procedures for the exercise of implementing powers conferred on the Commission reproduced below.

[73] Formerly Art. 146. Former Art. 146 substituted by Act of Accession of Austria, Finland and Sweden, Art. 12 ([1994] OJ C241) with effect from 1 January 1995. Previously inserted by Art. 8(43) TEU. Original Art. 146 repealed by Treaty establishing a single Council and a single Commission of the European Communities (Merger Treaty), Art. 7.

[74] For rotation of presidency, see Decision 95/2 ([1995] OJ L1/220) and Decision 2002/105 ([2002] OJ L39/17).

[75] Formerly Art. 147; inserted by Art. 8(44) TEU. Original Art. 147 repealed by Treaty establishing a single Council and a single Commission of the European Communities (Merger Treaty), Art. 7.

[76] Formerly Art. 148. Former Art. 148(2) substituted by Act of Accession of Austria, Finland and Sweden, Art. 15 (as substituted by Decision 95/1, Art. 8 ([1995] OJ L1/1)) with effect from 1 January 1995. For prospective amendments upon enlargement of the EU, see Protocol on enlargement of the EU annexed to the Treaty of Nice.

For their adoption, acts of the Council shall require at least:
— 62 votes in favour where this treaty requires them to be adopted on a proposal from the Commission,
— 62 votes in favour, cast by at least 10 members, in other cases.

3. Abstentions by members present in person or represented shall not prevent the adoption by the Council of acts which require unanimity.[77]

Article 206[78] **[Proxy voting]**

Where a vote is taken, any member of the Council may also act on behalf of not more than one other member. **2–209**

Article 207[79] **[COREPER; General Secretariat; Rules of Procedure]**

1. A committee consisting of the Permanent Representatives of the Member States shall be responsible for preparing the work of the Council and for carrying out the tasks assigned to it by the Council. The Committee may adopt procedural decisions in cases provided for in the Council's Rules of Procedure. **2–210**

2. The Council shall be assisted by a General Secretariat, under the responsibility of a Secretary-General, High Representative for the common foreign and security policy, who shall be assisted by a Deputy Secretary-General responsible for the running of the General Secretariat. The Secretary-General and the Deputy Secretary-General shall be appointed by the Council, acting by a qualified majority. The Council shall decide on the organisation of the General Secretariat.[80]

3. The Council shall adopt its Rules of Procedure.

For the purpose of applying Article 255(3), the Council shall elaborate in these Rules the conditions under which the public shall have access to Council documents.[81] For the purpose of this paragraph, the Council shall define the cases in which it is to be regarded as acting in its legislative capacity, with a view to allowing greater access to documents in those cases, while at the same time preserving the effectiveness of its decision-making process.

In any event, when the Council acts in its legislative capacity, the results of votes and explanations of vote as well as statements in the minutes shall be made public.

Article 208[82] **[Council requests for Commission studies or proposals]**

The Council may request the Commission to undertake any studies the Council considers desirable for the attainment of the common objectives, and to submit to it any appropriate proposals. **2–211**

Article 209[83] **[Rules governing committees]**

The Council shall, after receiving an opinion from the Commission, determine the rules governing the committees provided for in this Treaty. **2–212**

[77] See also the so-called "Ioannina Compromise" (Council Decision of 29 March 1994, concerning the taking of Decision by qualified majority by the Council, as amended) reproduced below.

[78] Formerly Art. 150.

[79] Formerly Art. 151; replaced by Treaty of Amsterdam, Art. 2(39). Former Art. 151 previously inserted by Art. 8(46) TEU. Original Art. 151 repealed by Treaty establishing a single Council and a single Commission of the European Communities (Merger Treaty), Art. 7.

[80] Article 207(2) replaced by Treaty of Nice, Art. 2(20).

[81] For conditions of access to Council documents, see Annex II to the Rules of Procedure as set out in Council Decision 2002/682 ([2002] OJ L230/7).

[82] Formerly Art. 152.

[83] Formerly Art. 153.

Article 210[84] [Remuneration for Commission and Court members]

2–213 The Council shall, acting by a qualified majority, determine the salaries, allowances and pensions of the President and Members of the Commission, and of the President, Judges, Advocates General and Registrar of the Court of Justice and of the Members and Registrar of the Court of First Instance. It shall also, again by a qualified majority, determine any payment to be made instead of remuneration.

SECTION 3—THE COMMISSION

Article 211[85] [Functions of the Commission]

2–214 In order to ensure the proper functioning and development of the common market, the Commission shall:
— ensure that the provisions of this Treaty and the measures taken by the institutions pursuant thereto are applied;
— formulate recommendations or deliver opinions on matters dealt with in this Treaty, if it expressly so provides or if the Commission considers it necessary;
— have its own power of decision and participate in the shaping of measures taken by the Council and by the European Parliament in the manner provided for in this Treaty;
— exercise the powers conferred on it by the Council for the implementation of the rules laid down by the latter.

Article 212[86] [Commission annual general report]

2–215 The Commission shall publish annually, not later than one month before the opening of the session of the European Parliament, a general report on the activities of the Community.

Article 213[87] [Composition and independence of the Commission]

2–216 1. The Commission shall consist of 20 Members, who shall be chosen on the grounds of their general competence and whose independence is beyond doubt.

The number of Members of the Commission may be altered by the Council, acting unanimously.

Only nationals of Member States may be Members of the Commission.

The Commission must include at least one national of each of the Member States, but may not include more than two Members having the nationality of the same State.[88]

2. The Members of the Commission shall, in the general interest of the Community, be completely independent in the performance of their duties.

In the performance of these duties, they shall neither seek nor take instructions from any government or from any other body. They shall refrain from any action

[84] Article 210 replaced by Treaty of Nice, Art. 2(21). Formerly Art. 154; inserted by Art. 8(47) TEU. Original Art. 154 repealed by Treaty establishing a single Council and a single Commission of the European Communities (Merger Treaty), Art. 7.

[85] Formerly Art. 155.

[86] Formerly Art. 156; inserted by Art. 8(48) TEU. Original Art. 156 repealed by Treaty establishing a single Council and a single Commission of the European Communities (Merger Treaty), Art. 19.

[87] Formerly Art. 157. Former Art. 157 substituted by Act of Accession of Austria, Finland and Sweden, Art. 16 (as substituted by Decision 95/1, Art 9 ([1995] OJ L1/1)) with effect from 1 January 1995. Former Art. 157 previously inserted by Art. 8(48) TEU. Original Art. 157 repealed by Treaty establishing a single Council and a single Commission of the European Communities (Merger Treaty), Art. 19.

[88] For prospective amendment of Art. 213(1), see Protocol on enlargement of the EU annexed to Treaty of Nice.

incompatible with their duties. Each Member State undertakes to respect this principle and not to seek to influence the Members of the Commission in the performance of their tasks.

The Members of the Commission may not, during their term of office, engage in any other occupation, whether gainful or not. When entering upon their duties they shall give a solemn undertaking that, both during and after their term of office, they will respect the obligations arising therefrom and in particular their duty to behave with integrity and discretion as regards the acceptance, after they have ceased to hold office, of certain appointments or benefits. In the event of any breach of these obligations, the Court of Justice may, on application by the Council or the Commission, rule that the Member concerned be, according to the circumstances, either compulsorily retired in accordance with Article 216 or deprived of his right to a pension or other benefits in its stead.

Article 214[89] [Nomination, appointment and term of office of Commission]

1. The Members of the Commission shall be appointed, in accordance with the procedure referred to in paragraph 2, for a period of five years, subject, if need be, to Article 201. **2–217**

Their term of office shall be renewable.

2. The Council, meeting in the composition of Heads of State or Government and acting by a qualified majority, shall nominate the person it intends to appoint as President of the Commission; the nomination shall be approved by the European Parliament.

The Council, acting by a qualified majority and by common accord with the nominee for President, shall adopt the list of the other persons whom it intends to appoint as Members of the Commission, drawn up in accordance with the proposals made by each Member State.

The President and the other Members of the Commission thus nominated shall be subject as a body to a vote of approval by the European Parliament. After approval by the European Parliament, the President and the other Members of the Commission shall be appointed by the Council, acting by a qualified majority.[90]

Article 215[91] [Resignation, removal or death of Commissioners in office]

Apart from normal replacement, or death, the duties of a Member of the Commission shall end when he resigns or is compulsorily retired. **2–218**

A vacancy caused by resignation, compulsory retirement or death shall be filled for the remainder of the Member's term of office by a new Member appointed by the Council, acting by a qualified majority. The Council may, acting unanimously, decide that such a vacancy need not be filled.

In the event of resignation, compulsory retirement or death, the President shall be replaced for the remainder of his term of office. The procedure laid down in Article 214(2) shall be applicable for the replacement of the President.

Save in the case of compulsory retirement under Article 216, Members of the Commission shall remain in office until they have been replaced or until the

---

[89] Formerly Art. 158; former Art. 158(2), first and second sub-paragraphs replaced and former Art. 158(3) deleted respectively by Treaty of Amsterdam, Art. 2(40) and 6(I)(66). Former Art. 158 inserted by Art. 8(48) TEU. Original Art. 158 repealed by Treaty establishing a single Council and a single Commission of the European Communities (Merger Treaty), Art. 19.

[90] Article 214(2) replaced by Treaty of Nice, Art. 2(22).

[91] Article 215 replaced by Treaty of Nice, Art. 2(23). Formerly Art. 159; inserted by Art. 8(48) TEU. Original Art. 159 repealed by Treaty establishing a single Council and a single Commission of the European Communities (Merger Treaty), Art. 19.

Council has decided that the vacancy need not be filled, as provided for in the second paragraph of this Article.

Article 216[92] **[Grounds for removal of serving Commissioner]**

2–219 If any Member of the Commission no longer fulfils the conditions required for the performance of his duties or if he has been guilty of serious misconduct, the Court of Justice may, on application by the Council or the Commission, compulsorily retire him.

Article 217[93] **[Commission President]**

2–220 1. The Commission shall work under the political guidance of its President, who shall decide on its internal organisation in order to ensure that it acts consistently, efficiently and on the basis of collegiality.

2. The responsibilities incumbent upon the Commission shall be structured and allocated among its Members by its President. The President may reshuffle the allocation of those responsibilities during the Commission's term of office. The Members of the Commission shall carry out the duties devolved upon them by the President under his authority.

3. After obtaining the approval of the College, the President shall appoint Vice-Presidents from among its Members.

4. A Member of the Commission shall resign if the President so requests, after obtaining the approval of the College.

Article 218[94] **[Cooperation with Council; Rules of Procedure]**

2–221 1. The Council and the Commission shall consult each other and shall settle by common accord their methods of cooperation.

2. The Commission shall adopt its Rules of Procedure so as to ensure that both it and its departments operate in accordance with the provisions of this Treaty. It shall ensure that these rules are published.

Article 219[95] **[Voting; quorum]**

2–222 The Commission shall act by a majority of the number of Members provided for in Article 213.

A meeting of the Commission shall be valid only if the number of Members laid down in its Rules of Procedure is present.

SECTION 4—THE COURT OF JUSTICE

Article 220[96] **[Functions of the ECJ and CFI]**

2–223 The Court of Justice and the Court of First Instance, each within its jurisdiction, shall ensure that in the interpretation and application of this Treaty the law is observed.

[92] Formerly Art. 160; inserted by Art. 8(48) TEU. Original Art. 160 repealed by Treaty establishing a single Council and a single Commission of the European Communities (Merger Treaty), Art. 19.

[93] Article 217 replaced by Treaty of Nice, Art. 2(24). Formerly Art. 161; inserted by Art. 8(48) TEU. Original Art. 161 repealed by Treaty establishing a single Council and a single Commission of the European Communities (Merger Treaty), Art. 19.

[94] Formerly Art. 162; inserted by Art. 8(48) TEU. Original Art. 162 repealed by Treaty establishing a single Council and a single Commission of the European Communities (Merger Treaty), Art. 19.

[95] Article 219, first paragraph, deleted by Treaty of Nice, Art. 2(25). Formerly Art. 163; first paragraph inserted by Treaty of Amsterdam, Art. 2(41); remainder of former Art. 163 inserted by Art. 8(48) TEU. Original Art. 163 repealed by Treaty establishing a single Council and a single Commission of the European Communities (Merger Treaty), Art. 19.

[96] Article 220 replaced by Treaty of Nice, Art. 2(26). Formerly Art. 164.

In addition, judicial panels may be attached to the Court of First Instance under the conditions laid down in Article 225a in order to exercise, in certain specific areas, the judicial competence laid down in this Treaty.

Article 221[97] **[Judges and organisation of the court]**

The Court of Justice shall consist of one judge per Member State. **2–224**

The Court of Justice shall sit in chambers or in a Grand Chamber, in accordance with the rules laid down for that purpose in the Statute of the Court of Justice.

When provided for in the Statute, the Court of Justice may also sit as a full Court.

Article 222[98] **[Advocates General]**

The Court of Justice shall be assisted by eight Advocates General. Should the **2–225** Court of Justice so request, the Council, acting unanimously, may increase the number of Advocates General.

It shall be the duty of the Advocate General, acting with complete impartiality and independence, to make, in open court, reasoned submissions on cases which, in accordance with the Statute of the Court of Justice, require his involvement.

Article 223[99] **[Appointment of Judges, Advocates General and Registrar]**

The Judges and Advocates General of the Court of Justice shall be chosen from **2–226** persons whose independence is beyond doubt and who possess the qualifications required for appointment to the highest judicial offices in their respective countries or who are jurisconsults of recognised competence; they shall be appointed by common accord of the governments of the Member States for a term of six years. Every three years there shall be a partial replacement of the Judges and Advocates General, in accordance with the conditions laid down in the Statute of the Court of Justice.

The Judges shall elect the President of the Court of Justice from among their number for a term of three years. He may be re-elected.

Retiring Judges and Advocates General may be reappointed.

The Court of Justice shall appoint its Registrar and lay down the rules governing his service.

The Court of Justice shall establish its Rules of Procedure. Those Rules shall require the approval of the Council, acting by a qualified majority.

Article 224[1] **[Court of First Instance]**

The Court of First Instance shall comprise at least one judge per Member State. **2–227** The number of Judges shall be determined by the Statute of the Court of Justice.

[97] Article 221 replaced by Treaty of Nice, Art. 2(27). Formerly Art. 165. Former Art. 165 substituted by Act of Accession of Austria, Finland and Sweden, Art. 17, 18 (as substituted by Decision 95/1, Art. 10 ([1995] OJ L1/1)) with effect from 1 January 1995. Previously replaced by Art. 8(49) TEU. Previous Art. 165, first paragraph, amended earlier by Act of Accession of Spain and Portugal, Art. 17 ([1985] OJ L302/2). Previous Art. 165, third paragraph, amended by Decision 74/584, Art. 1 ([1974] OJ L318/22).

[98] Article 222 replaced by Treaty of Nice, Art. 2(28). Formerly Art. 166. Former Art. 166, first paragraph, amended by Treaty of Amsterdam, Art. 6(I)(67). Former Art. 166, first paragraph amended by Act of Accession of Austria, Finland and Sweden, Art. 20 (as substituted by Decision 95/1, Art. 11 ([1995] OJ L1/1)) with effect from 1 January 1995. Previously substituted by Act of Accession of Spain and Portugal, Art. 18 ([1985] OJ L320/9).

[99] Article 223 replaced by Treaty of Nice, Art. 2(29). Formerly Art. 167. Former Art. 167, second and third paragraphs, substituted by Act of Accession of Austria, Finland and Sweden, Art. 21 (as substituted by Decision 95/1, Art. 12 ([1995] OJ L1/1)) with effect from 1 January 1995; previously substituted by Act of Accession of Spain and Portugal, Art. 19 ([1985] OJ L320/9).

[1] Article 224 replaced by Treaty of Nice, Art. 2(30). Formerly Art. 168.

The Statute may provide for the Court of First Instance to be assisted by Advocates-General.

The members of the Court of First Instance shall be chosen from persons whose independence is beyond doubt and who possess the ability required for appointment to high judicial office. They shall be appointed by common accord of the governments of the Member States for a term of six years. The membership shall be partially renewed every three years. Retiring members shall be eligible for reappointment.

The Judges shall elect the President of the Court of First Instance from among their number for a term of three years. He may be re-elected.

The Court of First Instance shall appoint its Registrar and lay down the rules governing his service.

The Court of First Instance shall establish its Rules of Procedure in agreement with the Court of Justice. Those Rules shall require the approval of the Council, acting by a qualified majority.

Unless the Statute of the Court of Justice provides otherwise, the provisions of this Treaty relating to the Court of Justice shall apply to the Court of First Instance.

Article 225[2] **[Jurisdiction of Court of First Instance]**

2–228 1. The Court of First Instance shall have jurisdiction to hear and determine at first instance actions or proceedings referred to in Articles 230, 232, 235, 236 and 238, with the exception of those assigned to a judicial panel and those reserved in the Statute for the Court of Justice. The Statute may provide for the Court of First Instance to have jurisdiction for other classes of action or proceeding.

Decisions given by the Court of First Instance under this paragraph may be subject to a right of appeal to the Court of Justice on points of law only, under the conditions and within the limits laid down by the Statute.

2. The Court of First Instance shall have jurisdiction to hear and determine actions or proceedings brought against decisions of the judicial panels set up under Article 225a.

Decisions given by the Court of First Instance under this paragraph may exceptionally be subject to review by the Court of Justice, under the conditions and within the limits laid down by the Statute, where there is a serious risk of the unity or consistency of Community law being affected.

3. The Court of First Instance shall have jurisdiction to hear and determine questions referred for a preliminary ruling under Article 234, in specific areas laid down by the Statute.

Where the Court of First Instance considers that the case requires a decision of principle likely to affect the unity or consistency of Community law, it may refer the case to the Court of Justice for a ruling.

Decisions given by the Court of First Instance on questions referred for a preliminary ruling may exceptionally be subject to review by the Court of Justice, under the conditions and within the limits laid down by the Statute, where there is a serious risk of the unity or consistency of Community law being affected.

[2] Article 225 replaced by Treaty of Nice, Art. 2(31). Formerly Art. 168a; replaced by Art. 8(50) TEU. Previous Art. 168a added by Art. 11 SEA.

Article 225a[3] [Judicial panels]

The Council, acting unanimously on a proposal from the Commission and after consulting the European Parliament and the Court of Justice or at the request of the Court of Justice and after consulting the European Parliament and the Commission, may create judicial panels to hear and determine at first instance certain classes of action or proceeding brought in specific areas. **2–229**

The decision establishing a judicial panel shall lay down the rules on the organisation of the panel and the extent of the jurisdiction conferred upon it.

Decisions given by judicial panels may be subject to a right of appeal on points of law only or, when provided for in the decision establishing the panel, a right of appeal also on matters of fact, before the Court of First Instance.

The members of the judicial panels shall be chosen from persons whose independence is beyond doubt and who possess the ability required for appointment to judicial office. They shall be appointed by the Council, acting unanimously.

The judicial panels shall establish their Rules of Procedure in agreement with the Court of Justice. Those Rules shall require the approval of the Council, acting by a qualified majority.

Unless the decision establishing the judicial panel provides otherwise, the provisions of this Treaty relating to the Court of Justice and the provisions of the Statute of the Court of Justice shall apply to the judicial panels.

Article 226[4] [Enforcement proceedings brought by Commission]

If the Commission considers that a Member State has failed to fulfil an obligation under this Treaty, it shall deliver a reasoned opinion on the matter after giving the State concerned the opportunity to submit its observations. **2–230**

If the State concerned does not comply with the opinion within the period laid down by the Commission, the latter may bring the matter before the Court of Justice.

Article 227[5] [Enforcement proceedings brought by Member States]

A Member State which considers that another Member State has failed to fulfil an obligation under this Treaty may bring the matter before the Court of Justice. **2–231**

Before a Member State brings an action against another Member State for an alleged infringement of an obligation under this Treaty, it shall bring the matter before the Commission.

The Commission shall deliver a reasoned opinion after each of the States concerned has been given the opportunity to submit its own case and its observations on the other party's case both orally and in writing.

---

[3] Article 225a inserted by Treaty of Nice, Art. 2(32).

[4] Formerly Art. 169. For derogations from this procedure, see Art. 88(2) (state aid), Art. 95(9) (cases of improper use by Member States of powers in Art. 95 to maintain national laws even where harmonisation measure has been adopted) and Art. 298 (cases of improper use by Member States of powers to protect essential security interests or to deal with serious internal disturbances or international tension). Procedure excluded in cases of surveillance of budgetary discipline (Art. 104). EIB Board of Directors and Council of ECB to enjoy same powers as Commission under Art. 226 *vis-à-vis* Member States and national central banks respectively (Art. 237).

[5] Formerly Art. 170. For derogations from this procedure, see Art. 88(2) (state aid), Art. 95(9) (cases of improper use by Member States of powers in Art. 95 to maintain national laws even where harmonisation measure has been adopted) and Art. 298 (cases of improper use by Member States of powers to protect essential security interests or to deal with serious internal disturbances or international tension). Procedure excluded in cases of surveillance of budgetary discipline (Art. 104).

If the Commission has not delivered an opinion within three months of the date on which the matter was brought before it, the absence of such opinion shall not prevent the matter from being brought before the Court of Justice.

Article 228[6] **[Compliance with judgments in enforcement proceedings]**

2–232 1. If the Court of Justice finds that a Member State has failed to fulfil an obligation under this Treaty, the State shall be required to take the necessary measures to comply with the judgment of the Court of Justice.

2. If the Commission considers that the Member State concerned has not taken such measures it shall, after giving that state the opportunity to submit its observations, issue a reasoned opinion specifying the points on which the Member State concerned has not complied with the judgment of the Court of Justice.

If the Member State concerned fails to take the necessary measures to comply with the court's judgment within the time-limit laid down by the Commission, the latter may bring the case before the Court of Justice. In so doing it shall specify the amount of the lump sum or penalty payment to be paid by the Member State concerned which it considers appropriate in the circumstances. If the Court of Justice finds that the Member State concerned has not complied with its judgment it may impose a lump sum or penalty payment on it.

This procedure shall be without prejudice to Article 227.

Article 229[7] **[ECJ jurisdiction over penalties]**

2–233 Regulations adopted jointly by the European Parliament and the Council, and by the Council, pursuant to the provisions of this Treaty, may give the Court of Justice unlimited jurisdiction with regard to the penalties provided for in such regulations.

Article 229a[8] **[ECJ jurisdiction over EC industrial property right disputes]**

2–234 Without prejudice to the other provisions of this Treaty, the Council, acting unanimously on a proposal from the Commission and after consulting the European Parliament, may adopt provisions to confer jurisdiction, to the extent that it shall determine, on the Court of Justice in disputes relating to the application of acts adopted on the basis of this Treaty which create Community industrial property rights. The Council shall recommend those provisions to the Member States for adoption in accordance with their respective constitutional requirements.

Article 230[9] **[Judicial review of EC acts]**

2–235 The Court of Justice shall review the legality of acts adopted jointly by the European Parliament and the Council, of acts of the Council, of the Commission and of the ECB, other than recommendations and opinions, and of acts of the European Parliament intended to produce legal effects *vis-à-vis* third parties.

It shall for this purpose have jurisdiction in actions brought by a Member State, the European Parliament, the Council or the Commission on grounds of lack of competence, infringement of an essential procedural requirement, infringement of this Treaty or of any rule of law relating to its application, or misuse of powers.

[6] Formerly Art. 171; replaced by Art. 8(51) TEU.

[7] Formerly Art. 172; replaced by Art. 8(52) TEU.

[8] Article 229a inserted by Treaty of Nice, Art. 2(33).

[9] Article 230, second and third paragraphs replaced by single paragraph by Treaty of Nice, Art. 2(34). Formerly Art. 173; former third paragraph replaced by Treaty of Amsterdam, Art. 2(42); former Art. 173 replaced by Union Treaty, Art. 8(53) TEU. Acts of the ECB also subject to review (see Protocol (No. 18) on Statute of ESCB and ECB, Art. 35).

The Court of Justice shall have jurisdiction under the same conditions in actions brought by the Court of Auditors and by the ECB for the purpose of protecting their prerogatives.

Any natural or legal person may, under the same conditions, institute proceedings against a decision addressed to that person or against a decision which, although in the form of a regulation or a decision addressed to another person, is of direct and individual concern to the former.

The proceedings provided for in this Article shall be instituted within two months of the publication of the measure, or of its notification to the plaintiff, or, in the absence thereof, of the day on which it came to the knowledge of the latter, as the case may be.

Article 231[10] **[Annulment of EC acts]**

If the action is well founded, the Court of Justice shall declare the act concerned to be void. **2–236**

In the case of a regulation, however, the Court of Justice shall, if it considers this necessary, state which of the effects of the regulation which it has declared void shall be considered as definitive.

Article 232[11] **[Action for failure to act]**

Should the European Parliament, the Council or the Commission, in infringement of this Treaty, fail to act, the Member States and the other institutions of the Community may bring an action before the Court of Justice to have the infringement established. **2–237**

The action shall be admissible only if the institution concerned has first been called upon to act. If, within two months of being so called upon, the institution concerned has not defined its position, the action may be brought within a further period of two months.

Any natural or legal person may, under the conditions laid down in the preceding paragraphs, complain to the Court of Justice that an institution of the Community has failed to address to that person any act other than a recommendation or an opinion.

The Court of Justice shall have jurisdiction, under the same conditions, in actions or proceedings brought by the ECB in the areas falling within the latter's field of competence and in actions or proceedings brought against the latter.

Article 233[12] **[Requirement of institutions to give effect to judgments]**

The institution or institutions whose act has been declared void or whose failure to act has been declared contrary to this Treaty shall be required to take the necessary measures to comply with the judgment of the Court of Justice. **2–238**

This obligation shall not affect any obligation which may result from the application of the second paragraph of Article 288.

This Article shall also apply to the ECB.

Article 234[13] **[Preliminary rulings procedure]**

The Court of Justice shall have jurisdiction to give preliminary rulings concerning: **2–239**

(a) the interpretation of this Treaty;

---

[10] Formerly Art. 174.

[11] Formerly Art. 175; replaced by Art. 8(54) TEU. Omissions of the ECB also subject to review (see Protocol (No. 18) on Statute of ESCB and ECB, Art. 35).

[12] Formerly Art. 176; replaced by Art. 8(55) TEU.

[13] Formerly Art. 177; replaced by Art. 8(56) TEU. For jurisdiction of the Court in the context of Title IV of this Treaty, see Art. 68 above.

(b) the validity and interpretation of acts of the institutions of the Community and of the ECB;
(c) the interpretation of the statutes of bodies established by an act of the Council, where those statutes so provide.

Where such a question is raised before any court or tribunal of a Member State, that court or tribunal may, if it considers that a decision on the question is necessary to enable it to give judgment, request the Court of Justice to give a ruling thereon.

Where any such question is raised in a case pending before a court or tribunal of a Member State against whose decisions there is no judicial remedy under national law, that court or tribunal shall bring the matter before the Court of Justice.

Article 235[14] **[Disputes concerning non-contractual liability of EC]**

2–240 The Court of Justice shall have jurisdiction in disputes relating to compensation for damage provided for in the second paragraph of Article 288.

Article 236[15] **[Staff disputes with EC institutions]**

2–241 The Court of Justice shall have jurisdiction in any dispute between the Community and its servants within the limits and under the conditions laid down in the Staff Regulations or the Conditions of Employment.

Article 237[16] **[Disputes concerning EIB and national central banks]**

2–242 The Court of Justice shall, within the limits hereinafter laid down, have jurisdiction in disputes concerning:

(a) the fulfilment by Member States of obligations under the Statute of the European Investment Bank. In this connection, the Board of Directors of the Bank shall enjoy the powers conferred upon the Commission by Article 226;
(b) measures adopted by the Board of Governors of the European Investment Bank. In this connection, any Member State, the Commission or the Board of Directors of the Bank may institute proceedings under the conditions laid down in Article 230;
(c) measures adopted by the Board of Directors of the European Investment Bank. Proceedings against such measures may be instituted only by Member States or by the Commission, under the conditions laid down in Article 230, and solely on the grounds of non-compliance with the procedure provided for in Article 21(2), (5), (6) and (7) of the Statute of the Bank;
(d) the fulfilment by national central banks of obligations under this Treaty and the Statute of the ESCB. In this connection the powers of the Council of the ECB in respect of national central banks shall be the same as those conferred upon the Commission in respect of Member States by Article 226. If the Court of Justice finds that a national central bank has failed to fulfil an obligation under this Treaty, that bank shall be required to take the necessary measures to comply with the judgment of the Court of Justice.

Article 238[17] **[Jurisdiction conferred by Community contracts]**

2–243 The Court of Justice shall have jurisdiction to give judgment pursuant to any arbitration clause contained in a contract concluded by or on behalf of the Community, whether that contract be governed by public or private law.

[14] Formerly Art. 178.
[15] Formerly Art. 179.
[16] Formerly Art. 180; replaced by Art. 8(57) TEU.
[17] Formerly Art. 181.

Article 239[18] **[Special jurisdiction in disputes between Member States]**

The Court of Justice shall have jurisdiction in any dispute between Member States which relates to the subject matter of this Treaty if the dispute is submitted to it under a special agreement between the parties. **2–244**

Article 240[19] **[Jurisdiction of national courts in disputes to which EC is party]**

Save where jurisdiction is conferred on the Court of Justice by this Treaty, disputes to which the Community is a party shall not on that ground be excluded from the jurisdiction of the courts or tribunals of the Member States. **2–245**

Article 241[20] **[Plea of illegality]**

Notwithstanding the expiry of the period laid down in the fifth paragraph of Article 230, any party may, in proceedings in which a regulation adopted jointly by the European Parliament and the Council, or a regulation of the Council, of the Commission, or of the ECB is at issue, plead the grounds specified in the second paragraph of Article 230 in order to invoke before the Court of Justice the inapplicability of that regulation. **2–246**

Article 242[21] **[Possible suspension of Community acts]**

Actions brought before the Court of Justice shall not have suspensory effect. The Court of Justice may, however, if it considers that circumstances so require, order that application of the contested act be suspended. **2–247**

Article 243[22] **[Interim measures]**

The Court of Justice may in any cases before it prescribe any necessary interim measures. **2–248**

Article 244[23] **[Enforcement of judgments]**

The judgments of the Court of Justice shall be enforceable under the conditions laid down in Article 256. **2–249**

Article 245[24] **[Statute of the Court]**

The Statute of the Court of Justice shall be laid down in a separate Protocol. The Council, acting unanimously at the request of the Court of Justice and after **2–250**

[18] Formerly Art. 182. See also Art. 292 (Member States may submit disputes concerning the interpretation or application of the Treaty only to those methods of settlement provided for in the Treaty).

[19] Formerly Art. 183.

[20] Formerly Art. 184; replaced by Art. 8(58) TEU.

[21] Formerly Art. 185.

[22] Formerly Art. 186.

[23] Formerly Art. 187.

[24] Article 245 replaced by Treaty of Nice, Art. 2(35). The Protocol on the Statute of the Court of Justice annexed to this Treaty by the Treaty of Nice is set out later in this chapter. Formerly Art. 188; second paragraph, inserted by Art. 12 SEA.

consulting the European Parliament and the Commission, or at the request of the Commission and after consulting the European Parliament and the Court of Justice, may amend the provisions of the Statute, with the exception of Title I.

SECTION 5—THE COURT OF AUDITORS

Article 246[25] **[Function of Court of Auditors]**

2–251 The Court of Auditors shall carry out the audit.

Article 247[26] **[Membership and terms of office]**

2–252 1. The Court of Auditors shall consist of one national from each Member State.[27]

2. The Members of the Court of Auditors shall be chosen from among persons who belong or have belonged in their respective countries to external audit bodies or who are especially qualified for this office. Their independence must be beyond doubt.

3. The Members of the Court of Auditors shall be appointed for a term of six years. The Council, acting by a qualified majority after consulting the European Parliament, shall adopt the list of Members drawn up in accordance with the proposals made by each Member State. The term of office of the Members of the Court of Auditors shall be renewable.

They shall elect the President of the Court of Auditors from among their number for a term of three years. The President may be re-elected.[28]

4. The Members of the Court of Auditors shall, in the general interest of the Community, be completely independent in the performance of their duties.
In the performance of these duties, they shall neither seek nor take instructions from any government or from any other body. They shall refrain from any action incompatible with their duties.

5. The Members of the Court of Auditors may not, during their term of office, engage in any other occupation, whether gainful or not. When entering upon their duties they shall give a solemn undertaking that, both during and after their term of office, they will respect the obligations arising therefrom and in particular their duty to behave with integrity and discretion as regards the acceptance, after they have ceased to hold office, of certain appointments or benefits.

6. Apart from normal replacement, or death, the duties of a Member of the Court of Auditors shall end when he resigns, or is compulsorily retired by a ruling of the Court of Justice pursuant to paragraph 7.

The vacancy thus caused shall be filled for the remainder of the Member's term of office.

Save in the case of compulsory retirement, Members of the Court of Auditors shall remain in office until they have been replaced.

7. A Member of the Court of Auditors may be deprived of his office or of his right to a pension or other benefits in its stead only if the Court of Justice, at the request of the Court of Auditors, finds that he no longer fulfils the requisite conditions or meets the obligations arising from his office.

8. The Council, acting by a qualified majority, shall determine the conditions of employment of the President and the Members of the Court of Auditors and in

---

[25] Formerly Art. 188a; inserted by Art. 8(59) TEU.

[26] Formerly Art. 188b. Former Art. 188b(1) substituted by Act of Accession of Austria, Finland and Sweden, Art. 22 (as substituted in turn by Decision 95/1, Art. 13 ([1995] OJ L1/1)). Former Art. 188b(3), second sub-paragraph, deleted by Treaty of Amsterdam, Art. 6(I)(68). Former Art. 188b originally inserted by Art. 8(59) TEU.

[27] Article 247(1) replaced by Treaty of Nice, Art. 2(36)(a).

[28] Article 247(3) replaced by Treaty of Nice, Art. 2(36)(b).

particular their salaries, allowances and pensions. It shall also, by the same majority, determine any payment to be made instead of remuneration.

9. The provisions of the Protocol on the privileges and immunities of the European Communities applicable to the Judges of the Court of Justice shall also apply to the Members of the Court of Auditors.

Article 248[29] [Tasks of the Court of Auditors]

1. The Court of Auditors shall examine the accounts of all revenue and expenditure of the Community. It shall also examine the accounts of all revenue and expenditure of all bodies set up by the Community insofar as the relevant constituent instrument does not preclude such examination. **2–253**

The Court of Auditors shall provide the European Parliament and the Council with a statement of assurance as to the reliability of the accounts and the legality and regularity of the underlying transactions which shall be published in the *Official Journal of the European Union*. This statement may be supplemented by specific assessments for each major area of Community activity.[30]

2. The Court of Auditors shall examine whether all revenue has been received and all expenditure incurred in a lawful and regular manner and whether the financial management has been sound. In doing so, it shall report in particular on any cases of irregularity.

The audit of revenue shall be carried out on the basis both of the amounts established as due and the amounts actually paid to the Community.

The audit of expenditure shall be carried out on the basis both of commitments undertaken and payments made.

These audits may be carried out before the closure of accounts for the financial year in question.

3. The audit shall be based on records and, if necessary, performed on the spot in the other institutions of the Community, on the premises of any body which manages revenue or expenditure on behalf of the Community and in the Member States, including on the premises of any natural or legal person in receipt of payments from the budget. In the Member States the audit shall be carried out in liaison with national audit bodies or, if these do not have the necessary powers, with the competent national departments. The Court of Auditors and the national audit bodies of the Member States shall co-operate in a spirit of trust while maintaining their independence. These bodies or departments shall inform the Court of Auditors whether they intend to take part in the audit. The other institutions of the Community, any bodies managing revenue or expenditure on behalf of the Community, any natural or legal person in receipt of payments from the budget, and the national audit bodies or, if these do not have the necessary powers, the competent national departments, shall forward to the Court of Auditors, at its request, any document or information necessary to carry out its task.

In respect of the European Investment Bank's activity in managing Community expenditure and revenue, the Court's rights of access to information held by the Bank shall be governed by an agreement between the Court, the Bank and the Commission.[31] In the absence of an agreement, the Court shall nevertheless have

[29] Formerly Art. 188c. Former Art. 188c(1), second sub-paragraph, substituted by Treaty of Amsterdam, Art. 2(43)(a); former Art. 188c(2), first sub-paragraph, substituted by Treaty of Amsterdam, Art. 2(43)(b) and former Art. 188c(3) substituted by Treaty of Amsterdam, Art. 2(43)(c). Former Art. 188c originally inserted by Art. 8(59) TEU.

[30] Article 248(1) replaced by Treaty of Nice, Art. 2(37)(a).

[31] See Declaration (No. 33) on Article [248(3)] of the EC Treaty annexed to the Final Act of the Treaty of Amsterdam.

access to information necessary for the audit of Community expenditure and revenue managed by the Bank.

4. The Court of Auditors shall draw up an annual report after the close of each financial year. It shall be forwarded to the other institutions of the Community and shall be published, together with the replies of these institutions to the observations of the Court of Auditors, in the *Official Journal of the European Union*.

The Court of Auditors may also, at any time, submit observations, particularly in the form of special reports, on specific questions and deliver opinions at the request of one of the other institutions of the Community.

It shall adopt its annual reports, special reports or opinions by a majority of its Members. However, it may establish internal chambers in order to adopt certain categories of reports or opinions under the conditions laid down by its Rules of Procedure.

It shall assist the European Parliament and the Council in exercising their powers of control over the implementation of the budget.

The Court of Auditors shall draw up its Rules of Procedure. Those rules shall require the approval of the Council, acting by a qualified majority.[32]

CHAPTER 2—PROVISIONS COMMON TO SEVERAL INSTITUTIONS

Article 249[33] [EC legislation]

2–254 In order to carry out their task and in accordance with the provisions of this Treaty, the European Parliament acting jointly with the Council, the Council and the Commission shall make regulations and issue directives, take decisions, make recommendations or deliver opinions.

A regulation shall have general application. It shall be binding in its entirety and directly applicable in all Member States.

A directive shall be binding, as to the result to be achieved, upon each Member State to which it is addressed, but shall leave to the national authorities the choice of form and methods.

A decision shall be binding in its entirety upon those to whom it is addressed.

Recommendations and opinions shall have no binding force.

Article 250[34] [Amendments to Commission proposals]

2–255 1. Where, in pursuance of this Treaty, the Council acts on a proposal from the Commission, unanimity shall be required for an act constituting an amendment to that proposal, subject to Article 251(4) and (5).

2. As long as the Council has not acted, the Commission may alter its proposal at any time during the procedures leading to the adoption of a Community act.

[32] Article 248(4) replaced by Treaty of Nice, Art. 2(37)(b).

[33] Formerly Art. 189; replaced by Art. 8(60) TEU. See Art. 110 and Protocol (No. 18) on the Statute of the ESCB and of the ECB, Art. 34 for rule-making powers of ECB.

[34] Formerly Art. 189a; inserted by Art. 8(61) TEU.

[35] Formerly Art. 189b; replaced by Treaty of Amsterdam, Art. 2(44). Previously inserted by Art. 8(61) TEU. See Joint Declaration of 4 May 1999 on the practical arrangements for the co-decision procedure, reproduced below; and Declaration (No. 34) on respect for time-limits under the co-decision procedure annexed to the Final Act of the Treaty of Amsterdam.

Article 251[35] **[Legislative process: co-decision procedure]**

1. Where reference is made in this Treaty to this Article for the adoption of an act,[36] the following procedure shall apply. **2–256**

2. The Commission shall submit a proposal to the European Parliament and the Council.

The Council, acting by a qualified majority after obtaining the opinion of the European Parliament,

— if it approves all the amendments contained in the European Parliament's opinion, may adopt the proposed act thus amended;
— if the European Parliament does not propose any amendments, may adopt the proposed act;
— shall otherwise adopt a common position and communicate it to the European Parliament. The Council shall inform the European Parliament fully of the reasons which led it to adopt its common position. The Commission shall inform the European Parliament fully of its position.

If, within three months of such communication, the European Parliament:

— approves the common position or has not taken a decision, the act in question shall be deemed to have been adopted in accordance with that common position;
— rejects, by an absolute majority of its component members, the common position, the proposed act shall be deemed not to have been adopted;
— proposes amendments to the common position by an absolute majority of its component members, the amended text shall be forwarded to the Council and to the Commission, which shall deliver an opinion on those amendments.

3. If, within three months of the matter being referred to it, the Council, acting by a qualified majority, approves all the amendments of the European Parliament, the act in question shall be deemed to have been adopted in the form of the common position thus amended; however, the Council shall act unanimously on the amendments on which the Commission has delivered a negative opinion. If the Council does not approve all the amendments, the President of the Council, in agreement with the President of the European Parliament, shall within six weeks convene a meeting of the Conciliation Committee.

4. The Conciliation Committee, which shall be composed of the members of the Council or their representatives and an equal number of representatives of the European Parliament, shall have the task of reaching agreement on a joint text, by a qualified majority of the members of the Council or their representatives and by a majority of the representatives of the European Parliament. The Commission shall take part in the Conciliation Committee's proceedings and shall take all the necessary initiatives with a view to reconciling the positions of the European Parliament and the Council. In fulfilling this task, the Conciliation Committee shall address the common position on the basis of the amendments proposed by the European Parliament.

5. If, within six weeks of its being convened, the Conciliation Committee approves a joint text, the European Parliament, acting by an absolute majority of the votes cast, and the Council, acting by a qualified majority, shall each have a period of six weeks from that approval in which to adopt the act in question in accordance with the joint text. If either of the two institutions fails to approve the proposed act within that period, it shall be deemed not to have been adopted.

[36] For substantive areas to which co-decision procedure applies, see Art. 12 (discrimination on grounds of nationality), 18(2) and 40 (free movement), 42 (social security), 44(1) freedom of establishment), 46(2) (restrictions on the freedom of establishment), 47(1), (2) (mutual recognition of qualifications), 67(2), (4) (Title IV measures), 71(1) (transport), 95(1) (internal market measures), 129 (co-operation on employment), 135 (customs co-operation), 137(2) (social policy), 141(3) (equal pay), 148 (European Social Fund), 149(4) (education), 150(4) (vocational training), 151(5) (culture), 152(4) (public health), 153(4) (consumer protection), 156 (trans-European networks), 162 (ERDF), 166(1) and 172 (research and technological development), 175(1) and (3) (environment), 179(1) (development co-operation), 280 (protection of EC financial interests), 285(1) (statistics), 286(1) (data protection).

6. Where the Conciliation Committee does not approve a joint text, the proposed act shall be deemed not to have been adopted.

7. The periods of three months and six weeks referred to in this Article shall be extended by a maximum of one month and two weeks respectively at the initiative of the European Parliament or the Council.

Article 252[37] **[Legislative procedure: cooperation procedure]**

2–257 Where reference is made in this Treaty to this Article for the adoption of an act,[38] the following procedure shall apply:

(a) The Council, acting by a qualified majority on a proposal from the Commission and after obtaining the opinion of the European Parliament, shall adopt a common position.

(b) The Council's common position shall be communicated to the European Parliament. The Council and the Commission shall inform the European Parliament fully of the reasons which led the Council to adopt its common position and also of the Commission's position.
If, within three months of such communication, the European Parliament approves this common position or has not taken a decision within that period, the Council shall definitively adopt the act in question in accordance with the common position.

(c) The European Parliament may, within the period of three months referred to in point (b), by an absolute majority of its component members, propose amendments to the Council's common position. The European Parliament may also, by the same majority, reject the Council's common position. The result of the proceedings shall be transmitted to the Council and the Commission.
If the European Parliament has rejected the Council's common position, unanimity shall be required for the Council to act on a second reading.

(d) The Commission shall, within a period of one month, re-examine the proposal on the basis of which the Council adopted its common position, by taking into account the amendments proposed by the European Parliament.
The Commission shall forward to the Council, at the same time as its re-examined proposal, the amendments of the European Parliament which it has not accepted, and shall express its opinion on them. The Council may adopt these amendments unanimously.

(e) The Council, acting by a qualified majority, shall adopt the proposal as re-examined by the Commission.
Unanimity shall be required for the Council to amend the proposal as re-examined by the Commission.

(f) In the cases referred to in points (c), (d) and (e), the Council shall be required to act within a period of three months. If no decision is taken within this period, the Commission proposal shall be deemed not to have been adopted.

(g) The periods referred to in points (b) and (f) may be extended by a maximum of one month by common accord between the Council and the European Parliament.

Article 253[39] **[Statement of reasons]**

2–258 Regulations, directives and decisions adopted jointly by the European Parliament and the Council, and such acts adopted by the Council or the Commission, shall state the reasons on which they are based and shall refer to any proposals or opinions which were required to be obtained pursuant to this Treaty.

---

[37] Formerly Art. 189c; inserted by Art. 8(61) TEU.

[38] For substantive areas to which cooperation procedure applies, see Art. 99(5) (cooperation on economic policy—multilateral surveillance measures), 102(2) (prohibition of privileged access to financial institutions), 103(2) (no liability for government commitments) and 106(2) (denominations and technical specifications of single currency coins).

[39] Formerly Art. 190; replaced by Art. 8(62) TEU. For application of Art. 253 to acts of ECB, see Protocol (No. 18) on the Statute of the ESCB and of the ECB, Art. 34.2.

Article 254[40] [Signature, publication, entry into force of EC measures]

1. Regulations, directives and decisions adopted in accordance with the procedure referred to in Article 251 shall be signed by the President of the European Parliament and by the President of the Council and published in the *Official Journal of the European Union*[41]. They shall enter into force on the date specified in them or, in the absence thereof, on the twentieth day following that of their publication. **2–259**

2. Regulations of the Council and of the Commission, as well as directives of those institutions which are addressed to all Member States, shall be published in the *Official Journal of the European Union*[42]. They shall enter into force on the date specified in them or, in the absence thereof, on the twentieth day following that of their publication.

3. Other directives, and decisions, shall be notified to those to whom they are addressed and shall take effect upon such notification.

Article 255[43] [Public access to documents of the institutions]

1. Any citizen of the Union, and any natural or legal person residing or having its registered office in a Member State, shall have a right of access to European Parliament, Council and Commission documents, subject to the principles and the conditions to be defined in accordance with paragraphs 2 and 3. **2–260**

2. General principles and limits on grounds of public or private interest governing this right of access to documents shall be determined by the Council, acting in accordance with the procedure referred to in Article 251 within two years of the entry into force of the Treaty of Amsterdam.

3. Each institution referred to above shall elaborate in its own Rules of Procedure specific provisions regarding access to its documents.

Article 256[44] [Enforcement of Community decisions imposing fines]

Decisions of the Council or of the Commission which impose a pecuniary obligation on persons other than States, shall be enforceable. **2–261**

Enforcement shall be governed by the rules of civil procedure in force in the State in the territory of which it is carried out. The order for its enforcement shall be appended to the decision, without other formality than verification of the authenticity of the decision, by the national authority which the government of each Member State shall designate for this purpose and shall make known to the Commission and to the Court of Justice.

When these formalities have been completed on application by the party concerned, the latter may proceed to enforcement in accordance with the national law, by bringing the matter directly before the competent authority.

Enforcement may be suspended only by a decision of the Court of Justice. However, the courts of the country concerned shall have jurisdiction over complaints that enforcement is being carried out in an irregular manner.

[40] Formerly Art. 191; replaced by Art. 8(63) TEU. For application of Art. 254 to acts of ECB, see Protocol (No. 18) on the Statute of the ESCB and of the ECB, Art. 34.2.

[41] The words "*Official Journal of the European Union*" replaced by Treaty of Nice, Art. 2(38).

[42] The words "*Official Journal of the European Union*" replaced by Treaty of Nice, Art. 2(38).

[43] Formerly Art. 191a; inserted by Treaty of Amsterdam, Art. 2(45). For application of Art. 255 to acts of ECB, see Protocol (No. 18) on the Statute of the ESCB and of the ECB, Art. 34.2. On public access to EC documents, see below. See also, Declaration (No. 35) on Article [255(1)] of the EC Treaty annexed to the Final Act of the Treaty of Amsterdam.

[44] Formerly Art. 192.

CHAPTER 3—THE ECONOMIC AND SOCIAL COMMITTEE

Article 257[45] [Establishment of the ESC]

2–262 An Economic and Social Committee is hereby established. It shall have advisory status.

The Committee shall consist of representatives of the various economic and social components of organised civil society, and in particular representatives of producers, farmers, carriers, workers, dealers, craftsmen, professional occupations, consumers and the general interest.

Article 258[46] [Membership of ESC]

2–263 The number of members of the Economic and Social Committee shall not exceed 350.

The number of members of the Committee shall be as follows:

Belgium	12
Denmark	9
Germany	24
Greece	12
Spain	21
France	24
Ireland	9
Italy	24
Luxembourg	6
Netherlands	12
Austria	12
Portugal	12
Finland	9
Sweden	12
United Kingdom	24

The members of the Committee may not be bound by any mandatory instructions. They shall be completely independent in the performance of their duties, in the general interest of the Community.

The Council, acting by a qualified majority, shall determine the allowances of members of the Committee.

Article 259[47] [Composition of ESC]

2–264 1. The members of the Committee shall be appointed for four years, on proposals from the Member States. The Council, acting by a qualified majority, shall adopt the list of members drawn up in accordance with the proposals made by each Member State. The term of office of the members of the Committee shall be renewable.[48]

---

[45] Article 257 replaced by Treaty of Nice, Art. 2(39). Formerly Art. 193. Functions conferred on ESC by EC and EAEC Treaties exercised by single committee, to which provisions of Art. 257 apply (see Treaty of Amsterdam, Art. 9(2)).

[46] Article 258 replaced by Treaty of Nice, Art. 2(40). Formerly Art. 194; substituted by Act of Accession of Austria, Finland and Sweden, Art. 23 (as replaced by Decision 95/1, Art. 14 ([1995] OJ L1/1)). Previously replaced by Art. 8(64) TEU.

[47] Formerly Art. 195.

[48] Article 259(1) replaced by Treaty of Nice, Art. 2(41).

2. The Council shall consult the Commission. It may obtain the opinion of European bodies which are representative of the various economic and social sectors to which the activities of the Community are of concern.

Article 260[49] **[Election of officers; Rules of Procedure]**

The Committee shall elect its chairman and officers from among its members for a term of two years. **2–265**

It shall adopt its Rules of Procedure.

The Committee shall be convened by its chairman at the request of the Council or of the Commission. It may also meet on its own initiative.

Article 261[50] **[Specialised sections and sub-committees]**

The Committee shall include specialised sections for the principal fields covered by this Treaty. **2–266**

These specialised sections shall operate within the general terms of reference of the Committee. They may not be consulted independently of the Committee.

Sub-committees may also be established within the Committee to prepare on specific questions or in specific fields, draft opinions to be submitted to the Committee for its consideration.

The Rules of Procedure shall lay down the methods of composition and the terms of reference of the specialised sections and of the sub-committees.

Article 262[51] **[Consultation of ESC]**

The Committee must be consulted by the Council or by the Commission where this Treaty so provides. The Committee may be consulted by these institutions in all cases in which they consider it appropriate. It may issue an opinion on its own initiative in cases in which it considers such action appropriate. **2–267**

The Council or the Commission shall, if it considers it necessary, set the Committee, for the submission of its opinion, a time-limit which may not be less than one month from the date on which the chairman receives notification to this effect. Upon expiry of the time-limit, the absence of an opinion shall not prevent further action.

The opinion of the Committee and that of the specialised section, together with a record of the proceedings, shall be forwarded to the Council and to the Commission.

The Committee may be consulted by the European Parliament.

CHAPTER 4—THE COMMITTEE OF THE REGIONS

Article 263[52] **[Establishment of COR]**

A Committee, hereinafter referred to as "the Committee of the Regions", consisting of representatives of regional and local bodies who either hold a regional or local authority electoral mandate or are politically accountable to an elected assembly, is hereby established with advisory status. **2–268**

The number of members of the Committee of the Regions shall not exceed 350.

---

[49] Formerly Art. 196; replaced by Art. 8(65) TEU.

[50] Formerly Art. 197; second paragraph deleted by Treaty of Amsterdam, Art. 6(I)(68). Functions conferred on ESC by EC and EAEC Treaties exercised by single committee, to which provisions of Art. 261 apply (see Treaty of Amsterdam, Art. 9(2)).

[51] Formerly Art. 198; fourth paragraph added by Treaty of Amsterdam, Art. 2(46). Former Art. 198 previously replaced by Art. 8(66) TEU.

[52] Article 263 replaced by Treaty of Nice, Art. 2(42). Formerly Art. 198a; third paragraph replaced by Treaty of Amsterdam, Art. 2(47). Former Art. 198a substituted by Act of Accession of Austria, Finland and Sweden, Art. 24 (as substituted by Decision 95/1, Art. 15 ([1995] OJ L1/1)); previously Art. 198a inserted by Union Treaty, art. G(67).

The number of members of the Committee shall be as follows:

Belgium	12
Denmark	9
Germany	24
Greece	12
Spain	21
France	24
Ireland	9
Italy	24
Luxembourg	6
Netherlands	12
Austria	12
Portugal	12
Finland	9
Sweden	12
United Kingdom	24

The members of the Committee and an equal number of alternate members shall be appointed for four years, on proposals from the respective Member States. Their term of office shall be renewable. The Council, acting by a qualified majority, shall adopt the list of members and alternate members drawn up in accordance with the proposals made by each Member State. When the mandate referred to in the first paragraph on the basis of which they were proposed comes to an end, the term of office of members of the Committee shall terminate automatically and they shall then be replaced for the remainder of the said term of office in accordance with the same procedure. No member of the Committee shall at the same time be a Member of the European Parliament.

The members of the Committee may not be bound by any mandatory instructions. They shall be completely independent in the performance of their duties, in the general interest of the Community.

Article 264[53] **[Election of officers; Rules of Procedure]**

2–269 The Committee of the Regions shall elect its chairman and officers from among its members for a term of two years.

It shall adopt its Rules of Procedure.

The Committee shall be convened by its chairman at the request of the Council or of the Commission. It may also meet on its own initiative.

Article 265[54] **[Consultation of COR]**

2–270 The Committee of the Regions shall be consulted by the Council or by the Commission where this Treaty so provides and in all other cases, in particular those which concern cross-border cooperation, in which one of these two institutions considers it appropriate.

The Council or the Commission shall, if it considers it necessary, set the Committee, for the submission of its opinion, a time-limit which may not be less than one month from the date on which the chairman receives notification to this effect. Upon expiry of the time-limit, the absence of an opinion shall not prevent further action.

Where the Economic and Social Committee is consulted pursuant to Article 262, the Committee of the Regions shall be informed by the Council or the

[53] Formerly Art. 198b; second paragraph replaced by Treaty of Amsterdam, Art. 2(48). Former Art. 198b originally inserted by Art. 8(67) TEU.

[54] Formerly Art. 198c; first and fourth paragraphs replaced by Treaty of Amsterdam, Art. 2(49)(a) and (b) respectively. Former Art. 198c originally inserted by Art. 8(67) TEU.

Commission of the request for an opinion. Where it considers that specific regional interests are involved, the Committee of the Regions may issue an opinion on the matter.

The Committee of the Regions may be consulted by the European Parliament.

It may issue an opinion on its own initiative in cases in which it considers such action appropriate.

The opinion of the Committee, together with a record of the proceedings, shall be forwarded to the Council and to the Commission.

CHAPTER 5—THE EUROPEAN INVESTMENT BANK

Article 266[55] [Legal personality of EIB; membership]

The European Investment Bank shall have legal personality. **2–271**

The members of the European Investment Bank shall be the Member States.

The Statute of the European Investment Bank is laid down in a Protocol annexed to this Treaty.[56] The Council, acting unanimously, at the request of the European Investment Bank and after consulting the European Parliament and the Commission, or at the request of the Commission and after consulting the European Parliament and the European Investment Bank, may amend Articles 4, 11 and 12 and Article 18(5) of the Statute of the Bank.

Article 267[57] [Task of the EIB]

The task of the European Investment Bank shall be to contribute, by having **2–272** recourse to the capital market and utilising its own resources, to the balanced and steady development of the common market in the interest of the Community.

For this purpose the Bank shall, operating on a non-profit-making basis, grant loans and give guarantees which facilitate the financing of the following projects in all sectors of the economy:

(a) projects for developing less-developed regions;

(b) projects for modernising or converting undertakings or for developing fresh activities called for by the progressive establishment of the common market, where these projects are of such a size or nature that they cannot be entirely financed by the various means available in the individual Member States;

(c) projects of common interest to several Member States which are of such a size or nature that they cannot be entirely financed by the various means available in the individual Member States.

In carrying out its task, the Bank shall facilitate the financing of investment programmes in conjunction with assistance from the Structural Funds and other Community financial instruments.

TITLE II—FINANCIAL PROVISIONS

Article 268[58] [The budget]

All items of revenue and expenditure of the Community, including those relating **2–273** to the European Social Fund, shall be included in estimates to be drawn up for each financial year and shall be shown in the budget.

Administrative expenditure occasioned for the institutions by the provisions of the Treaty on European Union relating to common foreign and security policy and to cooperation in the fields of justice and home affairs shall be charged to the budget. The operational expenditure occasioned by the implementation of the said provisions may, under the conditions referred to therein, be charged to the budget.

[55] Article 266 replaced by Treaty of Nice, Art. 2(43). Formerly Art. 198d, inserted by Art. 8(68) TEU.

[56] See Protocol (No. 10) on the Statute of the EIB (1957) (not reproduced).

[57] Formerly Art. 198e, inserted by Art. 8(68) TEU.

[58] Formerly Art. 199, replaced by Art. 8(69) TEU.

The revenue and expenditure shown in the budget shall be in balance.

Article 269[59] **[Finance from own resources]**

2–274 Without prejudice to other revenue, the budget shall be financed wholly from own resources.

The Council, acting unanimously on a proposal from the Commission and after consulting the European Parliament, shall lay down provisions relating to the system of own resources of the Community, which it shall recommend to the Member States for adoption in accordance with their respective constitutional requirements.

Article 270[60] **[New measures must be supportable from own resources]**

2–275 With a view to maintaining budgetary discipline, the Commission shall not make any proposal for a Community act, or alter its proposals, or adopt any implementing measure which is likely to have appreciable implications for the budget without providing the assurance that that proposal or that measure is capable of being financed within the limit of the Community's own resources arising under provisions laid down by the Council pursuant to Article 269.

Article 271[61] **[Community expenditure]**

2–276 The expenditure shown in the budget shall be authorised for one financial year, unless the regulations made pursuant to Article 279 provide otherwise.

In accordance with conditions to be laid down pursuant to Article 279, any appropriations, other than those relating to staff expenditure, that are unexpended at the end of the financial year may be carried forward to the next financial year only.

Appropriations shall be classified under different chapters grouping items of expenditure according to their nature or purpose and subdivided, as far as may be necessary, in accordance with the regulations made pursuant to Article 279.

The expenditure of the European Parliament, the Council, the Commission and the Court of Justice shall be set out in separate parts of the budget, without prejudice to special arrangements for certain common items of expenditure.

Article 272[62] **[Budget procedure]**

2–277 1. The financial year shall run from 1 January to 31 December.

2. Each institution of the Community shall, before 1 July, draw up estimates of its expenditure. The Commission shall consolidate these estimates in a preliminary draft budget. It shall attach thereto an opinion which may contain different estimates.

The preliminary draft budget shall contain an estimate of revenue and an estimate of expenditure.

3. The Commission shall place the preliminary draft budget before the Council not later than 1 September of the year preceding that in which the budget is to be implemented.

The Council shall consult the Commission and, where appropriate, the other institutions concerned whenever it intends to depart from the preliminary draft budget.

[59] Formerly Art. 201, replaced by Art. 8(71) TEU.
[60] Formerly Art. 201a, inserted by Art. 8(72) TEU.
[61] Formerly Art. 202.
[62] Formerly Art. 203; substituted by Art. 12 of the Treaty amending certain financial provisions of the Treaties establishing the European Communities (Second Budgetary Treaty) ([1977] OJ L359/1) with effect from 1 June 1977.

The Council, acting by a qualified majority, shall establish the draft budget and forward it to the European Parliament.

4. The draft budget shall be placed before the European Parliament not later than 5 October of the year preceding that in which the budget is to be implemented.

The European Parliament shall have the right to amend the draft budget, acting by a majority of its Members, and to propose to the Council, acting by an absolute majority of the votes cast, modifications to the draft budget relating to expenditure necessarily resulting from this Treaty or from acts adopted in accordance therewith.

If, within 45 days of the draft budget being placed before it, the European Parliament has given its approval, the budget shall stand as finally adopted. If within this period the European Parliament has not amended the draft budget nor proposed any modifications thereto, the budget shall be deemed to be finally adopted.

If within this period the European Parliament has adopted amendments or proposed modifications, the draft budget together with the amendments or proposed modifications shall be forwarded to the Council.

5. After discussing the draft budget with the Commission and, where appropriate, with the other institutions concerned, the Council shall act under the following conditions:

(a) the Council may, acting by a qualified majority, modify any of the amendments adopted by the European Parliament;

(b) with regard to the proposed modifications:

— where a modification proposed by the European Parliament does not have the effect of increasing the total amount of the expenditure of an institution, owing in particular to the fact that the increase in expenditure which it would involve would be expressly compensated by one or more proposed modifications correspondingly reducing expenditure, the Council may, acting by a qualified majority, reject the proposed modification. In the absence of a decision to reject it, the proposed modification shall stand as accepted;

— where a modification proposed by the European Parliament has the effect of increasing the total amount of the expenditure of an institution, the Council may, acting by a qualified majority, accept this proposed modification. In the absence of a decision to accept it, the proposed modification shall stand as rejected;

— where, in pursuance of one of the two preceding sub-paragraphs, the Council has rejected a proposed modification, it may, acting by a qualified majority, either retain the amount shown in the draft budget or fix another amount.

The draft budget shall be modified on the basis of the proposed modifications accepted by the Council.

If, within 15 days of the draft being placed before it, the Council has not modified any of the amendments adopted by the European Parliament and if the modifications proposed by the latter have been accepted, the budget shall be deemed to be finally adopted. The Council shall inform the European Parliament that it has not modified any of the amendments and that the proposed modifications have been accepted.

If within this period the Council has modified one or more of the amendments adopted by the European Parliament or if the modifications proposed by the latter have been rejected or modified, the modified draft budget shall again be forwarded to the European Parliament. The Council shall inform the European Parliament of the results of its deliberations.

6. Within 15 days of the draft budget being placed before it, the European Parliament, which shall have been notified of the action taken on its proposed modifications, may, acting by a majority of its Members and three fifths of the

votes cast, amend or reject the modifications to its amendments made by the Council and shall adopt the budget accordingly. If within this period the European Parliament has not acted, the budget shall be deemed to be finally adopted.

7. When the procedure provided for in this Article has been completed, the President of the European Parliament shall declare that the budget has been finally adopted.

8. However, the European Parliament, acting by a majority of its Members and two-thirds of the votes cast, may, if there are important reasons, reject the draft budget and ask for a new draft to be submitted to it.

9. A maximum rate of increase in relation to the expenditure of the same type to be incurred during the current year shall be fixed annually for the total expenditure other than that necessarily resulting from this treaty or from acts adopted in accordance therewith.

The Commission shall, after consulting the Economic Policy Committee, declare what this maximum rate is as it results from:

— the trend, in terms of volume, of the gross national product within the Community;
— the average variation in the budgets of the Member States; and
— the trend of the cost of living during the preceding financial year.

The maximum rate shall be communicated, before May 1, to all the institutions of the Community. The latter shall be required to conform to this during the budgetary procedure, subject to the provisions of the fourth and fifth sub-paragraphs of this paragraph.

If, in respect of expenditure other than that necessarily resulting from this Treaty or from acts adopted in accordance therewith, the actual rate of increase in the draft budget established by the Council is over half the maximum rate, the European Parliament may, exercising its right of amendment, further increase the total amount of that expenditure to a limit not exceeding half the maximum rate.

Where the European Parliament, the Council or the Commission consider that the activities of the Communities require that the rate determined according to the procedure laid down in this paragraph should be exceeded, another rate may be fixed by agreement between the Council, acting by a qualified majority, and the European Parliament, acting by a majority of its members and three-fifths of the votes cast.

10. Each institution shall exercise the powers conferred upon it by this Article, with due regard for the provisions of the Treaty and for acts adopted in accordance therewith, in particular those relating to the Communities' own resources and to the balance between revenue and expenditure.

Article 273[63] **[Limits on expenditure where budgets not adopted]**

2–278 If, at the beginning of a financial year, the budget has not yet been voted, a sum equivalent to not more than one-twelfth of the budget appropriations for the preceding financial year may be spent each month in respect of any chapter or other subdivision of the budget in accordance with the provisions of the regulations made pursuant to Article 279; this arrangement shall not, however, have the effect of placing at the disposal of the Commission appropriations in excess of one-twelfth of those provided for in the draft budget in course of preparation.

The Council may, acting by a qualified majority, provided that the other conditions laid down in the first sub-paragraph are observed, authorise expenditure in excess of one-twelfth.

[63] Formerly Art. 204; substituted by Art. 13 of the Treaty amending certain financial provisions of the Treaties establishing the European Communities (Second Budgetary Treaty) ([1977] OJ L359/1) with effect from 1 June 1977.

If the decision relates to expenditure which does not necessarily result from this Treaty or from acts adopted in accordance therewith, the Council shall forward it immediately to the European Parliament; within 30 days the European Parliament, acting by a majority of its members and three-fifths of the votes cast, may adopt a different decision on the expenditure in excess of the one-twelfth referred to in the first sub-paragraph. This part of the decision of the Council shall be suspended until the European Parliament has taken its decision. If within the said period the European Parliament has not taken a decision which differs from the decision of the Council, the latter shall be deemed to be finally adopted.

The decisions referred to in the second and third sub-paragraphs shall lay down the necessary measures relating to resources to ensure application of this Article.

Article 274[64] **[Implementation of budget by Commission]**

The Commission shall implement the budget, in accordance with the provisions of the regulations made pursuant to Article 279, on its own responsibility and within the limits of the appropriations, having regard to the principles of sound financial management. Member States shall co-operate with the Commission to ensure that the appropriations are used in accordance with the principles of sound financial management. **2–279**

The regulations shall lay down detailed rules for each institution concerning its part in effecting its own expenditure.

Within the budget, the Commission may, subject to the limits and conditions laid down in the regulations made pursuant to Article 279, transfer appropriations from one chapter to another or from one subdivision to another.

Article 275[65] **[Submission of annual accounts]**

The Commission shall submit annually to the Council and to the European Parliament the accounts of the preceding financial year relating to the implementation of the budget. The Commission shall also forward to them a financial statement of the assets and liabilities of the Community. **2–280**

Article 276[66] **[Discharge to Commission over budget implementation]**

1. The European Parliament, acting on a recommendation from the Council which shall act by a qualified majority, shall give a discharge to the Commission in respect of the implementation of the budget. To this end, the Council and the European Parliament in turn shall examine the accounts and the financial statement referred to in Article 275, the annual report by the Court of Auditors together with the replies of the institutions under audit to the observations of the Court of Auditors, the statement of assurance referred to in Article 248(1), second sub-paragraph and any relevant special reports by the Court of Auditors. **2–281**

2. Before giving a discharge to the Commission, or for any other purpose in connection with the exercise of its powers over the implementation of the budget, the European Parliament may ask to hear the Commission give evidence with regard to the execution of expenditure or the operation of financial control

[64] Formerly Art. 205; first paragraph, replaced by Treaty of Amsterdam, Art. 2(50). Former Art. 205 earlier replaced by Art. 8(73) TEU.

[65] Formerly Art 205a; substituted by Art. 14 of the Treaty amending certain financial provisions of the Treaties establishing the European Communities (Second Budgetary Treaty) ([1977] OJ L359/1) with effect from 1 June 1977.

[66] Formerly Art. 206; former Art. 206(1) replaced by Treaty of Amsterdam, Art. 2(51). Former Art. 206 previously replaced by Art. 8(74) TEU; amended by Act of Accession of Spain and Portugal, Art. 20; and substituted by Art. 15 of the Treaty amending certain financial provisions of the Treaties establishing the European Communities (Second Budgetary Treaty) ([1977] OJ L359/1) (with effect from1 June 1977).

systems. The Commission shall submit any necessary information to the European Parliament at the latter's request.

3. The Commission shall take all appropriate steps to act on the observations in the decisions giving discharge and on other observations by the European Parliament relating to the execution of expenditure, as well as on comments accompanying the recommendations on discharge adopted by the Council.

At the request of the European Parliament or the Council, the Commission shall report on the measures taken in the light of these observations and comments and in particular on the instructions given to the departments which are responsible for the implementation of the budget. These reports shall also be forwarded to the Court of Auditors.

Article 277[67] **[Budgetary unit of account]**

2–282 The budget shall be drawn up in the unit of account determined in accordance with the provisions of the regulations made pursuant to Article 279.[68]

Article 278[69] **[Currency transfers]**

2–283 The Commission may, provided it notifies the competent authorities of the Member States concerned, transfer into the currency of one of the Member States its holdings in the currency of another Member State, to the extent necessary to enable them to be used for purposes which come within the scope of this Treaty. The Commission shall as far as possible avoid making such transfers if it possesses cash or liquid assets in the currencies which it needs.

The Commission shall deal with each Member State through the authority designated by the State concerned. In carrying out financial operations the Commission shall employ the services of the bank of issue of the Member State concerned or of any other financial institution approved by that State.

Article 279[70] **[Measures for implementation of budget]**

2–284 1. The Council, acting unanimously on a proposal from the Commission and after consulting the European Parliament and obtaining the opinion of the Court of Auditors, shall:

(a) make Financial Regulations specifying in particular the procedure to be adopted for establishing and implementing the budget and for presenting and auditing accounts;
(b) lay down rules concerning the responsibility of financial controllers, authorising officers and accounting officers, and concerning appropriate arrangements for inspection.

From 1 January 2007, the Council shall act by a qualified majority on a proposal from the Commission and after consulting the European Parliament and obtaining the opinion of the Court of Auditors.

2. The Council, acting unanimously on a proposal from the Commission and after consulting the European Parliament and obtaining the opinion of the Court of Auditors, shall determine the methods and procedure whereby the budget revenue provided under the arrangements relating to the Community's own resources shall be made available to the Commission, and determine the measures to be applied, if need be, to meet cash requirements.

---

[67] Formerly Art. 207; second to fifth paragraphs deleted by Treaty of Amsterdam, Art. 6(I)(70).

[68] Regulation 3308/80 ([1980] OJ L345/1) substituted the ECU as unit of account in all Community legal instruments and Reg. 1103/97 ([1997] OJ L162/1) replaced references to the ECU in all legal instruments by references to the euro from 1 January 1999.

[69] Formerly Art. 208.

[70] Article 279 replaced by Treaty of Nice, Art. 2(44). Formerly Art. 209; replaced by Art. 8(76) TEU.

Article 280[71] **[Measures to protect EC financial interests]**

1. The Community and the Member States shall counter fraud and any other illegal activities affecting the financial interests of the Community through measures to be taken in accordance with this Article, which shall act as a deterrent and be such as to afford effective protection in the Member States. **2–285**

2. Member States shall take the same measures to counter fraud affecting the financial interests of the Community as they take to counter fraud affecting their own financial interests.

3. Without prejudice to other provisions of this Treaty, the Member States shall coordinate their action aimed at protecting the financial interests of the Community against fraud. To this end they shall organise, together with the Commission, close and regular cooperation between the competent authorities.

4. The Council, acting in accordance with the procedure referred to in Article 251, after consulting the Court of Auditors, shall adopt the necessary measures in the fields of the prevention of and fight against fraud affecting the financial interests of the Community with a view to affording effective and equivalent protection in the Member States. These measures shall not concern the application of national criminal law or the national administration of justice.

5. The Commission, in cooperation with Member States, shall each year submit to the European Parliament and to the Council a report on the measures taken for the implementation of this Article.

Part Six—General and Final Provisions

Article 281[72] **[EC to have legal personality]**

The Community shall have legal personality. **2–286**

Article 282[73] **[Legal capacity of EC in Member States]**

In each of the Member States, the Community shall enjoy the most extensive legal capacity accorded to legal persons under their laws; it may, in particular, acquire or dispose of movable and immovable property and may be a party to legal proceedings. To this end, the Community shall be represented by the Commission. **2–287**

Article 283[74] **[Staff Regulations]**

The Council shall, acting by a qualified majority on a proposal from the Commission and after consulting the other institutions concerned, lay down the Staff Regulations of officials of the European Communities and the conditions of employment of other servants of those Communities. **2–288**

Article 284[75] **[Commission powers of investigation]**

The Commission may, within the limits and under conditions laid down by the Council in accordance with the provisions of this Treaty, collect any information and carry out any checks required for the performance of the tasks entrusted to it. **2–289**

[71] Formerly Art. 209a; replaced by Treaty of Amsterdam, Art. 2(52). Previously replaced by Art. 8(77) TEU.

[72] Formerly Art. 210.

[73] Formerly Art. 211.

[74] Formerly Art. 212. Text of Art. 24(1), second paragraph, of Treaty establishing a single Council and a single Commission of the European Communities (Merger Treaty) (1965), inserted as Art. 212 of the EC Treaty by Treaty of Amsterdam, Art. 6(I)(71). Original Art. 212 repealed by Art. 24(2) of the Merger Treaty.

[75] Formerly Art. 213.

Article 285[76] [Production of Community statistics]

2–290 1. Without prejudice to Article 5 of the Protocol on the Statute of the European System of Central Banks and of the European Central Bank, the Council, acting in accordance with the procedure referred to in Article 251, shall adopt measures for the production of statistics where necessary for the performance of the activities of the Community.

2. The production of Community statistics shall conform to impartiality, reliability, objectivity, scientific independence, cost-effectiveness and statistical confidentiality; it shall not entail excessive burdens on economic operators.

Article 286[77] [Data protection]

2–291 1. From 1 January 1999, Community acts on the protection of individuals with regard to the processing of personal data and the free movement of such data shall apply to the institutions and bodies set up by, or on the basis of, this Treaty.

2. Before the date referred to in paragraph 1, the Council acting in accordance with the procedure referred to in Article 251, shall establish an independent supervisory body responsible for monitoring the application of such Community acts to Community institutions and bodies and shall adopt any other relevant provisions as appropriate.

Article 287[78] [Institutions' obligations of confidentiality]

2–292 The members of the institutions of the Community, the members of committees, and the officials and other servants of the Community shall be required, even after their duties have ceased, not to disclose information of the kind covered by the obligation of professional secrecy, in particular information about undertakings, their business relations or their cost components.

Article 288[79] [EC contractual and non-contractual liability]

2–293 The contractual liability of the Community shall be governed by the law applicable to the contract in question.

In the case of non-contractual liability, the Community shall, in accordance with the general principles common to the laws of the Member States, make good any damage caused by its institutions or by its servants in the performance of their duties.

The preceding paragraph shall apply under the same conditions to damage caused by the ECB or by its servants in the performance of their duties.

The personal liability of its servants towards the Community shall be governed by the provisions laid down in their Staff Regulations or in the Conditions of Employment applicable to them.

Article 289[80] [Seats of the institutions]

2–294 The seat of the institutions of the Community shall be determined by common accord of the governments of the Member States.

[76] Formerly Art. 213a; inserted by Treaty of Amsterdam, Art. 2(53).
[77] Formerly Art. 213b; inserted by Treaty of Amsterdam, Art. 2(54).
[78] Formerly Art. 214.
[79] Formerly Art. 215; replaced by Art. 6(78) TEU.
[80] Formerly Art. 216. See Protocol (No. 8) on the location of the seats of the institutions and of certain bodies and departments of the EC and Europol (1997).

Article 290[81] **[Working languages of the institutions]**

The rules governing the languages of the institutions of the Community shall, without prejudice to the provisions contained in the Statute of the Court of Justice, be determined by the Council, acting unanimously. **2–295**

Article 291[82] **[Privileges and immunities of the EC]**

The Community shall enjoy in the territories of the Member States such privileges and immunities as are necessary for the performance of its tasks, under the conditions laid down in the Protocol of 8 April 1965 on the privileges and immunities of the European Communities. The same shall apply to the European Central Bank, the European Monetary Institute, and the European Investment Bank. **2–296**

Article 292[83] **[Dispute settlement only in accordance with Treaty]**

Member States undertake not to submit a dispute concerning the interpretation or application of this Treaty to any method of settlement other than those provided for therein. **2–297**

Article 293[84] **[Additional scope of Member State cooperation]**

Member States shall, so far as is necessary, enter into negotiations with each other with a view to securing for the benefit of their nationals: **2–298**

— the protection of persons and the enjoyment and protection of rights under the same conditions as those accorded by each State to its own nationals;
— the abolition of double taxation within the Community;
— the mutual recognition of companies or firms within the meaning of the second paragraph of Article 48, the retention of legal personality in the event of transfer of their seat from one country to another, and the possibility of mergers between companies or firms governed by the laws of different countries;
— the simplification of formalities governing the reciprocal recognition and enforcement of judgments of courts or tribunals and of arbitration awards.

Article 294[85] **[Participation in company capital]**

Member States shall accord nationals of the other Member States the same treatment as their own nationals as regards participation in the capital of companies or firms within the meaning of Article 48, without prejudice to the application of the other provisions of this Treaty. **2–299**

---

[81] Article 290 replaced by Treaty of Nice, Art. 2(45). Formerly Art. 217. See Regulation 1/58 ([1952–1958] OJ Eng. Spec. Ed., p.59) (as amended by Acts of accession of Denmark, Ireland and the UK, Greece, Spain and Portugal, and Austria, Finland and Sweden) for determination of languages to be used by EC. Current official languages are: Danish, Dutch, English, Finnish, French, German, Greek, Italian, Portuguese, Spanish and Swedish.

[82] Formerly Art. 218. Text of Art. 28, first paragraph, of Treaty establishing a single Council and a single Commission of the European Communities (Merger Treaty), inserted as Art. 218 of the EC Treaty by Treaty of Amsterdam, Art. 6(I)(72). Original Art. 218 repealed by Art. 28 of the Merger Treaty. See further Protocol (No. 34) on the privileges and immunities of the European Communities (not reproduced).

[83] Formerly Art. 219.

[84] Formerly Art. 220.

[85] Formerly Art. 221; initial transitional wording removed by virtue of Treaty of Amsterdam, Art. 6(I)(73).

Article 295[86] **[Property ownership in Member States]**

2–300 This Treaty shall in no way prejudice the rules in Member States governing the system of property ownership.

Article 296[87] **[Essential security interests of Member States]**

2–301 1. The provisions of this Treaty shall not preclude the application of the following rules:

(a) no Member State shall be obliged to supply information the disclosure of which it considers contrary to the essential interests of its security;

(b) any Member State may take such measures as it considers necessary for the protection of the essential interests of its security which are connected with the production of or trade in arms, munitions and war material; such measures shall not adversely affect the conditions of competition in the common market regarding products which are not intended for specifically military purposes.

2. The Council may, acting unanimously on a proposal from the Commission, make changes to the list, which it drew up on 15 April 1958 of the products to which the provisions of paragraph 1(b) apply.

Article 297[88] **[Functioning of common market during political emergencies]**

2–302 Member States shall consult each other with a view to taking together the steps needed to prevent the functioning of the common market being affected by measures which a Member State may be called upon to take in the event of serious internal disturbances affecting the maintenance of law and order, in the event of war, serious international tension constituting a threat of war, or in order to carry out obligations it has accepted for the purpose of maintaining peace and international security.

Article 298[89] **[Minimising distortions of competition in emergencies]**

2–303 If measures taken in the circumstances referred to in Articles 296 and 297 have the effect of distorting the conditions of competition in the common market, the Commission shall, together with the State concerned, examine how these measures can be adjusted to the rules laid down in the Treaty.

By way of derogation from the procedure laid down in Articles 226 and 227, the Commission or any Member State may bring the matter directly before the Court of Justice if it considers that another Member State is making improper use of the powers provided for in Articles 296 and 297. The Court of Justice shall give its ruling in camera.

Article 299[90] **[Territorial scope of EC Treaty]**

2–304 1. This Treaty shall apply to the Kingdom of Belgium, the Kingdom of Denmark, the Federal Republic of Germany, the Hellenic Republic, the Kingdom of Spain, the French Republic, Ireland, the Italian Republic, the Grand Duchy of Luxembourg, the Kingdom of the Netherlands, the Republic of Austria,

---

[86] Formerly Art. 222. Permissible limitations on free movement of goods within EC include protection of industrial and commercial property (see Art. 30).

[87] Former Art. 223. Former Art. 223(2) and (3) merged as Art. 223(2) by Treaty of Amsterdam, Art. 6(I)(74).

[88] Formerly Art. 224.

[89] Formerly Art. 225.

[90] Formerly Art. 227.

the Portuguese Republic, the Republic of Finland, the Kingdom of Sweden and the United Kingdom of Great Britain and Northern Ireland.[91]

2. The provisions of this Treaty shall apply to the French overseas departments, the Azores, Madeira and the Canary Islands.

However, taking account of the structural social and economic situation of the French overseas departments, the Azores, Madeira and the Canary Islands, which is compounded by their remoteness, insularity, small size, difficult topography and climate, economic dependence on a few products, the permanence and combination of which severely restrain their development, the Council, acting by a qualified majority on a proposal from the Commission and after consulting the European Parliament, shall adopt specific measures aimed, in particular, at laying down the conditions of application of the present treaty to those regions, including common policies.

The Council shall, when adopting the relevant measures referred to in the second sub-paragraph, take into account areas such as customs and trade policies, fiscal policy, free zones, agriculture and fisheries policies, conditions for supply of raw materials and essential consumer goods, State aids and conditions of access to structural funds and to horizontal Community programmes.

The Council shall adopt the measures referred to in the second sub-paragraph taking into account the special characteristics and constraints of the outermost regions without undermining the integrity and the coherence of the Community legal order, including the internal market and common policies.[92]

3. The special arrangements for association set out in Part Four of this Treaty shall apply to the overseas countries and territories listed in Annex II to this Treaty.

This Treaty shall not apply to those overseas countries and territories having special relations with the United Kingdom of Great Britain and Northern Ireland which are not included in the aforementioned list.[93]

4. The provisions of this Treaty shall apply to the European territories for whose external relations a Member State is responsible.

5. The provisions of this Treaty shall apply to the Åland Islands in accordance with the provisions set out in Protocol No. 2 to the Act concerning the conditions of accession of the Republic of Austria, the Republic of Finland and the Kingdom of Sweden.[94]

6. Notwithstanding the preceding paragraphs:

(a) this Treaty shall not apply to the Faroe Islands;

(b) this Treaty shall not apply to the Sovereign Base Areas of the United Kingdom of Great Britain and Northern Ireland in Cyprus;

(c) this Treaty shall apply to the Channel Islands and the Isle of Man only to the extent necessary to ensure the implementation of the arrangements for those islands set out in the Treaty concerning the accession of new Member States to the European Economic Community and to the European Atomic Energy Community signed on 22 January 1972.[95]

---

[91] Former Art. 227(1) most recently substituted by Act of Accession of Austria, Finland and Sweden, Art. 27 (as substituted by Decision 95/1, Art. 18 ([1995] OJ L1/1)).

[92] Former Art. 227(2) replaced by Treaty of Amsterdam, Art. 2(55). Previously replaced by Art. 8(79) TEU.

[93] In former Art. 227(3), reference to Annex IV replaced by reference to Annex II by Treaty of Amsterdam, Art. 6(I)(76)(a). Second sub-paragraph added by Act of Accession of Denmark, Ireland and the UK, Art. 26(2).

[94] Former Art. 227(5) inserted and previous Art. 227(5) renumbered as Art. 227(6) by Treaty of Amsterdam, Art. 6(I)(76)(b) and (c) respectively. Previous Art. 227(5)(a) (Faroe Islands) replaced by Art. 8(79) TEU. Previous Art. 227(5)(d) (Åland Islands) deleted by Treaty of Amsterdam, Art. 6(I)(76)(c); originally added by Act of Accession of Austria, Finland and Sweden, Art. 28 (as substituted by Decision 95/1, Art. 19 ([1995] OJ L1/1).

[95] *ibid.*

Article 300[96] **[Negotiation and conclusion of international agreements]**

2–305 1. Where this Treaty provides for the conclusion of agreements between the Community and one or more States or international organisations, the Commission shall make recommendations to the Council, which shall authorise the Commission to open the necessary negotiations. The Commission shall conduct these negotiations in consultation with special committees appointed by the Council to assist it in this task and within the framework of such directives as the Council may issue to it.

In exercising the powers conferred upon it by this paragraph, the Council shall act by a qualified majority, except in the cases where the first sub-paragraph of paragraph 2 provides that the Council shall act unanimously.

2. Subject to the powers vested in the Commission in this field, the signing, which may be accompanied by a decision on provisional application before entry into force, and the conclusion of the agreements shall be decided on by the Council, acting by a qualified majority on a proposal from the Commission. The Council shall act unanimously when the agreement covers a field for which unanimity is required for the adoption of internal rules and for the agreements referred to in Article 310.

By way of derogation from the rules laid down in paragraph 3, the same procedures shall apply for a decision to suspend the application of an agreement, and for the purpose of establishing the positions to be adopted on behalf of the Community in a body set up by an agreement when that body is called upon to adopt decisions having legal effects, with the exception of decisions supplementing or amending the institutional framework of the agreement.

The European Parliament shall be immediately and fully informed of any decision under this paragraph concerning the provisional application or the suspension of agreements, or the establishment of the Community position in a body set up by an agreement.[97]

3. The Council shall conclude agreements after consulting the European Parliament, except for the agreements referred to in Article 133(3), including cases where the agreement covers a field for which the procedure referred to in Article 251 or that referred to in Article 252 is required for the adoption of internal rules. The European Parliament shall deliver its opinion within a time-limit which the Council may lay down according to the urgency of the matter. In the absence of an opinion within that time-limit, the Council may act.

By way of derogation from the previous sub-paragraph, agreements referred to in Article 310, other agreements establishing a specific institutional framework by organising cooperation procedures, agreements having important budgetary implications for the Community and agreements entailing amendment of an act adopted under the procedure referred to in Article 251 shall be concluded after the assent of the European Parliament has been obtained.

The Council and the European Parliament may, in an urgent situation, agree upon a time-limit for the assent.

4. When concluding an agreement, the Council may, by way of derogation from paragraph 2, authorise the Commission to approve modifications on behalf of the Community where the agreement provides for them to be adopted by a simplified procedure or by a body set up by the agreement; it may attach specific conditions to such authorisation.

5. When the Council envisages concluding an agreement which calls for amendments to this Treaty, the amendments must first be adopted in accordance with the procedure laid down in Article 48 of the Treaty on European Union.

[96] Formerly Art. 228. Former Art. 228(1), second sub-paragraph, and 228(2) replaced by Treaty of Amsterdam, Art. 2(56)(a) and (b) respectively. Original Art. 228 replaced by Art. 8(80) TEU.

[97] Article 300(2), second and third subparagraphs, replaced by Treaty of Nice, Art. 2(46)(a).

6. The European Parliament, the Council, the Commission or a Member State may obtain the opinion of the Court of Justice as to whether an agreement envisaged is compatible with the provisions of this Treaty. Where the opinion of the Court of Justice is adverse, the agreement may enter into force only in accordance with Article 48 of the Treaty on European Union.[98]

7. Agreements concluded under the conditions set out in this Article shall be binding on the institutions of the Community and on Member States.

Article 301[99] [Urgent economic measures arising from CFSP]

Where it is provided, in a common position or in a joint action adopted according to the provisions of the Treaty on European Union relating to the common foreign and security policy, for an action by the Community to interrupt or to reduce, in part or completely, economic relations with one or more third countries, the Council shall take the necessary urgent measures. The Council shall act by a qualified majority on a proposal from the Commission. **2–306**

Article 302[1] [Relations with UN and other international agencies]

It shall be for the Commission to ensure the maintenance of all appropriate relations with the organs of the United Nations and of its specialised agencies. **2–307**

The Commission shall also maintain such relations as are appropriate with all international organisations.

Article 303[2] [Cooperation with Council of Europe]

The Community shall establish all appropriate forms of cooperation with the Council of Europe. **2–308**

Article 304[3] [Cooperation with OECD]

The Community shall establish close cooperation with the Organisation for Economic Cooperation and Development, the details of which shall be determined by common accord. **2–309**

Article 305[4] [ECSC and EAEC Treaties unaffected by terms of EC Treaty]

1. The provisions of this Treaty shall not affect the provisions of the Treaty establishing the European Coal and Steel Community, in particular as regards the rights and obligations of Member States, the powers of the institutions of that Community and the rules laid down by that Treaty for the functioning of the common market in coal and steel. **2–310**

2. The provisions of this Treaty shall not derogate from those of the Treaty establishing the European Atomic Energy Community.

Article 306[5] [Benelux regional unions permitted]

The provisions of this Treaty shall not preclude the existence or completion of regional unions between Belgium and Luxembourg, or between Belgium, **2–311**

[98] Article 300(6) replaced by Treaty of Nice, Art. 2(46)(b).
[99] Formerly Art. 228a; inserted by Art. 8(81) TEU.
[1] Formerly Art. 229. In former Art. 229, first paragraph, the words "and of its specialised agencies." replaced by Treaty of Amsterdam, Art. 6(I)(77).
[2] Formerly Art. 230.
[3] Formerly Art. 231; replaced by Art. 8(82) TEU.
[4] Formerly Art. 232. Note that the ECSC Treaty expired on 23 July 2002.
[5] Formerly Art. 233.

Luxembourg and the Netherlands, to the extent that the objectives of these regional unions are not attained by application of this Treaty.

Article 307[6] **[Pre-existing agreements with third countries]**

2–312 The rights and obligations arising from agreements concluded before 1 January 1958 or, for acceding States, before the date of their accession, between one or more Member States on the one hand, and one or more third countries on the other, shall not be affected by the provisions of this Treaty.

To the extent that such agreements are not compatible with this Treaty, the Member State or States concerned shall take all appropriate steps to eliminate the incompatibilities established. Member States shall, where necessary, assist each other to this end and shall, where appropriate, adopt a common attitude.

In applying the agreements referred to in the first paragraph, Member States shall take into account the fact that the advantages accorded under this Treaty by each Member State form an integral part of the establishment of the Community and are thereby inseparably linked with the creation of common institutions, the conferring of powers upon them and the granting of the same advantages by all the other Member States.

Article 308[7] **[Additional powers to achieve Community objectives]**

2–313 If action by the Community should prove necessary to attain, in the course of the operation of the common market, one of the objectives of the Community and this Treaty has not provided the necessary powers, the Council shall, acting unanimously on a proposal from the Commission and after consulting the European Parliament, take the appropriate measures.

Article 309[8] **[Member States in serious and persistent breach of EU principles]**

2–314 1. Where a decision has been taken to suspend the voting rights of the representative of the government of a Member State in accordance with Article 7(3) of the Treaty on European Union, these voting rights shall also be suspended with regard to this Treaty.[9]

2. Moreover, where the existence of a serious and persistent breach by a Member State of principles mentioned in Article 6(1) of the Treaty on European Union has been determined in accordance with Article 7(2) of that Treaty, the Council, acting by a qualified majority, may decide to suspend certain of the rights deriving from the application of this Treaty to the Member State in question.[10] In doing so, the Council shall take into account the possible consequences of such a suspension on the rights and obligations of natural and legal persons.

The obligations of the Member State in question under this Treaty shall in any case continue to be binding on that State.

3. The Council, acting by a qualified majority, may decide subsequently to vary or revoke measures taken in accordance with paragraph 2 in response to changes in the situation which led to their being imposed.

4. When taking decisions referred to in paragraphs 2 and 3, the Council shall act without taking into account the votes of the representative of the government of

[6] Formerly Art. 234. In first paragraph, the words "before 1 January 1958 or, for acceding States, before the date of their accession" substituted by Treaty of Amsterdam, Art. 6(I)(78).

[7] Formerly Art. 235.

[8] Formerly Art. 236; inserted by Treaty of Amsterdam, Art. 2(57). Previous Art. 236 (proposals for amending treaty) repealed by Art. 8(83) TEU and superseded by Art. 48 TEU.

[9] Reference to Art. 7(3) replaced by Treaty of Nice, Art. 2(47)(a).

[10] Reference to Art. 7(2) replaced by Treaty of Nice, Art. 2(47)(b).

the Member State in question. By way of derogation from Article 205(2) a qualified majority shall be defined as the same proportion of the weighted votes of the members of the Council concerned as laid down in Article 205(2).

This paragraph shall also apply in the event of voting rights being suspended in accordance with paragraph 1. In such cases, a decision requiring unanimity shall be taken without the vote of the representative of the government of the Member State in question.

Article 310[11] [Association agreements]

The Community may conclude with one or more states or international organisations agreements establishing an association involving reciprocal rights and obligations, common action and special procedure. **2–315**

Article 311[12] [Protocols]

The Protocols annexed to this Treaty by common accord of the Member States shall form an integral part thereof. **2–316**

Article 312[13] [Duration of EC Treaty]

This Treaty is concluded for an unlimited period.

FINAL PROVISIONS **2–317**

Article 313[14] [Ratification and entry into force]

This Treaty shall be ratified by the high contracting parties in accordance with their respective constitutional requirements. The instruments of ratification shall be deposited with the Government of the Italian Republic. **2–318**

This Treaty shall enter into force on the first day of the month following the deposit of the instrument of ratification by the last signatory State to take this step. If, however, such deposit is made less than 15 days before the beginning of the following month, this Treaty shall not enter into force until the first day of the second month after the date of such deposit.

Article 314[15] [Authentic versions of the EC Treaty]

This Treaty, drawn up in a single original in the Dutch, French, German, and Italian languages, all four texts being equally authentic, shall be deposited in the archives of the Government of the Italian Republic, which shall transmit a certified copy to each of the governments of the other signatory states. **2–319**

Pursuant to the Accession Treaties, the Danish, English, Finnish, Greek, Irish, Portuguese, Spanish and Swedish versions of this Treaty shall also be authentic.

---

[11] Former Art. 238; replaced by Art. 8(84) TEU.
[12] former Art. 239.
[13] Formerly Art. 240.
[14] Formerly Art. 247.
[15] Formerly Art. 248; second paragraph added by Treaty of Amsterdam, Art. 6(I)(81).

Annexes

ANNEX I—LIST REFERRED TO IN ARTICLE 32 OF THIS TREATY[16]

2–320

1	2
Number in the Brussels nomenclature	Description of products
CHAPTER 1	Live animals
CHAPTER 2	Meat and edible meat offal
CHAPTER 3	Fish, crustaceans and molluscs
CHAPTER 4	Dairy produce; birds' eggs; natural honey
CHAPTER 5	
05.04	Guts, bladders and stomachs of animals (other than fish), whole and pieces thereof
05.15	Animal products not elsewhere specified or included; dead animals of Chapter 1 or Chapter 3, unfit for human consumption
CHAPTER 6	Live trees and other plants; bulbs, roots and the like; cut flowers and ornamental foliage
CHAPTER 7	Edible vegetables and certain roots and tubers
CHAPTER 8	Edible fruit and nuts; peel of melons or citrus fruits
CHAPTER 9	Coffee, tea and spices, excluding maté (heading no. 09.03)
CHAPTER 10	Cereals
CHAPTER 11	Products of the milling industry; malt and starches; gluten; inulin
CHAPTER 12	Oil seeds and oleaginous fruit; miscellaneous grains, seeds and fruit; industrial and medical plants; straw and fodder
CHAPTER 13	
ex 13.03	Pectin
CHAPTER 15	
15.01	Lard and other rendered pig fat; rendered poultry fat
15.02	Unrendered fats of bovine cattle sheep or goats; tallow (including "premier jus") produced from those fats
15.03	Lard stearin, oleostearin and tallow stearin; lard oil, oleo oil and tallow oil, not emulsified or mixed or prepared in any way
15.04	Fats and oil, of fish and marine mammals, whether or not refined
15.07	Fixed vegetable oils, fluid or solid, crude, refined or purified
15.12	Animal or vegetable fats and oils, hydrogenated, whether or not refined, but not further prepared
15.13	Margarine, imitation lard and other prepared edible fats
15.17	Residues resulting from the treatment of fatty substances or animal or vegetable waxes

[16] Formerly Annex II; renumbered as Annex I by Treaty of Amsterdam, Art. 6(II)(2). Headings 17.05, ex 22.08, ex 22.09 and ex 22.10 added by Regulation 7a, Art. 1 (OJ 1959–1962, Eng. Spec. Ed., p. 68); reference to Annex I substituted for reference to (former) Annex II by Treaty of Amsterdam, Art. 6(II)(2).

1	2
Number in the Brussels nomenclature	Description of products
CHAPTER 16	Preparations of meat, of fish, of crustaceans or molluscs
CHAPTER 17	
17.01	Beet sugar and cane sugar, solid
17.02	Other sugars; sugar syrups; artificial honey (whether or not mixed with natural honey); caramel
17.03	Molasses, whether or not decolourised
17.05	Flavoured or coloured sugars, syrups and molasses, but not including fruit juices containing added sugar in any proportion
CHAPTER 18	
18.01	Cocoa beans, whole or broken, raw or roasted
18.02	Cocoa shells, husks, skins and waste
CHAPTER 20	Preparations of vegetables, fruit or other parts of plants
CHAPTER 22	
22.04	Grape must, in fermentation or with fermentation arrested otherwise than by the addition of alcohol
22.05	Wine of fresh grapes; grape must with fermentation arrested by the addition of alcohol
22.07	Other fermented beverages (for example, cider, perry and mead)
ex 22.08 ex 22.09	Ethyl alcohol or neutral spirits, whether or not denatured, of any strength, obtained from agricultural products listed in Annex I to the Treaty, excluding liqueurs and other spirituous beverages and compound alcoholic preparations (known as "concentrated extracts") for the manufacture of beverages
22.10	Vinegar and substitutes for vinegar
CHAPTER 23	Residues and waste from the food industries; prepared animal fodder
CHAPTER 24	
24.01	Unmanufactured tobacco, tobacco refuse
CHAPTER 45	
45.01	Natural cork, unworked, crushed, granulated or ground; waste cork
CHAPTER 54	
54.01	Flax, raw or processes but not spun; flax tow and waste (including pulled or garnetted rags)
CHAPTER 57	
57.01	True hemp (*Cannabis sativa*), raw or processed but not spun; tow and waste of true hemp (including pulled or garnetted rags or ropes)

ANNEX II—OVERSEAS COUNTRIES AND TERRITORIES TO WHICH THE PROVISIONS OF PART FOUR OF THE TREATY APPLY[17]

2–321
— Greenland,
— New Caledonia and Dependencies,
— French Polynesia,
— French Southern and Antarctic Territories,
— Wallis and Futuna Islands,
— Mayotte,
— Saint Pierre and Miquelon,
— Aruba,
— Netherlands Antilles:
  — Bonaire,
  — Curaçao,
  — Saba,
  — Sint Eustatius,
  — Sint Maarten.
— Anguilla,
— Cayman Islands,
— Falkland Islands,
— South Georgia and the South Sandwich Islands,
— Montserrat,
— Pitcairn,
— Saint Helena and Dependencies,
— British Antarctic Territory,
— British Indian Ocean Territory,
— Turks and Caicos Islands,
— British Virgin Islands,
— Bermuda.

[17] Formerly Annex IV; renumbered as Annex II and text substituted by Treaty of Amsterdam, Art. 6(II)(4).

SELECTED PROTOCOLS

Protocols Annexed to the Treaty on European Union and the Treaty Establishing the European Community

PROTOCOL (NO. 2) INTEGRATING THE SCHENGEN *ACQUIS* INTO THE FRAMEWORK OF THE EUROPEAN UNION (1997)

(Not reproduced here—for full text see Treaty on European Union above) **2–322**

PROTOCOL (NO. 3) ON THE APPLICATION OF CERTAIN ASPECTS OF ARTICLE [14] OF THE TREATY ESTABLISHING THE EUROPEAN COMMUNITY TO THE UNITED KINGDOM AND TO IRELAND (1997)

(Not reproduced here—for full text see Treaty on European Union above) **2–323**

PROTOCOL (NO. 4) ON THE POSITION OF THE UNITED KINGDOM AND IRELAND (1997)

(Not reproduced here—for full text see Treaty on European Union above) **2–324**

PROTOCOL (NO. 5) ON THE POSITION OF DENMARK (1997)

(Not reproduced here—for full text see Treaty on European Union above) **2–325**

Protocols Annexed to the Treaty on European Union and the Treaties Establishing the European Community, the European Coal and Steel Community and the European Atomic Energy Community

PROTOCOL (NO. 6) ANNEXED TO THE TREATY ON EUROPEAN UNION AND TO THE TREATIES ESTABLISHING THE EUROPEAN COMMUNITIES (1992)

(Not reproduced here—for full text see Treaty on European Union above) **2–326**

PROTOCOL (NO. 8) ON THE LOCATION OF THE SEATS OF THE INSTITUTIONS AND OF CERTAIN BODIES AND DEPARTMENTS OF THE EUROPEAN COMMUNITIES AND OF EUROPOL (1997)

(Not reproduced here—for full text see Treaty on European Union above) **2–327**

PROTOCOL (NO. 9) ON THE ROLE OF NATIONAL PARLIAMENTS IN THE EUROPEAN UNION (1997)

(Not reproduced here—for full text see Treaty on European Union above) **2–328**

Protocols Annexed to the Treaty Establishing the European Community

PROTOCOL (NO. 16) ON THE ACQUISITION OF PROPERTY IN DENMARK (1992)

The High Contracting Parties, **2–329**
Desiring to settle certain particular problems relating to Denmark,

Have agreed upon the following provision, which shall be annexed to the Treaty establishing the European Community:

Notwithstanding the provisions of this Treaty, Denmark may maintain the existing legislation on the acquisition of second homes.

PROTOCOL (NO. 17) CONCERNING ARTICLE [141] OF THE TREATY ESTABLISHING THE EUROPEAN COMMUNITY (1992)

2–330 The High Contracting Parties,
Have agreed upon the following provision, which shall be annexed to the Treaty establishing the European Community:

For the purposes of Article [141] of this Treaty, benefits under occupational social security schemes shall not be considered as remuneration if and in so far as they are attributable to periods of employment prior to May 17, 1990, except in the case of workers or those claiming under them who have before that date initiated legal proceedings or introduced an equivalent claim under the applicable national law.

PROTOCOL (NO. 18) ON THE STATUTE OF THE EUROPEAN SYSTEM OF CENTRAL BANKS AND OF THE EUROPEAN CENTRAL BANK (1992)[18]

2–331 The High Contracting Parties,
Desiring to lay down the Statute of the European System of Central Banks and of the European Central Bank provided for in Article [8] of the Treaty establishing the European Community,

Have agreed upon the following provisions, which shall be annexed to the Treaty establishing the European Community:

CHAPTER I—CONSTITUTION OF THE ESCB

Article 1 The European System of Central Banks

2–332 1.1 The European System of Central Banks (ESCB) and the European Central Bank (ECB) shall be established in accordance with Article [8] of this Treaty; they shall perform their tasks and carry on their activities in accordance with the provisions of this Treaty and of this Statute.

1.2 In accordance with Article [107(1)] of this Treaty, the ESCB shall be composed of the ECB and of the central banks of the Member States ("national central banks"). The *Institut monétaire luxembourgeois* will be the central bank of Luxembourg.

CHAPTER II—OBJECTIVES AND TASKS OF THE ESCB

Article 2 Objectives

2–333 In accordance with Article [105(1)] of this Treaty, the primary objective of the ESCB shall be to maintain price stability. Without prejudice to the objective of

[18] For provisions of this Protocol not applying to the UK, see Protocol (No. 25) on certain provisions relating to the UK, point 8.

price stability, it shall support the general economic policies in the Community with a view to contributing to the achievement of the objectives of the Community as laid down in Article [2] of this Treaty. The ESCB shall act in accordance with the principle of an open market economy with free competition, favouring an efficient allocation of resources, and in compliance with the principles set out in Article [4] of this Treaty.

Article 3 Tasks

3.1 In accordance with Article [105(2)] of this Treaty, the basic tasks to be carried out through the ESCB shall be: **2–334**
- to define and implement the monetary policy of the Community;
- to conduct foreign exchange operations consistent with the provisions of Article 111 of this Treaty;
- to hold and manage the official foreign reserves of the Member States;
- to promote the smooth operation of payment systems.

3.2 In accordance with Article [105(3)] of this Treaty, the third indent of Article 3.1 shall be without prejudice to the holding and management by the governments of Member States of foreign exchange working balances.

3.3 In accordance with Article [105(5)] of this Treaty, the ESCB shall contribute to the smooth conduct of policies pursued by the competent authorities relating to the prudential supervision of credit institutions and the stability of the financial system.

Article 4 Advisory functions

In accordance with Article [105(4)] of this Treaty: **2–335**

(a) the ECB shall be consulted:
   - on any proposed Community act in its fields of competence;
   - by national authorities regarding any draft legislative provision in its fields of competence, but within the limits and under the conditions set out by the Council in accordance with the procedure laid down in Article 42;

(b) the ECB may submit opinions to the appropriate Community institutions or bodies or to national authorities on matters in its fields of competence.

Article 5 Collection of statistical information

5.1 In order to undertake the tasks of the ESCB, the ECB, assisted by the national central banks, shall collect the necessary statistical information either from the competent national authorities or directly from economic agents. For these purposes it shall cooperate with the Community institutions or bodies and with the competent authorities of the Member States or third countries and with international organisations. **2–336**

5.2 The national central banks shall carry out, to the extent possible, the tasks described in Article 5.1.

5.3 The ECB shall contribute to the harmonisation, where necessary, of the rules and practices governing the collection, compilation and distribution of statistics in the areas within its fields of competence.

5.4 The Council, in accordance with the procedure laid down in Article 42, shall define the natural and legal persons subject to reporting requirements, the confidentiality regime and the appropriate provisions for enforcement.

Article 6 International cooperation

6.1 In the field of international cooperation involving the tasks entrusted to the ESCB, the ECB shall decide how the ESCB shall be represented. **2–337**

6.2 The ECB and, subject to its approval, the national central banks may participate in international monetary institutions.

6.3 Articles 6.1 and 6.2 shall be without prejudice to Article [111(4)] of this Treaty.

CHAPTER III—ORGANISATION OF THE ESCB

Article 7 Independence

2–338 In accordance with Article [108] of this Treaty, when exercising the powers and carrying out the tasks and duties conferred upon them by this Treaty and this Statute, neither the ECB, nor a national central bank, nor any member of their decision-making bodies shall seek or take instructions from Community institutions or bodies, from any government of a Member State or from any other body. The Community institutions and bodies and the governments of the Member States undertake to respect this principle and not to seek to influence the members of the decision-making bodies of the ECB or of the national central banks in the performance of their tasks.

Article 8 Governing authorities

2–339 The ESCB shall be governed by the decision-making bodies of the ECB.

Article 9 The European Central Bank

2–340 9.1 The ECB which, in accordance with Article [107(2)] of this Treaty, shall have legal personality, shall enjoy in each of the Member States the most extensive legal capacity accorded to legal persons under its law; it may, in particular, acquire or dispose of movable and immovable property and may be a party to legal proceedings.

9.2 The ECB shall ensure that the tasks conferred upon the ESCB under Article [105(2), (3) and (5)] of this Treaty are implemented either by its own activities pursuant to this Statute or through the national central banks pursuant to Articles 12.1 and 14.

9.3 In accordance with Article [107(3)] of this Treaty, the decision-making bodies of the ECB shall be the Governing Council and the Executive Board.

Article 10 The Governing Council

2–341 10.1 In accordance with Article [112(1)] of this Treaty, the Governing Council shall comprise the members of the Executive Board of the ECB and the Governors of the national central banks.

10.2 Subject to Article 10.3, only members of the Governing Council present in person shall have the right to vote. By way of derogation from this rule, the Rules of Procedure referred to in Article 12.3 may lay down that members of the Governing Council may cast their vote by means of teleconferencing. These rules shall also provide that a member of the Governing Council who is prevented from voting for a prolonged period may appoint an alternate as a member of the Governing Council.

Subject to Article 10.3 and 11.3, each member of the Governing Council shall have one vote. Save as otherwise provided for in this Statute, the Governing Council shall act by a simple majority. In the event of a tie, the President shall have the casting vote.

In order for the Governing Council to vote, there shall be a quorum of two-thirds of the members. If the quorum is not met, the President may convene an extraordinary meeting at which decisions may be taken without regard to the quorum.

10.3 For any decisions to be taken under Articles 28, 29, 30, 32, 33 and 51, the votes in the Governing Council shall be weighted according to the national central banks' shares in the subscribed capital of the ECB. The weights of the votes of the members of the Executive Board shall be zero. A decision requiring a qualified majority shall be adopted if the votes cast in favour represent at least two-thirds of the subscribed capital of the ECB and represent at least half of the shareholders. If a Governor is unable to be present, he may nominate an alternate to cast his weighted vote.

10.4 The proceedings of the meetings shall be confidential. The Governing Council may decide to make the outcome of its deliberations public.

10.5 The Governing Council shall meet at least ten times a year.

10.6 Article 10.2 may be amended by the Council meeting in the composition of the Heads of State or Government, acting unanimously either on a recommendation from the ECB and after consulting the European Parliament and the Commission, or on a recommendation from the Commission and after consulting the European Parliament and the ECB. The Council shall recommend such amendments to the Member States for adoption. These amendments shall enter into force after having been ratified by all the Member States in accordance with their respective constitutional requirements.

A recommendation made by the ECB under this paragraph shall require a decision by the Governing Council acting unanimously.[19]

Article 11 The Executive Board

11.1 In accordance with Article [112(2)(a)] of this Treaty, the Executive Board shall comprise the President, the Vice-President and four other members. **2–342**

The members shall perform their duties on a full-time basis. No member shall engage in any occupation, whether gainful or not, unless exemption is exceptionally granted by the Governing Council.

11.2 In accordance with Article [112(2)(b)] of this Treaty, the President, the Vice-President and the other members of the Executive Board shall be appointed from among persons of recognised standing and professional experience in monetary or banking matters by common accord of the governments of the Member States at the level of the Heads of State or of Government, on a recommendation from the Council after it has consulted the European Parliament and the Governing Council.

Their term of office shall be eight years and shall not be renewable.

Only nationals of Member States may be members of the Executive Board.

11.3 The terms and conditions of employment of the members of the Executive Board, in particular their salaries, pensions and other social security benefits shall be the subject of contracts with the ECB and shall be fixed by the Governing Council on a proposal from a Committee comprising three members appointed by the Governing Council and three members appointed by the Council. The members of the Executive Board shall not have the right to vote on matters referred to in this paragraph.

11.4 If a member of the Executive Board no longer fulfils the conditions required for the performance of his duties or if he has been guilty of serious misconduct, the Court of Justice may, on application by the Governing Council or the Executive Board, compulsorily retire him.

11.5 Each member of the Executive Board present in person shall have the right to vote and shall have, for that purpose, one vote. Save as otherwise provided, the Executive Board shall act by a simple majority of the votes cast. In the event of a tie, the President shall have the casting vote. The voting arrangements shall be specified in the rules of procedure referred to in Article 12.3.

[19] Article 10.6 added by Treaty of Nice, Art. 5.

11.6 The Executive Board shall be responsible for the current business of the ECB.

11.7 Any vacancy on the Executive Board shall be filled by the appointment of a new member in accordance with Article 11.2.

Article 12 Responsibilities of the decision-making bodies

2–343 12.1 The Governing Council shall adopt the guidelines and take the decisions necessary to ensure the performance of the tasks entrusted to the ESCB under this Treaty and this Statute. The Governing Council shall formulate the monetary policy of the Community including, as appropriate, decisions relating to intermediate monetary objectives, key interest rates and the supply of reserves in the ESCB, and shall establish the necessary guidelines for their implementation.

The Executive Board shall implement monetary policy in accordance with the guidelines and decisions laid down by the Governing Council. In doing so the Executive Board shall give the necessary instructions to national central banks. In addition the Executive Board may have certain powers delegated to it where the Governing Council so decides.

To the extent deemed possible and appropriate and without prejudice to the provisions of this Article, the ECB shall have recourse to the national central banks to carry out operations which form part of the tasks of the ESCB.

12.2 The Executive Board shall have responsibility for the preparation of meetings of the Governing Council.

12.3 The Governing Council shall adopt rules of procedure which determine the internal organisation of the ECB and its decision-making bodies.

12.4 The Governing Council shall exercise the advisory functions referred to in Article 4.

12.5 The Governing Council shall take the decisions referred to in Article 6.

Article 13 The President

2–344 13.1 The President or, in his absence, the Vice-President shall chair the Governing Council and the Executive Board of the ECB.

13.2 Without prejudice to Article 39, the President or his nominee shall represent the ECB externally.

Article 14 National central banks

2–345 14.1 In accordance with Article [109] of this Treaty, each Member State shall ensure, at the latest at the date of the establishment of the ESCB, that its national legislation, including the statutes of its national central bank, is compatible with this Treaty and this Statute.

14.2 The statutes of the national central banks shall, in particular, provide that the term of office of a governor of a national central bank shall be no less than five years.

A governor may be relieved from office only if he no longer fulfils the conditions required for the performance of his duties or if he has been guilty of serious misconduct. A decision to this effect may be referred to the Court of Justice by the governor concerned or the Governing Council on grounds of infringement of this Treaty or of any rule of law relating to its application. Such proceedings shall be instituted within two months of the publication of the decision or of its notification to the plaintiff or, in the absence thereof, of the day on which it came to the knowledge of the latter, as the case may be.

14.3 The national central banks are an integral part of the ESCB and shall act in accordance with the guidelines and instructions of the ECB. The Governing

Council shall take the necessary steps to ensure compliance with the guidelines and instructions of the ECB, and shall require that any necessary information be given to it.

14.4 National central banks may perform functions other than those specified in the statute unless the Governing Council finds, by a majority of two-thirds of the votes cast, that these interfere with the objectives and tasks of the ESCB. Such functions shall be performed on the responsibility and liability of national central banks and shall not be regarded as being part of the functions of the ESCB.

Article 15 Reporting commitments

15.1 The ECB shall draw up and publish reports on the activities of the ESCB at least quarterly. **2–346**

15.2 A consolidated financial statement of the ESCB shall be published each week.

15.3 In accordance with Article [113(3)] of this Treaty, the ECB shall address an annual report on the activities of the ESCB and on the monetary policy of both the previous and the current year to the European Parliament, the Council and the Commission, and also to the European Council.

15.4 The reports and statements referred to in this Article shall be made available to interested parties free of charge.

Article 16 Bank notes

In accordance with Article [106(1)] of this Treaty, the Governing Council shall have the exclusive right to authorise the issue of bank notes within the Community. The ECB and the national central banks may issue such notes. The bank notes issued by the ECB and the national central banks shall be the only such notes to have the status of legal tender within the Community. **2–347**

The ECB shall respect as far as possible existing practices regarding the issue and design of bank notes.

CHAPTER IV—MONETARY FUNCTIONS AND OPERATIONS OF THE ESCB

Article 17 Accounts with the ECB and the national central banks

In order to conduct their operations, the ECB and the national central banks may open accounts for credit institutions, public entities and other market participants and accept assets, including book-entry securities, as collateral. **2–348**

Article 18 Open market and credit operations

18.1 In order to achieve the objectives of the ESCB and to carry out its tasks, the ECB and the national central banks may: **2–349**

— operate in the financial markets by buying and selling outright (spot and forward) or under repurchase agreement and by lending or borrowing claims and marketable instruments, whether in Community or in non-Community currencies, as well as precious metals;

— conduct credit operations with credit institutions and other market participants, with lending being based on adequate collateral.

18.2 The ECB shall establish general principles for open market and credit operations carried out by itself or the national central banks, including for the announcement of conditions under which they stand ready to enter into such transactions.

Article 19 Minimum reserves

2–350 19.1 Subject to Article 2, the ECB may require credit institutions established in Member States to hold minimum reserves on accounts with the ECB and national central banks in pursuance of monetary policy objectives. Regulations concerning the calculation and determination of the required minimum reserves may be established by the Governing Council. In cases of non-compliance the ECB shall be entitled to levy penalty interest and to impose other sanctions with comparable effect.

19.2 For the application of this Article, the Council shall, in accordance with the procedure laid down in Article 42, define the basis for minimum reserves and the maximum permissible ratios between those reserves and their basis, as well as the appropriate sanctions in cases of non-compliance.

Article 20 Other instruments of monetary control

2–351 The Governing Council may, by a majority of two-thirds of the votes cast, decide upon the use of such other operational methods of monetary control as it sees fit, respecting Article 2.

The Council shall, in accordance with the procedure laid down in Article 2, define the scope of such methods if they impose obligations on third parties.

Article 21 Operations with public entities

2–352 21.1 In accordance with Article 101 of this Treaty, overdrafts or any other type of credit facility with the ECB or with the national central banks in favour of Community institutions or bodies, central governments, regional, local or other public authorities, other bodies governed by public law or public undertakings of Member States shall be prohibited, as shall the purchase directly from them by the ECB or national central banks of debt instruments.

21.2 The ECB and national central banks may act as fiscal agents for the entities referred to in Article 21.1.

21.3 The provisions of this Article shall not apply to publicly-owned credit institutions which, in the context of the supply of reserves by central banks, shall be given the same treatment by national central banks and the ECB private credit institutions.

Article 22 Clearing and payment systems

2–353 The ECB and national central banks may provide facilities, and the ECB may make regulations, to ensure efficient and sound clearing and payment systems within the Community and with other countries.

Article 23 External operations

2–354 The ECB and national central banks may:

— establish relations with central banks and financial institutions in other countries and, where appropriate, with international organisations;
— acquire and sell spot and forward all types of foreign exchange assets and precious metals; the term "foreign exchange asset" shall include securities and all other assets in the currency of any country or units of account and in whatever form held;

— hold and manage the assets referred to in this Article;
— conduct all types of banking transactions in relations with third countries and international organisations, including borrowing and lending operations.

Article 24 Other operations

In addition to operations arising from their tasks, the ECB and national central banks may enter into operations for their administrative purposes or for their staff. **2–355**

CHAPTER V—PRUDENTIAL SUPERVISION

Article 25 Prudential supervision

25.1 The ECB may offer advice to and be consulted by the Council, the Commission and the competent authorities of the Member States on the scope and implementation of Community legislation relating to the prudential supervision of credit institutions and to the stability of the financial system. **2–356**

25.2 In accordance with any decision of the Council under Article [105(6)] of this Treaty, the ECB may perform specific tasks concerning policies relating to the prudential supervision of credit institutions and other financial institutions with the exception of insurance undertakings.

CHAPTER VI—FINANCIAL PROVISIONS OF THE ESCB

Article 26 Financial accounts

26.1 The financial year of the ECB and national central banks shall begin on the first day of January and end on the last day of December. **2–357**

26.2 The annual accounts of the ECB shall be drawn up by the Executive Board, in accordance with the principles established by the Governing Council. The accounts shall be approved by the Governing Council and shall thereafter be published.

26.3 For analytical and operational purposes, the Executive Board shall draw up a consolidated balance sheet of the ESCB, comprising those assets and liabilities of the national central banks that fall within the ESCB.

26.4 For the application of this Article, the Governing Council shall establish the necessary rules for standardising the accounting and reporting of operations undertaken by the national central banks.

Article 27 Auditing

27.1 The accounts of the ECB and national central banks shall be audited by independent external auditors recommended by the Governing Council and approved by the Council. The auditors shall have full power to examine all books and accounts of the ECB and national central banks and obtain full information about their transactions. **2–358**

27.2 The provisions of Article [247] of this Treaty shall only apply to an examination of the operational efficiency of the management of the ECB.

Article 28 Capital of the ECB

28.1 The capital of the ECB, which shall become operational upon its establishment, shall be ECU 5,000 million.[20] The capital may be increased by such amounts **2–359**

[20] See Art. 118 EC and Reg. 1103/97 ([1997] OJ L162/1) for replacement of the ECU by the euro as from 1 January 1999, as the unit of account of the EC institutions.

as may be decided by the Governing Council acting by the qualified majority provided for in Article 10.3, within the limits and under the conditions set by the Council under the procedure laid down in Article 42.

28.2 The national central banks shall be the sole subscribers to and holders of the capital of the ECB. The subscription of capital shall be according to the key established in accordance with Article 29.

28.3 The Governing Council, acting by the qualified majority provided for in Article 10.3, shall determine the extent to which and the form in which the capital shall be paid up.

28.4 Subject to Article 28.5, the shares of the national central banks in the subscribed capital of the ECB may not be transferred, pledged or attached.

28.5 If the key referred to in Article 29 is adjusted, the national central banks shall transfer among themselves capital shares to the extent necessary to ensure that the distribution of capital shares corresponds to the adjusted key. The Governing Council shall determine the terms and conditions of such transfers.

Article 29 Key for capital subscription

2–360 29.1 When in accordance with the procedure referred to in Article [111(1)] of this Treaty the ESCB and the ECB have been established, the key for subscription of the ECB's capital shall be established. Each national central bank shall be assigned a weighting in this key which shall be equal to the sum of:

— 50 per cent of the share of its respective Member State in the population of the Community in the penultimate year preceding the establishment of the ESCB;

— 50 per cent of the share of its respective Member State in the gross domestic product at market prices of the Community as recorded in the last five years preceding the penultimate year before the establishment of the ESCB.
The percentages shall be rounded up to the nearest multiple of 0.05 percentage points.

29.2 The statistical data to be used for the application of this Article shall be provided by the Commission in accordance with the rules adopted by the Council under the procedure provided for in Article 42.

29.3 The weightings assigned to the national central banks shall be adjusted every five years after the establishment of the ESCB by analogy with the provisions laid down in Article 29.1. The adjusted key shall apply with effect from the first day of the following year.

29.4 The Governing Council shall take all other measures necessary for the application of this Article.

Article 30 Transfer of foreign reserve assets to the ECB

2–361 30.1 Without prejudice to Article 28, the ECB shall be provided by the national central banks with foreign reserve assets, other than Member States' currencies, ECUs, IMF reserve positions and SDRs, up to an amount equivalent to ECU 50,000 million.[21] The Governing Council shall decide upon the proportion to be called up by the ECB following its establishment and the amounts called up at later dates. The ECB shall have the full right to hold and manage the foreign reserves that are transferred to it and to use them for the purposes set out in this Statute.

30.2 The contributions of each national central bank shall be fixed in proportion to its share in the subscribed capital of the ECB.

[21] See Art. 118 EC and Reg. 1103/97 ([1997] OJ L162/1) for replacement of the ECU by the euro as from 1 January 1999 as the unit of account of the EC institutions.

30.3 Each national central bank shall be credited by the ECB with a claim equivalent to its contribution. The Governing Council shall determine the denomination and remuneration of such claims.

30.4 Further calls of foreign reserve assets beyond the limit set in Article 30.1 may be effected by the ECB, in accordance with Article 30.2, within the limits and under the conditions set by the Council in accordance with the procedure laid down in Article 42.

30.5 The ECB may hold and manage IMF reserve positions and SDRs and provide for the pooling of such assets.

30.6 The Governing Council shall take all other measures necessary for the application of this Article.

Article 31 Foreign reserve assets held by national central banks

31.1 The national central banks shall be allowed to perform transactions in fulfilment of their obligations towards international organisations in accordance with Article 23. **2–362**

31.2 All other operations in foreign reserve assets remaining with the national central banks after the transfers referred to in Article 30, and Member States' transactions with their foreign exchange working balances shall, above a certain limit to be established within the framework of Article 31.3, be subject to approval by the ECB in order to ensure consistency with the exchange rate and monetary policies or the Community.

31.3 The Governing Council shall issue guidelines with a view to facilitating such operations.

Article 32 Allocation of monetary income of national central banks

32.1 The income accruing to the national central banks in the performance of the ESCB's monetary policy function (hereinafter referred to as "monetary income") shall be allocated at the end of each financial year in accordance with the provisions of this Article. **2–363**

32.2 Subject to Article 32.3, the amount of each national central bank's monetary income shall be equal to its annual income derived from its assets held against notes in circulation and deposit liabilities to credit institutions. These assets shall be earmarked by national central banks in accordance with guidelines to be established by the Governing Council.

32.3 If, after the start of the third stage, the balance sheet structures of the national central banks do not, in the judgment of the Governing Council, permit the application of Article 32.2, the Governing Council, acting by a qualified majority, may decide that, by way of derogation from Article 32.2, monetary income shall be measured according to an alternative method for a period of not more than five years.

32.4 The amount of each national central bank's monetary income shall be reduced by an amount equivalent to any interest paid by that central bank on its deposit liabilities to credit institutions in accordance with Article 19.
The Governing Council may decide that national central banks shall be indemnified against costs incurred in connection with the issue of bank notes or in exceptional circumstances for specific losses arising from monetary policy operations undertaken for the ESCB. Indemnification shall be in a form deemed appropriate in the judgement of the Governing Council; these amounts may be offset against the national central banks' monetary income.

32.5 The sum of the national central banks' monetary income shall be allocated to the national central banks in proportion to their paid-up shares in the capital of the

ECB, subject to any decision taken by the Governing Council pursuant to Article 33.2.

32.6 The clearing and settlement of the balances arising from the allocation of monetary income shall be carried out by the ECB in accordance with guidelines established by the Governing Council.

32.7 The Governing Council shall take all other measures necessary for the application of this Article.

Article 33 Allocation of net profits and losses of the ECB

2–364 33.1 The net profit of the ECB shall be transferred in the following order:
(a) an amount to be determined by the Governing Council, which may not exceed 20 per cent of the net profit, shall be transferred to the general reserve fund subject to a limit equal to 100 per cent of the capital;
(b) the remaining net profit shall be distributed to the shareholders of the ECB in proportion to their paid-up shares.

33.2 In the event of a loss incurred by the ECB, the shortfall may be offset against the general reserve fund of the ECB and, if necessary, following a decision by the Governing Council, against the monetary income of the relevant financial year in proportion and up to the amounts allocated to the national central banks in accordance with Article 32.5.

CHAPTER VII—GENERAL PROVISIONS

Article 34 Legal acts

2–365 34.1 In accordance with Article [110] of this Treaty, the ECB shall:
— make regulations to the extent necessary to implement the tasks defined in Article 3.1, first indent, Articles 19.1, 22 or 25.2 and in cases which shall be laid down in the acts of the Council referred to in Article 42;
— take decisions necessary for carrying out the tasks entrusted to the ESCB under this Treaty and this Statute;
— make recommendations and deliver opinions.

34.2 A regulation shall have general application. It shall be binding in its entirety and directly applicable in all Member States.

Recommendations and opinions shall have no binding force.

A decision shall be binding in its entirety upon those to whom it is addressed.

Articles 253 to 255 of this Treaty shall apply to regulations and decisions adopted by the ECB.

The ECB may decide to publish its decisions, recommendations and opinions.

34.3 Within the limits and under the conditions adopted by the Council under the procedure laid down in Article 42, the ECB shall be entitled to impose fines or periodic penalty payments on undertakings for failure to comply with obligations under its regulations and decisions.

Article 35 Judicial control and related matters

2–366 35.1 The acts or omissions of the ECB shall be open to review or interpretation by the Court of Justice in the cases and under the conditions laid down in this Treaty. The ECB may institute proceedings in the cases and under the conditions laid down in this Treaty.

35.2 Disputes between the ECB, on the one hand, and its creditors, debtors or any other person, on the other, shall be decided by the competent national courts, save where jurisdiction has been conferred upon the Court of Justice.

35.3 The ECB shall be subject to the liability regime provided for in Article [288] of this Treaty. The national central banks shall be liable according to their respective national laws.

35.4 The Court of Justice shall have jurisdiction to give judgment pursuant to any arbitration clause contained in a contract concluded by or on behalf of the ECB, whether that contract be governed by public or private law.

35.5 A decision of the ECB to bring an action before the Court of Justice shall be taken by the Governing Council.

35.6 The Court of Justice shall have jurisdiction in disputes concerning the fulfilment by a national central bank of obligations under this Statute. If the ECB considers that a national central bank has failed to fulfil an obligation under this Statute, it shall deliver a reasoned opinion on the matter after giving the national central bank concerned the opportunity to submit its observations. If the national central bank concerned does not comply with the opinion within the period laid down by the ECB, the latter may bring the matter before the Court of Justice.

Article 36 Staff

36.1 The Governing Council, on a proposal from the Executive Board, shall lay down the conditions of employment of the staff of the ECB. **2–367**

36.2 The Court of Justice shall have jurisdiction in any dispute between the ECB and its servants within the limits and under the conditions laid down in the conditions of employment.

Article 37 Seat

Before the end of 1992, the decision as to where the seat of the ECB will be established shall be taken by common accord of the governments of the Member States at the level of Heads of State or of Government.[22] **2–368**

Article 38 Professional secrecy

38.1 Members of the governing bodies and the staff of the ECB and the national central banks shall be required, even after their duties have ceased, not to disclose information of the kind covered by the obligation of professional secrecy. **2–369**

38.2 Persons having access to data covered by Community legislation imposing an obligation of secrecy shall be subject to such legislation.

Article 39 Signatories

The ECB shall be legally committed to third parties by the President or by two members of the Executive Board or by the signatures of two members of the staff of the ECB who have been duly authorised by the President to sign on behalf of the ECB. **2–370**

Article 40 Privileges and immunities

The ECB shall enjoy in the territories of the Member States such privileges and immunities as are necessary for the performance of its tasks, under the conditions laid down in the Protocol on the Privileges and Immunities of the European Communities.[23] **2–371**

[22] See Protocol (No. 8) on location of the seats of the institutions and of certain bodies and departments of the EC, point (i).

[23] Words omitted by Treaty of Amsterdam, Art. 6(III)(4). For application of the Protocol on the Privileges and Immunities of the European Communities to the ECB, see Art. 23 thereof as inserted by Treaty of Amsterdam, Art. 9(5).

CHAPTER VII—AMENDMENT OF THE STATUTE AND COMPLEMENTARY LEGISLATION

Article 41 Simplified amendment procedure

2–372 41.1 In accordance with Article [107(5)] of this Treaty, Articles 5.1, 5.2, 5.3, 17, 18, 19.1, 22, 23, 24, 26, 32.2, 32.3, 32.4, 32.6, 33.1(a) and 36 of this Statute may be amended by the Council, acting either by a qualified majority on a recommendation from the ECB and after consulting the Commission, or unanimously on a proposal from the Commission and after consulting the ECB. In either case the assent of the European Parliament shall be required.

41.2 A recommendation made by the ECB under this Article shall require a unanimous decision by the Governing Council.

Article 42 Complementary legislation

2–373 In accordance with Article [107(6)] of this Treaty, immediately after the decision on the date for the beginning of the third stage, the Council, acting by a qualified majority either on a proposal from the Commission and after consulting the European Parliament and the ECB, or on a recommendation from the ECB and after consulting the European Parliament and the Commission, shall adopt the provisions referred to in Articles 4, 5.4, 19.2, 20, 28.1, 29.2, 30.4 and 34.3 of this Statute.

CHAPTER IX—TRANSITIONAL AND OTHER PROVISIONS FOR THE ESCB

Article 43 General provisions

2–374 43.1 A derogation as referred to in Article 122(1) of this Treaty shall entail that the following Articles of this Statute shall not confer any rights or impose any obligations on the Member State concerned: 3, 6, 9.2, 12.1, 14.3, 16, 18, 19, 20, 22, 23, 26.2, 27, 30, 31, 32, 33, 34, 50 and 52.

43.2 The central banks of Member States with a derogation as specified in Article [122(1)] of this Treaty shall retain their powers in the field of monetary policy according to national law.

43.3 In accordance with Article [122(4)] of this Treaty, "Member States" shall be read as "Member States without a derogation" in the following Articles of this Statute: 3, 11.2, 19, 34.2 and 50.

43.4 "National central banks" shall be read as "central banks of Member States without a derogation" in the following Articles of this Statute: 9.2, 10.1, 10.3, 12.1, 16, 17, 18, 22, 23, 27, 30, 31, 32, 33.2 and 52.

43.5 "Shareholders" shall be read as "central banks of Member States without a derogation" in Articles 10.3 and 33.1.

43.6 "Subscribed capital of the ECB" shall be read as "capital of the ECB subscribed by the central banks of Member States without a derogation" in Articles 10.3 and 30.2.

Article 44 Transitional tasks of the ECB

2–375 The ECB shall take over those tasks of the EMI which, because of the derogations of one or more Member States, still have to be performed in the third stage.

The ECB shall give advice in the preparations for the abrogation of the derogations specified in Article [123] of this Treaty.

Article 45 The General Council of the ECB

2–376 45.1 Without prejudice to Article [107(3)] of this Treaty, the General Council shall be constituted as a third decision-making body of the ECB.

45.2 The General Council shall comprise the President and Vice-President of the ECB and the Governors of the national central banks. The other members of the Executive Board may participate, without having the right to vote, in meetings of the General Council.

45.3 The responsibilities of the General Council are listed in full in Article 47 of this statute.

Article 46 Rules of Procedure of the General Council

46.1 The President or, in his absence, the Vice-President of the ECB shall chair the General Council of the ECB. **2–377**

46.2 The President of the Council and a member of the Commission may participate, without having the right to vote, in meetings of the General Council.

46.3 The President shall prepare the meetings of the General Council.

46.4 By way of derogation from Article 12.3, the General Council shall adopt its Rules of Procedure.

46.5 The Secretariat of the General Council shall be provided by the ECB.

Article 47 Responsibilities of the General Council

47.1 The General Council shall: **2–378**
— perform the tasks referred to in Article 44;
— contribute to the advisory functions referred to in Articles 4 and 25.1.

47.2 The General Council shall contribute to:
— the collection of statistical information as referred to in Article 5;
— the reporting activities of the ECB as referred to in Article 15;
— the establishment of the necessary rules for the application of Article 26 as referred to in Article 26.4;
— the taking of all other measures necessary for the application of Article 29 as referred to in Article 29.4;
— the laying down of the conditions of employment of the staff of the ECB as referred to in Article 36.

47.3 The General Council shall contribute to the necessary preparations for irrevocably fixing the exchange rates of the currencies of Member States with a derogation against the currencies, or the single currency, of the Member States without a derogation, as referred to in Article 123(5) of this Treaty.

47.4 The General Council shall be informed by the President of the ECB of decisions of the Governing Council.

Article 48 Transitional provisions for the capital of the ECB

In accordance with Article 29.1 each national central bank shall be assigned a weighting in the key for subscription of the ECB's capital. By way of derogation from Article 28.3, central banks of Member States with a derogation shall not pay up their subscribed capital unless the General Council, acting by a majority representing at least two-thirds of the subscribed capital of the ECB and at least half of the shareholders, decides that a minimal percentage has to be paid up as a contribution to the operational costs of the ECB. **2–379**

Article 49 Deferred payment of capital, reserves and provisions of the ECB

49.1 The central bank of a Member State whose derogation has been abrogated shall pay up its subscribed share of the capital of the ECB to the same extent as the central banks of other Member States without a derogation, and shall transfer to **2–380** the ECB foreign reserve assets in accordance with Article 30.1. The sum to be transferred shall be determined by multiplying the ECU value at current exchange rates of the foreign reserve assets which have already been transferred to the ECB in accordance with Article 30.1, by the ratio between the number of shares subscribed by the national central bank concerned and the number of shares already paid up by the other national central banks.

49.2 In addition to the payment to be made in accordance with Article 49.1, the central bank concerned shall contribute to the reserves of the ECB, to those provisions equivalent to reserves, and to the amount still to be appropriated to the reserves and provisions corresponding to the balance of the profit and loss account as at December 31 of the year prior to the abrogation of the derogation. The sum to be contributed shall be determined by multiplying the amount of the reserves, as defined above and as stated in the approved balance sheet of the ECB, by the ratio between the number of shares subscribed by the central bank concerned and the number of shares already paid up by the other central banks.

Article 50 Initial appointment of the members of the Executive Board

2–381 When the Executive Board of the ECB is being established, the President, the Vice-President and the other members of the Executive Board shall be appointed by common accord of the governments of the Member States at the level of Heads of State or of Government, on a recommendation from the Council and after consulting the European Parliament and the Council of the EMI. The President of the Executive Board shall be appointed for eight years. By way of derogation from Article 11.2, the Vice-President shall be appointed for four years and the other members of the Executive Board for terms of office of between five and eight years. No term of office shall be renewable. The number of members of the Executive Board may be smaller than provided for in Article 11.1, but in no circumstance shall it be less than four.

Article 51 Derogation from Article 32

2–382 51.1 If, after the start of the third stage, the Governing Council decides that the application of Article 32 results in significant changes in national central banks' relative income positions, the amount of income to be allocated pursuant to Article 32 shall be reduced by a uniform percentage which shall not exceed 60 per cent in the first financial year after the start of the third stage and which shall decrease by at least 12 percentage points in each subsequent financial year.

51.2 Article 51.1 shall be applicable for not more than five financial years after the start of the third stage.

Article 52 Exchange of bank notes in Community currencies

2–383 Following the irrevocable fixing of exchange rates, the Governing Council shall take the necessary measures to ensure that bank notes denominated in currencies with irrevocably fixed exchange rates are exchanged by the national central banks at their respective par values.

Article 53 Applicability of the transitional provisions

2–384 If and as long as there are Member States with a derogation Articles 43 to 48 shall be applicable.

PROTOCOL (NO. 20) ON THE EXCESSIVE DEFICIT PROCEDURE (1992)

2–385 *The High Contracting Parties*,
Desiring to lay down the details of the excessive deficit procedure referred to in Article [104] of the Treaty establishing the European Community,

Have agreed upon the following provisions, which shall be annexed to the Treaty establishing the European Community:

Article 1 [Reference values]

The reference values referred to in Article [104(2)] of this Treaty are: **2–386**
— three per cent for the ratio of the planned or actual government deficit to gross domestic product at market prices;
— 60 per cent for the ratio of government debt to gross domestic product at market prices.

Article 2 [Definitions]

In Article 104 of this Treaty and in this Protocol: **2–387**
— government means general government, that is central government, regional or local government and social security funds, to the exclusion of commercial operations, as defined in the European System of Integrated Economic Accounts;
— deficit means net borrowing as defined in the European System of Integrated Economic Accounts;
— investment means gross fixed capital formation as defined in the European System of Integrated Economic Accounts;
— debt means total gross debt at nominal value outstanding at the end of the year and consolidated between and within the sectors of general government as defined in the first indent.

Article 3 [Responsibility of Member States]

In order to ensure the effectiveness of the excessive deficit procedure, the **2–388** governments of the Member States shall be responsible under this procedure for the deficits of general government as defined in the first indent of Article 2. The Member States shall ensure that national procedures in the budgetary area enable them to meet their obligations in this area deriving from this Treaty. The Member States shall report their planned and actual deficits and the levels of their debt promptly and regularly to the Commission.

Article 4 [Statistical data]

The statistical data to be used for the application of this Protocol shall be provided **2–389** by the Commission.

PROTOCOL (NO. 21) ON THE CONVERGENCE CRITERIA REFERRED TO IN ARTICLE 121 OF THE TREATY ESTABLISHING THE EUROPEAN COMMUNITY (1992)

The High Contracting Parties, **2–390**
Desiring to lay down the details of the convergence criteria which shall guide the Community in the decision making on the passage to the third stage of economic and monetary union, referred to in Article [121(1)] of this Treaty,
Have agreed upon the following provisions, which shall be annexed to the Treaty establishing the European Community:

Article 1 [Price stability]

The criterion on price stability referred to in the first indent of Article [121(1)] of **2–391** this Treaty shall mean that a Member State has a price performance that is sustainable and an average rate of inflation, observed over a period of one year before the examination, that does not exceed by more than 1 1/2 percentage points that of, at most, the three best performing Member States in terms of price stability. Inflation shall be measured by means of the consumer price index (CPI) on a comparable basis, taking into account differences in national definitions.

Article 2 [Government budgetary position]

2–392 The criterion on the government budgetary position referred to in the second indent of Article [121(1)] of this Treaty shall mean that at the time of the examination the Member State is not the subject of a Council decision under Article 104(6) of this Treaty that an excessive deficit exists.

Article 3 [Participation in ERM]

2–393 The criterion on participation in the Exchange Rate Mechanism of the European Monetary System referred to in the third indent of Article 121(1) of this Treaty shall mean that a Member State has respected the normal fluctuation margins provided for by the Exchange Rate Mechanism of the European Monetary System without severe tensions for at least the last two years before the examination. In particular, the Member State shall not have devalued its currency's bilateral central rate against any other Member State's currency on its own initiative for the same period.

Article 4 [Convergence of interest rates]

2–394 The criterion on the convergence of interest rates referred to in the fourth indent of Article 121(1) of this Treaty shall mean that, observed over a period of one year before the examination, a Member State has had an average nominal long-term interest rate that does not exceed by more than two percentage points that of, at most, the three best performing Member States in terms of price stability. Interest rates shall be measured on the basis of long-term government bonds or comparable securities, taking into account differences in national definitions.

Article 5 [Statistical data]

2–395 The statistical data to be used for the application of this Protocol shall be provided by the Commission.

Article 6 [Replacement of the Protocol]

2–396 The Council shall, acting unanimously on a proposal from the Commission and after consulting the European Parliament, the EMI or the ECB as the case may be, and the Committee referred to in Article [114], adopt appropriate provisions to lay down the details of the convergence criteria referred to in Article [121] of this Treaty, which shall then replace this Protocol.

PROTOCOL (NO. 22) ON DENMARK (1992)

2–397 *The High Contracting Parties*,
Desiring to settle certain particular problems relating to Denmark,
Have agreed upon the following provisions, which shall be annexed to the Treaty establishing the European Community:

The provisions of Article 14 of the Protocol on the Statute of the European System of Central Bank and of the European Central Bank shall not affect the right of the National Bank of Denmark to carry out its existing tasks concerning those parts of the Kingdom of Denmark which are not part of the Community.

PROTOCOL (NO. 25) ON CERTAIN PROVISIONS RELATING TO THE UNITED KINGDOM OF GREAT BRITAIN AND NORTHERN IRELAND (1992)

The High Contracting Parties, **2–398**

[1] Recognising that the United Kingdom shall not be obliged or committed to move to the third stage of Economic and Monetary Union without a separate decision to do so by its Government and Parliament,

[2] Noting the practice of the Government of the United Kingdom to fund its borrowing requirement by the sale of debt to the private sector,

Have agreed the following provisions, which shall be annexed to the Treaty establishing the European Community:

1. The United Kingdom shall notify the Council whether it intends to move to the third stage before the Council makes its assessment under Article [121(2)] of this Treaty.

Unless the United Kingdom notifies the Council that it intends to move to the third stage, it shall be under no obligation to do so.

If no date is set for the beginning of the third stage under Article [121(3)] of this Treaty, the United Kingdom may notify its intention to move to the third stage before 1 January 1998.

2. Paragraphs 3 to 9 shall have effect if the United Kingdom notifies the Council that it does not intend to move to the third stage.

3. The United Kingdom shall not be included among the majority of Member States which fulfil the necessary conditions referred to in the second indent of Article [121(2)] and the first indent of Article [121(3)] of this Treaty.

4. The United Kingdom shall retain its powers in the field of monetary policy according to national law.

5. Articles [4(2)], [104(1), (9) and (11)], [105(1) to (5)], [106], [108], [109], [110], [111], [112(1) and (2)(b)] and [123(4) and (5)] of this Treaty shall not apply to the United Kingdom. In these provisions references to the Community or the Member States shall not include the United Kingdom and references to national central banks shall not include the Bank of England.

6. Articles [116(4)] and [119] and [120] of this Treaty shall continue to apply to the United Kingdom. Articles [114(4)] and [124] shall apply to the United Kingdom as if it had a derogation.

7. The voting rights of the United Kingdom shall be suspended in respect of acts of the Council referred to in the Articles listed in paragraph 5. For this purpose the weighted votes of the United Kingdom shall be excluded from any calculation of a qualified majority under Article [122(5)] of this Treaty.

The United Kingdom shall also have no right to participate in the appointment of the President, the Vice-President and the other members of the Executive Board of the ECB under Articles [112(2)(b)] and [123(1)] of this Treaty.

8. Articles 3, 4, 6, 7, 9.2, 10.1, 10.3, 11.2, 12.1, 14, 16, 18 to 20, 22, 23, 26, 27, 30 to 34, 50 and 52 of the Protocol on the Statute of the European System of Central Banks and of the European Central Bank ("the Statute") shall not apply to the United Kingdom.

In those Articles, references to the Community or the Member States shall not include the United Kingdom and references to national central banks or shareholders shall not include the Bank of England.

References in Articles 10.3 and 30.2 of the Statute to "subscribed capital of the ECB" shall not include capital subscribed by the Bank of England.

9. Article [123(3)] of this Treaty and Articles 44 to 48 of the Statute shall have effect, whether or not there is any Member State with a derogation, subject to the following amendments:

(a) References in Article 44 to the tasks of the ECB and the EMI shall include those tasks that still need to be performed in the third stage owing to any decision of the United Kingdom not to move to that stage.

(b) In addition to the tasks referred to in Article 47 the ECB shall also give advice in relation to and contribute to the preparation of any decision of the Council with regard to the United Kingdom taken in accordance with paragraphs 10(a) and 10(c).
(c) The Bank of England shall pay up its subscription to the capital of the ECB as a contribution to its operational costs on the same basis as national central banks of Member States with a derogation.

10. If the United Kingdom does not move to the third stage, it may change its notification at any time after the beginning of that stage. In that event:
(a) The United Kingdom shall have the right to move to the third stage provided only that it satisfies the necessary conditions. The Council, acting at the request of the United Kingdom and under the conditions and in accordance with the procedure laid down in Article [122(2)] of this Treaty, shall decide whether it fulfils the necessary conditions.
(b) The Bank of England shall pay up its subscribed capital, transfer to the ECB foreign reserve assets and contribute to its reserves on the same basis as the national central bank of a Member State whose derogation has been abrogated.
(c) The Council, acting under the conditions and in accordance with the procedure laid down in Article [123(5)] of this Treaty, shall take all other necessary decisions to enable the United Kingdom to move to the third stage.

If the United Kingdom moves to the third stage pursuant to the provisions of this Protocol, paragraphs 3 to 9 shall cease to have effect.

11. Notwithstanding Articles [101] and [116(3)] of this Treaty and Article 21.1 of the Statute, the Government of the United Kingdom may maintain its ways and means facility with the Bank of England if and so long as the United Kingdom does not move to the third stage.

PROTOCOL (NO. 26) ON CERTAIN PROVISIONS RELATING TO DENMARK (1992)

2–399 *The High Contracting Parties*,

[1] Desiring to settle, in accordance with the general objectives of the Treaty establishing the European Community, certain particular problems existing at the present time,

[2] Taking into account that the Danish Constitution contains provisions which may imply a referendum in Denmark prior to Danish participation in the third stage of Economic and Monetary Union,

Have agreed on the following provisions, which shall be annexed to the Treaty establishing the European Community:

1. The Danish Government shall notify the Council of its position concerning participation in the third stage before the Council makes its assessment under Article [121(2)] of this Treaty.

2. In the event of a notification that Denmark will not participate in the third stage, Denmark shall have an exemption. The effect of the exemption shall be that all Articles and provisions of this Treaty and the Statute of the ESCB referring to a derogation shall be applicable to Denmark.

3. In such case, Denmark shall not be included among the majority of Member States which fulfil the necessary conditions referred to in the second indent of Article [121(2)] and the first indent of Article [121(3)] of this Treaty.

4. As for the abrogation of the exemption, the procedure referred to in Article [122(2)] shall only be initiated at the request of Denmark.

5. In the event of abrogation of the exemption status, the provisions of this protocol shall no longer be applicable.

PROTOCOL (NO. 28) ON ECONOMIC AND SOCIAL COHESION (1992)

The High Contracting Parties, 2–400

[1] Recalling that the Union has set itself the objective of promoting economic and social progress, *inter alia*, through the strengthening of economic and social cohesion;

[2] Recalling that Article 2 of this Treaty includes the task of promoting economic and social cohesion and solidarity between Member States and that the strengthening of economic and social cohesion figures among the activities of the Community listed in Article 3;

[3] Recalling that the provisions of Part Three, Title [XVII], on economic and social cohesion as a whole provide the legal basis for consolidating and further developing the Community's action in the field of economic and social cohesion, including the creation of a new fund;

[4] Recalling that the provisions of Part Three, Title [XV] on trans-European networks and Title [XIX] on environment envisage a Cohesion Fund to be set up before 31 December 1993;

[5] Stating their belief that progress towards Economic and Monetary Union will contribute to the economic growth of all Member States;

[6] Noting that the Community's Structural Funds are being doubled in real terms between 1987 and 1993, implying large transfers, especially as a proportion of GDP of the less prosperous Member States;

[7] Noting that the EIB is lending large and increasing amounts for the benefit of the poorer regions;

[8] Noting the desire for greater flexibility in the arrangements for allocations from the Structural Funds;

[9] Noting the desire for modulation of the levels of Community participation in programmes and projects in certain countries;

[10] Noting the proposal to take greater account of the relative prosperity of Member States in the system of own resources,

Reaffirm that the promotion of economic and social cohesion is vital to the full development and enduring success of the Community, and underline the importance of the inclusion of economic and social cohesion in Articles 2 and 3 of this Treaty;

Reaffirm their conviction that the Structural Funds should continue to play a considerable part in the achievement of Community objectives in the field of cohesion;

Reaffirm their conviction that the European Investment Bank should continue to devote the majority of its resources to the promotion of economic and social cohesion, and declare their willingness to review the capital needs of the European Investment Bank as soon as this is necessary for that purpose;

Reaffirm the need for a thorough evaluation of the operation and effectiveness of the Structural Funds in 1992, and the need to review, on that occasion, the appropriate size of these funds in the light of the tasks of the Community in the area of economic and social cohesion;

Agree that the Cohesion Fund to be set up before 31 December 1993, will provide Community financial contributions to projects in the fields of environment and trans-European networks in Member States with a per capita GNP of less than 90 per cent of the Community average which have a programme leading to the fulfilment of the conditions of economic convergence as set out in Article [104];

Declare their intention of allowing a greater margin of flexibility in allocating financing from the structural funds to specific needs not covered under the present Structural Funds regulations;

Declare their willingness to modulate the levels of Community participation in the context of programmes and projects of the Structural Funds, with a view to avoiding excessive increases in budgetary expenditure in the less prosperous Member States;

Recognise the need to monitor regularly the progress made towards achieving economic and social cohesion and state their willingness to study all necessary measures in this respect;

Declare their intention of taking greater account of the contributive capacity of individual Member States in the system of own resources, and of examining means of correcting, for the less prosperous Member States, regressive elements existing in the present own resources system;

Agree to annex this Protocol to this Treaty.

PROTOCOL (NO. 29) ON ASYLUM FOR NATIONALS OF MEMBER STATES OF THE EUROPEAN UNION (1997)

2–401 *The High Contracting Parties,*

[1] Whereas pursuant to the provisions of Article [6(2)] of the Treaty on European Union the Union shall respect fundamental rights as guaranteed by the European Convention for the Protection of Human Rights and Fundamental Freedoms signed in Rome on 4 November 1950;

[2] Whereas the Court of Justice of the European Communities has jurisdiction to ensure that in the interpretation and application of Article [6(2)] of the Treaty on European Union the law is observed by the European Community;

[3] Whereas pursuant to Article [49] of the Treaty on European Union any European state, when applying to become a member of the Union, must respect the principles set out in Article [6(1)] of the Treaty on European Union;

[4] Bearing in mind that Article [309] of the Treaty establishing the European Community establishes a mechanism for the suspension of certain rights in the event of a serious and persistent breach by a Member State of those principles;

[5] Recalling that each national of a Member State, as a citizen of the Union, enjoys a special status and protection which shall be guaranteed by the Member States in accordance with the provisions of Part Two of the Treaty establishing the European Community;

[6] Bearing in mind that the Treaty establishing the European Community establishes an area without internal frontiers and grants every citizen of the Union the right to move and reside freely within the territory of the Member States;

[7] Recalling that the question of extradition of nationals of Member States of the Union is addressed in the European Convention on Extradition of 13 December 1957 and the Convention of 27 September 1996 drawn up on the basis of Article [31] of the Treaty on European Union relating to extradition between the Member States of the European Union;

[8] Wishing to prevent the institution of asylum being resorted to for purposes alien to those for which it is intended;

[9] Whereas this Protocol respects the finality and the objectives of the Geneva Convention of 28 July 1951 relating to the status of refugees;

Have agreed upon the following provisions, which shall be annexed to the Treaty establishing the European Community.

Sole article

2–402 Given the level of protection of fundamental rights and freedoms by the Member States of the European Union, Member States shall be regarded as constituting safe countries of origin in respect of each other for all legal and practical purposes in relation to asylum matters. Accordingly, any application for asylum made by a national of a Member State may be taken into consideration or declared admissible for processing by another Member State only in the following cases:

(a) if the Member State of which the applicant is a national proceeds after the entry into force of the Treaty of Amsterdam, availing itself of the provisions of Article 15 of the Convention for the Protection of Human Rights and

Fundamental Freedoms, to take measures derogating in its territory from its obligations under that Convention;

(b) if the procedure referred to in Article [7(1)] of the Treaty on European Union has been initiated and until the Council takes a decision in respect thereof;

(c) if the Council, acting on the basis of Article [7(1)] of the Treaty on European Union, has determined, in respect of the Member State which the applicant is a national, the existence of a serious and persistent breach by that Member State of principles mentioned in Article [6(1)];

(d) if a Member State should so decide unilaterally in respect of the application of a national of another Member State; in that case the Council shall be immediately informed; the application shall be dealt with on the basis of the presumption that it is manifestly unfounded without affecting in any way, whatever the cases may be, the decision-making power of the Member State.[24]

PROTOCOL (NO. 30) ON THE APPLICATION OF THE PRINCIPLES OF SUBSIDIARITY AND PROPORTIONALITY (1997)[25]

The High Contracting Parties, 2–403

[1] Determined to establish the conditions for the application of the principles of subsidiarity and proportionality enshrined in article [5] of the Treaty establishing the European Community with a view to defining more precisely the criteria for applying them and to ensure their strict observance and consistent implementation by all institutions;

[2] Wishing to ensure that decisions are taken as closely as possible to the citizens of the Union;

[3] Taking account of the Interinstitutional Agreement of 25 October 1993 between the European Parliament, the Council and the Commission on procedures for implementing the principle of subsidiarity;

[4] Have confirmed that the conclusions of the Birmingham European Council on 16 October 1992 and the overall approach to the application of the subsidiarity principle agreed by the European Council meeting in Edinburgh on 11–12 December 1992 will continue to guide the action of the Union's institutions as well as the development of the application of the principle of subsidiarity, and, for this purpose,

Have agreed upon the following provisions which shall be annexed to the Treaty establishing the European Community:

(1) In exercising the powers conferred on it, each institution shall ensure that the principle of subsidiarity is complied with. It shall also ensure compliance with the principle of proportionality, according to which any action by the Community shall not go beyond what is necessary to achieve the objectives of the Treaty.

(2) The application of the principles of subsidiarity and proportionality shall respect the general provisions and the objectives of the Treaty, particularly as regards the maintaining in full of the *acquis communautaire* and the institutional balance; it shall not affect the principles developed by the Court of Justice regarding the relationship between national and Community law, and it should take into account Article [6(4)] of the Treaty on European Union, according to which "the Union shall provide itself with the means necessary to attain its objectives and carry through its policies".

(3) The principle of subsidiarity does not call into question the powers conferred on the European Community by the Treaty, as interpreted by the Court of Justice.

---

[24] See Declaration (No. 48) relating to the Protocol on asylum for nationals of Member States of the European Union annexed to the Final Act of the Treaty of Amsterdam and Declaration (No. 49) relating to sub-paragraph (d) of the sole article of the Protocol on asylum for nationals of Member States of the European Union annexed to the Final Act of the Treaty of Amsterdam.

[25] See Declaration (No. 43) relating to the Protocol on the application of the principles of subsidiarity and proportionality annexed to the Final Act of the Treaty of Amsterdam.

The criteria referred to in the second paragraph of Article [5] of the Treaty shall relate to areas for which the Community does not have exclusive competence. The principle of subsidiarity provides a guide as to how those powers are to be exercised at the Community level. Subsidiarity is a dynamic concept and should be applied in the light of the objectives set out in the Treaty. It allows Community action within the limits of its powers to be expanded where circumstances so require, and conversely, to be restricted or discontinued where it is no longer justified.

(4) For any proposed Community legislation, the reasons on which it is based shall be stated with a view to justifying its compliance with the principles of subsidiarity and proportionality; the reasons for concluding that a Community objective can be better achieved by the Community must be substantiated by qualitative or, wherever possible, quantitative indicators.

(5) For Community action to be justified, both aspects of the subsidiarity principle shall be met: the objectives of the proposed action cannot be sufficiently achieved by Member States' action in the framework of their national constitutional system and can therefore be better achieved by action on the part of the Community.

The following guidelines should be used in examining whether the abovementioned condition is fulfilled:

— the issue under consideration has transnational aspects which cannot be satisfactorily regulated by action by Member States;
— actions by Member States alone or lack of Community action would conflict with the requirements of the Treaty (such as the need to correct distortion of competition or avoid disguised restrictions on trade or strengthen economic and social cohesion) or would otherwise significantly damage Member States' interests;
— action at Community level would produce clear benefits by reason of its scale or effects compared with action at the level of the Member States.

(6) The form of Community action shall be as simple as possible, consistent with satisfactory achievement of the objective of the measure and the need for effective enforcement. The Community shall legislate only to the extent necessary. Other things being equal, directives should be preferred to regulations and framework directives to detailed measures. Directives as provided for in Article [249] of the Treaty, while binding upon each Member State to which they are addressed as to the result to be achieved, shall leave to the national authorities the choice of form and methods.

(7) Regarding the nature and the extent of Community action, Community measures should leave as much scope for national decision as possible, consistent with securing the aim of the measure and observing the requirements of the Treaty. While respecting Community law, care should be taken to respect well established national arrangements and the organisation and working of Member States' legal systems.

Where appropriate and subject to the need for proper enforcement, Community measures should provide Member States with alternative ways to achieve the objectives of the measures.

(8) Where the application of the principle of subsidiarity leads to no action being taken by the Community, Member States are required in their action to comply with the general rules laid down in Article [10] of the Treaty, by taking all appropriate measures to ensure fulfilment of their obligations under the Treaty and by abstaining from any measure which could jeopardise the attainment of the objectives of the Treaty.

(9) Without prejudice to its right of initiative, the Commission should:

— except in cases of particular urgency or confidentiality, consult widely before proposing legislation and, wherever appropriate, publish consultation documents;

— justify the relevance of its proposals with regard to the principle of subsidiarity; whenever necessary, the explanatory memorandum accompanying a proposal will give details in this respect. The financing of Community action in whole or in part from the Community budget shall require an explanation;
— take duly into account the need for any burden, whether financial or administrative, falling upon the Community, national governments, local authorities, economic operators and citizens, to be minimised and proportionate to the objective to be achieved;
— submit an annual report to the European Council, the European Parliament and the Council on the application of Article [5] of the Treaty. This annual report shall also be sent to the Committee of the Regions and to the Economic and Social Committee.

(10) The European Council shall take account of the Commission report referred to in the fourth indent of point 9 within the report on the progress achieved by the Union which it is required to submit to the European Parliament in accordance with Article [4] of the Treaty on European Union.

(11) While fully observing the procedures applicable, the European Parliament and the Council shall, as an integral part of the overall examination of Commission proposals, consider their consistency with Article [5] of the Treaty. This concerns the original Commission proposal as well as amendments which the European Parliament and the Council envisage making to the proposal.

(12) In the course of the procedures referred to in Articles [251] and [252] of the Treaty, the European Parliament shall be informed of the Council's position on the application of Article [5] of the Treaty, by way of a statement of the reasons which led the Council to adopt its common position. The Council shall inform the European Parliament of the reasons on the basis of which all or part of a Commission proposal is deemed to be inconsistent with Article [5] of the Treaty.

(13) Compliance with the principle of subsidiarity shall be reviewed in accordance with the rules laid down by the Treaty.

PROTOCOL (NO. 31) ON EXTERNAL RELATIONS OF THE MEMBER STATES WITH REGARD TO THE CROSSING OF EXTERNAL BORDERS (1997)

The High Contracting Parties, 2–404
Taking into account the need of the Member States to ensure effective controls at their external borders, in cooperation with third countries where appropriate,
Have agreed upon the following provision, which shall be annexed to the Treaty establishing the European Community,

The provisions on the measures on the crossing of external borders included in Article [62(2)(a)] of Title [IV] of the Treaty shall be without prejudice to the competence of Member States to negotiate or conclude agreements with third countries as long as they respect Community law and other relevant international agreements.

PROTOCOL (NO. 32) ON THE SYSTEM OF PUBLIC BROADCASTING IN THE MEMBER STATES (1997)

The High Contracting Parties, 2–405
Considering that the system of public broadcasting in the Member States is directly related to the democratic, social and cultural needs of each society and to the need to preserve media pluralism;
Have agreed upon the following interpretative provisions, which shall be annexed to the Treaty establishing the European Community,

The provisions of the Treaty establishing the European Community shall be without prejudice to the competence of Member States to provide for the funding of public service broadcasting insofar as such funding is granted to broadcasting organisations for the fulfilment of the public service remit as conferred, defined and organised by each Member State, and in so far as such funding does not affect trading conditions and competition in the Community to an extent which would be contrary to the common interest, while the realisation of the remit of that public service shall be taken into account.

PROTOCOL (NO. 33) ON PROTECTION AND WELFARE OF ANIMALS (1997)

2–406 *The High Contracting Parties*,
Desiring to ensure improved protection and respect for the welfare of animals as sentient beings;
Have agreed upon the following provision which shall be annexed to the Treaty establishing the European Community,

In formulating and implementing the Community's agriculture, transport, internal market and research policies, the Community and the Member States shall pay full regard to the welfare requirements of animals, while respecting the legislative or administrative provisions and customs of the Member States relating in particular to religious rites, cultural traditions and regional heritage.

Protocol Annexed by the Treaty of Nice to the Treaty on European Union and to the Treaties establishing the European Communities

PROTOCOL ON THE ENLARGEMENT OF THE EUROPEAN UNION (2001)

2–407 *The High Contracting Parties*
Have agreed upon the following provisions, which shall be annexed to the Treaty on European Union and to the Treaties establishing the European Communities:

Article 1 Repeal of the Protocol on the institutions

2–408 The Protocol on the institutions with the prospect of enlargement of the European Union, annexed to the Treaty on European Union and to the Treaties establishing the European Communities, is hereby repealed.

Article 2 Provisions concerning the European Parliament

2–409 1. On 1 January 2004 and with effect from the start of the 2004–2009 term, in Article 190(2) of the Treaty establishing the European Community and in Article 108(2) of the Treaty establishing the European Atomic Energy Community, the first subparagraph shall be replaced by the following:
"The number of representatives elected in each Member State shall be as follows:

Belgium	22
Denmark	13
Germany	99
Greece	22
Spain	50
France	72
Ireland	12
Italy	72

Luxembourg	6
Netherlands	25
Austria	17
Portugal	22
Finland	13
Sweden	18
United Kingdom	72"

2. Subject to paragraph 3, the total number of representatives in the European Parliament for the 2004–2009 term shall be equal to the number of representatives specified in Article 190(2) of the Treaty establishing the European Community and in Article 108(2) of the Treaty establishing the European Atomic Energy Community plus the number of representatives of the new Member States resulting from the accession treaties signed by 1 January 2004 at the latest.

3. If the total number of members referred to in paragraph 2 is less than 732, a pro rata correction shall be applied to the number of representatives to be elected in each Member State, so that the total number is as close as possible to 732, without such a correction leading to the number of representatives to be elected in each Member State being higher than that provided for in Article 190(2) of the Treaty establishing the European Community and in Article 108(2) of the Treaty establishing the European Atomic Energy Community for the 1999–2004 term.

The Council shall adopt a decision to that effect.

4. By way of derogation from the second paragraph of Article 189 of the Treaty establishing the European Community and from the second paragraph of Article 107 of the Treaty establishing the European Atomic Energy Community, in the event of the entry into force of accession treaties after the adoption of the Council decision provided for in the second subparagraph of paragraph 3 of this Article, the number of members of the European Parliament may temporarily exceed 732 for the period for which that decision applies. The same correction as that referred to in the first subparagraph of paragraph 3 of this Article shall be applied to the number of representatives to be elected in the Member States in question.

Article 3 Provisions concerning the weighting of votes in the Council

1. On 1 January 2005: **2–410**

(a) in Article 205 of the Treaty establishing the European Community and in Article 118 of the Treaty establishing the European Atomic Energy Community:

(i) paragraph 2 shall be replaced by the following:

"2. Where the Council is required to act by a qualified majority, the votes of its members shall be weighted as follows:

Belgium	12
Denmark	7
Germany	29
Greece	12
Spain	27
France	29
Ireland	7
Italy	29
Luxembourg	4
Netherlands	13
Austria	10
Portugal	12
Finland	7
Sweden	10
United Kingdom	29

Acts of the Council shall require for their adoption at least 169 votes in favour cast by a majority of the members where this Treaty requires them to be adopted on a proposal from the Commission.

In other cases, for their adoption acts of the Council shall require at least 169 votes in favour, cast by at least two-thirds of the members."

(ii) the following paragraph 4 shall be added:

"4. When a decision is to be adopted by the Council by a qualified majority, a member of the Council may request verification that the Member States constituting the qualified majority represent at least 62% of the total population of the Union. If that condition is shown not to have been met, the decision in question shall not be adopted."

(b) In Article 23(2) of the Treaty on European Union, the third subparagraph shall be replaced by the following text:

"The votes of the members of the Council shall be weighted in accordance with Article 205(2) of the Treaty establishing the European Community. For their adoption, decisions shall require at least 169 votes in favour cast by at least two-thirds of the members. When a decision is to be adopted by the Council by a qualified majority, a member of the Council may request verification that the Member States constituting the qualified majority represent at least 62% of the total population of the Union. If that condition is shown not to have been met, the decision in question shall not be adopted."

(c) In Article 34 of the Treaty on European Union, paragraph 3 shall be replaced by the following:

"3. Where the Council is required to act by a qualified majority, the votes of its members shall be weighted as laid down in Article 205(2) of the Treaty establishing the European Community, and for their adoption acts of the Council shall require at least 169 votes in favour, cast by at least two-thirds of the members. When a decision is to be adopted by the Council by a qualified majority, a member of the Council may request verification that the Member States constituting the qualified majority represent at least 62% of the total population of the Union. If that condition is shown not to have been met, the decision in question shall not be adopted."

2. At the time of each accession, the threshold referred to in the second subparagraph of Article 205(2) of the Treaty establishing the European Community and in the second subparagraph of Article 118(2) of the Treaty establishing the European Atomic Energy Community shall be calculated in such a way that the qualified majority threshold expressed in votes does not exceed the threshold resulting from the table in the Declaration on the enlargement of the European Union, included in the Final Act of the Conference which adopted the Treaty of Nice.[26]

Article 4 Provisions concerning the Commission

2–411 1. On 1 January 2005 and with effect from when the first Commission following that date takes up its duties, Article 213(1) of the Treaty establishing the European Community and Article 126(1) of the Treaty establishing the European Atomic Energy Community shall be replaced by the following:

"1. The Members of the Commission shall be chosen on the grounds of their general competence and their independence shall be beyond doubt.

The Commission shall include one national of each of the Member States.

The number of Members of the Commission may be altered by the Council, acting unanimously."

2. When the Union consists of 27 Member States, Article 213(1) of the Treaty establishing the European Community and Article 126(1) of the Treaty

[26] See Declaration 20.

establishing the European Atomic Energy Community shall be replaced by the following:

"1. The Members of the Commission shall be chosen on the grounds of their general competence and their independence shall be beyond doubt.

The number of Members of the Commission shall be less than the number of Member States. The Members of the Commission shall be chosen according to a rotation system based on the principle of equality, the implementing arrangements for which shall be adopted by the Council, acting unanimously.

The number of Members of the Commission shall be set by the Council, acting unanimously."

This amendment shall apply as from the date on which the first Commission following the date of accession of the twenty-seventh Member State of the Union takes up its duties.

3. The Council, acting unanimously after signing the treaty of accession of the twenty-seventh Member State of the Union, shall adopt:
— the number of Members of the Commission;
— the implementing arrangements for a rotation system based on the principle of equality containing all the criteria and rules necessary for determining the composition of successive colleges automatically on the basis of the following principles:
  (a) Member States shall be treated on a strictly equal footing as regards determination of the sequence of, and the time spent by, their nationals as Members of the Commission; consequently, the difference between the total number of terms of office held by nationals of any given pair of Member States may never be more than one;
  (b) subject to point (a), each successive college shall be so composed as to reflect satisfactorily the demographic and geographical range of all the Member States of the Union.

4. Any State which accedes to the Union shall be entitled, at the time of its accession, to have one of its nationals as a Member of the Commission until paragraph 2 applies.

Protocol Annexed by the Treaty of Nice to the Treaty on European Union, to the Treaty establishing the European Community and to the Treaty establishing the European Atomic Energy Community

PROTOCOL ON THE STATUTE OF THE COURT OF JUSTICE (2001)[27]

The High Contracting Parties 2–412
Desiring to lay down the Statute of the Court of Justice provided for in Article 245 of the Treaty establishing the European Community and in Article 160 of the Treaty establishing the European Atomic Energy Community,
Have agreed upon the following provisions, which shall be annexed to the Treaty on European Union, the Treaty establishing the European Community and the Treaty establishing the European Atomic Energy Community:

Article 1 [Constitution and functions]

The Court of Justice shall be constituted and shall function in accordance with the provisions of the Treaty on European Union (EU Treaty), of the Treaty 2–413

[27] Protocol replaced by virtue of Treaty of Nice, Art. 7.

establishing the European Community (EC Treaty), of the Treaty establishing the European Atomic Energy Community (EAEC Treaty) and of this Statute.

TITLE I—JUDGES AND ADVOCATES-GENERAL

Article 2 [Judicial oath]

2–414 Before taking up his duties each Judge shall, in open court, take an oath to perform his duties impartially and conscientiously and to preserve the secrecy of the deliberations of the Court.

Article 3 [Judicial immunity from legal proceedings]

2–415 The Judges shall be immune from legal proceedings. After they have ceased to hold office, they shall continue to enjoy immunity in respect of acts performed by them in their official capacity, including words spoken or written.

The Court, sitting as a full Court, may waive the immunity.

Where immunity has been waived and criminal proceedings are instituted against a Judge, he shall be tried, in any of the Member States, only by the court competent to judge the members of the highest national judiciary.

Articles 12 to 15 and Article 18 of the Protocol on the privileges and immunities of the European Communities shall apply to the Judges, Advocates-General, Registrar and Assistant Rapporteurs of the Court, without prejudice to the provisions relating to immunity from legal proceedings of Judges which are set out in the preceding paragraphs.

Article 4 [Holding other offices and positions]

2–416 The Judges may not hold any political or administrative office.

They may not engage in any occupation, whether gainful or not, unless exemption is exceptionally granted by the Council.

When taking up their duties, they shall give a solemn undertaking that, both during and after their term of office, they will respect the obligations arising therefrom, in particular the duty to behave with integrity and discretion as regards the acceptance, after they have ceased to hold office, of certain appointments or benefits.

Any doubt on this point shall be settled by decision of the Court.

Article 5 [Resignations of Judges]

2–417 Apart from normal replacement, or death, the duties of a Judge shall end when he resigns.

Where a Judge resigns, his letter of resignation shall be addressed to the President of the Court for transmission to the President of the Council. Upon this notification a vacancy shall arise on the bench.

Save where Article 6 applies, a Judge shall continue to hold office until his successor takes up his duties.

Article 6 [Removal of Judges from office]

2–418 A Judge may be deprived of his office or of his right to a pension or other benefits in its stead only if, in the unanimous opinion of the Judges and Advocates-General of the Court, he no longer fulfils the requisite conditions or meets the obligations arising from his office. The Judge concerned shall not take part in any such deliberations.

The Registrar of the Court shall communicate the decision of the Court to the President of the European Parliament and to the President of the Commission and shall notify it to the President of the Council.

In the case of a decision depriving a Judge of his office, a vacancy shall arise on the bench upon this latter notification.

Article 7 [Replacement Judges]

A Judge who is to replace a member of the Court whose term of office has not expired shall be appointed for the remainder of his predecessor's term. **2–419**

Article 8 [Application of rules to Advocates-General]

The provisions of Articles 2 to 7 shall apply to the Advocates-General. **2–420**

TITLE II—ORGANISATION

Article 9 [Triennial partial replacement of Judges and Advocates-General]

When, every three years, the Judges are partially replaced, eight and seven Judges shall be replaced alternately. **2–421**

When, every three years, the Advocates-General are partially replaced, four Advocates-General shall be replaced on each occasion.

Article 10 [Registrar's oath of office]

The Registrar shall take an oath before the Court to perform his duties impartially and conscientiously and to preserve the secrecy of the deliberations of the Court. **2–422**

Article 11 [Unavailability of Registrar]

The Court shall arrange for replacement of the Registrar on occasions when he is prevented from attending the Court. **2–423**

Article 12 [Court staff]

Officials and other servants shall be attached to the Court to enable it to function. They shall be responsible to the Registrar under the authority of the President. **2–424**

Article 13 [Assistant Rapporteurs]

On a proposal from the Court, the Council may, acting unanimously, provide for the appointment of Assistant Rapporteurs and lay down the rules governing their service. The Assistant Rapporteurs may be required, under conditions laid down in the Rules of Procedure, to participate in preparatory inquiries in cases pending before the Court and to cooperate with the Judge who acts as Rapporteur. **2–425**

The Assistant Rapporteurs shall be chosen from persons whose independence is beyond doubt and who possess the necessary legal qualifications; they shall be appointed by the Council. They shall take an oath before the Court to perform their duties impartially and conscientiously and to preserve the secrecy of the deliberations of the Court.

Article 14 [Residence requirement]

The Judges, the Advocates-General and the Registrar shall be required to reside at the place where the Court has its seat. **2–426**

Article 15 [Court sessions and vacations]

The Court shall remain permanently in session. The duration of the judicial vacations shall be determined by the Court with due regard to the needs of its business. **2–427**

Article 16 [Court chambers; sitting as full court]

The Court shall form chambers consisting of three and five Judges. The Judges shall elect the Presidents of the chambers from among their number. The **2–428**

Presidents of the chambers of five Judges shall be elected for three years. They may be re-elected once.

The Grand Chamber shall consist of eleven Judges. It shall be presided over by the President of the Court. The Presidents of the chambers of five Judges and other Judges appointed in accordance with the conditions laid down in the Rules of Procedure shall also form part of the Grand Chamber.

The Court shall sit in a Grand Chamber when a Member State or an institution of the Communities that is party to the proceedings so requests.

The Court shall sit as a full Court where cases are brought before it pursuant to Article 195(2), Article 213(2), Article 216 or Article 247(7) of the EC Treaty or Article 107d(2), Article 126(2), Article 129 or Article 160b(7) of the EAEC Treaty.

Moreover, where it considers that a case before it is of exceptional importance, the Court may decide, after hearing the Advocate-General, to refer the case to the full Court.

Article 17 [Quorum]

2–429 Decisions of the Court shall be valid only when an uneven number of its members is sitting in the deliberations.

Decisions of the chambers consisting of either three or five Judges shall be valid only if they are taken by three Judges.

Decisions of the Grand Chamber shall be valid only if nine Judges are sitting.

Decisions of the full Court shall be valid only if eleven Judges are sitting.

In the event of one of the Judges of a chamber being prevented from attending, a Judge of another chamber may be called upon to sit in accordance with conditions laid down in the Rules of Procedure.

Article 18 [Guarantee of impartiality]

2–430 No Judge or Advocate-General may take part in the disposal of any case in which he has previously taken part as agent or adviser or has acted for one of the parties, or in which he has been called upon to pronounce as a member of a court or tribunal, of a commission of inquiry or in any other capacity.

If, for some special reason, any Judge or Advocate-General considers that he should not take part in the judgment or examination of a particular case, he shall so inform the President. If, for some special reason, the President considers that any Judge or Advocate-General should not sit or make submissions in a particular case, he shall notify him accordingly.

Any difficulty arising as to the application of this Article shall be settled by decision of the Court.

A party may not apply for a change in the composition of the Court or of one of its chambers on the grounds of either the nationality of a Judge or the absence from the Court or from the chamber of a Judge of the nationality of that party.

TITLE III—PROCEDURE

Article 19 [Representation before the Court]

2–431 The Member States and the institutions of the Communities shall be represented before the Court by an agent appointed for each case; the agent may be assisted by an adviser or by a lawyer.

The States, other than the Member States, which are parties to the Agreement on the European Economic Area and also the EFTA Surveillance Authority referred to in that Agreement shall be represented in same manner.

Other parties must be represented by a lawyer.

Only a lawyer authorised to practise before a court of a Member State or of another State which is a party to the Agreement on the European Economic Area may represent or assist a party before the Court.

Such agents, advisers and lawyers shall, when they appear before the Court, enjoy the rights and immunities necessary to the independent exercise of their duties, under conditions laid down in the Rules of Procedure.

As regards such advisers and lawyers who appear before it, the Court shall have the powers normally accorded to courts of law, under conditions laid down in the Rules of Procedure.

University teachers being nationals of a Member State whose law accords them a right of audience shall have the same rights before the Court as are accorded by this Article to lawyers.

Article 20 [Written and oral procedure]

The procedure before the Court shall consist of two parts: written and oral. **2–432**

The written procedure shall consist of the communication to the parties and to the institutions of the Communities whose decisions are in dispute, of applications, statements of case, defences and observations, and of replies, if any, as well as of all papers and documents in support or of certified copies of them.

Communications shall be made by the Registrar in the order and within the time laid down in the Rules of Procedure.

The oral procedure shall consist of the reading of the report presented by a Judge acting as Rapporteur, the hearing by the Court of agents, advisers and lawyers and of the submissions of the Advocate-General, as well as the hearing, if any, of witnesses and experts.

Where it considers that the case raises no new point of law, the Court may decide, after hearing the Advocate-General, that the case shall be determined without a submission from the Advocate-General.

Article 21 [Procedure for bringing cases before the Court]

A case shall be brought before the Court by a written application addressed to the **2–433** Registrar. The application shall contain the applicant's name and permanent address and the description of the signatory, the name of the party or names of the parties against whom the application is made, the subject-matter of the dispute, the form of order sought and a brief statement of the pleas in law on which the application is based.

The application shall be accompanied, where appropriate, by the measure the annulment of which is sought or, in the circumstances referred to in Article 232 of the EC Treaty and Article 148 of the EAEC Treaty, by documentary evidence of the date on which an institution was, in accordance with those Articles, requested to act. If the documents are not submitted with the application, the Registrar shall ask the party concerned to produce them within a reasonable period, but in that event the rights of the party shall not lapse even if such documents are produced after the time-limit for bringing proceedings.

Article 22 [EAEC Treaty: appeals to the Court]

A case governed by Article 18 of the EAEC Treaty shall be brought before the **2–434** Court by an appeal addressed to the Registrar. The appeal shall contain the name and permanent address of the applicant and the description of the signatory, a reference to the decision against which the appeal is brought, the names of the respondents, the subject-matter of the dispute, the submissions and a brief statement of the grounds on which the appeal is based.

The appeal shall be accompanied by a certified copy of the decision of the Arbitration Committee which is contested.

If the Court rejects the appeal, the decision of the Arbitration Committee shall become final.

If the Court annuls the decision of the Arbitration Committee, the matter may be re-opened, where appropriate, on the initiative of one of the parties in the case, before the Arbitration Committee. The latter shall conform to any decisions on points of law given by the Court.

Article 23 [References for preliminary rulings]

2–435 In the cases governed by Article 35(1) of the EU Treaty, by Article 234 of the EC Treaty and by Article 150 of the EAEC Treaty, the decision of the court or tribunal of a Member State which suspends its proceedings and refers a case to the Court shall be notified to the Court by the court or tribunal concerned. The decision shall then be notified by the Registrar of the Court to the parties, to the Member States and to the Commission, and also to the Council or to the European Central Bank if the act the validity or interpretation of which is in dispute originates from one of them, and to the European Parliament and the Council if the act the validity or interpretation of which is in dispute was adopted jointly by those two institutions.

Within two months of this notification, the parties, the Member States, the Commission and, where appropriate, the European Parliament, the Council and the European Central Bank, shall be entitled to submit statements of case or written observations to the Court.

In the cases governed by Article 234 of the EC Treaty, the decision of the national court or tribunal shall, moreover, be notified by the Registrar of the Court to the States, other than the Member States, which are parties to the Agreement on the European Economic Area and also to the EFTA Surveillance Authority referred to in that Agreement which may, within two months of notification, where one of the fields of application of that Agreement is concerned, submit statements of case or written observations to the Court.

Article 24 [Providing documents and supplying information]

2–436 The Court may require the parties to produce all documents and to supply all information which the Court considers desirable. Formal note shall be taken of any refusal.

The Court may also require the Member States and institutions not being parties to the case to supply all information which the Court considers necessary for the proceedings.

Article 25 [Expert opinions]

2–437 The Court may at any time entrust any individual, body, authority, committee or other organisation it chooses with the task of giving an expert opinion.

Article 26 [Hearing of witnesses]

2–438 Witnesses may be heard under conditions laid down in the Rules of Procedure.

Article 27 [Failure of witnesses to appear]

2–439 With respect to defaulting witnesses the Court shall have the powers generally granted to courts and tribunals and may impose pecuniary penalties under conditions laid down in the Rules of Procedure.

Article 28 [Oath to be taken by witnesses and experts]

Witnesses and experts may be heard on oath taken in the form laid down in the Rules of Procedure or in the manner laid down by the law of the country of the witness or expert. **2–440**

Article 29 [Local hearing of witnesses]

The Court may order that a witness or expert be heard by the judicial authority of his place of permanent residence. **2–441**

The order shall be sent for implementation to the competent judicial authority under conditions laid down in the Rules of Procedure. The documents drawn up in compliance with the letters rogatory shall be returned to the Court under the same conditions.

The Court shall defray the expenses, without prejudice to the right to charge them, where appropriate, to the parties.

Article 30 [Perjury]

A Member State shall treat any violation of an oath by a witness or expert in the same manner as if the offence had been committed before one of its courts with jurisdiction in civil proceedings. At the instance of the Court, the Member State concerned shall prosecute the offender before its competent court. **2–442**

Article 31 [Public hearings]

The hearing in court shall be public, unless the Court, of its own motion or on application by the parties, decides otherwise for serious reasons. **2–443**

Article 32 [Direct examination by the Court]

During the hearings the Court may examine the experts, the witnesses and the parties themselves. The latter, however, may address the Court only through their representatives. **2–444**

Article 33 [Minutes of the hearing]

Minutes shall be made of each hearing and signed by the President and the Registrar. **2–445**

Article 34 [Case list]

The case list shall be established by the President. **2–446**

Article 35 [Confidentiality of Court deliberations]

The deliberations of the Court shall be and shall remain secret. **2–447**

Article 36 [Judicial reasoning]

Judgments shall state the reasons on which they are based. They shall contain the names of the Judges who took part in the deliberations. **2–448**

Article 37 [Delivery and signature of judgments]

2–449 Judgments shall be signed by the President and the Registrar. They shall be read in open court.

Article 38 [Costs]

2–450 The Court shall adjudicate upon costs.

Article 39 [Orders of the President of the Court]

2–451 The President of the Court may, by way of summary procedure, which may, in so far as necessary, differ from some of the rules contained in this Statute and which shall be laid down in the Rules of Procedure, adjudicate upon applications to suspend execution, as provided for in Article 242 of the EC Treaty and Article 157 of the EAEC Treaty, or to prescribe interim measures in pursuance of Article 243 of the EC Treaty or Article 158 of the EAEC Treaty, or to suspend enforcement in accordance with the fourth paragraph of Article 256 of the EC Treaty or the third paragraph of Article 164 of the EAEC Treaty.

Should the President be prevented from attending, his place shall be taken by another Judge under conditions laid down in the Rules of Procedure.

The ruling of the President or of the Judge replacing him shall be provisional and shall in no way prejudice the decision of the Court on the substance of the case.

Article 40 [Interventions in proceedings]

2–452 Member States and institutions of the Communities may intervene in cases before the Court.

The same right shall be open to any other person establishing an interest in the result of any case submitted to the Court, save in cases between Member States, between institutions of the Communities or between Member States and institutions of the Communities.

Without prejudice to the second paragraph, the States, other than the Member States, which are parties to the Agreement on the European Economic Area, and also the EFTA Surveillance Authority referred to in that Agreement, may intervene in cases before the Court where one of the fields of application that Agreement is concerned.

An application to intervene shall be limited to supporting the form of order sought by one of the parties.

Article 41 [Judgments in default]

2–453 Where the defending party, after having been duly summoned, fails to file written submissions in defence, judgment shall be given against that party by default. An objection may be lodged against the judgment within one month of it being notified. The objection shall not have the effect of staying enforcement of the judgment by default unless the Court decides otherwise.

Article 42 [Third-party proceedings]

2–454 Member States, institutions of the Communities and any other natural or legal persons may, in cases and under conditions to be determined by the Rules of Procedure, institute third-party proceedings to contest a judgment rendered without their being heard, where the judgment is prejudicial to their rights.

Article 43 [Applications for constructions of judgments]

2–455 If the meaning or scope of a judgment is in doubt, the Court shall construe it on application by any party or any institution of the Communities establishing an interest therein.

Article 44 [Applications for revisions of judgments]

An application for revision of a judgment may be made to the Court only on discovery of a fact which is of such a nature as to be a decisive factor, and which, when the judgment was given, was unknown to the Court and to the party claiming the revision. **2–456**

The revision shall be opened by a judgment of the Court expressly recording the existence of a new fact, recognising that it is of such a character as to lay the case open to revision and declaring the application admissible on this ground.

No application for revision may be made after the lapse of 10 years from the date of the judgment.

Article 45 [Periods of grace; expiry of time limits]

Periods of grace based on considerations of distance shall be determined by the Rules of Procedure. **2–457**

No right shall be prejudiced in consequence of the expiry of a time-limit if the party concerned proves the existence of unforeseeable circumstances or of force majeure.

Article 46 [Non-contractual liability: limitation period]

Proceedings against the Communities in matters arising from non-contractual liability shall be barred after a period of five years from the occurrence of the event giving rise thereto. The period of limitation shall be interrupted if proceedings are instituted before the Court or if prior to such proceedings an application is made by the aggrieved party to the relevant institution of the Communities. In the latter event the proceedings must be instituted within the period of two months provided for in Article 230 of the EC Treaty and Article 146 of the EAEC Treaty; the provisions of the second paragraph of Article 232 of the EC Treaty and the second paragraph of Article 148 of the EAEC Treaty, respectively, shall apply where appropriate. **2–458**

TITLE IV—THE COURT OF FIRST INSTANCE OF THE EUROPEAN COMMUNITIES

Article 47 [Members and organisation of the CFI]

Articles 2 to 8, Articles 14 and 15, the first, second, fourth and fifth paragraphs of Article 17 and Article 18 shall apply to the Court of First Instance and its members. The oath referred to in Article 2 shall be taken before the Court of Justice and the decisions referred to in Articles 3, 4 and 6 shall be adopted by that Court after hearing the Court of First Instance. **2–459**

The fourth paragraph of Article 3 and Articles 10, 11 and 14 shall apply to the Registrar of the Court of First Instance mutatis mutandis.

Article 48 [Composition of the CFI]

The Court of First Instance shall consist of 15 Judges. **2–460**

Article 49 [Role of Advocate-General]

The members of the Court of First Instance may be called upon to perform the task of an Advocate-General. **2–461**

It shall be the duty of the Advocate-General, acting with complete impartiality and independence, to make, in open court, reasoned submissions on certain cases brought before the Court of First Instance in order to assist the Court of First Instance in the performance of its task.

The criteria for selecting such cases, as well as the procedures for designating the Advocates-General, shall be laid down in the Rules of Procedure of the Court of First Instance.

A member called upon to perform the task of Advocate-General in a case may not take part in the judgment of the case.

Article 50 [Court chambers]

2–462 The Court of First Instance shall sit in chambers of three or five Judges. The Judges shall elect the Presidents of the chambers from among their number. The Presidents of the chambers of five Judges shall be elected for three years. They may be re-elected once.

The composition of the chambers and the assignment of cases to them shall be governed by the Rules of Procedure. In certain cases governed by the Rules of Procedure, the Court of First Instance may sit as a full court or be constituted by a single Judge.

The Rules of Procedure may also provide that the Court of First Instance may sit in a Grand Chamber in cases and under the conditions specified therein.

Article 51 [Matters reserved to the ECJ]

2–463 By way of exception to the rule laid down in Article 225(1) of the EC Treaty and Article 140a(1) of the EAEC Treaty, the Court of Justice shall have jurisdiction in actions brought by the Member States, by the institutions of the Communities and by the European Central Bank.

Article 52 [Officials]

2–464 The President of the Court of Justice and the President of the Court of First Instance shall determine, by common accord, the conditions under which officials and other servants attached to the Court of Justice shall render their services to the Court of First Instance to enable it to function. Certain officials or other servants shall be responsible to the Registrar of the Court of First Instance under the authority of the President of the Court of First Instance.

Article 53 [Procedure]

2–465 The procedure before the Court of First Instance shall be governed by Title III.

Such further and more detailed provisions as may be necessary shall be laid down in its Rules of Procedure. The Rules of Procedure may derogate from the fourth paragraph of Article 40 and from Article 41 in order to take account of the specific features of litigation in the field of intellectual property.

Notwithstanding the fourth paragraph of Article 20, the Advocate-General may make his reasoned submissions in writing.

Article 54 [Procedural interrelation between ECJ and CFI]

2–466 Where an application or other procedural document addressed to the Court of First Instance is lodged by mistake with the Registrar of the Court of Justice, it shall be transmitted immediately by that Registrar to the Registrar of the Court of First Instance; likewise, where an application or other procedural document addressed to the Court of Justice is lodged by mistake with the Registrar of the Court of First Instance, it shall be transmitted immediately by that Registrar to the Registrar of the Court of Justice.

Where the Court of First Instance finds that it does not have jurisdiction to hear and determine an action in respect of which the Court of Justice has jurisdiction, it shall refer that action to the Court of Justice; likewise, where the Court of Justice finds that an action falls within the jurisdiction of the Court of First Instance, it shall refer that action to the Court of First Instance, whereupon that Court may not decline jurisdiction.

Where the Court of Justice and the Court of First Instance are seised of cases in which the same relief is sought, the same issue of interpretation is raised or the validity of the same act is called in question, the Court of First Instance may, after hearing the parties, stay the proceedings before it until such time as the Court of Justice shall have delivered judgment. Where applications are made for the same act to be declared void, the Court of First Instance may also decline jurisdiction in order that the Court of Justice may rule on such applications. In the cases referred to in this paragraph, the Court of Justice may also decide to stay the proceedings before it; in that event, the proceedings before the Court of First Instance shall continue.

Article 55 [Notifications of decisions]

Final decisions of the Court of First Instance, decisions disposing of the substantive issues in part only or disposing of a procedural issue concerning a plea of lack of competence or inadmissibility, shall be notified by the Registrar of the Court of First Instance to all parties as well as all Member States and the institutions of the Communities even if they did not intervene in the case before the Court of First Instance. **2–467**

Article 56 [Appeals against final decisions]

An appeal may be brought before the Court of Justice, within two months of the notification of the decision appealed against, against final decisions of the Court of First Instance and decisions of that Court disposing of the substantive issues in part only or disposing of a procedural issue concerning a plea of lack of competence or inadmissibility. **2–468**

Such an appeal may be brought by any party which has been unsuccessful, in whole or in part, in its submissions. However, interveners other than the Member States and the institutions of the Communities may bring such an appeal only where the decision of the Court of First Instance directly affects them.

With the exception of cases relating to disputes between the Communities and their servants, an appeal may also be brought by Member States and institutions of the Communities which did not intervene in the proceedings before the Court of First Instance. Such Member States and institutions shall be in the same position as Member States or institutions which intervened at first instance.

Article 57 [Appeals: intervention, suspension and interim measures decisions]

Any person whose application to intervene has been dismissed by the Court of First Instance may appeal to the Court of Justice within two weeks from the notification of the decision dismissing the application. **2–469**

The parties to the proceedings may appeal to the Court of Justice against any decision of the Court of First Instance made pursuant to Article 242 or Article 243 or the fourth paragraph of Article 256 of the EC Treaty or Article 157 or Article 158 or the third paragraph of Article 164 of the EAEC Treaty within two months from their notification.

The appeal referred to in the first two paragraphs of this Article shall be heard and determined under the procedure referred to in Article 39.

Article 58 [Appeals to ECJ on points of law only]

An appeal to the Court of Justice shall be limited to points of law. It shall lie on the grounds of lack of competence of the Court of First Instance, a breach of **2–470** procedure before it which adversely affects the interests of the appellant as well as the infringement of Community law by the Court of First Instance.

No appeal shall lie regarding only the amount of the costs or the party ordered to pay them.

Article 59 [Appeal procedure]

2–471 Where an appeal is brought against a decision of the Court of First Instance, the procedure before the Court of Justice shall consist of a written part and an oral part. In accordance with conditions laid down in the Rules of Procedure, the Court of Justice, having heard the Advocate-General and the parties, may dispense with the oral procedure.

Article 60 [Temporal effect of appeals]

2–472 Without prejudice to Articles 242 and 243 of the EC Treaty or Articles 157 and 158 of the EAEC Treaty, an appeal shall not have suspensory effect.

By way of derogation from Article 244 of the EC Treaty and Article 159 of the EAEC Treaty, decisions of the Court of First Instance declaring a regulation to be void shall take effect only as from the date of expiry of the period referred to in the first paragraph of Article 56 of this Statute or, if an appeal shall have been brought within that period, as from the date of dismissal of the appeal, without prejudice, however, to the right of a party to apply to the Court of Justice, pursuant to Articles 242 and 243 of the EC Treaty or Articles 157 and 158 of the EAEC Treaty, for the suspension of the effects of the regulation which has been declared void or for the prescription of any other interim measure.

Article 61 [Successful appeals]

2–473 If the appeal is well founded, the Court of Justice shall quash the decision of the Court of First Instance. It may itself give final judgment in the matter, where the state of the proceedings so permits, or refer the case back to the Court of First Instance for judgment.

Where a case is referred back to the Court of First Instance, that Court shall be bound by the decision of the Court of Justice on points of law.

When an appeal brought by a Member State or an institution of the Communities, which did not intervene in the proceedings before the Court of First Instance, is well founded, the Court of Justice may, if it considers this necessary, state which of the effects of the decision of the Court of First Instance which has been quashed shall be considered as definitive in respect of the parties to the litigation.

Article 62 [ECJ power to review CFI decisions for consistency with Community law]

2–474 In the cases provided for in Article 225(2) and (3) of the EC Treaty and Article 140a(2) and (3) of the EAEC Treaty, where the First Advocate-General considers that there is a serious risk of the unity or consistency of Community law being affected, he may propose that the Court of Justice review the decision of the Court of First Instance.

The proposal must be made within one month of delivery of the decision by the Court of First Instance. Within one month of receiving the proposal made by the

First Advocate-General, the Court of Justice shall decide whether or not the decision should be reviewed.

TITLE V—FINAL PROVISIONS

Article 63 [Rules of Procedure]

The Rules of Procedure of the Court of Justice and of the Court of First Instance shall contain any provisions necessary for applying and, where required, supplementing this Statute. **2–475**

Article 64 [Language arrangements]

Until the rules governing the language arrangements applicable at the Court of Justice and the Court of First Instance have been adopted in this Statute, the provisions of the Rules of Procedure of the Court of Justice and of the Rules of Procedure of the Court of First Instance governing language arrangements shall continue to apply. Those provisions may only be amended or repealed in accordance with the procedure laid down for amending this Statute. **2–476**

Protocols Annexed by the Treaty of Nice to the Treaty establishing the European Community

PROTOCOL ON THE FINANCIAL CONSEQUENCES OF THE EXPIRY OF THE ECSC TREATY AND ON THE RESEARCH FUND FOR COAL AND STEEL (2001)

The High Contracting Parties,

[1] Desiring to settle certain questions relating to the expiry of the Treaty establishing the European Coal and Steel Community (ECSC); **2–477**

[2] Wishing to confer ownership of the ECSC funds on the European Community;

[3] Taking account of the desire to use these funds for research in sectors related to the coal and steel industry and therefore the necessity to provide for certain special rules in this regard;

Have agreed upon the following provisions, which shall be annexed to the Treaty establishing the European Community:

Article 1 [Transfer of assets and liabilities to EC]

1. All assets and liabilities of the ECSC, as they exist on 23 July 2002, shall be transferred to the European Community on 24 July 2002. **2–478**

2. The net worth of these assets and liabilities, as they appear in the balance sheet of the ECSC of 23 July 2002, subject to any increase or decrease which may occur as a result of the liquidation operations, shall be considered as assets intended for research in the sectors related to the coal and steel industry, referred to as the "ECSC in liquidation". On completion of the liquidation they shall be referred to as the "Assets of the Research Fund for Coal and Steel".

3. The revenue from these assets, referred to as the "Research Fund for Coal and Steel", shall be used exclusively for research, outside the research framework programme, in the sectors related to the coal and steel industry in accordance with the provisions of this Protocol and of acts adopted on the basis hereof.

Article 2 [Implementation]

The Council, acting unanimously on a proposal from the Commission and after consulting the European Parliament, shall adopt all the necessary provisions for the implementation of this Protocol, including essential principles and proper decision-making procedures, in particular for the adoption of multiannual financial guidelines for managing the assets of the Research Fund for Coal and **2–479**

Steel and technical guidelines for the research programme of the Research Fund for Coal and Steel.

Article 3 [Application of EC Treaty]

2–480 Except as otherwise provided in this Protocol and in the acts adopted on the basis hereof, the provisions of the Treaty establishing the European Community shall apply.

Article 4 [Effective date]

2–481 This Protocol shall apply from 24 July 2002.

PROTOCOL ON ARTICLE 67 OF THE TREATY ESTABLISHING THE EUROPEAN COMMUNITY (2002)

2–482 *The High Contracting Parties*
Have agreed upon the following provision, which shall be annexed to the Treaty establishing the European Community:

Sole Article [Majority voting on cooperation measures on visa etc. policy]

2–483 From 1 May 2004, the Council shall act by a qualified majority, on a proposal from the Commission and after consulting the European Parliament, in order to adopt the measures referred to in Article 66 of the Treaty establishing the European Community.

CHAPTER 3

AMENDING TREATIES

TREATY OF AMSTERDAM

AMENDING THE TREATY ON EUROPEAN UNION, THE TREATIES ESTABLISHING THE EUROPEAN COMMUNITIES AND CERTAIN RELATED ACTS

(2 October 1997)

([1997] OJ C340/01; Doc. Ref. 197D)

[**Editorial Note**—References below to provisions of the Treaty on European Union and the EC Treaty have been adjusted for convenience of use in line with Arts 6 and 12 of this Treaty.]

His Majesty the King of the Belgians, Her Majesty the Queen of Denmark, the President of the Federal Republic of Germany, the President of the Hellenic Republic, His Majesty the King of Spain, the President of the French Republic, the Commission authorised by article 14 of the Constitution of Ireland to exercise and perform the powers and functions of the President of Ireland, the President of the Italian Republic, His Royal Highness the Grand Duke of Luxembourg, Her Majesty the Queen of the Netherlands, the Federal President of the Republic of Austria, The President of the Portuguese Republic, The President of the Republic of Finland, His Majesty the King of Sweden, Her Majesty the Queen of the United Kingdom of Great Britain and Northern Ireland, **3–001**

Have resolved to amend the Treaty on European Union, the treaties establishing the European Communities and certain related acts, and to this end have designated as their Plenipotentiaries:

[Designation of plenipotentiaries omitted]

Who, having exchanged their full powers found in good and due form, *have agreed as follows:*

PART ONE—SUBSTANTIVE AMENDMENTS

Article 1 [Amendments to Union Treaty]

The Treaty on European Union shall be amended in accordance with the provisions of this Article) **3–002**

[Amendments not reproduced here]

Article 2 [Amendments to the EC Treaty]

The Treaty establishing the European Community shall be amended in accordance with the provisions of this Article. **3–003**

[Amendments not reproduced here]

...

PART TWO—SIMPLIFICATION

Article 6 [Rationalisation of the EC Treaty]

The Treaty establishing the European Community, including the Annexes and Protocols thereto, shall be amended in accordance with the provisions of this Article for the purpose of deleting lapsed provisions of the Treaty and adapting in consequence the text of certain of its provisions. **3–004**

[Amendments not reproduced here]

...

Article 9 [Common institutions]

3–005 1. Without prejudice to the paragraphs following hereinafter, which have as their purpose to retain the essential elements of their provisions, the Convention of 25 March 1957 on certain institutions common to the European Communities and the Treaty of 8 April 1965, establishing a Single Council and a Single Commission of the European Communities, but with the exception of the Protocol referred to in paragraph 5, shall be repealed.

2. The powers conferred on the European Parliament, the Council, the Commission, the Court of Justice and the Court of Auditors by the Treaty establishing the European Community, the Treaty establishing the European Coal and Steel Community and the Treaty establishing the European Atomic Energy Community shall be exercised by the single institutions under the conditions laid down respectively by the said Treaties and this Article.

The functions conferred on the Economic and Social Committee by the Treaty establishing the European Community and the Treaty establishing the European Atomic Energy Community shall be exercised by a single committee under the conditions laid down respectively by the said treaties. The provisions of Articles [257] and [261] of the Treaty establishing the European Community shall apply to that Committee.[1]

3. The officials and other staff of the European Communities shall form part of the single administration of those Communities and shall be governed by the provisions adopted pursuant to Article [283] of the Treaty establishing the European Community.[2]

...

6. The revenue and expenditure of the European Community, the administrative expenditure of the European Coal and Steel Community and the revenue relating thereto and the revenue and expenditure of the European Atomic Energy Community, except for those of the Supply Agency and Joint Undertakings, shall be shown in the budget of the European Communities, under the conditions laid down respectively in the Treaties establishing the three Communities.

7. Without prejudice to the application of Article [289] of the Treaty establishing the European Community,[3] Article 77 of the Treaty establishing the European Coal and Steel Community, Article 189 of the Treaty establishing the European Atomic Energy Community and the second paragraph of Article 1 of the Protocol on the Statute of the European Investment Bank, the representatives of the Governments of the Member States shall adopt by common accord the necessary provisions for the purpose of dealing with certain problems particular to the Grand Duchy of Luxembourg which arise from the creation of a Single Council and a Single Commission of the European Communities.

Article 10 [Continuity of legal effects][4]

3–006 1. The repeal or deletion in this part of lapsed provisions of the Treaty establishing the European Community, the Treaty establishing the European Coal and Steel

[1] Article 257 EC (formerly Art. 193)—establishment of ESC; Art. 261 EC (formerly Art. 197) —ESC specialised sections.

[2] Article 283 EC (formerly Art. 212) (text of former Treaty of April 8, 1965, establishing a Single Council and a Single Commission of the European Communities (or "Merger Treaty"), Art. 24(1))—staff of EC institutions.

[3] Article 289 EC (formerly Art. 216)—seats of the institutions.

[4] See below for Declaration No. 51 adopted by the Conference.

Community and the Treaty establishing the European Atomic Energy Community as in force before the entry into force of this Treaty of Amsterdam and the adaptation of certain of their provisions shall not bring about any change in the legal effects of the provisions of those Treaties, in particular the legal effects arising from the time-limits laid down by the said Treaties, nor of Accession Treaties.

2. There shall be no change in the legal effects of the Acts in force adopted on the basis of the said Treaties.

3. The position shall be the same as regards the repeal of the Convention of 25 March 1957 on certain institutions common to the European Communities and the repeal of the Treaty of 8 April 1965 establishing a Single Council and a Single Commission of the European Communities.

Article 11 [Continuity of powers of Court of Justice]

The provisions of the Treaty establishing the European Community, the Treaty **3–007** establishing the European Coal and Steel Community and the Treaty establishing the European Atomic Energy Community relating to the powers of the Court of Justice of the European Communities and to the exercise of those powers shall apply to the provisions of this part and to the Protocol on privileges and immunities referred to in Article 9(5).

Part Three—General and Final Provisions

Article 12 Consolidation of Treaty texts]

1. The Articles, Titles and Sections of the Treaty on European Union and of the **3–008** Treaty establishing the European Community, as amended by the provisions of this Treaty, shall be renumbered in accordance with the tables of equivalences set out in the Annex to this Treaty, which shall form an integral part thereof.

2. The cross references to Articles, Titles and Sections in the Treaty on European Union and in the Treaty establishing the European Community, as well as between them, shall be adapted in consequence. The same shall apply as regards references to Articles, Titles and Sections of those Treaties contained in the other Community treaties.

3. The references to the Articles, Titles and Sections of the Treaties referred to in paragraph 2 contained in other instruments or acts shall be understood as references to the Articles, Titles and Sections of the Treaties as renumbered pursuant to paragraph 1 and, respectively, to the paragraphs of the said Articles, as renumbered by certain provisions of Article 6.

4. References, contained in other instruments or acts, to paragraphs of Articles of the Treaties referred to in Articles 7 and 8 shall be understood as referring to those paragraphs as renumbered by certain provisions of the said Articles 7 and 8.

Article 13 [Treaty duration]

This Treaty is concluded for an unlimited period. **3–009**

Article 14 [Ratification process]

1. This Treaty shall be ratified by the High Contracting Parties in accordance with **3–010** their respective constitutional requirements. The instruments of ratification shall be deposited with the Government of the Italian Republic.

2. This Treaty shall enter into force on the first day of the second month following that in which the instrument of ratification is deposited by the last signatory State to fulfil that formality.[5]

[5] This Treaty entered into force as from 1 May 1999.

Article 15 [Languages]

3–011 This Treaty, drawn up in a single original in the Danish, Dutch, English, Finnish, French, German, Greek, Irish, Italian, Portuguese, Spanish and Swedish languages, the texts in each of these languages being equally authentic, shall be deposited in the archives of the Government of the Italian Republic, which will transmit a certified copy to each of the Governments of the other signatory States.

In witness whereof the undersigned plenipotentiaries have signed this Treaty. [Signatures not reproduced]

Done at Amsterdam on the second day of October in the year one thousand nine hundred and ninety seven.

ANNEX

3–012 Tables of equivalences referred to in Article 12 of the Treaty of Amsterdam

A. Treaty on European Union

Previous numbering	New numbering
Title I	Title I
Article A	Article 1
Article B	Article 2
Article C	Article 3
Article D	Article 4
Article E	Article 5
Article F	Article 6
Article F.1	Article 7
Title II	Title II
Article G	Article 8
Title III	Title III
Article H	Article 9
Title IV	Title IV
Article I	Article 10
Title V	Title V
Article J.1	Article 11
Article J.2	Article 12
Article J.3	Article 13
Article J.4	Article 14
Article J.5	Article 15
Article J.6	Article 16
Article J.7	Article 17
Article J.8	Article 18
Article J.9	Article 19
Article J.10	Article 20
Article J.11	Article 21
Article J.12	Article 22
Article J.13	Article 23
Article J.14	Article 24
Article J.15	Article 25
Article J.16	Article 26
Article J.17	Article 27
Article J.18	Article 28

Previous numbering	New numbering
Title VI	Title VI
Article K.1	Article 29
Article K.2	Article 30
Article K.3	Article 31
Article K.4	Article 32
Article K.5	Article 33
Article K.6	Article 34
Article K.7	Article 35
Article K.8	Article 36
Article K.9	Article 37
Article K.10	Article 38
Article K.11	Article 39
Article K.12	Article 40
Article K.13	Article 41
Article K.14	Article 42
Title VIa	Title VII
Article K.15	Article 43
Article K.16	Article 44
Article K.17	Article 45
Title VII	Title VIII
Article L	Article 46
Article M	Article 47
Article N	Article 48
Article O	Article 49
Article P	Article 50
Article Q	Article 51
Article R	Article 52
Article S	Article 53

B. Treaty establishing the European Community

Previous numbering	New numbering
Part One	Part One
Article 1	Article 1
Article 2	Article 2
Article 3	Article 3
Article 3a	Article 4
Article 3b	Article 5
Article 3c	Article 6
Article 4	Article 7
Article 4a	Article 8
Article 4b	Article 9
Article 5	Article 10
Article 5a	Article 11
Article 6	Article 12
Article 6a	Article 13
Article 7 (repealed)	—
Article 7a	Article 14
Article 7b (repealed)	—
Article 7c	Article 15
Article 7d	Article 16

Previous numbering	New numbering
Part Two	Part Two
Article 8	Article 17
Article 8a	Article 18
Article 8b	Article 19
Article 8c	Article 20
Article 8d	Article 21
Article 8e	Article 22
Part Three Title I	Part Three Title I
Article 9	Article 23
Article 10	Article 24
Article 11 (repealed)	—
Chapter 1	Chapter 1
Section 1 (deleted)	—
Article 12	Article 25
Article 13 (repealed)	—
Article 14 (repealed)	—
Article 15 (repealed)	—
Article 16 (repealed)	—
Article 17 (repealed)	—
Section 2 (deleted)	—
Article 18 (repealed)	—
Article 19 (repealed)	—
Article 20 (repealed)	—
Article 21 (repealed)	—
Article 22 (repealed)	—
Article 23 (repealed)	—
Article 24 (repealed)	—
Article 25 (repealed)	—
Article 26 (repealed)	—
Article 27 (repealed)	—
Article 28	Article 26
Article 29	Article 27
Chapter 2	Chapter 2
Article 30	Article 28
Article 31 (repealed)	—
Article 32 (repealed)	—
Article 33 (repealed)	—
Article 34	Article 29
Article 35 (repealed)	—
Article 36	Article 30
Article 37	Article 31
Title II	Title II
Article 38	Article 32
Article 39	Article 33
Article 40	Article 34
Article 41	Article 35
Article 42	Article 36
Article 43	Article 37
Article 44 (repealed)	—
Article 45 (repealed)	—
Article 46	Article 38
Article 47 (repealed)	—

Previous numbering	New numbering
Title III	Title III
Chapter 1	Chapter 1
Article 48	Article 39
Article 49	Article 40
Article 50	Article 41
Article 51	Article 43
Chapter 2	Chapter 2
Article 52	Article 43
Article 53 (repealed)	—
Article 54	Article 44
Article 55	Article 45
Article 56	Article 46
Article 57	Article 47
Article 58	Article 48
Chapter 3	Chapter 3
Article 59	Article 49
Article 60	Article 50
Article 61	Article 51
Article 62 (repealed)	—
Article 63	Article 52
Article 64	Article 53
Article 65	Article 54
Article 66	Article 55
Chapter 4	Chapter 4
Article 67 (repealed)	—
Article 68 (repealed)	—
Article 69 (repealed)	—
Article 70 (repealed)	—
Article 71 (repealed)	—
Article 72 (repealed)	—
Article 73 (repealed)	—
Article 73a (repealed)	—
Article 73b	Article 56
Article 73c	Article 57
Article 73d	Article 58
Article 73e (repealed)	—
Article 73f	Article 59
Article 73g	Article 60
Article 73h (repealed)	—
Title IIIa	Title IV
Article 73i	Article 61
Article 73j	Article 62
Article 73k	Article 63
Article 73l	Article 64
Article 73m	Article 65
Article 73n	Article 66
Article 73o	Article 67
Article 73p	Article 68
Article 73q	Article 69

Previous numbering	New numbering
Title IV	Title V
Article 74	Article 70
Article 75	Article 71
Article 76	Article 72
Article 77	Article 73
Article 78	Article 74
Article 79	Article 75
Article 80	Article 76
Article 81	Article 77
Article 82	Article 78
Article 83	Article 79
Article 84	Article 80
Title V Chapter 1 Section 1	Title VI Chapter 1 Section 1
Article 85	Article 81
Article 86	Article 82
Article 87	Article 83
Article 88	Article 84
Article 89	Article 85
Article 90	Article 86
Section 2 (deleted)	—
Article 91 (repealed)	—
Section 3	Section 2
Article 92	Article 87
Article 93	Article 88
Article 94	Article 89
Chapter 2	Chapter 2
Article 95	Article 90
Article 96	Article 91
Article 97 (repealed)	—
Article 98	Article 92
Article 99	Article 93
Chapter 3	Chapter 3
Article 100	Article 94
Article 100a	Article 95
Article 100b (repealed)	—
Article 100c (repealed)	—
Article 100d (repealed)	—
Article 101	Article 92
Article 102	Article 93
Title VI Chapter 1	Title VII Chapter 1
Article 102a	Article 98
Article 103	Article 99
Article 103a	Article 100
Article 104	Article 101
Article 104a	Article 102
Article 104b	Article 103
Article 104c	Article 104

Previous numbering	New numbering
Chapter 2 Article 105 Article 105a Article 106 Article 107 Article 108 Article 108a Article 109	Chapter 2 Article 105 Article 106 Article 107 Article 108 Article 109 Article 110 Article 111
Chapter 3 Article 109a Article 109b Article 109c Article 109d	Chapter 3 Article 112 Article 113 Article 114 Article 115
Chapter 4 Article 109e Article 109f Article 109g Article 109h Article 109i Article 109j Article 109k Article 109l Article 109m	Chapter 4 Article 116 Article 117 Article 118 Article 119 Article 120 Article 121 Article 122 Article 123 Article 124
Title VIa Article 109n Article 109o Article 109p Article 109q Article 109r Article 109s	Title VIII Article 125 Article 126 Article 127 Article 128 Article 129 Article 130
Title VII Article 110 Article 111 (repealed) Article 112 Article 113 Article 114 (repealed) Article 115	Title IX Article 131 — Article 132 Article 133 — Article 134
Title VIIa Article 116	Title X Article 135
Title VIII Chapter 1 Article 117 Article 118 Article 118a Article 118b Article 118c Article 119 Article 119a Article 120 Article 121 Article 122	Title XI Chapter 1 Article 136 Article 137 Article 138 Article 139 Article 140 Article 141 Article 142 Article 143 Article 144 Article 145

Previous numbering	New numbering
Chapter 2 Article 123 Article 124 Article 125	Chapter 2 Article 146 Article 147 Article 148
Chapter 3 Article 126 Article 127	Chapter 3 Article 149 Article 150
Title IX Article 128	Title XII Article 151
Title X Article 129	Title XIII Article 152
Title XI Article 129a	Title XIV Article 153
Title XII Article 129b Article 129c Article 129d	Title XV Article 154 Article 155 Article 156
Title XIII Article 130	Title XVI Article 157
Title XIV Article 130a Article 130b Article 130c Article 130d Article 130e	Title XVII Article 158 Article 159 Article 160 Article 161 Article 162
Title XV Article 130f Article 130g Article 130h Article 130i Article 130j Article 130k Article 130l Article 130m Article 130n Article 130o Article 130p Article 130q (repealed)	Title XVIII Article 163 Article 164 Article 165 Article 166 Article 167 Article 168 Article 169 Article 170 Article 171 Article 172 Article 173 —
Title XVI Article 130r Article 130s Article 130t	Title XIX Article 174 Article 175 Article 176

Previous numbering	New numbering
Title XVII	Title XX
Article 130u	Article 177
Article 130v	Article 178
Article 130w	Article 179
Article 130x	Article 180
Article 130y	Article 181
Part Four	Part Four
Article 131	Article 182
Article 132	Article 183
Article 133	Article 184
Article 134	Article 185
Article 135	Article 186
Article 136	Article 187
Article 136a	Article 188
Part Five Title I Chapter 1 Section 1	Part Five Title I Chapter 1 Section 1
Article 137	Article 189
Article 138	Article 190
Article 138a	Article 191
Article 138b	Article 192
Article 138c	Article 193
Article 138d	Article 194
Article 138e	Article 195
Article 139	Article 196
Article 140	Article 197
Article 141	Article 198
Article 142	Article 199
Article 143	Article 200
Article 144	Article 201
Section 2	Section 2
Article 145	Article 202
Article 146	Article 203
Article 147	Article 204
Article 148	Article 205
Article 149 (repealed)	—
Article 150	Article 206
Article 151	Article 207
Article 152	Article 208
Article 153	Article 209
Article 154	Article 210
Section 3	Section 3
Article 155	Article 211
Article 156	Article 212
Article 157	Article 213
Article 158	Article 214
Article 159	Article 215
Article 160	Article 216
Article 161	Article 217
Article 162	Article 218
Article 163	Article 219

Previous numbering	New numbering
Section 4	Section 4
Article 164	Article 220
Article 165	Article 221
Article 166	Article 222
Article 167	Article 223
Article 168	Article 224
Article 168a	Article 225
Article 169	Article 226
Article 170	Article 227
Article 171	Article 228
Article 172	Article 229
Article 173	Article 230
Article 174	Article 231
Article 175	Article 232
Article 176	Article 233
Article 177	Article 234
Article 178	Article 235
Article 179	Article 236
Article 180	Article 237
Article 181	Article 238
Article 182	Article 239
Article 183	Article 240
Article 184	Article 241
Article 185	Article 242
Article 186	Article 243
Article 187	Article 244
Article 188	Article 245
Section 5	Section 5
Article 188a	Article 246
Article 188b	Article 247
Article 188c	Article 248
Chapter 2	Chapter 2
Article 189	Article 249
Article 189a	Article 250
Article 189b	Article 251
Article 189c	Article 252
Article 190	Article 253
Article 191	Article 254
Article 191a	Article 255
Article 192	Article 256
Chapter 3	Chapter 3
Article 193	Article 257
Article 194	Article 258
Article 195	Article 259
Article 196	Article 260
Article 197	Article 261
Article 198	Article 262
Chapter 4	Chapter 4
Article 198a	Article 263
Article 198b	Article 264
Article 198c	Article 265

Previous numbering	New numbering
Chapter 5	Chapter 5
Article 198d	Article 266
Article 198e	Article 267
Title II	Title II
Article 199	Article 268
Article 200 (repealed)	—
Article 201	Article 269
Article 201a	Article 270
Article 202	Article 271
Article 203	Article 272
Article 204	Article 273
Article 205	Article 274
Article 205a	Article 275
Article 206	Article 276
Article 206a (repealed)	—
Article 207	Article 277
Article 208	Article 278
Article 209	Article 279
Article 209a	Article 280
Part Six	Part Six
Article 210	Article 281
Article 211	Article 282
Article 212	Article 283
Article 213	Article 284
Article 213a	Article 285
Article 213b	Article 286
Article 214	Article 287
Article 215	Article 288
Article 216	Article 289
Article 217	Article 290
Article 218	Article 291
Article 219	Article 292
Article 220	Article 293
Article 221	Article 294
Article 222	Article 295
Article 223	Article 296
Article 224	Article 297
Article 225	Article 298
Article 226 (repealed)	—
Article 227	Article 299
Article 228	Article 300
Article 228a	Article 301
Article 229	Article 302
Article 230	Article 303
Article 231	Article 304
Article 232	Article 305
Article 233	Article 306
Article 234	Article 307
Article 235	Article 308
Article 236	Article 309
Article 237 (repealed)	—
Article 238	Article 310
Article 239	Article 311
Article 240	Article 312

Previous numbering	New numbering
Part Six—*cont.*	Part Six—*cont.*
Article 241 (repealed)	—
Article 242 (repealed)	—
Article 243 (repealed)	—
Article 244 (repealed)	—
Article 245 (repealed)	—
Article 246 (repealed)	—
Final Provisions	Final Provisions
Article 247	Article 313
Article 248	Article 314

SELECTED DECLARATIONS ADOPTED BY THE CONFERENCE ANNEXED TO THE FINAL ACT

1. Declaration on the abolition of the death penalty

3–013 With reference to Article [6(2)] of the Treaty on European Union, the Conference recalls that Protocol No. 6 to the European Convention for the Protection of Human Rights and Fundamental Freedoms signed in Rome on 4 November 1950 and which has been signed and ratified by a large majority of Member States, provides for the abolition of the death penalty.

In this context, the Conference notes the fact that since the signature of the abovementioned Protocol on 28 April 1983 the death penalty has been abolished in most of the Member States of the Union and has not been applied in any of them.

4. Declaration on Articles [24] and [38] of the Treaty on European Union

3–014 The provisions of Articles [24] and [38][6] of the Treaty on European Union and any agreements resulting from them shall not imply any transfer of competence from the Member States to the European Union.

7. Declaration on Article [30] of the Treaty on European Union

3–015 Action in the field of police co-operation under Article [30][7] of the Treaty on European Union, including activities of Europol, shall be subject to appropriate judicial review by the competent national authorities in accordance with rules applicable in each Member State.

8. Declaration on Article [31(e)] of the Treaty on European Union

3–016 The Conference agrees that the provisions of Article [31(e)][8] of the Treaty on European Union shall not have the consequence of obliging a Member State whose legal system does not provide for minimum sentences to adopt them.

[6] Formerly Art. J.14 and K.10 respectively.
[7] Formerly Art. K.2.
[8] Formerly Art. K.3(e).

9. Declaration on Article [34](2) Of The Treaty On European Union

The Conference agrees that initiatives for measures referred to in Article [34](2)[9] of the Treaty on European Union and Acts adopted by the Council thereunder shall be published in the *Official Journal of the European Communities*, in accordance with the relevant Rules of Procedure of the Council and the Commission. **3–017**

10. Declaration on Article [35] of the Treaty on European Union[10]

The Conference notes that Member States may, when making a declaration pursuant to Article [35](2) of the Treaty on European Union, reserve the right to make provisions in their national law to the effect that, where a question relating to the validity or interpretation of an Act referred to in Article [35](1) is raised in a case pending before a national court or tribunal against whose decision there is no judicial remedy under national law, that court or tribunal will be required to refer the matter to the Court of Justice. **3–018**

11. Declaration on the status of churches and non-confessional organisations

The European Union respects and does not prejudice the status under national law of churches and religious associations or communities in the Member States. **3–019**

The European Union equally respects the status of philosophical and non-confessional organisations.

12. Declaration on environmental impact assessments

The Conference notes that the Commission undertakes to prepare environmental impact assessment studies when making proposals which may have significant environmental implications. **3–020**

13. Declaration on Article [16] of the Treaty establishing the European Community

The provisions of Article [16][11] of the Treaty establishing the European Community on public services shall be implemented with full respect for the jurisprudence of the Court of Justice, *inter alia*, as regards the principles of equality of treatment, quality and continuity of such services. **3–021**

15. Declaration on the preservation of the level of protection and security provided by the Schengen *acquis*

The Conference agrees that measures to be adopted by the Council, which will have the effect of replacing provisions on the abolition of checks at common borders contained in the 1990 Schengen Convention, should provide at least the same level of protection and security as under the aforementioned provisions of the Schengen Convention. **3–022**

16. Declaration on Article [62](2)(b) of the Treaty establishing the European Community

The Conference agrees that foreign policy considerations of the Union and the Member States shall be taken into account in the application of Article [62](2)(b)[12] of the Treaty establishing the European Community. **3–023**

---

[9] Formerly Art. K.6(2).
[10] Formerly Art. K.7.
[11] Formerly Art. 7d.
[12] Formerly Art. 73j(2)(b).

17. Declaration on Article [63] of the Treaty establishing the European Community[13]

3–024 Consultations shall be established with the United Nations High Commissioner for Refugees and other relevant international organisations on matters relating to asylum policy.

18. Declaration on Article [63](3)(a) of the Treaty establishing the European Community

3–025 The Conference agrees that Member States may negotiate and conclude agreements with third countries in the domains covered by Article [63](3)(a)[14] of the Treaty establishing the European Community as long as such agreements respect Community law.

19. Declaration on Article [64](1) of the Treaty establishing the European Community

3–026 The Conference agrees that Member States may take into account foreign policy considerations when exercising their responsibilities under Article [64](1)[15] of the Treaty establishing the European Community.

20. Declaration on Article [65] of the Treaty establishing the European Community

3–027 Measures adopted pursuant to Article [65][16] of the Treaty establishing the European Community shall not prevent any Member State from applying its constitutional rules relating to freedom of the press and freedom of expression in other media.

22. Declaration regarding persons with a disability

3–028 The Conference agrees that, in drawing up measures under Article [95][17] of the Treaty establishing the European Community, the institutions of the Community shall take account of the needs of persons with a disability.

23. Declaration on incentive measures referred to in Article [129] of the Treaty establishing the European Community

3–029 The Conference agrees that the incentive measures referred to in Article [129][18] of the Treaty establishing the European Community should always specify the following:

— the grounds for taking them based on an objective assessment of their need and the existence of an added value at Community level;
— their duration, which should not exceed five years;
— the maximum amount for their financing, which should reflect the incentive nature of such measures.

24. Declaration on Article [129] of the Treaty establishing the European Community

3–030 It is understood that any expenditure under Article [129][19] of the Treaty establishing the European Community will fall within Heading 3 of the financial perspectives.

[13] Formerly Art. 73k.
[14] Formerly Art. 73k(3)(a).
[15] Formerly Art. 73l.
[16] Formerly Art. 73m.
[17] Formerly Art. 100a.
[18] Formerly Art. 109r.
[19] *ibid.*

25. Declaration on Article [137] of the Treaty establishing the European Community

It is understood that any expenditure under Article [137][20] of the Treaty establishing the European Community will fall within Heading 3 of the financial perspectives. **3–031**

26. Declaration on Article [137](2) of the Treaty establishing the European Community

The High Contracting Parties note that in the discussions on Article [137](2)[21] of the Treaty establishing the European Community it was agreed that the Community does not intend, in laying down minimum requirements for the protection of the safety and health of employees, to discriminate in a manner unjustified by the circumstances against employees in small and medium-sized undertakings. **3–032**

27. Declaration on Article [139](2) of the Treaty establishing the European Community

The High Contracting Parties declare that the first of the arrangements for application of the agreements between management and labour at Community level—referred to in Article [139](2)[22] of the Treaty establishing the European Community—will consist in developing, by collective bargaining according to the rules of each Member State, the content of the agreements, and that consequently this arrangement implies no obligation on the Member States to apply the agreements directly or to work out rules for their transposition, nor any obligation to amend national legislation in force to facilitate their implementation. **3–033**

28. Declaration on Article [141](4) of the Treaty establishing the European Community

When adopting measures referred to in Article [141](4)[23] of the Treaty establishing the European Community, Member States should, in the first instance, aim at improving the situation of women in working life. **3–034**

29. Declaration on sport

The Conference emphasises the social significance of sport, in particular its role in forging identity and bringing people together. The Conference therefore calls on the bodies of the European Union to listen to sports associations when important questions affecting sport are at issue. In this connection, special consideration should be given to the particular characteristics of amateur sport. **3–035**

30. Declaration on island regions

The Conference recognises that island regions suffer from structural handicaps linked to their island status, the permanence of which impairs their economic and social development. **3–036**

---

[20] Formerly Art. 118.
[21] Formerly Art. 118(2).
[22] Formerly Art. 118b(2).
[23] Formerly Art. 119(4).

The Conference accordingly acknowledges that Community legislation must take account of these handicaps and that specific measures may be taken, where justified, in favour of these regions in order to integrate them better into the internal market on fair conditions.

33. Declaration on Article [248](3) of the Treaty establishing the European Community[24]

3–037 The Conference invites the Court of Auditors, the European Investment Bank and the Commission to maintain in force the present Tripartite Agreement. If a succeeding or amending text is required by any Party, they shall endeavour to reach agreement on such a text having regard to their respective interests.

34. Declaration on respect for time-limits under the co-decision procedure

3–038 The Conference calls on the European Parliament, the Council and the Commission to make every effort to ensure that the co-decision procedure operates as expeditiously as possible. It recalls the importance of strict respect for the deadlines set out in Article [251][25] of the Treaty establishing the European Community and confirms that recourse, provided for in paragraph 7 of that Article, to extension of the periods in question should be considered only when strictly necessary. In no case should the actual period between the second reading by the European Parliament and the outcome of the Conciliation Committee exceed nine months.

35. Declaration on Article [255](1) of the Treaty establishing the European Community

3–039 The Conference agrees that the principles and conditions referred to in Article [255](1)[26] of the Treaty establishing the European Community will allow a Member State to request the Commission or the Council not to communicate to third parties a document originating from that State without its prior agreement.

37. Declaration on public credit institutions in Germany

3–040 The Conference notes the Commission's opinion to the effect that the Community's existing competition rules allow services of general economic interest provided by public credit institutions existing in Germany and the facilities granted to them to compensate for the costs connected with such services to be taken into account in full. In this context, the way in which Germany enables local authorities to carry out their task of making available in their regions a comprehensive and efficient financial infrastructure is a matter for the organisation of that Member State. Such facilities may not adversely affect the conditions of competition to an extent beyond that required in order to perform these particular tasks and which is contrary to the interests of the Community.

The Conference recalls that the European Council has invited the Commission to examine whether similar cases exist in the other Member States, to apply as appropriate the same standards on similar cases and to inform the Council in its ECOFIN formation.

38. Declaration on voluntary service activities

3–041 The Conference recognises the important contribution made by voluntary service activities to developing social solidarity.

[24] Formerly Art. 188c(3).
[25] Formerly Art. 189b.
[26] Formerly Art. 191a.

The Community will encourage the European dimension of voluntary organisations with particular emphasis on the exchange of information and experiences as well as on the participation of the young and the elderly in voluntary work.

39. Declaration on the quality of the drafting of Community legislation

The Conference notes that the quality of the drafting of Community legislation is crucial if it is to be properly implemented by the competent national authorities and better understood by the public and in business circles. It recalls the conclusions on this subject reached by the Presidency of the European Council in Edinburgh on 11 and 12 December 1992 as well as the Council Resolution on the quality of drafting of Community legislation adopted on 8 June 1993 [1993] (OJ C166/1). **3–042**

The Conference considers that the three institutions involved in the procedure for adopting Community legislation, the European Parliament, the Council and the Commission, should lay down guidelines on the quality of drafting of the said legislation. It also stresses that Community legislation should be made more accessible and welcomes in this regard the adoption and first implementation of an accelerated working method for official codification of legislative texts, established by the Interinstitutional Agreement of 20 December 1994 [1996] (OJ C102/2).

Therefore, the Conference declares that the European Parliament, the Council and the Commission ought to:

- establish by common accord guidelines for improving the quality of the drafting of Community legislation and follow those guidelines when considering proposals for Community legislation or draft legislation, taking the internal organisational measures they deem necessary to ensure that these guidelines are properly applied;[27]
- make their best efforts to accelerate the codification of legislative texts.

41. Declaration on the provisions relating to transparency, access to documents and the fight against fraud

The Conference considers that the European Parliament, the Council and the Commission, when they act in pursuance of the Treaty establishing the European Coal and Steel Community and the Treaty establishing the European Atomic Energy Community, should draw guidance from the provisions relating to transparency, access to documents and the fight against fraud in force within the framework of the Treaty establishing the European Community. **3–043**

42. Declaration on the consolidation of the Treaties

The High Contracting Parties agreed that the technical work begun during the course of this Intergovernmental Conference shall continue as speedily as possible with the aim of drafting a consolidation of all the relevant treaties, including the Treaty on European Union. **3–044**

They agreed that the final results of this technical work, which shall be made public for illustrative purposes under the responsibility of the Secretary-General of the Council, shall have no legal value.

43. Declaration relating to the Protocol on the application of the principles of subsidiarity and proportionality

The High Contracting Parties confirm, on the one hand, the Declaration on the implementation of Community law annexed to the Final Act of the Treaty on **3–045**

[27] See the Interinstitutional Agreement of 22 December 1998, on common guidelines for drafting of Community legislation ([1999] OJ C73/1).

European Union and, on the other, the conclusions of the Essen European Council stating that the administrative implementation of Community law shall in principle be the responsibility of the Member States in accordance with their constitutional arrangements. This shall not affect the supervisory, monitoring and implementing powers of the Community Institutions as provided under Articles [202] and [211][28] of the Treaty establishing the European Community.

44. Declaration on Article 2 of the Protocol integrating the Schengen *acquis* into the framework of the European Union

3–046 The High Contracting Parties agree that the Council shall adopt all the necessary measures referred to in Article 2 of the Protocol integrating the Schengen *acquis* into the framework of the European Union upon the date of entry into force of the Treaty of Amsterdam. To that end, the necessary preparatory work shall be undertaken in due time in order to be completed prior to that date.

45. Declaration on Article 4 of the Protocol integrating the Schengen *acquis* into the framework of the European Union

3–047 The High Contracting Parties invite the Council to seek the opinion of the Commission before it decides on a request under Article 4 of the Protocol integrating the Schengen *acquis* into the framework of the European Union by Ireland or the United Kingdom of Great Britain and Northern Ireland to take part in some or all of the provisions of the Schengen *acquis*. They also undertake to make their best efforts with a view to allowing Ireland or the United Kingdom of Great Britain and Northern Ireland, if they so wish, to use the provisions of Article 4 of the said protocol so that the Council may be in a position to take the decisions referred to in that Article upon the date of entry into force of that protocol or at any time thereafter.

46. Declaration on Article 5 of the Protocol integrating the Schengen *acquis* into the framework of the European Union

3–048 The High Contracting Parties undertake to make all efforts in order to make action among all Member States possible in the domains of the Schengen *acquis*, in particular whenever Ireland and the United Kingdom of Great Britain and Northern Ireland have accepted some or all of the provisions of that *acquis* in accordance with Article 4 of the Protocol integrating the Schengen *acquis* into the framework of the European Union.

47. Declaration on Article 6 of the Protocol integrating the Schengen *acquis* into the framework of the European Union

3–049 The High Contracting Parties agree to take all necessary steps so that the Agreements referred to in Article 6 of the Protocol integrating the Schengen *acquis* into the framework of the European Union may enter into force on the same date as the date of entry into force of the Treaty of Amsterdam.

48. Declaration relating to the Protocol on asylum for nationals of Member States of the European Union

3–050 The Protocol on asylum for nationals of Member States of the European Union does not prejudice the right of each Member State to take the organisational

[28] Formerly Art. 145 and 155 respectively.

measures it deems necessary to fulfil its obligations under the Geneva Convention of 28 July 1951 relating to the status of refugees.

49. Declaration relating to sub-paragraph (d) of the Sole Article of the Protocol on asylum for nationals of Member States of the European Union

The Conference declares that, while recognising the importance of the Resolution of the Ministers of the Member States of the European Communities responsible for immigration of 30 November/1 December 1992, on manifestly unfounded applications for asylum and of the Resolution of the Council of 20 June 1995 on minimum guarantees for asylum procedures, the question of abuse of asylum procedures and appropriate rapid procedures to dispense with manifestly unfounded applications for asylum should be further examined with a view to introducing new improvements in order to accelerate these procedures. **3–051**

50. Declaration relating to the Protocol on the institutions with the prospect of enlargement of the European Union

Until the entry into force of the first enlargement it is agreed that the decision of the Council of 29 March 1994 ("the Ioannina Compromise")[29] will be extended and, by that date, a solution for the special case of Spain will be found. **3–052**

51. Declaration on Article 10 of the Treaty of Amsterdam

The Treaty of Amsterdam repeals and deletes lapsed provisions of the Treaty establishing the European Community, the Treaty establishing the European Coal and Steel Community and the Treaty establishing the European Atomic Energy Community as they were in force before the entry into force of the Treaty of Amsterdam and adapts certain of their provisions, including the insertion of certain provisions of the Treaty establishing a single Council and a single Commission of the European Communities and the Act concerning the election of the representatives of the European Parliament by direct universal suffrage. Those operations do not affect the "*acquis communautaire*". **3–053**

SELECTED DECLARATIONS OF WHICH THE CONFERENCE TOOK NOTE

1. Declaration by Austria and Luxembourg on credit institutions

Austria and Luxembourg consider that the Declaration on public credit institutions in Germany also applies to credit institutions in Austria and Luxembourg with a comparable organisational structure. **3–054**

2. Declaration by Denmark on Article [42] of the Treaty on European Union

Article [42][30] of the Treaty on European Union requires the unanimity of all members of the Council of the European Union, *i.e.* all Member States, for the adoption of any decision to apply the provisions of Title [IV][31] of the Treaty establishing the European Community on visas, asylum, immigration and other policies related to free movement of persons to action in areas referred to in Article [29].[32] Moreover, any unanimous Decision of the Council, before coming into force, will have to be adopted in each Member State, in accordance with its constitutional requirements. In Denmark, such adoption will, in the case of a transfer of sovereignty, as defined in the Danish constitution, require either a **3–055**

[29] See [1994] OJ L291/2; amended at [1995] OJ C1/1.
[30] Formerly Art. K.14.
[31] Formerly Title IIIa.
[32] Formerly Art. K.1.

majority of five-sixths of members of the Folketing or both a majority of the members of the Folketing and a majority of voters in a referendum.

3. Declaration by Germany, Austria and Belgium on subsidiarity

3–056 It is taken for granted by the German, Austrian and Belgian Governments that action by the European Community in accordance with the principle of subsidiarity not only concerns the Member States but also their entities to the extent that they have their own law-making powers conferred on them under national constitutional law.

4. Declaration by Ireland on Article 3 of the Protocol on the position of the United Kingdom and Ireland

3–057 Ireland declares that it intends to exercise its right under Article 3 of the Protocol on the position of the United Kingdom and Ireland to take part in the adoption of measures pursuant to Title [IV][33] of the Treaty establishing the European Community to the maximum extent compatible with the maintenance of its Common Travel Area with the United Kingdom. Ireland recalls that its participation in the Protocol on the application of certain aspects of Article [14][34] of the Treaty establishing the European Community reflects its wish to maintain its Common Travel Area with the United Kingdom in order to maximise freedom of movement into and out of Ireland.

5. Declaration by Belgium on the Protocol on asylum for nationals of Member States of the European Union

3–058 In approving the Protocol on asylum for nationals of Member States of the European Union, Belgium declares that, in accordance with its obligations under the 1951 Geneva Convention and the 1967 New York Protocol, it shall, in accordance with the provision set out in point (d) of the Sole Article of that Protocol, carry out an individual examination of any asylum request made by a national of another Member State.

7. Declaration by France concerning the situation of the overseas departments in the light of the Protocol integrating the Schengen *acquis* into the framework of the European Union

3–059 France considers that the implementation of the Protocol integrating the Schengen *acquis* into the framework of the European Union does not affect the geographical scope of the Convention implementing the Schengen Agreement of 14 June 1985, signed in Schengen on 19 June 1990 as it is defined by Article 138, first paragraph, of that Convention.

8. Declaration by Greece concerning the declaration on the status of churches and non-confessional organisations

3–060 With reference to the Declaration on the status of churches and non-confessional organisations, Greece recalls the Joint Declaration on Mount Athos annexed to the Final Act of the Treaty of Accession of Greece to the European Communities.

[33] Formerly Title IIIa.
[34] Formerly Art. 7a.

Treaty of Nice

Amending The Treaty on European Union, the Treaties Establishing the European Communities and Certain Related Acts

(26 February 2001)

([2001] OJ C80/1; Doc. Ref. 101C000)

[**Editorial note:** The Treaty of Nice entered into force on 1 February 2003. The amendments it makes to the Treaty on European Union and to the Treaty establishing the European Community have been included at the relevant points in those treaties and hence are not reproduced below. Similarly the texts of the protocols annexed by this treaty to those two treaties are reproduced in the chapter on the Treaty establishing the European Community and are not reproduced below.]

His Majesty the King of the Belgians, Her Majesty the Queen of Denmark, the President of the Federal Republic of Germany, the President of the Hellenic Republic, His Majesty the King of Spain, the President of the French Republic, the President of Ireland, the President of the Italian Republic, His Royal Highness the Grand Duke of Luxembourg, Her Majesty the Queen of the Netherlands, the Federal President of the Republic of Austria, the President of the Portuguese Republic, the President of the Republic of Finland, His Majesty the King of Sweden, Her Majesty the Queen of the United Kingdom of Great Britain and Northern Ireland, **3–061**

[1] Recalling the historic importance of the ending of the division of the European continent,

[2] Desiring to complete the process started by the Treaty of Amsterdam of preparing the institutions of the European Union to function in an enlarged Union,

[3] Determined on this basis to press ahead with the accession negotiations in order to bring them to a successful conclusion, in accordance with the procedure laid down in the Treaty on European Union,

Have resolved to amend the Treaty on European Union, the Treaties establishing the European Communities and certain related acts, and to this end have designated as their Plenipotentiaries:

[designation of Plenipotentiaries omitted]

Who, having exchanged their full powers found in good and due form, *have agreed as follows*:

PART ONE—SUBSTANTIVE AMENDMENTS

Article 1 [Amendments to the EU Treaty]

The Treaty on European Union shall be amended in accordance with the provisions of this Article. **3–062**

[Amendments not reproduced here]

Article 2 [Amendments to the EC Treaty]

The Treaty establishing the European Community shall be amended in accordance with the provisions of this Article. **3–063**

[Amendments not reproduced here]

...

Article 5 [Amendment to ESCB and ECB Protocol]

3–064 The Protocol on the Statute of the European System of Central Banks and of the European Central Bank shall be amended in accordance with the provisions of this Article.
[Amendment not reproduced here]
...

PART TWO—TRANSITIONAL AND FINAL PROVISIONS

Article 7 [Substitution of ECJ Protocols]

3–065 The Protocols on the Statute of the Court of Justice annexed to the Treaty establishing the European Community and to the Treaty establishing the European Atomic Energy Community are hereby repealed and replaced by the Protocol on the Statute of the Court of Justice annexed by this Treaty to the Treaty on European Union, to the Treaty establishing the European Community and to the Treaty establishing the European Atomic Energy Community.
...

Article 10 [Repeal of CFI decision]

3–066 Council Decision 88/591/ECSC, EEC, Euratom of 24 October 1988 establishing a Court of First Instance of the European Communities, as amended, is hereby repealed, with the exception of Article 3 insofar as the Court of First Instance exercises, pursuant to the said Article, the jurisdiction conferred on the Court of Justice by the Treaty establishing the European Coal and Steel Community.

Article 11 [Duration of Treaty]

3–067 This Treaty is concluded for an unlimited period.

Article 12 [Ratification and entry into force]

3–068 1. This Treaty shall be ratified by the High Contracting Parties in accordance with their respective constitutional requirements. The instruments of ratification shall be deposited with the Government of the Italian Republic.
2. This Treaty shall enter into force on the first day of the second month following that in which the instrument of ratification is deposited by the last signatory State to fulfil that formality.[35]

Article 13 [Authentic texts]

3–069 This Treaty, drawn up in a single original in the Danish, Dutch, English, Finnish, French, German, Greek, Irish, Italian, Portuguese, Spanish and Swedish languages, the texts in each of these languages being equally authentic, shall be deposited in the archives of the Government of the Italian Republic, which will transmit a certified copy to each of the governments of the other signatory States.

[35] Treaty of Nice entered into force 1 February 2003.

In witness whereof the undersigned Plenipotentiaries have signed this Treaty.

Done at Nice this twenty-sixth day of February in the year two thousand and one.
[Signatures of Plenipotentiaries omitted]

SELECTED DECLARATIONS ADOPTED BY THE CONFERENCE ANNEXED TO THE FINAL ACT

2. Declaration on Article 31(2) of the Treaty on European Union

The Conference recalls that: **3–070**

- the decision to set up a unit composed of national prosecutors, magistrates or police officers of equivalent competence, detached from each Member State (Eurojust), having the task of facilitating proper co-ordination between national prosecuting authorities and of supporting criminal investigations in organised crime cases, was provided for in the Presidency conclusions of the European Council at Tampere on 15 and 16 October 1999;
- the European Judicial Network was set up by Joint Action 98/428/JHA adopted by the Council on 29 June 1998 ([1998] OJ L191/4).

3. Declaration on Article 10 of the Treaty establishing the European Community

The Conference recalls that the duty of sincere cooperation which derives from **3–071** Article 10 of the Treaty establishing the European Community and governs relations between the Member States and the Community institutions also governs relations between the Community institutions themselves. In relations between those institutions, when it proves necessary, in the context of that duty of sincere cooperation, to facilitate the application of the provisions of the Treaty establishing the European Community, the European Parliament, the Council and the Commission may conclude interinstitutional agreements. Such agreements may not amend or supplement the provisions of the Treaty and may be concluded only with the agreement of these three institutions.

4. Declaration on the third paragraph of Article 21 of the Treaty establishing the European Community

The Conference calls upon the institutions and bodies referred to in the third **3–072** paragraph of Article 21 or in Article 7 to ensure that the reply to any written request by a citizen of the Union is made within a reasonable period.

5. Declaration on Article 67 of the Treaty establishing the European Community

The High Contracting Parties agree that the Council, in the decision it is required **3–073** to take pursuant to the second indent of Article 67(2):

- will decide, from 1 May 2004, to act in accordance with the procedure referred to in Article 251 in order to adopt the measures referred to in Article 62(3) and Article 63(3)(b);
- will decide to act in accordance with the procedure referred to in Article 251 in order to adopt the measures referred to in Article 62(2)(a) from the date on which agreement is reached on the scope of the measures concerning the crossing by persons of the external borders of the Member States.

The Council will, moreover, endeavour to make the procedure referred to in Article 251 applicable from 1 May 2004 or as soon as possible thereafter to the other areas covered by Title IV or to parts of them.

6. Declaration on Article 100 of the Treaty establishing the European Community

3–074 The Conference recalls that decisions regarding financial assistance, such as are provided for in Article 100 and are compatible with the "no bail-out" rule laid down in Article 103, must comply with the 2000–2006 financial perspective, and in particular paragraph 11 of the Interinstitutional Agreement of 6 May 1999 between the European Parliament, the Council and the Commission on budgetary discipline and improvement of the budgetary procedure, and with the corresponding provisions of future interinstitutional agreements and financial perspectives.

7. Declaration on Article 111 of the Treaty establishing the European Community

3–075 The Conference agrees that procedures shall be such as to enable all the Member States in the euro area to be fully involved in each stage of preparing the position of the Community at international level as regards issues of particular relevance to economic and monetary union.

8. Declaration on Article 137 of the Treaty establishing the European Community

3–076 The Conference agrees that any expenditure incurred by virtue of Article 137 is to be charged to heading 3 of the financial perspective.

9. Declaration on Article 175 of the Treaty establishing the European Community

3–077 The High Contracting Parties are determined to see the European Union play a leading role in promoting environmental protection in the Union and in international efforts pursuing the same objective at global level. Full use should be made of all possibilities offered by the Treaty with a view to pursuing this objective, including the use of incentives and instruments which are market-oriented and intended to promote sustainable development.

10. Declaration on Article 181a of the Treaty establishing the European Community

3–078 The Conference confirms that, without prejudice to other provisions of the Treaty establishing the European Community, balance-of-payments aid to third countries falls outside the scope of Article 181a.

11. Declaration on Article 191 of the Treaty establishing the European Community

3–079 The Conference recalls that the provisions of Article 191 do not imply any transfer of powers to the European Community and do not affect the application of the relevant national constitutional rules.

The funding for political parties at European level provided out of the budget of the European Communities may not be used to fund, either directly or indirectly, political parties at national level.

The provisions on the funding for political parties shall apply, on the same basis, to all the political forces represented in the European Parliament.

12. Declaration on Article 225 of the Treaty establishing the European Community

The Conference calls on the Court of Justice and the Commission to give overall **3–080** consideration as soon as possible to the division of jurisdiction between the Court of Justice and the Court of First Instance, in particular in the area of direct actions, and to submit suitable proposals for examination by the competent bodies as soon as the Treaty of Nice enters into force.

13. Declaration on Article 225(2) and (3) of the Treaty establishing the European Community

The Conference considers that the essential provisions of the review procedure in **3–081** Article 225(2) and (3) should be defined in the Statute of the Court of Justice. Those provisions should in particular specify:

- the role of the parties in proceedings before the Court of Justice, in order to safeguard their rights;
- the effect of the review procedure on the enforceability of the decision of the Court of First Instance;
- the effect of the Court of Justice decision on the dispute between the parties.

14. Declaration on Article 225(2) and (3) of the Treaty establishing the European Community

The Conference considers that when the Council adopts the provisions of the **3–082** Statute which are necessary to implement Article 225(2) and (3), it should put a procedure in place to ensure that the practical operation of those provisions is evaluated no later than three years after the entry into force of the Treaty of Nice.

15. Declaration on Article 225(3) of the Treaty establishing the European Community

The Conference considers that, in exceptional cases in which the Court of Justice **3–083** decides to review a decision of the Court of First Instance on a question referred for a preliminary ruling, it should act under an emergency procedure.

16. Declaration on Article 225a of the Treaty establishing the European Community

The Conference asks the Court of Justice and the Commission to prepare as **3–084** swiftly as possible a draft decision establishing a judicial panel which has jurisdiction to deliver judgments at first instance on disputes between the Community and its servants.

17. Declaration on Article 229a of the Treaty establishing the European Community

The Conference considers that Article 229a does not prejudge the choice of the **3–085** judicial framework which may be set up to deal with disputes relating to the application of acts adopted on the basis of the Treaty establishing the European Community which create Community industrial property rights.

18. Declaration on the Court of Auditors

3–086 The Conference invites the Court of Auditors and the national audit institutions to improve the framework and conditions for co-operation between them, while maintaining the autonomy of each. To that end, the President of the Court of Auditors may set up a contact committee with the chairmen of the national audit institutions.

19. Declaration on Article 10.6 of the Statute of the European System of Central Banks and of the European Central Bank

3–087 The Conference expects that a recommendation within the meaning of Article 10.6 of the Statute of the European System of Central Banks and of the European Central Bank will be presented as soon as possible.

20. Declaration on the enlargement of the European Union[36]

3–088 The common position to be adopted by the Member States at the accession conferences, as regards the distribution of seats at the European Parliament, the weighting of votes in the Council, the composition of the Economic and Social Committee and the composition of the Committee of the Regions will correspond to the following tables for a Union of 27 Member States.

1. The European Parliament

Member States	EP seats
Germany	99
United Kingdom	72
France	72
Italy	72
Spain	50
Poland	50
Romania	33
Netherlands	25
Greece	22
Czech Republic	20
Belgium	22
Hungary	20
Portugal	22
Sweden	18
Bulgaria	17
Austria	17
Slovakia	13
Denmark	13
Finland	13
Ireland	12
Lithuania	12
Latvia	8
Slovenia	7
Estonia	6

[36] The tables in this declaration take account only of those candidate countries with which accession negotiations have actually started.

Cyprus	6
Luxembourg	6
Malta	5
Total	**732**

2. The Weighting of Votes in the Council

Members of the Council	Weighted votes
Germany	29
United Kingdom	29
France	29
Italy	29
Spain	27
Poland	27
Romania	14
Netherlands	13
Greece	12
Czech Republic	12
Belgium	12
Hungary	12
Portugal	12
Sweden	10
Bulgaria	10
Austria	10
Slovakia	7
Denmark	7
Finland	7
Ireland	7
Lithuania	7
Latvia	4
Slovenia	4
Estonia	4
Cyprus	4
Luxembourg	4
Malta	3
Total	**345**

When a decision is to be adopted by the Council by a qualified majority, a member of the Council may request verification that the Member States constituting the qualified majority represent at least 62% of the total population of the Union. If that condition is shown not to have been met, the decision in question shall not be adopted.

3. The Economic and Social Committee

Member States	Members
Germany	24
United Kingdom	24
France	24
Italy	24
Spain	21
Poland	21
Romania	15
Netherlands	12
Greece	12
Czech Republic	12

Belgium	12
Hungary	12
Portugal	12
Sweden	12
Bulgaria	12
Austria	12
Slovakia	9
Denmark	9
Finland	9
Ireland	9
Lithuania	9
Latvia	7
Slovenia	7
Estonia	7
Cyprus	6
Luxembourg	6
Malta	5
Total	**344**

4. The Committee of the Regions

Member States	**Members**
Germany	24
United Kingdom	24
France	24
Italy	24
Spain	21
Poland	21
Romania	15
Netherlands	12
Greece	12
Czech Republic	12
Belgium	12
Hungary	12
Portugal	12
Sweden	12
Bulgaria	12
Austria	12
Slovakia	9
Denmark	9
Finland	9
Ireland	9
Lithuania	9
Latvia	7
Slovenia	7
Estonia	7
Cyprus	6
Luxembourg	6
Malta	5
Total	**344**

21. Declaration on the qualified majority threshold and the number of votes for a blocking minority in an enlarged Union

3–089 In so far as all the candidate countries listed in the Declaration on the enlargement of the European Union have not yet acceded to the Union when the new vote weightings take effect (1 January 2005), the threshold for a qualified majority will move, according to the pace of accessions, from a percentage below the current one to a maximum of 73.4 per cent. When all the candidate countries mentioned above have acceded, the blocking minority, in a Union of 27, will be raised to 91 votes, and the qualified majority threshold resulting from the table given in the Declaration on enlargement of the European Union will be automatically adjusted accordingly.

22. Declaration on the venue for European Councils

As from 2002, one European Council meeting per Presidency will be held in **3–090** Brussels. When the Union comprises 18 members, all European Council meetings will be held in Brussels.

23. Declaration on the future of the Union

1. Important reforms have been decided in Nice. The Conference welcomes the **3–091** successful conclusion of the Conference of Representatives of the Governments of the Member States and commits the Member States to pursue the early ratification of the Treaty of Nice.

2. It agrees that the conclusion of the Conference of Representatives of the Governments of the Member States opens the way for enlargement of the European Union and underlines that, with ratification of the Treaty of Nice, the European Union will have completed the institutional changes necessary for the accession of new Member States.

3. Having thus opened the way to enlargement, the Conference calls for a deeper and wider debate about the future of the European Union. In 2001, the Swedish and Belgian Presidencies, in co-operation with the Commission and involving the European Parliament, will encourage wide-ranging discussions with all interested parties: representatives of national parliaments and all those reflecting public opinion, namely political, economic and university circles, representatives of civil society, etc. The candidate States will be associated with this process in ways to be defined.

4. Following a report to be drawn up for the European Council in Göteborg in June 2001, the European Council, at its meeting in Laeken/Brussels in December 2001, will agree on a declaration containing appropriate initiatives for the continuation of this process.

5. The process should address, *inter alia*, the following questions:
- how to establish and monitor a more precise delimitation of powers between the European Union and the Member States, reflecting the principle of subsidiarity;
- the status of the Charter of Fundamental Rights of the European Union, proclaimed in Nice, in accordance with the conclusions of the European Council in Cologne;
- a simplification of the Treaties with a view to making them clearer and better understood without changing their meaning;
- the role of national parliaments in the European architecture.

6. Addressing the abovementioned issues, the Conference recognises the need to improve and to monitor the democratic legitimacy and transparency of the Union and its institutions, in order to bring them closer to the citizens of the Member States.

7. After these preparatory steps, the Conference agrees that a new Conference of the Representatives of the Governments of the Member States will be convened in 2004, to address the abovementioned items with a view to making corresponding changes to the Treaties.

8. The Conference of Member States shall not constitute any form of obstacle or pre-condition to the enlargement process. Moreover, those candidate States which have concluded accession negotiations with the Union will be invited to participate in the Conference. Those candidate States which have not concluded their accession negotiations will be invited as observers.

PART II: SPECIFIC TOPICS

CHAPTER 4

INSTITUTIONS

SECTION 1—LEGISLATION

Interinstitutional Agreement of 22 December 1998 on common guidelines for the quality of drafting of Community legislation

([1999] OJ C73/1; Doc. Ref. 31999Y0317(01))

The European Parliament, the Council of the European Union and The Commission of the European Communities,

Having regard to Declaration No. 39 on the quality of the drafting of Community legislation adopted on 2 October 1997 by the Intergovernmental Conference and annexed to the Final Act of the Treaty of Amsterdam, **4–001**

Whereas:

(1) clear, simple and precise drafting of Community legislative acts is essential if they are to be transparent and readily understandable by the public and economic operators. It is also a prerequisite for the proper implementation and uniform application of Community legislation in the Member States;

(2) according to the case law of the Court of Justice, the principle of legal certainty, which is part of the Community legal order, requires that Community legislation must be clear and precise and its application foreseeable by individuals. That requirement must be observed all the more strictly in the case of an act liable to have financial consequences and imposing obligations on individuals in order that those concerned may know precisely the extent of the obligations which it imposes on them;

(3) guidelines on the quality of drafting of Community legislation should therefore be adopted by common accord. These guidelines are intended as a guide for the Community institutions when they adopt legislative acts, and for those in the Community institutions who are involved in formulating and drafting such acts, whether at the stage of the initial text or that of the various amendments made to it in the course of the legislative procedure;

(4) these guidelines should be accompanied by measures to make sure that they are applied properly, with each institution adopting the relevant measures for its own use;

(5) the role played by the institutions' legal services, including their legal/linguistic experts, in improving the quality of drafting of Community legislative acts should be strengthened;

(6) these guidelines complement the efforts being made by the institutions to make Community legislation more accessible and easier to understand, particularly by means of the official codification of legislative acts, recasting and simplification of existing texts;

(7) these guidelines are to be regarded as instruments for internal use by the institutions. They are not legally binding,

Adopt these Guidelines by Common Accord:

General principles

1. Community legislative acts shall be drafted clearly, simply and precisely. **4–002**

2. The drafting of Community acts shall be appropriate to the type of act

concerned and, in particular, to whether or not it is binding (Regulation, Directive, Decision, recommendation or other act).

3. The drafting of acts shall take account of the persons to whom they are intended to apply, with a view to enabling them to identify their rights and obligations unambiguously, and of the persons responsible for putting the acts into effect.

4. Provisions of acts shall be concise and their content should be as homogeneous as possible. Overly long articles and sentences, unnecessarily convoluted wording and excessive use of abbreviations should be avoided.

5. Throughout the process leading to their adoption, draft acts shall be framed in terms and sentence structures which respect the multilingual nature of Community legislation concepts or terminology specific to any one national legal system are to be used with care.

6. The terminology used in a given act shall be consistent both internally and with acts already in force, especially in the same field. Identical concepts shall be expressed in the same terms, as far as possible without departing from their meaning in ordinary, legal or technical language.

Different parts of the act

4–003 7. All Community acts of general application shall be drafted according to a standard structure (title—preamble—enacting terms—annexes, where necessary).

8. The title of an act shall give as succinct and full an indication as possible of the subject matter which does not mislead the reader as to the content of the enacting terms. Where appropriate, the full title of the act may be followed by a short title.

9. The purpose of the citations is to set out the legal basis of the act and the main steps in the procedure leading to its adoption.

10. The purpose of the recitals is to set out concise reasons for the chief provisions of the enacting terms, without reproducing or paraphrasing them. They shall not contain normative provisions or political exhortations.

11. Each recital shall be numbered.

12. The enacting terms of a binding act shall not include provisions of a non-normative nature, such as wishes or political declarations, or those which repeat or paraphrase passages or articles from the Treaties or those which restate legal provisions already in force. Acts shall not include provisions which enunciate the content of other articles or repeat the title of the act.

13. Where appropriate, an article shall be included at the beginning of the enacting terms to define the subject matter and scope of the act.

14. Where the terms used in the act are not unambiguous, they should be defined together in a single article at the beginning of the act. The definitions shall not contain autonomous normative provisions.

15. As far as possible, the enacting terms shall have a standard structure (subject matter and scope—definitions—rights and obligations—provisions conferring implementing powers—procedural provisions—implementing measures—transitional and final provisions).

The enacting terms shall be subdivided into articles and, depending on their length and complexity, titles, chapters and sections. When an article contains a list, each item on the list should be identified by a number or a letter rather than an indent.

Internal and external references

16. References to other acts should be kept to a minimum. References shall indicate precisely the act or provision to which they refer. Circular references (references to an act or an article which itself refers back to the initial provision) and serial references (references to a provision which itself refers to another provision) shall also be avoided. **4–004**

17. A reference made in the enacting terms of a binding act to a non-binding Act shall not have the effect of making the latter binding. Should the drafters wish to render binding the whole or part of the content of the non-binding Act, its terms should as far as possible be set forth as part of the binding act.

Amending Acts

18. Every amendment of an act shall be clearly expressed. Amendments shall take the form of a text to be inserted in the act to be amended. Preference shall be given to replacing whole provisions (articles or subdivisions of articles) rather than inserting or deleting individual sentences, phrases or words. **4–005**

An amending act shall not contain autonomous substantive provisions which are not inserted in the act to be amended.

19. An Act not primarily intended to amend another act may set out, at the end, amendments of other acts which are a consequence of changes which it introduces. Where the consequential amendments are substantial, a separate amending act should be adopted.

Final provisions, repeals and annexes

20. Provisions laying down dates, time-limits, exceptions, derogations and extensions, transitional provisions (in particular those relating to the effects of the act on existing situations) and final provisions (entry into force, deadline for transposition and temporal application of the act) shall be drawn up in precise terms. **4–006**

Provisions on deadlines for the transposition and application of acts shall specify a date expressed as day/month/year. In the case of Directives, those deadlines shall be expressed in such a way as to guarantee an adequate period for transposition.

21. Obsolete acts and provisions shall be expressly repealed. The adoption of a new act should result in the express repeal of any act or provision rendered inapplicable or redundant by virtue of the new act.

22. Technical aspects of the act shall be contained in the annexes, to which individual reference shall be made in the enacting terms of the act and which shall not embody any new right or obligation not set forth in the enacting terms.

Annexes shall be drawn up in accordance with a standardised format,

Hereby Agree on the Following Implementing Measures:

The institutions shall take such measures relating to their internal organisation as they deem necessary in order to ensure that these guidelines are properly applied. **4–007**

In particular, the institutions:

(a) shall instruct their legal services to draw up, within one year after the publication of these guidelines, a joint practical guide for persons involved in the drafting of legislation;
(b) shall organise their respective internal procedures in such a way that their legal services, including their legal/linguistic experts, may, each for their own institution, make drafting suggestions in good time, with a view to applying these guidelines;
(c) shall foster the creation of drafting units within those bodies or departments within the institutions which are involved in the legislative process;
(d) shall ensure that their officials and other servants receive training in legal drafting, making them aware in particular of the effects of multilingualism on drafting quality;
(e) shall promote co-operation with the Member States with a view to improving understanding of the particular considerations to be taken into account when drafting texts;
(f) shall encourage the development and improvement of information technology tools for assisting legal drafting;
(g) shall foster collaboration between their respective departments responsible for ensuring the quality of drafting;
(h) shall instruct their respective legal services to draw up periodically, each for the institution to which it belongs, a report on the measures taken in pursuance of points (a) to (g).

Declaration by the European Parliament

4–008 The European Parliament considers that Community legislative acts must be self-explanatory and that the institutions and/or Member States must not adopt explanatory statements.

No provision is made for the adoption of explanatory statements in the Treaties and it is incompatible with the nature of Community law.

Council Statements

4–009 Like the European Parliament, the Council is of the opinion that legislative acts should be comprehensible in themselves. Recourse to statements interpreting legal acts should therefore be avoided where possible and the content of possible statements should, as appropriate, be included in the text of the act.

It should however be noted that insofar as they do not contradict the legislative Act concerned and they are made public (as provided for in [Article 207(3) of the EC Treaty]), such interpretative statements adopted by the Community legislator are compatible with Community law.

The Council finds it desirable that the general principles of good drafting which may be drawn from the "Common guidelines on the quality of drafting of Community legislation" serve, where appropriate, as an inspiration for the drafting of Acts adopted pursuant to Titles V and VI and of the Treaty on European Union.

The Council considers that, in order that the transparency of the Community decision-making process may be improved, it would be desirable for the Commission to provide in future for the statements of reasons accompanying its legislative proposals to be widely circulated to the public by the most appropriate means (for example, publication in the "C" series of the *Official Journal of the European Communities*, electronic distribution, or other).

The Council takes the view that, in addition to the adoption by the legislator of official codification of legislative acts, the Office for Official Publications of the European Communities should, with a view to improving access to Community legislation when the latter has been subject to frequent or substantial amendments, intensify its work of informally consolidating legislative acts and should improve the advertising of the availability of these texts. It would also be useful to examine with the other institutions the appropriateness of possible measures aimed at facilitating a more structured use of the recasting technique which combines the codification and the modifications of an Act in a single legislative text.

Interinstitutional Agreement of 28 November 2001 on a more structured use of the recasting technique for legal acts

([2002] OJ C77/1; Doc. Ref. 32002Q0328)

The European Parliament, the Council of the European Union and the Commission of the European Communities,
Whereas: **4–010**

(1) The European Council, meeting in Edinburgh in December 1992 underlined the importance for the Community of making Community legislation more accessible and comprehensible.

(2) On 20 December 1994 following the guidelines drawn up by the European Council, the European Parliament, the Council and the Commission concluded an Interinstitutional Agreement on an accelerated working method for official codification of legislative texts[1] with a view to substantially improving the readability of legal Acts which have been extensively amended.

(3) Experience shows, however, that despite the use of the accelerated method, the Commission's submission of official codification proposals and the legislature's adoption of official codification acts are often delayed, in particular because new amendments to the legal act in question have been adopted in the meanwhile, which leads to the codification work having to start all over again.

(4) It is therefore advisable, in particular with regard to frequently amended legal Acts, to use a legislative technique which enables amendments to, and codification of, Acts to be carried out within the framework of a single legislative text.

(5) In that context, where a substantive amendment has to be made to an earlier legal Act, the recasting technique permits the adoption of a single legislative text which simultaneously makes the desired amendment, codifies that amendment with the unchanged provisions of the earlier Act, and repeals that Act.

(6) Consequently, in so far as it prevents the proliferation of isolated amending acts which often make regulations difficult to understand, the recasting technique is an appropriate means of ensuring the readability of Community legislation on a permanent and universal basis.

(7) A more structured use of the recasting technique forms part of the measures undertaken by the institutions to make Community legislation more accessible, such as the adoption of the accelerated working method for official codification and the establishment of common guidelines for the quality of drafting of Community legislation through the Interinstitutional Agreement of 22 December 1998.[2]

(8) The European Council meeting in Helsinki in December 1999 wished an Interinstitutional Agreement on the use of the recasting technique to be concluded as quickly as possible by the European Parliament, the Councl and the Commission,

Have agreed as follows:

1. The aim of this Agreement is to lay down procedural rules enabling a more structured use to be made of the recasting technique pursuant to the Community's normal legislative process. **4–011**

[1] [1996] OJ C102/2.
[2] [1999] OJ C73/1.

2. Recasting shall consist in the adoption of a new legal act which incorporates in a single text both the substantive amendments which it makes to an earlier act and the unchanged provisions of that act. The new legal act replaces and repeals the earlier act.

3. A proposal for recasting submitted by the Commission shall deal with the substantive amendments which it makes to an earlier act. On a secondary level, the proposal shall include the codification of the unchanged provisions of the earlier act with those substantive amendments.

4. For the purposes of this Agreement:
— "earlier act" shall mean a legal act which is in force, and which may have been amended by one or more amending acts,
— "substantive amendment" shall mean any amendment which affects the substance of the earlier act as opposed to purely formal or editorial changes,
— "unchanged provision" shall mean any provision of the earlier act which, although it may be affected by purely formal or editorial changes, has not undergone any substantive amendment.

A new legal act shall not constitute a recast act if, with the exception of standardised provisions or wordings, it makes substantive amendments to all the provisions of the earlier act, which it replaces and repeals.

5. The Community's normal legislative process shall be complied with in full.

6. A proposal for recasting shall satisfy the following criteria:
(a) The explanatory memorandum accompanying the proposal shall:
  (i) state expressly that it relates to a proposal for recasting and explain the reasons for adopting such an approach;
  (ii) state the reasons for each proposed substantive amendment;
  (iii) specify which provisions of the earlier act remain unchanged.
(b) The proposed legislative text shall be presented in a way which:
  (i) enables the substantive amendments and new recitals to be clearly distinguished from the provisions and recitals which remain unchanged;
  (ii) with regard to the provisions and recitals which remain unchanged, is similar to the method used for presenting proposals for the official codification of legislative acts.

7. To ensure clarity and legal certainty, all recasting acts shall comply *inter alia*[3] with the following rules of legislative drafting:
(a) The first recital shall indicate that the new legal act constitutes a recasting of the earlier act.
(b) The article repealing the earlier Act shall provide that references to that Act shall be regarded as references to the recasting act and should be read in accordance with a correlation table annexed to the recasting Act.
(c) Moreover, in an act recasting a Directive:
  (i) the repealing article shall provide that Member States' obligations arising from the transposition period[4] and, where appropriate, the implementation period as set out in the Directive repealed by the recasting act shall not be affected by such repeal;
  (ii) the periods referred to in point (i) shall be set out in an annex in the form of a table;
  (iii) the article relating to the obligation to transpose[5] into national law a recast Directive shall refer only to those provisions which have undergone substantive amendment and which have been precisely identified as such.

---

[3] See, in particular, the Interinstitutional Agreement of 22 December 1998 on common guidelines for the quality of drafting of Community legislation (see above).

[4] That is, the period laid down for implementing the laws, regulations and administrative provisions necessary for complying with the provisions of the Directive.

[5] That is, the obligation to implement the laws, regulations and administrative provisions necessary for complying with the provisions of the Directive.

Those provisions which remain unchanged in the recast Directive shall be transposed in accordance with the earlier Directives.

8. Where, in the course of the legislative procedure, it appears necessary to introduce substantive amendments in the recasting Act to those provisions which remain unchanged in the Commission's proposal, such amendments shall be made to that Act in compliance with the procedure laid down by the Treaty according to the applicable legal basis.

9. A Consultative Working Party consisting of the respective legal services of the European Parliament, the Council and the Commission shall examine the proposal for recasting. It shall deliver an opinion as soon as possible for submission to the European Parliament, the Council and the Commission to the effect that the proposal does not comprise any substantive amendments other than those identified as such.

10. This agreement shall enter into force on the day following that of its publication in the *Official Journal of the European Communities*.

It shall apply to any proposal for recasting submitted from the date of its entry into force.

An assessment of the application of this Agreement shall take place three years after its entry into force. For this purpose the Legal Services of the institutions signatory to the Agreement shall submit an assessment report and propose, where appropriate, any changes required.

Declarations

Joint Declaration on point 2

The European Parliament, the Council and the Commission note that recasting may be either "vertical" (whereby the new legal Act replaces a single earlier act) or "horizontal" (whereby the new legal act replaces several parallel earlier acts relating to the same subject). **4–012**

Joint Declaration on point 4

The European Parliament, the Council and the Commission agree that, where an isolated amendment within a provision in fact amends the substance of that provision, such a provision shall be identified as having been amended in its entirety. **4–013**

Declaration of the European Parliament and the Council on point 6(b)

The European Parliament and the Council take note of the fact that the Commission provides for substantive amendments and any new recital to be identified by the use of "shaded" type in any COM document which it submits. **4–014**

Joint Declaration on point 9

The European Parliament, the Council and the Commission note that, for the purpose of giving proper effect to this Agreement, their Legal Services should have access to the appropriate human resources so that they have a sufficient number of representatives within the Consultative Working Party to enable the **4–015** proposals for recastings submitted by the Commission to be considered rapidly with a view to delivery of an opinion to the institutions as soon as possible.

SECTION 2—LEGISLATIVE PROCEDURE

Council Decision of 29 March 1994 concerning the taking of Decision by qualified majority by the Council

([1994] OJ C105/1; Doc. Ref. 31994D0413(01)

The Council of the European Union,
Decides:

Article 1 **[Compromise where substantial minority oppose adoption of measure by qualified majority]**

4–016 If Members of the Council representing a total of 23 to [25][6] votes indicate their intention to oppose the adoption by the Council of a Decision by qualified majority, the Council will do all in its power to reach, within a reasonable time and without prejudicing obligatory time-limits laid down by the Treaties and by secondary law, such as in Articles [251] and [252] of the Treaty establishing the European Community, a satisfactory solution that could be adopted by at least [65][7] votes. During this period, and always respecting the Rules of Procedure of the Council, the President undertakes, with the assistance of the Commission, any initiative necessary to facilitate a wider basis of agreement in the Council. The Members of the Council lend him their assistance.

Article 2 **[Publication]**

4–017 The present Decision shall be published in the *Official Journal of the European Communities*.

Joint declaration of 4 May 1999 on practical arrangements for the new co-decision procedure (Article 251 of the Treaty establishing the European Community)

([1999] OJ C148/1; Doc Ref. 31999Y0528(01))

Preamble

4–018 The European Parliament, the Council and the Commission, hereinafter referred to as the "institutions", note that the present practice of contacts between the Council Presidency, the Commission and the chairmen of the relevant committees and/or the rapporteurs of Parliament and between the co-chairmen of the Conciliation Committee has proved its worth. The institutions confirm that this practice should be extended to cover all stages of the co-decision procedure. The institutions undertake to examine their working methods with a view to making effective use of all the possibilities afforded by the new co-decision procedure. The institutions shall do what is necessary, in accordance with their rules of procedure, to promote reciprocal information about co-decision proceedings.

I. First Reading

4–019 1. The institutions shall co-operate in good faith with a view to reconciling their positions as far as possible so that wherever possible acts can be adopted at first reading.

---

[6] Figures substituted by Decision 95/101, Art. 1 ([1995] OJ C1/1) as from 1 January 1995.
[7] *ibid.*

2. The institutions shall ensure that their respective calendars of work are co-ordinated as far as possible in order to facilitate the conduct of proceedings at first reading in a coherent and convergent manner in the European Parliament and the Council. They shall establish appropriate contacts to monitor the progress of the work and analyze the degree of convergence.

3. The Commission shall ensure that such contacts are facilitated and shall exercise its right of initiative in a constructive manner with a view to making it easier to reconcile the positions of the European Parliament and the Council with due regard for the balance between the institutions and the role conferred on that institution by the Treaty.

II. Second Reading

1. In its statements of reasons the Council shall explain as clearly as possible the **4–020** reasons that have led it to adopt its common position. During its second reading the European Parliament shall take the greatest possible account of those reasons and of the Commission's opinion.

2. Appropriate contacts may be established with a view to achieving a better understanding of the respective positions and thus to bringing the legislative procedure to a conclusion as quickly as possible.

3. The Commission shall ensure that such contacts are facilitated and shall give its opinion with a view to reconciling the positions of the Council and the European Parliament, with due regard for the balance between the institutions and the role conferred on that institution by the Treaty.

III. Conciliation

1. The Conciliation Committee shall be convened by the President of the Council, **4–021** with the agreement of the President of the European Parliament and with due regard to the provisions of the Treaty.

2. The Commission shall take part in the conciliation proceedings and shall take all the necessary initiatives with a view to reconciling the positions of the European Parliament and the Council. Such initiatives may include, *inter alia*, draft compromise texts reflecting the positions of the Council and the European Parliament, with due regard to the role conferred upon the Commission by the Treaty.

3. The Committee shall be chaired jointly by the President of the European Parliament and the President of the Council. Committee meetings shall be chaired alternately by each co-chairman.

The dates and the agenda for the Committee's meetings shall be set jointly by the co-chairmen. The Commission shall be consulted on the dates envisaged. The European Parliament and the Council shall set aside, for guidance, appropriate dates for conciliation proceedings and shall notify the Commission thereof.

While respecting the Treaty provisions regarding time-limits, the European Parliament and the Council shall, as far as possible, take account of scheduling requirements, in particular those resulting from breaks in the institutions' activities and from European Parliament elections. In any case, the interruption of activities shall be as short as possible.

The Committee shall meet alternately at the premises of the European Parliament and those of the Council.

4. The Committee shall have available to it the Commission proposal, the Council's common position, the amendments proposed by the European Parliament, the Commission's opinion thereon and a joint working document by the European Parliament and Council delegations. The Commission shall, as a general rule, submit its opinion within two weeks of official receipt of the outcome

of Parliament's vote and at the latest by the commencement of conciliation proceedings.

5. The co-chairman may submit texts for the Committee's approval.

6. The detailed outcome of votes and, where appropriate, explanations of vote, taken within each delegation to the Conciliation Committee, shall be forwarded to the Committee.

7. Agreement on a joint text shall be established at a meeting of the Conciliation Committee or, subsequently, by an exchange of letters between the co-chairmen. Copies of such letters shall be forwarded to the Commission.

8. If the Committee reaches agreement on a joint text, it shall, after legal/linguistic finalisation, be submitted to the co-chairmen for approval.

9. The co-chairmen shall forward the approved joint text to the Presidents of the European Parliament and of the Council by means of a jointly signed letter. Where the Conciliation Committee is unable to agree on a joint text, the co-chairmen shall notify the Presidents of the European Parliament and of the Council thereof in a jointly signed letter. Such letters shall serve as minutes. Copies of such letters shall be forwarded to the Commission for information.

10. The General Secretariats of the Council and of the European Parliament shall act jointly as the Committee's secretariat, in association with the General Secretariat of the Commission.

IV. General Provisions

4–022 1. Should the European Parliament or the Council deem it essential to extend the time-limits referred to in Article 251 of the Treaty establishing the European Community, they shall notify the President of the other institution and the Commission thereof.

2. Texts shall be finalised by the legal/linguistic experts of the Parliament and of the Council acting in close co-operation and by mutual agreement.

3. Following the adoption of a legislative act under the co-decision procedure by the European Parliament and the Council, the text shall be submitted, for signature, to the President of the European Parliament and the President of the Council and to the Secretaries-General of the two institutions.

The jointly signed text shall be forwarded to the Official Journal for publication if possible within at most one month, and in any case as soon as possible.

4. If one of the institutions finds a clerical error in a text (or in any of the language versions), it shall immediately notify the other institutions. If the error is found in an Act that has not yet been adopted, the legal/linguistic services of the European Parliament and of the Council shall prepare the necessary corrigendum in close co-operation. Where the error is found in an Act that has already been adopted or published, the European Parliament and the Council shall adopt, by mutual agreement, a corrigendum drawn up under their respective procedures.

Council Decision 1999/468 of 28 June 1999 laying down the procedures for the exercise of implementing powers conferred on the Commission

([1999] OJ L184/23; Doc. Ref. 31999D0468)

The Council of the European Union,

4–023 Having regard to the Treaty establishing the European Community, and in particular the third indent of Article 202 thereof,

Having regard to the proposal from the Commission,[8]

[8] [1998] OJ C279/5.

Having regard to the opinion of the European Parliament,[9]

Whereas:

(1) in the instruments which it adopts, the Council has to confer on the Commission powers for the implementation of the rules which the Council lays down; the Council may impose certain requirements in respect of the exercise of these powers; it may also reserve to itself the right, in specific and substantiated cases, to exercise directly implementing powers;

(2) the Council adopted Decision 87/373 of 13 July 1987 laying down the procedures for the exercise of implementing powers conferred on the Commission,[10] that Decision has provided for a limited number of procedures for the exercise of such powers;

(3) declaration No. 31 annexed to the Final Act of the Intergovernmental Conference which adopted the Amsterdam Treaty calls on the Commission to submit to the Council a proposal amending Decision 87/373;

(4) for reasons of clarity, rather than amending Decision 87/373, it has been considered more appropriate to replace that Decision by a new Decision and, therefore, to repeal Decision 87/373;

(5) the first purpose of this Decision is, with a view to achieving greater consistency and predictability in the choice of type of committee, to provide for criteria relating to the choice of committee procedures, it being understood that such criteria are of a non-binding nature;

(6) in this regard, the management procedure should be followed as regards management measures such as those relating to the application of the common agricultural and common fisheries policies or to the implementation of programmes with substantial budgetary implications; such management measures should be taken by the Commission by a procedure ensuring decision-making within suitable periods; however, where non-urgent measures are referred to the Council, the Commission should exercise its discretion to defer application of the measures;

(7) the regulatory procedure should be followed as regards measures of general scope designed to apply essential provisions of basic instruments, including measures concerning the protection of the health or safety of humans, animals or plants, as well as measures designed to adapt or update certain non-essential provisions of a basic instrument; such implementing measures should be adopted by an effective procedure which complies in full with the Commission's right of initiative in legislative matters;

(8) the advisory procedure should be followed in any case in which it is considered to be the most appropriate; the advisory procedure will continue to be used in those cases where it currently applies;

(9) the second purpose of this Decision is to simplify the requirements for the exercise of implementing powers conferred on the Commission as well as to improve the involvement of the European Parliament in those cases where the basic instrument conferring implementation powers on the Commission was adopted in accordance with the procedure laid down in Article 251 of the Treaty; it has been accordingly considered appropriate to reduce the number of procedures as well as to adjust them in line with the respective powers of the institutions involved and notably to give the European Parliament an opportunity to have its views taken into consideration by, respectively, the Commission or the Council in cases where it considers that, respectively, a draft measure submitted to a committee or a proposal submitted to the Council under the regulatory procedure exceeds the implementing powers provided for in the basic instrument;

(10) the third purpose of this Decision is to improve information to the European Parliament by providing that the Commission should inform it on a regular basis of committee proceedings, that the Commission should transmit to it

[9] Opinion delivered on 6 May 1999.

[10] [1987] OJ L197/33.

documents related to activities of committees and inform it whenever the Commission transmits to the Council measures or proposals for measures to be taken;

(11) the fourth purpose of this Decision is to improve information to the public concerning committee procedures and therefore to make applicable to committees the principles and conditions on public access to documents applicable to the Commission, to provide for a list of all committees which assist the Commission in the exercise of implementing powers and for an annual report on the working of committees to be published as well as to provide for all references to documents related to committees which have been transmitted to the European Parliament to be made public in a register;

(12) the specific committee procedures created for the implementation of the common commercial policy and the competition rules laid down by the Treaties that are not currently based upon Decision 87/373 are not in any way affected by this Decision,

Has decided as follows:

Article 1 [Conferment of implementing powers on Commission]

4–024 Other than in specific and substantiated cases where the basic instrument reserves to the Council the right to exercise directly certain implementing powers itself, such powers shall be conferred on the Commission in accordance with the relevant provisions in the basic instrument. These provisions shall stipulate the essential elements of the powers thus conferred.

Where the basic instrument imposes specific procedural requirements for the adoption of implementing measures, such requirements shall be in conformity with the procedures provided for by Articles 3, 4, 5 and 6.

Article 2 [Choice of procedure for adopting implementing measures]

4–025 The choice of procedural methods for the adoption of implementing measures shall be guided by the following criteria:

(a) management measures, such as those relating to the application of the common agricultural and common fisheries policies, or to the implementation of programmes with substantial budgetary implications, should be adopted by use of the management procedure;

(b) measures of general scope designed to apply essential provisions of basic instruments, including measures concerning the protection of the health or safety of humans, animals or plants, should be adopted by use of the regulatory procedure; where a basic instrument stipulates that certain non-essential provisions of the instrument may be adapted or updated by way of implementing procedures, such measures should be adopted by use of the regulatory procedure;

(c) without prejudice to points (a) and (b), the advisory procedure shall be used in any case in which it is considered to be the most appropriate.

Article 3 Advisory procedure

4–026 1. The Commission shall be assisted by an advisory committee composed of the representatives of the Member States and chaired by the representative of the Commission.

2. The representative of the Commission shall submit to the committee a draft of the measures to be taken. The committee shall deliver its opinion on the draft, within a time-limit which the chairman may lay down according to the urgency of the matter, if necessary by taking a vote.

3. The opinion shall be recorded in the minutes; in addition, each Member State shall have the right to ask to have its position recorded in the minutes.

4. The Commission shall take the utmost account of the opinion delivered by the committee. It shall inform the committee of the manner in which the opinion has been taken into account.

Article 4 Management procedure

1. The Commission shall be assisted by a management committee composed of the representatives of the Member States and chaired by the representative of the Commission. **4–027**

2. The representative of the Commission shall submit to the committee a draft of the measures to be taken. The committee shall deliver its opinion on the draft within a time-limit which the chairman may lay down according to the urgency of the matter. The opinion shall be delivered by the majority laid down in Article 205(2) of the Treaty, in the case of decisions which the Council is required to adopt on a proposal from the Commission. The votes of the representatives of the Member States within the committee shall be weighted in the manner set out in that Article. The chairman shall not vote.

3. The Commission shall, without prejudice to Article 8, adopt measures which shall apply immediately. However, if these measures are not in accordance with the opinion of the committee, they shall be communicated by the Commission to the Council forthwith. In that event, the Commission may defer application of the measures which it has decided on for a period to be laid down in each basic instrument but which shall in no case exceed three months from the date of such communication.

4. The Council, acting by qualified majority, may take a different decision within the period provided for by paragraph 3.

Article 5 Regulatory procedure

1. The Commission shall be assisted by a regulatory committee composed of the representatives of the Member States and chaired by the representative of the Commission. **4–028**

2. The representative of the Commission shall submit to the committee a draft of the measures to be taken. The committee shall deliver its opinion on the draft within a time-limit which the chairman may lay down according to the urgency of the matter. The opinion shall be delivered by the majority laid down in Article 205(2) of the Treaty in the case of decisions which the Council is required to adopt on a proposal from the Commission. The votes of the representatives of the Member States within the committee shall be weighted in the manner set out in that Article. The chairman shall not vote.

3. The Commission shall, without prejudice to Article 8, adopt the measures envisaged if they are in accordance with the opinion of the committee.

4. If the measures envisaged are not in accordance with the opinion of the committee, or if no opinion is delivered, the Commission shall, without delay, submit to the Council a proposal relating to the measures to be taken and shall inform the European Parliament.

5. If the European Parliament considers that a proposal submitted by the Commission pursuant to a basic instrument adopted in accordance with the procedure laid down in Article 251 of the Treaty exceeds the implementing powers provided for in that basic instrument, it shall inform the Council of its position.

6. The Council may, where appropriate in view of any such position, act by qualified majority on the proposal, within a period to be laid down in each basic instrument but which shall in no case exceed three months from the date of referral to the Council.

If within that period the Council has indicated by qualified majority that it opposes the proposal, the Commission shall re-examine it. It may submit an amended proposal to the Council, re-submit its proposal or present a legislative proposal on the basis of the Treaty.

If on the expiry of that period the Council has neither adopted the proposed implementing act nor indicated its opposition to the proposal for implementing measures, the proposed implementing act shall be adopted by the Commission.

Article 6 Safeguard procedure

4–029 The following procedure may be applied where the basic instrument confers on the Commission the power to decide on safeguard measures:

(a) the Commission shall notify the Council and the Member States of any decision regarding safeguard measures. It may be stipulated that before adopting its decision, the Commission shall consult the Member States in accordance with procedures to be determined in each case;

(b) any Member State may refer the Commission's decision to the Council within a time-limit to be determined within the basic instrument in question;

(c) the Council, acting by a qualified majority, may take a different decision within a time-limit to be determined in the basic instrument in question. Alternatively, it may be stipulated in the basic instrument that the Council, acting by qualified majority, may confirm, amend or revoke the decision adopted by the Commission and that, if the Council has not taken a decision within the abovementioned time-limit, the decision of the Commission is deemed to be revoked.

Article 7 [Rules of procedure; access to documents; information to Parliament]

4–030 1. Each committee shall adopt its own rules of procedure on the proposal of its chairman, on the basis of standard rules of procedure which shall be published in the *Official Journal of the European Communities*.[11]

In so far as necessary existing committees shall adapt their rules of procedure to the standard rules of procedure.

2. The principles and conditions on public access to documents applicable to the Commission shall apply to the committees.

3. The European Parliament shall be informed by the Commission of committee proceedings on a regular basis. To that end, it shall receive agendas for committee meetings, draft measures submitted to the committees for the implementation of instruments adopted by the procedure provided for by Article 251 of the Treaty, and the results of voting and summary records of the meetings and lists of the authorities and organisations to which the persons designated by the Member States to represent them belong. The European Parliament shall also be kept informed whenever the Commission transmits to the Council measures or proposals for measures to be taken.

4. The Commission shall, within six months of the date on which this Decision takes effect, publish in the *Official Journal of the European Communities*, a list of all committees which assist the Commission in the exercise of implementing powers. This list shall specify, in relation to each committee, the basic instrument(s) under which the committee is established. From 2000 onwards, the Commission shall also publish an annual report on the working of committees.

5. The references of all documents sent to the European Parliament pursuant to paragraph 3 shall be made public in a register to be set up by the Commission in 2001.

[11] See [2001] OJ C38/3.

Article 8 [Draft measures exceeding implementing powers]

If the European Parliament indicates, in a Resolution setting out the grounds on which it is based, that draft implementing measures, the adoption of which is contemplated and which have been submitted to a committee pursuant to a basic instrument adopted under Article 251 of the Treaty, would exceed the implementing powers provided for in the basic instrument, the Commission shall re-examine the draft measures. Taking the Resolution into account and within the time-limits of the procedure under way, the Commission may submit new draft measures to the committee, continue with the procedure or submit a proposal to the European Parliament and the Council on the basis of the Treaty. **4–031**

The Commission shall inform the European Parliament and the committee of the action which it intends to take on the Resolution of the European Parliament and of its reasons for doing so.

Article 9 [Repeal]

Decision 87/373 shall be repealed. **4–032**

Article 10 [Effective date]

This Decision shall take effect on the day following that of its publication in the *Official Journal of the European Communities*.[12] **4–033**

Declarations on Council Decision 1999/468 of 28 June 1999 laying down the procedures for the exercise of implementing powers conferred on the Commission

([1999] OJ C203/1; Doc. Ref. 31999Y0717(01)

1. Commission Statement (ad Article 4)

Under the management procedure, the Commission would recall that its constant practice is to try to secure a satisfactory decision which will also muster the widest possible support within the Committee. **4–034**

The Commission will take account of the position of the members of the Committee and act in such a way as to avoid going against any predominant position which might emerge against the appropriateness of an implementing measure.

2. Council and Commission Statement

The Commission and the Council agree that provisions relating to committees assisting the Commission in the exercise of implementing powers provided for in application of Decision 87/373 should be adjusted without delay in order to align them with Articles 3, 4, 5 and 6 of Decision 1999/468 in accordance with the appropriate legislative procedures.[13] **4–035**

Such adjustment should be made as follows:

— current procedure I would be turned into the new advisory procedure

— current procedures II(a) and II(b) would be turned into the new management procedure

— current procedures III(a) and III(b) would be turned into the new regulatory procedure.

A modification of the type of committee provided for in a basic instrument should be made, on a case-by-case basis, in the course of normal revision of legislation, guided *inter alia* by the criteria provided for in Article 2.

[12] Effective date was 18 July 1999.

[13] For adaptations of provisions relating to committees assisting the Commission in exercising its implementing powers to Decision 1999/468, see Regulations 806/2003 and 807/2003 ([2003] OJ L122/1 and 36).

Such adjustment or modification should be made in compliance with the obligations incumbent on the Community institutions. It should not have the effect of jeopardising attainment of the objectives of the basic instrument or the effectiveness of Community action.

3. Commission Statement (ad Article 5)

4–036 In the review of proposals for implementing measures concerning particularly sensitive sectors, the Commission, in order to find a balanced solution, will act in such a way as to avoid going against any predominant position which might emerge within the Council against the appropriateness of an implementing measure.

Agreement between the European Parliament and the Commission on procedures for implementing Council Decision 1999/468 laying down the procedures for the exercise of implementing powers conferred on the Commission

([2000] OJ L256/19; Doc. Ref. 32000Q1010(01))

4–037 1. Pursuant to Article 7(3) of Decision 1999/468,[14] the European Parliament is to be informed by the Commission on a regular basis of the proceedings of the committees involved in committee procedures. To that end, it is to receive, at the same time as the members of the committees and on the same terms, the draft agendas for committee meetings, the draft implementing measures submitted to the committees under basic instruments adopted by the procedure provided for by Article 251 of the EC Treaty, and the results of voting and summary records of the meetings and lists of the authorities to which the persons designated by the Member States to represent them belong.

2. Furthermore, the Commission agrees to forward to the European Parliament, for information, at the request of the parliamentary committee responsible, specific draft measures for implementing basic instruments which, although not adopted under the co-decision procedure, are of particular importance to the European Parliament. Pursuant to the judgment of the Court of First Instance of the European Communities of 19 July 1999 (Case T-188/97, *Rothmans v. Commission*),[15] the European Parliament may request access to minutes of committee meetings.

3. The European Parliament and the Commission consider the following agreements superseded and thus of no effect in so far as they themselves are concerned: the 1988 Plumb/Delors agreement, the 1996 Samland/Williamson agreement and the 1994 *modus vivendi*.[16]

4. Once the appropriate technical arrangements have been made, the documents referred to in Article 7(3) of Decision 1999/468 will be forwarded electronically. Confidential documents will be processed in accordance with internal administrative procedures drawn up by each institution with a view to providing all the requisite guarantees.

5. Pursuant to Article 8 of Decision 1999/468, the European Parliament may indicate, in a resolution setting out the grounds on which it is based, that draft measures for implementing a basic instrument adopted by the procedure provided for by Article 251 of the Treaty exceed the implementing powers provided for in that basic instrument.

[14] [1999] OJ L184/23 (see above).
[15] [1999] ECR II-2463.
[16] [1996] OJ C102/1.

6. The European Parliament is to adopt such resolutions in plenary; it is to have a period of one month in which to do so, beginning on the date of receipt of the final draft of the implementing measures in the language versions submitted to the Commission.

7. In urgent cases, and in the case of measures relating to day-to-day administrative matters and/or having a limited period of validity, the time-limit will be shorter. That time-limit may be very short in extremely urgent cases, and in particular on public health grounds. The Member of the Commission responsible is to set the appropriate time-limit and to state the reason for that time-limit. The European Parliament may then use a procedure whereby application of Article 8 of Decision 1999/468, within the relevant time-limit, may be delegated to the parliamentary committee responsible.

8. Following adoption by the European Parliament of a resolution setting out the grounds on which it is based, the Member of the Commission responsible is to inform the European Parliament or, where appropriate, the parliamentary committee responsible, of the action the Commission intends to take thereon.

9. The European Parliament supports the aim and the procedures set out in Declaration No. 2 of the Council and the Commission.[17] That Declaration is aimed at simplifying Community implementing arrangements by bringing the committee procedures currently in force into line with those contained in Decision 1999/468.

SECTION 3—ACCESS TO DOCUMENTS

Regulation 1049/2001 of the European Parliament and of the Council of 30 May 2001, regarding public access to European Parliament, Council and Commission documents

([2001] OJ L145/43; Doc. Ref. 32001R1049)

The European Parliament and the Council of the European Union,

Having regard to the Treaty establishing the European Community, and in particular Article 255(2) thereof, **4–038**

Having regard to the proposal from the Commission,[18]

Acting in accordance with the procedure referred to in Article 251 of the Treaty,[19]

Whereas:

(1) The second sub-paragraph of Article 1 of the Treaty on European Union enshrines the concept of openness, stating that the Treaty marks a new stage in the process of creating an ever closer union among the peoples of Europe, in which decisions are taken as openly as possible and as closely as possible to the citizen.

(2) Openness enables citizens to participate more closely in the decision-making process and guarantees that the administration enjoys greater legitimacy and is more effective and more accountable to the citizen in a democratic system. Openness contributes to strengthening the principles of democracy and respect for fundamental rights as laid down in Article 6 of the EU Treaty and in the Charter of Fundamental Rights of the European Union.

(3) The conclusions of the European Council meetings held at Birmingham, Edinburgh and Copenhagen stressed the need to introduce greater transparency into the work of the Union institutions. This Regulation consolidates the

[17] [1999] OJ C203/1 (see above).

[18] [2000] OJ C177/70.

[19] Opinion of the European Parliament of 3 May 2001, and Council Decision of 28 May 2001.

initiatives that the institutions have already taken with a view to improving the transparency of the decision-making process.

(4) The purpose of this Regulation is to give the fullest possible effect to the right of public access to documents and to lay down the general principles and limits on such access in accordance with Article 255(2) of the EC Treaty.

(5) Since the question of access to documents is not covered by provisions of the Treaty establishing the European Coal and Steel Community and the Treaty establishing the European Atomic Energy Community, the European Parliament, the Council and the Commission should, in accordance with Declaration No. 41 attached to the Final Act of the Treaty of Amsterdam, draw guidance from this Regulation as regards documents concerning the activities covered by those two Treaties.

(6) Wider access should be granted to documents in cases where the institutions are acting in their legislative capacity, including under delegated powers, while at the same time preserving the effectiveness of the institutions' decision-making process. Such documents should be made directly accessible to the greatest possible extent.

(7) In accordance with Articles 28(1) and 41(1) of the EU Treaty, the right of access also applies to documents relating to the common foreign and security policy and to police and judicial co-operation in criminal matters. Each institution should respect its security rules.

(8) In order to ensure the full application of this Regulation to all activities of the Union, all agencies established by the institutions should apply the principles laid down in this Regulation.

(9) On account of their highly sensitive content, certain documents should be given special treatment. Arrangements for informing the European Parliament of the content of such documents should be made through interinstitutional agreement.

(10) In order to bring about greater openness in the work of the institutions, access to documents should be granted by the European Parliament, the Council and the Commission not only to documents drawn up by the institutions, but also to documents received by them. In this context, it is recalled that Declaration No. 35 attached to the Final Act of the Treaty of Amsterdam provides that a Member State may request the Commission or the Council not to communicate to third parties a document originating from that State without its prior agreement.

(11) In principle, all documents of the institutions should be accessible to the public. However, certain public and private interests should be protected by way of exceptions. The institutions should be entitled to protect their internal consultations and deliberations where necessary to safeguard their ability to carry out their tasks. In assessing the exceptions, the institutions should take account of the principles in Community legislation concerning the protection of personal data, in all areas of Union activities.

(12) All rules concerning access to documents of the institutions should be in conformity with this Regulation.

(13) In order to ensure that the right of access is fully respected, a two-stage administrative procedure should apply, with the additional possibility of court proceedings or complaints to the Ombudsman.

(14) Each institution should take the measures necessary to inform the public of the new provisions in force and to train its staff to assist citizens exercising their rights under this Regulation. In order to make it easier for citizens to exercise their rights, each institution should provide access to a register of documents.

(15) Even though it is neither the object nor the effect of this Regulation to amend national legislation on access to documents, it is nevertheless clear that, by virtue of the principle of loyal co-operation which governs relations between the institutions and the Member States, Member States should take care not to hamper the proper application of this Regulation and should respect the security rules of the institutions.

(16) This Regulation is without prejudice to existing rights of access to documents for Member States, judicial authorities or investigative bodies.

(17) In accordance with Article 255(3) of the EC Treaty, each institution lays down specific provisions regarding access to its documents in its rules of procedure. Council Decision 93/731 of 20 December 1993 on public access to Council documents,[20] Commission Decision 94/90/ECSC, EC, Euratom of 8 February 1994 on public access to Commission documents,[21] European Parliament Decision 97/632/ECSC, EC, Euratom of 10 July 1997 on public access to European Parliament documents,[22] and the rules on confidentiality of Schengen documents should therefore, if necessary, be modified or be repealed,

Have adopted this Regulation:

Article 1 Purpose

The purpose of this Regulation is: **4–039**

(a) to define the principles, conditions and limits on grounds of public or private interest governing the right of access to European Parliament, Council and Commission (hereinafter referred to as "the institutions") documents provided for in Article 255 of the EC Treaty in such a way as to ensure the widest possible access to documents,

(b) to establish rules ensuring the easiest possible exercise of this right, and

(c) to promote good administrative practice on access to documents.

Article 2 Beneficiaries and scope

1. Any citizen of the Union, and any natural or legal person residing or having its registered office in a Member State, has a right of access to documents of the institutions, subject to the principles, conditions and limits defined in this Regulation. **4–040**

2. The institutions may, subject to the same principles, conditions and limits, grant access to documents to any natural or legal person not residing or not having its registered office in a Member State.

3. This Regulation shall apply to all documents held by an institution, that is to say, documents drawn up or received by it and in its possession, in all areas of activity of the European Union.

4. Without prejudice to Articles 4 and 9, documents shall be made accessible to the public either following a written application or directly in electronic form or through a register. In particular, documents drawn up or received in the course of a legislative procedure shall be made directly accessible in accordance with Article 12.

5. Sensitive documents as defined in Article 9(1) shall be subject to special treatment in accordance with that Article.

6. This Regulation shall be without prejudice to rights of public access to documents held by the institutions which might follow from instruments of international law or acts of the institutions implementing them.

---

[20] [1993] OJ L340/43. Decision as last amended by Decision 2000/527 ([2000] OJ L212/9) repealed by Decision 2001/840 ([2001] OJ L313/40).

[21] [1994] OJ L46/58. Decision as amended by Decision 96/567 ([1996] OJ L247/45) repealed by Decision 2001/937 ([2001] OJ L345/94).

[22] [1997] OJ L263/27.

Article 3 Definitions

4–041 For the purpose of this Regulation:
(a) "document" shall mean any content whatever its medium (written on paper or stored in electronic form or as a sound, visual or audiovisual recording) concerning a matter relating to the policies, activities and decisions falling within the institution's sphere of responsibility;
(b) "third party" shall mean any natural or legal person, or any entity outside the institution concerned, including the Member States, other Community or non-Community institutions and bodies and third countries.

Article 4 Exceptions

4–042 1. The institutions shall refuse access to a document where disclosure would undermine the protection of:
(a) the public interest as regards:
— public security,
— defence and military matters,
— international relations,
— the financial, monetary or economic policy of the Community or a Member State;
(b) privacy and the integrity of the individual, in particular in accordance with Community legislation regarding the protection of personal data.

2. The institutions shall refuse access to a document where disclosure would undermine the protection of:
— commercial interests of a natural or legal person, including intellectual property,
— court proceedings and legal advice,
— the purpose of inspections, investigations and audits,
unless there is an overriding public interest in disclosure.

3. Access to a document, drawn up by an institution for internal use or received by an institution, which relates to a matter where the decision has not been taken by the institution, shall be refused if disclosure of the document would seriously undermine the institution's decision-making process, unless there is an overriding public interest in disclosure.

Access to a document containing opinions for internal use as part of deliberations and preliminary consultations within the institution concerned shall be refused even after the decision has been taken if disclosure of the document would seriously undermine the institution's decision-making process, unless there is an overriding public interest in disclosure.

4. As regards third-party documents, the institution shall consult the third party with a view to assessing whether an exception in paragraph 1 or 2 is applicable, unless it is clear that the document shall or shall not be disclosed.

5. A Member State may request the institution not to disclose a document originating from that Member State without its prior agreement.

6. If only parts of the requested document are covered by any of the exceptions, the remaining parts of the document shall be released.

7. The exceptions as laid down in paragraphs 1 to 3 shall only apply for the period during which protection is justified on the basis of the content of the document. The exceptions may apply for a maximum period of 30 years. In the case of documents covered by the exceptions relating to privacy or commercial interests

and in the case of sensitive documents, the exceptions may, if necessary, continue to apply after this period.

Article 5 Documents in the Member States

Where a Member State receives a request for a document in its possession, originating from an institution, unless it is clear that the document shall or shall not be disclosed, the Member State shall consult with the institution concerned in order to take a decision that does not jeopardise the attainment of the objectives of this Regulation. **4–043**

The Member State may instead refer the request to the institution.

Article 6 Applications

1. Applications for access to a document shall be made in any written form, including electronic form, in one of the languages referred to in Article 314 of the EC Treaty and in a sufficiently precise manner to enable the institution to identify the document. The applicant is not obliged to state reasons for the application. **4–044**

2. If an application is not sufficiently precise, the institution shall ask the applicant to clarify the application and shall assist the applicant in doing so, for example, by providing information on the use of the public registers of documents.

3. In the event of an application relating to a very long document or to a very large number of documents, the institution concerned may confer with the applicant informally, with a view to finding a fair solution.

4. The institutions shall provide information and assistance to citizens on how and where applications for access to documents can be made.

Article 7 Processing of initial applications

1. An application for access to a document shall be handled promptly. An acknowledgement of receipt shall be sent to the applicant. Within 15 working days from registration of the application, the institution shall either grant access to the document requested and provide access in accordance with Article 10 within that period or, in a written reply, state the reasons for the total or partial refusal and inform the applicant of his or her right to make a confirmatory application in accordance with paragraph 2 of this Article. **4–045**

2. In the event of a total or partial refusal, the applicant may, within 15 working days of receiving the institution's reply, make a confirmatory application asking the institution to reconsider its position.

3. In exceptional cases, for example in the event of an application relating to a very long document or to a very large number of documents, the time-limit provided for in paragraph 1 may be extended by 15 working days, provided that the applicant is notified in advance and that detailed reasons are given.

4. Failure by the institution to reply within the prescribed time-limit shall entitle the applicant to make a confirmatory application.

Article 8 Processing of confirmatory applications

1. A confirmatory application shall be handled promptly. Within 15 working days from registration of such an application, the institution shall either grant access to the document requested and provide access in accordance with Article 10 within that period or, in a written reply, state the reasons for the total or partial refusal. In the event of a total or partial refusal, the institution shall inform the applicant of the remedies open to him or her, namely instituting court proceedings against the institution and/or making a complaint to the Ombudsman, under the conditions laid down in Articles 230 and 195 of the EC Treaty, respectively. **4–046**

2. In exceptional cases, for example in the event of an application relating to a very long document or to a very large number of documents, the time-limit provided for in paragraph 1 may be extended by 15 working days, provided that the applicant is notified in advance and that detailed reasons are given.

3. Failure by the institution to reply within the prescribed time-limit shall be considered as a negative reply and entitle the applicant to institute court proceedings against the institution and/or make a complaint to the Ombudsman, under the relevant provisions of the EC Treaty.

Article 9 Treatment of sensitive documents

4–047 1. Sensitive documents are documents originating from the institutions or the agencies established by them, from Member States, third countries or International Organisations, classified as "TRÈS SECRET/TOP SECRET", "SECRET" or "CONFIDENTIEL" in accordance with the rules of the institution concerned, which protect essential interests of the European Union or of one or more of its Member States in the areas covered by Article 4(1)(a), notably public security, defence and military matters.

2. Applications for access to sensitive documents under the procedures laid down in Articles 7 and 8 shall be handled only by those persons who have a right to acquaint themselves with those documents. These persons shall also, without prejudice to Article 11(2), assess which references to sensitive documents could be made in the public register.

3. Sensitive documents shall be recorded in the register or released only with the consent of the originator.

4. An institution which decides to refuse access to a sensitive document shall give the reasons for its decision in a manner which does not harm the interests protected in Article 4.

5. Member States shall take appropriate measures to ensure that when handling applications for sensitive documents the principles in this Article and Article 4 are respected.

6. The rules of the institutions concerning sensitive documents shall be made public.

7. The Commission and the Council shall inform the European Parliament regarding sensitive documents in accordance with arrangements agreed between the institutions.

Article 10 Access following an application

4–048 1. The applicant shall have access to documents either by consulting them on the spot or by receiving a copy, including, where available, an electronic copy, according to the applicant's preference. The cost of producing and sending copies may be charged to the applicant. This charge shall not exceed the real cost of producing and sending the copies. Consultation on the spot, copies of less than 20 A4 pages and direct access in electronic form or through the register shall be free of charge.

2. If a document has already been released by the institution concerned and is easily accessible to the applicant, the institution may fulfil its obligation of granting access to documents by informing the applicant how to obtain the requested document.

3. Documents shall be supplied in an existing version and format (including electronically or in an alternative format such as Braille, large print or tape) with full regard to the applicant's preference.

Article 11 Registers

1. To make citizens' rights under this Regulation effective, each institution shall provide public access to a register of documents. Access to the register should be provided in electronic form. References to documents shall be recorded in the register without delay. **4–049**

2. For each document the register shall contain a reference number (including, where applicable, the interinstitutional reference), the subject matter and/or a short description of the content of the document and the date on which it was received or drawn up and recorded in the register. References shall be made in a manner which does not undermine protection of the interests in Article 4.

3. The institutions shall immediately take the measures necessary to establish a register which shall be operational by 3 June 2002.

Article 12 Direct access in electronic form or through a register

1. The institutions shall as far as possible make documents directly accessible to the public in electronic form or through a register in accordance with the rules of the institution concerned. **4–050**

2. In particular, legislative documents, that is to say, documents drawn up or received in the course of procedures for the adoption of acts which are legally binding in or for the Member States, should, subject to Articles 4 and 9, be made directly accessible.

3. Where possible, other documents, notably documents relating to the development of policy or strategy, should be made directly accessible.

4. Where direct access is not given through the register, the register shall as far as possible indicate where the document is located.

Article 13 Publication in the *Official Journal*

1. In addition to the acts referred to in Article 254(1) and (2) of the EC Treaty and the first paragraph of Article 163 of the Euratom Treaty, the following documents shall, subject to Articles 4 and 9 of this Regulation, be published in the *Official Journal*: **4–051**

(a) Commission proposals;
(b) common positions adopted by the Council in accordance with the procedures referred to in Articles 251 and 252 of the EC Treaty and the reasons underlying those common positions, as well as the European Parliament's positions in these procedures;
(c) framework decisions and decisions referred to in Article 34(2) of the EU Treaty;
(d) conventions established by the Council in accordance with Article 34(2) of the EU Treaty;
(e) conventions signed between Member States on the basis of Article 293 of the EC Treaty;
(f) international agreements concluded by the Community or in accordance with Article 24 of the EU Treaty.

2. As far as possible, the following documents shall be published in the *Official Journal*:

(a) initiatives presented to the Council by a Member State pursuant to Article 67(1) of the EC Treaty or pursuant to Article 34(2) of the EU Treaty;
(b) common positions referred to in Article 34(2) of the EU Treaty;
(c) directives other than those referred to in Article 254(1) and (2) of the EC Treaty, decisions other than those referred to in Article 254(1) of the EC Treaty, recommendations and opinions.

3. Each institution may in its rules of procedure establish which further documents shall be published in the *Official Journal*.

Article 14 Information

4–052 1. Each institution shall take the requisite measures to inform the public of the rights they enjoy under this Regulation.

2. The Member States shall cooperate with the institutions in providing information to the citizens.

Article 15 Administrative practice in the institutions

4–053 1. The institutions shall develop good administrative practices in order to facilitate the exercise of the right of access guaranteed by this Regulation.

2. The institutions shall establish an interinstitutional committee to examine best practice, address possible conflicts and discuss future developments on public access to documents.

Article 16 Reproduction of documents

4–054 This Regulation shall be without prejudice to any existing rules on copyright which may limit a third party's right to reproduce or exploit released documents.

Article 17 Reports

4–055 1. Each institution shall publish annually a report for the preceding year including the number of cases in which the institution refused to grant access to documents, the reasons for such refusals and the number of sensitive documents not recorded in the register.

2. At the latest by 31 January 2004, the Commission shall publish a report on the implementation of the principles of this Regulation and shall make recommendations, including, if appropriate, proposals for the revision of this Regulation and an action programme of measures to be taken by the institutions.

Article 18 Application measures

4–056 1. Each institution shall adapt its rules of procedure to the provisions of this Regulation. The adaptations shall take effect from 3 December 2001.[23]

2. Within six months of the entry into force of this Regulation, the Commission shall examine the conformity of Council Regulation (EEC, Euratom) 354/83 of 1 February 1983 concerning the opening to the public of the historical archives of the European Economic Community and the European Atomic Energy Community[24] with this Regulation in order to ensure the preservation and archiving of documents to the fullest extent possible.

3. Within six months of the entry into force of this Regulation, the Commission shall examine the conformity of the existing rules on access to documents with this Regulation.

Article 19 Entry into force

4–057 This Regulation shall enter into force on the third day following that of its publication in the *Official Journal of the European Communities*.[25]

---

[23] See Parliament's Rules of Procedure, 15th Edition (February 2003) ([2003] OJ L61/1), r.172, Decision 2002/682 adopting the Council's Rules of Procedure ([2002] OJ L230/7), Art. 10 and Annex II, and the Annex to Decision 2001/937 amending the Commission's Rules of Procedure ([2001] OJ L345/94).

[24] [1983] OJ L43/1.

[25] The date of entry into force was 3 June 2001.

It shall be applicable from 3 December 2001.

This Regulation shall be binding in its entirety and directly applicable in all Member States.

SECTION 4—THE COURTS

Rules of Procedure of the Court of Justice of the European Communities of 19 June 1991

([1991] OJ L176/7; Corrigendum at [1992] OJ L383/117; Doc. Ref. 31991Q0704(02))[26]

The Court of Justice,

Having regard to the powers conferred on the Court of Justice by the Treaty establishing the European Coal and Steel Community, the Treaty establishing the EC and the Treaty establishing the European Atomic Energy Community (Euratom), **4–058**

Having regard to Article 55 of the Protocol on the Statute of the Court of Justice of the European Coal and Steel Community,

Having regard to the third paragraph of Article [245] of the Treaty establishing the [European Community],

Having regard to the third paragraph of Article 160 of the Treaty establishing the European Atomic Energy Community (Euratom),

Whereas it is necessary to revise the text of its Rules of Procedure in the various languages in order to ensure coherence and uniformity between those language versions;

With the unanimous approval of that revision, given by the Council on 29 April 1991;

And whereas, after the numerous amendments to its Rules of Procedure, it is necessary, in the interests of clarity and simplicity to establish a coherent authentic text,

With the unanimous approval of the Council, given on 7 June 1991,

Replaces its Rules of Procedure by the following Rules:

INTERPRETATION

Article 1 [Definitions]

[In these Rules: **4–059**

"Union Treaty" means the Treaty on European Union,

"EC Treaty" means the Treaty establishing the European Community,

"EAEC Treaty" means the Treaty establishing the European Atomic Energy Community,

"Statute" means the Protocol on the Statute of the Court of Justice,[27]

---

[26] Rules of Procedure subsequently amended at [1995] OJ L44/61 (to adjust the Rules for the entry into force of the Treaty on European Union and the EEA Agreement), [1997] OJ L103/1 and 3 (to adjust the Rules, *inter alia*, for the accession of Austria, Finland and Sweden), [2000] OJ L122/43 (*inter alia* to provide for accelerated procedures and to adapt the Rules to amendments introduced the Treaty of Amsterdam), [2000] OJ L322/1 (to allow for expedited procedures in urgent cases, to reduce the time-limit for intervention in direct actions and to provide rules on sending documents by fax), [2001] OJ L119/1 (to provide for copies of the application and defence to be sent to the European Parliament where it is not a party to a case to enable it to assess if the inapplicability of an act adopted by the Parliament and Council is being invoked), [2002] OJ L272/24 (to lay down rules applicable to languages to be used where non-Member States participate in preliminary rulings procedures in agreed areas) and [2003] OJ L147/17 (to adjust the Rules of Procedure to take account of the entry into force of the Treaty of Nice which, inter alia, substituted a single Protocol of the Statute of the Court of Justice annexed to the Union, EC and EAEC Treaties as from 1 February 2003).

[27] Reproduced in full text in Chapter 2 above.

"EEA Agreement" means the Agreement on the European Economic Area.
For the purposes of these Rules:
— "institutions" means the institutions of the Communities and bodies which are established by the Treaties, or by an Act adopted in implementation thereof, and which may be parties before the Court,
— "EFTA Surveillance Authority" means the surveillance authority referred to in the EEA Agreement.][28]

TITLE I—ORGANISATION OF THE COURT

CHAPTER 1—JUDGES AND ADVOCATES GENERAL

Article 2 [Judicial term of office defined]

4–060 The term of office of a Judge shall begin on the date laid down in his instrument of appointment. In the absence of any provisions regarding the date, the term shall begin on the date of the instrument.

Article 3 [Judicial oath and declaration]

4–061 1. Before taking up his duties, a Judge shall at the first public sitting of the Court which he attends after his appointment take the following oath:

> "I swear that I will perform my duties impartially and conscientiously. I swear that I will preserve the secrecy of the deliberations of the Court."

2. Immediately after taking the oath, a Judge shall sign a declaration by which he solemnly undertakes that, both during and after his term of office, he will respect the obligations arising therefrom, and in particular the duty to behave with integrity and discretion as regards the acceptance, after he has ceased to hold office, of certain appointments and benefits.

Article 4 [Procedure to decide if conditions of office still fulfilled]

4–062 When the Court is called upon to decide whether a Judge no longer fulfils the requisite conditions or no longer meets the obligations arising from his office, the President shall invite the Judge concerned to make representations to the Court, in closed session and in the absence of the Registrar.

Article 5 [Application to Advocates General]

4–063 Articles 2, 3 and 4 of these Rules shall apply to Advocates General.

Article 6 [Precedence]

4–064 Judges and Advocates General shall rank equally in precedence according to their seniority in office.

Where there is equal seniority in office, precedence shall be determined by age.

Retiring Judges and Advocates General who are reappointed shall retain their former precedence.

[28] Article 1 replaced by amendments to the Rules of Procedure ([2003] OJ L147/17) Art. 1(1) with effect from 1 August 2003.

CHAPTER 2—PRESIDENCY OF THE COURT AND CONSTITUTION OF THE CHAMBERS

Article 7 [Election of President]

1. The Judges shall, immediately after the partial replacement provided for in Article [223][29] of the [EC Treaty [. . .][30] and Article 139 of the Euratom Treaty],[31] elect one of their number as President of the Court for a term of three years. **4–065**

2. If the office of the President of the Court falls vacant before the normal date of expiry thereof, the Court shall elect a successor for the remainder of the term.

3. The elections provided for in this Article shall be by secret ballot. If a Judge obtains an absolute majority he shall be elected. If no Judge obtains an absolute majority, a second ballot shall be held and the Judge obtaining the most votes shall be elected. Where two or more Judges obtain an equal number of votes the oldest of them shall be deemed elected.

Article 8 [Functions of President]

The President shall direct the judicial business and the administration of the Court; he shall preside at hearings and deliberations. **4–066**

Article 9 [Chambers of Court]

1. The Court shall set up Chambers [of five and three Judges][32] in accordance with [Article 16 of the Statute][33] and shall decide which Judges shall be attached to them. **4–067**

[The assignment of Judges to Chambers][34] shall be published in the *Official Journal* [*of the European Union*].[35]

2. As soon as an application initiating proceedings has been lodged, the President of the Court shall assign the case to one of the Chambers [of three Judges][36] for any preparatory inquiries and shall designate a Judge from that Chamber to act as Rapporteur.

3. For cases assigned to a formation of the Court in accordance with Article 44(3), the word "Court" in these Rules shall mean that formation.[37]

4. In cases [assigned to a Chamber of five or three Judges][38] the powers of the President of the Court shall be exercised by the President of the Chamber.

Article 10 [Presidents of Chambers and First Advocate General]

[1. The Judges shall, immediately after the election of the President of the Court, elect the Presidents of the Chambers of five Judges for a term of three years. **4–068**

---

[29] Word substituted by amendments to Rules of Procedure ([2000] OJ L122/43) Art. 1(13) with effect from 1 July 2000.

[30] Words deleted by amendments to the Rules of Procedure ([2003] OJ L147/17) Art. 1(2) with effect from 1 August 2003.

[31] Term "EC Treaty" replaced and order in which Treaties are cited replaced by amendments to Rules of Procedure ([1995] OJ L44/61) Art. 1(11) with effect from 1 April 1995.

[32] Words added by amendments to the Rules of Procedure ([2003] OJ L147/17) Art. 1(3)(a) with effect from 1 August 2003.

[33] Words replaced by amendments to the Rules of Procedure ([2003] OJ L147/17) Art. 1(3)(a) with effect from 1 August 2003.

[34] Words replaced by amendments to the Rules of Procedure ([2003] OJ L147/17) Art. 1(3)(b) with effect from 1 August 2003.

[35] *ibid.*

[36] Words added by amendments to the Rules of Procedure ([2003] OJ L147/17) Art. 1(4) with effect from 1 August 2003.

[37] Article 9(3) replaced by amendments to the Rules of Procedure ([2003] OJ L147/17) Art. 1(5) with effect from 1 August 2003.

[38] Words replaced and former first subparagraph deleted by amendments to the Rules of Procedure ([2003] OJ L147/17) Art. 1(6) with effect from 1 August 2003.

The Judges shall elect the Presidents of the Chambers of three Judges for a period of one year.

The Court shall appoint for a period of one year the First Advocate General. The provisions of Article 7(2) and (3) shall apply.

Appointments made in pursuance of this paragraph shall be published in the *Official Journal of the European Union*.][39]

2. The First Advocate General shall assign each case to an Advocate General as soon as the Judge-Rapporteur has been designated by the President. He shall take the necessary steps if an Advocate General is absent or prevented from acting.

Article 11 [Procedure in absence of Court President/Presidents of Chambers]

4–069 When the President of the Court is absent or prevented from attending or when the office of President is vacant, the functions of President shall be exercised by a President of a Chamber [of five Judges][40] according to the order of precedence laid down in Article 6 of these Rules.

[When the President of the Court and the Presidents of the Chambers of five Judges are all prevented from attending at the same time, or their posts are vacant at the same time, the functions of President shall be exercised by one of the Presidents of the Chambers of three Judges according to the order of precedence laid down in Article 6 of these Rules.][41]

If the President of the Court and [all the Presidents of Chambers][42] are all prevented from attending at the same time, or their posts are vacant at the same time, the functions of President shall be exercised by one of the other Judges according to the order of precedence laid down in Article 6 of these Rules.

[CHAPTER 2(A)—FORMATIONS OF THE COURT

Article 11(a) [Full Court, Grand Chamber and Chambers]

4–070 The Court shall sit in the following formations:
— the full Court, composed of all the Judges,
— the Grand Chamber, composed of eleven Judges in accordance with Article 11(b),
— Chambers composed of five or three Judges in accordance with Article 11(c).

Article 11(b) [Composition of Grand Chamber]

4–071 1. For each case the Grand Chamber shall be composed of the President of the Court, the Presidents of the Chambers of five Judges, the Judge-Rapporteur and the number of Judges necessary to reach eleven. The last-mentioned Judges shall be designated from the list referred to in paragraph (2), following the order laid down therein, the starting-point moving on by one name at each general meeting of the Court.

2. After the election of the President of the Court and of the Presidents of the Chambers of five Judges, a list of the other Judges shall be drawn up for the purposes of determining the composition of the Grand Chamber. That list shall follow the order laid down in Article 6 of these Rules, alternating with the reverse

[39] Article 10(1) replaced by amendments to the Rules of Procedure ([2003] OJ L147/17) Art. 1(7) with effect from 1 August 2003.

[40] Words added by amendments to the Rules of Procedure ([2003] OJ L147/17) Art. 1(8)(a) with effect from 1 August 2003.

[41] Second subparagraph added by amendments to the Rules of Procedure ([2003] OJ L147/17) Art. 1(8)(b) with effect from 1 August 2003.

[42] Words replaced by amendments to the Rules of Procedure ([2003] OJ L147/17) Art. 1(8)(c) with effect from 1 August 2003.

order: the first Judge on that list shall be the first according to the order laid down in that Article, the second Judge shall be the last according to that order, the third Judge shall be the second according to that order, the fourth Judge the penultimate according to that order, and so on.

The list shall be published in the *Official Journal of the European Union.*

Article 11(c) [Composition of Chambers]

1. The Chambers of five Judges and three Judges shall, for each case, be composed of the President of the Chamber, the Judge-Rapporteur and the number of Judges required to attain the number of five and three Judges respectively. Those last-mentioned Judges shall be designated from the lists referred to in paragraph (2) and following the order laid down in them, the starting-point being moved on by one name at each general meeting of the Court. **4–072**

2. For the composition of the Chambers of five Judges, after the election of the Presidents of those Chambers lists shall be drawn up including all the Judges attached to the Chamber concerned, with the exception of its President. The lists shall be drawn up in the same way as the list referred to in Article 11(b)(2).

For the composition of the Chambers of three Judges, after the election of the Presidents of those Chambers lists shall be drawn up including all the Judges attached to the Chamber concerned, with the exception of its President. The lists shall be drawn up according to the order laid down in Article 6 of these Rules.

The lists referred to in this paragraph shall be published in the *Official Journal of the European Union.*

Article 11(d) [Procedure in joined cases]

Where the Court considers that several cases must be heard and determined together by one and the same formation of the Court, the composition of that formation shall be that fixed for the case in respect of which the preliminary report was first examined. **4–073**

Article 11(e) [Deputising for absentee Court members]

When a member of the formation determining a case is prevented from attending, he shall be replaced by a Judge according to the order of the lists referred to in Article 11(b)(2) or 11(c)(2). **4–074**

When the President of the Court is prevented from attending, the functions of the President of the Grand Chamber shall be exercised in accordance with the provisions of Article 11.

When the President of a Chamber of five Judges is prevented from attending, the functions of President of the Chamber shall be exercised by a President of a Chamber of three Judges, where necessary according to the order laid down in Article 6 of these Rules or, if that Chamber does not include a President of a Chamber of three Judges, by one of the other Judges according to the order laid down in Article 6.

When the President of a Chamber of three Judges is prevented from attending, the functions of President of the Chamber shall be exercised by a Judge of that Chamber according to the order laid down in Article 6 of these Rules.][43]

[43] Chapter 2(a) inserted by amendments to the Rules of Procedure ([2003] OJ L147/17) Art. 1(9) with effect from 1 August 2003.

CHAPTER 3—REGISTRY

SECTION 1—THE REGISTRAR AND ASSISTANT REGISTRARS

Article 12 [Registrar]

4–075 1. The Court shall appoint the Registrar. Two weeks before the date fixed for making the appointment, the President shall inform the Members of the Court of the applications which have been made for the post.

2. An application shall be accompanied by full details of the candidate's age, nationality, university degrees, knowledge of any languages, present and past occupations and experience, if any, in judicial and international fields.

3. The appointment shall be made following the procedure laid down in Article 7(3) of these Rules.

4. The Registrar shall be appointed for a term of six years. He may be reappointed.

5. The Registrar shall take the oath in accordance with Article 3 of these Rules.

6. The Registrar may be deprived of his office only if he no longer fulfils the requisite conditions or no longer meets the obligations arising from his office the Court shall take its decision after giving the Registrar an opportunity to make representations.

7. If the office of Registrar falls vacant before the normal date of expiry of the term thereof, the Court shall appoint a new Registrar for a term of six years.

Article 13 [Assistant Registrars]

4–076 The Court may, following the procedure laid down in respect of the Registrar, appoint one or more Assistant Registrars to assist the Registrar and to take his place in so far as the Instructions to the Registrar referred to in Article 15 of these Rules allow.

Article 14 [Absence of Registrar and Assistant Registrars]

4–077 Where the Registrar and the Assistant Registrars are absent or prevented from attending or their posts are vacant, the President shall designate an official or other servant to carry out the duties of Registrar.

Article 15 [Instructions to Registrar]

4–078 Instructions to the Registrar shall be adopted by the Court acting on a proposal from the President.

Article 16 [Court Register]

4–079 1. There shall be kept in the Registry, under the control of the Registrar, a register initialled by the President, in which all pleadings and supporting documents shall be entered in the order in which they are lodged.

2. When a document has been registered, the Registrar shall make a note to that effect on the original and, if a party so requests, on any copy submitted for the purpose.

3. Entries in the register and the notes provided for in the preceding paragraph shall be authentic.

4. Rules for keeping the register shall be prescribed by the Instructions to the Registrar referred to in Article 15 of these Rules.

5. Persons having an interest may consult the register at the Registry and may obtain copies or extracts on payment of a charge on a scale fixed by the Court on a proposal from the Registrar.

The parties to a case may on payment of the appropriate charge also obtain copies of pleadings and authenticated copies of judgments and orders.

6. Notice shall be given in the *Official Journal [of the European Union]*[44] of the date of registration of an application initiating proceedings, the names and addresses of the parties, the subject-matter of the proceedings, the form of order sought by the applicant and a summary of the pleas in law and of the main supporting arguments.

7. Where the Council or the Commission is not a party to a case, the Court shall send to it copies of the application and of the defence, without the annexes thereto, to enable it to assess whether the inapplicability of one of its acts is being invoked under Article [241][45] of the [EC Treaty [...][46] or Article 156 of the Euratom Treaty].[47] [Copies of the application and of the defence shall likewise be sent to the European Parliament, to enable it to assess whether the inapplicability of an act adopted jointly by that institution and by the Council is being invoked under Article 241 of the EC Treaty.][48]

Article 17 [Other functions of Registrar]

1. The Registrar shall be responsible, under the authority of the President, for the acceptance, transmission and custody of documents and for effecting service as provided for by these Rules. **4–080**

[2. The Registrar shall assist the Court, the President and the Presidents of Chambers and the Judges in all their official functions.][49]

Article 18 [Court Seals; records and publications]

The Registrar shall have custody of the seals. He shall be responsible for the records and be in charge of the publications of the Court. **4–081**

Article 19 [Attendance at sittings]

Subject to Articles 4 and 27 of these Rules, the Registrar shall attend the sittings of the Court and of the Chambers. **4–082**

SECTION 2—OTHER DEPARTMENTS

Article 20 [Officials and other servants]

1. The officials and other servants of the Court shall be appointed in accordance with the provisions of the Staff Regulations. **4–083**

2. Before taking up his duties, an official shall take the following oath before the President, in the presence of the Registrar:

> "I swear that I will perform loyally, discreetly and conscientiously the duties assigned to me by the Court of Justice of the European Communities."

[44] Words replaced by amendments to the Rules of Procedure ([2003] OJ L147/17) Art. 1(10) with effect from 1 August 2003.

[45] Word substituted by amendments to Rules of Procedure ([2000] OJ L122/43) Art. 1(13) with effect from 1 July 2000.

[46] Words omitted by amendments to the Rules of Procedure ([2003] OJ L147/17) Art. 1(11) with effect from 1 August 2003.

[47] Term "EC Treaty" replaced and order in which Treaties are cited replaced by amendments to Rules of Procedure ([1995] OJ L44/61) Art. 1(11) with effect from 1 April 1995.

[48] Words inserted by amendments to Rules of Procedure ([2001] OJ L119/1) Art. 1 with effect from 1 June 2001.

[49] Article 17(2) replaced by amendments to the Rules of Procedure ([2003] OJ L147/17) Art. 1(12) with effect from 1 August 2003.

Article 21 [Organisation of Court departments]

4–084 The organisation of the departments of the Court shall be laid down, and may be modified, by the Court on a proposal from the Registrar.

Article 22 [Translation service]

4–085 The Court shall set up a translating service staffed by experts with adequate legal training and a thorough knowledge of several official languages of the Court.

Article 23 [Court administration, financial management and accounts]

4–086 The Registrar shall be responsible, under the authority of the President, for the administration of the Court, its financial management and its accounts; he shall be assisted in this by an administrator.

CHAPTER 4—ASSISTANT RAPPORTEURS

Article 24 [Appointment of Assistant Rapporteurs]

4–087 1. Where the Court is of the opinion that the consideration of, and preparatory inquiries in, cases before it so require, it shall, pursuant to [Article 13 of the Statute],[50] propose the appointment of Assistant Rapporteurs.

2. Assistant Rapporteurs shall in particular:
— assist the President in connection with applications for the adoption of interim measures
— assist the Judge-Rapporteurs in their work.

3. In the performance of their duties the Assistant Rapporteurs shall be responsible to the President of the Court, the President of a Chamber or a Judge-Rapporteur, as the case may be.

4. Before taking up his duties, an Assistant Rapporteur shall take before the Court the oath set out in Article 3 of these Rules.

CHAPTER 5—THE WORKING OF THE COURT

Article 25 [Court sittings]

4–088 1. The dates and times of the sittings of the [Grand Chamber and of the full Court][51] shall be fixed by the President.
2. The dates and times of the sittings of the Chambers [of five and three Judges][52] shall be fixed by their respective Presidents.
3. The Court [may][53] choose to hold one or more sittings in a place other than that in which the Court has its seat.

Article 26 [Quorum]

4–089 1. Where, by reason of a Judge being absent or prevented from attending, there is an even number of Judges, the most junior Judge within the meaning of Article 6 of these Rules shall abstain from taking part in the deliberations unless he is the

[50] Words replaced by amendments to the Rules of Procedure ([2003] OJ L147/17) Art. 1(13) with effect from 1 August 2003.
[51] Word replaced by amendments to the Rules of Procedure ([2003] OJ L147/17) Art. 1(14) with effect from 1 August 2003.
[52] Words added by amendments to the Rules of Procedure ([2003] OJ L147/17) Art. 1(15) with effect from 1 August 2003.
[53] Words replaced by amendments to the Rules of Procedure ([2003] OJ L147/17) Art. 1(16) with effect from 1 August 2003.

Judge-Rapporteur. In that case the Judge immediately senior to him shall abstain from taking part in the deliberations.

[2. If, after the [Grand Chamber or full Court][54] has been convened, it is found that the quorum referred to in [the third or fourth paragraph of Article 17 of the Statute][55] has not been attained, the President shall adjourn the sitting until there is a quorum.

3. If, in [any Chamber of five or three Judges],[56] the quorum referred to in [the second paragraph of Article 17 of the Statute][57] has not been attained [and if it is not possible to replace the Judges prevented from attending in accordance with Article 11(e)],[58] the President of that Chamber shall so inform the President of the Court who shall designate another Judge to complete the Chamber.][59]

Article 27 [Deliberations and decisions]

1. The Court [shall deliberate][60] in closed session. **4–090**

2. Only those Judges who were present at the oral proceedings and the Assistant Rapporteur, if any, entrusted with the consideration of the case may take part in the deliberations.

3. Every Judge taking part in the deliberations shall state his opinion and the reasons for it.

4. Any Judge may require that any questions be formulated in the language of his choice and communicated in writing to the Court [...][61] before being put to the vote.

5. The conclusions reached by the majority of the Judges after final discussion shall determine the decision of the Court. Votes shall be cast in reverse order to the order of precedence laid down in Article 6 of these Rules.

6. Differences of view on the substance, wording or order of questions, or on the interpretation of the voting shall be settled by decision of the Court [...].[62]

7. Where the deliberations of the Court concern questions of its own administration, the Advocates General shall take part and have a vote. The Registrar shall be present, unless the Court decides to the contrary.

---

[54] Word replaced by amendments to the Rules of Procedure ([2003] OJ L147/17) Art. 1(17)(a) with effect from 1 August 2003.

[55] Words replaced by amendments to the Rules of Procedure ([2003] OJ L147/17) Art. 1(17)(b) with effect from 1 August 2003.

[56] Words replaced by amendments to the Rules of Procedure ([2003] OJ L147/17) Art. 1(18)(a) with effect from 1 August 2003.

[57] Words replaced by amendments to the Rules of Procedure ([2003] OJ L147/17) Art. 1(18)(b) with effect from 1 August 2003.

[58] Words added by amendments to the Rules of Procedure ([2003] OJ L147/17) Art. 1(18)(c) with effect from 1 August 2003.

[59] Article 26(2) and (3) replaced by amendments to Rules of Procedure ([1997] OJ L103/1) Art. 1(1) with effect from 1 June 1997.

[60] Words replaced by amendments to the Rules of Procedure ([2003] OJ L147/17) Art. 1(19) with effect from 1 August 2003.

[61] Words deleted by amendments to the Rules of Procedure ([2003] OJ L147/17) Art. 1(20) with effect from 1 August 2003.

[62] Words deleted by amendments to the Rules of Procedure ([2003] OJ L147/17) Art. 1(21) with effect from 1 August 2003.

8. Where the Court sits without the Registrar being present it shall, if necessary, instruct the most junior Judge within the meaning of Article 6 of these Rules to draw up minutes. The minutes shall be signed by that Judge and by the President.

Article 28 [Court vacations]

4–091 1. Subject to any special decision of the Court, its vacations shall be as follows:
— from 18 December to 10 January,
— from the Sunday before Easter to the second Sunday after Easter,
— from 15 July to 15 September.

During the vacations, the functions of President shall be exercised at the place where the Court has its seat either by the President himself, keeping in touch with the Registrar, or by a President of Chamber or other Judge invited by the President to take his place.

2. In a case of urgency, the President may convene the Judges and the Advocates General during the vacations.

3. The Court shall observe the official holidays of the place where it has its seat.

4. The Court may, in proper circumstances, grant leave of absence to any Judge or Advocate General.

CHAPTER 6—LANGUAGES

Article 29 [Language of the case]

4–092 [1. The language of a case shall be Danish, Dutch, English, Finnish, French, German, Greek, Irish, Italian, Portuguese, Spanish or Swedish.][63]

[2. The language of the case shall be chosen by the applicant, except that:
(a) where the defendant is a Member State or a natural or legal person having the nationality of a Member State, the language of the case shall be the official language of that State; where that State has more than one official language, the applicant may choose between them;
(b) at the joint request of the parties, the use of another of the languages mentioned in paragraph 1 for all or part of the proceedings may be authorised;
(c) at the request of one of the parties, and after the opposite party and the Advocate General have been heard, the use of another of the languages mentioned in paragraph 1 as the language of the case for all or part of the proceedings may be authorised by way of derogation from sub-paragraphs (a) and (b); such a request may not be submitted by an institution of the European Communities.

In cases to which Article 103 of these Rules applies, the language of the case shall be the language of the national court or tribunal which refers the matter to the Court. At the duly substantiated request of one of the parties to the main proceedings, and after the opposite party and the Advocate General have been heard, the use of another of the languages mentioned in paragraph 1 may be authorised for the oral procedure.

Requests as above may be decided on by the President; the latter may and, where he wishes to accede to a request without the agreement of all the parties, must refer the request to the Court.][64]

---

[63] Article 29(1) replaced by amendments to Rules of Procedure ([1997] OJ L103/1) Art. 1(2) with effect from 1 June 1997.

[64] Article 29(2) replaced by amendments to Rules of Procedure ([1997] OJ L103/1) Art. 1(3) (as corrected at [1997] OJ L351/72) with effect from 1 June 1997.

3. The language of the case shall in particular be used in the written and oral pleadings of the parties and in supporting documents, and also in the minutes and decisions of the Court.

Any supporting documents expressed in another language must be accompanied by a translation into the language of the case.

In the case of lengthy documents, translations may be confined to extracts. However, the Court [...][65] may, of its own motion or at the request of a party, at any time call for a complete or fuller translation.

Notwithstanding the foregoing provisions, a Member State shall be entitled to use its official language when intervening in a case before the Court or when taking part in any reference of a kind mentioned in Article 103. This provision shall apply both to written statements and to oral addresses. The Registrar shall cause any such statement or address to be translated into the language of the case.

[The States, other than the Member States, which are parties to the EEA Agreement, and also the EFTA Surveillance Authority, may be authorised to use one of the languages mentioned in paragraph 1, other than the language of the case, when they intervene in a case before the Court or participate in preliminary ruling proceedings envisaged by [Article 23 of the Statute].[66] This provision shall apply both to written statements and oral addresses. The Registrar shall cause any such statement or address to be translated into the language of the case.][67]

[Non-member States taking part in proceedings for a preliminary ruling pursuant to [the fourth paragraph of Article 23 of the Statute][68] may be authorised to use one of the languages mentioned in paragraph 1 of this Article other than the language of the case. This provision shall apply both to written documents and to oral statements. The Registrar shall in each case arrange for their translation into the language of the case.][69]

4. Where a witness or expert states that he is unable adequately to express himself in one of the languages referred to in paragraph (1) of this Article, the Court [...][70] may authorise him to give his evidence in another language. The Registrar shall arrange for translation into the language of the case.

5. The President of the Court and the Presidents of Chambers in conducting oral proceedings, the Judge-Rapporteur both in his preliminary report and in his report for the hearing, Judges and Advocates General in putting questions and Advocates General in delivering their opinions may use one of the languages referred to in paragraph 1 of this Article other than the language of the case. The Registrar shall arrange for translation into the language of the case.

Article 30 [Translation into other official languages]

1. The Registrar shall, at the request of any Judge, of the Advocate General or of a party, arrange for anything said or written in the course of the proceedings before the Court [...][71] to be translated into the languages he chooses from those referred to in Article 29(1). **4–093**

[65] Words deleted by amendments to the Rules of Procedure ([2003] OJ L147/17) Art. 1(22)(a) with effect from 1 August 2003.

[66] Words replaced by amendments to the Rules of Procedure ([2003] OJ L147/17) Art. 1(22)(b) with effect from 1 August 2003.

[67] Words added by amendments to Rules of Procedure ([1995] OJ L44/61) Art. 1(2) with effect from 1 April 1995.

[68] Words replaced by amendments to the Rules of Procedure ([2003] OJ L147/17) Art. 1(22)(c) with effect from 1 August 2003.

[69] Final subparagraph of Art.29(3) added by amendment to Rules of Procedure ([2002] OJ L272/24) Art.1(1) with effect from 10 October 2002.

[70] Words deleted by amendments to the Rules of Procedure ([2003] OJ L147/17) Art. 1(23) with effect from 1 August 2003.

[71] Words deleted by amendments to the Rules of Procedure ([2003] OJ L147/17) Art. 1(24) with effect from 1 August 2003.

2. Publications of the Court shall be issued in the languages referred to in Article 1 of Council Regulation 1.[72]

Article 31 [Authenticity of documents]

4–094 The texts of documents drawn up in the language of the case or in any other language authorised by the Court pursuant to Article 29 of these Rules shall be authentic.

CHAPTER 7—RIGHTS AND OBLIGATIONS OF AGENTS, ADVISERS AND LAWYERS

Article 32 [Immunity from suit and other privileges]

4–095 [1. Agents, advisers and lawyers appearing before the Court or before any judicial authority to which the Court has addressed letters rogatory, shall enjoy immunity in respect of words spoken or written by them concerning the case or the parties.][73]

2. Agents, advisers and lawyers shall enjoy the following further privileges and facilities:

(a) papers and documents relating to the proceedings shall be exempt from both search and seizure in the event of a dispute the customs officials or police may seal those papers and documents they shall then be immediately forwarded to the Court for inspection in the presence of the Registrar and of the person concerned;

(b) agents, advisers and lawyers shall be entitled to such allocation of foreign currency as may be necessary for the performance of their duties;

(c) agents, advisers and lawyers shall be entitled to travel in the course of duty without hindrance.

Article 33 [Proof of status]

4–096 [In order to qualify for the privileges, immunities and facilities specified in Article 32, persons entitled to them shall furnish proof of their status as follows:

(a) agents shall produce an official document issued by the party for whom they act, and shall forward without delay a copy thereof to the Registrar;

(b) advisers and lawyers shall produce a certificate signed by the Registrar. The validity of this certificate shall be limited to a specified period, which may be extended or curtailed according to the length of the proceedings.][74]

Article 34 [Waiver of immunity]

4–097 The privileges, immunities and facilities specified in Article 32 of these Rules are granted exclusively in the interests of the proper conduct of proceedings.

The Court may waive the immunity where it considers that the proper conduct of proceedings will not be hindered thereby.

Article 35 [Exclusion from proceedings]

4–098 1. Any adviser or lawyer whose conduct towards the Court, [...][75] a Judge, an Advocate General or the Registrar is incompatible with the dignity of the Court, or who uses his rights for purposes other than those for which they were granted,

[72] Regulation 1/58 ([1952–1958] OJ, Eng. Spec. Ed., p.59) (as amended) determines languages to be used by the EC.

[73] Article 32(1) substituted by amendments to Rules of Procedure ([1995] OJ L44/61) Art. 1(3) with effect from 1 April 1995.

[74] Article 33 substituted by amendments to Rules of Procedure ([1995] OJ L44/61) Art. 1(4) with effect from 1 April 1995.

[75] Words deleted by amendments to the Rules of Procedure ([2003] OJ L147/17) Art. 1(25)(a) with effect from 1 August 2003.

may at any time be excluded from the proceedings by an order of the Court [. . .],[76] after the Advocate General has been heard the person concerned shall be given an opportunity to defend himself.

The order shall have immediate effect.

2. Where an adviser or lawyer is excluded from the proceedings, the proceedings shall be suspended for a period fixed by the President in order to allow the party concerned to appoint another adviser or lawyer.

3. Decisions taken under this Article may be rescinded.

Article 36 [University teachers]

The provisions of this Chapter shall apply to university teachers who have a right of audience before the Court in accordance with [Article 19 of the Statute].[77] **4–099**

Title II—Procedure

CHAPTER 1—WRITTEN PROCEDURE

Article 37 [Pleadings]

1. The original of every pleading must be signed by the party's agent or lawyer. The original, accompanied by all annexes referred to therein, shall be lodged together with five copies for the Court and a copy for every other party to the proceedings. Copies shall be certified by the party lodging them. **4–100**

2. Institutions shall in addition produce, within time-limits laid down by the Court, translations of all pleadings into the other languages provided for by Article 1 of Council Regulation 1.[78] The second subparagraph of paragraph 1 of this Article shall apply.

3. All pleadings shall bear a date. In the reckoning of time-limits for taking steps in proceedings, only the date of lodgment at the Registry shall be taken into account.

4. To every pleading there shall be annexed a file containing the documents relied on in support of it, together with a schedule listing them.

5. Where in view of the length of a document only extracts from it are annexed to the pleading, the whole document or a full copy of it shall be lodged at the Registry.

[6. Without prejudice to the provisions of paragraphs 1 to 5, the date on which a copy of the signed original of a pleading, including the schedule of documents referred to in paragraph 4, is received at the Registry by telefax or other technical means of communication available to the Court shall be deemed to be the date of lodgment for the purposes of compliance with the time-limits for taking steps in proceedings, provided that the signed original of the pleading, accompanied by the annexes and copies referred to in the second sub-paragraph of paragraph 1 above, is lodged at the Registry no later than ten days thereafter.][79]

[76] Words deleted by amendments to the Rules of Procedure ([2003] OJ L147/17) Art. 1(25)(b) with effect from 1 August 2003.

[77] Words replaced by amendments to the Rules of Procedure ([2003] OJ L147/17) Art. 1(26) with effect from 1 August 2003.

[78] Regulation 1/58 ([1952–1958] OJ, Eng. Spec. Ed., p.59) (as amended) determines languages to be used by the EC.

[79] Article 37(6) added by amendments to Rules of Procedure ([2000] OJ L322/1) Art. 1(1) from 1 February 2001.

Article 38 [Written applications to Registrar]

4–101 1. An application of the kind referred to in [Article 21 of the Statute][80] shall state:
(a) the name and address of the applicant;
(b) the designation of the party against whom the application is made;
(c) the subject-matter of the proceedings and a summary of the pleas in law on which the application is based;
(d) the form of order sought by the applicant;
(e) where appropriate, the nature of any evidence offered in support.

2. For the purpose of the proceedings, the application shall state an address for service in the place where the Court has its seat and the name of the person who is authorised and has expressed willingness to accept service.

[In addition to, or instead of, specifying an address for service as referred to in the first subparagraph, the application may state that the lawyer or agent agrees that service is to be effected on him by telefax or other technical means of communication.][81]

If the application does not comply [with the requirements referred to in the first and second sub-paragraphs],[82] all service on the party concerned for the purpose of the proceedings shall be effected, for so long as the defect has not been cured, by registered letter addressed to the agent or lawyer of that party. By way of derogation from Article 79[(1)],[83] service shall then be deemed to be duly effected by the lodging of the registered letter at the post office of the place where the Court has its seat.

[3. The lawyer acting for a party must lodge at the Registry a certificate that he is authorised to practise before a court of a Member State or of another State which is a party to the EEA Agreement.][84]

4. The application shall be accompanied, where appropriate, by the documents specified in [the second paragraph of Article 21 of the Statute].[85]

5. An application made by a legal person governed by private law shall be accompanied by:
(a) the instrument or instruments constituting or regulating that legal person or a recent extract from the register of companies, firms or associations or any other proof of its existence in law;
(b) proof that the authority granted to the applicant's lawyer has been properly conferred on him by someone authorised for the purpose.

6. An application submitted under Articles [238 and 239][86] of the [EC Treaty [...][87] and Articles 153 and 154 of the Euratom Treaty][88] shall be accompanied by a copy

[80] Words replaced by amendments to the Rules of Procedure ([2003] OJ L147/17) Art. 1(27) with effect from 1 August 2003.
[81] Words inserted by amendments to Rules of Procedure ([2000] OJ L322/1) Art. 1(2) from 1 February 2001.
[82] Words substituted by Rules of Procedure ([2000] OJ L322/1) Art. 1(2) from 1 February 2001.
[83] Word inserted by Rules of Procedure ([2000] OJ L322/1) Art. 1(2) from 1 February 2001.
[84] Article 38(3) substituted by amendments to Rules of Procedure ([1995] OJ L44/61) Art. 1(5) with effect from 1 April 1995.
[85] Words replaced by amendments to the Rules of Procedure ([2003] OJ L147/17) Art. 1(28) with effect from 1 August 2003.
[86] Words substituted by amendments to Rules of Procedure ([2000] OJ L122/43) Art. 1(13) from 1 July 2000.
[87] Words deleted by amendments to the Rules of Procedure ([2003] OJ L147/17) Art. 1(29) with effect from 1 August 2003.
[88] Term "EC Treaty" replaced and order in which Treaties are cited replaced by amendments to Rules of Procedure ([1995] OJ L44/61) Art. 1(11) with effect from 1 April 1995.

of the arbitration clause contained in the contract governed by private or public law entered into by the Communities or on their behalf, or, as the case may be, by a copy of the special agreement concluded between the Member States concerned.

7. If an application does not comply with the requirements set out in paragraphs 3 to 6 of this Article, the Registrar shall prescribe a reasonable period within which the applicant is to comply with them whether by putting the application itself in order or by producing any of the abovementioned documents. If the applicant fails to put the application in order or to produce the required documents within the time prescribed, the Court shall, after hearing the Advocate General, decide whether the non-compliance with these conditions renders the application formally inadmissible.

Article 39 [Service on defendant]

The application shall be served on the defendant. In a case where Article 38(7) applies, service shall be effected as soon as the application has been put in order or the Court has declared it admissible notwithstanding the failure to observe the formal requirements set out in that Article. **4–102**

Article 40 [Lodging of defence]

1. Within one month after service on him of the application, the defendant shall lodge a defence, stating: **4–103**
(a) the name and address of the defendant;
(b) the arguments of fact and law relied on;
(c) the form of order sought by the defendant;
(d) the nature of any evidence offered by him.
The provisions of Article 38(2) to (5) of these Rules shall apply to the defence.

2. The time-limit laid down in paragraph 1 of this Article may be extended by the President on a reasoned application by the defendant.

Article 41 [Reply and rejoinder]

1. The application initiating the proceedings and the defence may be supplemented by a reply from the applicant and by a rejoinder from the defendant. **4–104**

2. The President shall fix the time-limits within which these pleadings are to be lodged.

Article 42 [New evidence and pleas]

1. In reply or rejoinder a party may offer further evidence. The party must, however, give reasons for the delay in offering it. **4–105**

2. No new plea in law may be introduced in the course of proceedings unless it is based on matters of law or of fact which come to light in the course of the procedure.

If in the course of the procedure one of the parties puts forward a new plea in law which is so based, the President may, even after the expiry of the normal procedural time-limits, acting on a report of the Judge-Rapporteur and after hearing the Advocate General, allow the other party time to answer on that plea.

The decision on the admissibility of the plea shall be reserved for the final judgment.

Article 43 [Joinder of cases]

The President may, at any time, after hearing the parties and the Advocate General, if the assignment referred to in Article 10(2) has taken place, order that **4–106** two or more cases concerning the same subject-matter shall, on account of the connection between them, be joined for the purposes of the written or oral procedure or of the final judgment. The cases may subsequently be disjoined. [The President may refer these matters to the Court.][89]

[CHAPTER 1(A)—THE PRELIMINARY REPORT AND ASSIGNMENT OF CASES TO FORMATIONS

Article 44 [Judge-Rapporteur's report; basis of case assignment]

4–107 1. The President shall fix a date on which the Judge-Rapporteur is to present his preliminary report to the general meeting of the Court, either:

(a) after the rejoinder has been lodged; or
(b) where no reply or no rejoinder has been lodged within the time-limit fixed in accordance with Article 41(2); or
(c) where the party concerned has waived his right to lodge a reply or rejoinder; or
(d) where the expedited procedure referred to in Article 62(a)is to be applied, when the President fixes a date for the hearing.

2. The preliminary report shall contain recommendations as to whether a preparatory inquiry or any other preparatory step should be undertaken and as to the formation to which the case should be assigned. It shall also contain the Judge-Rapporteur's recommendation, if any, as to whether to dispense with a hearing as provided for in Article 44a and as to whether to dispense with an opinion of the Advocate General pursuant to the fifth subparagraph of Article 20 of the Statute.

The Court shall decide, after hearing the Advocate General, what action to take upon the recommendations of the Judge-Rapporteur.

3. The Court shall assign to the Chambers of five and three Judges any case brought before it in so far as the difficulty or importance of the case or particular circumstances are not such as to require that it should be assigned to the Grand Chamber.

However, a case may not be assigned to a Chamber of five or three Judges if a Member State or an institution of the Communities, being a party to the proceedings, has requested that the case be decided by the Grand Chamber. For the purposes of this provision, "party to the proceedings" means any Member State or any institution which is a party to or an intervener in the proceedings or which has submitted written observations in any reference of a kind mentioned in Article 103. A request such as that referred to in this subparagraph may not be made in proceedings between the Communities and their servants.

The Court shall sit as a full Court where cases are brought before it pursuant to the provisions referred to in the fourth paragraph of Article 16 of the Statute. It may assign a case to the full Court where, in accordance with the fifth paragraph of Article 16 of the Statute, it considers that the case is of exceptional importance.

4. The formation to which a case has been assigned may, at any stage of the proceedings, refer the case back to the Court in order that it may be reassigned to a formation composed of a greater number of Judges.

5. Where a preparatory inquiry has been opened, the formation determining the case may, if it does not undertake it itself, assign the inquiry to the Chamber referred to in Article 9(2) of these Rules.

Where the oral procedure is opened without an inquiry, the President of the formation determining the case shall fix the opening date.][90]

[89] Words added by amendments to Rules of Procedure ([1997] OJ L103/1) Art. 1(4) with effect from 1 June 1997.

[90] Replaced by amendments to the Rules of Procedure ([2003] OJ L147/17) Art. 1(30) with effect from 1 August 2003.

[Article 44a [Oral hearings]

Without prejudice to any special provisions laid down in these Rules, the procedure before the Court shall also include an oral part. However, after the pleadings referred to in Article 40(1) and, as the case may be, in Article 41(1) have been lodged, the Court, acting on a report from the Judge-Rapporteur and after hearing the Advocate General, and if none of the parties has submitted an application setting out the reasons for which he wishes to be heard, may decide otherwise. The application shall be submitted within a period of one month from notification to the party of the close of the written procedure. That period may be extended by the President.][91] **4–108**

CHAPTER 2—[PREPARATORY INQUIRIES AND OTHER PREPARATORY MEASURES][92]

SECTION 1—MEASURES OF INQUIRY

Article 45 [Court orders] **4–109**

1. The Court, after hearing the Advocate General, shall prescribe the measures of inquiry that it considers appropriate by means of an order setting out the facts to be proved. Before the Court decides on the measures of inquiry referred to in paragraph 2(c), (d) and (e) the parties shall be heard.
The order shall be served on the parties.

2. Without prejudice to Articles [24 and 25 of the Statute],[93] the following measures of inquiry may be adopted:
(a) the personal appearance of the parties;
(b) a request for information and production of documents;
(c) oral testimony;
(d) the commissioning of an expert's report;
(e) an inspection of the place or thing in question.

3. The measures of inquiry which the Court has ordered may be conducted by the Court itself, or be assigned to the Judge-Rapporteur.
The Advocate General shall take part in the measures of inquiry.

4. Evidence may be submitted in rebuttal and previous evidence may be amplified.

Article 46 [Powers of Chambers to which preparatory inquiry assigned]

1. A Chamber to which a preparatory inquiry has been assigned may exercise the powers vested in the Court by Articles 45 and 47 to 53 of these Rules the powers vested in the President of the Court may be exercised by the President of the Chamber. **4–110**

2. Articles 56 and 57 of these Rules shall apply to proceedings before the Chamber.

3. The parties shall be entitled to attend the measures of inquiry.

SECTION 2—THE SUMMONING AND EXAMINATION OF WITNESSES AND EXPERTS

Article 47 [Summoning and appearance of witnesses]

1. The Court may, either of its own motion or on application by a party, and after hearing the Advocate General, order that certain facts be proved by witnesses. The order of the Court shall set out the facts to be established. **4–111**

---

[91] Article 44a inserted by amendments to Rules of Procedure ([2000] OJ L122/43) Art. 1(2) with effect from 1 July 2000.

[92] Words substituted by amendments to Rules of Procedure ([2000] OJ L122/43) Art. 1(3) with effect from 1 July 2000.

[93] Words replaced by amendments to the Rules of Procedure ([2003] OJ L147/17) Art. 1(31) with effect from 1 August 2003.

The Court may summon a witness of its own motion or on application by a party or at the instance of the Advocate General.

An application by a party for the examination of a witness shall state precisely about what facts and for what reasons the witness should be examined.

2. The witness shall be summoned by an order of the Court containing the following information:

(a) the surname, forenames, description and address of the witness;

(b) an indication of the facts about which the witness is to be examined;

(c) where appropriate, particulars of the arrangements made by the Court for reimbursement of expenses incurred by the witness, and of the penalties which may be imposed on defaulting witnesses.

The order shall be served on the parties and the witnesses.

3. The Court may make the summoning of a witness for whose examination a party has applied conditional upon the deposit with the cashier of the Court of a sum sufficient to cover the taxed costs thereof the Court shall fix the amount of the payment.

The cashier shall advance the funds necessary in connection with the examination of any witness summoned by the Court of its own motion.

4. After the identity of the witness has been established, the President shall inform him that he will be required to vouch the truth of his evidence in the manner laid down in these Rules.

The witness shall give his evidence to the Court, the parties having been given notice to attend. After the witness has given his main evidence the President may, at the request of a party or of his own motion, put questions to him.

The other Judges and the Advocate General may do likewise.

Subject to the control of the President, questions may be put to witnesses by the representatives of the parties.

5. After giving his evidence, the witness shall take the following oath:

> "I swear that I have spoken the truth, the whole truth and nothing but the truth."

The Court may, after hearing the parties, exempt a witness from taking the oath.

6. The Registrar shall draw up minutes in which the evidence of each witness is reproduced.

The minutes shall be signed by the President or by the Judge-Rapporteur responsible for conducting the examination of the witness, and by the Registrar. Before the minutes are thus signed, witnesses must be given an opportunity to check the content of the minutes and to sign them.

The minutes shall constitute an official record.

Article 48 [Failure of witnesses to appear]

4–112 1. Witnesses who have been duly summoned shall obey the summons and attend for examination.

2. If a witness who has been duly summoned fails to appear before the Court, the Court may impose upon him a pecuniary penalty not exceeding ECU 5,000[94] and may order that a further summons be served on the witness at his own expense.

The same penalty may be imposed upon a witness who, without good reason, refuses to give evidence or to take the oath or where appropriate to make a solemn affirmation equivalent thereto.

3. If the witness proffers a valid excuse to the Court, the pecuniary penalty imposed on him may be cancelled. The pecuniary penalty imposed may be

[94] References to the ECU in all legal instruments replaced by reference to the euro with effect from 1 January 1999 (see Regulation 1103/97, [1997] OJ L162/1).

reduced at the request of the witness where he establishes that it is disproportionate to his income.

4. Penalties imposed and other measures ordered under this Article shall be enforced in accordance with Articles [244 and 256][95] of the [EC Treaty [...][96] and Articles 159 and 164 of the Euratom Treaty].[97]

Article 49 [Expert evidence]

1. The Court may order that an expert's report be obtained. The order appointing the expert shall define his task and set a time-limit within which he is to make his report. **4–113**

2. The expert shall receive a copy of the order, together with all the documents necessary for carrying out his task. He shall be under the supervision of the Judge-Rapporteur, who may be present during his investigation and who shall be kept informed of his progress in carrying out his task.
The Court may request the parties or one of them to lodge security for the costs of the expert's report.

3. At the request of the expert, the Court may order the examination of witnesses. Their examination shall be carried out in accordance with Article 47 of these Rules.

4. The expert may give his opinion only on points which have been expressly referred to him.

5. After the expert has made his report, the Court may order that he be examined, the parties having been given notice to attend.
Subject to the control of the President, questions may be put to the expert by the representatives of the parties.

6. After making his report, the expert shall take the following oath before the Court:

"I swear that I have conscientiously and impartially carried out my task."

The Court may, after hearing the parties, exempt the expert from taking the oath.

Article 50 [Objection to witness or expert]

1. If one of the parties objects to a witness or to an expert on the ground that he is not a competent or proper person to act as witness or expert or for any other reason, or if a witness or expert refuses to give evidence, to take the oath or to make a solemn affirmation equivalent thereto, the matter shall be resolved by the Court. **4–114**

2. An objection to a witness or to an expert shall be raised within two weeks after service of the order summoning the witness or appointing the expert the statement of objection must set out the grounds of objection and indicate the nature of any evidence offered.

Article 51 [Payments to witnesses and experts]

1. Witnesses and experts shall be entitled to reimbursement of their travel and subsistence expenses. The cashier of the Court may make a payment to them towards these expenses in advance. **4–115**

[95] Words substituted by amendments to Rules of Procedure ([2000] OJ L122/43) Art. 1(13) from 1 July 2000.

[96] Words deleted by amendments to the Rules of Procedure ([2003] OJ L147/17) Art. 1(32) with effect from 1 August 2003.

[97] Term "EC Treaty" replaced and order in which Treaties are cited replaced by amendments to Rules of Procedure ([1995] OJ L44/61) Art. 1(11) with effect from 1 April 1995.

2. Witnesses shall be entitled to compensation for loss of earnings, and experts to fees for their services. The cashier of the Court shall pay witnesses and experts their compensation or fees after they have carried out their respective duties or tasks.

Article 52 [Letters rogatory]

4–116 The Court may, on application by a party or of its own motion, issue letters rogatory for the examination of witnesses or experts, as provided for in the supplementary rules mentioned in Article 125 of these Rules.

Article 53 [Minutes of hearings]

4–117 1. The Registrar shall draw up minutes of every hearing. The minutes shall be signed by the President and by the Registrar and shall constitute an official record.

2. The parties may inspect the minutes and any expert's report at the Registry and obtain copies at their own expense.

SECTION 3—CLOSURE OF THE PREPARATORY INQUIRY

Article 54 [Fixing date for opening oral procedure]

4–118 Unless the Court prescribes a period within which the parties may lodge written observations, the President shall fix the date for the opening of the oral procedure after the preparatory inquiry has been completed.

Where a period had been prescribed for the lodging of written observations, the President shall fix the date for the opening of the oral procedure after that period has expired.

[SECTION 4—REQUESTS FOR INFORMATION AND DOCUMENTATION

Article 54a [Information requests by Judge-Rapporteur or Advocate General]

4–119 The Judge-Rapporteur and the Advocate General may request the parties to submit within a specified period all such information relating to the facts, and all such documents or other particulars, as they may consider relevant. The information and/or documents provided shall be communicated to the other parties.][98]

CHAPTER 3—ORAL PROCEDURE

Article 55 [Order of handling cases]

4–120 1. Subject to the priority of decisions provided for in Article 85 of these Rules, the Court shall deal with the cases before it in the order in which the preparatory inquiries in them have been completed. Where the preparatory inquiries in several cases are completed simultaneously, the order in which they are to be dealt with shall be determined by the dates of entry in the register of the applications initiating them respectively.

2. The President may in special circumstances order that a case be given priority over others.

The President may in special circumstances, after hearing the parties and the Advocate General, either on his own initiative or at the request of one of the

[98] Section 4 inserted by amendments to Rules of Procedure ([2000] OJ L122/43) Art. 1(4) with effect from 1 July 2000.

parties, defer a case to be dealt with at a later date. On a joint application by the parties the President may order that a case be deferred.

Article 56 [Conduct of hearing]

1. The proceedings shall be opened and directed by the President, who shall be responsible for the proper conduct of the hearing. **4–121**

2. The oral proceedings in cases heard in camera shall not be published.

Article 57 [Direct examination by Court members]

The President may in the course of the hearing put questions to the agents, advisers or lawyers of the parties. **4–122**

The other Judges and the Advocate General may do likewise.

Article 58 [No personal appearances]

A party may address the Court only through his agent, adviser or lawyer. **4–123**

Article 59 [Advocate General's opinion; closure of oral procedure]

1. The Advocate General shall deliver his opinion orally at the end of the oral procedure. **4–124**

2. After the Advocate General has delivered his opinion, the President shall declare the oral procedure closed.

Article 60 [Measures of enquiry post-Advocate General's opinion]

The Court may at any time, in accordance with Article 45(1), after hearing the Advocate General, order any measure of inquiry to be taken or that a previous inquiry be repeated or expanded. The Court may direct the Chamber or the Judge-Rapporteur to carry out the measures so ordered. **4–125**

Article 61 [Possible reopening of oral procedure]

The Court may after hearing the Advocate General order the reopening of the oral procedure. **4–126**

Article 62 [Minutes of hearings]

1. The Registrar shall draw up minutes of every hearing. The minutes shall be signed by the President and by the Registrar and shall constitute an official record. **4–127**

2. The parties may inspect the minutes at the Registry and obtain copies at their own expense.

[CHAPTER 3A—EXPEDITED PROCEDURES

Article 62a [Exceptional procedure]

1. On application by the applicant or the defendant, the President may exceptionally decide, on the basis of a recommendation by the Judge-Rapporteur and after hearing the other party and the Advocate General, that a case is to be determined pursuant to an expedited procedure derogating from the provisions of these Rules, where the particular urgency of the case requires the Court to give its ruling with the minimum of delay. **4–128**

An application for a case to be decided under an expedited procedure shall be made by a separate document lodged at the same time as the application initiating the proceedings or the defence, as the case may be.

2. Under the expedited procedure, the originating application and the defence may be supplemented by a reply and a rejoinder only if the President considers this to be necessary.

An intervener may lodge a statement in intervention only if the President considers this to be necessary.

3. Once the defence has been lodged or, if the decision to adjudicate under an expedited procedure is not made until after that pleading has been lodged, once that decision has been taken, the President shall fix a date for the hearing, which shall be communicated forthwith to the parties. He may postpone the date of the hearing where the organisation of measures of inquiry or of other preparatory measures so requires.

Without prejudice to Article 42, the parties may supplement their arguments and offer further evidence in the course of the oral procedure. They must, however, give reasons for the delay in offering such further evidence.

4. The Court shall give its ruling after hearing the Advocate General.][99]

CHAPTER 4—JUDGMENTS

Article 63 [Content of judgments]

4–129 The judgment shall contain:

— a statement that it is the judgment of the Court,
— the date of its delivery,
— the names of the President and of the Judges taking part in it,
— the name of the Advocate General,
— the name of the Registrar,
— the description of the parties,
— the names of the agents, advisers and lawyers of the parties,
— a statement of the forms of order sought by the parties,
— a statement that the Advocate General has been heard,
— a summary of the facts,
— the grounds for the decision,
— the operative part of the judgment, including the decision as to costs.

Article 64 [Delivery and recording of judgments]

4–130 1. The judgment shall be delivered in open court the parties shall be given notice to attend to hear it.

2. The original of the judgment, signed by the President, by the Judges who took part in the deliberations and by the Registrar, shall be sealed and deposited at the Registry the parties shall be served with certified copies of the judgment.

3. The Registrar shall record on the original of the judgment the date on which it was delivered.

Article 65 [Binding effect of judgment]

4–131 The judgment shall be binding from the date of its delivery.

Article 66 [Rectification of judgments]

4–132 1. Without prejudice to the provisions relating to the interpretation of judgments the Court may, of its own motion or on application by a party made within two weeks after the delivery of a judgment, rectify clerical mistakes, errors in calculation and obvious slips in it.

[99] Chapter 3a inserted by amendments to Rules of Procedure ([2000] OJ L322/1) Art. 1(4) with effect from 1 February 2001.

2. The parties, whom the Registrar shall duly notify, may lodge written observations within a period prescribed by the President.

3. The Court shall take its decision in closed session after hearing the Advocate General.

4. The original of the rectification order shall be annexed to the original of the rectified judgment. A note of this order shall be made in the margin of the original of the rectified judgment.

Article 67 [Supplementary judgments]

If the Court should omit to give a decision on a specific head of claim or on costs, any party may within a month after service of the judgment apply to the Court to supplement its judgment. **4–133**

The application shall be served on the opposite party and the President shall prescribe a period within which that party may lodge written observations.

After these observations have been lodged, the Court shall, after hearing the Advocate General, decide both on the admissibility and on the substance of the application.

Article 68 [Reports of cases]

The Registrar shall arrange for the publication of reports of cases before the Court. **4–134**

CHAPTER 5—COSTS

Article 69 [Decisions on costs]

1. A decision as to costs shall be given in the final judgment or in the order which closes the proceedings. **4–135**

2. The unsuccessful party shall be ordered to pay the costs if they have been applied for in the successful party's pleadings.

Where there are several unsuccessful parties the Court shall decide how the costs are to be shared.

3. Where each party succeeds on some and fails on other heads, or where the circumstances are exceptional, the Court may order that the costs be shared or that the parties bear their own costs.

The Court may order a party, even if successful, to pay costs which the Court considers that party to have unreasonably or vexatiously caused the opposite party to incur.

4. The Member States and institutions which intervene in the proceedings shall bear their own costs.

[The States, other than the Member States, which are parties to the EEA Agreement, and also the EFTA Surveillance Authority, shall bear their own costs if they intervene in the proceedings.

The Court may order an intervener other than those mentioned in the preceding sub-paragraphs to bear his own costs.][1]

5. A party who discontinues or withdraws from proceedings shall be ordered to pay the costs if they have been applied for in the other party's [observations on the discontinuance].[2] However, upon application by the party who discontinues or

[1] New second sub-paragraph inserted and existing second sub-paragraph becomes third sub-paragraph by virtue of amendments to Rules of Procedure ([1995] OJ L44/61) Art. 1(6) with effect from 1 April 1995.

[2] Words inserted by amendments to Rules of Procedure ([1997] OJ L103/1) Art. 1(5) with effect from 1 June 1997.

withdraws from proceedings, the costs shall be borne by the other party if this appears justified by the conduct of that party.

Where the parties have come to an agreement on costs, the decision as to costs shall be in accordance with that agreement.

[If costs are not applied for, the parties shall bear their own costs.][3]

6. Where a case does not proceed to judgment the costs shall be in the discretion of the Court.

Article 70 [Costs of institutions in staff cases]

4–136 Without prejudice to the second sub-paragraph of Article 69(3) of these Rules, in proceedings between the Communities and their servants the institutions shall bear their own costs.

Article 71 [Costs of enforcement]

4–137 Costs necessarily incurred by a party in enforcing a judgment or order of the Court shall be refunded by the opposite party on the scale in force in the State where the enforcement takes place.

Article 72 [Avoidable Court costs or excessive translation costs]

4–138 Proceedings before the Court shall be free of charge, except that:

(a) where a party has caused the Court to incur avoidable costs the Court may, after hearing the Advocate General, order that party to refund them;

(b) where copying or translation work is carried out at the request of a party, the cost shall, in so far as the Registrar considers it excessive, be paid for by that party on the scale of charges referred to in Article 16(5) of these Rules.

Article 73 [Witness costs and other necessary expenses]

4–139 Without prejudice to the preceding Article, the following shall be regarded as recoverable costs:

(a) sums payable to witnesses and experts under Article 51 of these Rules

(b) expenses necessarily incurred by the parties for the purpose of the proceedings, in particular the travel and subsistence expenses and the remuneration of agents, advisers or lawyers.

Article 74 [Orders in disputes over recoverable costs]

4–140 1. If there is a dispute concerning the costs to be recovered, the Chamber [referred to in Article 9(2) of the Rules][4] to which the case has been assigned shall, on application by the party concerned and after hearing the opposite party and the Advocate General, make an order, from which no appeal shall lie.

2. The parties may, for the purposes of enforcement, apply for an authenticated copy of the order.

Article 75 [Currency of payment]

4–141 1. Sums due from the cashier of the Court shall be paid in the currency of the country where the Court has its seat.

At the request of the person entitled to any sum, it shall be paid in the currency of the country where the expenses to be refunded were incurred or where the steps in respect of which payment is due were taken.

[3] Words replaced by amendments to Rules of Procedure ([1997] OJ L103/1) Art. 1(5) with effect from 1 June 1997.

[4] Words added by amendments to the Rules of Procedure ([2003] OJ L147/17) Art. 1(33) with effect from 1 August 2003.

2. Other debtors shall make payment in the currency of their country of origin.

3. Conversions of currency shall be made at the official rates of exchange ruling on the day of payment in the country where the Court has its seat.

CHAPTER 6—LEGAL AID

Article 76 [Applications for legal aid]

1. A party who is wholly or in part unable to meet the costs of the proceedings may at any time apply for legal aid. **4–142**

The application shall be accompanied by evidence of the applicant's need of assistance, and in particular by a document from the competent authority certifying his lack of means.

2. If the application is made prior to proceedings which the applicant wishes to commence, it shall briefly state the subject of such proceedings.

The application need not be made through a lawyer.

3. The President shall designate a Judge to act as Rapporteur. The Chamber [of three Judges][5] to which the latter belongs shall, after considering the written observations of the opposite party and after hearing the Advocate General, decide whether legal aid should be granted in full or in part, or whether it should be refused. The Chamber shall consider whether there is manifestly no cause of action.

The Chamber shall make an order without giving reasons, and no appeal shall lie therefrom.

4. The Chamber may at any time, either of its own motion or on application, withdraw legal aid if the circumstances which led to its being granted alter during the proceedings.

5. Where legal aid is granted, the cashier of the Court shall advance the funds necessary to meet the expenses.

In its decision as to costs the Court may order the payment to the cashier of the Court of the whole or any part of amounts advanced as legal aid.

The Registrar shall take steps to obtain the recovery of these sums from the party ordered to pay them.

CHAPTER 7—DISCONTINUANCE

Article 77 [Out-of-Court settlements]

If, before the Court has given its decision, the parties reach a settlement of their dispute and intimate to the Court the abandonment of their claims, the President shall order the case to be removed from the register and shall give a decision as to costs in accordance with Article 69(5), having regard to any proposals made by the parties on the matter. **4–143**

This provision shall not apply to proceedings under Articles [230 and 232][6] of the [EC Treaty [. . .][7] and Articles 146 and 148 of the Euratom Treaty].[8]

[5] Words added by amendments to the Rules of Procedure ([2003] OJ L147/17) Art. 1(34) with effect from 1 August 2003.

[6] Words substituted by amendments to Rules of Procedure ([2000] OJ L122/43) Art. 1(13) with effect from 1 July 2000.

[7] Words deleted by amendments to the Rules of Procedure ([2003] OJ L147/17) Art. 1(35) with effect from 1 August 2003.

[8] Term "EC Treaty" replaced and order in which Treaties are cited replaced by amendments to Rules of Procedure ([1995] OJ L44/61) Art. 1(11) with effect from 1 April 1995.

Article 78 [Requests to discontinue proceedings]

4–144 If the applicant informs the Court in writing that he wishes to discontinue the proceedings, the President shall order the case to be removed from the register and shall give a decision as to costs in accordance with Article 69(5).

CHAPTER 8—SERVICE

[Article 79 [Service of documents]

4–145 1. Where these Rules require that a document be served on a person, the Registrar shall ensure that service is effected at that person's address for service either by the dispatch of a copy of the document by registered post with a form for acknowledgement of receipt or by personal delivery of the copy against a receipt.

The Registrar shall prepare and certify the copies of documents to be served, save where the parties themselves supply the copies in accordance with Article 37(1) of these Rules.

2. Where, in accordance with the second sub-paragraph of Article 38(2), the addressee has agreed that service is to be effected on him by telefax or other technical means of communication, any procedural document other than a judgment or order of the Court may be served by the transmission of a copy of the document by such means.

Where, for technical reasons or on account of the nature or length of the document, such transmission is impossible or impracticable, the document shall be served, if the addressee has failed to state an address for service, at his address in accordance with the procedures laid down in paragraph 1 of this article. The addressee shall be so advised by telefax or other technical means of communication. Service shall then be deemed to have been effected on the addressee by registered post on the tenth day following the lodging of the registered letter at the post office of the place where the Court has its seat, unless it is shown by the acknowledgement of receipt that the letter was received on a different date or the addressee informs the Registrar, within three weeks of being advised by telefax or other technical means of communication, that the document to be served has not reached him.][9]

CHAPTER 9—TIME-LIMITS

Article 80 [Calculation of time-limits]

4–146 1. Any period of time prescribed by [the Union Treaty, the EC Treaty and the EAEC Treaty, the Statute of the Court][10] or these Rules for the taking of any procedural step shall be reckoned as follows:

(a) where a period expressed in days, weeks, months or years is to be calculated from the moment at which an event occurs or an action takes place, the day during which that event occurs or that action takes place shall not be counted as falling within the period in question;

(b) a period expressed in weeks, months or in years shall end with the expiry of whichever day in the last week, month or year is the same day of the week, or falls on the same date, as the day during which the event or action from which the period is to be calculated occurred or took place. If, in a period expressed in months or in years, the day on which it should expire does not occur in the last month, the period shall end with the expiry of the last day of that month;

(c) where a period is expressed in months and days, it shall first be reckoned in whole months, then in days;

(d) periods shall include official holidays, Sundays and Saturdays;

[9] Text of Art. 79 renumbered as Art. 79(1) and Art. 79(2) inserted by amendments to Rules of Procedure ([2000] OJ L322/1) Art. 1(5) from 1 February 2001.

[10] Words replaced by amendments to the Rules of Procedure ([2003] OJ L147/17) Art. 1(36) with effect from 1 August 2003.

(e) periods shall not be suspended during the judicial vacations.

2. If the period would otherwise end on a Saturday, Sunday or an official holiday, it shall be extended until the end of the first following working day.

A list of official holidays drawn up by the Court shall be published in the *Official Journal* [*of the European Union*].[11]

Article 81 [Calculation of limitation periods]

[1. Where the period of time allowed for initiating proceedings against a measure adopted by an institution runs from the publication of that measure, that period shall be calculated, for the purposes of Article 80(1)(a), from the end of the 14th day after publication thereof in the *Official Journal* [*of the European Union*].[12]][13] **4–147**

[2. The prescribed time-limits shall be extended on account of distance by a single period of ten days.][14]

Article 82 [Extension of time-limits]

Any time-limit prescribed pursuant to these Rules may be extended by whoever prescribed it. **4–148**

The President and the Presidents of Chambers may delegate to the Registrar power of signature for the purpose of fixing time-limits which, pursuant to these Rules, it falls to them to prescribe or of extending such time-limits.

CHAPTER 10—STAY OF PROCEEDINGS

Article 82a [Circumstances and duration of stay]

1. The proceedings may be stayed: **4–149**
(a) in the circumstances specified in [the third paragraph of Article 54 of the Statute],[15] by order of the Court [...][16] made after hearing the Advocate General;
(b) in all other cases, by decision of the President adopted after hearing the Advocate General and, save in the case of references for a preliminary ruling as referred to in Article 103, the parties.

The proceedings may be resumed by order or decision, following the same procedure. The orders or decisions referred to in this paragraph shall be served on the parties.

2. The stay of proceedings shall take effect on the date indicated in the order or decision of stay or, in the absence of such indication, on the date of that order or decision.

While proceedings are stayed time shall cease to run for the purposes of prescribed time-limits for all parties.

3. Where the order or decision of stay does not fix the length of stay, it shall end on the date indicated in the order or decision of resumption or, in the absence of such indication, on the date of the order or decision of resumption.

---

[11] Words replaced by amendments to the Rules of Procedure ([2003] OJ L147/17) Art. 1(37) with effect from 1 August 2003.

[12] Words replaced by amendments to the Rules of Procedure ([2003] OJ L147/17) Art. 1(38) with effect from 1 August 2003.

[13] Article 81(1) replaced by amendments to Rules of Procedure ([1997] OJ L103/1) Art. 1(6) with effect from 1 June 1997.

[14] Article 81(2) substituted by amendments to Rules of Procedure ([2000] OJ L322/1) Art. 1(6) with effect from 1 February 2001.

[15] Words replaced by amendments to the Rules of Procedure ([2003] OJ L147/17) Art. 1(39) with effect from 1 August 2003.

[16] Words deleted by amendments to the Rules of Procedure ([2003] OJ L147/17) Art. 1(39) with effect from 1 August 2003.

From the date of resumption time shall begin to run afresh for the purposes of the time-limits.

Title III—Special Forms of Procedure

CHAPTER 1—SUSPENSION OF OPERATION OR ENFORCEMENT AND OTHER INTERIM MEASURES

Article 83 [Applications to suspend measures or adopt other interim measures]

4–150 1. An application to suspend the operation of any measure adopted by an institution, made pursuant to Article [242][17] of the [EC Treaty [...][18] and Article 157 of the Euratom Treaty],[19] shall be admissible only if the applicant is challenging that measure in proceedings before the Court.

An application for the adoption of any other interim measure referred to in Article [243][20] of the [EC Treaty [...][21] and Article 158 of the Euratom Treaty],[22] shall be admissible only if it is made by a party to a case before the Court and relates to that case.

2. An application of a kind referred to in paragraph 1 of this Article shall state the subject-matter of the proceedings, the circumstances giving rise to urgency and the pleas of fact and law establishing a prima facie case for the interim measures applied for.

3. The application shall be made by a separate document and in accordance with the provisions of Articles 37 and 38 of these Rules.

Article 84 [Service on other party]

4–151 1. The application shall be served on the opposite party, and the President shall prescribe a short period within which that party may submit written or oral observations.

2. The President may order a preparatory inquiry.

The President may grant the application even before the observations of the opposite party have been submitted. This decision may be varied or cancelled even without any application being made by any party.

Article 85 [Decision on application]

4–152 The President shall either decide on the application himself or refer it to the Court.

---

[17] Words substituted by amendments to Rules of Procedure ([2000] OJ L122/43) Art. 1(13) with effect from 1 July 2000.

[18] Words deleted by amendments to the Rules of Procedure ([2003] OJ L147/17) Art. 1(40)(a) with effect from 1 August 2003.

[19] Term "EC Treaty" replaced and order in which Treaties are cited replaced by amendments to Rules of Procedure ([1995] OJ L44/61) Art. 1(11) with effect from 1 April 1995.

[20] Words substituted by amendments to Rules of Procedure ([2000] OJ L122/43) Art. 1(13) with effect from 1 July 2000.

[21] Words deleted by amendments to the Rules of Procedure ([2003] OJ L147/17) Art. 1(40)(b) with effect from 1 August 2003.

[22] Term "EC Treaty" replaced and order in which Treaties are cited replaced by amendments to Rules of Procedure ([1995] OJ L44/61) Art. 1(11) with effect from 1 April 1995.

If the President is absent or prevented from attending, Article 11 of these Rules shall apply.

Where the application is referred to it, the Court shall postpone all other cases, and shall give a decision after hearing the Advocate General. Article 84 shall apply.

Article 86 [Orders for interim measures]

1. The decision on the application shall take the form of a reasoned order, from which no appeal shall lie. The order shall be served on the parties forthwith. **4–153**

2. The enforcement of the order may be made conditional on the lodging by the applicant of security, of an amount and nature to be fixed in the light of the circumstances.

3. Unless the order fixes the date on which the interim measure is to lapse, the measure shall lapse when final judgment is delivered.

4. The order shall have only an interim effect, and shall be without prejudice to the decision of the Court on the substance of the case.

Article 87 [Variation or cancellation of order]

On application by a party, the order may at any time be varied or cancelled on account of a change in circumstances. **4–154**

Article 88 [New applications for measures]

Rejection of an application for an interim measure shall not bar the party who made it from making a further application on the basis of new facts. **4–155**

Article 89 [Suspension of enforcement of Court decisions or other measures]

The provisions of this Chapter shall apply to applications to suspend the enforcement of a decision of the Court or of any measure adopted by another institution, submitted pursuant to Articles [244 and 256][23] of the [EC Treaty [. . .][24] and Articles 159 and 164 of the Euratom Treaty].[25] **4–156**

The order granting the application shall fix, where appropriate, a date on which the interim measure is to lapse.

Article 90 [Warrants for inspection under Euratom Treaty]

[Not reproduced] **4–157**

CHAPTER 2—PRELIMINARY ISSUES

Article 91 [Applications for rulings on preliminary issues]

1. A party applying to the Court for a decision on a preliminary objection or other preliminary plea not going to the substance of the case shall make the application by a separate document. **4–158**

The application must state the pleas of fact and law relied on and the form of order sought by the applicant any supporting documents must be annexed to it.

[23] Words substituted by amendments to Rules of Procedure ([2000] OJ L122/43) Art. 1(13) with effect from 1 July 2000.

[24] Words deleted by amendments to the Rules of Procedure ([2003] OJ L147/17) Art. 1(41) with effect from 1 August 2003.

[25] Term "EC Treaty" replaced and order in which Treaties are cited replaced by amendments to Rules of Procedure ([1995] OJ L44/61) Art. 1(11) with effect from 1 April 1995.

2. As soon as the application has been lodged, the President shall prescribe a period within which the opposite party may lodge a document containing a statement of the form of order sought by that party and its pleas in law.

3. Unless the Court decides otherwise, the remainder of the proceedings shall be oral.

4. The Court shall, after hearing the Advocate General, decide on the application or reserve its decision for the final judgment.

If the Court refuses the application or reserves its decision, the President shall prescribe new time-limits for the further steps in the proceedings.

Article 92 [Inadmissible cases or bars to proceeding]

4–159 1. Where it is clear that the Court has no jurisdiction to take cognisance of an action or where the action is manifestly inadmissible, the Court may, by reasoned order, after hearing the Advocate General and without taking further steps in the proceedings, give a decision on the action.

[2. The Court may at any time of its own motion consider whether there exists any absolute bar to proceeding with a case or declare, after hearing the parties, that the action has become devoid of purpose and that there is no need to adjudicate on it; it shall give its decision in accordance with Article 91(3) and (4) of these Rules.][26]

CHAPTER 3—INTERVENTION

Article 93 [Applications to intervene in proceedings]

4–160 1. An application to intervene must be made within [six weeks][27] of the publication of the notice referred to in Article 16(6) of these Rules.

The application shall contain:

(a) the description of the case;
(b) the description of the parties;
(c) the name and address of the intervener;
(d) the intervener's address for service at the place where the Court has its seat;
(e) the form of order sought, by one or more of the parties, in support of which the intervener is applying for leave to intervene;
[(f) a statement of the circumstances establishing the right to intervene, where the application is submitted pursuant to [the second or third paragraph of Article 40 of this Statute].[28]

The intervener shall be represented in accordance with [Article 19 of the Statute][29].][30]

Articles 37 and 38 of these Rules shall apply.

2. The application shall be served on the parties.

The President shall give the parties an opportunity to submit their written or oral observations before deciding on the application.

The President shall decide on the application by order or shall refer the application to the Court.

3. If the President allows the intervention, the intervener shall receive a copy of every document served on the parties. The President may, however, on application by one of the parties, omit secret or confidential documents.

4. The intervener must accept the case as he finds it at the time of his intervention.

[26] Article 92(2) replaced by amendments to Rules of Procedure ([1997] OJ L103/1) Art. 1(7) with effect from 1 June 1997.

[27] Words substituted by Rules of Procedure ([2000] OJ L322/1) Art. 1(7)(a) from 1 February 2001.

[28] Words replaced by amendments to the Rules of Procedure ([2003] OJ L147/17) Art. 1(42)(a) with effect from 1 August 2003.

[29] Words replaced by amendments to the Rules of Procedure ([2003] OJ L147/17) Art. 1(42)(b) with effect from 1 August 2003.

[30] Point (f) of second sub-paragraph and third sub-paragraph substituted by amendments to Rules of Procedure ([1995] OJ L44/61) Art. 1(7) with effect from 1 April 1995.

5. The President shall prescribe a period within which the intervener may submit a statement in intervention.

The statement in intervention shall contain:

(a) a statement of the form of order sought by the intervener in support of or opposing, in whole or in part, the form of order sought by one of the parties;
(b) the pleas in law and arguments relied on by the intervener;
(c) where appropriate, the nature of any evidence offered.

6. After the statement in intervention has been lodged, the President shall, where necessary, prescribe a time-limit within which the parties may reply to that statement.

[7. Consideration may be given to an application to intervene which is made after the expiry of the period prescribed in paragraph 1 but before the decision to open the oral procedure provided for in Article 44(3). In that event, if the President allows the intervention, the intervener may, on the basis of the Report for the Hearing communicated to him, submit his observations during the oral procedure, if that procedure takes place.][31]

CHAPTER 4—JUDGMENTS BY DEFAULT AND APPLICATIONS TO SET THEM ASIDE

Article 94 [Applications for judgment by default]

1. If a defendant on whom an application initiating proceedings has been duly served fails to lodge a defence to the application in the proper form within the time prescribed, the applicant may apply for judgment by default. **4–161**

The application shall be served on the defendant. [The Court may decide to open the oral procedure on the application.][32]

2. Before giving judgment by default the Court shall, after hearing the Advocate General, consider whether the application initiating proceedings is admissible, whether the appropriate formalities have been complied with, and whether the application appears well founded. The Court may order a preparatory inquiry.

3. A judgment by default shall be enforceable. The Court may, however, grant a stay of execution until the Court has given its decision on any application under paragraph 4 to set aside the judgment, or it may make execution subject to the provision of security of an amount and nature to be fixed in the light of the circumstances this security shall be released if no such application is made or if the application fails.

4. Application may be made to set aside a judgment by default.

The application to set aside the judgment must be made within one month from the date of service of the judgment and must be lodged in the form prescribed by Articles 37 and 38 of these Rules.

5. After the application has been served, the President shall prescribe a period within which the other party may submit his written observations.

The proceedings shall be conducted in accordance with Article 44 *et seq.* of these Rules.

6. The Court shall decide by way of a judgment which may not be set aside. The original of this judgment shall be annexed to the original of the judgment by default. A note of the judgment on the application to set aside shall be made in the margin of the original of the judgment by default.

[...][33]

[31] Article 93(7) inserted by amendments to Rules of Procedure ([2000] OJ L322/1) Art. 1(7)(b) with effect from 1 February 2001.

[32] Words replaced by amendments to Rules of Procedure ([1997] OJ L103/1) Art. 1(8) with effect from 1 June 1997.

[33] Former Chapter 5 governing assignment of cases to Chambers repealed by amendments to the Rules of Procedure ([2003] OJ L147/17) Art. 1(43) with effect from 1 August 2003.

Chapter 6—Exceptional Review Procedures

Section 1—Third-Party Proceedings

Article 97 [Applications initiating third-party proceedings]

4–162 1. Articles 37 and 38 of these Rules shall apply to an application initiating third-party proceedings. In addition such an application shall:
(a) specify the judgment contested;
(b) state how that judgment is prejudicial to the rights of the third party;
(c) indicate the reasons for which the third party was unable to take part in the original case.

The application must be made against all the parties to the original case.

Where the judgment has been published in the *Official Journal* [*of the European Union*],[34] the application must be lodged within two months of the publication.

2. The Court may, on application by the third party, order a stay of execution of the judgment. The provisions of Title III, Chapter I, of these Rules shall apply.

3. The contested judgment shall be varied on the points on which the submissions of the third party are upheld.

The original of the judgment in the third-party proceedings shall be annexed to the original of the contested judgment. A note of the judgment in the third-party proceedings shall be made in the margin of the original of the contested judgment.

SECTION 2—REVISION

Article 98 [Timing of applications for revision of judgment]

4–163 An application for revision of a judgment shall be made within three months of the date on which the facts on which the application is based came to the applicant's knowledge.

Article 99 [Content of application for revision]

4–164 1. Articles 37 and 38 of these Rules shall apply to an application for revision. In addition such an application shall:
(a) specify the judgment contested;
(b) indicate the points on which the judgment is contested;
(c) set out the facts on which the application is based;
(d) indicate the nature of the evidence to show that there are facts justifying revision of the judgment, and that the time-limit laid down in Article 98 has been observed.

2. The application must be made against all parties to the case in which the contested judgment was given.

Article 100 [Decisions on admissibility of applications]

4–165 1. Without prejudice to its decision on the substance, the Court, in closed session, shall, after hearing the Advocate General and having regard to the written observations of the parties, give in the form of a judgment its decision on the admissibility of the application.

2. If the Court finds the application admissible, it shall proceed to consider the substance of the application and shall give its decision in the form of a judgment in accordance with these Rules.

3. The original of the revising judgment shall be annexed to the original of the judgment revised. A note of the revising judgment shall be made in the margin of the original of the judgment revised.

---

[34] Words replaced by amendments to the Rules of Procedure ([2003] OJ L147/17) Art. 1(44) with effect from 1 August 2003.

CHAPTER 7—APPEALS AGAINST DECISIONS OF THE ARBITRATION COMMITTEE

Article 101 [Appeals from arbitration under Euratom Treaty]

[Not reproduced] **4–166**

CHAPTER 8—INTERPRETATION OF JUDGMENTS

Article 102 [Applications for interpretation of judgments]

1. An application for interpretation of a judgment shall be made in accordance with Articles 37 and 38 of these Rules. In addition it shall specify: **4–167**
(a) the judgment in question;
(b) the passages of which interpretation is sought.
The application must be made against all the parties to the case in which the judgment was given.

2. The Court shall give its decision in the form of a judgment after having given the parties an opportunity to submit their observations and after hearing the Advocate General.

The original of the interpreting judgment shall be annexed to the original of the judgment interpreted. A note of the interpreting judgment shall be made in the margin of the original of the judgment interpreted.

CHAPTER 9—PRELIMINARY RULINGS AND OTHER REFERENCES FOR INTERPRETATION

Article 103 [Procedure for references for preliminary rulings or interpretation]

1. In cases governed by [Article 23 of the Statute],[35] the procedure shall be governed by the provisions of these Rules, subject to adaptations necessitated by the nature of the reference for a preliminary ruling. **4–168**

2. The provisions of paragraph 1 shall apply to the references for a preliminary ruling provided for in the Protocol concerning the interpretation by the Court of Justice of the Convention of 29 February 1968 on the mutual recognition of companies and legal persons and the Protocol concerning the interpretation by the Court of Justice of the Convention of 27 September 1968 on jurisdiction and the enforcement of judgments in civil and commercial matters, signed at Luxembourg on 3 June 1971, and to the references provided for by Article 4 of the latter Protocol.

The provisions of paragraph 1 shall apply also to references for interpretation provided for by other existing or future agreements.

[...][36]

Article 104 [Decisions to refer; representation; reasoned orders etc.]

1. The decisions of national courts or tribunals referred to in Article 103 shall be communicated to the Member States in the original version, accompanied by a translation into the official language of the State to which they are addressed. **4–169**

[In the cases governed by [the third paragraph of Article 23 of the Statute],[37] the decisions of national courts or tribunals shall be notified to the States, other than the Member States, which are parties to the EEA Agreement, and also to the EFTA Surveillance Authority, in the original version, accompanied by a

---

[35] Words replaced by amendments to the Rules of Procedure ([2003] OJ L147/17) Art. 1(45)(a) with effect from 1 August 2003.

[36] Article 103(3) repealed by amendments to the Rules of Procedure ([2003] OJ L147/17) Art. 1(45)(b) with effect from 1 August 2003.

[37] Words replaced by amendments to the Rules of Procedure ([2003] OJ L147/17) Art. 1(46)(a) with effect from 1 August 2003.

translation into one of the languages mentioned in Article 29(1), to be chosen by the addressee of the notification.][38]

[Where a non-member State has the right to take part in proceedings for a preliminary ruling pursuant to [the fourth paragraph of Article 23 of the Statute],[39] the original version of the decision of the national court or tribunal shall be communicated to it together with a translation into one of the languages mentioned in Article 29(1), to be chosen by the non-member State concerned.][40]

2. As regards the representation and attendance of the parties to the main proceedings in the preliminary ruling procedure the Court shall take account of the rules of procedure of the national court or tribunal which made the reference.

[3. Where a question referred to the Court for a preliminary ruling is identical to a question on which the Court has already ruled, where the answer to such a question may be clearly deduced from existing case law or where the answer to the question admits of no reasonable doubt, the Court may, after informing the court or tribunal which referred the question to it, after hearing any observations submitted by the persons referred to in [Article 23 of the Statute][41] and after hearing the Advocate General, give its decision by reasoned order in which, if appropriate, reference is made to its previous judgment or to the relevant case-law.][42]

[4. Without prejudice to paragraph 3 of this Article, the procedure before the Court in the case of a reference for a preliminary ruling shall also include an oral part.

However, after the statements of case or written observations referred to in [Article 23 of the Statute][43] have been submitted, the Court, acting on a report from the Judge-Rapporteur, after informing the persons who under the aforementioned provisions are entitled to submit such statements or observations, may, after hearing the Advocate General, decide otherwise, provided that none of those persons has submitted an application setting out the reasons for which he wishes to be heard. The application shall be submitted within a period of one month from service on the party or person of the written statements of case or written observations which have been lodged. That period may be extended by the President.][44]

[5. The Court may, after hearing the Advocate General, request clarification from the national court.][45]

[6.][46] It shall be for the national court or tribunal to decide as to the costs of the reference.

In special circumstances the Court may grant, by way of legal aid, assistance for the purpose of facilitating the representation or attendance of a party.

---

[38] Words added by amendments to Rules of Procedure ([1995] OJ L44/61) Art. 1(9) with effect from 1 April 1995.

[39] Words replaced by amendments to the Rules of Procedure ([2003] OJ L147/17) Art. 1(46)(b) with effect from 1 August 2003.

[40] Fourth subparagraph of Art.104(1) added by amendment to Rules of Procedure ([2002] OJ L272/24) Art.1(1) with effect from 10 October 2002.

[41] Words replaced by amendments to the Rules of Procedure ([2003] OJ L147/17) Art. 1(46)(c) with effect from 1 August 2003.

[42] Article 104(3) substituted by amendments to Rules of Procedure ([2000] OJ L122/43) Art. 1(6) with effect from 1 July 2000.

[43] Words replaced by amendments to the Rules of Procedure ([2003] OJ L147/17) Art. 1(46)(c) with effect from 1 August 2003.

[44] Article 104(4) substituted by amendments to Rules of Procedure ([2000] OJ L122/43) Art. 1(7) with effect from 1 July 2000.

[45] Article 104(5) inserted by amendments to Rules of Procedure ([2000] OJ L122/43) Art. 1(8) with effect from 1 July 2000.

[46] Article 104(5) renumbered as Art. 104(6) by amendments to Rules of Procedure ([2000] OJ L122/43) Art. 1(8) with effect from 1 July 2000.

[Article 104a [Accelerated procedure in exceptional cases]

At the request of the national court, the President may exceptionally decide, on a proposal from the Judge-Rapporteur and after hearing the Advocate General, to apply an accelerated procedure derogating from the provisions of these Rules to a reference for a preliminary ruling, where the circumstances referred to establish that a ruling on the question put to the Court is a matter of exceptional urgency. **4–170**

In that event, the President may immediately fix the date for the hearing, which shall be notified to the parties in the main proceedings and to the other persons referred to in [Article 23 of the Statute][47] when the decision making the reference is served.

The parties and other interested persons referred to in the preceding paragraph may lodge statements of case or written observations within a period prescribed by the President, which shall be not less than 15 days. The President may request the parties and other interested persons to restrict the matters addressed in their statement of case or written observations to the essential points of law raised by the question referred.

The statements of case or written observations, if any, shall be notified to the parties and to the other persons referred to above prior to the hearing.

The Court shall rule after hearing the Advocate General.][48]

CHAPTER 10—SPECIAL PROCEDURES UNDER ARTICLES 103 TO 105 OF THE EURATOM TREATY

Article 105 [Rulings on agreements or conventions with third countries]

[Not reproduced] **4–171**

Article 106 [Rulings on compatibility of existing agreements]

[Not reproduced] **4–172**

CHAPTER 11—OPINIONS

Article 107 [Compatibility of international agreements with EC Treaty; powers to conclude such agreements]

1. [A request by the European Parliament for an opinion pursuant to Article 300 of the EC Treaty shall be served on the Council, on the Commission and on the Member States. Such a request by the Council shall be served on the Commission and on the European Parliament. Such a request by the Commission shall be served on the Council, on the European Parliament and on the Member States. Such a request by a Member State shall be served on the Council, on the Commission, on the European Parliament and on the other Member States.][49] **4–173**

The President shall prescribe a period within which the institutions and Member States which have been served with a request may submit their written observations.

2. The Opinion may deal not only with the question whether the envisaged agreement is compatible with the provisions of the [EC Treaty][50] but also with the

[47] Words replaced by amendments to the Rules of Procedure ([2003] OJ L147/17) Art. 1(47) with effect from 1 August 2003.

[48] Article 104a inserted by amendments to Rules of Procedure ([2000] OJ L122/43) Art. 1(9) with effect from 1 July 2000.

[49] Article 107(1), first subparagraph replaced by amendments to the Rules of Procedure ([2003] OJ L147/17) Art. 1(48) with effect from 1 August 2003.

[50] Term "EC Treaty" replaced by amendments to Rules of Procedure ([1995] OJ L44/61) Art. 1(11) with effect from 1 April 1995.

question whether the Community or any Community institution has the power to enter into that agreement.

Article 108 [Procedure]

4–174 1. As soon as the request for an Opinion has been lodged, the President shall designate a Judge to act as Rapporteur.

2. The Court sitting in closed session shall, after hearing the Advocates General, deliver a reasoned Opinion.

[3. The Opinion, signed by the President, by the Judges who took part in the deliberations and by the Registrar, shall be served on the Council, the Commission, the European Parliament and the Member States.][51]
[...][52]

[CHAPTER 12—REQUESTS FOR INTERPRETATION UNDER ARTICLE 68 OF THE EC TREATY

Article 109a [Measures establishing common area of freedom, security and justice]

4–175 1. A request for a ruling on a question of interpretation under Article 68(3) of the EC Treaty shall be served on the Commission and the Member States if the request is submitted by the Council, on the Council and the Member States if the request is submitted by the Commission and on the Council, the Commission and the other Member States if the request is submitted by a Member State.

The President shall prescribe a time-limit within which the institutions and the Member States on which the request has been served are to submit their written observations.

2. As soon as the request referred to in paragraph 1 has been submitted, the President shall designate the Judge-Rapporteur. The First Advocate General shall thereupon assign the request to an Advocate General.

3. The Court shall, after the Advocate General has delivered his opinion, give its decision on the request by way of judgment.

The procedure relating to the request shall include an oral part where a Member State or one of the institutions referred to in paragraph 1 so requests.

CHAPTER 13—SETTLEMENT OF THE DISPUTES REFERRED TO IN ARTICLE 35 OF THE UNION TREATY

Article 109b [Measures on police and judicial cooperation in criminal matters]

4–176 1. In the case of disputes between Member States as referred to in Article 35(7) of the Union Treaty, the matter shall be brought before the Court by an application by a party to the dispute. The application shall be served on the other Member States and on the Commission.

In the case of disputes between Member States and the Commission as referred to in Article 35(7) of the Union Treaty, the matter shall be brought before the Court by an application by a party to the dispute. The application shall be served on the other Member States, the Council and the Commission if it was made by a Member State. The application shall be served on the Member States and on the Council if it was made by the Commission.

The President shall prescribe a time-limit within which the institutions and the Member States on which the application has been served are to submit their written observations.

[51] Article 108(3) replaced by amendments to Rules of Procedure ([1997] OJ L103/1) Art. 1(10) with effect from 1 June 1997.

[52] Former Art.109 repealed by amendments to the Rules of Procedure ([2003] OJ L147/17) Art. 1(49) with effect from 1 August 2003.

2. As soon as the application referred to in paragraph 1 has been submitted, the President shall designate the Judge-Rapporteur. The First Advocate General shall thereupon assign the application to an Advocate General.

3. The Court shall, after the Advocate General has delivered his opinion, give its ruling on the dispute by way of judgment.

The procedure relating to the application shall include an oral part where a Member State or one of the institutions referred to in paragraph 1 so requests.

4. The same procedure shall apply where an agreement concluded between the Member States confers jurisdiction on the Court to rule on a dispute between Member States or between Member States and an institution.][53]

Title IV—Appeals Against Decisions of the Court of First Instance

Article 110 [Language of the case]

Without prejudice to the arrangements laid down in Article 29(2)(b) and (c) and the fourth sub-paragraph of Article 29(3) of these Rules, in appeals against decisions of the Court of First Instance as referred to in [Articles 56 and 57 of the Statute],[54] the language of the case shall be the language of the decision of the Court of First Instance against which the appeal is brought. **4–177**

Article 111 [Lodging appeals]

1. An appeal shall be brought by lodging an application at the Registry of the Court of Justice or of the Court of First Instance. **4–178**

2. The Registry of the Court of First Instance shall immediately transmit to the Registry of the Court of Justice the papers in the case at first instance and, where necessary, the appeal.

Article 112 [Contents of appeal]

1. An appeal shall contain: **4–179**

(a) the name and address of the appellant;
(b) the names of the other parties to the proceedings before the Court of First Instance;
(c) the pleas in law and legal arguments relied on;
(d) the form or order sought by the appellant.

Article 37 and Article 38(2) and (3) of these Rules shall apply to appeals.

2. The decision of the Court of First Instance appealed against shall be attached to the appeal. The appeal shall state the date on which the decision appealed against was notified to the appellant.

3. If an appeal does not comply with Article 38(3) or with paragraph 2 of this Article, Article 38(7) of these Rules shall apply.

Article 113 [Object of appeal]

1. An appeal may seek: **4–180**

— to set aside, in whole or in part, the decision of the Court of First Instance;
— the same form of order, in whole or in part, as that sought at first instance and shall not seek a different form of order.

2. The subject-matter of the proceedings before the Court of First Instance may not be changed in the appeal.

[53] Chapters 12 and 13 inserted by amendments to Rules of Procedure ([2000] OJ L122/43) Art. 1(10) with effect from 1 July 2000.

[54] Words replaced by amendments to the Rules of Procedure ([2003] OJ L147/17) Art. 1(50) with effect from 1 August 2003.

Article 114 [Notice of appeal]

4–181 Notice of the appeal shall be served on all the parties to the proceedings before the Court of First Instance. Article 39 of these Rules shall apply.

Article 115 [Response to appeal]

4–182 1. Any party to the proceedings before the Court of First Instance may lodge a response within two months after service on him of notice of the appeal. The time-limit for lodging a response shall not be extended.

2. A response shall contain:
(a) the name and address of the party lodging it;
(b) the date on which notice of the appeal was served on him;
(c) the pleas in law and legal arguments relied on;
(d) the form of order sought by the respondent.
[Article 37 and Article 38(2) and (3) of these Rules shall apply.][55]

Article 116 [Object of response]

4–183 1. A response may seek:
— to dismiss, in whole or in part, the appeal or to set aside, in whole or in part, the decision of the Court of First Instance;
— the same form of order, in whole or in part, as that sought at first instance and shall not seek a different form of order.

2. The subject-matter of the proceedings before the Court of First Instance may not be changed in the response.

Article 117 [Replies and rejoinders]

4–184 [1. The appeal and the response may be supplemented by a reply and a rejoinder where the President, on application made by the appellant within seven days of service of the response, considers such further pleading necessary and expressly allows the submission of a reply in order to enable the appellant to put forward his point of view or in order to provide a basis for the decision on the appeal. The President shall prescribe the date by which the reply is to be submitted and, upon service of that pleading, the date by which the rejoinder is to be submitted.][56]

2. Where the response seeks to set aside, in whole or in part, the decision of the Court of First Instance on a plea in law which was not raised in the appeal, the appellant or any other party may submit a reply on that plea alone within two months of the service of the response in question. Paragraph 1 shall apply to any further pleading following such a reply.

3. [...][57]

Article 118 [Application of procedural rules to appeals]

4–185 Subject to the following provisions, Articles 42(2), 43, 44, 55 to 90, 93, 95 to 100 and 102 of these Rules shall apply to the procedure before the Court of Justice on appeal from a decision of the Court of First Instance.

[55] Words substituted by amendments to Rules of Procedure ([2000] OJ L322/1) Art. 1(8) with effect from 1 February 2001.

[56] Article 117(1) substituted by amendments to Rules of Procedure ([2000] OJ L322/1) Art. 1(9)(a) with effect from 1 February 2001.

[57] Article 117(3) repealed by amendments to Rules of Procedure ([2000] OJ L322/1) Art. 1(9)(b) as from 1 February 2001.

Article 119 [Dismissal of appeal by reasoned order]

Where the appeal is, in whole or in part, clearly inadmissible or clearly unfounded, the Court may at any time, acting on a report from the Judge-Rapporteur and after hearing the Advocate General, by reasoned order dismiss the appeal in whole or in part. **4–186**

[Article 120 [Dispensing with oral procedure]

After the submission of pleadings as provided for in Article 115(1) and, if any, Article 117(1) and (2) of these Rules, the Court, acting on a report from the Judge-Rapporteur and after hearing the Advocate General and the parties, may decide to dispense with the oral part of the procedure unless one of the parties submits an application setting out the reasons for which he wishes to be heard. The application shall be submitted within a period of one month from notification to the party of the close of the written procedure. That period may be extended by the President.][58] **4–187**

[Article 121 [Presentation of Judge-Rapporteur's preliminary report]

The report referred to in Article 44(2) shall be presented to the Court after the pleadings provided for in Article 115(1) and, where appropriate, Article 117(1) and (2) have been lodged. Where no such pleadings are lodged, the same procedure shall apply after the expiry of the period prescribed for lodging them.][59] **4–188**

Article 122 [Costs]

Where the appeal is unfounded or where the appeal is well founded and the Court itself gives final judgment in the case, the Court shall make a decision as to costs. **4–189**

In proceedings between the Communities and their servants:

— Article 70 of these Rules shall apply only to appeals brought by institutions;
— by way of derogation from Article 69(2) of these Rules, the Court may, in appeals brought by officials or other servants of an institution, order the parties to share the costs where equity so requires.

If the appeal is withdrawn Article 69(5) shall apply.

When an appeal brought by a Member State or an institution which did not intervene in the proceedings before the Court of First Instance is well founded, the Court of Justice may order that the parties share the costs or that the successful appellant pay the costs which the appeal has caused an unsuccessful party to incur.

Article 123 [Applications to intervene in appeal proceedings]

[An application to intervene made to the Court in appeal proceedings shall be lodged before the expiry of a period of one month running from the publication referred to in Article 16(6).][60] **4–190**

[Title V—Procedures Provided for by the EEA Agreement

Article 123a [Disputes on interpretation of EEA provisions corresponding to EC measures]

1. In the case governed by Article 111(3) of the EEA Agreement,[61] the matter shall be brought before the Court by a request submitted by the Contracting **4–191**

---

[58] Article 120 substituted by amendments to Rules of Procedure ([2000] OJ L122/43) Art. 1(11) with effect from 1 July 2000.

[59] Article 121 substituted by amendments to Rules of Procedure ([2000] OJ L322/1) Art. 1(10) with effect from 1 February 2001.

[60] Article 123 replaced by amendments to Rules of Procedure ([1997] OJ L103/1) Art. 1(11) with effect from 1 June 1997.

[61] For text of the EEA Agreement, see [1994] OJ L1/27.

Parties to the dispute. The request shall be served on the other Contracting Parties, on the Commission, on the EFTA Surveillance Authority and, where appropriate, on the other persons to whom a reference for a preliminary ruling raising the same question of interpretation of Community legislation would be notified.

The President shall prescribe a period within which the Contracting Parties and the other persons on whom the request has been served may submit written observations. The request shall be made in one of the languages mentioned in Article 29(1). Paragraphs 3 and 5 of that Article shall apply. The provisions of Article 104(1) shall apply *mutatis mutandis*.

2. As soon as the request referred to in paragraph 1 of this Article has been submitted, the President shall appoint a Judge-Rapporteur. The First Advocate General shall, immediately afterwards, assign the request to an Advocate General.

The Court shall, after hearing the Advocate General, give a reasoned decision on the request in closed session.

3. The decision of the Court, signed by the President, by the Judges who took part in the deliberations and by the Registrar, shall be served on the Contracting Parties and on the other persons referred to in paragraph 1.

Article 123b [Requests for preliminary rulings from EFTA State courts]

4–192 In the case governed by Article 1 of Protocol 34 to the EEA Agreement, the request of a court or tribunal of an EFTA State shall be served on the parties to the case, on the Contracting Parties, on the Commission, on the EFTA Surveillance Authority and, where appropriate, on the other persons to whom a reference for a preliminary ruling raising the same question of interpretation of Community legislation would be notified.

If the request is not submitted in one of the languages mentioned in Article 29(1), it shall be accompanied by a translation into one of those languages.

Within two months of this notification, the parties to the case, the Contracting Parties and the other persons referred to in the first paragraph shall be entitled to submit statements of case or written observations.

The procedure shall be governed by the provisions of these Rules, subject to the adaptations called for by the nature of the request.][62]

Miscellaneous Provisions

Article 124 [Instructions to witnesses or experts]

4–193 1. The President shall instruct any person who is required to take an oath before the Court, as witness or expert, to tell the truth or to carry out his task conscientiously and impartially, as the case may be, and shall warn him of the criminal liability provided for in his national law in the event of any breach of this duty.

2. The witness shall take the oath either in accordance with the first sub-paragraph of Article 47(5) of these Rules or in the manner laid down by his national law.

Where his national law provides the opportunity to make, in judicial proceedings, a solemn affirmation equivalent to an oath as well as or instead of taking an

[62] Title V inserted by amendments to Rules of Procedure ([1995] OJ L44/61) Art. 1(10) with effect from 1 April 1995.

oath, the witness may make such an affirmation under the conditions and in the form prescribed in his national law.

Where his national law provides neither for taking an oath nor for making a solemn affirmation, the procedure described in paragraph 1 shall be followed.

3. Paragraph 2 shall apply *mutatis mutandis* to experts, a reference to the first sub-paragraph of Article 49(6) replacing in this case the reference to the first sub-paragraph of Article 47(5) of these Rules.

Article 125 [Supplementary rules]

Subject to the provisions of [Article 223 of the EC Treaty and Article 160 of the EAEC Treaty][63] and after consultation with the governments concerned, the Court shall adopt supplementary rules concerning its practice in relation to: **4–194**

(a) letters rogatory;
(b) applications for legal aid;
(c) reports of perjury by witnesses or experts, delivered pursuant to [Article 30 of the EC Statute].[64]

[Article 125a [Practice directions]

The Court may issue practice directions relating in particular to the preparation and conduct of the hearings before it and to the lodging of written statements of case or written observations.][65] **4–195**

Article 126 [Prior rules superseded]

These Rules replace the Rules of Procedure of the Court of Justice of the European Communities adopted on 4 December 1974 (*Official Journal of the European Communities* No. L350 of 28 December 1974, p.1) as last amended on 15 May 1991. **4–196**

Article 127 [Publication and entry into force]

These Rules, which are authentic in the languages mentioned in Article 29(1) of these Rules, shall be published in the *Official Journal* [*of the European Union*][66] and shall enter into force on the first day of the second month following their publication. **4–197**

Annex I—Decision on Official Holidays

The Court of Justice of the European Communities,

Having regard to Article 80(2) of the Rules of Procedure, which requires the Court to draw up a list of official holidays: **4–198**

Decides:

Article 1 [Designated official holidays]

For the purposes of Article 80(2) of the Rules of Procedure the following shall be official holidays: **4–199**

63 Words replaced by amendments to the Rules of Procedure ([2003] OJ L147/17) Art. 1(51) with effect from 1 August 2003.

64 *ibid.*

65 Article 125a inserted by amendments to Rules of Procedure ([2000] OJ L122/43) Art. 1(12) from 1 July 2000. For practice directions, see [2003] OJ L98/9.

66 Words replaced by amendments to the Rules of Procedure ([2003] OJ L147/17) Art. 1(52) with effect from 1 August 2003.

— New Year's Day
— Easter Monday
— 1 May
— Ascension Day
— Whit Monday
— 23 June
— 24 June, where 23 June is a Sunday
— 15 August
— 1 November
— 25 December
— 26 December.

The official holidays referred to in the first paragraph hereof shall be those observed at the place where the Court of Justice has its seat.

Article 2 **[Calculation of time-limits using designated holidays only]**

4–200 Article 80(2) of the Rules of Procedure shall apply only to the official holidays mentioned in Article 1 of this Decision.

Article 3 **[Entry into force]**

4–201 This Decision, which shall constitute Annex I to the Rules of Procedure, shall enter into force on the same day as those Rules.

It shall be published in the *Official Journal of the European Communities*.

Annex II—Decision on Extension of Time-Limits on Account of Distance

The Court of Justice of the European Communities,

4–202 Having regard to Article 81(2) of the Rules of Procedure relating to the extension, on account of distance, of prescribed time-limits
Decides:

Article 1 **[Extension of procedural time-limits]**

4–203 In order to take account of distance, procedural time-limits for all parties save those habitually resident in the Grand Duchy of Luxembourg shall be extended as follows:

— for the Kingdom of Belgium: two days,
— for the Federal Republic of Germany, the European territory of the French Republic and the European territory of the Kingdom of the Netherlands: six days,
[— for the European territory of the Kingdom of Denmark, for the Kingdom of Spain, for Ireland, for the Hellenic Republic, for the Italian Republic, for the Republic of Austria, for the Portuguese Republic (with the exception of the Azores and Madeira), for the Republic of Finland, for the Kingdom of Sweden and for the United Kingdom: 10 days,][67]
— for other European countries and territories: two weeks,
— for the autonomous regions of the Azores and Madeira of the Portuguese Republic: three weeks,
— for other countries, departments and territories: one month.

[67] Third indent replaced by Decision of the Court of Justice amending Annex II to the Rules of Procedure ([1997] OJ L103/3) Art. 1 with effect from 19 April 1997, in order to provide for extension of time-limits on account of distance for residents of Austria, Finland and Sweden.

Article 2 [Entry into force]

This Decision, which shall constitute Annex II to the Rules of Procedure, shall enter into force on the same day as those Rules. **4–204**

It shall be published in the *Official Journal of the European Communities*.

CHAPTER 5

FREE MOVEMENT OF GOODS

Commission Directive 70/50 of 22 December 1969, based on the provisions of [former] Article 33(7), on the abolition of measures which have an effect equivalent to quantitative restrictions on imports and are not covered by other provisions adopted in pursuance of the [EC] Treaty

([1970] OJ (I), Eng. Spec. Ed., p.17; Doc. Ref. 31970L0050)

The Commission of the European Communities, **5–001**

Having regard to the provisions of the Treaty establishing the [European Community], and in particular [former] Article 33(7)[1] thereof;

[1] Whereas for the purpose of Article [28] *et seq*. "measures" means laws, regulations, administrative provisions, administrative practices, and all instruments issuing from a public authority, including recommendations;

[2] Whereas for the purposes of this Directive "administrative practices" means any standard and regularly followed procedure of a public authority; whereas "recommendations" means any instruments issuing from a public authority which, while not legally binding on the addressees thereof, cause them to pursue a certain conduct;

[3] Whereas the formalities to which imports are subject do not as a general rule have an effect equivalent to that of quantitative restrictions and, consequently, are not covered by this Directive;

[4] Whereas certain measures adopted by Member States, other than those applicable equally to domestic and imported products, which were operative at the date of entry into force of the Treaty and are not covered by other provisions adopted in pursuance of the Treaty, either preclude importation or make it more difficult or costly than the disposal of domestic production;

[5] Whereas such measures must be considered to include those which make access of imported products to the domestic market, at any marketing stage, subject to a condition which is not laid down for domestic products or to a condition differing from that laid down for domestic products, and more difficult to satisfy, so that a burden is thus placed on imported products only;

[6] Whereas such measures must also be considered to include those which, at any marketing stage, grant to domestic products a preference, other than an aid, to which conditions may or may not be attached, and where such measures totally or partially preclude the disposal of imported products;

[7] Whereas such measures hinder imports which could otherwise take place, and thus have an effect equivalent to quantitative restrictions on imports;

[8] Whereas effects on the free movement of goods of measures which relate to the marketing of products and which apply equally to domestic and imported products are not as a general rule equivalent to those of quantitative restrictions, since such effects are normally inherent in the disparities between rules applied by Member States in this respect;

[9] Whereas, however, such measures may have a restrictive effect on the free movement of goods over and above that which is intrinsic to such rules;

[10] Whereas such is the case where imports are either precluded or made more difficult or costly than the disposal of domestic production and where such effect is not necessary for the attainment of an objective within the scope of the powers for

---

[1] Provision repealed by Treaty of Amsterdam, Art. 6(I)(20), with effect from 1 May 1999.

the regulation of trade left to Member States by the Treaty; whereas such is in particular the case where the said objective can be attained just as effectively by other means which are less of a hindrance to trade; whereas such is also the case where the restrictive effect of these provisions on the free movement of goods is out of proportion to their purpose;

[11] Whereas these measures accordingly have an effect equivalent to that of quantitative restrictions on imports;

[12] Whereas the customs union cannot be achieved without the abolition of such measures having an equivalent effect to quantitative restrictions on imports;

[13] Whereas Member States must abolish all measures having equivalent effect by the end of the transitional period at the latest, even if no Commission Directive expressly requires them to do so;

[14] Whereas the provisions concerning the abolition of quantitative restrictions and measures having equivalent effect between Member States apply both to products originating in and exported by Member States and to products originating in third countries and put into free circulation in the other Member States;

[15] Whereas [former] Article 33(7) does not apply to measures of the kind referred to which fall under other provisions of the Treaty, and in particular those which fall under Articles [31(1)] and [former] 44[2] of the Treaty or form an integral part of a national organisation of an agricultural market;

[16] Whereas [former] Article 33(7) does not apply to the charges and taxation referred to in Article [25] *et seq.* and Article [90] *et seq.* or to the aids mentioned in Article [88];

[17] Whereas the provisions of [former] Article 33(7) do not prevent the application, in particular, of Articles [30] and [296];

Has adopted this Directive:

Article 1 [Abolition of obstacles to trade]

5–002 The purpose of this Directive is to abolish the measures referred to in Articles 2 and 3, which were operative at the date of entry into force of the [EC] Treaty.

Article 2 [Types of measure to be abolished]

5–003 1. This Directive covers measures, other than those applicable equally to domestic or imported products, which hinder imports which could otherwise take place, including measures which make importation more difficult or costly than the disposal of domestic production.

2. In particular, it covers measures which make imports or the disposal, at any marketing stage, of imported products subject to a condition—other than a formality—which is required in respect of imported products only, or a condition differing from that required for domestic products and more difficult to satisfy. Equally, it covers, in particular, measures which favour domestic products or grant them a preference, other than an aid, to which conditions may or may not be attached.

3. The measures referred to must be taken to include those measures which:

(a) lay down, for imported products only, minimum or maximum prices below or above which imports are prohibited, reduced or made subject to conditions liable to hinder importation;

(b) lay down less favourable prices for imported products than for domestic products;

(c) fix profit margins or any other price components for imported products only or fix these differently for domestic products and for imported products, to the detriment of the latter;

[2] Provision repealed by Treaty of Amsterdam, Art. 6(I)(28), with effect from 1 May 1999.

(d) preclude any increase in the price of the imported product corresponding to the supplementary costs and charges inherent in importation;
(e) fix the prices of products solely on the basis of the cost price or the quality of domestic products at such a level as to create a hindrance to importation;
(f) lower the value of an imported product, in particular by causing a reduction in its intrinsic value, or increase its costs;
(g) make access of imported products to the domestic market conditional upon having an agent or representative in the territory of the importing Member State;
(h) lay down conditions of payment in respect of imported products only, or subject imported products to conditions which are different from those laid down for domestic products and more difficult to satisfy;
(i) require, for imports only, the giving of guarantees or making of payments on account;
(j) subject imported products only to conditions, in respect, in particular of shape, size, weight, composition, presentation, identification or putting up, or subject imported products to conditions which are different from those for domestic products and more difficult to satisfy;
(k) hinder the purchase by private individuals of imported products only, or encourage, require or give preference to the purchase of domestic products only;
(l) totally or partially preclude the use of national facilities or equipment in respect of imported products only, or totally or partially confine the use of such facilities or equipment to domestic products only;
(m) prohibit or limit publicity in respect of imported products only, or totally or partially confine publicity to domestic products only;
(n) prohibit, limit or require stocking in respect of imported products only; totally or partially confine the use of stocking facilities to domestic products only, or make the stocking of imported products subject to conditions which are different from those required for domestic products and more difficult to satisfy;
(o) make importation subject to the granting of reciprocity by one or more Member States;
(p) prescribe that imported products are to conform, totally or partially, to rules other than those of the importing country;
(q) specify time-limits for imported products which are insufficient or excessive in relation to the normal course of the various transactions to which these time-limits apply;
(r) subject imported products to controls or, other than those inherent in the customs clearance procedure, to which domestic products are not subject or which are stricter in respect of imported products than they are in respect of domestic products, without this being necessary in order to ensure equivalent protection;
(s) confine names which are not indicative of origin or source to domestic products only.

Article 3 [Other obstacles to trade]

This Directive also covers measures governing the marketing of products which deal, in particular, with shape, size, weight, composition, presentation, identification or putting up and which are equally applicable to domestic and imported products, where the restrictive effect of such measures on the free movement of goods exceeds the effects intrinsic to trade rules. **5–004**

This is the case, in particular, where:

— the restrictive effects on the free movement of goods are out of proportion to their purpose;

— the same objective can be attained by other means which are less of a hindrance to trade.

Article 4 [Duty to abolish measures obstructing intra-Community trade]

5–005 1. Member States shall take all necessary steps in respect of products which must be allowed to enjoy free movement pursuant to Articles [23] and [24] of the Treaty to abolish measures having an effect equivalent to quantitative restrictions on imports and covered by this Directive.

2. Member States shall inform the Commission of measures taken pursuant to this Directive.

Article 5 [Exclusions]

5–006 1. This Directive does not apply to measures:

(a) which fall under Article [31(1)] of the [EC] Treaty;
(b) which are referred to in [former] Article 44 of the [EC] Treaty or form an integral part of a national organisation of an agricultural market not yet replaced by a common organisation.

2. This Directive shall apply without prejudice to the application, in particular, of Articles [30] and [296] of the [EC] Treaty.

Article 6 [Addressees]

5–007 This Directive is addressed to the Member States.

Communication from the Commission concerning the consequences of the judgment given by the Court of Justice on 20 February 1979, in Case 120/78 ("*Cassis de Dijon*")

([1980] OJ C256/2; Doc. Ref. 31980Y1003(01))

5–008 The following is the text of a letter which has been sent to the Member States; the European Parliament and the Council have also been notified of it.

In the Commission's Communication of 6 November 1978 on "Safeguarding free trade within the Community", it was emphasised that the free movement of goods is being affected by a growing number of restrictive measures.

The judgment delivered by the Court of Justice on 20 February 1979 in Case 120/78 (the "Cassis de Dijon" case),[3] and recently reaffirmed in the judgment of 26 June 1980 in Case 788/79,[4] has given the Commission some interpretative guidance enabling it to monitor more strictly the application of the Treaty rules on the free movement of goods, particularly Articles [28] to [30] of the [EC] Treaty.

The Court gives a very general definition of the barriers to free trade which are prohibited by the provisions of Article [28] *et seq.* of the [EC] Treaty. These are taken to include "any national measure capable of hindering, directly or indirectly, actually or potentially, intra-Community trade".

In its judgment of 20 February 1979 the Court indicates the scope of this definition as it applies to technical and commercial rules.

Any product lawfully produced and marketed in one Member State must, in principle, be admitted to the market of any other Member State.

Technical and commercial rules, even those equally applicable to national and imported products, may create barriers to trade only where those rules are necessary to satisfy mandatory requirements and to serve a purpose which is in the

[3] *Rewe-Zentrale AG v Bundesmonopolverwaltung für Branntwein* (Case 120/78) [1979] ECR 649.
[4] *Gilli and Andres* (Case 788/79) [1980] ECR 2071.

general interest and for which they are an essential guarantee. This purpose must be such as to take precedence over the requirements of the free movement of goods, which constitutes one of the fundamental rules of the Community.

The conclusions in terms of policy which the Commission draws from this new guidance are set out below.

Whereas Member States may, with respect to domestic products and in the absence of relevant Community provisions, regulate the terms on which such products are marketed, the case is different for products imported from other Member States.

Any product imported from another Member State must in principle be admitted to the territory of the importing Member State if it has been lawfully produced, that is, conforms to rules and processes of manufacture that are customarily and traditionally accepted in the exporting country, and is marketed in the territory of the latter.

This principle implies that Member States, when drawing up commercial or technical rules liable to affect the free movement of goods, may not take an exclusively national viewpoint and take account only of requirements confined to domestic products. The proper functioning of the common market demands that each Member State also give consideration to the legitimate requirements of the other Member States.

Only under very strict conditions does the Court accept exceptions to this principle; barriers to trade resulting from differences between commercial and technical rules are only admissible:

— if the rules are necessary, that is appropriate and not excessive, in order to satisfy mandatory requirements (public health, protection of consumers or the environment, the fairness of commercial transactions, etc.);
— if the rules serve a purpose in the general interest which is compelling enough to justify an exception to a fundamental rule of the Treaty such as the free movement of goods;
— if the rules are essential for such a purpose to be attained, *i.e.* are the means which are the most appropriate and at the same time least hinder trade.

The Court's interpretation has induced the Commission to set out a number of guidelines.

The principles deduced by the Court imply that a Member State may not in principle prohibit the sale in its territory of a product lawfully produced and marketed in another Member State even if the product is produced according to technical or quality requirements which differ from those imposed on its domestic products. Where a product "suitably and satisfactorily" fulfils the legitimate objective of a Member State's own rules (public safety, protection of the consumer or the environment, etc.), the importing country cannot justify prohibiting its sale in its territory by claiming that the way it fulfils the objective is different from that imposed on domestic products.

In such a case, an absolute prohibition of sale could not be considered "necessary" to satisfy a "mandatory requirement" because it would not be an "essential guarantee" in the sense defined in the Court's judgment.

The Commission will therefore have to tackle a whole body of commercial rules which lay down that products manufactured and marketed in one Member State must fulfil technical or qualitative conditions in order to be admitted to the market of another and specifically in all cases where the trade barriers occasioned by such rules are inadmissible according to the very strict criteria set out by the Court.

The Commission is referring in particular to rules covering the composition, designation, presentation and packaging of products as well as rules requiring compliance with certain technical standards.

The Commission's work of harmonisation will henceforth have to be directed mainly at national laws having an impact on the functioning of the common market where barriers to trade to be removed arise from national provisions which are admissible under the criteria set by the Court.

The Commission will be concentrating on sectors deserving priority because of their economic relevance to the creation of a single internal market.

To forestall later difficulties, the Commission will be informing Member States of potential objections, under the terms of Community law, to provisions they may be considering introducing which come to the attention of the Commission.

It will be producing suggestions soon on the procedures to be followed in such cases.

The Commission is confident that this approach will secure greater freedom of trade for the Community's manufacturers, so strengthening the industrial base of the Community, while meeting the expectations of consumers.

Council Regulation 2679/98 of 7 December 1998, on the functioning of the internal market in relation to the free movement of goods among the Member States

([1998] OJ L337/8; Doc. Ref. 31998R2679)

The Council of the European Union,

5–009 Having regard to the Treaty establishing the European Community, and in particular Article 235 thereof,

Having regard to the proposal from the Commission,[5]

Having regard to the opinion of the European Parliament,[6]

Having regard to the opinion of the Economic and Social Committee[7]:

(1) Whereas, as provided for in Article [14] of the Treaty, the internal market comprises an area without internal frontiers in which, in particular, the free movement of goods is ensured in accordance with Articles [28] to [30] of the Treaty;

(2) Whereas breaches of this principle, such as occur when in a given Member State the free movement of goods is obstructed by actions of private individuals, may cause grave disruption to the proper functioning of the internal market and inflict serious losses on the individuals affected;

(3) Whereas, in order to ensure fulfilment of the obligations arising from the Treaty, and, in particular, to ensure the proper functioning of the internal market, Member States should, on the one hand, abstain from adopting measures or engaging in conduct liable to constitute an obstacle to trade and, on the other hand, take all necessary and proportionate measures with a view to facilitating the free movement of goods in their territory;

(4) Whereas such measures must not affect the exercise of fundamental rights, including the right or freedom to strike;

(5) Whereas this Regulation does not prevent any actions which may be necessary in certain cases at Community level to respond to problems in the functioning of the internal market, taking into account, where appropriate, the application of this Regulation;

(6) Whereas Member States have exclusive competence as regards the maintenance of public order and the safeguarding of internal security as well as in determining whether, when and which measures are necessary and proportionate in order to facilitate the free movement of goods in their territory in a given situation;

(7) Whereas there should be adequate and rapid exchange of information between the Member States and the Commission on obstacles to the free movement of goods;

(8) Whereas a Member State on the territory of which obstacles to the free movement of goods occur should take all necessary and proportionate measures

[5] [1998] OJ C10/14.

[6] [1998] OJ C359.

[7] [1998] OJ C214/90.

to restore as soon as possible the free movement of goods in their territory in order to avoid the risk that the disruption or loss in question will continue, increase or intensify and that there may be a breakdown in trade and in the contractual relations which underlie it; whereas such Member State should inform the Commission and, if requested, other Member States of the measures it has taken or intends to take in order to fulfil this objective

(9) Whereas the Commission, in fulfilment of its duty under the Treaty, should notify the Member State concerned of its view that a breach has occurred and the Member State should respond to that notification;

(10) Whereas the Treaty provides for no powers, other than those in Article [308] thereof, for the adoption of this Regulation,

Has adopted this Regulation:

Article 1 [Definitions]

For the purpose of this Regulation:

1. The term "obstacle" shall mean an obstacle to the free movement of goods among Member States which is attributable to a Member State, whether it involves action or inaction on its part, which may constitute a breach of Articles [28] to [30] of the Treaty and which: **5–010**

(a) leads to serious disruption of the free movement of goods by physically or otherwise preventing, delaying or diverting their import into, export from or transport across a Member State,
(b) causes serious loss to the individuals affected, and
(c) requires immediate action in order to prevent any continuation, increase or intensification of the disruption or loss in question.

2. The term "inaction" shall cover the case when the competent authorities of a Member State, in the presence of an obstacle caused by actions taken by private individuals, fail to take all necessary and proportionate measures within their powers with a view to removing the obstacle and ensuring the free movement of goods in their territory.

Article 2 [Fundamental rights unaffected]

This Regulation may not be interpreted as affecting in any way the exercise of fundamental rights as recognised in Member States, including the right or freedom to strike. These rights may also include the right or freedom to take other actions covered by the specific industrial relations systems in Member States. **5–011**

Article 3 [Establishing the nature of the obstacle to trade]

1. When an obstacle occurs or when there is a threat thereof **5–012**

(a) any Member State (whether or not it is the Member State concerned) which has relevant information shall immediately transmit it to the Commission, and
(b) the Commission shall immediately transmit to the Member States that information and any information from any other source which it may consider relevant.

2. The Member State concerned shall respond as soon as possible to requests for information from the Commission and from other Member States concerning the nature of the obstacle or threat and the action which it has taken or proposes to take. Information exchange between Member States shall also be transmitted to the Commission.

Article 4 [Duty to ensure free movement of goods]

1. When an obstacle occurs, and subject to Article 2, the Member State concerned shall **5–013**

(a) take all necessary and proportionate measures so that the free movement of goods is assured in the territory of the Member State in accordance with the Treaty, and
(b) inform the Commission of the actions which its authorities have taken or intend to take.

2. The Commission shall immediately transmit the information received under paragraph 1(b) to the other Member States.

Article 5 [Role of the Commission]

5–014 1. Where the Commission considers that an obstacle is occurring in a Member State, it shall notify the Member State concerned of the reasons that have led the Commission to such a conclusion and shall request the Member State to take all necessary and proportionate measures to remove the said obstacle within a period which it shall determine with reference to the urgency of the case.

2. In reaching its conclusion, the Commission shall have regard to Article 2.

3. The Commission may publish in the *Official Journal of the European Communities* the text of the notification which it has sent to the Member State concerned and shall immediately transmit the text to any party which requests it.

4. The Member State shall, within five working days of receipt of the text, either:
— inform the Commission of the steps which it has taken or intends to take to implement paragraph 1, or
— communicate a reasoned submission as to why there is no obstacle constituting a breach of Articles [28] to [30] of the Treaty.

5. In exceptional cases, the Commission may allow an extension of the deadline mentioned in paragraph 4 if the Member State submits a duly substantiated request and the grounds cited are deemed acceptable.

This Regulation shall be binding in its entirety and directly applicable in all Member States.

Chapter 6

FREE MOVEMENT OF PERSONS

SECTION 1—FREE MOVEMENT AND RIGHTS OF RESIDENCE

Council Directive 64/221 of 25 February 1964 on the co-ordination of special measures concerning the movement and residence of foreign nationals which are justified on grounds of public policy, public security or public health

([1963—1964] OJ, Eng. Spec. Ed., p.117; Doc. Ref. 31964L0221)

The Council of the European Economic Community, **6–001**

Having regard to the Treaty establishing the European Economic Community, and in particular [former] Article 56(2) thereof,

Having regard to Council Regulation 15 of 16 August 1961[1] on initial measures to bring about free movement of workers within the Community, and in particular Article 47 thereof,

Having regard to Council Directive of 16 August 1961[2] on administrative procedures and practices governing the entry into and employment and residence in a Member State of workers and their families from other Member States of the Community,

Having regard to the General Programmes[3] for the abolition of restrictions on freedom of establishment and on freedom to provide services, and in particular Title II of each such programme,

Having regard to the Council Directive of 25 February 1964[4] on the abolition of restrictions on movement and residence within the Community for nationals of Member States with regard to establishment and the provision of services,

Having regard to the proposal from the Commission,

Having regard to the Opinion of the European Parliament,[5]

Having regard to the Opinion of the Economic and Social Committee,[6]

[1] Whereas co-ordination of provisions laid down by law, regulation or administrative action which provide for special treatment for foreign nationals on grounds of public policy, public security or public health should in the first place deal with the conditions for entry and residence of nationals of Member States moving within the Community either in order to pursue activities as employed or self-employed persons, or as recipients of services;

[2] Whereas such co-ordination presupposes in particular an approximation of the procedures followed in each Member State when invoking grounds of public policy, public security or public health in matters connected with the movement or residence of foreign nationals;

[3] Whereas, in each Member State, nationals of other Member States should have adequate legal remedies available to them in respect of the decisions of the administration in such matters;

[4] Whereas it would be of little practical use to compile a list of diseases and disabilities which might endanger public health, public policy or public security and it would be difficult to make such a list exhaustive whereas it is sufficient to classify such diseases and disabilities in groups,

---

1 [1961] JO 57/1073.
2 [1961] JO 80/1513.
3 [1962] JO 2/32 and 36.
4 [1964] JO 56/845.
5 [1962] JO 134/2861.
6 [1964] JO 56/856.

Has adopted this Directive:

Article 1 [Personal scope of the Directive]

6–002 1. The provisions of this Directive shall apply to any national of a Member State who resides in or travels to another Member State of the Community, either in order to pursue an activity as an employed or self-employed person, or as a recipient of services.[7]

2. These provisions shall apply also to the spouse and to members of the family who come within the provisions of the regulations and directives adopted in this field in pursuance of the Treaty.

Article 2 [Scope of the Directive]

6–003 1. This Directive relates to all measures concerning entry into their territory, issue or renewal of residence permits, or expulsion from their territory, taken by Member States on grounds of public policy, public security or public health.

2. Such grounds shall not be invoked to service economic ends.

Article 3 [Public policy and public security]

6–004 1. Measures taken on grounds of public policy or of public security shall be based exclusively on the personal conduct of the individual concerned.

2. Previous criminal convictions shall not in themselves constitute grounds for the taking of such measures.

3. Expiry of the identity card or passport used by the person concerned to enter the host country and to obtain a residence permit shall not justify expulsion from the territory.

4. The State which issued the identity card or passport shall allow the holder of such document to re-enter its territory without any formality even if the document is no longer valid or the nationality of the holder is in dispute.

Article 4 [Public health]

6–005 1. The only diseases or disabilities justifying refusal of entry into a territory or refusal to issue a first residence permit shall be those listed in the Annex to this Directive.

2. Diseases or disabilities occurring after a first residence permit has been issued shall not justify refusal to renew the residence permit or expulsion from the territory.

3. Member States shall not introduce new provisions or practices which are more restrictive than those in force at the date of notification of this Directive.

Article 5 [Grant or refusal of first residence permits]

6–006 1. A decision to grant or to refuse a first residence permit shall be taken as soon as possible and in any event not later than six months from the date of application for the permit.

The person concerned shall be allowed to remain temporarily in the territory pending a decision either to grant or to refuse a residence permit.

2. The host country may, in cases where this is considered essential, request the Member State of origin of the applicant, and if need be other Member States, to

[7] See Directive 75/35 below for application of Directive 64/221 to self-employed and members of their families with right to remain in host State.

provide information concerning any previous police record. Such enquiries shall not be made as a matter of routine. The Member State consulted shall give its reply within two months.

Article 6 [Right to be informed of grounds of decision]

The person concerned shall be informed of the grounds of public policy, public security, or public health upon which the decision taken in his case is based, unless this is contrary to the interests of the security of the State involved. **6–007**

Article 7 [Notification of refusal to issue/renew permit]

The person concerned shall be officially notified of any decision to refuse the issue or renewal of a residence permit or to expel him from the territory. The period allowed for leaving the territory shall be stated in this notification. Save in cases of urgency, this period shall be not less than fifteen days if the person concerned has not yet been granted a residence permit and not less than one month in all other cases. **6–008**

Article 8 [Legal remedies]

The person concerned shall have the same legal remedies in respect of any decision concerning entry, or refusing the issue or renewal of a residence permit, or ordering expulsion from the territory, as are available to nationals of the State concerned in respect of acts of the administration. **6–009**

Article 9 [Due process]

1. Where there is no right of appeal to a court of law, or where such appeal may be only in respect of the legal validity of the decision, or where the appeal cannot have suspensory effect, a decision refusing renewal of a residence permit or ordering the expulsion of the holder of a residence permit from the territory shall not be taken by the administrative authority, save in cases of urgency, until an opinion has been obtained from a competent authority of the host country before which the person concerned enjoys such rights of defence and of assistance or representation as the domestic law of that country provides for. **6–010**

This authority shall not be the same as that empowered to take the decision refusing renewal of the residence permit or ordering expulsion.

2. Any decision refusing the issue of a first residence permit or ordering expulsion of the person concerned before the issue of the permit shall, where that person so requests, be referred for consideration to the authority whose prior opinion is required under paragraph 1. The person concerned shall then be entitled to submit his defence in person, except where this would be contrary to the interests of national security.

Article 10 [Implementation by Member States]

1. Member States shall within six months of notification of this Directive put into force the measures necessary to comply with its provisions and shall forthwith inform the Commission thereof.

2. Member States shall ensure that the texts of the main provisions of national law which they adopt in the field governed by this Directive are communicated to the Commission. **6–011**

Article 11 [Addressees]

6–012 This Directive is addressed to the Member States.

ANNEX

A. Diseases which might endanger public health:

6–013 1. Diseases subject to quarantine listed in International Health Regulation No. 2 of the World Health Organisation of 25 May 1951;

2. Tuberculosis of the respiratory system in an active state or showing a tendency to develop;

3. Syphilis;

4. Other infectious diseases or contagious parasitic diseases if they are the subject of provisions for the protection of nationals of the host country.

B. Diseases and disabilities which might threaten public policy or public security:

6–014 1. Drug addiction;

2. Profound mental disturbance manifest conditions of psychotic disturbance with agitation, delirium, hallucinations or confusion.

Council Directive 68/360 of 15 October 1968 on the abolition of restrictions on movement and residence within the Community for workers of Member States and their families

([1968(I)] OJ, Eng Spec. Ed., p.485; Doc. Ref. 31968L0360)

6–015 *The Council of the European Communities,*
Having regard to the Treaty establishing the [European Community], and in particular Article [40] thereof,

Having regard to the proposal from the Commission,

Having regard to the Opinion of the European Parliament,[8]

Having regard to the Opinion of the Economic and Social Committee,[9]

[1] Whereas Council Regulation 1612/68[10] fixed the provisions governing freedom of movement for workers within the Community; whereas, consequently, measures should be adopted for the abolition of restrictions which still exist concerning movement and residence within the Community, which conform to the rights and privileges accorded by the said Regulation to nationals of any Member State who move in order to pursue activities as employed persons and to members of their families;

[2] Whereas the rules applicable to residence should, as far as possible, bring the position of workers from other Member States and members of their families into line with that of nationals;

[3] Whereas the co-ordination of special measures relating to the movement and residence of foreign nationals, justified on grounds of public policy, public security of public health, is the subject of the Council Directive of 25 February 1964[11] adopted in application of [former] Article 56(2) of the Treaty,

---

8 [1967] JO 268/10.
9 [1967] JO 298/10.
10 [1968(I)] OJ, Eng. Spec. Ed., p. 475 (see above).
11 Directive 64/221, [1963–1964] OJ, Eng. Spec. Ed., p.117 (see above)

Has adopted this Directive:

Article 1 **[Duty to abolish restrictions on movement and residence]**

Member States shall, acting as provided in this Directive, abolish restrictions on the movement and residence of nationals of the said States and of members of their families to whom Regulation 1612/68 applies. **6–016**

Article 2 **[Right to leave home country; issue of passports or identity cards]**

1. Member States shall grant the nationals referred to in Article 1 the right to leave their territory in order to take up activities as employed persons and to pursue such activities in the territory of another Member State. Such right shall be exercised simply on production of a valid identity card or passport. Members of the family shall enjoy the same right as the national on whom they are dependent. **6–017**

2. Member States shall, acting in accordance with their laws, issue to such nationals, or renew, an identity card or passport, which shall state in particular the holder's nationality.

3. The passport must be valid at least for all Member States and for countries through which the holder must pass when travelling between Member States. Where a passport is the only document on which the holder may lawfully leave the country, its period of validity shall be not less than five years.

4. Member States may not demand from the nationals referred to in Article 1 any exit visa or any equivalent document.

Article 3 **[Entry into host country]**

1. Member States shall allow the persons referred to in Article 1 to enter their territory simply on production of a valid identity card or passport. **6–018**

2. No entry visa or equivalent document may be demanded save from members of the family who are not nationals of a Member State. Member States shall accord to such persons every facility for obtaining any necessary visas.

Article 4 **[Grant of right of residence]**

1. Member States shall grant the right of residence in their territory to the persons referred to in Article 1 who are able to produce the documents listed in paragraph 3. **6–019**

2. As proof of the right of residence, a document entitled "Residence Permit for a National of a Member State of the EEC" shall be issued. This document must include a statement that it has been issued pursuant to Regulation 1612/68 and to the measures taken by the Member States for the implementation of the present Directive. The text of such statement is given in the Annex to this Directive.

3. For the issue of a Residence Permit for a National of a Member State of the EEC, Member States may require only the production of the following documents;

— by the worker:
(a) the document with which he entered their territory;
(b) a confirmation of engagement from the employer or a certificate of employment;
— by the members of the worker's family:
(c) the document with which they entered the territory;
(d) a document issued by the competent authority of the State of origin or the State whence they came, proving their relationship;
(e) in the cases referred to in Article 10(1) and (2) of Regulation 1612/68, a document issued by the competent authority of the State of origin or the State whence they came, testifying that they are dependent on the worker or that they live under his roof in such country.

4. A member of the family who is not a national of a Member State shall be issued with a residence document which shall have the same validity as that issued to the worker on whom he is dependent.

Article 5 [Employment not hindered by incomplete residence permit formalities]

6–020 Completion of the formalities for obtaining a residence permit shall not hinder the immediate beginning of employment under a contract concluded by the applicants.

Article 6 [Validity of residence permit]

6–021 1. The residence permit:
(a) must be valid throughout the territory of the Member State which issued it;
(b) must be valid for at least five years from the date of issue and be automatically renewable.

2. Breaks in residence not exceeding six consecutive months and absence on military service shall not affect the validity of a residence permit.

3. Where a worker is employed for a period exceeding three months but not exceeding a year in the service of an employer in the host State or in the employ of a person providing services, the host Member State shall issue him a temporary residence permit, the validity of which may be limited to the expected period of the employment.

Subject to the provisions of Article 8(1)(c), a temporary residence permit shall be issued also to a seasonal worker employed for a period of more than three months. The period of employment must be shown in the documents referred to in paragraph 4(3)(b).

Article 7 [Effect of incapacity for work or unemployment]

6–022 1. A valid residence permit may not be withdrawn from a worker solely on the grounds that he is no longer in employment, either because he is temporarily incapable of work as a result of illness or accident, or because he is involuntarily unemployed, this being duly confirmed by the competent employment office.

2. When the residence permit is renewed for the first time, the period of residence may be restricted, but not to less than twelve months, where the worker has been involuntarily unemployed in the Member State for more than twelve consecutive months.

Article 8 [Special cases]

1. Member States shall, without issuing a residence permit, recognise the right of residence in their territory of: 6–023

(a) a worker pursuing an activity as an employed person, where the activity is not expected to last for more than three months. The document with which the person concerned entered the territory and a statement by the employer on the expected duration of the employment shall be sufficient to cover his stay; a statement by the employer shall not, however, be required in the case of workers coming within the provisions of the Council Directive of 25 February 1964[12] on the attainment of freedom of establishment and freedom to provide services in respect of the activities of intermediaries in commerce, industry and small craft industries.

(b) a worker who, while having his residence in the territory of a Member State to which he returns as a rule, each day or at least once a week, is employed in the territory of another Member State. The competent authority of the State where he is employed may issue such worker with a special permit valid for five years and automatically renewable

(c) a seasonal worker who holds a contract of employment stamped by the competent authority of the Member State on whose territory he has come to pursue his activity.

2. In all cases referred to in paragraph 1, the competent authorities of the host Member State may require the worker to report his presence in the territory.

Article 9 [Provision of permits and visas]

1. The residence documents granted to nationals of a Member State of the EEC referred to in this Directive shall be issued and renewed free of charge or on payment of an amount not exceeding the dues and taxes charged for the issue of identity cards to nationals. 6–024

2. The visa referred to in Article 3(2) and the stamp referred to in Article 8(1)(c) shall be free of charge.

3. Member States shall take the necessary steps to simplify as much as possible the formalities and procedure for obtaining the documents mentioned in paragraph 1.

Article 10 [Limited power of Member States to derogate]

Member States shall not derogate from the provisions of this Directive save on grounds of public policy, public security or public health. 6–025

Article 11 [Workers under ECSC and Euratom Treaties]

[Not reproduced]. 6–026

Article 12 [Implementation]

1. Member States shall, within nine months of notification of this Directive, bring into force the measures necessary to comply with its provisions and shall forthwith inform the Commission thereof. 6–027

2. They shall notify the Commission of amendments made to provisions imposed by law, regulation or administrative action for the simplification of the formalities

[12] [1964] JO 56/869.

and procedure for issuing such documents as are still necessary for the entry, exit and residence of workers and members of their families.

Article 13 [Transitional provision]

6–028 [Not reproduced]

Article 14 [Addressees]

6–029 This Directive is addressed to the Member States.

Annex

6–030 Text of the statement referred to in Article 4(2):
"This permit is issued pursuant to Regulation (EEC) No. 1612/68 of the Council of the European Communities of 15 October 1968 and to the measures taken in implementation of the Council Directive of 15 October 1968.
In accordance with the provisions of the above-mentioned Regulation, the holder of this permit has the right to take up and pursue an activity as an employed person in ....[13][13] territory under the same conditions as ....[13][14] workers."

Council Regulation 1612/68 of 15 October 1968 on freedom of movement for workers within the Community

([1968(I)] OJ, Eng. Spec. Ed., p.475; Doc. Ref. 31968R16120)

6–031 *The Council of the European Communities,*
Having regard to the Treaty establishing the [European Community], and in particular Article [40] thereof;

Having regard to the proposal from the Commission,

Having regard to the Opinion of the European Parliament,[15]

Having regard to the Opinion of the Economic and Social Committee,[16]

[1] Whereas freedom of movement for workers should be secured within the Community by the end of the transitional period at the latest; whereas the attainment of this objective entails the abolition of any discrimination based on nationality between workers of the Member States as regards employment, remuneration and other conditions of work and employment, as well as the right of such workers to move freely within the Community in order to pursue activities as employed persons subject to any limitations justified on grounds of public policy, public security or public health;

[2] Whereas by reason in particular of the early establishment of the customs union and in order to ensure the simultaneous completion of the principal foundations of the Community, provisions should be adopted to enable the objectives laid down in Articles 48 and 49 of the Treaty in the field of freedom of movement to be achieved and to perfect measures adopted successively under Regulation 15[17] on the first steps for attainment of freedom of movement and under Council Regulation 38/54[18] of 25 March 1964, on freedom of movement for workers within the Community;

---

[13] [Austrian, Belgian, British, Danish, Finnish, German, Greek, Irish, French, Italian, Luxembourg, Netherlands, Norwegian, Portuguese, Spanish, Swedish, according to the country issuing the permit.]

[14] Words substituted by Act of Accession of Austria, Finland and Sweden Annex 1/04/B (as adapted by Decision 1/95) as from 1 January 1995. Text of the statement otherwise unamended.

[15] [1967] JO 268/9.

[16] [1967] JO 298/10.

[17] [1961] JO 57/1073.

[18] [1964] JO 62/965.

[3] Whereas freedom of movement constitutes a fundamental right of workers and their families; whereas mobility of labour within the Community must be one of the means by which the worker is guaranteed the possibility of improving his living and working conditions and promoting his social advancement, while helping to satisfy the requirements of the economies of the Member States; whereas the right of all workers in the Member States to pursue the activity of their choice within the Community should be affirmed;

[4] Whereas such right must be enjoyed without discrimination by permanent, seasonal and frontier workers and by those who pursue their activities for the purpose of providing services;

[5] Whereas the right of freedom of movement, in order that it may be exercised, by objective standards, in freedom and dignity, requires that equality of treatment shall be ensured in fact and in law in respect of all matters relating to the actual pursuit of activities as employed persons and to eligibility for housing, and also that obstacles to the mobility of workers shall be eliminated, in particular as regards the worker's right to be joined by his family and the conditions for the integration of that family into the host country;

[6] Whereas the principle of non-discrimination between Community workers entails that all nationals of Member States have the same priority as regards employment as is enjoyed by national workers;

[7] Whereas it is necessary to strengthen the machinery for vacancy clearance, in particular by developing direct co-operation between the central employment services and also between the regional services, as well as by increasing and co-ordinating the exchange of information in order to ensure in a general way a clearer picture of the labour market; whereas workers wishing to move should also be regularly informed of living and working conditions whereas, furthermore, measures should be provided for the case where a Member State undergoes or foresees disturbances on its labour market which may seriously threaten the standard of living and level of employment in a region or an industry; whereas for this purpose the exchange of information, aimed at discouraging workers from moving to such a region or industry, constitutes the method to be applied in the first place but, where necessary, it should be possible to strengthen the results of such exchange of information by temporarily suspending the abovementioned machinery, any such decision to be taken at Community level;

[8] Whereas close links exist between freedom of movement for workers, employment and vocational training, particularly where the latter aims at putting workers in a position to take up offers of employment from other regions of the Community whereas such links make it necessary that the problems arising in this connection should no longer be studied in isolation but viewed as inter-dependent, account also being taken of the problems of employment at the regional level and whereas it is therefore necessary to direct the efforts of Member States toward co-ordinating their employment policies at Community level;

[9] Whereas the Council, by its Decision of 15 October 1968,[19] made Articles [39] and [40] of the Treaty and also the measures taken in implementation thereof applicable to the French overseas departments,

Has adopted this Regulation:

Part I—Employment and Workers' Families

Title I—Eligibility for Employment

Article 1 [Right to take up employment in host State]

1. Any national of a Member State, shall, irrespective of his place of residence, have the right to take up an activity as an employed person, and to pursue such **6–032**

[19] Decision 68/359, [1968(I)] OJ, Eng. Spec. Ed., p.474.

activity, within the territory of another Member State in accordance with the provisions laid down by law, regulation or administrative action governing the employment of nationals of that State.

2. He shall, in particular, have the right to take up available employment in the territory of another Member State with the same priority as nationals of that State.

Article 2 [Freedom to conclude employment contracts]

6–033 Any national of a Member State and any employer pursuing an activity in the territory of a Member State may exchange their applications for and offers of employment, and may conclude and perform contracts of employment in accordance with the provisions in force laid down by law, regulation or administrative action, without any discrimination resulting therefrom.

Article 3 [Discrimination in national employment law prohibited]

6–034 1. Under this Regulation, provisions laid down by law, regulation or administrative action or administrative practices of a Member State shall not apply:

— where they limit application for and offers of employment, or the right of foreign nationals to take up and pursue employment or subject these to conditions not applicable in respect of their own nationals; or

— where, though applicable irrespective of nationality, their exclusive or principal aim or effect is to keep nationals of other Member States away from the employment offered.

This provision shall not apply to conditions relating to linguistic knowledge required by reason of the nature of the post to be filled.

2. There shall be included in particular among the provisions or practices of a Member State referred to in the first sub-paragraph of paragraph 1 those which:

(a) prescribe a special recruitment procedure for foreign nationals;

(b) limit or restrict the advertising of vacancies in the press or through any other medium or subject it to conditions other than those applicable in respect of employers pursuing their activities in the territory of that Member State;

(c) subject eligibility for employment to conditions of registration with employment offices or impede recruitment of individual workers, where persons who do not reside in the territory of that State are concerned.

Article 4 [Quotas for overseas workers inapplicable to EC nationals]

6–035 1. Provisions laid down by law, regulation or administrative action of the Member States which restrict by number or percentage the employment of foreign nationals in any undertaking, branch of activity or region, or at a national level, shall not apply to nationals of the other Member States.

2. When in a Member State the granting of any benefit to undertakings is subject to a minimum percentage of national workers being employed, nationals of the other Member States shall be counted as national workers, subject to the provisions of the Council Directive of 15 October 1963.[20]

Article 5 [Assistance in seeking employment in host State]

6–036 A national of a Member State who seeks employment in the territory of another Member State shall receive the same assistance there as that afforded by the employment offices in that State to their own nationals seeking employment.

[20] [1963] JO 159/2661.

Article 6 [Medical, vocational or other criteria for employment]

1. The engagement and recruitment of a national of one Member State for a post in another Member State shall not depend on medical, vocational or other criteria which are discriminatory on grounds of nationality by comparison with those applied to nationals of the other Member State who wish to pursue the same activity. **6–037**

2. Nevertheless, a national who holds an offer in his name from an employer in a Member State other than that of which he is a national may have to undergo a vocational test, if the employer expressly requests this when making his offer of employment.

Title II—Employment and Equality of Treatment

Article 7 [Conditions of employment; social/tax advantages; access to training]

1. A worker who is a national of a Member State may not, in the territory of another Member State, be treated differently from national workers by reason of his nationality in respect of any conditions of employment and work, in particular as regards remuneration, dismissal, and should he become unemployed, reinstatement or re-employment. **6–038**

2. He shall enjoy the same social and tax advantages as national workers.

3. He shall also, by virtue of the same right and under the same conditions as national workers, have access to training in vocational schools and retraining centres.

4. Any clause of a collective or individual agreement or of any other collective regulation concerning eligibility for employment, employment, remuneration and other conditions of work or dismissal shall be null and void in so far as it lays down or authorises discriminatory conditions in respect of workers who are nationals of the other Member States.

Article 8 [Trade union rights; access to posts governed by public law]

1. A worker who is a national of a Member State and who is employed in the territory of another Member State shall enjoy equality of treatment as regards membership of trade unions and the exercise of rights attaching thereto, including the right to vote [and to be eligible for the administration or management posts of a trade union][21]; he may be excluded from taking part in the management of bodies governed by public law and from holding an office governed by public law. Furthermore, he shall have the right of eligibility for workers' representative bodies in the undertaking. The provisions of this Article shall not affect laws or regulations in certain Member States which grant more extensive rights to workers coming from the other Member States. **6–039**

2. [...][22]

Article 9 [Access to housing]

1. A worker who is a national of a Member State and who is employed in the territory of another Member State shall enjoy all the rights and benefits accorded to national workers in matters of housing, including ownership of the housing he needs. **6–040**

2. Such worker may, with the same right as nationals, put his name down on the housing lists in the region in which he is employed, where such lists exist he shall enjoy the resultant benefits and priorities.

[21] Words inserted by Regulation 312/76 Art. 1(1) as from 17 February 1976.
[22] Article 8(2) repealed by Regulation 312/76 Art. 1(2) as from 17 February 1976.

If his family has remained in the country whence he came, they shall be considered for this purpose as residing in the said region, where national workers benefit from a similar presumption.

Title III—Workers' Families

Article 10 [Which family members entitled to join worker in host State]

6–041 1. The following shall, irrespective of their nationality, have the right to install themselves with a worker who is a national of one Member State and who is employed in the territory of another Member State:

(a) his spouse and their descendants who are under the age of 21 years or are dependants;
(b) dependent relatives in the ascending line of the worker and his spouse.

2. Member States shall facilitate the admission of any member of the family not coming within the provisions of paragraph 1 if dependent on the worker referred to above or living under his roof in the country whence he comes.

3. For the purposes of paragraphs 1 and 2, the worker must have available for his family housing considered as normal for national workers in the region where he is employed; this provision, however must not give rise to discrimination between national workers and workers from the other Member States.

6–042 **Article 11 [Rights of family members to take up employment]**

Where a national of a Member State is pursuing an activity as an employed or self-employed person in the territory of another Member State, his spouse and those of the children who are under the age of 21 years or dependent on him shall have the right to take up any activity as an employed person throughout the territory of that same State, even if they are not nationals of any Member State.

Article 12 [Access of children to education and training]

6–043 The children of a national of a Member State who is or has been employed in the territory of another Member State shall be admitted to that State's general educational, apprenticeship and vocational training courses under the same conditions as the nationals of that State, if such children are residing in its territory.

Member States shall encourage all efforts to enable such children to attend these courses under the best possible conditions.

Part II—Clearance of Vacancies and Applications for Employment

6–044 **Articles 13–23** [Not reproduced].

Part III—Committees for Ensuring Close Co-operation between the Member States in Matters Concerning the Freedom of Movement of Workers and their Employment

6–045 **Articles 24–37** [Not reproduced].

Part IV—Transitional and Final Provisions

Title I—Transitional Provisions

Articles 38–41

[Not reproduced]. **6–046**

Title II—Final Provisions

Article 42 [Relationship of Regulation to other provisions]

1. This Regulation shall not affect the provisions of the Treaty establishing the European Coal and Steel Community which relate to workers with recognised qualifications in coalmining or steelmaking, nor those of the Treaty establishing the European Atomic Energy Community which deal with eligibility for skilled employment in the field of nuclear energy, nor any measures taken in pursuance of those Treaties. **6–047**

Nevertheless, this Regulation shall apply to categories of workers referred to in the first sub-paragraph and to members of their families in so far as their legal position is not governed by the above-mentioned Treaties or measures.

2. This Regulation shall not affect measures taken in accordance with Article 51 of the Treaty.

3. This Regulation shall not affect the obligations of Member States arising out of:
— special relations or future agreements with certain non-European countries or territories, based on institutional ties existing at the time of the entry into force of this Regulation; or
— agreements in existence at the time of the entry into force of this Regulation with certain non-European countries or territories, based on institutional ties between them.

Workers from such countries or territories who, in accordance with this provision, are pursuing activities as employed persons in the territory of one of those Member States may not invoke the benefit of the provisions of this Regulation in the territory of the other Member States.

Article 43 [Member State agreements to be notified to Commission]

Member States shall, for information purposes, communicate to the Commission the texts of agreements, conventions or arrangements concluded between them in the manpower field between the date of their being signed and that of their entry into force. **6–048**

Article 44 [Implementation measures]

The Commission shall adopt measures pursuant to this Regulation for its implementation. To this end it shall act in close co-operation with the central public authorities of the Member States. **6–049**

Article 45 [Removing restrictions on eligibility for employment]

The Commission shall submit to the Council proposals aimed at abolishing, in accordance with the conditions of the Treaty, restrictions on eligibility for **6–050** employment of workers who are nationals of Member States, where the absence of mutual recognition of diplomas, certificates or other evidence of formal qualifications may prevent freedom of movement for workers.

Article 46 [Budget]

6–051 [Not reproduced].

Article 47 [Territorial and personal scope of Regulation]

6–052 This Regulation shall apply to the territories of the Member States and to their nationals, without prejudice to Articles 2, 3, 10 and 11.

Article 48 [Repeal]

6–053 Regulation 38/64 shall cease to have effect when this Regulation enters into force.

This Regulation shall be binding in its entirety and directly applicable in all Member States.

ANNEX

6–054 [...][23]

Commission Regulation 1251/70 of 29 June 1970 on the right of workers to remain in the territory of a Member State after having been employed in that State

(1970(II) OJ, Eng. Spec. Ed., p.402; Doc. Ref. 31970R1251)

6–055 *The Commission of the European Communities,*

Having regard to the Treaty establishing the [European Community], and in particular Article [39](3)(d) thereof, and Article 2 of the Protocol on the Grand Duchy of Luxembourg,

Having regard to the Opinion of the European Parliament,[24]

[1] Whereas Council Regulation 1612/68[25] of 15 October 1968 and Council Directive 68/360 of 15 October 1968[26] enabled freedom of movement for workers to be secured at the end of a series of measures to be achieved progressively; whereas the right of residence acquired by workers in active employment has as a corollary the right, granted by the Treaty to such workers, to remain in the territory of a Member State after having been employed in that State; whereas it is important to lay down the conditions for the exercise of such right;

[2] Whereas the said Council Regulation and Council Directive contain the appropriate provisions concerning the right of workers to reside in the territory of a Member State for the purposes of employment; whereas the right to remain, referred to in Article [39](3)(d) of the Treaty is interpreted therefore as the right of the worker to maintain his residence in the territory of a Member State when he ceases to be employed there;

[3] Whereas the mobility of labour in the Community requires that workers may be employed successively in several Member States without thereby being placed at a disadvantage;

[4] Whereas it is important, in the first place, to guarantee to the worker residing in the territory of a Member State the right to remain in that territory

[23] Annex repealed by Regulation 2434/92 Art. 1(8) as from 27 August 1992.
[24] [1970] JO C65/16.
[25] [1968(I)] OJ, Eng. Spec. Ed., p.475 (see above).
[26] [1968(I)] OJ, Eng. Spec. Ed., p.485 (see above).

when he ceases to be employed in that State because he has reached retirement age or by reason of permanent incapacity to work; whereas, however, it is equally important to ensure that right for the worker who, after a period of employment and residence in the territory of a Member State, works as an employed person in the territory of another Member State, while still retaining his residence in the territory of the first State;

[5] Whereas, to determine the conditions under which the right to remain arises, account should be taken of the reasons which have led to the termination of employment in the territory of the Member State concerned and, in particular, of the difference between retirement, the normal and foreseeable end of working life, and incapacity to work which leads to a premature and unforeseeable termination of activity; whereas special conditions must be laid down where termination of activity is the result of an accident at work or occupational disease, or where the worker's spouse is or was a national of the Member State concerned;

[6] Whereas the worker who has reached the end of his working life should have sufficient time in which to decide where he wishes to establish his final residence;

[7] Whereas the exercise by the worker of the right to remain entails that such right shall be extended to members of his family; whereas in the case of the death of the worker during his working life, maintenance of the right of residence of the members of his family must also be recognised and be the subject of special conditions;

[8] Whereas persons to whom the right to remain applies must enjoy equality of treatment with national workers who have ceased their working lives,

Has adopted this Regulation:

Article 1 [Personal scope of the Regulation]

The provisions of this Regulation shall apply to nationals of a Member State who have worked as employed persons in the territory of another Member State and to members of their families, as defined in Article 10 of Council Regulation 1612/68 on freedom of movement for workers within the Community. **6–056**

Article 2 [Those with a right to remain]

1. The following shall have the right to remain permanently in the territory of a Member State: **6–057**

(a) a worker who, at the time of termination of his activity, has reached the age laid down by the law of that Member State for entitlement to an old-age pension and who has been employed in that State for at least the last twelve months and has resided there continuously for more than three years;

(b) a worker who, having resided continuously in the territory of that State for more than two years, ceases to work there as an employed person as a result of permanent incapacity to work. If such incapacity is the result of an accident at work or an occupational disease entitling him to a pension for which an institution of that State is entirely or partially responsible, no condition shall be imposed as to length of residence;

(c) a worker who, after three years' continuous employment and residence in the territory of that State, works as an employed person in the territory of another Member State, while retaining his residence in the territory of the first State, to which he returns, as a rule, each day or at least once a week.

Periods of employment completed in this way in the territory of the other Member State shall, for the purposes of entitlement to the rights referred to in sub-paragraphs (a) and (b), be considered as having been completed in the territory of the State of residence.

2. The conditions as to length of residence and employment laid down in paragraph 1(a) and the condition as to length of residence laid down in paragraph 1(b) shall not apply if the worker's spouse is a national of the Member State concerned or has lost the nationality of that State by marriage to that worker.

Article 3 [Members of a worker's family]

6–058 1. The members of a worker's family referred to in Article 1 of this Regulation who are residing with him in the territory of a Member State shall be entitled to remain there permanently if the worker has acquired the right to remain in the territory of that State in accordance with Article 2, and to do so even after his death.

2. If, however, the worker dies during his working life and before having acquired the right to remain in the territory of the State concerned, members of his family shall be entitled to remain there permanently on condition that:

— the worker, on the date of his decease, had resided continuously in the territory of that Member State for at least two years; or
— his death resulted from an accident at work or an occupational disease; or
— the surviving spouse is a national of the State of residence or lost the nationality of that State by marriage to that worker.

Article 4 [Proof of continuity of residence; periods of unemployment or absence]

6–059 1. Continuity of residence as provided for in Articles 2(1) and 3(2) may be attested by any means of proof in use in the country of residence. It shall not be affected by temporary absences not exceeding a total of three months per year, nor by longer absences due to compliance with the obligations of military service.

2. Periods of involuntary unemployment, duly recorded by the competent employment office, and absences due to illness or accident shall be considered as periods of employment within the meaning of Article 2(1).

Article 5 [Exercise of the right to remain]

6–060 1. The person entitled to the right to remain shall be allowed to exercise it within two years from the time of becoming entitled to such right pursuant to Article 2(1)(a) and (b) and Article 3. During such period he may leave the territory of the Member State without adversely affecting such right.

2. No formality shall be required on the part of the person concerned in respect of the exercise of the right to remain.

Article 6 [Entitlement to residence permit]

6–061 1. Persons coming under the provisions of this Regulation shall be entitled to a residence permit which:

(a) shall be issued and renewed free of charge or on payment of a sum not exceeding the dues and taxes payable by nationals for the issue or renewal identity documents;
(b) must be valid throughout the territory of the Member State issuing it;
(c) must be valid for at least five years and be renewable automatically.

2. Periods of non-residence not exceeding six consecutive months shall not affect the validity of the residence permit.

Article 7 [Right to equal treatment]

6–062 The right to equality of treatment, established by Council Regulation 1612/68, shall apply also to persons coming under the provisions of this Regulation.

Article 8 [More favourable Member State laws; later re-admission]

6–063 1. This Regulation shall not affect any provisions laid down by law, regulation or administrative action of one Member State which would be more favourable to nationals of other Member States.

2. Member States shall facilitate re-admission to their territories of workers who have left those territories after having resided there permanently for a long period and having been employed there and who wish to return there when they have reached retirement age or are permanently incapacitated for work.

Article 9 [Position of Luxembourg]

1. The Commission may, taking account of developments in the demographic situation of the Grand Duchy of Luxembourg, lay down, at the request of that State, different conditions from those provided for in this Regulation, in respect of the exercise of the right to remain in Luxembourg territory. **6–064**

2. Within two months after the request supplying all appropriate details has been put before it, the Commission shall take a decision, stating the reasons on which it is based.

It shall notify the Grand Duchy of Luxembourg of such decision and inform the other Member States thereof.

This Regulation shall be binding in its entirety and directly applicable in all Member States.

Council Directive 73/148 of 21 May 1973 on the abolition of restrictions on movement and residence within the Community for nationals of Member States with regard to establishment and the provision of services

([1973] OJ L172/14; Doc. Ref. 31973L0148)

The Council of the European Communities **6–065**

Having regard to the Treaty establishing the [European Community], and in particular Article [44(1)] and Article [52(1)] thereof,

Having regard to the General Programmes for the abolition of restrictions on freedom of establishment and freedom to provide services,[27] and in particular Title II thereof,

Having regard to the proposal from the Commission,

Having regard to the Opinion of the European Parliament,[28]

Having regard to the Opinion of the Economic and Social Committee,[29]

[1] Whereas freedom of movement of persons as provided for in the Treaty and the General Programmes for the abolition of restrictions on freedom of establishment and on freedom to provide services entails the abolition of restrictions on movement and residence within the Community for nationals of Member States wishing to establish themselves or to provide services within the territory of another Member State;

[2] Whereas freedom of establishment can be fully attained only if a right of permanent residence is granted to the persons who are to enjoy freedom of establishment; whereas freedom to provide services entails that persons providing and receiving services should have the right of residence for the time during which the services are being provided;

[3] Whereas Council Directive of 25 February 1964[30] on the abolition of restrictions on movement and residence within the Community for nationals of Member States with regard to establishment and the provision of services laid down the rules applicable in this area to activities as self-employed persons;

[4] Whereas Council Directive of 15 October 1968[31] on the abolition of restrictions on movement and residence within the Community for workers of

---

27 [1959–1962] OJ, Eng. Spec. Ed., pp.3 and 7.

28 [1972] JO C19/5.

29 [1972] JO C67/7.

30 [1964] JO 56/845.

31 [1968(I)] OJ, Eng. Spec. Ed., p.485 (see above).

Member States and their families, which replaced the Directive of 25 March 1964[32] bearing the same title, has in the meantime amended the rules applicable to employed persons;

[5] Whereas the provisions concerning movement and residence within the Community of self-employed persons and their families should likewise be improved;

[6] Whereas the co-ordination of special measures concerning the movement and residence of foreign nationals, justified on grounds of public policy, public security or public health, is already the subject of the Council Directive of 25 February 1964[33];

Has adopted this Directive:

Article 1 [Personal scope of Directive]

6–066 1. The Member States shall, acting as provided in this Directive, abolish restrictions on the movement and residence of:

(a) nationals of a Member State who are established or who wish to establish themselves in another Member State in order to pursue activities as self-employed persons, or who wish to provide services in that State;
(b) nationals of Member States wishing to go to another Member State as recipients of services;
(c) the spouse and the children under twenty-one years of age of such nationals, irrespective of their nationality;
(d) the relatives in the ascending and descending lines of such nationals and of the spouse of such nationals, which relatives are dependent on them, irrespective of their nationality.

2. Member States shall favour the admission of any other member of the family of a national referred to in paragraph 1(a) or (b) or of the spouse of that national, which member is dependent on that national or spouse of that national or who in the country of origin was living under the same roof.

Article 2 [Right to leave home State; issue of passports and identity cards]

6–067 1. Member States shall grant the persons referred to in Article 1 the right to leave their territory. Such right shall be exercised simply on production of a valid identity card or passport. Members of the family shall enjoy the same right as the national on whom they are dependent.

2. Member States shall, acting in accordance with their laws, issue to their nationals, or renew, an identity card or passport, which shall state in particular the holder's nationality.

3. The passport must be valid at least for all Member States and for countries through which the holder must pass when travelling between Member States. Where a passport is the only document on which the holder may lawfully leave the country, its period of validity shall be not less than five years.

4. Member States may not demand from the persons referred to in Article 1 any exit visa or any equivalent requirement.

Article 3 [Right to enter host State]

6–068 1. Member States shall grant to the persons referred to in Article 1 right to enter their territory merely on production of a valid identity card or passport.

2. No entry visa or equivalent requirement may be demanded save in respect of members of the family who do have the nationality of a Member State. Member States shall afford to such persons every facility for obtaining any necessary visas.

[32] [1964] JO 62/981.
[33] [1964] JO 56/850.

Article 4 [Rights of residence in host State]

1. Each Member State shall grant the right of permanent residence to nationals of other Member States who establish themselves within its territory in order to pursue activities as self-employed persons, when the restrictions on these activities have been abolished pursuant to the Treaty. **6–069**

As proof of the right of residence, a document entitled "Residence Permit for a National of a Member State of the European Communities" shall be issued. This document shall be valid for not less than five years from the date of issue and shall be automatically renewable.

Breaks in residence not exceeding six consecutive months and absence on military service shall not affect the validity of a residence permit.

A valid residence permit may not be withdrawn from a national referred to in Article 1(1)(a) solely on the grounds that he is no longer in employment because he is temporarily incapable of work as a result of illness or accident.

Any national of a Member State who is not specified in the first sub-paragraph but who is authorised under the laws of another Member State to pursue an activity within its territory shall be granted a right of abode for a period not less than that of the authorisation granted for the pursuit of the activity in question.

However, any national referred to in sub-paragraph 1 and to whom the provisions of the preceding sub-paragraph apply as a result of a change of employment shall retain his residence permit until the date on which it expires.

2. The right of residence for persons providing and receiving services shall be of equal duration with the period during which the services are provided.

Where such period exceeds three months, the Member State in the territory of which the services are performed shall issue a right of abode as proof of the right of residence.

Where the period does not exceed three months, the identity card or passport with which the person concerned entered the territory shall be sufficient to cover his stay. The Member State may, however, require the person concerned to report his presence in the territory.

3. A member of the family who is not a national of a Member State shall be issued with a residence document which shall have the same validity as that issued to the national on whom he is dependent.

Article 5 [Territorial extent of right of residence]

The right of residence shall be effective throughout the territory of the Member State concerned. **6–070**

Article 6 [Formalities for applicants for residence permit or right of abode]

An applicant for a residence permit or right of abode shall not be required by a Member State to produce anything other than the following, namely: **6–071**

(a) the identity card or passport with which he or she entered its territory;
(b) proof that he or she comes within one of the classes of person referred to in Articles 1 and 4.

Article 7 [Provision of residence documents and visas]

1. The residence documents granted to nationals of a Member State shall be issued and renewed free of charge or on payment of an amount not exceeding the dues **6–072**

and taxes charged for the issue of identity cards to nationals. These provisions shall also apply to documents and certificates required for the issue and renewal of such residence documents.

2. The visas referred to in Article 3(2) shall be free of charge.

3. Member States shall take the necessary steps to simplify as much as possible the formalities and the procedure for obtaining the documents mentioned in paragraph 1.

Article 8 [Limited grounds for Member State derogation]

6–073 Member States shall not derogate from the provisions of this Directive save on grounds of public policy, public security or public health.

Article 9 [Implementation]

6–074 1. Member States shall, within six months of notification of this Directive, bring into force the measures necessary to comply with its provisions and shall forthwith inform the Commission thereof.

2. They shall notify the Commission of amendments made to provisions imposed by law, regulation or administrative action for the simplification with regard to establishment and the provision of services of the formalities and procedure for issuing such documents as are still necessary for the movement and residence of persons referred to in Article 1.

Article 10 [Transitional provisions]

6–075 [Not reproduced].

Article 11 [Addressees]

6–076 This Directive is addressed to the Member States.

Council Directive 75/34 of 17 December 1974 concerning the right of nationals of a Member State to remain in the territory of another Member State after having pursued therein an activity in a self-employed capacity

([1975] OJ L14/10; Doc. Ref. 31975L0034)

6–077 *The Council of the European Communities,*

Having regard to the Treaty establishing the [European Community], and in particular Article [308] thereof,

Having regard to the General Programme for the abolition of restrictions on freedom of establishment,[34] and in particular Title II thereof,

Having regard to the proposal from the Commission,

Having regard to the Opinion of the European Parliament,[35]

Having regard to the Opinion of the Economic and Social Committee,[36]

[1] Whereas pursuant to Council Directive 73/148[37] of 21 May 1973 on the abolition of restrictions on movement and residence within the Community for nationals of Member States with regard to establishment and the provision of services, each Member State grants the right of permanent residence to nationals of other Member States who establish themselves within its territory in order to pursue activities as self-employed persons, when the restrictions on these activities have been abolished pursuant to the Treaty;

[34] [1959–1962] OJ Eng. Spec. Ed., p.7.
[35] [1973] OJ C14/20.
[36] [1972] JO C142/12.
[37] [1973] OJ L172/14.

[2] Whereas it is normal for a person to prolong a period of permanent residence in the territory of a Member State by remaining there after having pursued an activity there; whereas the absence of a right so to remain in such circumstances is an obstacle to the attainment of freedom of establishment; whereas, as regards employed persons, the conditions under which such a right may be exercised have already been laid down by Regulation 1251/70,[38]

[3] Whereas Article [39](3)(d) of the Treaty recognises the right of workers to remain in the territory of a Member State after having been employed in that State; whereas Article [44(1)] does not expressly provide a similar right for self-employed persons; whereas, nevertheless, the nature of establishment, together with attachments formed to the countries in which they have pursued their activities, means that such persons have a definite interest in enjoying the same right to remain as that granted to workers; whereas in justification of this measure reference should be made to the Treaty provision enabling it to be taken;

[4] Whereas freedom of establishment within the Community requires that nationals of Member States may pursue self-employed activities in several Member States in succession without thereby being placed at a disadvantage;

[5] Whereas a national of a Member State residing in the territory of another Member State should be guaranteed the right to remain in that territory when he ceases to pursue an activity as a self-employed person in that State because he has reached retirement age or by reason of permanent incapacity to work; whereas such a right should also be guaranteed to the national of a Member State who, after a period of activity in a self-employed capacity and residence in the territory of a second Member State, pursues an activity in the territory of a third Member State, while still retaining his residence in the territory of the second State;

[6] Whereas, to determine the conditions under which the right to remain arises, account should be taken of the reasons which have led to the termination of activity in the territory of the Member State concerned and, in particular, of the difference between retirement, the normal and foreseeable end of working life, and permanent incapacity to work which leads to a premature and unforeseeable termination of activity; whereas special conditions must be laid down where the spouse is or was a national of the Member State concerned, or where termination of activity is the result of an accident at work or occupational illness;

[7] Whereas a national of a Member State who has reached the end of his working life, after working in a self-employed capacity in the territory of another Member State, should have sufficient time in which to decide where he wishes to establish his final residence;

[8] Whereas the exercise of the right to remain by a national of a Member State working in a self-employed capacity entails extension of such right to the members of his family; whereas in the case of the death of a national of a Member State working in a self-employed capacity during his working life the right of residence of the members of his family must also be recognised and be the subject of special conditions;

[9] Whereas persons to whom the right to remain applies must enjoy equality of treatment with nationals of the State concerned who have reached the end of their working lives,

Has adopted this Directive:

Article 1 [Removal of restrictions to remain in host State]

Member States shall, under the conditions laid down in this Directive, abolish restrictions on the right to remain in their territory in favour of nationals of another Member State who have pursued activities as self-employed persons in their territory, and members of their families, as defined in Article 1 of Directive 73/148. **6–078**

[38] [1970(II)] OJ, Eng. Spec. Ed., p.402.

Article 2 [Personal scope of Directive]

6–079 1. Each Member State shall recognise the right to remain permanently in its territory of:

(a) any person who, at the time of termination of his activity, has reached the age laid down by the law of that State for entitlement to an old-age pension and who has pursued his activity in that State for at least the previous 12 months and has resided there continuously for more than three years.

Where the law of that Member State does not grant the right to an old-age pension to certain categories of self-employed workers, the age requirement shall be considered as satisfied when the beneficiary reaches 65 years of age;

(b) any person who, having resided continuously in the territory of that State for more than two years, ceases to pursue his activity there as a result of permanent incapacity to work.

If such incapacity is the result of an accident at work or an occupational illness entitling him to a pension which is payable in whole or in part by an institution of that State no condition shall be imposed as to length of residence;

(c) any person who, after three years' continuous activity and residence in the territory of that State, pursues his activity in the territory of another Member State, while retaining his residence in the territory of the first State, to which he returns, as a rule, each day or at least once a week.

Periods of activity so completed in the territory of the other Member State shall, for the purposes of entitlement to the rights referred to in (a) and (b), be considered as having been completed in the territory of the State of residence.

2. The conditions as to length of residence and activity laid down in paragraph 1(a) and the condition as to length of residence laid down in paragraph 1(b) shall not apply if the spouse of the self-employed person is a national of the Member State concerned or has lost the nationality of that State by marriage to that person.

Article 3 [Rights of family to remain in host State]

6–080 1. Each Member State shall recognise the right of the members of the self-employed person's family referred to in Article 1 who are residing with him in the territory of that State to remain there permanently, if the person concerned has acquired the right to remain in the territory of that State in accordance with Article 2. This provision shall continue to apply even after the death of the person concerned.

2. If, however, the self-employed person dies during his working life and before having acquired the right to remain in the territory of the State concerned, that State shall recognise the right of the members of his family to remain there permanently on condition that:

— the person concerned, on the date of his decease, had resided continuously in its territory for at least two years; or
— his death resulted from an accident at work or an occupational illness; or
— the surviving spouse is a national of that State or lost such nationality by marriage to the person concerned.

Article 4 [Continuity of residence; periods of inactivity]

6–081 1. Continuity of residence as provided for in Articles 2(1) and 3(2) may be attested by any means of proof in use in the country of residence. It may not be affected by temporary absences not exceeding a total of three months per year, nor by longer absences due to compliance with the obligations of military service.

2. Periods of inactivity due to circumstances outside the control of the person concerned or of inactivity owing to illness or accident must be considered as periods of activity within the meaning of Article 2(1).

Article 5 [Exercise of right to remain]

1. Member States shall allow the person entitled to the right to remain to exercise such right within two years from the time of becoming entitled thereto pursuant to Article 2(1)(a) and (b) and Article 3. During this period the beneficiary must be able to leave the territory of the Member State without adversely affecting such right. **6–082**

2. Member States shall not require the person concerned to comply with any particular formality in order to exercise the right to remain.

Article 6 [Right to residence permit]

1. Member States shall recognise the right of persons having the right to remain in their territory to a residence permit, which must: **6–083**

(a) be issued and renewed free of charge or on payment of a sum not exceeding the dues and taxes payable by nationals for the issue or renewal of identity cards;
(b) be valid throughout the territory of the Member State issuing it;
(c) be valid for five years and renewable automatically.

2. Periods of non-residence not exceeding six consecutive months and longer absences due to compliance with the obligations of military service may not affect the validity of a residence permit.

Article 7 [Right to equal treatment]

Member States shall apply to persons having the right to remain in their territory the right of equality of treatment recognised by the Council Directives on the abolition of restrictions on freedom of establishment pursuant to Title III of the General Programme which provides for such abolition. **6–084**

Article 8 [More favourable Member State laws; later re-admission]

1. This Directive shall not affect any provisions laid down by law, regulation or administrative action of any Member State which would be more favourable to nationals of other Member States. **6–085**

2. Member States shall facilitate re-admission to their territories of self-employed persons who left those territories after having resided there permanently for a long period while pursuing an activity there and who wish to return when they have reached retirement age as defined in Article 2(1)(a) or are permanently incapacitated for work.

Article 9 [Limited grounds for Member State derogation]

Member States may not derogate from the provisions of this Directive save on grounds of public policy, public security or public health. **6–086**

Article 10 [Implementation]

1. Member States shall, within twelve months of notification of this Directive, bring into force the measures necessary to comply with its provisions and shall forthwith inform the Commission thereof. **6–087**

2. Following notification of this Directive, Member States shall further ensure that the Commission is informed, in sufficient time for it to submit its comments, of all proposed laws, regulations or administrative provisions which they intend to adopt in the field covered by this Directive.

Article 11 [Addressees]

6–088 This Directive is addressed to the Member States.

Council Directive 75/35 of 17 December 1974 extending the scope of Directive 64/221 on the co-ordination of special measures concerning the movement and residence of foreign nationals which are justified on grounds of public policy, public security or public health to include nationals of a Member State who exercise the right to remain in the territory of another Member State after having pursued therein an activity in a self-employed capacity

([1975] OJ L14/14; Doc. Ref. 31975L0035)

6–089 *The Council of the European Communities,*

Having regard to the Treaty establishing the European Economic Community, and in particular Article 56 (2) and Article 235 thereof;

Having regard to the proposal from the Commission;

Having regard to the Opinion of the European Parliament[39];

Having regard to the Opinion of the Economic and Social Committee[40];

[1] Whereas Directive 64/221[41] co-ordinated special measures concerning the movement and residence of foreign nationals which are justified on grounds of public policy, public security or public health and whereas Directive 75/34[42] laid down conditions for the exercise of the right of nationals of a Member State to remain in the territory of another Member State after having pursued therein an activity in a self-employed capacity;

[2] Whereas Directive 64/221 should therefore apply to persons to whom Directive 75/34 applies,

Has adopted this Directive:

Article 1 [Extension of Directive 64/221]

6–090 Directive 64/221 shall apply to nationals of Member States and members of their families who have the right to remain in the territory of a Member State pursuant to Directive 75/34.

Article 2 [Implementation]

6–091 Member States shall, within 12 months of notification of this Directive, bring into force the measures necessary to comply with its provisions and shall forthwith inform the Commission thereof.

Article 3 [Addressees]

6–092 This Directive is addressed to the Member States.

Council Directive 90/364 of 28 June 1990 on the right of residence

([1990] OJ L180/26; Doc. Ref. 31990L0364)

6–093 *The Council of the European Communities,*

Having regard to the Treaty establishing the [European Community], and in particular Article [308] thereof,

---

[39] [1973] OJ C14/21.

[40] [1972] OJ C142/10.

[41] [1963–1964] OJ, Eng. Spec. Ed., p.117 (see above).

[42] [1975] OJ L14/10 (see above).

Having regard to the proposal from the Commission,[43]
Having regard to the opinion of the European Parliament,[44]
Having regard to the opinion of the Economic and Social Committee,[45]

[1] Whereas Article 3(c) of the Treaty provides that the activities of the Community shall include, as provided in the Treaty, the abolition, as between Member States, of obstacles to freedom of movement for persons,

[2] Whereas [former] Article 8a of the Treaty[46] provides that the internal market must be established by 31 December 1992; whereas the internal market comprises an area without internal frontiers in which the free movement of goods, persons, services and capital is ensured in accordance with the provisions of the Treaty;

[3] Whereas national provisions on the right of nationals of the Member States to reside in a Member State other than their own must be harmonised to ensure such freedom of movement;

[4] Whereas beneficiaries of the right of residence must not become an unreasonable burden on the public finances of the host Member State;

[5] Whereas this right can only be genuinely exercised if it is also granted to members of the family;

[6] Whereas the beneficiaries of this Directive should be covered by administrative arrangements similar to those laid down in particular in Directive 68/360[47] and Directive 64/221,[48]

[7] Whereas the Treaty does not provide, for the action concerned, powers other than those of Article [308],

Has adopted this Directive:

Article 1 [Personal scope of the Directive]

1. Member States shall grant the right of residence to nationals of Member States who do not enjoy this right under other provisions of Community law and to members of their families as defined in paragraph 2, provided that they themselves and the members of their families are covered by sickness insurance in respect of all risks in the host Member State and have sufficient resources to avoid becoming a burden on the social assistance system of the host Member State during their period of residence. The resources referred to in the first sub-paragraph shall be deemed sufficient where they are higher than the level of resources below which the host Member State may grant social assistance to its nationals, taking into account the personal circumstances of the applicant and, where appropriate, the personal circumstances of persons admitted pursuant to paragraph 2. **6–094**

Where the second sub-paragraph cannot be applied in a Member State, the resources of the applicant shall be deemed sufficient if they are higher than the level of the minimum social security pension paid by the host Member State.

2. The following shall, irrespective of their nationality, have the right to install themselves in another Member State with the holder of the right of residence:
(a) his or her spouse and their descendants who are dependants;
(b) dependent relatives in the ascending line of the holder of the right of residence and his or her spouse.

Article 2 [Exercise of rights]

1. Exercise of the right of residence shall be evidenced by means of the issue of a document known as a "Residence permit for a national of a Member State of the **6–095**

[43] [1989] OJ C191/5 and [1990] OJ C26/22.
[44] Opinion delivered on 13 June 1990.
[45] [1989] OJ C329/25.
[46] See now Art. 18 of the Treaty for right of free movement and residence.
[47] [1968(I)] OJ, Eng. Spec. Ed., p.485 (see above).
[48] [1963–1964] OJ, Eng. Spec. Ed., p.117 (see above).

EEC", the validity of which may be limited to five years on a renewable basis. However, the Member States may, when they deem it to be necessary, require revalidation of the permit at the end of the first two years of residence. Where a member of the family does not hold the nationality of a Member State, he or she shall be issued with a residence document of the same validity as that issued to the national on whom he or she depends.

For the purpose of issuing the residence permit or document, the Member State may require only that the applicant present a valid identity card or passport and provide proof that he or she meets the conditions laid down in Article 1.

2. Articles 2, 3, 6(1)(a) and (2) and Article 9 of Directive 68/360 shall apply *mutatis mutandis* to the beneficiaries of this Directive.

The spouse and the dependent children of a national of a Member State entitled to the right of residence within the territory of a Member State shall be entitled to take up any employed or self-employed activity anywhere within the territory of that Member State, even if they are not nationals of a Member State.

Member States shall not derogate from the provisions of this Directive save on grounds of public policy, public security or public health. In that event, Directive 64/221 shall apply.

3. This Directive shall not affect existing law on the acquisition of second homes.

Article 3 [Duration of right of residence]

6–096 The right of residence shall remain for as long as beneficiaries of that right fulfil the conditions laid down in Article 1.

Article 4 [Regular reports on application of Directive]

6–097 The Commission shall, not more than three years after the date of implementation of this Directive, and at three-yearly intervals thereafter, draw up a report on the application of this Directive and submit it to the European Parliament and the Council.

Article 5 [Implementation]

6–098 Member States shall bring into force the laws, regulations and administrative provisions necessary to comply with this Directive not later than 30 June 1992. They shall forthwith inform the Commission thereof.

Article 6 [Addressees]

6–099 This Directive is addressed to the Member States.

Council Directive 90/365 of 28 June 1990 on the right of residence for employees and self-employed persons who have ceased their occupational activity

([1990] OJ L180/28; Doc. Ref. 31990L0365)

6–100 *The Council of the European Communities,*

Having regard to the Treaty establishing the [European Community], and in particular Article [308] thereof,

Having regard to the proposal from the Commission,[49]

Having regard to the opinion of the European Parliament,[50]

[49] [1989] OJ C191/3 and [1990] OJ C26/19.

[50] Opinion delivered on 13 June 1990.

Having regard to the opinion of the Economic and Social Committee,[51]

[1] Whereas Article 3(c) of the Treaty provides that the activities of the Community shall include, as provided in the Treaty, the abolition, as between Member States, of obstacles to freedom of movement for persons;

[2] Whereas [former] Article 8a of the Treaty[52] provides that the internal market must be established by 31 December 1992; whereas the internal market comprises an area without internal frontiers in which the free movement of goods, persons, services and capital is ensured, in accordance with the provisions of the Treaty;

[3] Whereas Articles [39] and [43] of the Treaty provide for freedom of movement for workers and self-employed persons, which entails the right of residence in the Member States in which they pursue their occupational activity; whereas it is desirable that this right of residence also be granted to persons who have ceased their occupational activity even if they have not exercised their right to freedom of movement during their working life;

[4] Whereas beneficiaries of the right of residence must not become an unreasonable burden on the public finances of the host Member State;

[5] Whereas under Article 10 of Regulation 1408/71,[53] as amended by Regulation 1390/81,[54] recipients of invalidity or old age cash benefits or pensions for accidents at work or occupational diseases are entitled to continue to receive these benefits and pensions even if they reside in the territory of a Member State other than that in which the institution responsible for payment is situated;

[6] Whereas this right can only be genuinely exercised if it is also granted to members of the family;

[7] Whereas the beneficiaries of this Directive should be covered by administrative arrangements similar to those laid down in particular by Directive 68/630[55] and Directive 64/221[56];

[8] Whereas the Treaty does not provide, for the action concerned, powers other than those of Article [308];

Has adopted this Directive:

Article 1 [Personal scope of the Directive]

1. Member States shall grant the right of residence to nationals of Member States who have pursued an activity as an employee or self-employed person and to members of their families as defined in paragraph 2, provided that they are recipients of an invalidity or early retirement pension, or old age benefits, or of a pension in respect of an industrial accident or disease of an amount sufficient to avoid becoming a burden on the social security system of the host Member State during their period of residence and provided they are covered by sickness insurance in respect of all risks in the host Member State. **6–101**

The resources of the applicant shall be deemed sufficient where they are higher than the level of resources below which the host Member State may grant social assistance to its nationals, taking into account the personal circumstances of persons admitted pursuant to paragraph 2.

Where the second sub-paragraph cannot be applied in a Member State, the resources of the applicant shall be deemed sufficient if they are higher than the level of the minimum social security pension paid by the host Member State.

2. The following shall, irrespective of their nationality, have the right to install themselves in another Member State with the holder of the right of residence:

(a) his or her spouse and their descendants who are dependants;

---

[51] [1989] OJ C329/25.

[52] See now Art. 18 of the Treaty for right of free movement and residence.

[53] [1971(II)] OJ, Eng. Spec. Ed., p.416.

[54] [1981] OJ L143/1.

[55] [1968(I)] OJ, Eng. Spec. Ed., p.485 (see above).

[56] [1963–1964] OJ, Eng. Spec. Ed., p.117 (see above).

(b) dependent relatives in the ascending line of the holder of the right of residence and his or her spouse.

Article 2 **[Exercise of rights]**

6–102 1. Exercise of the right of residence shall be evidenced by means of the issue of a document known as a "Residence permit for a national of a Member State of the EEC", whose validity may be limited to five years on a renewable basis. However, the Member States may, when they deem it to be necessary, require revalidation of the permit at the end of the first two years of residence. Where a member of the family does not hold the nationality of a Member State, he or she shall be issued with a residence document of the same validity as that issued to the national on whom he or she depends.

For the purposes of issuing the residence permit or document, the Member State may require only that the applicant present a valid identity card or passport and provide proof that he or she meets the conditions laid down in Article 1.

2. Articles 2, 3, 6(1)(a) and (2) and Article 9 of Directive 68/360 shall apply *mutatis mutandis* to the beneficiaries of this Directive.

The spouse and the dependent children of a national of a Member State entitled to the right of residence within the territory of a Member State shall be entitled to take up any employed or self-employed activity anywhere within the territory of that Member State, even if they are not nationals of a Member State.

Member States shall not derogate from the provisions of this Directive save on grounds of public policy, public security or public health. In that event, Directive 64/221 shall apply.

3. This Directive shall not affect existing law on the acquisition of second homes.

Article 3 **[Duration of right of residence]**

6–103 The right of residence shall remain for as long as beneficiaries of that right fulfil the conditions laid down in Article 1.

Article 4 **[Regular reports on application of Directive]**

6–104 The Commission shall, not more than three years after the date of implementation of this Directive, and at three-yearly intervals thereafter, draw up a report on the application of this Directive and submit it to the European Parliament and the Council.

Article 5 **[Implementation]**

6–105 Member States shall bring into force the laws, regulations and administrative provisions necessary to comply with this Directive not later than 30 June 1992. They shall forthwith inform the Commission thereof.

Article 6 **[Addressees]**

6–106 This Directive is addressed to the Member States.

Council Directive 93/96 of 29 October 1993 on the right of residence for students

([1993] OJ L317/59; Doc. Ref. 31993L0096)

6–107 *The Council of the European Communities,*
Having regard to the Treaty establishing the [European Community], and in particular the second paragraph of [former] Article 7[57] thereof,

[57] See now Art. 12 of the Treaty. Measures are now adopted using the co-decision procedure rather than the co-operation procedure.

Having regard to the proposal from the Commission,[58]
In co-operation with the European Parliament,[59]
Having regard to the opinion of the Economic and Social Committee,[60]

[1] Whereas Article 3(c) of the Treaty provides that the activities of the Community shall include, as provided in the Treaty, the abolition, as between Member States, of obstacles to freedom of movement for persons;

[2] Whereas [former] Article 8a of the Treaty[61] provides that the internal market must be established by 31 December 1992; whereas the internal market comprises an area without internal frontiers in which the free movement of goods, persons, services and capital is ensured in accordance with the provisions of the Treaty;

[3]Whereas, as the Court of Justice has held, [former] Articles 128 and 7[62] of the Treaty prohibit any discrimination between nationals of the Member States as regards access to vocational training in the Community; whereas access by a national of one Member State to vocational training in another Member State implies, for that national, a right of residence in that other Member State;

[4] Whereas, accordingly, in order to guarantee access to vocational training, the conditions likely to facilitate the effective exercise of that right of residence should be laid down;

[5] Whereas the right of residence for students forms part of a set of related measures designed to promote vocational training;

[6] Whereas beneficiaries of the right of residence must not become an unreasonable burden on the public finances of the host Member State;

[7] Whereas, in the present state of Community law, as established by the case law of the Court of Justice, assistance granted to students, does not fall within the scope of the Treaty within the meaning of Article [12] thereof;

[8] Whereas the right of residence can only be genuinely exercised if it is also granted to the spouse and their dependent children;

[9] Whereas the beneficiaries of this Directive should be covered by administrative arrangements similar to those laid down in particular in Council Directive 68/360 of 15 October 1968 on the abolition of restrictions on movement and residence within the Community for workers of Member States and their families[63] and Council Directive 64/221 of 25 February 1964 on the co-ordination of special measures concerning the movement and residence of foreign nationals which are justified on grounds of public policy, public security or public health[64];

[10] Whereas this Directive does not apply to students who enjoy the right of residence by virtue of the fact that they are or have been effectively engaged in economic activities or are members of the family of a migrant worker;

[11] Whereas, by its judgment of 7 July 1992 in Case C-295/90,[65] the Court of Justice annulled Council Directive 90/366 of 28 June 1990 on the right of residence for students,[66] while maintaining the effects of the annulled Directive until the entry into force of a directive adopted on the appropriate legal basis;

[12] Whereas the effects of Directive 90/366 should be maintained during the period up to 31 December 1993, the date by which Member States are to have adopted the laws, regulations and administrative provisions necessary to comply with this Directive,

---

[58] [1993] OJ C166/16.
[59] [1993] OJ C255/70 and [1993] OJ C315.
[60] [1993] OJ C304/1.
[61] See now Art. 18 of the Treaty for right of free movement and residence.
[62] See now Art. 150 of the Treaty for vocational training policy and Art. 12 for prohibition of discrimination based on nationality.
[63] [1968(I)] OJ, Eng. Spec. Ed., p.485 (see above).
[64] [1963–1964] OJ, Eng. Spec. Ed., p.117 (see above).
[65] *European Parliament v EC Council* (Case C-295/90) [1992] ECR I-4193.
[66] [1990] OJ L180/30.

Has adopted this Directive:

Article 1 [Personal scope of the Directive]

6–108 In order to lay down conditions to facilitate the exercise of the right of residence and with a view to guaranteeing access to vocational training in a non-discriminatory manner for a national of a Member State who has been accepted to attend a vocational training course in another Member State, the Member States shall recognise the right of residence for any student who is a national of a Member State and who does not enjoy that right under other provisions of Community law, and for the student's spouse and their dependent children, where the student assures the relevant national authority, by means of a declaration or by such alternative means as the student may choose that are at least equivalent, that he has sufficient resources to avoid becoming a burden on the social assistance system of the host Member State during their period of residence, provided that the student is enrolled in a recognised educational establishment for the principal purpose of following a vocational training course there and that he is covered by sickness insurance in respect of all risks in the host Member State.

Article 2 [Exercise of rights]

6–109 1. The right of residence shall be restricted to the duration of the course of studies in question.

The right of residence shall be evidenced by means of the issue of a document known as a "residence permit for a national of a Member State of the Community", the validity of which may be limited to the duration of the course of studies or to one year where the course lasts longer in the latter event it shall be renewable annually. Where a member of the family does not hold the nationality of a Member State, he or she shall be issued with a residence document of the same validity as that issued to the national on whom he or she depends.

For the purpose of issuing the residence permit or document, the Member State may require only that the applicant present a valid identity card or passport and provide proof that he or she meets the conditions laid down in Article 1.

2. Articles 2, 3 and 9 of Directive 68/360 shall apply *mutatis mutandis* to the beneficiaries of this Directive.

The spouse and the dependent children of a national of a Member State entitled to the right of residence within the territory of a Member State shall be entitled to take up any employed or self-employed activity anywhere within the territory of that Member State, even if they are not nationals of a Member State.

Member States shall not derogate from the provisions of this Directive save on grounds of public policy, public security or public health; in that event, Articles 2 to 9 of Directive 64/221 shall apply.

Article 3 [No right to maintenance grants from host State]

6–110 This Directive shall not establish any entitlement to the payment of maintenance grants by the host Member State on the part of students benefiting from the right of residence.

Article 4 [Duration of right of residence]

6–111 The right of residence shall remain for as long as beneficiaries of that right fulfil the conditions laid down in Article 1.

Article 5 [Regular report on application of Directive]

6–112 The Commission shall, not more than three years after the date of implementation of this Directive, and at three-yearly intervals thereafter, draw up a report on the application of this Directive and submit it to the European Parliament and the Council.

The Commission shall pay particular attention to any difficulties to which the implementation of Article 1 might give rise in the Member States it shall, if appropriate, submit proposals to the Council with the aim of remedying such difficulties.

Article 6 [Implementation]

Member States shall bring into force the laws, regulations and administrative provisions necessary to comply with this Directive not later than 31 December 1993. They shall forthwith inform the Commission thereof. **6–113**

For the period preceding that date, the effects of Directive 90/366 shall be maintained.

When Member States adopt those measures, they shall contain a reference to this Directive or shall be accompanied by such a reference on the occasion of their official publication. The methods of making such references shall be laid down by the Member States.

Article 7 [Addressees]

This Directive is addressed to the Member States. **6–114**

SECTION 2—MUTUAL RECOGNITION OF QUALIFICATIONS

Council Directive 89/48 of 21 December 1988, on a general system for the recognition of higher-education diplomas awarded on completion of professional education and training of at least three years' duration[67]

([1989] OJ L19/16; Doc. Ref. 31989L0048)

The Council of the European Communities, **6–115**

Having regard to the Treaty establishing the [European Community], and in particular Articles [40], [47](1) and [55] thereof,

Having regard to the proposal from the Commission,[68]

In co-operation with the European Parliament,[69]

Having regard to the opinion of the Economic and Social Committee,[70]

[1] Whereas, pursuant to Article 3(c) of the Treaty the abolition, as between Member States, of obstacles to freedom of movement for persons and services constitutes one of the objectives of the Community; whereas, for nationals of the Member States, this means in particular the possibility of pursuing a profession, whether in a self-employed or employed capacity, in a Member State other than that in which they acquired their professional qualifications;

[2] Whereas the provisions so far adopted by the Council, and pursuant to which Member States recognise mutually and for professional purposes higher-education diplomas issued within their territory, concern only a few professions; whereas the level and duration of the education and training governing access to those professions have been regulated in a similar fashion in all the Member States or have been the subject of the minimal harmonisation needed to establish sectoral systems for the mutual recognition of diplomas;

[3] Whereas, in order to provide a rapid response to the expectations of nationals of Community countries who hold higher-education diplomas awarded

[67] For the mechanism for the recognition of qualifications in respect of certain professional activities not covered by this directive and Directive 92/51 below, see Directive 1999/42 ([1999] OJ L201/77).

[68] [1985] OJ C217/3, and [1986] OJ C143/7.

[69] [1985] OJ C345/80, and [1988] OJ C309. Co-operation procedure used for adoption of EC measures in this context before the Union Treaty substituted the co-decision procedure from 1 November 1993.

[70] [1986] OJ C75/5.

on completion of professional education and training issued in a Member State other than that in which they wish to pursue their profession, another method of recognition of such diplomas should also be put in place such as to enable those concerned to pursue all those professional activities which in a host Member State are dependent on the completion of post-secondary education and training, provided they hold such a diploma preparing them for those activities awarded on completion of a course of studies lasting at least three years and issued in another Member State;

[4] Whereas this objective can be achieved by the introduction of a general system for the recognition of higher-education diplomas awarded on completion of professional education and training of at least three years' duration;

[5] Whereas, for those professions for the pursuit of which the Community has not laid down the necessary minimum level of qualification, Member States reserve the option of fixing such a level with a view to guaranteeing the quality of services provided in their territory; whereas, however, they may not, without infringing their obligations laid down in Article [10] of the Treaty, require a national of a Member State to obtain those qualifications which in general they determine only by reference to diplomas issued under their own national education systems, where the person concerned has already acquired all or part of those qualifications in another Member State; whereas, as a result, any host Member State in which a profession is regulated is required to take account of qualifications acquired in another Member State and to determine whether those qualifications correspond to the qualifications which the Member State concerned requires;

[6] Whereas collaboration between the Member States is appropriate in order to facilitate their compliance with those obligations; whereas, therefore, the means of organising such collaboration should be established;

[7] Whereas the term "regulated professional activity" should be defined so as to take account of differing national sociological situations whereas the term should cover not only professional activities access to which is subject, in a Member State, to the possession of a diploma, but also professional activities, access to which is unrestricted when they are practised under a professional title reserved for the holders of certain qualifications; whereas the professional associations and organisations which confer such titles on their members and are recognised by the public authorities cannot invoke their private status to avoid application of the system provided for by this Directive;

[8] Whereas it is also necessary to determine the characteristics of the professional experience or adaptation period which the host Member State may require of the person concerned in addition to the higher-education diploma, where the person's qualifications do not correspond to those laid down by national provisions;

[9] Whereas an aptitude test may also be introduced in place of the adaptation period; whereas the effect of both will be to improve the existing situation with regard to the mutual recognition of diplomas between Member States and therefore to facilitate the free movement of persons within the Community; whereas their function is to assess the ability of the migrant, who is a person who has already received his professional training in another Member State, to adapt to this new professional environment; whereas, from the migrant's point of view, an aptitude test will have the advantage of reducing the length of the practice period; whereas, in principle, the choice between the adaptation period and the aptitude test should be made by the migrant; whereas, however, the nature of certain professions is such that Member States must be allowed to prescribe, under certain conditions, either the adaptation period or the test; whereas, in particular, the differences between the legal systems of the Member States, whilst they may vary in extent from one Member State to another, warrant special provisions since, as a rule, the education or training attested by the diploma, certificate or other evidence of formal qualifications in a field of law in the

Member State of origin does not cover the legal knowledge required in the host Member State with respect to the corresponding legal field;

[10] Whereas, moreover, the general system for the recognition of higher-education diplomas is intended neither to amend the rules, including those relating to professional ethics, applicable to any person pursuing a profession in the territory of a Member State nor to exclude migrants from the application of those rules; whereas that system is confined to laying down appropriate arrangements to ensure that migrants comply with the professional rules of the host Member State;

[11] Whereas Articles [40], [47](1) and [55] of the Treaty empower the Community to adopt provisions necessary for the introduction and operation of such a system;

[12] Whereas the general system for the recognition of higher-education diplomas is entirely without prejudice to the application of Article [39](4) and Article [45] of the Treaty;

[13] Whereas such a system, by strengthening the right of a Community national to use his professional skills in any Member State, supplements and reinforces his right to acquire such skills wherever he wishes;

[14] Whereas this system should be evaluated, after being in force for a certain time, to determine how efficiently it operates and in particular how it can be improved or its field of application extended,

Has adopted this Directive:

Article 1 [Definitions]

For the purposes of this Directive the following definitions shall apply: **6–116**

(a) diploma: any diploma, certificate or other evidence of formal qualifications or any set of such diplomas, certificates or other evidence:

— which has been awarded by a competent authority in a Member State, designated in accordance with its own laws, regulations or administrative provisions;

[— which shows that the holder has successfully completed a post-secondary course of at least three years' duration, or of an equivalent duration part-time, at a university or establishment of higher education or another establishment of equivalent level and, where appropriate, that he has successfully completed the professional training required in addition to the post-secondary course, and][71]

— which shows that the holder has the professional qualifications required for the taking up or pursuit of a regulated profession in that Member State,

provided that the education and training attested by the diploma, certificate or other evidence of formal qualifications were received mainly in the Community, or the holder thereof has three years' professional experience certified by the Member State which recognised a third-country diploma, certificate or other evidence of formal qualifications.

The following shall be treated in the same way as a diploma, within the meaning of the first sub-paragraph: any diploma, certificate or other evidence of formal qualifications or any set of such diplomas, certificates or other evidence awarded by a competent authority in a Member State if it is awarded on the successful completion of education and training received in the Community and recognised by a competent authority in that Member State as being of an equivalent level and if it confers the same rights in respect of the taking up and pursuit of a regulated profession in that Member State;

(b) host Member State: any Member State in which a national of a Member State applies to pursue a profession subject to regulation in that Member State, other than the State in which he obtained his diploma or first pursued the profession in question;

[71] Words substituted by Directive 2001/19 Art. 1(1)(a) as from 31 July 2001.

(c) regulated profession: the regulated professional activity or range of activities which constitute this profession in a Member State;

(d) regulated professional activity: a professional activity, in so far as the taking up or pursuit of such activity or one of its modes of pursuit in a Member State is subject, directly or indirectly by virtue of laws, regulations or administrative provisions, to the possession of a diploma. The following in particular shall constitute a mode of pursuit of a regulated professional activity:

— pursuit of an activity under a professional title, in so far as the use of such a title is reserved to the holders of a diploma governed by laws, regulations or administrative provisions,

— pursuit of a professional activity relating to health, in so far as remuneration and/or reimbursement for such an activity is subject by virtue of national social security arrangements to the possession of a diploma.

Where the first sub-paragraph does not apply, a professional activity shall be deemed to be a regulated professional activity if it is pursued by the members of an association or organisation the purpose of which is, in particular, to promote and maintain a high standard in the professional field concerned and which, to achieve that purpose, is recognised in a special form by a Member State and:

— awards a diploma to its members,

— ensures that its members respect the rules of professional conduct which it prescribes, and

— confers on them the right to use a title or designatory letters, or to benefit from a status corresponding to that diploma.

A non-exhaustive list of associations or organisations which, when this Directive is adopted, satisfy the conditions of the second sub-paragraph is contained in the Annex. Whenever a Member State grants the recognition referred to in the second sub-paragraph to an association or organisation, it shall inform the Commission thereof, which shall publish this information in the *Official Journal of the European Communities*;

(d) [a regulated education and training: any education and training which:

— pursuit of an activity under a professional title, in so far as the use of such a title is reserved to the holders of a diploma governed by laws, regulations or administrative provisions,

— is directly geared to the practice of a defined profession, and

— comprises a post-secondary course of at least three years' duration, or an equivalent duration part-time, at a university or higher education establishment or in another establishment of equivalent level and, where appropriate, the professional training, professional traineeship or professional practice required in addition to the post-secondary course; the structure and level of the professional training, professional traineeship or professional practice shall be determined by the laws, regulations or administrative provisions of the Member State concerned or monitored or approved by the authority designated for that purpose.][72]

(e) professional experience: the actual and lawful pursuit of the profession concerned in a Member State;

(f) adaptation period: the pursuit of a regulated profession in the host Member State under the responsibility of a qualified member of that profession, such period of supervised practice possibly being accompanied by further training. This period of supervised practice shall be the subject of an assessment. The detailed rules governing the adaptation period and its assessment as well as the status of a migrant person under supervision shall be laid down by the competent authority in the host Member States;

[72] Article 1(d) (*sic*) inserted by Directive 2001/19 Art. 1(1)(b) as from 31 July 2001.

(g) aptitude test: a test limited to the professional knowledge of the applicant, made by the competent authorities of the host Member State with the aim of assessing the ability of the applicant to pursue a regulated profession in that Member State.

In order to permit this test to be carried out, the competent authorities shall draw up a list of subjects which, on the basis of a comparison of the education and training required in the Member State and that received by the applicant, are not covered by the diploma or other evidence of formal qualifications possessed by the applicant.

The aptitude test must take account of the fact that the applicant is a qualified professional in the Member State of origin or the Member State from which he comes. It shall cover subjects to be selected from those on the list, knowledge of which is essential in order to be able to exercise the profession in the host Member State. The test may also include knowledge of the professional rules applicable to the activities in question in the host Member State. The detailed application of the aptitude test shall be determined by the competent authorities of that State with due regard to the rules of Community law.

The status, in the host Member State, of the applicant who wishes to prepare himself for the aptitude test in that State shall be determined by the competent authorities in that State.

Article 2 [Personal scope of the Directive]

This Directive shall apply to any national of a Member State wishing to pursue a regulated profession in a host Member State in a self-employed capacity or as an employed person. **6–117**

This Directive shall not apply to professions which are the subject of a separate Directive establishing arrangements for the mutual recognition of diplomas by Member States.

Article 3 [Access to regulated profession in host State]

Where, in a host Member State, the taking up or pursuit of a regulated profession is subject to possession of a diploma, the competent authority may not, on the grounds of inadequate qualifications, refuse to authorise a national of a Member State to take up or pursue that profession on the same conditions as apply to its own nationals: **6–118**

(a) if the applicant holds the diploma required in another Member State for the taking up or pursuit of the profession in question in its territory, such diploma having been awarded in a Member State; or

(b) if the applicant has pursued the profession in question full-time for two years during the previous ten years in another Member State which does not regulate that profession, within the meaning of Article 1(c) and the first sub-paragraph of Article 1 (d), and possesses evidence of one or more formal qualifications:

— which have been awarded by a competent authority in a Member State, designated in accordance with the laws, regulations or administrative provisions of such State,

— which show that the holder has successfully completed a post-secondary course of at least three years' duration, or of an equivalent duration part-time, at a university or establishment of higher education or another establishment of similar level of a Member State and, where appropriate, that he has successfully completed the professional training required in addition to the post-secondary course, and

— which have prepared the holder for the pursuit of his profession.

[If the host Member State intends to require the applicant to complete an adaptation period or take an aptitude test, it must first examine whether the knowledge acquired by the applicant in the course of his professional experience is such that it fully or partly covers the substantial difference referred to in the first sub-paragraph.][73]

The following shall be treated in the same way as the evidence of formal qualifications referred to in the first sub-paragraph: any formal qualifications or any set of such formal qualifications awarded by a competent authority in a Member State if it is awarded on the successful completion of training received in the Community and is recognised by that Member State as being of an equivalent level, provided that the other Member States and the Commission have been notified of this recognition.

Article 4 [Professional experience; adaptation periods; aptitude tests]

6–119 1. Notwithstanding Article 3, the host Member State may also require the applicant:

(a) to provide evidence of professional experience, where the duration of the education and training adduced in support of his application, as laid down in Article 3(a) and (b), is at least one year less than that required in the host Member State. In this event, the period of professional experience required:

— may not exceed twice the shortfall in duration of education and training where the shortfall relates to post-secondary studies and/or to a period of probationary practice carried out under the control of a supervising professional person and ending with an examination,

— may not exceed the shortfall where the shortfall relates to professional practice acquired with the assistance of a qualified member of the profession.

In the case of diplomas within the meaning of the last sub-paragraph of Article 1(a), the duration of education and training recognised as being of an equivalent level shall be determined as for the education and training defined in the first sub-paragraph of Article 1(a).

When applying these provisions, account must be taken of the professional experience referred to in Article 3(b).

At all events, the professional experience required may not exceed four years;

(b) to complete an adaptation period not exceeding three years or take an aptitude test:

— where the matters covered by the education and training he has received as laid down in Article 3(a) and (b), differ substantially from those covered by the diploma required in the host Member State, or

— where, in the case referred to in Article 3(a), the profession regulated in the host Member State comprises one or more regulated professional activities which are not in the profession regulated in the Member State from which the applicant originates or comes and that difference corresponds to specific education and training required in the host Member State and covers matters which differ substantially from those covered by the diploma adduced by the applicant, or

— where, in the case referred to in Article 3(b), the profession regulated in the host Member State comprises one or more regulated professional activities which are not in the profession pursued by the applicant in the Member State from which he originates or comes, and that difference corresponds to specific education and training required in the host Member State and covers matters which differ substantially from those covered by the evidence of formal qualifications adduced by the applicant.

---

[73] Words inserted by Directive 2001/19 Art. 1(2) as from 31 July 2001.

[If the host Member State intends to require the applicant to complete an adaptation period or take an aptitude test, it must first examine whether the knowledge acquired by the applicant in the course of his professional experience is such that it fully or partly covers the substantial difference referred to in the first sub-paragraph.][74]

Should the host Member State make use of this possibility, it must give the applicant the right to choose between an adaptation period and an aptitude test. By way of derogation from this principle, for professions whose practice requires precise knowledge of national law and in respect of which the provision of advice and/or assistance concerning national law is an essential and constant aspect of the professional activity, the host Member State may stipulate either an adaptation period or an aptitude test. Where the host Member State intends to introduce derogations for other professions as regards an applicant's right to choose, the procedure laid down in Article 10 shall apply.

2. However, the host Member State may not apply the provisions of paragraph 1(a) and (b) cumulatively.

Article 5 [Professional practice in host State]

Without prejudice to Articles 3 and 4, a host Member State may allow the applicant, with a view to improving his possibilities of adapting to the professional environment in that State, to undergo there, on the basis of equivalence, that part of his professional education and training represented by professional practice, acquired with the assistance of a qualified member of the profession, which he has not undergone in his Member State of origin or the Member State from which he has come. **6–120**

Article 6 [Proof of equivalence to professional requirements in host State]

1. Where the competent authority of a host Member State requires of persons wishing to take up a regulated profession proof that they are of good character or repute or that they have not been declared bankrupt, or suspends or prohibits the pursuit of that profession in the event of serious professional misconduct or a criminal offence, that State shall accept as sufficient evidence, in respect of nationals of Member States wishing to pursue that profession in its territory, the production of documents issued by competent authorities in the Member State of origin or the Member State from which the foreign national comes showing that those requirements are met. **6–121**

Where the competent authorities of the Member State of origin or of the Member State from which the foreign national comes do not issue the documents referred to in the first sub-paragraph, such documents shall be replaced by a declaration on oath—or, in States where there is no provision for declaration on oath, by a solemn declaration—made by the person concerned before a competent judicial or administrative authority or, where appropriate, a notary or qualified professional body of the Member State of origin or the Member State from which the person comes; such authority or notary shall issue a certificate attesting the authenticity of the declaration on oath or solemn declaration.

2. Where the competent authority of a host Member State requires of nationals of that Member State wishing to take up or pursue a regulated profession a certificate of physical or mental health, that authority shall accept as sufficient evidence in this respect the production of the document required in the Member State of origin or the Member State from which the foreign national comes.

Where the Member State of origin or the Member State from which the foreign national comes does not impose any requirements of this nature on those wishing to take up or pursue the profession in question, the host Member State shall accept

[74] Words inserted by Directive 2001/19 Art. 1(3) as from 31 July 2001.

from such nationals a certificate issued by a competent authority in that State corresponding to the certificates issued in the host Member State.

3. The competent authorities of host Member States may require that the documents and certificates referred to in paragraphs 1 and 2 are presented no more than three months after their date of issue.

4. Where the competent authority of a host Member State requires nationals of that Member State wishing to take up or pursue a regulated profession to take an oath or make a solemn declaration and where the form of such oath or declaration cannot be used by nationals of other Member States, that authority shall ensure that an appropriate and equivalent form of oath or declaration is offered to the person concerned.

5. [Where proof of financial standing is required in order to take up or pursue a regulated profession in the host Member State, that Member State shall regard certificates issued by banks in the Member State of origin or in the Member State from where the foreign national comes as equivalent to those issued in its own territory.

6. Where the competent authority of the host Member State requires of its own nationals wishing to take up or pursue a regulated profession proof that they are insured against the financial risks arising from their professional liability, that Member State shall accept certificates issued by insurance undertakings of other Member States as equivalent to those issued in its own territory. Such certificates shall state that the insurer has complied with the laws and regulations in force in the host Member State regarding the terms and extent of cover. They may not be presented more than three months after their date of issue.][75]

Article 7 [Use of professional and academic titles/designations]

6–122 1. The competent authorities of host Member States shall recognise the right of nationals of Member States who fulfil the conditions for the taking up and pursuit of a regulated profession in their territory to use the professional title of the host Member State corresponding to that profession.

2. The competent authorities of host Member States shall recognise the right of nationals of Member States who fulfil the conditions for the taking up and pursuit of a regulated profession in their territory to use their lawful academic title and, where appropriate, the abbreviation thereof deriving from their Member State of origin or the Member State from which they come, in the language of that State. Host Member State may require this title to be followed by the name and location of the establishment or examining board which awarded it.

3. Where a profession is regulated in the host Member State by an association or organisation referred to in Article 1(d), nationals of Member States shall only be entitled to use the professional title or designatory letters conferred by that organisation or association on proof of membership.

Where the association or organisation makes membership subject to certain qualification requirements, it may apply these to nationals of other Member States who are in possession of a diploma within the meaning of Article 1(a) or a formal qualification within the meaning of Article 3(b) only in accordance with this Directive, in particular Articles 3 and 4.

Article 8 [Decisions on applications to pursue regulated professions]

6–123 1. The host Member State shall accept as proof that the conditions laid down in Articles 3 and 4 are satisfied the certificates and documents issued by the competent authorities in the Member States, which the person concerned shall submit in support of his application to pursue the profession concerned.

[75] Words inserted by Directive 2001/19 Art. 1(4) as from 31 July 2001.

2. The procedure for examining an application to pursue a regulated profession shall be completed as soon as possible and the outcome communicated in a reasoned decision of the competent authority in the host Member State not later than four months after presentation of all the documents relating to the person concerned. A remedy shall be available against this decision, or the absence thereof, before a court or tribunal in accordance with the provisions of national law.

Article 9 **[Designation of competent authorities; Member State coordinators]**

1. Member States shall designate, within the period provided for in Article 12, the competent authorities empowered to receive the applications and take the decisions referred to in this Directive. They shall communicate this information to the other Member States and to the Commission. **6–124**

2. Each Member State shall designate a person responsible for co-ordinating the activities of the authorities referred to in paragraph 1 and shall inform the other Member States and the Commission to that effect. His role shall be to promote uniform application of this Directive to all the professions concerned. A co-ordinating group shall be set up under the aegis of the Commission, composed of the co-ordinators appointed by each Member State or their deputies and chaired by a representative of the Commission.

The task of this group shall be:

[— to facilitate the implementation of this Directive, in particular by adopting and publishing opinions on the questions referred to it by the Commission,][76]

— to collect all useful information for its application in the Member States.

The group may be consulted by the Commission on any changes to the existing system that may contemplated.

3. Member States shall take measures to provide the necessary information on the recognition of diplomas within the framework of this Directive. They may be assisted in this task by the information centre on the academic recognition of diplomas and periods of study established by the Member States within the framework of the Resolution of the Council and the Ministers of Education meeting within the Council of 9 February 1976,[77] and, where appropriate, the relevant professional associations or organisations. The Commission shall take the necessary initiatives to ensure the development and coordination of the communication of the necessary information.

Article 10 **[Procedure when choice of adaptation period or aptitude test not offered]**

1. If, pursuant to the third sentence of the second sub-paragraph of Article 4(1)(b), a Member State proposes not to grant applicants the right to choose between an adaptation period and an aptitude test in respect of a profession within the meaning of this Directive, it shall immediately communicate to the Commission the corresponding draft provision. It shall at the same time notify the Commission of the grounds which make the enactment of such a provision necessary. **6–125**

The Commission shall immediately notify the other Member States of any draft it has received it may also consult the co-ordinating group referred to in Article 9(2) of the draft.

2. Without prejudice to the possibility for the Commission and the other Member States of making comments on the draft, the Member State may adopt the

[76] Words substituted by Directive 2001/19 Art. 1(5) as from 31 July 2001.

[77] [1976] OJ C38/1.

provision only if the Commission has not taken a decision to the contrary within three months.

3. At the request of a Member State or the Commission, Member States shall communicate to them, without delay, the definitive text of a provision arising from the application of this Article.

Article 11 [Member state reports on application of system]

6–126 Following the expiry of the period provided for in Article 12, Member States shall communicate to the Commission, every two years, a report on the application of the system introduced.

In addition to general remarks, this report shall contain a statistical summary of the decisions taken and a description of the main problems arising from application of the Directive.

Article 12 [Implementation]

6–127 Member States shall take the measures necessarily to comply with this Directive within two years of its notification.[78] They shall forthwith inform the Commission thereof.

Member States shall communicate to the Commission the texts of the main provisions of national law which they adopt in the field governed by this Directive.

Article 13 [Review of system]

6–128 Five years at the latest following the date specified in Article 12, the Commission shall report to the European Parliament and the Council on the state of application of the general system for the recognition of higher-education diplomas awarded on completion of professional education and training of at least three years' duration.

After conducting all necessary consultations, the Commission shall, on this occasion, present its conclusions as to any changes that need to be made to the system as it stands. At the same time the Commission shall, where appropriate, submit proposals for improvements in the present system in the interest of further facilitating the freedom of movement, right of establishment and freedom to provide services of the persons covered by this Directive.

6–129 **Article 14 [Addressees]**

This Directive is addressed to the Member States.

ANNEX

6–130 List of professional associations or organisations which satisfy the conditions of the second sub-paragraph of Article 1(d)

Ireland[79]

1. The Institute of Chartered Accountants in Ireland[80]
2. The Institute of Certified Public Accountants in Ireland[81]

[78] This Directive was notified to Member States on 4 January 1989.

[79] Irish nationals are also members of the following United Kingdom chartered bodies: Institute of Chartered Accountants in England and Wales; Institute of Chartered Accountants of Scotland; Institute of Actuaries; Faculty of Actuaries; The Chartered Institute of Management Accountants; Institute of Chartered Secretaries and Administrators; Royal Town Planning Institute; Royal Institution of Chartered Surveyors; Chartered Institute of Building.

[80] For the purposes of the activity of auditing only.

[81] *ibid.*

3. The Association of Certified Accountants[82]
4. Institution of Engineers of Ireland
5. Irish Planning Institute

United Kingdom

1. Institute of Chartered Accountants in England and Wales
2. Institute of Chartered Accountants of Scotland
3. Institute of Chartered Accountants in Ireland
4. Chartered Association of Certified Accountants
5. Chartered Institute of Loss Adjusters
6. Chartered Institute of Management Accountants
7. Institute of Chartered Secretaries and Administrators
8. Chartered Insurance Institute
9. Institute of Actuaries
10. Faculty of Actuaries
11. Chartered Institute of Bankers
12. Institute of Bankers in Scotland
13. Royal Institution of Chartered Surveyors
14. Royal Town Planning Institute
15. Chartered Society of Physiotherapy
16. Royal Society of Chemistry
17. British Psychological Society
18. Library Association
19. Institute of Chartered Foresters
20. Chartered Institute of Building
21. Engineering Council
22. Institute of Energy
23. Institution of Structural Engineers
24. Institution of Civil Engineers
25. Institution of Mining Engineers
26. Institution of Mining and Metallurgy
27. Institution of Electrical Engineers
28. Institution of Gas Engineers
29. Institution of Mechanical Engineers
30. Institution of Chemical Engineers
31. Institution of Production Engineers
32. Institution of Marine Engineers
33. Royal Institution of Naval Architects
34. Royal Aeronautical Society
35. Institute of Metals
36. Chartered Institution of Building Services Engineers
37. Institute of Measurement and Control
38. British Computer Society

Statement by the Council and the Commission

Re Article 9(1) **6–131**

"The Council and the Commission agree that professional bodies and higher-education establishments should be consulted or be involved in an appropriate way in the decision-making process."

[82] *ibid.*

Council Recommendation 89/49 of 21 December 1988 concerning nationals of Member States who hold a diploma conferred in a third State

([1989] OJ L19/24; Doc. Ref. 31989H00490)

6–132 *The Council of the European Communities,*
Approving Council Directive 89/48 of 21 December 1988 on a general system for the recognition of higher-education diplomas awarded on completion of professional education and training of at least three years' duration,[83]

Noting that this Directive refers only to diplomas, certificates and other evidence of formal qualifications awarded in Member States to nationals of Member States,

Anxious, however, to take account of the special position of nationals of Member States who hold diplomas, certificates or other evidence of formal qualifications awarded in third States and who are thus in a position comparable to one of those described in Article 3 of the Directive,

Hereby recommends:

that the Governments of the Member States should allow the persons referred to above to take up and pursue regulated professions within the Community by recognising these diplomas, certificates and other evidence of formal qualifications in their territories.

Council Directive 92/51 of 18 June 1992 on a second general system for the recognition of professional education and training to supplement Directive 89/48

([1992] OJ L209/25; Corrigenda at [1995] OJ L17/20 and [1995] OJ L30/40; Doc Ref. 31992L0051)

6–133 *The Council of the European Communities,*
Having regard to the Treaty establishing the European Economic Community, particular Articles [40], [47](1) and [55] thereof,

Having regard to the proposal from the Commission,[84]

In co-operation with the European Parliament,[85]

Having regard to the opinion of the Economic and Social Committee,[86]

(1) Whereas, pursuant to Article [14] of the Treaty, the internal market shall comprise an area without internal frontiers and whereas, pursuant to Article 3(c) of the Treaty, the abolition, as between Member States, of obstacles to freedom of movement for persons and services constitutes one of the objectives of the Community; whereas, for nationals of the Member States, this means in particular the possibility of pursuing a profession, whether in a self-employed or employed capacity, in a Member State other than that in which they acquired their professional qualifications;

(2) Whereas, for those professions for the pursuit of which the Community has not laid down the necessary minimum level of qualification, Member States reserve the option of fixing such a level with a view to guaranteeing the quality of services provided in their territory; whereas, however, they may not, without disregarding their obligations laid down in Articles [10], [39], [43] and [49] of the

[83] [1989] OJ L19/16 (see above).
[84] [1989] OJ C263/1 and [1990] OJ C217/4.
[85] [1990] OJ C149/149, and [1992] OJ C150.
[86] [1990] OJ C75/11.

Treaty, require a national of a Member State to obtain those qualifications which in general they determine only by reference to those issued under their own national education and training systems, where the person concerned has already acquired all or part of those qualifications in another Member State; whereas, as a result, any host Member State in which a profession is regulated is required to take account of qualifications acquired in another Member State and to determine whether those qualifications correspond to the qualifications which the Member State concerned requires;

(3) Whereas Council Directive 89/48 of 21 December 1988 on a general system for the recognition of higher education diplomas awarded on completion of professional education and training of at least three years' duration[87] facilitates compliance with such obligations; whereas, however, it is limited to higher education;

(4) Whereas, in order to facilitate the pursuit of all those professional activities which in a host Member State are dependent on the completion of a certain level of education and training, a second general system should be introduced to complement the first;

(5) Whereas the complementary general system must be based on the same principles and contain *mutatis mutandis* the same rules as the initial general system;

(6) Whereas this Directive is not applicable to those regulated professions which are covered by specific Directives principally concerned with introducing mutual recognition of training courses completed before entry into professional life;

(7) Whereas neither is it applicable, furthermore, to those activities covered by specific Directives principally intended to introduce recognition of technical skills based on experience acquired in another Member State; whereas certain of those Directives apply solely to the pursuit of activities in a self-employed capacity; whereas, in order to ensure that the pursuit of such activities as an employed person does not fall within the scope of this Directive, whereby the pursuit of the same activity would be subject to different legal recognition arrangements depending on whether it was pursued in a self-employed capacity or as an employed person, those Directives should be made applicable to persons pursuing the activities in question as employed persons;

(8) Whereas the complementary general system is entirely without prejudice to the application of Article [39](4) and Article [45] of the Treaty;

(9) Whereas this complementary system must cover the levels of education and training not covered by the initial general system, namely that corresponding to other post-secondary education and training courses and other equivalent education and training, and that corresponding to long or short secondary courses, possibly complemented by professional training or experience;

(10) Whereas, where in most Member States pursuit of a given regulated profession is subject to either very short training or the possession of certain personal attributes or merely general knowledge, the normal mechanisms for recognition under this Directive may be excessively cumbersome whereas in such cases there should be provision for simplified mechanisms;

(11) Whereas account should also be taken of the professional training system in the United Kingdom whereby standards for levels of performance for all professional activities are established via the "National Framework of Vocational Qualifications";

(12) Whereas in some Member States there are only relatively few regulated professions; whereas, however, training for professions which are not regulated may be specifically geared to the pursuit of the profession, with the structure and level of training being monitored or approved by the competent authorities of the

[87] [1989] OJ L19/16.

Member State concerned; whereas this provides guarantees equivalent to those provided in connection with a regulated profession;

(13) Whereas the competent authorities of the host Member State should be allowed to determine, in accordance with the relevant provisions of Community law, the detailed rules necessary for implementation of the adaptation period and the aptitude test;

(14) Whereas, since it covers two levels of education and training and since the initial general system covers a third level, the complementary general system must lay down whether and under what conditions a person possessing a certain level of education and training may pursue, in another Member State, a profession the qualifications for which are regulated at a different level;

(15) Whereas, for the pursuit of certain professions, certain Member States require the possession of a diploma within the meaning of Directive 89/48, while for the same profession other Member States require the completion of professional education or training with a different structure; whereas certain kinds of education and training, while not of a post-secondary nature of minimum duration within the meaning of this Directive, nevertheless result in a comparable professional level and prepare the person for similar responsibilities and activities; whereas such education and training should therefore be classed in the same category as that attested by a diploma; whereas such education and training is very varied and this classification can be achieved only by listing the courses in question whereas such classification would, where appropriate, establish the recognition of equivalence between such education and training and that covered by Directive 89/48; whereas some regulated education and training should also be classed at diploma level in a second list;

(16) Whereas, in view of the constantly changing organisation of professional training, there should be a procedure for amending those lists;

(17) Whereas, since it covers occupations the pursuit of which is dependent on the possession of professional or vocational education and training qualifications of secondary level and generally requires manual skills, the complementary general system must also provide for the recognition of such qualifications even where they have been acquired solely through professional experience in a Member State which does not regulate such professions;

(18) Whereas the aim of this general system, like the first general system, is to eliminate obstacles to the taking up and pursuit of regulated professions; whereas work carried out pursuant to Council Decision 85/368 of 16 July 1985 on the comparability of vocational training qualifications between the Member States of the European Community,[88] while pursuing a different objective from the elimination of legal obstacles to freedom of movement, namely that of improving the transparency of the labour market, must be used, where appropriate, in the application of this Directive, particularly where it could provide information on the subject, content and duration of professional training;

(19) Whereas professional bodies and professional educational and training establishments should, where appropriate, be consulted or be involved in an appropriate way in the decision-making process;

(20) Whereas, like the initial system, such a system, by strengthening the right of a Community national to use his occupational skills in any Member State, supplements and reinforces his right to acquire such skills wherever he wishes;

(21) Whereas the two systems should be evaluated, after a certain period of application, in order to determine how efficiently they operate and, in particular, how they can both be improved,

[88] [1985] OJ L199/56.

Has adopted this Directive:

CHAPTER I—DEFINITIONS

Article 1 **[Definitions]**

For the purposes of this Directive, the following definitions shall apply: **6–134**

(a) *diploma*: any evidence of education and training or any set of such evidence:

— which has been awarded by a competent authority in a Member State, designated in accordance with the laws, regulations or administrative provisions of that State,

— which shows that the holder has successfully completed:

(i) either a post-secondary course other than that referred to in the second indent of Article 1(a) of Directive 89/48, of at least one year's duration or of equivalent duration on a part-time basis, one of the conditions of entry of which is, as a general rule, the successful completion of the secondary course required to obtain entry to university or higher education, as well as the professional training which may be required in addition to that post-secondary course;

(ii) or one of the education and training courses in Annex C,[89] and

— which shows that the holder has the professional qualifications required for the taking up or pursuit of a regulated profession in that Member State,

provided that the education and training attested by this evidence was received mainly in the Community, or outside the Community at teaching establishments which provide education and training in accordance with the laws, regulations or administrative provisions of a Member State, or that the holder thereof has three years' professional experience certified by the Member State which recognised third-country evidence of education and training.

The following shall be treated in the same way as a diploma within the meaning of the first sub-paragraph: any evidence of education and training or any set of such evidence awarded by a competent authority in a Member State if it is awarded on the successful completion of education and training received in the Community and recognised by a competent authority in that Member State as being of an equivalent level and if it confers the same rights in respect of the taking up and pursuit of a regulated profession in that Member State;

(b) *certificate*: any evidence of education and training or any set of such evidence:

— which has been awarded by a competent authority in a Member State, designated in accordance with the laws, regulations or administrative provisions of that State,

— which shows that the holder, after having followed a secondary course, has completed:

either a course of education or training other than courses referred to in point (a), provided at an educational or training establishment or on the job, or in combination at an educational or training establishment and on the job, and complemented, where appropriate, by the probationary or professional practice required in addition to this course,

or the probationary or professional practice required in addition to this secondary course, or

— which shows that the holder, after having followed a secondary course of a technical or vocational nature has completed, where necessary,

---

[89] Annex C not reproduced. The Annex lists recognised training courses in the following fields in different Member States: paramedical and childcare; master craftsmen; seafaring; the technical sector; and UK courses accredited as NVQs or SVQs.

either a course of education or training as referred to in the previous indent, or the probationary or professional practice required in addition to this secondary course of a technical or vocational nature and

— which shows that the holder has the professional qualifications required for the taking up or pursuit of a regulated profession in that Member State,

provided that the education and training attested by this evidence was received mainly in the Community, or outside the Community at teaching establishments which provide education and training in accordance with the laws, regulations or administrative provisions of a Member State, or that the holder thereof has two years' professional experience certified by the Member State which recognised third-country evidence of education and training.

The following shall be treated in the same way as a certificate, within the meaning of the first sub-paragraph: any evidence of education and training or any set of such evidence awarded by a competent authority in a Member State if it is awarded on the successful completion of education and training received in the Community and recognised by a competent authority in a Member State as being of an equivalent level and if it confers the same rights in respect of the taking up and pursuit of a regulated profession in that Member State;

(c) *attestation of competence*: any evidence of qualifications:

— attesting to education and training not forming part of a set constituting a diploma within the meaning of Directive 89/48 or a diploma or certificate within the meaning of this Directive, or

— awarded following an assessment of the personal qualities, aptitudes or knowledge which it is considered essential that the applicant have for the pursuit of a profession by an authority designated in accordance with the laws, regulations or administrative provisions of a Member State, without proof of prior education and training being required;

(d) *host Member State*: any Member State in which a national of a Member State applies to pursue a profession subject to regulation in that Member State, other than the State in which he obtained his evidence of education and training or attestation of competence or first pursued the profession in question;

(e) *regulated profession*: the regulated professional activity or range of activities which constitute this profession in a Member State;

(f) *regulated professional activity*: a professional activity the taking up or pursuit of which, or one of its modes of pursuit in a Member State, is subject, directly or indirectly, by virtue of laws, regulations or administrative provisions, to the possession of evidence of education and training or an attestation of competence. The following in particular shall constitute a mode of pursuit of a regulated professional activity:

— pursuit of an activity under a professional title, in so far as the use of such a title is reserved to the holders of evidence of education and training or an attestation of competence governed by laws, regulations or administrative provisions,

— pursuit of a professional activity relating to health, in so far as remuneration and/or reimbursement for such an activity is subject by virtue of national social security arrangements to the possession of evidence of education and training or an attestation of competence.

Where the first sub-paragraph does not apply, a professional activity shall be deemed to be a regulated professional activity if it is pursued by the members of an association or organisation the purpose of which is, in particular, to promote and maintain a high standard in the professional field concerned and which, to achieve that purpose, is recognised in a special form by a Member State and:

— awards evidence of education and training to its members,
— ensures that its members respect the rules of professional conduct which it prescribes, and
— confers on them the right to use a professional title or designatory letters, or to benefit from a status corresponding to that education and training.

Whenever a Member State grants the recognition referred to in the second sub-paragraph to an association or organisation which satisfies the conditions of that sub-paragraph, it shall inform the Commission thereof;

(g) *regulated education and training*: any education and training which:
— is specifically geared to the pursuit of a given profession, and
— comprises a course or courses complemented, where appropriate, by professional training or probationary or professional practice, the structure and level of which are determined by the laws, regulations or administrative provisions of that Member State or which are monitored or approved by the authority designated for that purpose;

(h) *professional experience*: the actual and lawful pursuit of the profession concerned in a Member State;

(i) *adaptation period*: the pursuit of a regulated profession in the host Member State under the responsibility of a qualified member of that profession, such period of supervised practice possibly being accompanied by further education and training. This period of supervised practice shall be the subject of an assessment. The detailed rules governing the adaptation period and its assessment shall be laid down by the competent authorities in the host Member State.

The status enjoyed in the host Member State by the person undergoing the period of supervised practice, in particular in the matter of right of residence as well as of obligations, social rights and benefits, allowances and remuneration, shall be established by the competent authorities in that Member State in accordance with applicable Community law;

(j) *aptitude test*: a test limited to the professional knowledge of the applicant, made by the competent authorities of the host Member State with the aim of assessing the ability of the applicant to pursue a regulated profession in that Member State.

In order to permit this test to be carried out, the competent authorities shall draw up a list of subjects which, on the basis of a comparison of the education and training required in the Member State and that received by the applicant, are not covered by the evidence of education and training possessed by the applicant. These subjects may cover both theoretical knowledge and practical skills required for the pursuit of the profession.

This aptitude test must take account of the fact that the applicant is a qualified professional in the Member State of origin or the Member State from which he comes. It shall cover subjects to be selected from those on the list referred to in the second sub-paragraph, knowledge of which is essential to the pursuit of the profession in the host Member State. The test may also include knowledge of the professional rules applicable to the activities in question in the host Member State. The detailed application of the aptitude test shall be determined by the competent authorities of that State.

The status in the host Member State of the applicant who wishes to prepare himself for the aptitude test in that State shall be determined by the competent authorities in that State, in accordance with applicable Community law.

CHAPTER II—SCOPE

Article 2 [Individuals, professions and activities covered][90]

6–135 This Directive shall apply to any national of a Member State wishing to pursue a regulated profession in a host Member State in a self-employed capacity or as an employed person.

This Directive shall apply to neither professions which are the subject of a specific Directive establishing arrangements for the mutual recognition of diplomas by Member States, nor activities covered by a Directive listed in Annex A.[91]

The Directives listed in Annex B shall be made applicable to the pursuit as an employed person of the activities covered by those Directives.[92]

CHAPTER III—SYSTEM FOR RECOGNITION WHERE A HOST MEMBER STATE REQUIRES POSSESSION OF A DIPLOMA WITHIN THE MEANING OF THIS DIRECTIVE OR DIRECTIVE 89/48

Article 3 [Possession of equivalent diploma or professional experience plus education and training]

6–136 Without prejudice to Directive 89/48, where, in a host Member State, the taking up or pursuit of a regulated profession is subject to possession of a diploma, as defined in this Directive or in Directive 89/48, the competent authority may not, on the grounds of inadequate qualifications, refuse to authorise a national of a Member State to take up or pursue that profession on the same conditions as those which apply to its own nationals:

(a) if the applicant holds the diploma, as defined in this Directive or in Directive 89/48, required in another Member State for the taking up or pursuit of the profession in question in its territory, such diploma having been awarded in a Member State; or

(b) if the applicant has pursued the profession in question full-time for two years, or for an equivalent period on a part-time basis, during the previous 10 years in another Member State which does not regulate that profession within the meaning of either Article 1(e) and the first sub-paragraph of Article 1(f) of this Directive or Article 1(c) and the first sub-paragraph of Article 1(d) of Directive 89/48, and possesses evidence of education and training which:

— has been awarded by a competent authority in a Member State, designated in accordance with the laws, regulations or administrative provisions of that State, and

— either shows that the holder has successfully completed a post-secondary course, other than that referred to in the second indent of Article 1(a) of Directive 89/48, of at least one year's duration, or of equivalent duration on a part-time basis, one of the conditions of entry of which is, as a general rule, the successful completion of the secondary course required to obtain entry to university or higher education, as well as any professional training which is an integral part of that post-secondary course,

— or attests to regulated education and training referred to in Annex D,[93] and

— has prepared the holder for the pursuit of his profession.

However, the two years' professional experience referred to above may not be required where the evidence of education and training held by the applicant and referred to in this point is awarded on completion of regulated education and training.

---

[90] For the mechanism for the recognition of qualifications in respect of certain professional activities not covered by this Directive and Directive 89/48 above see Directive 1999/42 ([1999] OJ L201/77).

[91] Annex A not reproduced.

[92] Annex B not reproduced.

[93] Annex D not reproduced. The Annex lists courses in several Member States having a special structure.

The following shall be treated in the same way as the evidence of education and training referred to in the first sub-paragraph of this point: any evidence of education and training or any set of such evidence awarded by a competent authority in a Member State if it is awarded on the completion of education and training received in the Community and is recognised by that Member State as being of an equivalent level, provided that the other Member States and the Commission have been notified of this recognition.

By way of derogation from the first sub-paragraph of this Article, the host Member State is not required to apply this Article where the taking up or pursuit of a regulated profession is subject in its country to possession of a diploma as defined in Directive 89/48, one of the conditions for the issue of which shall be the completion of a post-secondary course of more than four years' duration.

Article 4 [Evidence of professional experience; adaptation periods and aptitude tests]

1. Notwithstanding Article 3, the host Member State may also require the applicant: **6–137**

(a) to provide evidence of professional experience, where the duration of the education and training adduced in support of his application, as laid down in points (a) and (b) of the first sub-paragraph of Article 3, is at least one year less than that required in the host Member State. In this event, the period of professional experience required may not exceed:
- twice the shortfall in duration of education and training where the shortfall relates to a post-secondary course and/or to a period of probationary practice carried out under the control of a supervising professional person and ending with an examination,
- the shortfall where the shortfall relates to professional practice acquired with the assistance of a qualified member of the profession concerned.

In the case of diplomas within the meaning of the second sub-paragraph of Article 1(a), the duration of education and training recognised as being of an equivalent level shall be determined as for the education and training defined in the first sub-paragraph of Article 1(a).

When these provisions are applied, account must be taken of the professional experience referred to in point (b) of the first sub-paragraph of Article 3.

In any event, the professional experience required may not exceed four years.

Professional experience may not, however, be required of an applicant holding a diploma attesting to a post-secondary course as referred to in the second indent of Article 1(a) or a diploma as defined in Article 1(a) of Directive 89/48 who wishes to pursue his profession in a host Member State which requires the possession of a diploma attesting to one of the courses of education and training as referred to in Annex C;

(b) to complete an adaptation period not exceeding three years or take an aptitude test where:
- the theoretical and/or practical matters covered by the education and training which he has received as laid down in points (a) or (b) of the first sub-paragraph of Article 3 differ substantially from those covered by the diploma, as defined in this Directive or in Directive 89/48, required in the host Member State, or
- in the case referred to in point (a) of the first sub-paragraph of Article 3, the profession regulated in the host Member State comprises one or more regulated professional activities which do not form part of the profession regulated in the Member State from which the applicant originates or comes and that difference corresponds to specific education and training required in the host Member State and covers theoretical and/or practical matters which differ substantially from those covered by the diploma, as defined in this Directive or in Directive 89/48, adduced by the applicant, or

— in the case referred to in point (b) of the first sub-paragraph of Article 3, the profession regulated in the host Member State comprises one or more regulated professional activities which do not form part of the profession pursued by the applicant in the Member State from which he originates or comes, and that difference corresponds to specific education and training required in the host Member State and covers theoretical and/or practical matters which differ substantially from those covered by the evidence of education and training adduced by the applicant.

[If the host Member State intends to require the applicant to complete an adaptation period or take an aptitude test, it must examine first whether the knowledge acquired by the applicant in the course of his professional experience is such that it fully or partly covers the substantial difference referred to in the first sub-paragraph.][94]

Should the host Member State make use of this possibility, it must give the applicant the right to choose between an adaptation period and an aptitude test. Where the host Member State, which requires a diploma as defined in Directive 89/48 or in this Directive, intends to introduce derogations from an applicant's right to choose, the procedure laid down in Article 14 shall apply.

By way of derogation from the second sub-paragraph of this point, the host Member State may reserve the right to choose between the adaptation period and the aptitude test if

— a profession is involved the pursuit of which requires a precise knowledge of national law and in respect of which the provision of advice and/or assistance concerning national law is an essential and constant feature of the professional activity, or

— where the host Member State makes access to the profession or its pursuit subject to the possession of a diploma as defined in Directive 89/48, one of the conditions for the award of which is the completion of a post-secondary course of more than three years' duration or an equivalent period on a part-time basis and the applicant holds either a diploma as defined in this Directive or evidence of education and training within the meaning of point (b) of the first sub-paragraph of Article 3 and not covered by Article 3(b) of Directive 89/48.

2. However, the host Member State may not apply the provisions of paragraph 1(a) and (b) cumulatively.

CHAPTER IV—SYSTEM FOR RECOGNITION WHERE A HOST MEMBER STATE REQUIRES POSSESSION OF A DIPLOMA AND THE APPLICANT IS THE HOLDER OF A CERTIFICATE OR HAS RECEIVED CORRESPONDING EDUCATION AND TRAINING

Article 5 [Possession of certificate or professional experience plus education and training]

6–138 Where, in a host Member State, the taking up or pursuit of a regulated profession is subject to possession of a diploma, the competent authority may not, on the grounds of inadequate qualifications, refuse to authorise a national of a Member State to take up or pursue that profession on the same conditions as those which apply to its own nationals:

(a) if the applicant holds the certificate required in another Member State for the taking up or pursuit of the same profession in its territory, such certificate having been awarded in a Member State; or

(b) if the applicant has pursued the same profession full-time for two years during the previous 10 years in another Member State which does not regulate that profession, within the meaning of Article 1(e) and the first sub-paragraph of Article 1(f), and possesses evidence of education and training:

[94] Words inserted by Directive 2001/19 Art. 2(1) as from 31 July 2001.

— which has been awarded by a competent authority in a Member State, designated in accordance with the laws, regulations or administrative provisions of that State, and
— which shows that the holder, after having followed a secondary course, has completed:
either a course of professional education or training other than courses referred to in point (a), provided at an educational or training establishment or on the job, or in combination at an educational or training establishment and on the job and complemented, where appropriate, by the probationary or professional practice which is an integral part of that training course,
or the probationary or professional practice which is an integral part of that secondary course, or
— which shows that the holder, after having followed a secondary course of a technical or vocational nature has completed, where necessary,
either a course of professional education or training as referred to in the previous indent,
or the period of probationary or professional practice which is an integral part of that secondary course of a technical or vocational nature and
— which has prepared the holder for the pursuit of this profession.

However, the two years' professional experience referred to above may not be required where the evidence of education and training held by the applicant and referred to in this point is awarded on completion of regulated education and training.

Nevertheless, the host Member State may require the applicant to undergo an adaptation period not exceeding three years or take an aptitude test. The host Member State must give the applicant the right to choose between an adaptation period and an aptitude test.

[If the host Member State intends to require the applicant to complete an adaptation period or take an aptitude test, it must first examine whether knowledge acquired by the applicant in the course of his professional experience is such that it fully or partly covers the substantial difference between the diploma and the certificate.][95]

Where the host Member State intends to introduce derogations from an applicant's right to choose, the procedure laid down in Article 14 shall apply.

CHAPTER V—SYSTEM FOR RECOGNITION WHERE A HOST MEMBER STATE REQUIRES POSSESSION OF A CERTIFICATE

Article 6 [Possession of equivalent certificate/diploma or professional experience plus education and training]

Where, in the host Member State, the taking up or pursuit of a regulated profession is subject to possession of a certificate, the competent authority may not, on the grounds of inadequate qualifications, refuse to authorise a national of a Member State to take up or pursue that profession on the same conditions as those which apply to its own nationals: **6–139**

(a) if the applicant holds the diploma, as defined in this Directive or in Directive 89/48, or the certificate required in another Member State for the taking up or pursuit of the profession in question in its territory, such diploma having been awarded in a Member State; or
(b) if the applicant has pursued the profession in question full-time for two years or for an equivalent period on a part-time basis during the previous 10 years in another Member State which does not regulate that profession, within the meaning of Article 1(e) and the first sub-paragraph of Article 1(f), and possesses evidence of education and training:

[95] Words inserted by Directive 2001/19 Art. 2(2) as from 31 July 2001.

— which has been awarded by a competent authority in a Member State, designated in accordance with the laws, regulations or administrative provisions of that State, and
— which shows that the holder has successfully completed a post-secondary course other than that referred to in the second indent of Article 1(a) of Directive 89/48, of at least one year's duration or of equivalent duration on a part-time basis, one of the conditions of entry of which is, as a general rule, the completion of the secondary course required to obtain entry to university or higher education, as well as any professional training which is an integral part of that post-secondary course, or
— which shows that the holder, after having followed a secondary course, has completed:
either a course of education or training for a profession other than courses referred to in point (a), provided at an educational establishment or on the job, or in combination at an educational establishment and on the job and complemented, where appropriate, by the probationary or professional practice which is an integral part of that training course,
or the probationary or professional practice which is an integral part of that secondary course, or
— which shows that the holder, after having followed a secondary course of a technical or vocational nature has completed, where necessary,
either a course of education or training for a profession as referred to in the previous indent,
or the period of probationary or professional practice which is an integral part of that secondary course of a technical or vocational nature, and
— which has prepared the holder for the pursuit of this profession.

However, the two years' professional experience referred to above may not be required where the evidence of education and training held by the applicant and referred to in this point is awarded on completion or regulated education and training.

(c) if the applicant who does not hold any diploma, certificate or other evidence of education and training within the meaning of Article 3(b) or of point (b) of this Article has pursued the profession in question full-time for three consecutive years, or for an equivalent period on a part-time basis, during the previous 10 years in another Member State which does not regulate that profession within the meaning of Article 1(e) and the first sub-paragraph of Article 1(f).

The following shall be treated in the same way as the evidence of education and training referred to under (b) in the first sub-paragraph: any evidence of education and training or any set of such evidence awarded by a competent authority in a Member State if it is awarded on the completion of education and training received in the Community and is recognised by that Member State as being of an equivalent level, provided that the other Member States and the Commission have been notified of this recognition.

Article 7 **[Adaptation periods and aptitude tests]**

6–140 Without prejudice to Article 6, a host Member State may also require the applicant to:

(a) complete an adaptation period not exceeding two years or to take an aptitude test when the education and training which he received in accordance with points (a) and (b) of the first sub-paragraph of Article 6 relates to theoretical or practical matters differing substantially from those covered by the certificate required in the host Member State, or where there are differences in the fields of activity characterised in the host Member State by specific education and training relating to theoretical or practical matters differing substantially from those covered by the applicant's evidence of formal qualifications.

[If the host Member State intends to require the applicant to complete an adaptation period or take an aptitude test, it must first examine whether knowledge acquired by the applicant in the course of his professional experience is such that it fully or partly covers the substantial difference referred to in the first sub-paragraph.][96]

Should the host Member State make use of this possibility, it must give the applicant the right to choose between an adaptation period and an aptitude test. Where the host Member State which requires a certificate intends to introduce derogations as regards an applicant's right to choose, the procedure laid down in Article 14 shall apply;

(b) undergo an adaptation period not exceeding two years or take an aptitude test where, in the instance referred to in point (c) of the first sub-paragraph of Article 6, he does not hold a diploma, certificate or other evidence of education and training. The host Member State may reserve the right to choose between an adaptation period and an aptitude test.

CHAPTER VI—SPECIAL SYSTEMS FOR RECOGNITION OF OTHER QUALIFICATIONS

Article 8 [Equivalent attestation of competence or proof of qualifications plus giving guarantees of health etc.]

Where, in the host Member State, the taking up or pursuit of a regulated **6–141**
profession is subject to possession of an attestation of competence, the competent authority may not, on the grounds of inadequate qualifications, refuse to authorise a national of a Member State to take up or pursue that profession on the same conditions as those which apply to its own nationals:

(a) if the applicant holds the attestation of competence required in another Member State for the taking up or pursuit of the same profession in its territory, such attestation having been awarded in a Member State; or

(b) if the applicant provides proof of qualifications obtained in other Member States,

and giving guarantees, in particular in the matter of health, safety, environmental protection and consumer protection, equivalent to those required by the laws, regulations or administrative provisions of the host Member State.

If the applicant does not provide proof of such an attestation or of such qualifications the laws, regulations or administrative provisions of the host Member State shall apply.

Article 9 [Evidence of general education]

Where, in the host Member State, the taking up or pursuit of a regulated **6–142**
profession is subject only to possession of evidence of education attesting to general education at primary or secondary school level, the competent authority may not, on the grounds of inadequate qualifications, refuse to authorise a national of a Member State to take up or pursue that profession on the same conditions as those which apply to its own nationals if the applicant possesses formal qualifications of the corresponding level, awarded in another Member State.

This evidence of formal qualifications must have been awarded by a competent authority in that Member State, designated in accordance with its own laws, regulations or administrative provisions.

[96] Words inserted by Directive 2001/19 Art. 2(3) as from 31 July 2001.

CHAPTER VII—OTHER MEASURES TO FACILITATE THE EFFECTIVE EXERCISE OF THE RIGHT OF ESTABLISHMENT, FREEDOM TO PROVIDE SERVICES AND FREEDOM OF MOVEMENT OF EMPLOYED PERSONS

Article 10 [Other conditions governing access to regulated profession]

6–143 1. Where the competent authority of the host Member State requires of persons wishing to take up a regulated profession proof that they are of good character or repute or that they have not been declared bankrupt, or suspends or prohibits the pursuit of that profession in the event of serious professional misconduct or a criminal offence, that State shall accept as sufficient evidence, in respect of nationals of Member States wishing to pursue that profession in its territory, the production of documents issued by competent authorities in the Member State of origin or the Member State from which the foreign national comes showing that those requirements are met.

Where the competent authorities of the Member State of origin or of the Member State from which the foreign national comes do not issue the documents referred to in the first sub-paragraph, such documents shall be replaced by a declaration on oath—or, in Member States where there is no provision for declaration on oath, by a solemn declaration—made by the person concerned before a competent judicial or administrative authority or, where appropriate, a notary or qualified professional body of the Member State of origin or the Member State from which the person comes; such authority or notary shall issue written confirmation attesting the authenticity of the declaration on oath or solemn declaration.

2. Where the competent authority of the host Member State requires of nationals of that Member State wishing to take up or pursue a regulated profession a statement of physical of mental health, that authority shall accept as sufficient evidence in this respect the production of the document required in the Member State of origin or the Member State from which the foreign national comes.

Where the Member State of origin or the Member State from which the foreign national comes does not impose any requirements of this nature on those wishing to take up or pursue the profession in question, the host Member State shall accept from such nationals a statement issued by a competent authority in that State corresponding to the statement issued in the host Member State.

3. The competent authority of the host Member State may require that the documents and statements referred to in paragraphs 1 and 2 are presented no more than three months after their date of issue.

4. Where the competent authority of the host Member State requires nationals of that Member State wishing to take up or pursue a regulated profession to take an oath or make solemn declaration and where the form of such oath or declaration cannot be used by nationals of other Member States, that authority shall ensure that an appropriate and equivalent form of oath or declaration is offered to the person concerned.

[5. Where proof of financial standing is required in order to take up or pursue a regulated profession in the host Member State, that Member State shall regard certificates issued by banks in the Member State of origin or in the Member State from where the foreign national comes as equivalent to those issued in its own territory.

6. Where the competent authority of the host Member State requires of its own nationals wishing to take up or pursue a regulated profession proof that they are insured against the financial risks arising from their professional liability, that Member State shall accept certificates issued by insurance undertakings of other Member States as equivalent to those issued in its own territory. Such certificates shall state that the insurer has complied with the laws and regulations in force in

the host Member State regarding the terms and extent of cover. They may not be presented more than three months after their date of issue.][97]

Article 11 [Professional and academic titles]

1. The competent authorities of host Member States shall recognise the right of nationals of Member States who fulfil the conditions for the taking up and pursuit of a regulated profession in their territory to use the professional title of the host Member State corresponding to that profession. **6–144**

2. The competent authority of the host Member State shall recognise the right of nationals of Member States who fulfil the conditions for the taking up and pursuit of a regulated profession in the territory to use their lawful academic title and, where appropriate, the abbreviation thereof deriving from their Member State of origin or the Member State from which they come, in the language of that State. The host Member State may require this title to be followed by the name and location of the establishment or examining board which awarded it.

3. Where a profession is regulated in the host Member State by an association or organisation referred to in Article 1(f), nationals of Member States shall be entitled to use the professional title or designatory letters conferred by that organisation or association only on proof of membership.

Where the association or organisation makes membership subject to certain qualification requirements, it may apply these to nationals of other Member States who are in possession of a diploma within the meaning of Article 1(a), a certificate within the meaning of Article 1(b) or evidence of education and training or qualification within the meaning of point (b) of the first sub-paragraph of Article 3, point (b) of the first sub-paragraph of Article 5 or Article 9 in accordance only with this Directive, in particular Articles 3, 4 and 5.

Article 12 [Decisions on applications to pursue regulated professions]

1. The host Member State shall accept as means of proof that the conditions laid down in Articles 3 to 9 are satisfied the documents issued by the competent authorities in the Member States, which the person concerned shall submit in support of his application to pursue the profession concerned. **6–145**

2. The procedure for examining an application to pursue a regulated profession shall be completed as soon as possible and the outcome communicated in a reasoned decision of the competent authority in the host Member State not later than four months after presentation of all the documents relating to the person concerned. A remedy shall be available against this decision or the absence thereof, before a court or tribunal in accordance with the provisions of national law.

CHAPTER VIII—PROCEDURE FOR CO-ORDINATION

Article 13 [Designation of competent authorities; Member State co-ordinators]

1. Member States shall designate, within the period provided for in Article 17, the competent authorities empowered to receive the applications and take the **6–146**

[97] Article 10(5) and (6) inserted by Directive 2001/19 Art. 2(4) as from 31 July 2001.

decisions referred to in this Directive. They shall communicate this information to the other Member States and to the Commission.

2. Each Member State shall designate a person responsible for co-ordinating the activities of the authorities referred to in paragraph 1 and shall inform the other Member States and the Commission to that effect. His role shall be to promote uniform application of this Directive to all the professions concerned. This co-ordinator shall be a member of the co-ordinating group set up under the aegis of the Commission by Article 9(2) of Directive 89/48.

The co-ordinating group set up under the aforementioned provision of Directive 89/48 shall also be required to:

[— facilitate the implementation of this Directive, in particular by adopting and publishing opinions on the questions referred to it by the Commission,][98]

— collect all useful information for its application in the Member States, particularly information relating to the establishment of an indicative list of regulated professions and to the disparities between the qualifications awarded in the Member States with a view to assisting the competent authorities of the Member States in their task of assessing whether substantial differences exist.

The group may be consulted by the Commission on any changes to the existing system which may be contemplated.

3. The Member States shall take measures to provide the necessary information on the recognition of diplomas and certificates and on other conditions governing the taking up of the regulated professions within the framework of this Directive. To carry out this task they may call upon the existing information networks and, where appropriate, the relevant professional associations or organisations. The Commission shall take the necessary initiatives to ensure the development and co-ordination of the communication of the necessary information.

CHAPTER IX—PROCEDURE FOR DEROGATING FROM THE RIGHT TO CHOOSE BETWEEN ADAPTATION PERIOD AND APTITUDE TEST

Article 14 [Procedure when choice of adaptation period or aptitude test not offered]

6–147 1. If, pursuant to the second sentence of the second sub-paragraph of Article 4(1)(b), the third sub-paragraph of Article 5, or the second sentence of the second sub-paragraph of Article 7(a), a Member State proposes not to grant applicants the right to choose between an adaptation period and an aptitude test, it shall immediately communicate to the Commission the corresponding draft provision. It shall at the same time notify the Commission of the grounds which make the enactment of such a provision necessary.

The Commission shall immediately notify the other Member States of any draft which it has received it may also consult the co-ordinating group referred to in Article 13(2) on the draft.

2. Without prejudice to the possibility for the Commission and the other Member States to make comments on the draft, the Member State may adopt the provision only if the Commission has not taken a decision to the contrary within three months.

3. At the request of a Member State or the Commission, Member States shall communicate to them, without delay, the definitive text of any provision arising from the application of this Article.

98 Words substituted by Directive 2001/19 Art. 2(5) as from 31 July 2001.

CHAPTER X—PROCEDURE FOR AMENDING ANNEXES C AND D

Article 15 [Amendments to education and training courses]

[Not reproduced]. **6–148**

CHAPTER XI—OTHER PROVISIONS

Article 16 [Regular Member State reports on the application of the system]

Following the expiry of the period provided for in Article 17, Member States shall **6–149** communicate to the Commission, every two years, a report on the application of the system introduced.

In addition to general remarks, this report shall contain a statistical summary of the decisions taken and a description of the main problems arising from the application of this Directive.

Article 17 [Implementation]

1. Member States shall adopt the laws, regulations and administrative provisions **6–150** necessary for them to comply with this Directive before 18 June 1994. They shall forthwith inform the Commission thereof.

When Member States adopt these measures, the latter shall include a reference to this Directive or be accompanied by such reference at the time of their official publication. The methods of making such a reference shall be laid down by the Member States.

2. Member States shall communicate to the Commission the texts of the main provisions of national law which they adopt in the field governed by this Directive.

Article 18 [Review]

Five years at the latest following the date specified in Article 17, the Commission **6–151** shall report to the European Parliament, the Council and the Economic and Social Committee on the progress of the application of this Directive.

After conducting all necessary consultations, the Commission shall present its conclusions as to any changes which need to be made to this Directive. At the same time the Commission shall, where appropriate, submit proposals for improving the existing rules in the interest of facilitating freedom of movement, right of establishment and freedom to provide services.

Article 19 [Addressees]

This Directive is addressed to the Member States. **6–152**

ANNEX A

List of the Directives referred to in the second sub-paragraph of Article 2:

[Not reproduced]. **6–153**

Annex B

List of the Directives referred to in Article 2, third sub-paragraph:

6–154 [Not reproduced].

Annex C

List of courses having a special structure as referred to in point (ii) of the second indent of the first sub-paragraph of Article 1(a):

[Not reproduced].

Annex D

List of courses having a special structure as referred to in the third indent of point (b) of the first sub-paragraph of Article 3

6–155 [Not reproduced].

SECTION 3—LAWYERS

Council Directive 77/249 of 22 March 1977 to facilitate the effective exercise by lawyers of freedom to provide services

([1977] OJ L78/17; Doc. Ref. 31977L0249)

The Council of the European Communities,

6–156 Having regard to the Treaty establishing the European Economic Community, and in particular Articles [47] and [55] thereof,

Having regard to the proposal from the Commission,

Having regard to the opinion of the European Parliament,[99]

Having regard to the opinion of the Economic and Social Committee,[1]

[1] Whereas, pursuant to the Treaty, any restriction on the provision of services which is based on nationality or on conditions of residence has been prohibited since the end of the transitional period;

[2] Whereas this Directive deals only with measures to facilitate the effective pursuit of the activities of lawyers by way of provision of services; whereas more detailed measures will be necessary to facilitate the effective exercise of the right of establishment;

[3] Whereas if lawyers are to exercise effectively the freedom to provide services host Member States must recognise as lawyers those persons practising the profession in the various Member States,

[4] Whereas, since this Directive solely concerns provision of services and does not contain provisions on the mutual recognition of diplomas, a person to whom the Directive applies must adopt the professional title used in the Member State in which he is established, hereinafter referred to as "the Member State from which he comes",

Has adopted this Directive:

Article 1 [Legal services]

6–157 1. This Directive shall apply, within the limits and under the conditions laid down herein, to the activities of lawyers pursued by way of provision of services.

Notwithstanding anything contained in this Directive, Member States may reserve to prescribed categories of lawyers the preparation of formal documents

[99] [1972] JO C103/19 and [1976] OJ C53/33. Note that measures on mutual recognition are now subject to the co-decision procedure rather than the consultation procedure in force at the time that this Directive was adopted.

[1] [1970] JO C36/37 and [1976] OJ C50/17.

for obtaining title to administer estates of deceased persons, and the drafting of formal documents creating or transferring interests in land.

2. "Lawyer" means any person entitled to pursue his professional activities under one of the following designations:

[*Belgium*	Avocat/Advocaat
Denmark	Advokat
Germany	Rechtsanwalt
Greece	Dikigoros
Spain	Abogado
France	Avocat
Ireland	Barrister Solicitor
Italy	Avvocato
Luxembourg	Avocat-avoué
The Netherlands	Advocaat
Austria	Rechstanwalt
Portugal	Advogado
Finland	Asianajaja/Advokat
Sweden	Advocat
United Kingdom	Barrister Solicitor][2]

Article 2 [Recognition]

Each Member State shall recognise as a lawyer for the purpose of pursuing the activities specified in Article 1(1) any person listed in paragraph 2 of that Article. **6–158**

Article 3 [Home State professional title to be used]

A person referred to in Article 1 shall adopt the professional title used in the Member State from which he comes, expressed in the language or one of the languages, of that State, with an indication of the professional organisation by which he is authorised to practise or the court of law before which he is entitled to practise pursuant to the laws of that State. **6–159**

Article 4 [Compliance with local rules and rules of professional conduct]

1. Activities relating to the representation of a client in legal proceedings or before public authorities shall be pursued in each host Member State under the conditions laid down for lawyers established in that State, with the exception of any conditions requiring residence, or registration with a professional organisation, in that State. **6–160**

2. A lawyer pursuing these activities shall observe the rules of professional conduct of the host Member State, without prejudice to his obligations in the Member State from which he comes.

[2] Table as amended by Acts of Accession of Greece, of Spain and Portugal and of Austria, Finland and Sweden.

3. When these activities are pursued in the United Kingdom, "rules of professional conduct of the host Member State" means the rules of professional conduct applicable to solicitors, where such activities are not reserved for barristers and advocates. Otherwise the rules of professional conduct applicable to the latter shall apply. However, barristers from Ireland shall always be subject to the rules of professional conduct applicable in the United Kingdom to barristers and advocates.

When these activities are pursued in Ireland "rules of professional conduct of the host Member State" means, in so far as they govern the oral presentation of a case in court, the rules of professional conduct applicable to barristers. In all other cases the rules of professional conduct applicable to solicitors shall apply. However, barristers and advocates from the United Kingdom shall always be subject to the rules of professional conduct applicable in Ireland to barristers.

4. A lawyer pursuing activities other than those referred to in paragraph 1 shall remain subject to the conditions and rules of professional conduct of the Member State from which he comes without prejudice to respect for the rules, whatever their source, which govern the profession in the host Member State, especially those concerning the incompatibility of the exercise of the activities of a lawyer with the exercise of other activities in that State, professional secrecy, relations with other lawyers, the prohibition on the same lawyer acting for parties with mutually conflicting interests, and publicity. The latter rules are applicable only if they are capable of being observed by a lawyer who is not established in the host Member State and to the extent to which their observance is objectively justified to ensure, in that State, the proper exercise of a lawyer's activities, the standing of the profession and respect for the rules concerning incompatibility.

Article 5 [Additional pre-conditions host States may impose]

6–161 For the pursuit of activities relating to the representation of a client in legal proceedings, a Member State may require lawyers to whom Article 1 applies:

— to be introduced, in accordance with local rules or customs, to the presiding judge and, where appropriate, to the President of the relevant Bar in the host Member State;

— to work in conjunction with a lawyer who practises before the judicial authority in question and who would, where necessary, be answerable to that authority, or with an "avoué" or "procuratore" practising before it.

Article 6 [Employed lawyers representing employer in legal proceedings]

6–162 Any Member State may exclude lawyers who are in the salaried employment of a public or private undertaking from pursuing activities relating to the representation of that undertaking in legal proceedings in so far as lawyers established in that State are not permitted to pursue those activities.

Article 7 [Proof of qualification; failure to comply with local rules]

6–163 1. The competent authority of the host Member State may request the person providing the services to establish his qualifications as a lawyer.

2. In the event of non-compliance with the obligations referred to in Article 4 and in force in the host Member State, the competent authority of the latter shall determine in accordance with its own rules and procedures the consequences of such non-compliance, and to this end may obtain any appropriate professional information concerning the person providing services. It shall notify the competent authority of the Member State from which the person comes of any decision taken. Such exchanges shall not affect the confidential nature of the information supplied.

Article 8 [Implementation]

1. Member States shall bring into force the measures necessary to comply with this Directive within two years of its notification and shall forthwith inform the Commission thereof. **6–164**

2. Member States shall communicate to the Commission the texts of the main provisions of national law which they adopt in the field covered by this Directive.

Article 9 [Addressees]

This Directive is addressed to the Member States. **6–165**

Directive 98/5 of the European Parliament and of the Council of 16 February 1998 to facilitate practice of the profession of lawyer on a permanent basis in a Member State other than that in which the qualification was obtained

([1998] OJ L77/36; Doc. Ref. 31998L0005)

The European Parliament and the Council of the European Union, **6–166**

Having regard to the Treaty establishing the European Community, and in particular Article [40], Article [47](1) and the [former] first and third sentences of [what is now] Article [47(2)] thereof,

Having regard to the proposal from the Commission,[3]

Having regard to the Opinion of the Economic and Social Committee,[4]

Acting in accordance with the procedure laid down in Article [251] of the Treaty,[5]

(1) Whereas, pursuant to Article [14] of the Treaty, the internal market is to comprise an area without internal frontiers; whereas, pursuant to Article 3(c) of the Treaty, the abolition, as between Member States, of obstacles to freedom of movement for persons and services constitutes one of the objectives of the Community; whereas, for nationals of the Member States, this means among other things the possibility of practising a profession, whether in a self-employed or a salaried capacity, in a Member State other than that in which they obtained their professional qualifications;

(2) Whereas, pursuant to Council Directive 89/48 of 21 December 1988 on a general system for the recognition of higher-education diplomas awarded on completion of professional education and training of at least three years' duration,[6] a lawyer who is fully qualified in one Member State may already ask to have his diploma recognised with a view to establishing himself in another Member State in order to practise the profession of lawyer there under the professional title used in that State; whereas the objective of Directive 89/48 is to ensure that a lawyer is integrated into the profession in the host Member State, and the Directive seeks neither to modify the rules regulating the profession in that State nor to remove such a lawyer from the ambit of those rules;

(3) Whereas while some lawyers may become quickly integrated into the profession in the host Member State, *inter alia* by passing an aptitude test as provided for in Directive 89/48, other fully qualified lawyers should be able to achieve such integration after a certain period of professional practice in the host Member State under their home-country professional titles or else continue to practise under their home-country professional titles;

(4) Whereas at the end of that period the lawyer should be able to integrate into the profession in the host Member States after verification that the possesses professional experience in that Member State;

---

[3] [1995] OJ C128/6 and [1996] OJ C355/19.

[4] [1995] OJ C256/14.

[5] Opinion of the European Parliament of 19 June 1996 ([1996] OJ C198/85), Council Common Position of 24 July 1997 ([1997] OJ C297/6), Decision of the European Parliament of 19 November 1997 (Council Decision of 15 December 1997).

[6] [1989] OJ L19/16.

(5) Whereas action along these lines is justified at Community level not only because, compared with the general system for the recognition of diplomas, it provides lawyers with an easier means whereby they can integrate into the profession in a host Member State, but also because, by enabling lawyers to practise under their home-country professional titles on a permanent basis in a host Member State, it meets the needs of consumers of legal services who, owing to the increasing trade flows resulting, in particular, from the internal market, seek advice when carrying out cross-border transactions in which international law, Community law and domestic laws often overlap;

(6) Whereas action is also justified at Community level because only a few Member States already permit in their territory the pursuit of activities of lawyers, otherwise than by way of provision of services, by lawyers from other Member States practising under their home-country professional titles; whereas, however, in the Member States where this possibility exists, the practical details concerning, for example, the area of activity and the obligation to register with the competent authorities differ considerably; whereas such a diversity of situations leads to inequalities and distortions in competition between lawyers from the Member States and constitutes an obstacle to freedom of movement; whereas only a directive laying down the conditions governing practice of the profession, otherwise than by way of provision of services, by lawyers practising under their home-country professional titles is capable of resolving these difficulties and of affording the same opportunities to lawyers and consumers of legal services in all Member States;

(7) Whereas, in keeping with its objective, this Directive does not lay down any rules concerning purely domestic situations, and where it does affect national rules regulating the legal profession it does so no more than is necessary to achieve its purpose effectively; whereas it is without prejudice in particular to national legislation governing access to and practice of the profession of lawyer under the professional title used in the host Member State;

(8) Whereas lawyers covered by the Directive should be required to register with the competent authority in the host Member State in order that that authority may ensure that they comply with the rules of professional conduct in force in that State; whereas the effect of such registration as regards the jurisdictions in which, and the levels and types of court before which, lawyers may practise is determined by the law applicable to lawyers in the host Member State;

(9) Whereas lawyers who are not integrated into the profession in the host Member State should practise in that State under their home-country professional titles so as to ensure that consumers are properly informed and to distinguish between such lawyers and lawyers from the host Member State practising under the professional title used there;

(10) Whereas lawyers covered by this Directive should be permitted to give legal advice in particular on the law of their home Member States, on Community law, on international law and on the law of the host Member State; whereas this is already allowed as regards the provision of services under Council Directive 77/249 of 22 March 1977 to facilitate the effective exercise by lawyers of freedom to provide services[7]; whereas, however, provision should be made, as in Directive 77/249, for the option of excluding from the activities of lawyers practising under their home-country professional titles in the United Kingdom and Ireland the preparation of certain formal documents in the conveyancing and probate spheres; whereas this Directive in no way affects the provisions under which, in every Member State, certain activities are reserved for professions other than the legal profession; whereas the provision in Directive 77/249 concerning the possibility of the host Member State to require a lawyer practising under his home-country professional title to work in conjunction with a local lawyer when representing or defending a client in legal proceedings should also be

[7] [1977] OJ L78/17. Directive as last amended by the 1994 Act of Accession.

incorporated in this Directive; whereas that requirement must be interpreted in the light of the case law of the Court of Justice of the European Communities, in particular its judgment of 25 February 1988 in Case 427/85, *Commission v Germany*[8];

(11) Whereas to ensure the smooth operation of the justice system Member States should be allowed, by means of specific rules, to reserve access to their highest courts to specialist lawyers, without hindering the integration of Member States' lawyers fulfilling the necessary requirements;

(12) Whereas a lawyer registered under his home-country professional title in the host Member State must remain registered with the competent authority in his home Member State if he is to retain his status of lawyer and be covered by this Directive; whereas for that reason close collaboration between the competent authorities is indispensable, in particular in connection with any disciplinary proceedings;

(13) Whereas lawyers covered by this Directive, whether salaried or self-employed in their home Member States, may practise as salaried lawyers in the host Member State, where that Member State offers that possibility to its own lawyers;

(14) Whereas the purpose pursued by this Directive in enabling lawyers to practise in another Member State under their home-country professional titles is also to make it easier for them to obtain the professional title of that host Member State; whereas under Articles [39] and [43] of the Treaty as interpreted by the Court of Justice the host Member State must take into consideration any professional experience gained in its territory; whereas after effectively and regularly pursuing in the host Member State an activity in the law of that State including Community law for a period of three years, a lawyer may reasonably be assumed to have gained the aptitude necessary to become fully integrated into the legal profession there; whereas at the end of that period the lawyer who can, subject to verification, furnish evidence of his professional competence in the host Member State should be able to obtain the professional title of that Member State; whereas if the period of effective and regular professional activity of at least three years includes a shorter period of practice in the law of the host Member State, the authority shall also take into consideration any other knowledge of that State's law, which it may verify during an interview; whereas if evidence of fulfilment of these conditions is not provided, the decision taken by the competent authority of the host State not to grant the State's professional title under the facilitation arrangements linked to those conditions must be substantiated and subject to appeal under national law;

(15) Whereas, for economic and professional reasons, the growing tendency for lawyers in the Community to practise jointly, including in the form of associations, has become a reality; whereas the fact that lawyers belong to a grouping in their home Member State should not be used as a pretext to prevent or deter them from establishing themselves in the host Member State; whereas Member States should be allowed, however, to take appropriate measures with the legitimate aim of safeguarding the profession's independence; whereas certain guarantees should be provided in those Member States which permit joint practice,

Have adopted this Directive:

Article 1 Object, scope and definitions

1. The purpose of this Directive is to facilitate practice of the profession of lawyer on a permanent basis in a self-employed or salaried capacity in a Member State other than that in which the professional qualification was obtained. **6–167**

[8] [1988] ECR 1123.

2. For the purposes of this Directive:

(a) *"lawyer"* means any person who is a national of a Member State and who is authorised to pursue his professional activities under one of the following professional titles:

Belgium	Avocat/Advocaat/Rechtsanwalt
Denmark	Advokat
Germany	Rechtsanwalt
Greece	Dikigoros
Spain	Abogado/Advocat/Avogado/ Abokatu
France	Avocat
Ireland	Barrister/Solicitor
Italy	Avvocato
Luxembourg	Avocat
The Netherlands	Advocaat
Austria	Rechstanwalt
Portugal	Advogado
Finland	Asianajaja/Advokat
Sweden	Advocat
United Kingdom	Advocate/Barrister/Solicitor

(b) *"home Member State"* means the Member State in which a lawyer acquired the right to use one of the professional titles referred to in (a) before practising the profession of lawyer in another Member State;

(c) *"host Member State"* means the Member State in which a lawyer practises pursuant to this Directive;

(d) *"home-country professional title"* means the professional title used in the Member State in which a lawyer acquired the right to use that title before practising the profession of lawyer in the host Member State;

(e) *"grouping"* means any entity, with or without legal personality, formed under the law of a Member State, within which lawyers pursue their professional activities jointly under a joint name;

(f) *"relevant professional title"* or *"relevant profession"* means the professional title or profession governed by the competent authority with whom a lawyer has registered under Article 3, and *"competent authority"* means that authority.

3. This Directive shall apply both to lawyers practising in a self-employed capacity and to lawyers practising in a salarial capacity in the home Member State and, subject to Article 8, in the host Member State.

4. Practice of the profession of lawyer within the meaning of this Directive shall not include the provision of services, which is covered by Directive 77/249.

Article 2 Right to practise under the home-country professional title

6–168 Any lawyer shall be entitled to pursue on a permanent basis, in any other Member State under his home-country professional title, the activities specified in Article 5. Integration into the profession of lawyer in the host Member State shall be subject to Article 10.

Article 3 Registration with the competent authority

1. A lawyer who wishes to practise in a Member State other than that in which he obtained his professional qualification shall register with the competent authority in that State. **6–169**

2. The competent authority in the host Member State shall register the lawyer upon presentation of a certificate attesting to his registration with the competent authority in the home Member State. It may require that, when presented by the competent authority of the home Member State, the certificate be not more than three months old. It shall inform the competent authority in the home Member State of the registration.

3. For the purpose of applying paragraph 1:

— in the United Kingdom and Ireland, lawyers practising under a professional title other than those used in the United Kingdom or Ireland shall register either with the authority responsible for the profession of barrister or advocate or with the authority responsible for the profession of solicitor,

— in the United Kingdom, the authority responsible for a barrister from Ireland shall be that responsible for the profession of barrister or advocate, and the authority responsible for a solicitor from Ireland shall be that responsible for the profession of solicitor,

— in Ireland, the authority responsible for a barrister or an advocate from the United Kingdom shall be that responsible for the profession of barrister, and the authority responsible for a solicitor from the United Kingdom shall be that responsible for the profession of solicitor.

4. Where the relevant competent authority in a host Member State publishes the names of lawyers registered with it, it shall also publish the names of lawyers registered pursuant to this Directive.

Article 4 Practice under the home-country professional title

1. A lawyer practising in a host Member State under his home-country professional title shall do so under that title, which must be expressed in the official language or one of the official languages of his home Member State, in an intelligible manner and in such a way as to avoid confusion with the professional title of the host Member State. **6–170**

2. For the purpose of applying paragraph 1, a host Member State may require a lawyer practising under his home-country professional title to indicate the professional body of which he is a member in his home Member State or the judicial authority before which he is entitled to practise pursuant to the laws of his home Member State. A host Member State may also require a lawyer practising under his home-country professional title to include a reference to his registration with the competent authority in that State.

Article 5 Area of activity

1. Subject to paragraphs 2 and 3, a lawyer practising under his home-country professional title carries on the same professional activities as a lawyer practising under the relevant professional title used in the host Member State and may, *inter alia*, give advice on the law of his home Member State, on Community law, on international law and on the law of the host Member State. He shall in any event comply with the rules of procedure applicable in the national courts. **6–171**

2. Member States which authorise in their territory a prescribed category of lawyers to prepare deeds for obtaining title to administer estates of deceased persons and for creating or transferring interests in land which, in other Member States, are reserved for professions other than that of lawyer may exclude from such activities lawyers practising under a home-country professional title conferred in one of the latter Member States.

3. For the pursuit of activities relating to the representation or defence of a client in legal proceedings and insofar as the law of the host Member State reserves such activities to lawyers practising under the professional title of that State, the latter may require lawyers practising under their home-country professional titles to work in conjunction with a lawyer who practises before the judicial authority in question and who would, where necessary, be answerable to that authority or with an "avoué" practising before it.

Nevertheless, in order to ensure the smooth operation of the justice system, Member States may lay down specific rules for access to supreme courts, such as the use of specialist lawyers.

Article 6 Rules of professional conduct applicable

6–172 1. Irrespective of the rules of professional conduct to which he is subject in his home Member State, a lawyer practising under his home-country professional title shall be subject to the same rules of professional conduct as lawyers practising under the relevant professional title of the host Member State in respect of all the activities he pursues in its territory.

2. Lawyers practising under their home-country professional titles shall be granted appropriate representation in the professional associations of the host Member State. Such representation shall involve at least the right to vote in elections to those associations' governing bodies.

3. The host Member State may require a lawyer practising under his home-country professional title either to take out professional indemnity insurance or to become a member of a professional guarantee fund in accordance with the rules which that State lays down for professional activities pursued in its territory. Nevertheless, a lawyer practising under his home-country professional title shall be exempted from that requirement if he can prove that he is covered by insurance taken out or a guarantee provided in accordance with the rules of his home Member State, insofar as such insurance or guarantee is equivalent in terms of the conditions and extent of cover. Where the equivalence is only partial, the competent authority in the host Member State may require that additional insurance or an additional guarantee be contracted to cover the elements which are not already covered by the insurance or guarantee contracted in accordance with the rules of the home Member State.

Article 7 Disciplinary proceedings

6–173 1. In the event of failure by a lawyer practising under his home-country professional title to fulfil the obligations in force in the host Member State, the rules of procedure, penalties and remedies provided for in the host Member State shall apply.

2. Before initiating disciplinary proceedings against a lawyer practising under his home-country professional title, the competent authority in the host Member State shall inform the competent authority in the home Member State as soon as possible, furnishing it with all the relevant details.

The first sub-paragraph shall apply *mutatis mutandis* where disciplinary proceedings are initiated by the competent authority of the home Member State, which shall inform the competent authority of the host Member State(s) accordingly.

3. Without prejudice to the decision-making power of the competent authority in the host Member State, that authority shall co-operate throughout the disciplinary proceedings with the competent authority in the home Member State. In particular, the host Member State shall take the measures necessary to ensure that the competent authority in the home Member State can make submissions to the bodies responsible for hearing any appeal.

4. The competent authority in the home Member State shall decide what action to take, under its own procedural and substantive rules, in the light of a decision of the competent authority in the host Member State concerning a lawyer practising under his home-country professional title.

5. Although it is not a prerequisite for the decision of the competent authority in the host Member State, the temporary or permanent withdrawal by the competent authority in the home Member State of the authorisation to practise the profession shall automatically lead to the lawyer concerned being temporarily or permanently prohibited from practising under his home-country professional title in the host Member State.

Article 8 Salaried practice

A lawyer registered in a host Member State under his home-country professional title may practise as a salaried lawyer in the employ of another lawyer, an association or firm of lawyers, or a public or private enterprise to the extent that the host Member State so permits for lawyers registered under the professional title used in that State. **6–174**

Article 9 Statement of reasons and remedies

Decisions not to effect the registration referred to in Article 3 or to cancel such registration and decisions imposing disciplinary measures shall state the reasons on which they are based. **6–175**

A remedy shall be available against such decisions before a court or tribunal in accordance with the provisions of domestic law.

Article 10 Like treatment as a lawyer of the host Member State

1. A lawyer practising under his home-country professional title who has effectively and regularly pursued for a period of at least three years an activity in the host Member State in the law of that State including Community law shall, with a view to gaining admission to the profession of lawyer in the host Member State, be exempted from the conditions set out in Article 4(1)(b) of Directive 89/48. "*Effective and regular pursuit*" means actual exercise of the activity without any interruption other than that resulting from the events of everyday life. **6–176**

It shall be for the lawyer concerned to furnish the competent authority in the host Member State with proof of such effective regular pursuit for a period of at least three years of an activity in the law of the host Member State. To that end:

(a) the lawyer shall provide the competent authority in the host Member State with any relevant information and documentation, notably on the number of matters he has dealt with and their nature;

(b) the competent authority of the host Member State may verify the effective and regular nature of the activity pursued and may, if need be, request the lawyer to provide, orally or in writing, clarification of or further details on the information and documentation mentioned in point (a).

Reasons shall be given for a decision by the competent authority in the host Member State not to grant an exemption where proof is not provided that the requirements laid down in the first sub-paragraph have been fulfilled, and the decision shall be subject to appeal under domestic law.

2. A lawyer practising under his home-country professional title in a host Member State may, at any time, apply to have his diploma recognised in accordance with Directive 89/48 with a view to gaining admission to the profession of lawyer in the host Member State and practising it under the professional title corresponding to the profession in that Member State.

3. A lawyer practising under his home-country professional title who has effectively and regularly pursued a professional activity in the host Member State

for a period of at least three years but for a lesser period in the law of that Member State may obtain from the competent authority of that State admission to the profession of lawyer in the host Member State and the right to practise it under the professional title corresponding to the profession in that Member State, without having to meet the conditions referred to in Article 4(1)(b) of Directive 89/48, under the conditions and in accordance with the procedures set out below:

(a) The competent authority of the host Member State shall take into account the effective and regular professional activity pursued during the above-mentioned period and any knowledge and professional experience of the law of the host Member State, and any attendance at lectures or seminars on the law of the host Member State, including the rules regulating professional practice and conduct.

(b) The lawyer shall provide the competent authority of the host Member State with any relevant information and documentation, in particular on the matters he has dealt with. Assessment of the lawyer's effective and regular activity in the host Member State and assessment of his capacity to continue the activity he has pursued there shall be carried out by means of an interview with the competent authority of the host Member State in order to verify the regular and effective nature of the activity pursued.

Reasons shall be given for a decision by the competent authority in the host Member State not to grant authorisation where proof is not provided that the requirements laid down in the first sub-paragraph have been fulfilled, and the decision shall be subject to appeal under domestic law.

4. The competent authority of the host Member State may, by reasoned decision subject to appeal under domestic law, refuse to allow the lawyer the benefit of the provisions of this Article if it considers that this would be against public policy, in a particular because of disciplinary proceedings, complaints or incidents of any kind.

5. The representatives of the competent authority entrusted with consideration of the application shall preserve the confidentiality of any information received.

6. A lawyer who gains admission to the profession of lawyer in the host Member State in accordance with paragraphs 1, 2 and 3 shall be entitled to use his home-country professional title, expressed in the official language or one of the official languages of his home Member State, alongside the professional title corresponding to the profession of lawyer in the host Member State.

Article 11 Joint practice

6–177 Where joint practice is authorised in respect of lawyers carrying on their activities under the relevant professional title in the host Member State, the following provisions shall apply in respect of lawyers wishing to carry on activities under that title or registering with the competent authority:

(1) One or more lawyers who belong to the same grouping in their home Member State and who practise under their home-country professional title in a host Member State may pursue their professional activities in a branch or agency of their grouping in the host Member State. However, where the fundamental rules governing that grouping in the home Member State are incompatible with the fundamental rules laid down by law, regulation or administrative action in the host Member State, the latter rules shall prevail insofar as compliance therewith is justified by the public interest in protecting clients and third parties.

(2) Each Member State shall afford two or more lawyers from the same grouping or the same home Member State who practise in its territory under their home-country professional titles access to a form of joint practice. If the host Member State gives its lawyers a choice between several forms of joint practice, those same forms shall also be made available to the

aforementioned lawyers. The manner in which such lawyers practise jointly in the host Member State shall be governed by the laws, regulations and administrative provisions of that State.

(3) The host Member State shall take the measures necessary to permit joint practice also between:

(a) several lawyers from different Member States practising under their home-country professional titles;

(b) one or more lawyers covered by point (a) and one or more lawyers from the host Member State.

The manner in which such lawyers practice jointly in the host Member State shall be governed by the laws, regulations and administrative provisions of that State.

(4) A lawyer who wishes to practise under his home-country professional title shall inform the competent authority in the host Member State of the fact that he is a member of a grouping in his home Member State and furnish any relevant information on that grouping.

(5) Notwithstanding points 1 to 4, a host Member State, insofar as it prohibits lawyers practising under its own relevant professional title from practising the profession of lawyer within a grouping in which some persons are not members of the profession, may refuse to allow a lawyer registered under his home-country professional title to practice in its territory in his capacity as a member of his grouping. The grouping is deemed to include persons who are not members of the profession if

— the capital of the grouping is held entirely or partly, or

— the name under which it practises is used, or

— the decision-making power in that grouping is exercised, *de facto* or *de jure*, by persons who do not have the status of lawyer within the meaning of Article 1(2).

Where the fundamental rules governing a grouping of lawyers in the home Member State are incompatible with the rules in force in the host Member State or with the provisions of the first sub-paragraph, the host Member State may oppose the opening of a branch or agency within its territory without the restrictions laid down in point (1).

Article 12 Name of the grouping

Whatever the manner in which lawyers practise under their home-country **6–178**
professional titles in the host Member State, they may employ the name of any grouping to which they belong in their home Member State.

The host Member State may require that, in addition to the name referred to in the first sub-paragraph, mention be made of the legal form of the grouping in the home Member State and/or of the names of any members of the grouping practising in the host Member State.

Article 13 Co-operation between the competent authorities in the home and host Member States and confidentiality

In order to facilitate the application of this Directive and to prevent its provisions **6–179**
from being misapplied for the sole purpose of circumventing the rules applicable in the host Member State, the competent authority in the host Member State and the competent authority in the home Member State shall collaborate closely and afford each other mutual assistance.

They shall preserve the confidentiality of the information they exchange.

Article 14 Designation of the competent authorities

Member States shall designate the competent authorities empowered to receive **6–180**
the applications and to take the decisions referred to in this Directive by 14 March

2000. They shall communicate this information to the other Member States and to the Commission.

Article 15 Report by the Commission

6–181 Ten years at the latest from the entry into force of this Directive, the Commission shall report to the European Parliament and to the Council on progress in the implementation of the Directive.

After having held all the necessary consultations, it shall on that occasion present its conclusions and any amendments which could be made to the existing system.

Article 16 Implementation

6–182 1. Member States shall bring into force the laws, regulations and administrative provisions necessary to comply with this Directive by 14 March 2000. They shall forthwith inform the Commission thereof.

When Member States adopt these measures, they shall contain a reference to this Directive or shall be accompanied by such reference on the occasion of their official publication. The methods of making such reference shall be adopted by Member States.

2. Member States shall communicate to the Commission the texts of the main provisions of domestic law which they adopt in the field covered by this Directive.

Article 17 Entry into force

6–183 This Directive shall enter into force on the date of its publication in the *Official Journal of the European Communities*.

Article 18 Addressees

6–184 This Directive is addressed to the Member States.

SECTION 4—POSTING OF WORKERS ABROAD

Directive 96/71 of the European Parliament and of the Council of 16 December 1996 concerning the posting of workers in the framework of the provision of services

([1997] OJ L18/1; Doc. Ref. 31996L0071)

The European Parliament and the Council of the European Union,

6–185 Having regard to the Treaty establishing the European Community, and in particular Articles [47](2) and [55] thereof,

Having regard to the proposal from the Commission,[9]

Having regard to the opinion of the Economic and Social Committee,[10]

Acting in accordance with the procedure laid down in Article [251] of the Treaty,[11]

(1) Whereas, pursuant to Article 3(c) of the Treaty, the abolition, as between Member States, of obstacles to the free movement of persons and services constitutes one of the objectives of the Community;

(2) Whereas, for the provision of services, any restrictions based on nationality or residence requirements are prohibited under the Treaty with effect from the end of the transitional period;

---

[9] [1991] OJ C225/6 and [1993] OJ C187/5.

[10] [1992] OJ C49/41.

[11] Opinion of the European Parliament of 10 February 1993 ([1993] OJ C72/78), Council common position of 3 June 1996 ([1996] OJ C220/1) and Decision of the European Parliament of 18 September 1996, Council Decision of 24 September 1996.

(3) Whereas the completion of the internal market offers a dynamic environment for the transnational provision of services, prompting a growing number of undertakings to post employees abroad temporarily to perform work in the territory of a Member State other than the State in which they are habitually employed;

(4) Whereas the provision of services may take the form either of performance of work by an undertaking on its account and under its direction, under a contract concluded between that undertaking and the party for whom the services are intended, or of the hiring-out of workers for use by an undertaking in the framework of a public or a private contract;

(5) Whereas any such promotion of the transnational provision of services requires a climate of fair competition and measures guaranteeing respect for the rights of workers;

(6) Whereas the transnationalisation of the employment relationship raises problems with regard to the legislation applicable to the employment relationship; whereas it is in the interests of the parties to lay down the terms and conditions governing the employment relationship envisaged;

(7) Whereas the Rome Convention of 19 June 1980 on the law applicable to contractual obligations,[12] signed by 12 Member States, entered into force on 1 April 1991 in the majority of Member States;

(8) Whereas Article 3 of that Convention provides, as a general rule, for the free choice of law made by the parties; whereas, in the absence of choice, the contract is to be governed, according to Article 6(2), by the law of the country, in which the employee habitually carries out his work in performance of the contract, even if he is temporarily employed in another country, or, if the employee does not habitually carry out his work in any one country, by the law of the country in which the place of business through which he was engaged is situated, unless it appears from the circumstances as a whole that the contract is more closely connected with another country, in which case the contract is to be governed by the law of that country;

(9) Whereas, according to Article 6(1) of the said Convention, the choice of law made by the parties is not to have the result of depriving the employee of the protection afforded to him by the mandatory rules of the law which would be applicable under paragraph 2 of that Article in the absence of choice;

(10) Whereas Article 7 of the said Convention lays down, subject to certain conditions, that effect may be given, concurrently with the law declared applicable, to the mandatory rules of the law of another country, in particular the law of the Member State within whose territory the worker is temporarily posted;

(11) Whereas, according to the principle of precedence of Community law laid down in its Article 20, the said Convention does not affect the application of provisions which, in relation to a particular matter, lay down choice-of-law rules relating to contractual obligations and which are or will be contained in acts of the institutions of the European Communities or in national laws harmonised in implementation of such acts;

(12) Whereas Community law does not preclude Member States from applying their legislation, or collective agreements entered into by employers and labour, to any person who is employed, even temporarily, within their territory, although his employer is established in another Member State; whereas Community law does not forbid Member States to guarantee the observance of those rules by the appropriate means;

(13) Whereas the laws of the Member States must be co-ordinated in order to lay down a nucleus of mandatory rules for minimum protection to be observed in the host country by employers who post workers to perform temporary work in

---

[12] [1980] OJ L266/1.

the territory of a Member State where the services are provided; whereas such co-ordination can be achieved only by means of Community law;

(14) Whereas a "hard core" of clearly defined protective rules should be observed by the provider of the services notwithstanding the duration of the worker's posting;

(15) Whereas it should be laid down that, in certain clearly defined cases of assembly and/or installation of goods, the provisions on minimum rates of pay and minimum paid annual holidays do not apply;

(16) Whereas there should also be some flexibility in application of the provisions concerning minimum rates of pay and the minimum length of paid annual holidays; whereas, when the length of the posting is not more than one month, Member States may, under certain conditions, derogate from the provisions concerning minimum rates of pay or provide for the possibility of derogation by means of collective agreements; whereas, where the amount of work to be done is not significant, Member States may derogate from the provisions concerning minimum rates of pay and the minimum length of paid annual holidays;

(17) Whereas the mandatory rules for minimum protection in force in the host country must not prevent the application of terms and conditions of employment which are more favourable to workers;

(18) Whereas the principle that undertakings established outside the Community must not receive more favourable treatment than undertakings established in the territory of a Member State should be upheld;

(19) Whereas, without prejudice to other provisions of Community law, this Directive does not entail the obligation to give legal recognition to the existence of temporary employment undertakings, nor does it prejudice the application by Member States of their laws concerning the hiring-out of workers and temporary employment undertakings to undertakings not established in their territory but operating therein in the framework of the provision of services;

(20) Whereas this Directive does not affect either the agreements concluded by the Community with third countries or the laws of Member States concerning the access to their territory of third-country providers of services; whereas this Directive is also without prejudice to national laws relating to the entry, residence and access to employment of third-country workers;

(21) Whereas Council Regulation 1408/71 of 14 June 1971 on the application of social security schemes to employed persons and their families moving within the Community[13] lays down the provisions applicable with regard to social security benefits and contributions;

(22) Whereas this Directive is without prejudice to the law of the Member States concerning collective action to defend the interests of trades and professions;

(23) Whereas competent bodies in different Member States must co-operate with each other in the application of this Directive; whereas Member States must provide for appropriate remedies in the event of failure to comply with this Directive;

(24) Whereas it is necessary to guarantee proper application of this Directive and to that end to make provision for close collaboration between the Commission and the Member States;

(25) Whereas five years after adoption of this Directive at the latest the Commission must review the detailed rules for implementing this Directive with a view to proposing, where appropriate, the necessary amendments,

[13] [1971(II)] OJ, Eng. Spec. Ed., p.416. Regulation as last amended by Regulation 3096/95 ([1995] OJ L335/10).

Have adopted this Directive:

Article 1 Scope

1. This Directive shall apply to undertakings established in a Member State which, in the framework of the transnational provision of services, post workers, in accordance with paragraph 3, to the territory of a Member State. **6–186**

2. This Directive shall not apply to merchant navy undertakings as regards seagoing personnel.

3. This Directive shall apply to the extent that the undertakings referred to in paragraph 1 take one of the following transnational measures:
(a) post workers to the territory of a Member State on their account and under their direction, under a contract concluded between the undertaking making the posting and the party for whom the services are intended, operating in that Member State, provided there is an employment relationship between the undertaking making the posting and the worker during the period of posting; or
(b) post workers to an establishment or to an undertaking owned by the group in the territory of a Member State, provided there is an employment relationship between the undertaking making the posting and the worker during the period of posting; or
(c) being a temporary employment undertaking or placement agency, hire out a worker to a user undertaking established or operating in the territory of a Member State, provided there is an employment relationship between the temporary employment undertaking or placement agency and the worker during the period of posting.

4. Undertakings established in a non-member State must not be given more favourable treatment than undertakings established in a Member State.

Article 2 Definition

1. For the purposes of this Directive, "posted worker" means a worker who, for a limited period, carries out his work in the territory of a Member State other than the State in which he normally works. **6–187**

2. For the purposes of this Directive, the definition of a worker is that which applies in the law of the Member State to whose territory the worker is posted.

Article 3 Terms and conditions of employment

1. Member States shall ensure that, whatever the law applicable to the employment relationship, the undertakings referred to in Article 1(1) guarantee workers posted to their territory the terms and conditions of employment covering the following matters which, in the Member State where the work is carried out, are laid down: **6–188**
— by law, regulation or administrative provision, and/or
— by collective agreements or arbitration awards which have been declared universally applicable within the meaning of paragraph 8, insofar as they concern the activities referred to in the Annex:
  (a) maximum work periods and minimum rest periods;
  (b) minimum paid annual holidays;

(c) the minimum rates of pay, including overtime rates; this point does not apply to supplementary occupational retirement pension schemes;
(d) the conditions of hiring-out of workers, in particular the supply of workers by temporary employment undertakings;
(e) health, safety and hygiene at work;
(f) protective measures with regard to the terms and conditions of employment of pregnant women or women who have recently given birth, of children and of young people;
(g) equality of treatment between men and women and other provisions on non-discrimination.

For the purposes of this Directive, the concept of minimum rates of pay referred to in paragraph 1(c) is defined by the national law and/or practice of the Member State to whose territory the worker is posted.

2. In the case of initial assembly and/or first installation of goods where this is an integral part of a contract for the supply of goods and necessary for taking the goods supplied into use and carried out by the skilled and/or specialist workers of the supplying undertaking, the first sub-paragraph of paragraph 1(b) and (c) shall not apply, if the period of posting does not exceed eight days. This provision shall not apply to activities in the field of building work listed in the Annex.

3. Member States may, after consulting employers and labour, in accordance with the traditions and practices of each Member State, decide not to apply the first sub-paragraph of paragraph 1(c) in the cases referred to in Article 1(3)(a) and (b) when the length of the posting does not exceed one month.

4. Member States may, in accordance with national laws and/or practices, provide that exemptions may be made from the first sub-paragraph of paragraph 1(c) in the cases referred to in Article 1(3)(a) and (b) and from a decision by a Member State within the meaning of paragraph 3 of this Article, by means of collective agreements within the meaning of paragraph 8 of this Article, concerning one or more sectors of activity, where the length of the posting does not exceed one month.

5. Member States may provide for exemptions to be granted from the first sub-paragraph of paragraph 1(b) and (c) in the cases referred to in Article 1(3)(a) and (b) on the grounds that the amount of work to be done is not significant. Member States availing themselves of the option referred to in the first sub-paragraph shall lay down the criteria which the work to be performed must meet in order to be considered as "non-significant".

6. The length of the posting shall be calculated on the basis of a reference period of one year from the beginning of the posting. For the purpose of such calculations, account shall be taken of any previous periods for which the post has been filled by a posted worker.

7. Paragraphs 1 to 6 shall not prevent application of terms and conditions of employment which are more favourable to workers.

Allowances specific to the posting shall be considered to be part of the minimum wage, unless they are paid in reimbursement of expenditure actually incurred on account of the posting, such as expenditure on travel, board and lodging.

8. "Collective agreements or arbitration awards which have been declared universally applicable" means collective agreements or arbitration awards which must be observed by all undertakings in the geographical area and in the profession or industry concerned.

In the absence of a system for declaring collective agreements or arbitration awards to be of universal application within the meaning of the first sub-paragraph, Member States may, if they so decide, base themselves on:

— collective agreements or arbitration awards which are generally applicable to all similar undertakings in the geographical area and in the profession or industry concerned, and/or

— collective agreements which have been concluded by the most representative employers' and labour organisations at national level and which are applied throughout national territory,

provided that their application to the undertakings referred to in Article 1(1) ensures equality of treatment on matters listed in the first sub-paragraph of paragraph 1 of this Article between those undertakings and the other undertakings referred to in this sub-paragraph which are in a similar position.

Equality of treatment, within the meaning of this Article, shall be deemed to exist where national undertakings in a similar position:

— are subject, in the place in question or in the sector concerned, to the same obligations as posting undertakings as regards the matters listed in the first sub-paragraph of paragraph 1, and

— are required to fulfil such obligations with the same effects.

9. Member States may provide that the undertakings referred to in Article 1(1) must guarantee workers referred to in Article 1(3)(c) the terms and conditions which apply to temporary workers in the Member State where the work is carried out.

10. This Directive shall not preclude the application by Member States, in compliance with the Treaty, to national undertakings and to the undertakings of other States, on a basis of equality of treatment, of:

— terms and conditions of employment on matters other than those referred to in the first sub-paragraph of paragraph 1 in the case of public policy provisions,

— terms and conditions of employment laid down in the collective agreements or arbitration awards within the meaning of paragraph 8 and concerning activities other than those referred to in the Annex.

Article 4 Cooperation on information

1. For the purposes of implementing this Directive, Member States shall, in accordance with national legislation and/or practice, designate one or more liaison offices or one or more competent national bodies. **6–189**

2. Member States shall make provision for cooperation between the public authorities which, in accordance with national legislation, are responsible for monitoring the terms and conditions of employment referred to in Article 3. Such cooperation shall in particular consist in replying to reasoned requests from those authorities for information on the transnational hiring-out of workers, including manifest abuses or possible cases of unlawful transnational activities.

The Commission and the public authorities referred to in the first sub-paragraph shall cooperate closely in order to examine any difficulties which might arise in the application of Article 3(10).

Mutual administrative assistance shall be provided free of charge.

3. Each Member State shall take the appropriate measures to make the information on the terms and conditions of employment referred to in Article 3 generally available.

4. Each Member State shall notify the other Member States and the Commission of the liaison offices and/or competent bodies referred to in paragraph 1.

Article 5 Measures

6–190 Member States shall take appropriate measures in the event of failure to comply with this Directive. They shall in particular ensure that adequate procedures are available to workers and/or their representatives for the enforcement of obligations under this Directive.

Article 6 Jurisdiction

6–191 In order to enforce the right to the terms and conditions of employment guaranteed in Article 3, judicial proceedings may be instituted in the Member State in whose territory the worker is or was posted, without prejudice, where applicable, to the right, under existing international conventions on jurisdiction, to institute proceedings in another State.

Article 7 Implementation

6–192 Member States shall adopt the laws, regulations and administrative provisions necessary to comply with this Directive by 16 December 1999 at the latest. They shall forthwith inform the Commission thereof. When Member States adopt these provisions, they shall contain a reference to this Directive or shall be accompanied by such reference on the occasion of their official publication. The methods of making such reference shall be laid down by Member States.

Article 8 Commission review

6–193 By 16 December 2001 at the latest, the Commission shall review the operation of this Directive with a view to proposing the necessary amendments to the Council where appropriate.

Article 9 [Addressees]

6–194 This Directive is addressed to the Member States.

Annex

6–195 The activities mentioned in Article 3(1), second indent, include all building work relating to the construction, repair, upkeep, alteration or demolition of buildings, and in particular the following work:

1. excavation
2. earthmoving
3. actual building work
4. assembly and dismantling of prefabricated elements
5. fitting out or installation
6. alterations
7. renovation
8. repairs
9. dismantling
10. demolition
11. maintenance
12. upkeep, painting and cleaning work
13. improvements.

SECTION 5—SOCIAL SECURITY FOR MIGRANT WORKERS

Council Regulation 1408/71 of 14 June 1971 on the application of social security schemes to employed persons, to self-employed persons and to members of their families moving within the Community

([1997] OJ L28/1; Doc. Ref. 31997R0118)[14]

The Council of the European Union,

Having regard to the Treaty establishing the European Community, and in particular Articles [42] and [308] thereof, **6–196**

Having regard to the proposal from the Commission,

Having regard to the opinion of the European Parliament,

Having regard to the opinion of the Economic and Social Committee,

[1] Whereas the provisions for coordination of national security legislations fall within the framework of freedom of movement for workers who are nationals of Member States and should contribute towards the improvement of their standard of living and conditions of employment;

[2] Whereas freedom of movement for persons, which is one of the cornerstones of the Community, is not confined to employed persons but also extends to self-employed persons in the framework of the freedom of establishment and the freedom to supply services;

[3] Whereas the considerable differences existing between national legislations as regards the persons to whom they apply make it preferable to establish the principle that the Regulation applies to all persons insured under social security schemes for employed persons and for self-employed persons or by virtue of pursuing employment or self-employment;

[4] Whereas it is necessary to respect the special characteristics of national social security legislations and to draw up only a system of coordination;

[5] Whereas it is necessary, within the framework of that coordination, to guarantee within the Community equality of treatment under the various national legislations to workers living in the Member States and their dependants and their survivors;

[6] Whereas the provisions for coordination must guarantee that workers moving within the Community and their dependants and their survivors retain the rights and the advantages acquired and in the course of being acquired;

[7] Whereas these objectives must be attained in particular by aggregation of all the periods taken into account under the various national legislations for the purpose of acquiring and retaining the right to benefits and of calculating the amount of benefits, and by the provision of benefits for the various categories of persons covered by the Regulation regardless of their place of residence within the Community;

[8] Whereas employed persons and self-employed persons moving within the Community should be subject to the social security scheme of only one single Member State in order to avoid overlapping of national legislations applicable and the complications which could result therefrom;

[9] Whereas the instances in which a person should be subject simultaneously to the legislation of two Member States as an exception to the general rule should be as limited in number and scope as possible;

[10] Whereas with a view to guaranteeing the equality of treatment of all workers occupied on the territory of a Member State as effectively as possible, it is appropriate to determine as the legislation applicable, as a general rule, that of the

[14] Note: the text reproduced below is derived from a consolidated version of Regulation 1408/71 as reproduced in Annex A, Pt I to Regulation 118/97 ([1997] OJ L28/1) and incorporates amendments made up to April 2003.

Member State in which the person concerned pursues employment or self-employment;

[11] Whereas in certain situations which justify other criteria of applicability, it is possible to derogate from this general rule;

[12] Whereas certain benefits foreseen under national laws may fall simultaneously within social security and social assistance, because of the personal scope of their application, their objectives and their manner of application, it is necessary to lay down a system of coordination, which takes into account the special characteristics of the benefits concerned, that should be included in the Regulation in order to protect the interests of migrant workers in accordance with the provisions of the Treaty;

[13] Whereas such benefits should be granted, in respect of persons falling within the scope of this Regulation, solely in accordance with the legislation of the country of residence of the person concerned or of the members of his or her family, with such aggregation of periods of residence completed in any other Member State as is necessary and without discrimination on grounds of nationality;

[14] Whereas it is necessary to lay down specific rules, in particular in the field of sickness and unemployment, for frontier workers and seasonal workers, taking account of the specific nature of their situation;

[15] Whereas in the field of sickness and maternity benefits, it is necessary to guarantee the protection of persons living or staying in a Member State other than the competent Member State;

[16] Whereas the specific position of pension claimants and pensioners and the members of their families calls for the provisions governing sickness insurance to adapted to their situation;

[17] Whereas for invalidity benefits a system of coordination should be drawn up which respects the specific characteristics of national legislations; whereas it is therefore necessary to make a distinction between legislations under which the amount of invalidity benefit is independent of the length of insurance and legislations under which the amount depends on the aforementioned length;

[18] Whereas the differences between the schemes in the Member States call for the adoption of rules of coordination which are applicable in the case of aggravation of invalidity;

[19] Whereas it is expedient that a system for the award of old-age benefits and survivors benefits be worked out where the employed or self-employed person has been subject to the legislation of one or more Member States;

[20] Whereas there is a need to determine the amount of a pension calculated in accordance with the method used for aggregation and pro rata calculation and guaranteed by Community law where the application of national legislation, including provisions concerning reduction, suspension or withdrawal, is less favourable than the aforementioned method;

[21] Whereas, to protect migrant workers and their survivors against an excessively stringent application of the national provisions concerning reduction, suspension or withdrawal, it is necessary to include provisions laying down strict rules for the application of these provisions;

[22] Whereas, in respect of benefits for accidents at work and occupational diseases, it is necessary, for the purpose of affording protection, that rules be laid down covering the situation of persons residing or staying in a Member State other than the competent Member State;

[23] Whereas it is necessary to lay down specific provisions for death grants;

[24] Whereas, in order to secure mobility of labour under improved conditions, it is necessary henceforth to ensure closer coordination between the unemployment insurance schemes and the unemployment assistance schemes of all the Member States;

[25] Whereas it is therefore particularly appropriate, in order to facilitate search for employment in the various Member States, to grant to an unemployed worker,

for a limited period, the unemployment benefits provided for by the legislation of the Member State to which he was last subject;

[26] Whereas, with a view to determining the legislation applicable to family benefits, the criterion of employment ensures equal treatment between all workers subject to the same legislation;

[27] Whereas, in order to avoid unwarranted overlapping of benefits, there is a need to provide for rules of priority in the case of overlapping of the right to family benefits under the legislation of the competent State and under the legislation of the country of residence of the members of the family;

[28] Whereas the legislations of the Member States differ from each other and are specific in nature, it is considered necessary to draw up specific rules for the coordination of the national schemes providing benefits for dependent children of pensioners and for orphans;

[29] Whereas it is necessary to establish an Administrative Commission consisting of a government representative from each of the Member States, charged in particular with dealing with all administrative questions or questions of interpretation arising from the provisions of this Regulation, and to further cooperation between the Member States;

[30] Whereas it is desirable, within the framework of an Advisory Committee, to have the representatives of workers and employers examine the issues treated by the Administrative Commission;

[31] Whereas it is necessary to lay down special provisions which correspond to the special characteristics of the national legislations in order to facilitate the application of the rules of coordination,

Has adopted this Regulation:

Title I—General Provisions

Article 1 Definitions

For the purpose of this Regulation: **6–197**

(a) "employed person" and "self-employed person" mean respectively:

[(i) any person who is insured, compulsorily or on an optional continued basis, for one or more of the contingencies covered by the branches of a social security scheme for employed or self-employed persons or by a special scheme for civil servants;][15]

(ii) any person who is compulsorily insured for one or more of the contingencies covered by the branches of social security dealt with in this Regulation, under a social security dealt with in this Regulation, under a social security scheme for all residents or for the whole working population, if such person:

— can be identified as an employed or self-employed person by virtue of the manner in which such scheme is administered or financed, or,

— failing such criteria, is insured for some other contingency specified in Annex I under a scheme for employed or self-employed persons, or under a scheme referred to in (iii), either compulsorily or on an optional continued basis, or, where no such scheme exists in the Member State concerned, complies with the definition given in Annex I;

(iii) any person who is compulsorily insured for several of the contingencies covered by the branches dealt with in this Regulation, under a standard social security scheme for the whole rural population in accordance with the criteria laid down in Annex I;

(iv) any person who is voluntarily insured for one or more of the contingencies covered by the branches dealt with in this Regulation, under a social security scheme of a Member State for employed or self-employed persons or for all residents or for certain categories of residents:

---

[15] Words replaced by Regulation 1606/98, Art. 1(1)(a) as from 25 October 1998.

— if such person carries out an activity as an employed or self-employed person, or
— if such person has previously been compulsorily insured for the same contingency under a scheme for employed or self-employed persons for the same Member State;

(b) "frontier worker" means any employed or self-employed person who pursues his occupation in the territory of a Member State and resides in the territory of another Member State to which he returns as a rule daily or at least once a week; however, a frontier worker who is posted elsewhere in the territory of the same or another Member State by the undertaking to which he is normally attached, or who engages in the provision of services elsewhere in the territory of the same or another Member State, shall retain the status of frontier worker for a period not exceeding four months, even if he is prevented, during that period, from returning daily or at least once a week to the place where he resides;

(c) "seasonal worker" means any employed person who goes to the territory of a Member State other than the one in which he is resident to do work there of a seasonal nature for an undertaking or an employer of that State for a period which may on no account exceed eight months, and who stays in the territory of the said State for the duration of this work; work of a seasonal nature shall be taken to mean work which, being dependent on the succession of the seasons, automatically recurs each year;

[(ca) "student" means any person other than an employed or self-employed person or a member of his family or survivor within the meaning of this Regulation who studies or receives vocational training leading to a qualification officially recognised by the authorities of a Member State, and is insured under a general social security scheme or a special social security scheme applicable to students;][16]

(d) "refugee" shall have the meaning assigned to it in Article 1 of the Convention of the Status of Refugees, signed at Geneva on 28 July 1951;

(e) "stateless person" shall have the meaning assigned to it in Article 1 of the Convention on the Status of Stateless Persons, signed in New York on 28 September 1954;

(f) (i) "member of the family" means any person defined or recognised as a member of the family or designated as a member of the household by the legislation under which benefits are provided or, in the cases referred to in Articles 22(1)(a) and 31, by the legislation of the Member State in whose territory such person resides; where, however, the said legislations regard as a member of the family or a member of the household only a person living under the same roof as the [employed or self-employed person or student],[17] this condition shall be considered satisfied if the person in question is mainly dependent on that person. [Where the legislation of a Member State does not enable members of the family to be distinguished from the other persons to whom it applies, the term "member of the family" shall have the meaning given to it in Annex I];[18]

(ii) where, however, the benefits concerned are benefits for disabled persons granted under the legislation of a Member State to all nationals of that State who fulfil the prescribed conditions, the term "member of the family" means at least the spouse of an [employed or self-employed person or student][19] and the children of such person who are either minors or dependent upon such person;

[16] Words inserted by Regulation 307/1999, Art. 1(1)(a) as from 1 May 1999.
[17] Words replaced by Regulation 307/1999, Art. 1(1)(b) as from 1 May 1999.
[18] Words replaced by Regulation 1290/97 Art. 1, point 1 as from 4 October 1997.
[19] Words replaced by Regulation 307/1999, Art. 1(1)(b) as from 1 May 1999.

(g) "survivor" means any person defined or recognised as such by the legislation under which the benefits are granted; where, however, the said legislation regards as a survivor only a person who was living under the same roof as the deceased, this condition shall be considered satisfied if such person was mainly dependent on the deceased;

(h) "residence" means habitual residence;

(i) "stay" means temporary residence;

(j) "legislation" means in respect of each Member State statutes, regulations and other provisions and all other implementing measures, present or future, relating to the branches and schemes of social security covered by Article 4(1) and (2) or those special non-contributory benefits covered by Article 4(2a).

The term excludes provisions of existing or future industrial agreements, whether or not they have been the subject of a decision by the authorities rendering them compulsory or extending their scope. However, in so far as such provisions:

(i) serve to put into effect compulsory insurance imposed by the laws and regulations referred to in the preceding sub-paragraph; or

(ii) set up a scheme administered by the same institution as that which administers the schemes set up by the laws and regulations referred to in the preceding sub-paragraph,

the limitation on the term may at any time be lifted by a declaration of the Member State concerned specifying the schemes of such a kind to which this Regulation applies. Such a declaration shall be notified and published in accordance with the provisions of Article 97.

The provisions of the preceding sub-paragraph shall not have the effect of exempting from the application of this Regulation the schemes to which Regulation No. 3 applied.

The term "legislation" also excludes provisions governing special schemes for self-employed persons the creation of which is left to the initiatives of those concerned or which apply only to a part of the territory of the Member State concerned, irrespective of whether or not the authorities decided to make them compulsory or extend their scope. The special schemes in question are specified in Annex II;

[(ja) "special scheme for civil servants" means any social security scheme which is different from the general social security scheme applicable to employed persons in the Member States concerned and to which all, or certain categories of, civil servants or persons treated as such are directly subject;][20]

(k) "social security convention" means any bilateral or multilateral instrument which binds or will bind two or more Member States exclusively, and any other multilateral instrument which binds or will bind at least two Member States and one or more other States in the field of social security, for all or part of the branches and schemes set out in Article 4(1) and (2), together with agreements, of whatever kind, concluded pursuant to the said instruments;

(l) "competent authority" means, in respect of each Member State, the Minister, Ministers or other equivalent authority responsible for social security schemes throughout or in any part of the territory of the State in question;

(m) "Administrative Commission" means the Commission referred to in Article 80;

(n) "institution" means, in respect of each Member State, the body or authority responsible for administering all or part of the legislation;

(o) "competent institution" means:

(i) the institution with which the person concerned is insured at the time of the application for benefit; or

[20] Words inserted by Regulation 1606/98, Art. 1(1)(b) as from 25 October 1998.

(ii) the institution from which the person concerned is entitled or would be entitled to benefits if he or a member or members of his family were resident in the territory of the Member State in which the institution is situated; or

(iii) the institution designated by the competent authority of the Member State concerned; or

(iv) in the case of a scheme relating to an employer's liability in respect of the benefits set out in Article 4(1), either the employer or the insurer involved or, in default thereof, a body or authority designated by the competent authority of the Member State concerned;

(p) "institution of the place of residence" and "institution of the place of stay" mean respectively the institution which is competent to provide benefits in the place where the person concerned resides and the institution which is competent to provide benefits in the place where the person concerned is staying, under the legislation administered by that institution or, where no such institution exists, the institution designated by the competent authority of the Member State in question;

(q) "competent State" means the Member State in whose territory the competent institution is situated;

(r) "periods of insurance" means periods of contribution or period of employment or self-employment as defined or recognised as periods of insurance by the legislation under which they were completed or considered as completed, and all periods treated as such, where they are regarded by the said legislation as equivalent to periods of insurance; [periods completed under a special scheme for civil servants are also considered as periods of insurance;][21]

(s) "periods of employment" and "periods of self-employment" mean periods so defined or recognised by the legislation under which they were completed, and all periods treated as such, where they are regarded by the said legislation as equivalent to periods of employment or of self-employment; [periods completed under a special scheme for civil servants are also considered as periods of employment;][22]

(sa) "periods of residence" means periods as defined or recognised as such by the legislation under which they were completed or considered as completed;

(t) "benefits" and "pensions" mean all benefits and pensions, including all elements thereof payable out of public funds, revalorisation increases and supplementary allowances, subject to the provisions of Title III, as also lump-sum benefits which may be paid in lieu of pensions, and payments made by way of reimbursement of contributions;

(u) (i) the term "family benefits" means all benefits in kind or in cash intended to meet family expenses under the legislation provided for in Article 4(1)(h), excluding the special childbirth or adoption allowances referred to in Annex II;

(ii) "family allowances" means periodical cash benefits granted exclusively by reference to the number and, where appropriate, the age of members of the family;

(v) death grants means any once-for-all payment in the event of death exclusive of the lump-sum benefits referred to in sub-paragraph (t).

[Article 2 Persons covered

6–198 1. This Regulation shall apply to employed or self-employed persons and to students who are or have been subject to the legislation of one or more Member States and who are nationals of one of the Member States or who are stateless

[21] Words inserted by Regulation 16076/98, Art. 1(1)(c) as from 25 October 1998.

[22] Words inserted by Regulation 1606/98, Art. 1(1)(d) as from 25 October 1998.

persons or refugees residing within the territory of one of the Member States, as well as to the members of their families and their survivors.

2. This Regulation shall apply to the survivors of employed or self-employed persons and of students who have been subject to the legislation of one or more Member States, irrespective of the nationality of such persons, where their survivors are nationals of one of the Member States, or stateless persons or refugees residing within the territory of one of the Member States.][23]

Article 3 Equality of treatment

1. Subject to the special provisions of this Regulation, persons resident in the territory of one of the Member States to whom this Regulation applies shall be subject to the same obligations and enjoy the same benefits under the legislation of any Member State as the nationals of the State. **6–199**

2. The provisions of paragraph 1 shall apply to the right to elect members of the organs of social security institutions or to participate in their nomination, but shall not affect the legislative provisions of any Member State relating to eligibility or methods of nomination of persons concerned to those organs.

3. Save as provided in Annex III, the provisions of social security conventions which remain in force pursuant to Article 7(2)(c) and the provisions of conventions concluded pursuant to Article 8(1), shall apply to all persons to whom this Regulation applies.

Article 4 Matters covered

1. This Regulation shall apply to all legislation concerning the following branches of social security: **6–200**
(a) sickness and maternity benefits;
(b) invalidity benefits, including those intended for the maintenance or improvement of earning capacity;
(c) old-age benefits;
(d) survivors' benefits;
(e) benefits in respect of accidents at work and occupational diseases;
(f) death grants;
(g) unemployment benefits;
(h) family benefits.

2. This Regulation shall apply to all general and special social security schemes, whether contributory or non-contributory, and to schemes concerning the liability of an employer or shipowner in respect of the benefits referred to in paragraph 1.

2a. This Regulation shall also apply to special non-contributory benefits which are provided under legislation or schemes other than those referred to in paragraph 1 or excluded by virtue of paragraph 4, where such benefits are intended:
(a) either to provide supplementary, substitute or ancillary cover agaisnt the risks covered by the branches of social security referred to in paragraph 1(a) to (h); or
(b) solely as specific protection for the disabled.

[23] Article 2 replaced by Regulation 307/1999 Art. 1(2) as from 1 May 1999. With effect from 1 June 2003, the provisions of Regulations 1408/71 and 574/72 are extended to nationals of third countries who are not already covered by those provisions solely on the ground of their nationality, as well as to members of their families and to their survivors (see Regulation 859/2003, [2003] OJ L124/1). This depends on the individuals being legally resident in the territory of a Member State.

2b. This Regulation shall not apply to the provisions in the legislation of a Member State concerning special non-contributory benefits, referred to in Annex II, Section III, the validity of which is confined to part of its territory.

3. The provisions of Title III of this Regulation shall not, however, affect the legislative provisions of any Member State concerning a shipowner's liability.

4. This Regulation shall not apply to social and medical assistance, to benefit schemes for victims of war or its consequences [...].[24]

Article 5 Declarations by the Member States on the scope of this Regulation

6–201 The Member States shall specify the legislation and schemes referred to in Article 4(1) and (2), the special non-contributory benefits referred to in Article 4(2a), the minimum benefits referred to in Article 50 and the benefits referred to in Articles 77 and 78 in declarations to be notified and published in accordance with Article 97.

Article 6 Social security conventions replaced by this Regulation

6–202 Subject to the provisions of Article 7, 8 and 46(4) this Regulation shall, as regards persons and matters which it covers, replace the provisions of any social security convention binding either;

(a) two or more Member States exclusively, or
(b) at least two Member States and one or more other States, where settlement of the cases concerned does not involve any institution of one of the latter States.

Article 7 International provisions not affected by this Regulation

6–203 1. This Regulation shall not affect obligations arising from:

(a) any convention adopted by the International Labour Conference which, after ratification by one or more Member States, has entered into force;
(b) the European Interim Agreements on Social Security of 11 December 1953 concluded between the Member States of the Council of Europe.

2. The provisions of Article 6 notwithstanding, the following shall continue to apply:

(a) the provisions of the Agreements of 27 July 1950 and 30 November 1979 concerning social security for Rhine boatmen;
(b) the provisions of the European Convention of 9 July 1956 concerning social security for workers in international transport;
(c) the provisions of the social security conventions listed in Annex III.

Article 8 Conclusion of conventions between Member States

6–204 1. Two or more Member States may, as need arises, conclude conventions with each other based on the principles and in the spirit of this Regulation.

2. Each Member State shall notify, in accordance with the provisions of Article 97(1), any convention concluded with another Member State under the provisions of paragraph 1.

Article 9 Admission to voluntary or optional continued insurance

6–205 1. The provisions of the legislation of any Member State which make admission to voluntary or optional continued insurance conditional upon residence in the

[24] Words deleted by Regulation 1606/98, Art. 1(3) as from 25 October 1998.

territory of that State shall not apply to persons resident in the territory of another Member State, provided that at some time in their past working life they were subject to the legislation of the first State as employed or as self-employed persons.

2. Where under the legislation of a Member State, admission to voluntary or optional continued insurance is conditional upon completion of periods of insurance, the periods of insurance or residence completed under the legislation of another Member State shall be taken into account, to the extent required, as if they were completed under the legislation of the first State.

Article 9a Prolongation of the reference period

Where, under the legislation of a Member State, recognition of entitlement to a benefit is conditional upon completion of a minimum period of insurance during a specific period preceding the contingency insured against (reference period) and where the aforementioned legislation provides that the periods during which the benefits have been granted under the legislation of that Member State or periods devoted to the upbringing of children in the territory of that Member State shall give rise to prolongation of the reference period, periods during which invalidity pensions or old-age pensions or sickness benefits, unemployment benefits or benefits for accidents at work (except for pensions) have been awarded under the legislation of another Member State and periods devoted to the upbringing of children in the territory of another Member State shall likewise give rise to prolongation of the aforesaid reference period. **6–206**

Article 10 Waiving of residence clauses—Effect of compulsory insurance on reimbursement of contributions

1. Save as otherwise provided in this Regulation invalidity, old-age or survivors' cash benefits, pensions for accidents at work or occupational diseases and death grants acquired under the legislation of one or more Member States shall not be subject to any reduction, modification, suspension, withdrawal or confiscation by reason of the fact that the recipient resides in the territory of a Member State other than that in which the institution responsible for payment is situated. **6–207**

The first sub-paragraph shall also apply to lump-sum benefits granted in cases of remarriage of a surviving spouse who was entitled to a survivors' pension.

2. Where under the legislation of a Member State reimbursement of contributions is conditional upon the person concerned having ceased to be subject to compulsory insurance, this condition shall not be considered satisfied as long as the person concerned is subject to compulsory insurance [...][25] under the legislation of another Member State.

Article 10a Special non-contributory benefits

1. Notwithstanding the provisions of Article 10 and Title III, persons to whom this Regulation applies shall be granted the special non-contributory cash benefits referred to in Article 4(2a) exclusively in the territory of the Member State in which they reside, in accordance with the legislation of that State, provided that such benefits are listed in Annex IIa. Such benefits shall be granted by and at the expense of the institution of the place of residence. **6–208**

2. The institution of a Member State under whose legislation entitlement to benefits covered by paragraph 1 is subject to the completion of periods of employment, self-employment or residence shall regard, to the extent necessary, periods of employment, self-employment or residence completed in the territory

[25] Words deleted by Regulation 307/1999, Art. 1(4) as from 1 May 1999.

of any other Member State as periods completed in the territory of the first Member State.

3. Where entitlement to a benefit covered by paragraph 1 but granted in the form of a supplement is subject, under the legislation of a Member State, to receipt of a benefit covered by Article 4(1)(a) to (h), and no such benefit is due under that legislation, any corresponding benefit granted under the legislation of any other Member State shall be treated as a benefit granted under the legislation of the first Member State for the purposes of entitlement to the supplement.

4. Where the granting of a disability or invalidity benefit covered by paragraph 1 is subject, under the legislation of a Member State, to the condition that the disability or invalidity should be diagnosed for the first time in the territory of that Member State, this condition shall be deemed to be fulfilled where such diagnosis is made for the first time in the territory of another Member State.

Article 11 Revalorisation of benefits

6–209 Rules for revalorisation provided by the legislation of a Member State shall apply to benefits due under that legislation taking into account the provisions of this Regulation.

Article 12 Prevention of overlapping of benefits

6–210 1. This Regulation can neither confer nor maintain the right to several benefits of the same kind for one and the same period of compulsory insurance. However, this provision shall not apply to benefits in respect of invalidity, old age, death (pensions) or occupational disease whch are awarded by the institutions of two or more Member States, in accordance with the provisions of Articles 41, 43(2) and (3), 46, 50 and 51 or Article 60(1)(b).

2. Save as otherwise provided in this Regulation, the provisions of the legislations of a Member State governing the reduction, suspension or withdrawal of benefits in cases of overlapping with other social security benefits or any other form of income may be invoked even where such benefits were acquired under the legislation of another Member State or where such income was acquired in the territory of another Member State.

3. The provisions of the legislation of a Member State for reduction, suspension or withdrawal of benefit in the case of a person in receipt of invalidity benefits or anticipatory old-age benefits pursuing a professional or trade activity may be invoked against such person even though he is pursuing his activity in the territory of another Member State.

4. An invalidity pension payable under Netherlands legislation shall, in case where the Netherlands institution is bound under the provisions of Article 57(5) or 60(2)(b) to contribute also to the cost of benefits for occupational disease granted under the legislation of another Member State, be reduced by the amount payable to the institution of the other Member State which is responsible for granting the benefits for occupational disease.

Title II—Determination of the Legislation Applicable

Article 13 General rules

6–211 [1. Subject to Articles 14c and 14f, persons to whom this Regulation applies shall be subject to the legislation of a single Member State only. That legislation shall be determined in accordance with the provisions of this Title.][26]

[26] Words replaced by Regulation 1606/98, Art. 1(4) as from 25 October 1998.

2. Subject to Articles 14 to 17:

(a) a person employed in the territory of one Member State shall be subject to the legislation of that State even if he resides in the territory of another Member State or if the registered office or place of business of the undertaking or individual employing him is situated in the territory of another Member State;

(b) a person who is self-employed in the territory of one Member State shall be subjected to the legislation of that State even if he resides in the territory of another Member State;

(c) a person employed on board a vessel flying the flag of a Member State shall be subject to the legislation of the State;

(d) civil servants and persons treated as such shall be subject to the legislation of the Member State to which the administration employing them is subject;

(e) a person called up or recalled for service in the armed forces, or for civilian service, of a Member State shall be subject to the legislation of that State. If entitlement under that legislation is subject to the completion of periods of insurance before entry into or after release from such military or civilian service, periods of insurance completed under the legislation of any other Member State shall be taken into account, to the extent necessary, as if they were periods of insurance completed under the legislation of the first State. The employed or self-employed person called up or recalled for service in the armed forces or for civilian service shall retain the status of employed or self-employed person;

(f) a person to whom the legislation of a Member State ceases to be applicable, without the legislation of another Member State becoming applicable to him in accordance with one of the rules laid down in the aforegoing sub-paragraphs or in accordance with one of the exceptions or special provisions laid down in Articles 14 to 17 shall be subject to the legislation of the Member State in whose territory he resides in accordance with the provisions of that legislation alone.

Article 14 Special rules applicable to persons, other than mariners, engaged in paid employment

Article 13(2)(a) shall apply subject to the following exceptions and circumstances: **6–212**

1.(a) A person employed in the territory of a Member State by an undertaking to which he is normally attached who is posted by that undertaking to the territory of another Member State to perform work there for that undertaking shall continue to be subject to the legislation of the first Member State, provided that the ancipated duration of that work does not exceed 12 months and that he is not sent to replace another person who has completed his term of posting.

(b) If the duration of the work to be done extends beyond the duration originally anticipated, owing to unforeseeable circumstances, and exceeds 12 months, the legislation of the first Member State shall continue to apply until the completion of such work, provided that the competent authority of the Member State in whose territory the person concerned is posted or the body designated by that authority gives its consent; such consent must be requested before the end of the initial 12-month period. Such consent cannot, however, be given for a period exceeding 12 months.

2. A person normally employed in the territory of two or more Member States shall be subject to the legislation determined as follows:

(a) A person who is a member of the travelling or flying personnel of an undertaking which, for hire or reward or on its own account, operates international transport services for passengers or goods by rail, road, air or inland waterway and has its registered office or place of business in the territory of a Member State shall be subject to the legislation of the latter State, with the following restrictions:

(i) where the said undertaking has a branch or permanent representation in the territory of a Member State other than that in which it has its registered office or place of business, a person employed by such branch or permanent representation shall be subject to the legislation of the Member State in whose territory such branch or permanent representataion is situated;

(ii) where a person is employed principally in the territory of the Member State in which he resides, he shall be subject to the legislation of that State, even if the undertaking which employs him has no registered office or place of business or branch or permanent representation in that territory.

(b) A person other than that referred to in (a) shall be subject:

(i) to the legislation of the Member State in those territory he resides, if he pursues his activity partly in that territory or if he is attached to several undertakings or several employers who have their registered offices or places of business in the territory of different Member States;

(ii) to the legislation of the Member State in whose territory is situated the registered office or place of business of the undertaking or individual employing him, if he does not reside in the territory of any of the Member States where he is pursuing his activity.

3. A person who is employed in the territory of one Member State by an undertaking which has its registered office or place of business in the territory of another Member State and which straddles the common frontier of these States shall be subject to the legislation of the Member State in whose territory the undertaking has its registered office or place of business.

Article 14a Special rules applicable to persons, other than mariners, who are self-employed

6–213 Article 13(2)(b) shall apply subject to the following exceptions and circumstances:

1.(a) A person normally self-employed in the territory of a Member State and who performs work in the territory of another Member State shall continue to be subject to the legislation of the first Member State, provided that the anticipated duration of the work does not exceed 12 months.

(b) If the duration of the work to be done extends beyond the duration originally anticipated, owing to unforeseeable circumstances, and exceeds 12 months, the legislation of the first Member State shall continue to apply until the completion of such work, provided that the competent authority of the Member State in whose territory the person concerned has entered to perform the work in question or the body appointed by that authority gives its consent; such consent must be requested before the end of the initial 12-month period. Such consent cannot, however, be given for a period exceeding 12 months.

2. A person normally self-employed in the territory of two or more Member States shall be subject to the legislation of the Member State in whose territory he resides if he pursues any part of his activity in the territory of that Member State. If he does not pursue any activity in the territory of the Member State in which he resides, he shall be subject to the legislation of the Member State in whose territory he pursues his main activity. The criteria used to determine the principal activity are laid down in the Regulation referred to in Article 98.

3. A person who is self-employed in an undertaking which has its registered office or place of business in the territory of one Member State and which straddles the common frontier of two Member States shall be subject to the legislation of the Member State in whose territory the undertaking has its registered office or place of business.

4. If the legislation to which a person should be subject in accordance with paragraph 2 or 3 does not enable that person, even on a voluntary basis, to join a

pension scheme, the person concerned shall be subject to the legislation of the other Member State which would apply apart from these particular provisions, or should the legislations of two or more Member States apply in this way, he shall be subject to the legislation decided on by common agreement amongst the Member States concerned or their competent authorities.

Article 14b Special rules application to mariners

[Not reproduced]. **6–214**

Article 14c Special rules applicable to persons who are simultaneously employed in the territory of one Member State and self-employed in the territory of another Member State

A person who is simultaneously employed in the territory of one Member State **6–215** and self-employed in the territory of another Member State shall be subject:

(a) save as otherwise provided in sub-paragraph (b) to the legislation of the Member State in the territory of which he is engaged in paid employment or, where he pursues such an activity in the territory of two or more Member States, to the legislation determined in accordance with Article 14(2) or (3);

(b) in the cases mentiioned in Annex VII:
- to the legislation of the Member State in the territory of which he is engaged in paid employment, that legislation having been determined in accordance with the provisions of Article 14(2) or (3), where he pursues such an activity in the territory of two or more Member States, and
- to the legislation of the Member State in the territory of which he is self-employed, that legislation having been determined in accordance with article 14a(2), (3) or (4), where he pursues such an activity in the territory of two or more Member States.

Article 14d Miscellaneous provisions

[1. The person referred to in Article 14(2) and (3), Article 14a(2), (3) and (4), **6–216** Article 14c(a) and Article 14e shall be treated, for the purposes of application of the legislation laid down in accordance with these provisions, as if he pursued all his professional activity or activities in the territory of the Member State concerned.][27]

2. The person referred to in Article 14c(b) shall be treated, for the purposes of determining the rates of contributions to be charged to self-employed workers under the legislation of the Member State in whose territory he is self-employed, as if he pursued his paid employment in the territory of the Member State concerned.

3. The provisions of the legislation of a Member State under which a pensioner who is pursuing a professional or trade activity is not subject to compulsory insurance in respect of such activity shall also apply to a pensioner whose pension was acquired under the legislation of another Member State, unless the person concerned expressly asks to be so subject by applying to the institution designated by the competent authority of the first Member State and named in Annex 10 to the Regulation referred to in Article 98.

[Article 14e Special rules applicable to persons insured in a special scheme for civil servants who are simultaneously employed and/or self-employed in the territory of one or more other Member States

A person who is simultaneously employed as a civil servant or a person treated as **6–217** such and insured in a special scheme for civil servants in one Member State and

[27] Words replaced by Regulation 1606/98, Art. 1(5) as from 25 October 1998.

who is employed and/or self-employed in the territory of one or more other Member States shall be subject to the legislation of the Member State in which he is insured in a special scheme for civil servants.

Article 14f **Special rules applicable to civil servants simultaneously employed in more than one Member State and insured in one of these States in a special scheme**

6–218 A person who is simultaneously employed in two or more Member States as a civil servant or person treated as such and insured in at least one of those Member States in a special scheme for civil servants shall be subject to the legislation of each of these Member States.][28]

Article 15 **Rules concerning voluntary insurance or optional continued insurance**

6–219 1. Articles 13 to 14d shall not apply to voluntary insurance or to optional continued insurance unless, in respect of one of the branches referred to in Article 4, there exists in any Member State only a voluntary scheme of insurance.

2. Where application of the legislations of two or more Member States entails overlapping of insurance:
— under a compulsory insurance scheme and one or more voluntary or optional continued insurance schemes, the person concerned shall be subject exclusively to the compulsory insurance scheme;
— under two or more voluntary or optional continued insurance schemes, the person concerned may join only the voluntary or optional continued insurance scheme for which he has opted.

3. However, in respect of invalidity, old age and death (pensions), the person concerned may join the voluntary or optional continued insurance scheme of a Member State, even if he is compulsorily subject to the legislation of another Member State, to the extent that such overlapping is explicitly or implicitly admitted in the first Member State.

Article 16 **Special rules regarding persons employed by diplomatic missions and consular posts, and auxiliary staff of the European Communities**

6–220 [Not reproduced].

Article 17 **Exceptions to Articles 13 to 16**

6–221 Two or more Member States, the competent authorities of these States or the bodies designated by these authorities may by common agreement provide for exceptions to the provisions of Articles 13 to 16 in the interest of certain categories of persons or of certain persons.

Article 17a **Special rules concerning recipients of pensions due under the legislation of one or more Member State**

6–222 The recipient of a pension due under the legislation of a Member State or of pensions due under the legislation of several Member States who resides in the

[28] Article 14e and 14f inserted by Regulation 1606/98, Art. 1(6) as from 25 October 1998.

territory of another Member State may at his request be exempted from the legislation of the latter State provided that he is not subject to that legislation because of the pursuit of an occupation.

Title III—Special Provisions Relating to the Various Categories of Benefits

CHAPTER I—SICKNESS AND MATERNITY

SECTION 1—COMMON PROVISIONS

Article 18 Aggregation of periods of insurance, employment or residence

1. The competent institution of a Member State whose legislation makes the acquisition, retention or recovery of the rights to benefits conditional upon the completion of periods of insurance, employment or residence shall, to the extent necessary, take account of periods of insurance, employment or residence completed under the legislation of any other Member State as if they were periods completed under the legislation which it administers. **6–223**

2. The provisions of paragraph 1 shall apply to seasonal workers, even in respect of periods prior to any break in insurance exceeding the period allowed by the legislation of the competent State, provided, however, that the person concerned has not ceased to be insured for a period exceeding four months.

SECTION 2—EMPLOYED OR SELF-EMPLOYED PERSONS AND MEMBERS OF THEIR FAMILIES

Article 19 Residence in a Member State other than the competent State—General rules

1. An employed or self-employed person residing in the territory of a Member State other than the competent State, who satisfies the conditions of the legislation of the competent State for entitlement to benefits, taking account where appropriate of the provisions of Article 18, shall receive in the State in which he is resident: **6–224**

(a) benefits in kind provided on behalf of the competent institution by the institution of the place of residence in accordance with the provisions of the legislation administered by that institution as though he were insured with it;
(b) cash benefits provided by the competent institution in accordance with the legislation which it administers. However, by agreement between the competent institution and the institution of the place of residence, such benefits may be provided by the latter institution on behalf of the former, in accordance with the legislation of the competent State.

2. The provisions of paragraph 1 shall apply by analogy to members of the family who reside in the territory of a Member State other than the competent State in so far as they are not entitled to such benefits under the legislation of the State in whose territory they reside.

Where the members of the family reside in the territory of a Member State under whose legislation the right to receive benefits in kind is not subject to condition of insurance or employment, benefits in kind which they receive shall be considered as being on behalf of the institution with which the employed or self-employed person is insured, unless the spouse or the person looking after the children pursues a professional or trade activity in the territory of the said Member State.

Article 20 Frontier workers and members of their families—Special rules

A frontier worker may also obtain benefits in the territory of the competent State. **6–225**
Such benefits shall be provided by the competent institution in accordance with

the provisions of the legislation of that State, as though the person concerned were resident in that State. Members of his family may receive benefits under the same conditions; however, receipt of such benefits shall, except in urgent cases, be conditional upon an agreement between the States concerned or between the competent authorities of those States or, in its absence, on prior authorisation by the competent institution.

Article 21 Stay in or transfer of residence to the competent State

6–226 The employed or self-employed person referred to in Article 19(1) who is staying in the territory of the competent State shall receive benefits in accordance with the provisions of the legislation of that State as though he were resident there, even if he has already received benefits for the same case of sickness or maternity before his stay.

2. Paragraph 1 shall apply by analogy to the members of the family referred to in Article 19(2). However, where the latter reside in the territory of a Member State other than the one in whose territory the employed or self-employed person resides, benefits in kind shall be provided by the institution of the place of stay on behalf of the institution of the place of residence of the persons concerned.

3. Paragraphs 1 and 2 shall not apply to frontier workers and the members of their families.

4. An employed or self-employed person and members of his family referred to in Article 19 who transfer their residence to the territory of the competent State shall receive benefits in accordance with the provisions of the legislation of that State even if they have already received benefits for the same case of sickness or maternity before transferring their residence.

Article 22 Stay outside the competent State—Return to or transfer of residence to another Member State during sickness or maternity—Need to go to another Member State in order to receive appropriate treatment

6–227 1. An employed or self-employed person who satisfies the conditions of the legislation of the competent State for entitlement to benefits, taking account where appropriate of the provisions of Article 18, and:
(a) whose condition necessitates immediate benefits during a stay in the territory of another Member State; or
(b) who, having become entitled to benefits chargeable to the competent institution, is authorised by that institution to return to the territory of the Member State where he resides, or to transfer his residence to the territory of another Member State; or
(c) who is authorised by the competent institution to go to the territory of another Member State to receive there the treatment appropriate to his condition,

shall be entitled:
(i) to benefits in kind provided on behalf of the competent institution by the institution of the place of stay or residence in accordance with the provisions of the legislation which it administers, as though he were insured with it; the length of the period during which benefits are provided shall be governed, however, by the legislation of the competent State;
(ii) to cash benefits provided by the competent institution in accordance with the provisions of the legislation which it administers. However, by agreement between the competent institution and the institution of the place of stay or

residence, such benefits may be provided by the latter institution on behalf of the former, in accordance with the provisions of the legislation of the competent State.

2. The authorisation required under paragraph 1(b) may be refused only if it is established that movement of the person concerned would be prejudicial to his state of health or the receipt of medical treatment.

The authorisation required under paragraph 1(c) may not be refused where the treatment in question is among the benefits provided for by the legislation of the Member State on whose territory the person concerned resided and where he cannot be given such treatment within the time normally necessary for obtaining the treatment in question in the Member State of residence taking account of his current state of health and the probable course of the disease.

3. The provisions of paragraphs 1 and 2 shall apply by analogy to members of the family of an employed or self-employed person.

However, for the purpose of applying paragraph 1(a) and (c)(i) to the members of the family referred to in Article 19(2) who reside in the territory of a Member State other than the one in whose territory the employed or self-employed person resides:

(a) benefits in kind shall be provided on behalf of the institution of the Member State in whose territory the members of the family are residing by the institution of the place of stay in accordance with the provisions of the legislation which it administers as if the employed or self-employed person were insured there. The period during which benefits are provided shall, however, be that laid down under the legislation of the Member State in whose territory the members of the family are residing;

(b) the authorisation required under paragraph 1(c) shall be issued by the institution of the Member State in whose territory the members of the family are residing.

4. The fact that the provisions of paragraph 1 apply to an employed or self-employed person shall not affect the right to benefit of members of his family.

Article 22a Special rules for certain categories of persons

Notwithstanding Article 2 of the Regulation, Article 22(1)(a) and (c) shall also apply to persons who are nationals of a Member State and are insured under the legislation of a Member State and to the members of their families residing with them. **6–228**

Article 22b Employment in a Member State other than the competent State—Stay in the State of employment

The employed or self-employed person referred to in Article 13(2)(d), 14, 14a, 14b, 14c(a) or 17, and members of the family accompanying him, shall benefit from the provisions of Article 22(1)(a) for any condition requiring benefits during a stay in the territory of the Member State in which the worker is employed or whose flag the vessel aboard which the worker is employed is flying. **6–229**

[...][29]

Article 23 Calculation of cash benefits

1. The competent institution of a Member State whose legislation provides that the calculation of cash benefits shall be based on average earnings or on average contributions, shall determine such average earnings or contributions exclusively by reference to earnings or contributions completed under the said legislation. **6–230**

[29] Article 22c deleted by Regulation 307/1999, Art. 1(5) as from 1 May 1999; previously inserted by Regulation 1290/97, Art. 1, point 3 as from 4 October 1997 (but in the case of those studying or receiving vocational training in the Netherlands, no later than 1 January 1999).

2. The competent institution of a Member State whose legislation provides that the calculation of cash benefits shall be based on standard earnings, shall take account exclusively of the standard earnings or, where appropriate, of the average of standard earnings for the periods completed under the said legislation.

3. The competent institution of a Member State under whose legislation the amount of cash benefits varies with the number of members of the family, shall also take into account the members of the family of the person concerned who are resident in the territory of another Member State as if they were resident in the territory of the competent State.

Article 24 Substantial benefits in kind

6–231 1. Where the right of an employed or self-employed person or a member of his family to a prosthesis, a major appliance or other substantial benefits in kind has been recognised by the institution of a Member State before he becomes insured with the institution of another Member State, the said employed or self-employed person shall receive such benefits at the expense of the first institution, even if they are granted after he becomes insured with the second institution.

2. The Administrative Commission shall draw up the list of benefits to which the provisions of paragraph 1 apply.

SECTION 3—UNEMPLOYED PERSONS AND MEMBERS OF THEIR FAMILIES

Article 25 [Entitlement to benefits in kind and cash benefits]

6–232 1. An unemployed person who was formerly employed or self-employed, to whom the provisions of Article 69(1) or the second sentence of Article 71(1)(b)(ii) apply, and who satisfies the conditions of the legislation of the competent State for entitlement to benefits in kind and in cash, taking account where appropriate of the provisions of Article 18, shall receive for the period provided under Article 69(1)(c):

(a) benefits in kind provided on behalf of the competent institution by the institution of the Member State in which he seeks employment in accordance with the provisions of the legislation which the latter institution administers, as though he were insured with it;

(b) cash benefits provided by the competent institution in accordance with the provisions of the legislation which it administers. However, by agreement between the competent institution and the institution of the Member State in which the unemployed person seeks employment, benefits may be provided by the latter institution on behalf of the former institution in accordance with the provisions of the legislation of the competent State. Unemployment benefits under Article 69(1) shall not be granted for the period during which cash benefits are received.

2. A totally unemployed person who was formerly employed and to whom the provisions of Article 71(1)(a)(ii) or the first sentence of Article 71(1)(b)(ii) apply, shall receive benefits in kind and in cash in accordance with the provisions of the legislation of the Member State in whose territory he resides, as though he had been subject to that legislation during his last employment, taking account where appropriate of the provisions of Article 18; the cost of such benefits shall be met by the institution of the country of residence.

3. Where an unemployed person satisfies the conditions of the legislation of the Member State which is responsible for the cost of unemployment benefits for entitlement to sickness and maternity benefits, taking account where appropriate of the provisions of Article 18, the members of his family shall receive these benefits, irrespective of the Member State in whose territory they reside or are staying. Such benefits shall be provided:

(i) with regard to the benefits in kind, by the institution of the place of residence or stay in accordance with the provisions of the legislation which it administers, on behalf of the competent institution of the Member State which is responsible for the cost of unemployment benefits;
(ii) with regard to cash benefits, by the competent institution of the Member State which is responsible for the cost of unemployment benefits, in accordance with the legislation which it administers.

4. Without prejudice to any provisions of the legislation of a Member State which permit an extension of the period during which sickness benefits may be granted, the period provided for in paragraph 1 may, in cases of *force majeure*, be extended by the competent institution within the limit fixed by the legislation administered by that institution.

Article 25a Contributions payable by wholly unemployed persons

The institution which is responsible for granting benefits in kind and cash benefits to the unemployed persons referred to in Article 25(2) and which belongs to a Member State whose legislation provides for deduction of contributions payable by unemployed persons to cover sickness and maternity benefits shall be authorised to make such deductions in accordance with the provisions of its legislation. **6–233**

SECTION 4—PENSION CLAIMANTS AND MEMBERS OF THEIR FAMILIES

[Article 26 not reproduced] **6–234**

SECTION 5—PENSIONERS AND MEMBERS OF THEIR FAMILIES

[Articles 27 to 34 not reproduced] **6–235**

[SECTION 5A—PERSONS WHO STUDY OR RECEIVE VOCATIONAL TRAINING AND MEMBERS OF THEIR FAMILIES

Article 34a Special provisions for students and members of their families

The provisions of Article 18, Article 19, Article 22(1)(a) and (c), the second sub-paragraph of Article 22(2), Article 22(3), Article 23, Article 24 and of Sections 6 and 7 shall apply by analogy to students and to members of their families, as appropriate. **6–236**

Article 34b Common provisions

A person, as referred to in Article 22(1) and (3) and in Article 34a, who stays in a Member State other than the competent State to study there or receive vocational training leading to a qualification officially recognised by the authorities of a Member State, and the members of his family accompanying him during his stay, shall be covered by the provisions of Article 22(1)(a) for any conditions necessitating benefits during the stay in the territory of the Member State where such person is studying or in training.][30] **6–237**

[30] Section 5a inserted by Regulation 307/1999, Art. 1(6) as from 1 May 1999.

SECTION 6—MISCELLANEOUS PROVISIONS

Article 35 Scheme applicable where there are a number of schemes in the country of residence or stay—Previous illness—Maximum period during which benefits are granted

6–238 1. Subject to paragraph 2, where the legislation of the country of stay or residence contains several sickness or maternity insurance schemes, the provisions applicable under Article 19, 21(1), 22, 25, 26, 28(1), 29(1) or 31 shall be those of the scheme covering manual workers in the steel industry. Where, however, the said legislation includes a special scheme for workers in mines and similar undertakings, the provisions of such scheme shall apply to that category of workers and members of their families provided the institution of the place of stay or residence to which application is made is competent to administer such scheme.

2. Where the legislation of the country of stay or residence includes one or more special schemes, covering all or most occupational categories of self-employed persons, which grant benefits in kind less favourable than those granted to employed persons, the provisions applicable to the person concerned and the members of his family pursuant to Articles 19(1)(a) and (2), 22(1) (under (i)) and (3), 28(1)(a) and 31(a) shall be those of the scheme or schemes determined by the implementing Regulation referred to in Article 98:
(a) where, in the competent State, the person concerned is insured under a special scheme for self-employed persons which also grants less favourable benefits in kind than those granted to employed persons, or
(b) where a person in receipt of one or more pensions is, under the pensions legislation of the competent Member State or Member States, entitled only to the benefits in kind provided for by a special scheme for self-employed persons which also grants less favourable benefits in kind than those granted to employed persons.

3. Where, under the legislation of a Member State, the granting of benefits is conditional upon the origin of the illness, that conditions [shall not apply to persons][31] to whom this Regulation applies, regardless of the Member State in whose territory they reside.

4. Where the legislation of a Member State fixes a maximum period for the granting of benefits, the institution which administers that legislation may, where appropriate, take account of the period during which the benefits have already been provided by the institution of another Member State for the same case of sickness or maternity.

SECTION 7—REIMBURSEMENT BETWEEN INSTITUTIONS

Article 36 [Refunds for benefits in kind]

6–239 1. Benefits in kind provided in accordance with the provisions of this chapter by the institution of one Member State on behalf of the institution of another Member State shall be fully refunded.

2. The refunds referred to in paragraph 1 shall be determined and made in accordance with the procedure provided for by the implementing Regulation referred to in Article 98, either on production of proof of actual expenditure or on the basis of lump-sum payments.

In the latter case, the lump-sum payments shall be such as to ensure that the refund is as close as possible to actual expenditure.

3. Two or more Member States, or the competent authorities of those States, may provide for other methods of reimbursement or may waive all reimbursement between institutions under their jurisdiction.

[31] Words replaced by Regulation 307/1999, Art. 1(7) as from 1 May 1999.

CHAPTER 2—INVALIDITY

[Articles 37 to 43a not reproduced] **6–240**

CHAPTER 3—OLD AGE AND DEATH (PENSIONS)

Article 44 General provisions for the award of benefits where an employed or self-employed person has been subject to the legislation of two or more Member States

1. The rights to benefits of an employed or self-employed person who has been subject to the legislation of two or more Member States, or of his survivors, shall be determined in accordance with the provisions of this Chapter. **6–241**

2. Save as otherwise provided in Article 49, the processing of a claim for an award submitted by the person concerned shall have regard to all the legislations to which the employed or self-employed person has been subject. Exception shall be made to this rule if the person concerned expressly asks for postponement of the award of old-age benefits to which he would be entitled under the legislation of one or more Member States.

[3. This chapter shall not apply to increases in or supplements to pensions in respect of children or to orphans' pensions to be granted in accordance with the provisions of Chapter 8.][32]

Article 45 Consideration of periods of insurance or of residence completed under the legislations to which an employed person or self-employed person was subject, for the acquisition, retention or recovery of the right to benefits

1. Where the legislation of a Member State makes the acquisition, retention or recovery of the right to benefits, under a scheme which is not a special scheme within the meaning of paragraph 2 or 3, subject to the completion of periods of insurance or of residence, the competent institution of that Member State shall take account, where necessary, of the periods of insurance or of residence completed under the legislation of any other Member State, be it under a general scheme or under a special scheme and either as an employed person or a self-employed person. For that purpose, it shall take account of these periods as if they had completed under its own legislation. **6–242**

2. Where the legislation of a Member State makes the granting of certain benefits conditional upon the periods of insurance having been completed only in an occupation which is subject to a special scheme for employed persons or, where appropriate, in a specific employment, periods completed under the legislation of other Member States shall be taken into account for the granting of these benefits only if completed under a corresponding scheme or, failing that, in the same occupation or, where appropriate, in the same employment. If, account having been taken of the periods thus completed, the person concerned does not satisfy the conditions for receipt of these benefits, these periods shall be taken into account for the granting of the benefits under the general scheme or, failing that, under the scheme applicable to manual or clerical workers, as the case may be, subject to the condition that the person has been affiliated to one or other of these schemes.

3. Where the legislation of a Member State makes the granting of certain benefits conditional upon the periods of insurance having been completed only in an occupation subject to a special scheme for self-employed persons, periods completed under the legislations of other Member States shall be taken into

[32] Words replaced by Regulation 1399/1999, Art. 1(1) as from 1 September 1999; previously replaced by Regulation 1606/98, Art. 1(8)(a) as from 25 October 1998.

account for the granting of these benefits only if completed under a corresponding scheme or, failing that, in the same occupation. The special schemes for self-employed persons referred to in this paragraph are listed in Annex IV, part B, for each Member State concerned. If, account having been taken of the periods referred to in this paragraph, the person concerned does not satisfy the conditions for receipt of these benefits, these periods shall be taken into account for the granting of the benefits under the general scheme or, failing this, under the scheme applicable to manual or clerical workers, as the case may be, subject to the condition that the person concerned has been affiliated to one or other of these schemes.

4. The periods of insurance completed under a special scheme of a Member State shall be taken into account under the general scheme or, failing that, under the scheme applicable to manual or clerical workers, as the case may be, of another Member State for the acquisition, retention or recovery of the right to benefits, subject to the condition that the person concerned has been affiliated to one or other of these schemes, even if these periods have already been taken into account in the latter State under a scheme referred to in paragraph 2 or in the first sentence of paragraph 3.

5. Where the legislation of a Member State makes the acquisition, retention of recovery of the right to benefits conditional upon the person concerned being insured at the time of the materialisation of the risk, this condition shall be regarded as having been satisfied in the case of insurance under the legislation of another Member State, in accordance with the procedures provided in Annex VI for each Member State concerned.

6. A period of full employment of a worker to whom Article 81(1)(a)(ii) or (b)(ii), first sentence, applies shall be taken into account by the competent institution of the Member State in whose territory the worker concerned resides in accordance with the legislation administered by that institution, as if that legislation applied to him during his last employment.

Where that institution applies legislation providing for deduction of contributions payable by unemployed persons to cover old age pensions and death, it shall be authorised to make such deductions in accordance with the provisions of its legislation.

If the period of full unemployment in the country of residence of the person concerned can be taken into account only if contribution periods have been completed in that country, this condition shall be deemed to be fulfilled if the contribution periods have been completed in another Member State.

Article 46 Award of benefits

6–243 1. Where the conditions required by the legislation of a Member State for entitlement to benefits have been satisfied without having to apply Article 45 or Article 40(3), the following rules shall apply:

(a) the competent institution shall calculate the amount of the benefit that would be due:

(i) on the one hand, only under the provisions of the legislation which it administers;

(ii) on the other hand, pursuant to paragraph 2;

(b) the competent institution may, however, waive the calculation to be carried out in accordance with (a)(ii) if the result of this calculation, apart from differences arising from the use of round figures, is equal to or lower than the result of the calculation carried out in accordance with (a)(i), in so far as that institution does not apply any legislation containing rules against overlapping as referred to in Articles 46b and 46c or if the aforementioned institution applies a legislation containing rules against overlapping in the case referred to in Article 46c, provided that the said legislation lays down that benefits of a different kind shall be taken into consideration only on the basis of the relation of the periods of insurance or of residence completed under that legislation alone to the periods of insurance or of residence required by that legislation in order to qualify for full benefit entitlement.

Annex IV, part C, lists for each Member State concerned the cases where the two calculations would lead to a result of this kind.

2. Where the conditions required by the legislation of a Member State for entitlement to benefits are satisfied only after application of Article 45 and or Article 40(3), the following rules shall apply:

(a) the competent institution shall calculate the theoretical amount of the benefit to which the person concerned could lay claim provided all periods of insurance and/or of residence, which have been completed under the legislation of the Member States to which the employed person or self-employed person was subject, have been completed in the State in question under the legislation which it administers on the date of the award of the benefit. If, under this legislation, the amount of the benefit is independent of the duration of the periods completed, the amount shall be regarded as being the theoretical amount referred to in this paragraph;

(b) the competent institution shall subsequently determine the actual amount of the benefit on the basis of the theoretical amount referred to in the preceding paragraph in accordance with the ratio of the duration of the periods of insurance or of residence completed before the materialisation of the risk under the legislation which it administers to the total duration of the periods of insurance and of residence completed before the materialisation of the risk under the legislations of all the Member States concerned.

3. The person concerned shall be entitled to the highest amount calculated in accordance with paragraphs 1 and 2 from the competent institution of each Member State without prejudice to any application of the provisions concerning reduction, suspension or withdrawal provided for by the legislation under which this benefit is due.

Where that is the case, the comparison to be carried out shall relate to the amounts determined after the application of the said provisions.

4. When, in the case of invalidity, old-age or survivor's pensions, the total of the benefits due from the competent institutions of two or more Member States under the provisions of a multilateral social security convention referred to in Article 6(b) does not exceed the total which would be due from such Member States under paragraphs 1 to 3, the person concerned shall benefit from the provisions of this Chapter.

Article 46a General provisions relating to reduction, suspension or withdrawal applicable to benefits in respect of invalidity, old age or survivors under the legislations of the Member States

1. For the purposes of the Chapter, overlapping or benefits of the same kind shall have the following meaning: all overlapping of benefits in respect of invalidity, old age and survivors calculated or provided on the basis of periods of insurance and/or residence completed by one and the same person. **6–244**

2. For the purposes of this Chapter, overlapping of benefits of different kinds means all overlapping of benefits that cannot be regarded as being of the same kind within the meaning of paragraph 1.

3. The following rules shall be applicable for the application of provisions on reduction, suspension or withdrawal laid down by the legislation of a Member State in the case of overlapping of a benefit in respect of invalidity, old age or survivors with a benefit of the same kind or a benefit of a different kind or with other income:

(a) account shall be taken of the benefits acquired under the legislation of another Member State or of other income acquired in another Member State only where the legislation of the first Member State provides for the taking into account of benefits or income acquired abroad;
(b) account shall be taken of the amount of benefits to be granted by another Member State before deductions of taxes, social security contributions and other individual levies or deductions;
(c) no account shall be taken of the amount of benefits acquired under the legislation of another Member State which are awarded on the basis of voluntary insurance or continued optional insurance;
(d) where provisions on reduction, suspension or withdrawal are applicable under the legislation of only one Member State on account of the fact that the person concerned receives benefits of a similar or different kind payable under the legislation of other Member States or other income acquired within the territory of other Member States, the benefit payable under the legislation of the first Member State may be reduced only within the limit of the amount of the benefits payable under the legislation or the income acquired within the territory of other Member States.

Article 46b Special provisions applicable in the case of overlapping of benefits of the same kind under the legislation of two or more Member States

6–245 1. The provisions on reduction, suspension or withdrawal laid down by the legislation of a Member State shall not be applicable to a benefit calculated in accordance with Article 46(2).

2. The provisions on reduction, suspension or withdrawal laid down by the legislation of a Member State shall apply to a benefit calculated in accordance with Article 46(1)(a)(i) only if the benefit concerned is:
(a) either a benefit, which is referred to in Annex IV, part D, the amount of which does not depend on the length of the periods of insurance of residence completed, or
(b) a benefit, the amount of which is determined on the basis of a credited period deemed to have been completed between the date on which the risk materialised and a later date. In the latter case, the said provisions shall apply in the case of overlapping of such a benefit:
(i) either with a benefit of the same kind, except where an agreement has been concluded between two or more Member States providing that one and the same credited period may not be taken into account two or more times;
(ii) or with a benefit of the type referred to in (a).
The benefits referred to in (a) and (b) and agreements are mentioned in Annex IV, part D.

Article 46c Special provisions applicable in the case of overlapping of one or more benefits referred to in Article 46a(1) with one or more benefits of a different kind or with other income, where two or more Member States are concerned

6–246 1. If the receipt of benefits of a different kind or other income entails the reduction, suspension or withdrawal of two or more benefits referred to in Article 46(1)(a)(i), the amounts which would not be paid in strict application of the provisions concerning reduction, suspension or withdrawal provided for by the legislation of the Member States concerned shall be divided by the number of benefits subject to reduction, suspension or withdrawal.

2. Where the benefit in question is calculated in accordance with Article 46(2), the benefit or benefits of a different kind from other Member States or other income and all other elements provided for by the legislation of the Member State for the

application of the provisions in the respect of reduction, suspension or withdrawal shall be taken into account in proportion to the periods of insurance and/or residence referred to in Article 46(2)(b), and shall be used for the calculation of the said benefit.

3. If the receipt of benefits of a different kind or of other income entails the reduction, suspension or withdrawal of one or more benefits referred to in Article 46(1)(a)(i), and of one or more benefits referred to in Article 46(2), the following rules shall apply:

(a) where in a case of a benefit or benefits referred to in Article 46(1)(a)(i), the amounts which would not be paid in strict application of the provisions concerning reduction, suspension or withdrawal provided for by the legislation of the Member States concerned shall be divided by the number of benefits subject to reduction, suspension or withdrawal;

(b) where in a case of a benefit or benefits calculated in accordance with Article 46(2), the reduction, suspension or withdrawal shall be carried out in accordance with paragraph 2.

4. Where, in the case referred to in paragraphs 1 and 3(a), the legislation of a Member State provides that, for the application of provisions concerning reduction, suspension or withdrawal, account shall be taken of benefits of a different kind and/or other income and all other elements in proportion to the periods of insurance referred to in Article 46(2)(b), the division provided for in the said paragraphs shall not apply in respect of that Member State.

5. All the abovementioned provisions shall apply *mutatis mutandis* where the legislation of one or more Member States provides that the right to a benefit cannot be acquired in the case where the person concerned is in receipt of a benefit of a different kind, payable under the legislation of another Member State, or of other income.

Article 47 Additional provisions for the calculation of benefits

1. For the calculation of the theoretical and pro rata amounts referred to in Article 46(2), the following rules shall apply: **6–247**

(a) where the total length of the periods of insurance and of residence completed before the risk materialised under the legislations of all the Member States concerned is longer than the maximum period required by the legislation of one of these States for receipt of full benefit, the competent institution of that State shall take into consideration this maximum period instead of the total length of the periods completed; this method of calculation must not result in the imposition on that institution of the cost of a benefit greater than the full benefit provided for by the legislation which it administers. This provision shall not apply to benefits, the amount of which does not depend on the length of insurance;

(b) the procedure for taking account of overlapping periods is laid down in the implementing Regulation referred to in Article 98;

(c) where, under the legislation of a Member State, benefits are calculated on the basis of average earnings, an average contribution, an average increase or on the relation which existed, during the periods of insurance, between the claimant's gross earnings and the average gross earnings of all insured persons other than apprentices, such average figures or relations shall be determined by the competent institution of that State solely on the basis of the periods of insurance completed under the legislation of the said State, or the gross earnings received by the person concerned during those periods only;

(d) where, under the legislation of a Member State, benefits are calculated on the basis of the amount of earnings, contributions or increases, the competent institution of the State shall determine the earnings, contributions and increases to be taken into account in respect of the periods of insurance or residence completed under the legislation of other Member States on the basis of the average earnings, contributions or increases recorded in respect of the periods of insurance completed under the legislation which it administers;

(e) where, under the legislation of a Member State, benefits are calculated on the basis of standard earnings or a fixed amount, the competent institutions of that State shall consider the standard earnings or the fixed amount to be taken into account by it in respect of periods of insurance or residence completed under the legislations of other Member States as being equal to the standard earnings or fixed amount or, where appropriate, to the average of the standard earnings or the fixed amount corresponding to the periods of insurance completed under the legislation which it administers;

(f) where, under the legislation of a Member State, benefits are calculated for some periods on the basis of the amount of earnings and, for other periods, on the basis of standard earnings or a fixed amount, the competent institution of that State shall, in respect of periods of insurance or residence completed under the legislations of other Member States, take into account the earnings or fixed amounts determined in accordance with the provisions referred to in (d) or (e) or, as appropriate, the average of these earnings or fixed amounts, where benefits are calculated on the basis of standard earnings or a fixed amount for all the periods completed under the legislation which it administers, the competent institution shall consider the earnings to be taken into account in respect of the periods of insurance or residence completed under the legislations of other Member States as being equal to the national earnings corresponding to the standard earnings or fixed amounts;

(g) where, under the legislation of a Member State, benefits are calculated on the basis of average contributions, the competent institution shall determine that average by reference only to those periods of insurance completed under the legislation of the said State.

2. The provisions of the legislation of a Member State concerning the revalorisation of the factors taken into account for the calculation of benefits shall apply, as appropriate, to the factors to be taken into account by the competent institution of that State, in accordance with paragraph 1, in respect of the periods of insurance or residence completed under the legislation of other Member States.

3. If, under the legislation of a Member State, the amount of benefits is determined taking into account the existence of members of the family other than children, the competent institution of that State shall also take into consideration those members of the family of the person concerned who are residing in the territory of another Member State as if they were residing in the territory of the competent State.

4. If the legislation which the competent institution of a Member State administers requires a salary to be taken into account for the calculation of benefits, where the first and second sub-paragraphs of Article 45(6) have been applied, and if, in this Member State, only periods of full unemployment with benefit in accordance with Article 71(1)(a)(ii) or the first sentence of Article 71(1)(b)(ii) are taken into consideration for the payment of pensions, the competent institution of that Member State shall pay the pension on the basis of the salary it used as the reference for providing that unemployment benefit in accordance with the legislation which it administers.

Article 48 Periods of insurance or of residence of less than one year

6–248 1. Notwithstanding Article 46(2), the institution of a Member State shall not be required to award benefits in respect of periods completed under the legislation it administers which are taken into account when the risk materialises, if:

— the duration of the said periods does not amount to one year, and
— taking only these periods into consideration, no right to benefit is acquired by virtue of the provisions of that legislation.

2. The competent institution of each of the Member States concerned shall take into account the periods referred to in paragraph 1, for the purposes of applying Article 46(2) excepting sub-paragraph (b).

3. If the effect of applying paragraph 1 would be to relieve all the institutions of the Member States concerned of their obligations, benefits shall be awarded exclusively under the legislation of the last of those States whose conditions are satisfied, as if all the periods of insurance and residence completed and taken into account in accordance with Article 45(1) to (4) had been completed under the legislation of that State.

Article 49 Calculation of benefits where the person concerned does not simultaneously satisfy the conditions laid down by all the legislations under which periods of insurance or of residence have been completed or when he has expressly requested a postponement of the award of old-age benefits

1. If, at a given time, the person concerned does not satisfy the conditions laid down for the provisions of benefits by all the legislations of the Member States to which he has been subject, taking into account where appropriate Article 45 and/or Article 40(3), but satisfies the conditions or one or more of them only, the following provisions shall apply: **6–249**

(a) each of the competent institutions administering a legislation whose conditions are satisfied shall calculate the amount of the benefit due, in accordance with Article 46;
(b) however:
 (i) if the person concerned satisfies the conditions of at least two legislations without having recourse to periods of insurance or residence completed under the legislations whose conditions are not satisfied, these periods shall not be taken into account for the purposes of Article 46(2) unless taking account of the said periods makes it possible to determine a higher amount of benefit;
 (ii) if the person concerned satisfies the conditions of one legislation only without having recourse to periods of insurance or residence completed under the legislations whose conditions are not satisfied, the amount of the benefit due shall, in accordance with Article 46(1)(a)(i), be calculated only in accordance with the provisions of the legislation whose conditions are satisfied, taking account of the periods completed under that legislation only, unless taking account of the periods completed under the legislations whose conditions are not satisfied makes it possible, in accordance with Article 46(1)(a)(ii), to determine a higher amount of benefit.

The provisions of this paragraph shall apply *mutatis mutandis* where the person concerned has expressly requested the postponement of the award of old-age benefits, in accordance with the second sentence of Article 44(2).

2. The benefit or benefits awarded under one or more of the legislations in question, in the case referred to in paragraph 1, shall be recalculated automatically in accordance with Article 46, as and when the conditions required by one or more of the other legislations to which the person concerned has been subject are satisfied, taking into account, where appropriate, Article 45 and taking into account once again, where appropriate, paragraph 1. This paragraph shall apply *mutatis mutandis* where a person requests the award of old-age benefits acquired under the legislation of one or more Member States which had until then been postponed in accordance with the second sentence of Article 44(2).

3. A recalculation shall automatically be made in accordance with paragraph 1, without prejudice to Article 40(2), where the conditions required by one or more of the legislations concerned are no longer satisfied.

Article 50 Award of a supplement where the total of benefits payable under the legislations of the various Member States does not amount to the minimum laid down by the legislation of the State in whose territory the recipient resides

6–250 A recipient of benefits to whom this Chapter applies may not, in the State in whose territory he resides and under whose legislation a benefit is payable to him, be awarded a benefit which is less than the minimum benefit fixed by that legislation for a period of insurance or residence equal to all the periods of insurance or residence equal to all the periods of insurance taken into account for the payment in accordance with the preceding Articles. The competent institution of that State shall, if necessary, pay him throughout the period of his residence in its territory a supplement equal to the difference between the total of the benefits payable under this Chapter and the amount of the minimum benefit.

Article 51 Revalorisation and recalculation of benefits

6–251 1. If, by reason of an increase in the cost of living or changes in the level of wages or salaries or other reasons for adjustment, the benefits of the States concerned are altered by a fixed percentage or amount, such perentage or amount must be applied directly to the benefits determined under Article 46, without the need for a recalculation in accordance with that Article.

2. On the other hand, if the method of determining benefits or the rules for calculating benefits should be altered, a recalculation shall be carried out in accordance with Article 46.

[Article 51a Persons covered by a special scheme for civil servants][33]

6–252 [Not reproduced]

CHAPTER 4—ACCIDENTS AT WORK AND OCCUPATIONAL DISEASES

SECTION 1—RIGHT TO BENEFITS

Article 52 Residence in a Member State other than the competent State—General rules

6–253 An employed or self-employed person who sustains an accident at work or contracts an occupational disease, and who is residing in the territory of a Member State other than the competent State, shall receive in the State in which he is residing:

(a) benefits in kind, provided on behalf of the competent institution by the institutions of his place of residence in accordance with the provisions of the legislation which it administers as if he were insured with it;

(b) cash benefits provided by the competent institution in accordance with the provisions of the legislation which it administers. However, by agreement between the competent institution and the institution of the place of residence, these benefits may be provided by the latter institution on behalf of the former in accordance with the legislation of the competent State.

Article 53 Frontier workers—Special rule

6–254 A frontier worker may also obtain benefits in the territory of the competent State. Such benefits shall be provided by the competent institution in accordance with

[33] Article 51a inserted by Regulation 1606/98, Art. 1(8)(b) as from 25 October 1998.

the provisions of the legislation of that State, as if the person concerned were residing there.

Article 54 Stay in or transfer or residence to the competent State

1. An employed or self-employed person covered by Article 52 who is staying in the territory of the competent State shall receive benefits in accordance with the provisions of the legislation of that State, even if he has already received benefits before his stay. This provision shall not, however, apply to frontier workers. **6–255**

2. An employed or self-employed person covered by Article 52 who transfers his place of residence to the territory of the competent State shall receive benefits in accordance with the provisions of the legislation of that State, even if he has already received benefits before transferring his residence.

Article 55 Stay outside the competent State—Return to or transfer of residence to another Member State after sustaining an accident or contracting an occupational disease—Need to go to another Member State in order to receive appropriate treatment

1. An employed or self-employed person who sustains an accident at work or contracts an occupational disease and: **6–256**
(a) who is staying in the territory of a Member State other than the competent State; or
(b) who, after having become entitled to benefits chargeable to the competent institution, is authorised by that institution to return to the territory of the Member State where he is resident, or to transfer his place of residence to the territory of another Member State; or
(c) who is authorised by the competent institution to go to the territory of another Member State in order to receive there the treatment appropriate to his condition;

shall be entitled:
(i) to benefits in kind provided on behalf of the competent institution by the institution of the place of stay or residence in accordance with the provisions of the legislation administered by that institution as though he were insured with it, the period during which benefits are provided shall, however, be governed by the legislation of the competent State;
(ii) to cash benefits provided by the competent institution in accordance with the legislation which it administers. However, by agreement between the competent institution and the institution of the place of stay or residence, those benefits may be provided by the latter institution on behalf of the former institution, in accordance with the legislation of the competent State.

2. The authorisation required under paragraph 1(b) may be refused only if it is established that movement of the person concerned would be prejudicial to his state of health or to the medical treatment being given.

The authorisation required under paragraph 1(c) may not be refused where the treatment in question cannot be given to the person concerned in the territory of the Member State in which he resides.

Article 56 Accidents while travelling

An accident while travelling which occurs in the territory of a Member State other than the competent State shall be deemed to have occurred in the territory of the competent State. **6–257**

Article 57 Benefits for an occupational disease where the person concerned has been exposed to the same risk in several Member States

6–258 1. When a person who has contracted an occupational disease has, under the legislation of two or more Member States, pursued an activity which by its nature is likely to cause that disease, the benefits that he or his survivors may claim shall be awarded exclusively under the legislation of the last of those States whose conditions are satisfied, taking into account, where appropriate, paragraphs 2 to 5.

2. If, under the legislation of a Member State, the granting of benefits in respect of an occupational disease is subject to the condition that the disease in question was first diagnosed within its territory, such condition shall be deemed to be satisfied if the disease was first diagnosed in the territory of another Member State.

3. If, under the legislation of a Member State, the granting of benefits in respect of an occupational disease is subject to the condition that the disease in question was diagnosed within a specific time-limit following cessation of the last activity which was likely to cause such a disease, the competent institution of that State, when checking the time at which such activity was pursued, shall take into account, to the extent necessary, similar activities pursued under the legislation of any other Member State, as if they had been pursued under the legislation of the first State.

4. If, under the legislation of a Member State, the granting of benefits in respect of an occupational disease is subject to the condition that an activity likely to cause the disease in question was pursued for a certain length of time, the competent institution of the State shall take into account, to the extent necessary, periods during which such activity was pursued under the legislation of any other Member State, as if it had been pursued under the legislation of the first State.

5. In cases of sclerogenic pneumoconiosis, the cost of cash benefits, including pensions, shall be divided among the competent institutions of the Member States in whose territory the person concerned pursued an activity likely to cause the disease. This division shall be carried out on the basis of the ratio which the length of the periods of old-age insurance or residence referred to in Article 45(1) completed under the legislation of each of the States bears to the total length of the periods of old-age insurance or residence completed under the legislation of all the States at the dates on which the benefits commenced.

6. The Council shall determine unanimously, on a proposal from the Commission, the occupational diseases to which the provisions of paragraph 5 shall be extended.

Article 58 Calculation of cash benefits

6–259 1. The competent institution of a Member State whose legislation provides that the calculation of cash benefits shall be based on average earnings shall determine such average earnings exclusively by reference to earnings confirmed as having been paid during the periods completed under the said legislation.

2. The competent institution of a Member State whose legislation provides that the calculation of cash benefits shall be based on standard earnings shall take account exclusively of the standard earnings, or where appropriate, of the average of standard earnings for the periods completed under the said legislation.

3. The competent institution of a Member State whose legislation provides that the amount of cash benefits shall vary with the number of members in the family

shall take into account also the members of the family of the person concerned who are residing in the territory of another Member State, as if they were residing in the territory of the competent State.

Article 59 **Costs of transporting a person who has sustained an accident at work or is suffering from an occupational disease**

1. The competent institution of a Member State whose legislation provides for meeting the costs of transporting a person who has sustained an accident at work or is suffering from an occupational disease, either to his place of residence or to a hospital, shall meet such costs to the corresponding place in the territory of another Member State where the person resides, provided that that institution gives prior authorisation for such transport, duly taking into account the reasons justifying it. Such authorisation shall not be required in the case of a frontier worker. **6–260**

2. The competent institution of a Member State whose legislation provides for the costs of transporting the body of a person killed in an accident at work to the place of burial shall, in accordance with the provisions of the legislation which it administers, meet such costs to the corresponding place in the territory of another Member State, where the person was residing at the time of the accident.

SECTION 2—AGGRAVATION OF AN OCCUPATIONAL DISEASE FOR WHICH THE BENEFIT HAS BEEN AWARDED

Article 60 **[Taking account of aggravation of occupational disease]**

1. In the event of aggravation of an occupational disease for which an employed or self-employed person has received or is receiving benefit under the legislation of a Member State, the following rules shall apply: **6–261**

(a) if the person concerned has not, while in receipt of benefits, been engaged in an occupation under the legislation of another Member State likely to cause or aggravate the disease in question, the competent institution of the first Member State shall be bound to meet the cost of the benefits under the provisions of the legislation which it administers taking into account the aggravation;

(b) if the person concerned, while in receipt of benefits, has pursued such an activity under the legislation of another Member State, the competent institution of the first Member State shall be bound to meet the cost of the benefits under the legislation which it administers without taking the aggravation into account. The competent institution of the second Member State shall grant a supplement to the person concerned, the amount of which shall be equal to the difference between the amount of benefits due after the aggravation and the amount which would have been due prior to the aggravation under the legislation which it administers if the disease in question had occurred under the legislation of that Member State;

(c) if, in the case covered by sub-paragraph (b), an employed or self-employed person suffering from sclerogenic pneumoconiosis or from a disease determined under Article 57(6) is not entitled to benefits under the legislation of the second Member State, the competent institution of the first Member State shall be bound to provide benefits under the legislation which it administers, taking the aggravation into account. The competent institution of the second Member State shall, however, meet the cost of the difference between the amount of cash benefits, including pensions, due from the competent institution of the first Member State, taking the aggravation into account, and the amount of the corresponding benefits which were due prior to the aggravation;

(d) the provisions for reduction, suspension or withdrawal laid down by the legislation of a Member State shall not apply to persons receiving benefits awarded by institutions of two Member States in accordance with sub-paragraph (b).

2. In the event of aggravation of an occupational disease giving rise to the application of the provisions of Article 57(5), the following provisions shall apply:

(a) the competent institution which granted the benefits in accordance with the provisions of Article 57(1) shall be bound to provide benefits under the legislation which it administers taking the aggravation into account;

(b) the cost of cash benefits, including pensions, shall continue to be divided between the institutions which shared the costs of former benefits in accordance with the provisions of Article 57(5). Where, however, the person has again pursued an activity likely to cause or to aggravate the occupational disease in question, either under the legislation of one of the Member States in which he had already pursued an activity of the same nature or under the legislation of another Member State, the competent institution of such State shall meet the cost of the difference between the amount of benefits due, taking account of the aggravation, and the amount of benefits due prior to the aggravation.

SECTION 3—MISCELLANEOUS PROVISIONS

Article 61 Rules for taking into account the special features of certain legislations

6–262 1. If there is no insurance against accidents at work or occupational diseases in the territory of the Member State in which the person concerned happens to be, or if such insurance exists but there is no institution responsible for providing benefits in kind, those benefits shall be provided by the institution of the place of stay or residence responsible for providing benefit in kind in the event of sickness.

2. Where the legislation of the competent State makes wholly cost-free benefits in kind conditional upon use of the medical service organised by the employer, benefits in kind provided in the cases referred to in Articles 52 and 55(1) shall be deemed to have been provided by such a medical service.

3. Where the legislation of the competent State includes a scheme relating to the obligations of the employer, benefits in kind provided in the case referred to in Articles 52 and 55(1) shall be deemed to have been provided at the request of the competent institution.

4. Where the nature of the scheme of the competent State relating to compensation for accidents at work is not that of compulsory insurance, the provision of benefits in kind shall be made directly by the employer or by the insurer involved.

5. Where the legislation of a Member State provides expressly or by implication that accidents at work or occupational diseases which have occurred or have been confirmed previously shall be taken into consideration in order to assess the degree of incapacity, to establish a right to any benefit, or to determine the amount of benefit, the competent institution of that Member State shall also take into consideration accidents at work or occupational diseases which have occurred or have been confirmed previously under the legislation of another Member State as if they had occurred or had been confirmed under the legislation which it administers.

6. Where the legislation of a Member State provides expressly or by implication that accidents at work or occupational diseases which have occurred or have been confirmed subsequently shall be taken into consideration in order to assess the degree of incapacity, to establish the right to any benefit, or to determine the amount of such benefit, the competent institution of that Member State shall also

take into consideration accidents at work or occupational diseases which have occurred or have been confirmed subsequently under the legislation of another Member State, as if they had occurred or had been confirmed under the legislation which it administers, but only where:

(1) no compensation is due in respect of the accident at work or the occupational disease which had occurred or had been confirmed previously under the legislaton which it administers; and

(2) no compensation is due by virtue of the legislation of the other Member State under which the accident at work or the occupational disease occurred or was confirmed subsequently, account having been taken of the provisions of paragraph 5, in respect of that accident at work or that occupational disease:

Article 62 Scheme applicable where there are several schemes in the country of stay or residence—Maximum duration of benefits

1. If the legislation of the country of stay or residence has several insurance schemes, the provisions applicable to employed or self-employed persons covered by Article 52 or 55(1) shall be those of the scheme for manual workers in the steel industry. However, if that legislation includes a special scheme for workers in mines and similar undertakings, the provisions of that scheme shall apply to that category of workers where the institution of the place of stay or residence to which they submit their claim is competent to administer that scheme. **6–263**

2. If the legislation of a Member State fixes a maximum period during which benefits may be granted, the institution which administers that legislation may take into account any period during which the benefits have already been provided by the institution of another Member State.

SECTION 4—REIMBURSEMENTS BETWEEN INSTITUTIONS

Article 63 [Obligation to reimburse benefits in kind]

1. The competent institution shall be obliged to reimburse the amount of benefits in kind provided on its behalf in accordance with the provisions of Articles 52 and 55(1). **6–264**

2. The reimbursements referred to in paragraph 1 shall be determined and made in accordance with the procedures laid down by the implementing Regulation referred to in Article 98, on proof of actual expenditure.

3. Two or more Member States, or the competent authorities of such States, may provide for other methods of reimbursement or waive reimbursement between the institutions coming under their jurisdiction.

[SECTION 5—STUDENTS

Article 63a [Application to students]

The provisions of Sections 1 to 4 shall apply by analogy to students.][34] **6–265**

CHAPTER 5—DEATH GRANTS

[Articles 64 to 66 not reproduced] **6–266**

CHAPTER 6—UNEMPLOYMENT BENEFITS

SECTION 1—COMMON PROVISIONS

Article 67 Aggregation of periods of insurance or employment

1. The competent institution of a Member State whose legislation makes the acquisition, retention or recovery of the right to benefits subject to the completion **6–267**

[34] Section 5 inserted by Regulation 307/1999, Art. 1(8) as from 1 May 1999.

of periods of insurance shall take into account, to the extent necessary, periods of insurance or employment completed as an employed person under the legislation of any other Member State, as though they were periods of insurance completed under the legislation which it administers, provided, however, that the periods of employment would have been counted as periods of insurance had they been completed under that legislation.

2. The competent institution of a Member State whose legislation makes the acquisition, retention or recovery of the right to benefits subject to the completion of periods of employment shall take into account, to the extent necessary, periods of insurance or employment completed as an employed person under the legislation of any other Member State, as though they were periods of employment completed under the legislation which it administers.

3. Except in the cases referred to in Article 71(1)(a)(ii) and (b)(ii), application of the provisions of paragraphs 1 and 2 shall be subject to the condition that the person concerned should have completed lastly:
— in the case of paragraph 1, periods of insurance,
— in the case of paragraph 2, periods of employment,
in accordance with the provisions of the legislation under which the benefits are claimed.

4. Where the length of the period during which benefits may be granted depends on the length of periods of insurance or employment, the provisions of paragraph 1 or 2 shall apply, as appropriate.

Article 68 Calculation of benefits

6–268 1. The competent institution of a Member State whose legislation provides that the calculation of benefits should be based on the amount of the previous wage or salary shall take into account exclusively the wage or salary received by the person concerned in respect of his last employment in the territory of that State. However, if the person concerned had been in his last employment in that territory for less than four weeks, the benefits shall be calculated on the basis of the normal wage or salary corresponding, in the place where the unemployed person is residing or staying, to an equivalent or similar employment to his last employment in the territory of another Member State.

2. The competent institution of a Member State whose legislation provides that the amount of benefits varies with the number of members of the family, shall take into account also members of the family of the person concerned who are residing in the territory of another Member State, as though they were residing in the territory of the competent State. This provision shall not apply if, in the country of residence of the members of the family, another person is entitled to unemployment benefits for the calculation of which the members of the family are taken into consideration.

SECTION 2—UNEMPLOYED PERSONS GOING TO A MEMBER STATE OTHER THAN THE COMPETENT STATE

Article 69 Conditions and limits for the retention of the right to benefits

6–269 1. An employed or self-employed person who is wholly unemployed and who satisfies the conditions of the legislation of a Member State for entitlement to benefits and who goes to one or more other Member States in order to seek employment there shall retain his entitlement to such benefits under the following conditions and within the following limits:

(a) Before his departure, he must have been registered as a person seeking work and have remained available to the employment services of the competent State for at least four weeks after becoming unemployed. However, the competent services or institutions may authorise his departure before such time has expired.

(b) He must register as a person seeking work with the employment services of each of the Member States to which he goes and be subject to the control procedure organised therein. This condition shall be considered satisfied for the period before registration if the person concerned registered within seven days of the date when he ceased to be available to the employment services of the State he left. In exceptional cases, this period may be extended by the competent services or institutions.

(c) Entitlement to benefits shall continue for a maximum period of three months from the date when the person concerned ceased to be available to the employment services of the State which he left, provided that the total duration of the benefits does not exceed the duration of the period of benefits he was entitled to under the legislation of that State. In the case of a seasonal worker such duration shall, moreover, be limited to the period remaining until the end of the season for which he was engaged.

2. If the person concerned returns to the competent State before the expiry of the period during which he is entitled to benefits under the provision of paragraph 1(c), he shall continue to be entitled to benefits under the legislation of that State; he shall lose all entitlement to benefits under the legislation of the competent State if he does not return there before the expiry of that period. In exceptional cases, this time-limit may be extended by the competent services or institutions.

3. The provisions of paragraph 1 may be invoked only once between two periods of employment.

4. Where the competent State is Belgium, an unemployed person who returns there after the expiry of the three-month period laid down in paragraph 1(c), shall not requalify for benefits in that country until he has been employed there for at least three months.

Article 70 Provision of benefits and reimbursements

1. In the cases referred to in Article 69(1), benefits shall be provided by the institution of each of the States to which an unemployed person goes to seek employment. **6–270**

The competent institution of the Member State to whose legislation an employed or self-employed person was subject at the time of his last employment shall be obliged to reimburse the amount of such benefits.

2. The reimbursements referred to in paragraph 1 shall be determined and made in accordance with the procedure laid down by the implementing Regulation referred to in Article 98, on proof of actual expenditure, or by lump sum payments.

3. Two or more Member States, or the competent authorities of those States, may provide for other methods of reimbursement or payment, or may waive all reimbursement between the institutions coming under their jurisdiction.

SECTION 3—UNEMPLOYED PERSONS WHO, DURING THEIR LAST EMPLOYMENT, WERE RESIDING IN A MEMBER STATE OTHER THAN THE COMPETENT STATE

Article 71 [Entitlement to benefit]

1. An unemployed person who was formerly employed and who, during his last employment, was residing in the territory of a Member State other than the competent State shall receive benefits in accordance with the following provisions: **6–271**

(a) (i) A frontier worker who is partially or intermittently unemployed in the undertaking which employs him, shall receive benefits in accordance with the provisions of the legislation of the competent State as if he were residing in the territory of that State; these benefits shall be provided by the competent institution.

(ii) A frontier worker who is wholly unemployed shall receive benefits in accordance with the provisions of the legislation of the Member State in whose territory he resides as though he had been subject to that legislation while last employed; these benefits shall be provided by the institution of the place of residence at its own expense.

(b) (i) An employed person, other than a frontier worker, who is partially, intermittently or wholly unemployed and who remains available to his employer or to the employment services in the territory of the competent State shall receive benefits in accordance with the provisions of the legislation of that State as though he were residing in its territory; these benefits shall be provided by the competent institution.

(ii) An employed person, other than a frontier worker, who is wholly unemployed and who makes himself available for work to the employment services in the territory of the Member State in which he resides, or who returns to that territory, shall receive benefits in accordance with the legislation of that State as if he had last been employed there; the institution fo the place of residence shall provide such benefits at its own expense. However, if such an employed person has become entitled to benefits at the expense of the competent institution of the Member State to whose legislation he was last subject, he shall receive benefits under the provisions of Article 69. Receipt of benefits under the legislation of the State in which he resides shall be suspended for any period during which the unemployed person may, under the provisions of Article 69, make a claim for benefits under the legislation to which he was last subject.

2. An unemployed person may not claim benefits under the legislation of the Member State in whose territory he resides while he is entitled to benefits under the provisions of paragraph 1(a)(i) or (b)(i).

[SECTION 4—PERSONS COVERED BY A SPECIAL SCHEME FOR CIVIL SERVANTS

Article 71a **[Application of provisions to special civil service schemes]**

6–272 1. The provisions of Sections 1 and 2 shall apply by analogy to persons covered by a special unemployment scheme for civil servants.

2. The provisions of Section 3 shall not apply to persons covered by a special unemployment scheme for civil servants. An unemployed person who is covered by a special unemployment scheme for civil servants, who is partially or wholly unemployed, and who, during his last employment, was residing in the territory of a Member State other than the competent State, shall receive benefits in accordance with the provisions of the legislation of the competent State as if he were residing in the territory of that State; these benefits shall be provided by the competent institution, at its expense.][35]

CHAPTER 7—FAMILY BENEFITS

Article 72 **Aggregation of periods of insurance, employment or self-employment**

6–273 Where the legislation of a Member State makes acquisition of the right to benefits conditional upon completion of periods of insurance, employment or self-employment, the competent institution of that State shall take into account for

[35] Section 4 inserted by Regulation 1606/98, Art. 1(9) as from 25 October 1998.

this purpose, to the extent necessary, periods of insurance, employment or self-employment completed in any other Member State, as if they were periods completed under the legislation which it administers.

Article 72a Employed persons who have become fully unemployed

An employed person who has become fully unemployed and to whom Article 71(1)(a)(ii) or (b)(ii), first sentence, apply shall, for the members of his family residing in the territory of the same Member State as he, receive family benefits in accordance with the legislation of the State, as if he had been subject to that legislation during his last employment, taking account, where appropriate, of the provisions of Article 72. These benefits shall be provided by, and at the expense of, the institution of the place of residence. **6–274**

Where that institution applies legislation providing for deduction of contributions payable by unemployed persons to cover family benefits, it shall be authorised to make such deductions in accordance with the provisions of its legislation.

Article 73 Employed or self-employed persons the members of whose families reside in a Member State other than the competent State

An employed or self-employed person subject to the legislation of a Member State shall be entitled, in respect of the members of his family who are residing in another Member State, to the family benefits provided for by the legislation of the former State, as if they were residing in that State, subject to the provisions of Annex VI. **6–275**

Article 74 Unemployed persons the members of whose families reside in a Member State other than the competent State

An unemployed person who was formerly employed or self-employed and who draws unemployment benefits under the legislation of a Member State shall be entitled, in respect of the members of his family residing in another Member State, to the family benefits provided for by the legislation of the former State, as if they were residing in that State, subject to the provisions of Annex VI. **6–276**

Article 75 Provisions of benefits

1. Family benefits shall be provided, in the cases referred to in Article 73, by the competent institution of the State to the legislation of which the employed or self-employed person is subject and, in the cases referred to in Article 74, by the competent institution of the State under the legislation of which an unemployed person who was formerly employed or self-employed receives unemployment benefits. They shall be provided in accordance with the provisions administered by such institutions, whether or not the natural or legal person to whom such benefits are payable is residing or staying in the territory of the competent State or in that of another Member State. **6–277**

2. However, if the family benefits are not used by the person to whom they should be provided for the maintenance of the members of the family, the competent institution shall discharge its legal obligations by providing the said benefits to the natural or legal person actually maintaining the members of the family, at the request of, and through the agency of, the institution of their place of residence or of the designated institution or body appointed for this purpose by the competent authority of the country of their residence.

3. Two or more Member States may agree, in accordance with the provisions of Article 8, that the competent institution shall provide the family benefits due under the legislation of those States or of one of those States to the natural or legal person actually maintaining the members of the family, either directly or through the agency of the institution of their place of residence.

Article 76 Rules or priority in cases of overlapping entitlement to family benefits under the legislation of the competent State and under the legislation of the Member State of residence of the members of the family

6–278 1. Where, during the same period, for the same family member and by reason of carrying on an occupation, family benefits are provided for by the legislation of the Member State in whose territory the members of the family are residing, entitlement to the family benefits due in accordance with the legislation of another Member State, if appropriate under Article 73 or 74, shall be suspended up to the amount provided for in the legislation of the first Member State.

2. If an application for benefits is not made in the Member States in whose territory the members of the family are residing, the competent institution of the other Member State may apply the provisions of paragraph 1 as if benefits were granted in the first Member State.

[Article 76a Students

6–279 The provisions of Article 72 shall apply by analogy to students.][36]

CHAPTER 8—BENEFITS FOR DEPENDENT CHILDREN OF PENSIONERS AND FOR ORPHANS

6–280 [Articles 77 to 79a not reproduced.]

TITLE IV—ADMINISTRATIVE COMMISSION ON SOCIAL SECURITY FOR MIGRANT WORKERS

Articles 80–81

6–281 [Not reproduced].

TITLE V—ADVISORY COMMITTEE ON SOCIAL SECURITY FOR MIGRANT WORKERS

Articles 82–83

6–282 [Not reproduced]

TITLE VI—MISCELLANEOUS PROVISIONS

Articles 84–92

6–283 [Not reproduced].

Article 93 Rights of institutions responsible for benefits against liable third parties

6–284 1. If a person receives benefits under the legislation of one Member State in respect of an injury resulting from an occurrence in the territory of another State, any rights of the institution responsible for benefits against a third party bound to compensate for the injury shall be governed by the following rules:

[36] Article 76a inserted by Regulation 307/1999, Art. 1(10) as from 1 May 1999.

(a) Where the institution responsible for benefits is, by virtue of the legislation which it administers, subrogated to the rights which the recipient has against the third party, such subrogation shall be recognised by each Member State.
(b) Where the said institution has direct rights against the third party, such rights shall be recognised by each Member State.

2. If a person receives benefits under the legislation of one Member State in respect of an injury resulting from an occurrence in the territory of another Member State, the provisions of the said legislation which determine in which cases the civil liability of employers or of the persons employed by them is to be excluded shall apply with regard to the said person or to the competent institution.

The provisions of paragraph 1 shall also apply to any rights of the institution responsible for benefit against an employer or the persons employed by him in cases where their liability is not excluded.

3. Where, in accordance with the provisions of Article 36(3) and/or Article 63(3), two or more Member States or the competent authorities of those States have concluded an agreement to waive reimbursement between institutions under their jurisdiction, any rights arising against a liable third party shall be governed by the following rules:
(a) Where the institution of the Member State of stay or residence awards benefits to a person in respect of an injury which was sustained within its territory, that institution, in accordance with the legislation which it administers, shall excercise the right to subrogation or direct action against the third party liable to provide compensation for the injury.
(b) For the purpose of implementing (a):
  (i) the person receiving benefits shall be deemed to be insured with the institution of the place of stay of residence, and
  (ii) that institution shall be deemed to be the debtor institution.
(c) The provisions of paragraphs 1 and 2 shall remain applicable in respect of any benefits not covered by the waiver agreement referred to in this paragraph.

Title VII—Transitional and Final Provisions

Articles 94–97

[Not reproduced] **6–285**

Article 98 Implementing Regulation

A further Regulation shall lay down the procedure for implementing this Regulation.[37] **6–286**

[37] Note: See Regulation 574/72 fixing the procedure for implementing Regulation 1408/71 on the application of social security schemes to employed persons and their families moving within the Community, the most recent consolidated text of which is reproduced in Annex A, Pt II to Regulation 118/97 (1997 OJ L28/1). It has been amended on seven occasions since publication of this consolidated version.

Chapter 7

COMPETITION

Council Regulation 17 of 6 February 1962: First Regulation implementing Articles [81] and [82] of the Treaty[1]

([1959–1962] OJ Eng. Spec. Ed., p.87; Doc. Ref. 31962R0017)

The Council of the European Economic Community, 7–001

Having regard to the Treaty establishing the [European Community], and in particular Article [83] thereof,

Having regard to the proposal from the Commission,

Having regard to the Opinion of the Economic and Social Committee,

Having regard to the Opinion of the European Parliament,

[1] Whereas, in order to establish a system ensuring that competition shall not be distorted in the common market, it is necessary to provide for balanced application of Articles [81] and [82] in a uniform manner in the Member States;

[2] Whereas in establishing the rules for applying Article [81(3)] account must be taken of the need to ensure effective supervision and to simplify administration to the greatest possible extent;

[3] Whereas it is accordingly necessary to make it obligatory, as a general principle, for undertakings which seek application of Article [81(3)] to notify to the Commission their agreements, decisions and concerted practices;

[4] Whereas, on the one hand, such agreements, decisions and concerted practices are probably very numerous and cannot therefore all be examined at the same time and, on the other hand, some of them have special features which may make them less prejudicial to the development of the common market;

[5] Whereas there is consequently a need to make more flexible arrangements for the time being in respect of certain categories of agreement, decision and concerted practice without prejudging their validity under Article [81];

[6] Whereas it may be in the interest of undertakings to know whether any agreements, decisions or practices to which they are party, or propose to become party, may lead to action on the part of the Commission pursuant to Article [81(1)] or Article [82];

[7] Whereas, in order to secure uniform application of Articles [81] and [82] in the common market, rules must be made under which the Commission, acting in close and constant liaison with the competent authorities of the Member States, may take the requisite measures for applying those Articles;

[8] Whereas for this purpose the Commission must have the cooperation of the competent authorities of the Member States and be empowered, throughout the common market, to require such information to be supplied and to undertake such investigations as are necessary to bring to light any agreement, decision or concerted practice prohibited by Article [81(1)] or any abuse of a dominant position prohibited by Article [82];

[9] Whereas, in order to carry out its duty of ensuring that the provisions of the Treaty are applied, the Commission must be empowered to address to undertakings or associations of undertakings recommendations and decisions for the purpose of bringing to an end infringements of Articles [81] and [82];

---

[1] Regulation 17/62 is to be repealed as from 1 May 2004, with the exception of Art. 8(3) which will continue to apply to decisions adopted pursuant to Art. 81(3) of the Treaty prior to that date and until the date of expiry of those decisions, by virtue of Regulation 1/2003, Art. 43(1) ([2003] OJ L1/1). References to Regulation No. 17 will, after 1 May 2003, be construed as references to Regulation 1/2003 (Regulation 1/2003, Art. 43(3)).

[10] Whereas compliance with Articles [81] and [82] and the fulfilment of obligations imposed on undertakings and associations of undertakings under this Regulation must be enforceable by means of fines and periodic penalty payments;

[11] Whereas undertakings concerned must be accorded the right to be heard by the Commission, third parties whose interests may be affected by a decision must be given the opportunity of submitting their comments beforehand, and it must be ensured that wide publicity is given to decisions taken;

[12] Whereas all decisions taken by the Commission under this Regulation are subject to review by the Court of Justice under the conditions specified in the Treaty whereas it is moreover desirable to confer upon the Court of Justice, pursuant to Article [229], unlimited jurisdiction in respect of decisions under which the Commission imposes fines or periodic penalty payments;

[13] Whereas this Regulation may enter into force without prejudice to any other provisions that may hereafter be adopted pursuant to Article [83],

Has adopted this Regulation:

Article 1

7–002 **Basic provision**Without prejudice to Articles 6, 7 and 23 of this Regulation, agreements, decisions and concerted practices of the kind described in Article [81(1)] of the Treaty and the abuse of a dominant position in the market, within the meaning of Article [82] of the Treaty, shall be prohibited, no prior decision to that effect being required.

Article 2 Negative clearance

7–003 Upon application by the undertakings or associations of undertakings concerned, the Commission may certify that, on the basis of the facts in its possession, there are no grounds under Article [81(1)] or Article [82] of the Treaty for action on its part in respect of an agreement, decision or practice.[2]

Article 3 Termination of infringements

7–004 1. Where the Commission, upon application or upon its own initiative, finds that there is infringement of Article [81] or Article [82] of the Treaty, it may by decision require the undertakings or associations of undertakings concerned to bring such infringement to an end.

2. Those entitled to make application are:

(a) Member States

(b) natural or legal persons who claim a legitimate interest.

3. Without prejudice to the other provisions of this Regulation, the Commission may, before taking a decision under paragraph 1, address to the undertakings or associations of undertakings concerned recommendations for termination of the infringement.

Article 4 Notification of new agreements, decisions and practices

7–005 1. Agreements, decisions and concerted practices of the kind described in Article [81(1)] of the Treaty which come into existence after the entry into force of this Regulation and in respect of which the parties seek application of Article [81(3)] must be notified to the Commission. Until they have been notified, no decision in application of Article [81(3)] may be taken.[3]

[2] See Commission Notice on procedures concerning applications for negative clearance pursuant to Art. 2 of Council Reg. 17 ([1982] OJ C343/4).

[3] See Commission Notice on procedures concerning notifications pursuant to Art. 4 of Council Reg. 17 ([1983] OJ C295/6).

2. [Paragraph 1 shall not apply to agreements, decisions and concerted practices where:][4]

(1) the only parties thereto are undertakings from one Member State and the agreements, decisions or practices do not relate either to imports or to exports between Member States

[(2)

(a) the agreements or concerted practices are entered into by two or more undertakings, each operating, for the purposes of the agreement, at a different level of the production or distribution chain, and relate to the conditions under which the parties may purchase, sell or resell certain goods or services;

(b) not more than two undertakings are party thereto, and the agreements only impose restrictions on the exercise of the rights of the assignee or user of industrial property rights, in particular patents, utility models, designs or trade marks, or of the person entitled under a contract to the assignment, or grant, of the right to use a method of manufacture or knowledge relating to the use and to the application of industrial processes.][5]

(3) they have as their sole object:

(a) the development or uniform application of standards or types or

[(b) joint research and development][6]

[(c) specialisation in the manufacture of products, including agreements necessary for achieving this

— where the products which are the subject of specialisation do not, in a substantial part of the common market, represent more than 15% of the volume of business done in identical products or those considered by consumers to be similar by reason of their characteristics, price and use, and

— where the total annual turnover of the participating undertakings does not exceed 200 million units of account.

These agreements, decisions and practices may be notified to the Commission.][7]

Article 5 Notification of existing agreements, decisions and practices

1. Agreements, decisions and concerted practices of the kind described in Article [81(1)] of the Treaty which are in existence at the date of entry into force of this Regulation and in respect of which the parties seek application of Article [81(3)] shall be notified to the Commission [before 1 November 1962].[8] [However, notwithstanding the foregoing provisions, any agreements, decisions and concerted practices to which not more than two undertakings are party shall be notified before 1 February 1963.][9] **7–006**

2. Paragraph 1 shall not apply to agreements, decisions or concerted practices falling within Article 4(2) ; these may be notified to the Commission.

Article 6 Decisions pursuant to Article [81(3)]

1. Whenever the Commission takes a decision pursuant to Article [81(3)] of the Treaty, it shall specify therein the date from which the decision shall take effect. Such date shall not be earlier than the date of notification. **7–007**

2. The second sentence of paragraph 1 shall not apply to agreements, decisions or concerted practices falling within Article 4(2) and Article 5(2), nor to those falling

[4] Words substituted by Reg. 2822/71 sole Art. as from 18 January 1972.

[5] Article 4(2)(2) substituted by Reg. 1216/99 Art. 1 ([1999] OJ L148/5) as from 18 June 1999.

[6] Words substituted by Reg. 2822/71 sole Art. as from 18 January 1972.

[7] Article 4(3)(c) inserted by Reg. 2822/71 sole Art. as from 18 January 1972.

[8] Words substituted by Reg. 59/62 Art. 1(1) as from 11 July 1962.

[9] Words inserted by Reg. 59/62 Art. 1(2) as from 11 July 1962.

within Article 5(1) which have been notified within the time limit specified in Article 5(1).

Article 7 Special provisions for existing agreements, decisions and practices

7–008 1. Where agreements, decisions and concerted practices in existence at the date of entry into force of this Regulation and notified [within the time limits specified in Article 5(1)][10] do not satisfy the requirements of Article [81(3)] of the Treaty and the undertakings or associations of undertakings concerned cease to give effect to them or modify them in such manner that they no longer fall within the prohibition contained in Article [81(1)] or that they satisfy the requirements of Article [81(3)], the prohibition contained in Article [81(1)] shall apply only for a period fixed by the Commission. A decision by the Commission pursuant to the foregoing sentence shall not apply as against undertakings and associations of undertakings which did not expressly consent to the notification.

2. Paragraph 1 shall apply to agreements, decisions and concerted practices falling within Article 4(2) which are in existence at the date of entry into force of this Regulation if they are notified [before 1 January 1967].[11]

7–009 **Article 8 Duration and revocation of decisions under Article [81(3)]**

1. A decision in application of Article [81(3)] of the Treaty shall be issued for a specified period and conditions and obligations may be attached thereto.

2. A decision may on application be renewed if the requirements of Article [81(3)] of the Treaty continue to be satisfied.

3. The Commission may revoke or amend its decision or prohibit specified acts by the parties:
(a) where there has been a change in any of the facts which were basic to the making of the decision
(b) where the parties commit a breach of any obligation attached to the decision
(c) where the decision is based on incorrect information or was induced by deceit
(d) where the parties abuse the exemption from the provisions of Article [81(1)] of the Treaty granted to them by the decision.

In cases to which sub-paragraphs (b), (c) or (d) apply, the decision may be revoked with retroactive effect.

Article 9 Powers

7–010 1. Subject to review of its decision by the Court of Justice, the Commission shall have sole power to declare Article [81(1)] inapplicable pursuant to Article [81(3)] of the Treaty.

2. The Commission shall have power to apply Article [81(1)] and Article [82] of the Treaty this power may be exercised notwithstanding that the time-limits specified in Article 5(1) and in Article 7(2) relating to notification have not expired.

3. As long as the Commission has not initiated any procedure under Articles 2, 3 or 6, the authorities of the Member States shall remain competent to apply Article [81(1)] and Article [82] in accordance with Article [84] of the Treaty they shall remain competent in this respect notwithstanding that the time-limits specified in Article 5(1) and in Article 7(2) relating to notification have not expired.

Article 10 Liaison with the authorities of the Member States

7–011 1. The Commission shall forthwith transmit to the competent authorities of the Member States a copy of the applications and notifications together with copies of

[10] Words substituted by Reg. 59/62 Art. 1(3) as from 11 July 1962.
[11] Words substituted by Reg. 118/63 Art. 1 as from 8 November 1963.

the most important documents lodged with the Commission for the purpose of establishing the existence of infringements of Articles [81] or [82] of the Treaty or of obtaining negative clearance or a decision in application of Article [81(3)].

2. The Commission shall carry out the procedure set out in paragraph 1 in close and constant liaison with the competent authorities of the Member States such authorities shall have the right to express their views upon that procedure.

3. An Advisory Committee on Restrictive Practices and Monopolies shall be consulted prior to the taking of any decision following upon a procedure under paragraph 1, and of any decision concerning the renewal, amendment or revocation of a decision pursuant to Article [81(3)] of the Treaty.

4. The Advisory Committee shall be composed of officials competent in the matter of restrictive practices and monopolies. Each Member State shall appoint an official to represent it who, if prevented from attending, may be replaced by another official.

5. The consultation shall take place at a joint meeting convened by the Commission such meeting shall be held not earlier than 14 days after dispatch of the notice convening it. The notice shall, in respect of each case to be examined, be accompanied by a summary of the case together with an indication of the most important documents, and a preliminary draft decision.

6. The Advisory Committee may deliver an opinion notwithstanding that some of its members or their alternates are not present. A report of the outcome of the consultative proceedings shall be annexed to the draft decision. It shall not be made public.

Article 11 Requests for information

1. In carrying out the duties assigned to it by Article [85] and by provisions adopted under Article [83] of the Treaty, the Commission may obtain all necessary information from the Governments and competent authorities of the Member States and from undertakings and associations of undertakings. **7–012**

2. When sending a request for information to an undertaking or association of undertakings, the Commission shall at the same time forward a copy of the request to the competent authority of the Member State in whose territory the seat of the undertaking or association of undertakings is situated.

3. In its request the Commission shall state the legal basis and the purpose of the request and also the penalties provided for in Article 15(1)(b) for supplying incorrect information.

4. The owners of the undertakings or their representatives and, in the case of legal persons, companies or firms, or of associations having no legal personality, the persons authorised to represent them by law or by their constitution shall supply the information requested.

5. Where an undertaking or association of undertakings does not supply the information requested within the time-limit fixed by the Commission, or supplies incomplete information, the Commission shall by decision require the information to be supplied. The decision shall specify what information is required, fix an appropriate time-limit within which it is to be supplied and indicate the penalties provided for in Article 15(1)(b) and Article 16(1)(c) and the right to have the decision reviewed by the Court of Justice.

6. The Commission shall at the same time forward a copy of its decision to the competent authority of the Member State in whose territory the seat of the undertaking or association of undertakings is situated.

Article 12 Inquiry into sectors of the economy

7–013 1. If in any sector of the economy the trend of trade between Member States, price movements, inflexibility of prices or other circumstances suggest that in the economic sector concerned competition is being restricted or distorted within the common market, the Commission may decide to conduct a general inquiry into that economic sector and in the course thereof may request undertakings in the sector concerned to supply the information necessary for giving effect to the principles formulated in Articles [81] and [82] of the Treaty and for carrying out the duties entrusted to the Commission.

2. The Commission may in particular request every undertaking or association of undertakings in the economic sector concerned to communicate to it all agreements, decisions and concerted practices which are exempt from notification by virtue of Article 4(2) and Article 5(2).

3. When making inquiries pursuant to paragraph 2, the Commission shall also request undertakings or groups of undertakings whose size suggests that they occupy a dominant position within the common market or a substantial part thereof to supply to the Commission such particulars of the structure of the undertakings and of their behaviour as are requisite to an appraisal of their position in the light of Article [82] of the Treaty.

4. Article 10(3) to (6) and Articles 11, 13 and 14 shall apply correspondingly.

Article 13 Investigations by the authorities of the Member States

7–014 1. At the request of the Commission, the competent authorities of the Member States shall undertake the investigations which the Commission considers to be necessary under Article 14(1), or which it has ordered by decision pursuant to Article 14(3). The officials of the competent authorities of the Member States responsible for conducting these investigations shall exercise their powers upon production of an authorisation in writing issued by the competent authority of the Member State in whose territory the investigation is to be made. Such authorisation shall specify the subject matter and purpose of the investigation.

2. If so requested by the Commission or by the competent authority of the Member State in whose territory the investigation is to be made, the officials of the Commission may assist the officials of such authorities in carrying out their duties.

Article 14 Investigating powers of the Commission

7–015 1. In carrying out the duties assigned to it by Article [85] and by provisions adopted under Article [83] of the Treaty, the Commission may undertake all necessary investigations into undertakings and associations of undertakings. To this end the officials authorised by the Commission are empowered:

(a) to examine the books and other business records
(b) to take copies of or extracts from the books and business records
(c) to ask for oral explanations on the spot
(d) to enter any premises land and means of transport of undertakings.

2. The officials of the Commission authorised for the purpose of these investigations shall exercise their powers upon production of an authorisation in writing specifying the subject matter and purpose of the investigation and the penalties provided for in Article 15(1)(c) in cases where production of the required books or other business records is incomplete. In good time before the investigation, the Commission shall inform the competent authority of the Member State in whose territory the same is to be made of the investigation and of the identity of the authorised officials.[12]

[12] See Explanatory Note to authorisation to investigate under Art. 14(2) of Council Reg. 17 (*Thirteenth Report on Competition Policy* (1983), p.270).

3. Undertakings and associations of undertakings shall submit to investigations ordered by decision of the Commission. The decision shall specify the subject matter and purpose of the investigation, appoint the date on which it is to begin and indicate the penalties provided for in Article 15(1)(c) and Article 16(1)(d) and the right to have the decision reviewed by the Court of Justice.[13]

4. The Commission shall take decisions referred to in paragraph 3 after consultation with the competent authority of the Member State in whose territory the investigation is to be made.

5. Officials of the competent authority of the Member State in whose territory the investigation is to be made may, at the request of such authority or of the Commission, assist the officials of the Commission in carrying out their duties.

6. Where an undertaking opposes an investigation ordered pursuant to this Article, the Member State concerned shall afford the necessary assistance to the officials authorised by the Commission to enable them to make their investigation. Member States shall, after consultation with the Commission, take the necessary measures to this end before 1 October 1962.

Article 15 Fines

1. The Commission may by decision impose on undertakings or associations of undertakings fines of from 100 to 5,000 units of account where, intentionally or negligently: **7–016**

(a) they supply incorrect or misleading information in an application pursuant to Article 2 or in a notification pursuant to Articles 4 or 5 or
(b) they supply incorrect information in response to a request made pursuant to Article 11(3) or (5) or to Article 12, or do not supply information within the time limit fixed by a decision taken under Article 11(5) ; or
(c) they produce the required books or other business records in incomplete form during investigations under Article 13 or 14, or refuse to submit to an investigation ordered by decision issued in implementation of Article 14(3).

2. The Commission may by decision impose on undertakings or associations of undertakings fines of from 1,000 to 1,000,000 units of account, or a sum in excess thereof but not exceeding 10 per cent of the turnover in the preceding business year of each of the undertakings participating in the infringement where, either intentionally or negligently:
(a) they infringe Article [81(1)] or Article [82] of the Treaty or
(b) they commit a breach of any obligation imposed pursuant to Article 8(1).
In fixing the amount of the fine, regard shall be had both to the gravity and to the duration of the infringement.[14]

3. Article 10(3) to (6) shall apply.

4. Decisions taken pursuant to paragraphs 1 and 2 shall not be of a criminal law nature.

5. The fines provided for in paragraph 2(a) shall not be imposed in respect of acts taking place:

---

[13] See Explanatory Note to authorisation to investigate in execution of a Commission Decision under Art. 14(3) of Council Reg. 17 (*Thirteenth Report on Competition Policy* (1983), p.271).

[14] See further, Guidelines on the method of setting fines imposed pursuant to Art. 15(2) of Reg. 17 and Art. 65(5) of the ECSC Treaty ([1998] OJ C9/3) and Commission Notice on immunity from fines and reduction of fines in cartel cases ([2002] OJ C45/3).

(a) after notification to the Commission and before its decision in application of Article [81(3)] of the Treaty, provided they fall within the limits of the activity described in the notification
(b) before notification and in the course of agreements, decisions or concerted practices in existence at the date of entry into force of this Regulation, provided that notification was effected within the time-limits specified in Article 5(1) and Article 7(2).

6. Paragraph 5 shall not have effect where the Commission has informed the undertakings concerned that after preliminary examination it is of opinion that Article [81(1)] of the Treaty applies and that application of Article [81(3)] is not justified.

Article 16 Periodic penalty payments

7–017 1. The Commission may by decision impose on undertakings or associations of undertakings periodic penalty payments of from 50 to 1,000 units of account per day, calculated from the date appointed by the decision, in order to compel them:
(a) to put an end to an infringement of Article [81] or [82] of the Treaty, in accordance with a decision taken pursuant to Article 3 of this Regulation;
(b) to refrain from any act prohibited under Article 8(3);
(c) to supply complete and correct information which it has requested by decision taken pursuant to Article 11(5);
(d) to submit to an investigation which it has ordered by decision taken pursuant to Article 14(3).

2. Where the undertakings or associations of undertakings have satisfied the obligation which it was the purpose of the periodic penalty payment to enforce, the Commission may fix the total amount of the periodic penalty payment at a lower figure than that which would arise under the original decision.

3. Article 10(3) to (6) shall apply.

Article 17 Review by the Court of Justice

7–018 The Court of Justice shall have unlimited jurisdiction within the meaning of Article [229] of the Treaty to review decisions whereby the Commission has fixed a fine or periodic penalty payment it may cancel, reduce or increase the fine or periodic penalty payment imposed.

Article 18 Unit of account

7–019 For the purposes of applying Articles 15 to 17 the unit of account shall be that adopted in drawing up the budget of the Community in accordance with Articles [277] and [279] of the Treaty.[15]

Article 19 Hearing of the parties and of third persons

7–020 1. Before taking decisions as provided for in Articles 2, 3, 6, 7, 8, 15 and 16, the Commission shall give the undertakings or associations of undertakings concerned the opportunity of being heard on the matters to which the Commission has taken objection.

2. If the Commission or the competent authorities of the Member States consider it necessary, they may also hear other natural or legal persons. Applications to be heard on the part of such persons shall, where they show a sufficient interest, be granted.

[15] The unit of account presently used is the euro; see Reg. 3308/80 ([1980] OJ L345/1) and Reg. 1103/97 ([1997] OJ L162/1).

3. Where the Commission intends to give negative clearance pursuant to Article 2 or take a decision in application of Article [81(3)] of the Treaty, it shall publish a summary of the relevant application or notification and invite all interested third parties to submit their observations within a time-limit which it shall fix being not less than one month. Publication shall have regard to the legitimate interest of undertakings in the protection of their business secrets.

Article 20 Professional secrecy

1. Information acquired as a result of the application of Articles 11, 12, 13 and 14 shall be used only for the purpose of the relevant request or investigation. **7–021**

2. Without prejudice to the provisions of Articles 19 and 21, the Commission and the competent authorities of the Member States, their officials and other servants shall not disclose information acquired by them as a result of the application of this Regulation and of the kind covered by the obligation of professional secrecy.

3. The provisions of paragraphs 1 and 2 shall not prevent publication of general information or surveys which do not contain information of undertakings.

Article 21 Publication of decisions

1. The Commission shall publish the decisions which it takes pursuant to Articles 2, 3, 6, 7 and 8. **7–022**

2. The publication shall state the names of the parties and the main content of the decision it shall have regard to the legitimate interest of undertakings in the protection of their business secrets.

Article 22 Special provisions

1. The Commission shall submit to the Council proposals for making certain categories of agreement, decision and concerted practice falling within Article 4(2) or Article 5(2) compulsorily notifiable under Article 4 or 5. **7–023**

2. Within one year from the date of entry into force of this Regulation, the Council shall examine, on a proposal from the Commission, what special provisions might be made for exempting from the provisions of this Regulation agreements, decisions and concerted practices falling within Article 4(2) or Article 5(2).

Article 23 Transitional provisions applicable to decisions of authorities of the Member States

1. Agreements, decisions and concerted practices of the kind described in Article [81(1)] of the Treaty to which, before the entry into force of this Regulation, the competent authority of a Member State has declared Article [81(1)] to be inapplicable pursuant to Article [81(3)] shall not be subject to compulsory notification under Article 5. The decision of the competent authority of the Member State shall be deemed to be a decision within the meaning of Article 6 it shall cease to be valid upon expiration of the period fixed by such authority but in any event not more than three years after the entry into force of this Regulation. Article 8(3) shall apply. **7–024**

2. Applications for renewal of decisions of the kind described in paragraph 1 shall be decided upon by the Commission in accordance with Article 8(2).

Article 24 Implementing provisions

The Commission shall have power to adopt implementing provisions concerning the form, content and other details of applications pursuant to Articles 2 and 3 and **7–025** of notifications pursuant to Articles 4 and 5, and concerning hearings pursuant to Article 19(1) and (2).[16]

Article 25 [Application of regulation to new Member States]

7–026 1. As regards agreements, Decisions and concerted practices to which Article [81] of the Treaty applies by virtue of accession, the date of accession shall be substituted for the date of entry into force of this Regulation in every place where reference is made in this Regulation to this latter date.

2. Agreements, Decisions and concerted practices existing at the date of accession to which Article [81] of the Treaty applies by virtue of accession shall be notified pursuant to Article 5(1) or Article 7(1) and (2) within six months from the date of accession.

3. Fines under Article 15(2)(a) shall not be imposed in respect of any act prior to notification of the agreements, Decisions and practices to which paragraph 2 applies and which have been notified within the period therein specified.

4. New Member States shall take the measures referred to in Article 14(6) within six months from the date of accession after consulting the Commission.][17]

[5. The provisions of paragraphs 1 to 4 above still apply in the same way in the case of the accession of the Hellenic Republic, the Kingdom of Spain and of the Portuguese Republic.][18]

[6. The provisions of paragraphs 1 to 4 still apply in the same way in the case of the accession of Austria, Finland, Norway and Sweden. However, they do not apply to agreements, decisions and concerted practices which at the date of accession already fall under Article 53 of the EEA Agreement.][19]

This Regulation shall be binding in its entirety and directly applicable in all Member States.

Council Regulation 4064/89 of 21 December 1989, on the control of concentrations between undertakings

([1990] OJ L257/13,[20] corrigendum [1998] OJ L3/16; Doc. Ref. 31989R4064)

7–027 *The Council of the European Communities*,
Having regard to the Treaty establishing the [European Community], and in particular Articles [83] and [308] thereof,

Having regard to the proposal from the Commission,[21]

Having regard to the opinion of the European Parliament,[22]

Having regard to the opinion of the Economic and Social Committee,[23]

(1) Whereas, for the achievement of the aims of the Treaty establishing the [European Community], Article [3(g)] gives the Community the objective of

[16] Current implementing regulations: Reg. 3385/94 on form, content and other details of applications and notifications ([1994] OJ L377/28); Reg. 2842/98 on hearings under art. 19(1) and (2) ([1998] OJ L354/18) (see below).

[17] Article 25 inserted by Act of Accession of Denmark, Ireland and the UK, Annex I(V) para. 1 (OJ Spec. Ed., 27 March 1972, p.92) as from 1 January 1973.

[18] Article 25(5) substituted by Act of Accession of Spain and Portugal, Annex I(IV) para. 5 ([1985] OJ L302/165) as from 1 January 1986; originally inserted by Act of Accession of Greece, Annex I(V) para. 1 ([1979] OJ L291/93) as from 1 January 1981.

[19] Article 25(6) inserted by Act of Accession of Austria, Finland and Sweden Annex I(III)(B) ([1994] OJ C241/57) para. 1 as from 1 January 1995.

[20] Regulation 4064/89 was originally published at [1989] OJ L395/1, but that version was replaced by the version published at [1990] OJ L257/13 because of various errors.

[21] [1988] OJ C130/4.

[22] [1988] OJ C309/55.

[23] [1988] OJ C208/11.

instituting "a system ensuring that competition in the common market is not distorted";

(2) Whereas this system is essential for the achievement of the internal market by 1992 and its further development;

(3) Whereas the dismantling of internal frontiers is resulting and will continue to result in major corporate reorganisations in the Community, particularly in the form of concentrations;

(4) Whereas such a development must be welcomed as being in line with the requirements of dynamic competition and capable of increasing the competitiveness of European industry, improving the conditions of growth and raising the standard of living in the Community;

(5) Whereas, however, it must be ensured that the process of reorganization does not result in lasting damage to competition whereas Community law must therefore include provisions governing those concentrations which may significantly impede effective competition in the common market or in a substantial part of it;

(6) Whereas Articles [81] and [82], while applicable, according to the case law of the Court of Justice, to certain concentrations, are not, however, sufficient to control all operations which may prove to be incompatible with the system of undistorted competition envisaged in the Treaty;

(7) Whereas a new legal instrument should therefore be created in the form of a Regulation to permit effective control of all concentrations from the point of view of their effect on the structure of competition in the Community and to be the only instrument applicable to such concentrations;

(8) Whereas this Regulation should therefore be based not only on Article [83] but, principally, on Article [308] of the Treaty, under which the Community may give itself the additional powers of action necessary for the attainment of its objectives, including with regard to concentrations on the markets for agricultural products listed in Annex [I] to the Treaty;

(9) Whereas the provisions to be adopted in this Regulation should apply to significant structural changes the impact of which on the market goes beyond the national borders of any one Member State;

(10) Whereas the scope of application of this Regulation should therefore be defined according to the geographical area of activity of the undertakings concerned and be limited by quantitative thresholds in order to cover those concentrations which have a Community dimension whereas, at the end of an initial phase of the application of this Regulation, these thresholds should be reviewed in the light of the experience gained;

(11) Whereas a concentration with a Community dimension exists where the combined aggregate turnover of the undertakings concerned exceeds given levels worldwide and within the Community and where at least two of the undertakings concerned have their sole or main fields of activities in different Member States or where, although the undertakings in question act mainly in one and the same Member State, at least one of them has substantial operations in at least one other Member State whereas that is also the case where the concentrations are effected by undertakings which do not have their principal fields of activities in the Community but which have substantial operations there;[24]

(12) Whereas the arrangements to be introduced for the control of concentrations should, without prejudice to Article [86(2)] of the Treaty, respect the principle of non-discrimination between the public and the private sectors whereas, in the public sector, calculation of the turnover of an undertaking concerned in a concentration needs, therefore, to take account of undertakings

[24] See also recital 3 of the preamble to Regulation 1310/97 amending Regulation 4064/89 ([1997] OJ L180/1): "Whereas additional criteria should be established for the application of Community merger control ... whereas those criteria should consist of new thresholds established in terms of the total turnover of the undertakings concerned achieved world-wide, at Community level and in at least three Member States".

making up an economic unit with an independent power of decision, irrespective of the way in which their capital is held or of the rules of administrative supervision applicable to them;

(13) Whereas it is necessary to establish whether concentrations with a Community dimension are compatible or not with the common market from the point of view of the need to maintain and develop effective competition in the common market whereas, in so doing, the Commission must place its appraisal within the general framework of the achievement of the fundamental objectives referred to in Article 2 of the Treaty, including that of strengthening the Community's economic and social cohesion, referred to in Article [158];

(14) Whereas this Regulation should establish the principle that a concentration with a Community dimension which creates or strengthens a position as a result of which effective competition in the common market or in a substantial part of it is significantly impeded is to be declared incompatible with the common market;

(15) Whereas concentrations which, by reason of the limited market share of the undertakings concerned, are not liable to impede effective competition may be presumed to be compatible with the common market whereas, without prejudice to Articles [81] and [82] of the Treaty, an indication to this effect exists, in particular, where the market share of the undertakings concerned does not exceed 25 per cent either in the common market or in a substantial part of it;

(16) Whereas the Commission should have the task of taking all the decisions necessary to establish whether or not concentrations with a Community dimension are compatible with the common market, as well as decisions designed to restore effective competition;

(17) Whereas to ensure effective control undertakings should be obliged to give prior notification of concentrations with a Community dimension and provision should be made for the suspension of concentrations for a limited period, and for the possibility of extending or waiving a suspension where necessary whereas in the interests of legal certainty the validity of transactions must nevertheless be protected as much as necessary;

(18) Whereas a period within which the Commission must initiate proceedings in respect of a notified concentration and periods within which it must give a final decision on the compatibility or incompatibility with the common market of a notified concentration should be laid down;

(19) Whereas the undertakings concerned must be afforded the right to be heard by the Commission when proceedings have been initiated whereas the members of the management and supervisory bodies and the recognised representatives of the employees of the undertakings concerned, and third parties showing a legitimate interest, must also be given the opportunity to be heard;

(20) Whereas the Commission should act in close and constant liaison with the competent authorities of the Member States from which it obtains comments and information;

(21) Whereas, for the purposes of this Regulation, and in accordance with the case law of the Court of Justice, the Commission must be afforded the assistance of the Member States and must also be empowered to require information to be given and to carry out the necessary investigations in order to appraise concentrations;

(22) Whereas compliance with this Regulation must be enforceable by means of fines and periodic penalty payments whereas the Court of Justice should be given unlimited jurisdiction in that regard pursuant to Article [229] of the Treaty;

(23) Whereas it is appropriate to define the concept of concentration in such a manner as to cover only operations bringing about a lasting change in the structure of the undertakings concerned whereas it is therefore necessary to exclude from the scope of this Regulation those operations which have as their object or effect the coordination of the competitive behaviour of undertakings which remain independent, since such operations fall to be examined under the appropriate

provisions of the Regulations implementing Articles [81] and [82] of the Treaty whereas it is appropriate to make this distinction specifically in the case of the creation of joint ventures;[25]

(24) Whereas there is no coordination of competitive behaviour within the meaning of this Regulation where two or more undertakings agree to acquire jointly control of one or more other undertakings with the object and effect of sharing amongst themselves such undertakings or their assets;

(25) Whereas this Regulation should still apply where the undertakings concerned accept restrictions directly related and necessary to the implementation of the concentration;

(26) Whereas the Commission should be given exclusive competence to apply this Regulation, subject to review by the Court of Justice;

(27) Whereas the Member States may not apply their national legislation on competition to concentrations with a Community dimension, unless this Regulation makes provision therefor whereas the relevant powers of national authorities should be limited to cases where, failing intervention by the Commission, effective competition is likely to be significantly impeded within the territory of a Member State and where the competition interests of that Member State cannot be sufficiently protected otherwise by this Regulation whereas the Member States concerned must act promptly in such cases whereas this Regulation cannot, because of the diversity of national law, fix a single deadline for the adoption of remedies;

(28) Whereas, furthermore, the exclusive application of this Regulation to concentrations with a Community dimension is without prejudice to Article [296] of the Treaty, and does not prevent the Member States from taking appropriate measures to protect legitimate interests other than those pursued by this Regulation, provided that such measures are compatible with the general principles and other provisions of Community law;

(29) Whereas concentrations not covered by this Regulation come, in principle, within the jurisdiction of the Member States whereas, however, the Commission should have the power to act, at the request of a Member State concerned, in cases where effective competition could be significantly impeded within that Member State's territory;[26]

(30) Whereas the conditions in which concentrations involving Community undertakings are carried out in non-member countries should be observed, and provision should be made for the possibility of the Council giving the Commission an appropriate mandate for negotiation with a view to obtaining non-discriminatory treatment for Community undertakings;

---

[25] See also recital 5 of the preamble to Regulation 1310/97 amending Regulation 4064/89 ([1997] OJ L180/1): "Whereas it is appropriate to define the concept of concentration in such a manner as to cover operations bringing about a lasting change in the structure of the undertakings concerned; whereas in the specific case of joint ventures it is appropriate to include within the scope and procedure of Regulation 4064/89 all full-function joint ventures; whereas, in addition to the dominance test set out in Article 2 of that Regulation, it should be provided that the Commission apply the criteria of Article [81(1) and (3)] of the Treaty to such joint ventures, to the extent that their creation has as its direct consequence an appreciable restriction of competition between undertakings that remain independent; whereas, if the effects of such joint ventures on the market are primarily structural, Article [81(1)] does not as a general rule apply; whereas Article [81(1)] may apply if two or more parent companies remain active in the market of the joint venture, or, possibly, if the creation of the joint venture has as its object or effect the prevention, restriction or distortion of competition between the parent companies in upstream, downstream or neighbouring markets; whereas, in this context, the appraisal of all competition aspects of the creation of the joint venture must be made within the same procedure".

[26] See also recital 13 of the preamble to Regulation 1310/97 amending Regulation 4064/89 ([1997] OJ L180/1): "Whereas it should be expressly provided that two or more Member States may make a joint request pursuant to Article 22 of Regulation 4064/89; whereas to ensure effective control, provision should be made for the suspension of concentrations referred to the Commission by one or more Member States".

(31) Whereas this Regulation in no way detracts from the collective rights of employees as recognised in the undertakings concerned,
Has adopted this Regulation:

Article 1

7–028 **Scope**
[1. Without prejudice to Article 22 this Regulation shall apply to all concentrations with a Community dimension as defined in paragraphs 2 and 3].[27]

2. For the purposes of this Regulation, a concentration has a Community dimension where:
(a) the combined aggregate worldwide turnover of all the undertakings concerned[28] is more than [EUR][29] 5,000 million, and
(b) the aggregate Community-wide turnover of each of at least two of the undertakings concerned is more than [EUR] 250 million,
unless each of the undertakings concerned achieves more than two-thirds of its aggregate Community-wide turnover within one and the same Member State.

[3. For the purposes of this Regulation, a concentration that does not meet the thresholds laid down in paragraph 2 has a Community dimension where:
(a) the combined aggregate worldwide turnover of all the undertakings concerned is more than [EUR] 2,500 million;
(b) in each of at least three Member States, the combined aggregate turnover of all the undertakings concerned is more than [EUR] 100 million;
(c) in each of at least three Member States included for the purpose of point (b), the aggregate turnover of each of at least two of the undertakings concerned is more than [EUR] 25 million; and
(d) the aggregate Community-wide turnover of each of at least two of the undertakings concerned is more than [EUR] 100 million;
unless each of the undertakings concerned achieves more than two-thirds of its aggregate Community-wide turnover within one and the same Member State.][30]

[4. Before 1 July 2000 the Commission shall report to the Council on the operation of the thresholds and criteria set out in paragraphs 2 and 3.

5. Following the report referred to in paragraph 4 and on a proposal from the Commission, the Council, acting by a qualified majority, may revise the thresholds and criteria mentioned in paragraph 3.][31]

Article 2 Appraisal of concentrations

7–029 1. Concentrations within the scope of this Regulation shall be appraised in accordance with the following provisions with a view to establishing whether or not they are compatible with the common market.
In making this appraisal, the Commission shall take into account:

[27] Article 1(1) replaced by Reg. 1310/97 Art. 1(1)(a) ([1997] OJ L180/1, as corrected at [1998] OJ L40/17) as from 1 March 1998.
[28] See Commission Notice on the concept of undertakings concerned under Council Reg. 4064/89 on the control of concentrations between undertakings ([1998] OJ C66/14).
[29] References to ECU replaced with references to euros (EUR) by Regulation 1103/97 Art. 2 ([1997] OJ L162/1) as from 1 January 1999.
[30] Article 1(3) replaced by Reg. 1310/97 Art. 1(1)(b) as from 1 March 1998.
[31] Article 1(4) and (5) added by Reg. 1310/97 Art. 1(1)(c) as from 1 March 1998.

(a) the need to maintain and develop effective competition within the common market in view of, among other things, the structure of all the markets concerned and the actual or potential competition from undertakings located either within or outwith the Community;
(b) the market position of the undertakings concerned and their economic and financial power, the alternatives available to suppliers and users, their access to supplies or markets, any legal or other barriers to entry, supply and demand trends for the relevant goods and services, the interests of the intermediate and ultimate consumers, and the development of technical and economic progress provided that it is to consumers' advantage and does not form an obstacle to competition.

2. A concentration which does not create or strengthen a dominant position as a result of which effective competition would be significantly impeded in the common market or in a substantial part of it shall be declared compatible with the common market.

3. A concentration which creates or strengthens a dominant position as a result of which effective competition would be significantly impeded in the common market or in a substantial part of it shall be declared incompatible with the common market.

[4. To the extent that the creation of a joint venture constituting a concentration pursuant to Article 3 has as its object or effect the coordination of the competitive behaviour of undertakings that remain independent, such coordination shall be appraised in accordance with the criteria of Article [81 (1) and (3)] of the Treaty, with a view to establishing whether or not the operation is compatible with the common market.

In making this appraisal, the Commission shall take into account in particular:
— whether two or more parent companies retain to a significant extent activities in the same market as the joint venture or in a market which is downstream or upstream from that of the joint venture or in a neighbouring market closely related to this market,
— whether the coordination which is the direct consequence of the creation of the joint venture affords the undertakings concerned the possibility of eliminating competition in respect of a substantial part of the products or services in question.][32]

Article 3 **Definition of concentration**

1. A concentration shall be deemed to arise where: 7–030
(a) two or more previously independent undertakings merge, or
(b) — one or more persons already controlling at least one undertaking, or
— one or more undertakings acquire, whether by purchase of securities or assets, by contract or by any other means, direct or indirect control of the whole or parts of one or more other undertakings.[33]

2. [. . .][34]
The creation of a joint venture performing on a lasting basis all the functions of an autonomous economic entity, [. . .],[35] shall constitute a concentration within the meaning of paragraph 1(b).[36]

---

[32] Article 2(4) added by Reg. 1310/97 Art. 1(2) as from 1 March 1998.
[33] See Commission Notice on the concept of concentration under Council Reg. 4064/89 on the control of concentrations between undertakings ([1998] OJ C66/5).
[34] First sub-paragraph deleted by Reg. 1310/97 Art. 1(3)(a) as from 1 March 1998.
[35] Words deleted by Reg. 1310/97 Art. 1(3)(b) as from 1 March 1998.
[36] See Commission Notice on the concept of full-function joint ventures under Council Reg. 4064/89 on the control of concentrations between undertakings ([1998] OJ C66/1).

3. For the purposes of this Regulation, control shall be constituted by rights, contracts or any other means which, either separately or in combination and having regard to the considerations of fact or law involved, confer the possibility of exercising decisive influence on an undertaking, in particular by:
(a) ownership or the right to use all or part of the assets of an undertaking,
(b) rights or contracts which confer decisive influence on the composition, voting or decisions of the organs of an undertaking.

4. Control is acquired by persons or undertakings which:
(a) are holders of the rights or entitled to rights under the contracts concerned, or
(b) while not being holders of such rights or entitled to rights under such contracts, have the power to exercise the rights deriving therefrom.

5. A concentration shall not be deemed to arise where:
(a) credit institutions or other financial institutions or insurance companies, the normal activities of which include transactions and dealing in securities for their own account or for the account of others, hold on a temporary basis securities which they have acquired in an undertaking with a view to reselling them, provided that they do not exercise voting rights in respect of those securities with a view to determining the competitive behaviour of that undertaking or provided that they exercise such voting rights only with a view to preparing the disposal of all or part of that undertaking or of its assets or the disposal of those securities and that any such disposal takes place within one year of the date of acquisition that period may be extended by the Commission on request where such institutions or companies can show that the disposal was not reasonably possible within the period set;
(b) control is acquired by an office-holder according to the law of a Member State relating to liquidation, winding up, insolvency, cessation of payments, compositions or analogous proceedings;
(c) the operations referred to in paragraph 1(b) are carried out by the financial holding companies referred to in Article 5(3) of the Fourth Council Directive 78/660 of 25 July 1978, on the annual accounts of certain types of companies,[37] as last amended by Directive 84/569,[38] provided however that the voting rights in respect of the holding are exercised, in particular in relation to the appointment of members of the management and supervisory bodies of the undertakings in which they have holdings, only to maintain the full value of those investments and not to determine directly or indirectly the competitive conduct of those undertakings.

Article 4 Prior notification of concentrations

7–031 1. Concentrations with a Community dimension defined in this Regulation shall be notified to the Commission not more than one week after the conclusion of the agreement, or the announcement of the public bid, or the acquisition of a controlling interest. That week shall begin when the first of those events occurs.

2. A concentration which consists of a merger within the meaning of Article 3(1)(a) or in the acquisition of joint control within the meaning of Article 3(1)(b) shall be notified jointly by the parties to the merger or by those acquiring joint control as the case may be. In all other cases, the notification shall be effected by the person or undertaking acquiring control of the whole or parts of one or more undertakings.

3. Where the Commission finds that a notified concentration falls within the scope of this Regulation, it shall publish the fact of the notification, at the same time

[37] [1978] OJ L222/11.
[38] [1984] OJ L314/28.

indicating the names of the parties, the nature of the concentration and the economic sectors involved. The Commission shall take account of the legitimate interest of undertakings in the protection of their business secrets.

Article 5 Calculation of turnover[39]

1. Aggregate turnover within the meaning of Article 1(2) shall comprise the amounts derived by the undertakings concerned[40] in the preceding financial year from the sale of products and the provision of services falling within the undertakings' ordinary activities after deduction of sales rebates and of value added tax and other taxes directly related to turnover. The aggregate turnover of an undertaking concerned shall not include the sale of products or the provision of services between any of the undertakings referred to in paragraph 4. **7–032**

Turnover, in the Community or in a Member State, shall comprise products sold and services provided to undertakings or consumers, in the Community or in that Member State as the case may be.

2. By way of derogation from paragraph 1, where the concentration consists in the acquisition of parts, whether or not constituted as legal entities, of one or more undertakings, only the turnover relating to the parts which are the subject of the transaction shall be taken into account with regard to the seller or sellers.

However, two or more transactions within the meaning of the first subparagraph which take place within a two-year period between the same persons or undertakings shall be treated as one and the same concentration arising on the date of the last transaction.

[3. In place of turnover the following shall be used:

(a) for credit institutions and other financial institutions, as regards Article 1(2) and (3), the sum of the following income items as defined in Council Directive 86/635 of 8 December 1986, on the annual accounts and consolidated accounts of banks and other financial institutions,[41] after deduction of value added tax and other taxes directly related to those items, where appropriate:
   (i) interest income and similar income;
   (ii) income from securities:
      — income from shares and other variable yield securities,
      — income from participating interests,
      — income from shares in affiliated undertakings;
   (iii) commissions receivable;
   (iv) net profit on financial operations;
   (v) other operating income.

   The turnover of a credit or financial institution in the Community or in a Member State shall comprise the income items, as defined above, which are received by the branch or division of that institution established in the Community or in the Member State in question, as the case may be;

(b) for insurance undertakings, the value of gross premiums written which shall comprise all amounts received and receivable in respect of insurance contracts issued by or on behalf of the insurance undertakings, including also outgoing reinsurance premiums, and after deduction of taxes and parafiscal contributions or levies charged by reference to the amounts of individual premiums or the total volume of premiums; as regards Article 1(2)(b) and (3)(b), (c) and (d) and the final part of Article 1(2) and (3), gross premiums received from Community residents and from residents of one Member State respectively shall be taken into account.][42]

---

[39] See Commission Notice on the calculation of turnover under Council Reg. 4064/89 on the control of concentrations between undertakings ([1998] OJ C66/25).

[40] See Commission Notice on the concept of undertakings concerned under Council Reg. 4064/89 on the control of concentrations between undertakings ([1998] OJ C66/14).

[41] [1986] OJ L372/1.

[42] Article 5(3) replaced by Reg. 1310/97 Art. 1(4) first indent as from 1 March 1998.

4. [Without prejudice to paragraph 2, the aggregate turnover of an undertaking concerned within the meaning of Article 1 (2) and (3) shall be calculated by adding together the respective turnovers of the following:][43]

(a) the undertaking concerned;
(b) those undertakings in which the undertaking concerned, directly or indirectly:
    — owns more than half the capital or business assets, or
    — has the power to exercise more than half the voting rights, or
    — has the power to appoint more than half the members of the supervisory board, the administrative board or bodies legally representing the undertakings, or
    — has the right to manage the undertakings' affairs;
(c) those undertakings which have in the undertaking concerned the rights or powers listed in (b);
(d) those undertakings in which an undertaking as referred to in (c) has the rights or powers listed in (b);
(e) those undertakings in which two or more undertakings as referred to in (a) to (d) jointly have the rights or powers listed in (b).

5. [Where undertakings concerned by the concentration jointly have the rights or powers listed in paragraph 4 (b), in calculating the aggregate turnover of the undertakings concerned for the purposes of Article 1 (2) and (3):][44]

(a) no account shall be taken of the turnover resulting from the sale of products or the provision of services between the joint undertaking and each of the undertakings concerned or any other undertaking connected with any one of them, as set out in paragraph 4(b) to (e);
(b) account shall be taken of the turnover resulting from the sale of products and the provision of services between the joint undertaking and any third undertakings. This turnover shall be apportioned equally amongst the undertakings concerned.

Article 6 Examination of the notification and initiation of proceedings

7–033 1. The Commission shall examine the notification as soon as it is received.

(a) Where it concludes that the concentration notified does not fall within the scope of this Regulation, it shall record that finding by means of a decision.
(b) Where it finds that the concentration notified, although falling within the scope of this Regulation, does not raise serious doubts as to its compatibility with the common market, it shall decide not to oppose it and shall declare that it is compatible with the common market.
    [The decision declaring the concentration compatible shall also cover restrictions directly related and necessary to the implementation of the concentration.][45, 46]
(c) [Without prejudice to paragraph 2, where the Commission finds that the concentration notified falls within the scope of this Regulation and raises serious doubts as to its compatibility with the common market, it shall decide to initiate proceedings.][47]

[2. Where the Commission finds that, following modification by the undertakings concerned, a notified concentration no longer raises serious doubts within the meaning of paragraph 1(c), it may decide to declare the concentration compatible with the common market pursuant to paragraph 1(b).

[43] Words replaced by Reg. 1310/97 Art. 1(4) second indent as from 1 March 1998.
[44] Words replaced by Reg. 1310/97 Art. 1(4) third indent as from 1 March 1998.
[45] Sub-paragraph added by Reg. 1310/97 Art. 1(5)(a) first indent as from 1 March 1998.
[46] See Commission Notice on restrictions directly related and necessary to concentrations ([2001] OJ C188/5). See also Commission Notice on a simplified procedure for treatment of certain concentrations under Council Reg. 4064/89 ([2000] OJ C217/32).
[47] Point (c) replaced by Reg. 1310/97 Art. 1(5)(a) second indent as from 1 March 1998.

The Commission may attach to its decision under paragraph 1 (b) conditions and obligations intended to ensure that the undertakings concerned comply with the commitments they have entered into *vis-à-vis* the Commission with a view to rendering the concentration compatible with the common market.

3. The Commission may revoke the decision it has taken pursuant to paragraph 1(a) or (b) where:
(a) the decision is based on incorrect information for which one of the undertakings is responsible or where it has been obtained by deceit, or
(b) the undertakings concerned commit a breach of an obligation attached to the decision.

4. In the cases referred to in paragraph 3, the Commission may take a decision under paragraph 1, without being bound by the deadlines referred to in Article 10(1).][48]

[5.][49] The Commission shall notify its decision to the undertakings concerned and the competent authorities of the Member States without delay.

Article 7 Suspension of concentrations

[1. A concentration as defined in Article 1 shall not be put into effect either before its notification or until it as been declared compatible with the common market pursuant to a decision under Article 6(1)(b) or Article 8(2) or on the basis of a presumption according to Article 10 (6).][50] **7–034**

2. [. . .][51]

3. [Paragraph 1][52] shall not prevent the implementation of a public bid which has been notified to the Commission in accordance with Article 4(1), provided that the acquirer does not exercise the voting rights attached to the securities in question or does so only to maintain the full value of those investments and on the basis of a derogation granted by the Commission under paragraph 4.

[4. The Commission may, on request, grant a derogation from the obligations imposed in paragraphs 1 or 3. The request to grant a derogation must be reasoned. In deciding on the request, the Commission shall take into account *inter alia* the effects of the suspension on one or more undertakings concerned by a concentration or on a third party and the threat to competition posed by the concentration. That derogation may be made subject to conditions and obligations in order to ensure conditions of effective competition. A derogation may be applied for and granted at any time, even before notification or after the transaction.][53]

[5. The validity of any transaction carried out in contravention of paragraph 1 shall be dependent on a decision pursuant to Article 6(1)(b) or Article 8(2) or (3) or on a presumption pursuant to Article 10(6).

This Article shall, however, have no effect on the validity of transactions in securities including those convertible into other securities admitted to trading on a market which is regulated and supervised by authorities recognised by public bodies, operates regularly and is accessible directly or indirectly to the public, unless the buyer and seller knew or ought to have known that the transaction was carried out in contravention of paragraph 1.][54]

[48] Article 6(2), (3) and (4) added by Reg. 1310/97 Art. 1(5)(b) as from 1 March 1998.
[49] Article 6(2) renumbered as Art. 6(5) by Reg. 1310/97 Art. 1(5)(c) as from 1 March 1998.
[50] Article 7(1) replaced by Reg. 1310/97 Art. 1(6)(a) as from 1 March 1998.
[51] Article 7(2) deleted by Reg. 1310/97 Art. 1(6)(b) as from 1 March 1998.
[52] Words replaced by Reg. 1310/97 Art. 1(6)(c) as from 1 March 1998.
[53] Article 7(4) replaced by Reg. 1310/97 Art. 1(6)(d) as from 1 March 1998.
[54] Article 7(5) replaced by Reg. 1310/97 Art. 1(6)(e) as from 1 March 1998.

Article 8 Powers of decision of the Commission

7–035 1. Without prejudice to Article 9, all proceedings initiated pursuant to Article 6(1)(c) shall be closed by means of a decision as provided for in paragraphs 2 to 5.

[2. Where the Commission finds that, following modification by the undertakings concerned if necessary, a notified concentration fulfils the criterion laid down in Article 2(2) and, in the cases referred to in Article 2(4), the criteria laid down in Article [81(3)] of the Treaty, it shall issue a decision declaring the concentration compatible with the common market.[55]

It may attach to its decision conditions and obligations intended to ensure that the undertakings concerned comply with the commitments they have entered into *vis-à-vis* the Commission with a view to rendering the concentration compatible with the common market. The decision declaring the concentration compatible with the common market shall also cover restrictions directly related and necessary to the implementation of the concentration.][56, 57]

[3. Where the Commission finds that a concentration fulfils the criterion defined in Article 2(3) or, in the cases referred to in Article 2(4), does not fulfil the criteria laid down in Article [81(3)] of the Treaty, it shall issue a decision declaring that the concentration is incompatible with the common market.][58]

4. Where a concentration has already been implemented, the Commission may, in a decision pursuant to paragraph 3 or by separate decision, require the undertakings or assets brought together to be separated or the cessation of joint control or any other action that may be appropriate in order to restore conditions of effective competition.

5. The Commission may revoke the decision it has taken pursuant to paragraph 2 where:

(a) the declaration of compatibility is based on incorrect information for which one of the undertakings is responsible or where it has been obtained by deceit or
(b) the undertakings concerned commit a breach of an obligation attached to the decision.

6. In the cases referred to in paragraph 5, the Commission may take a decision under paragraph 3, without being bound by the deadline referred to in Article 10(3).

Article 9 Referral to the competent authorities of the Member States

7–036 1. The Commission may, by means of a decision notified without delay to the undertakings concerned and the competent authorities of the other Member States, refer a notified concentration to the competent authorities of the Member State concerned in the following circumstances.

[2. Within three weeks of the date of receipt of the copy of the notification a Member State may inform the Commission, which shall inform the undertakings concerned, that:

(a) a concentration threatens to create or to strengthen a dominant position as a result of which effective competition will be significantly impeded on a market within that Member State, which presents all the characteristics of a distinct market, or

[55] See Commission Notice on remedies acceptable under Council Reg. 4064/89 and under Commission Reg. 447/98 ([2001] OJ C68/3).

[56] Article 8(2) replaced by Reg. 1310/97 Art. 1(7)(a) as from 1 March 1998.

[57] See Commission Notice on restrictions directly related and necessary to concentrations ([2001] OJ C188/5).

[58] Article 8(3) replaced by Reg. 1310/97 Art. 1(7)(b) as from 1 March 1998.

(b) a concentration affects competition on a market within that Member State, which presents all the characteristics of a distinct market and which does not constitute a substantial part of the common market.][59]

3. If the Commission considers that, having regard to the market for the products or services in question and the geographical reference market within the meaning of paragraph 7, there is such a distinct market and that such a threat exists, either:
(a) it shall itself deal with the case in order to maintain or restore effective competition on the market concerned or
(b) [it shall refer the whole or part of the case to the competent authorities of the Member State concerned with a view to the application of that State's national competition law.][60]

If, however, the Commission considers that such a distinct market or threat does not exist it shall adopt a decision to that effect which it shall address to the Member State concerned.

[In cases where a Member State informs the Commission that a concentration affects competition in a distinct market within its territory that does not form a substantial part of the common market, the Commission shall refer the whole or part of the case relating to the distinct market concerned, if it considers that such a distinct market is affected.][61]

4. A decision to refer or not to refer pursuant to paragraph 3 shall be taken:
(a) as a general rule within the six-week period provided for in Article 10(1), second sub-paragraph, where the Commission, pursuant to Article 6(1)(b), has not initiated proceedings, or
(b) within three months at most of the notification of the concentration concerned where the Commission has initiated proceedings under Article 6(1)(c), without taking the preparatory steps in order to adopt the necessary measures under Article 8(2), second sub-paragraph, (3) or (4) to maintain or restore effective competition on the market concerned.

5. If within the three months referred to in paragraph 4(b) the Commission, despite a reminder from the Member State concerned, has not taken a decision on referral in accordance with paragraph 3 nor has taken the preparatory steps referred to in paragraph 4(b), it shall be deemed to have taken a decision to refer the case to the Member State concerned in accordance with paragraph 3(b).

6. The publication of any report or the announcement of the findings of the examination of the concentration by the competent authority of the Member State concerned shall be effected not more than four months after the Commission's referral.

7. The geographical reference market shall consist of the area in which the undertakings concerned are involved in the supply and demand of products or services, in which the conditions of competition are sufficiently homogeneous and which can be distinguished from neighbouring areas because, in particular, conditions of competition are appreciably different in those areas. This assessment should take account in particular of the nature and characteristics of the products or services concerned, of the existence of entry barriers or of consumer preferences, of appreciable differences of the undertakings' market shares between the area concerned and neighbouring areas or of substantial price differences.

8. In applying the provisions of this Article, the Member State concerned may take only the measures strictly necessary to safeguard or restore effective competition on the market concerned.

[59] Article 9(2) replaced by Reg. 1310/97 Art. 1(8)(a) as from 1 March 1998.
[60] Article 9(3)(b) replaced by Reg. 1310/97 Art. 1(8)(b) first indent as from 1 March 1998.
[61] Sub-paragraph added by Reg. 1310/97 Art. 1(8)(b) second indent as from 1 March 1998.

9. In accordance with the relevant provisions of the Treaty, any Member State may appeal to the Court of Justice, and in particular request the application of Article [243], for the purpose of applying its national competition law.

[10. This Article may be re-examined at the same time as the thresholds referred to in Article 1.][62]

Article 10 Time-limits for initiating proceedings and for decisions

7–037 1. The decisions referred to in Article 6(1) must be taken within one month at most. That period shall begin on the day following that of the receipt of a notification or, if the information to be supplied with the notification is incomplete, on the day following that of the receipt of the complete information.

That period shall be increased to six weeks if the Commission receives a request from a Member State in accordance with Article 9(2) [or where, after notification of a concentration, the undertakings concerned submit commitments pursuant to Article 6(2), which are intended by the parties to form the basis for a decision pursuant to Article 6(1)(b)].[63]

2. Decisions taken pursuant to Article 8(2) concerning notified concentrations must be taken as soon as it appears that the serious doubts referred to in Article 6(1)(c) have been removed, particularly as a result of modifications made by the undertakings concerned, and at the latest by the deadline laid down in paragraph 3.

3. Without prejudice to Article 8(6), decisions taken pursuant to Article 8(3) concerning notified concentrations must be taken within not more than four months of the date on which proceedings are initiated.

4. [The periods set by paragraphs 1 and 3][64] shall exceptionally be suspended where, owing to circumstances for which one of the undertakings involved in the concentration is responsible, the Commission has had to request information by decision pursuant to Article 11 or to order an investigation by decision pursuant to Article 13.

5. Where the Court of Justice gives a Judgement which annuls the whole or part of a Commission decision taken under this Regulation, the periods laid down in this Regulation shall start again from the date of the Judgement.

6. Where the Commission has not taken a decision in accordance with Article 6(1)(b) or (c) or Article 8(2) or (3) within the deadlines set in paragraphs 1 and 3 respectively, the concentration shall be deemed to have been declared compatible with the common market, without prejudice to Article 9.

Article 11 Requests for information

7–038 1. In carrying out the duties assigned to it by this Regulation, the Commission may obtain all necessary information from the Governments and competent authorities of the Member States, from the persons referred to in Article 3(1)(b), and from undertakings and associations of undertakings.

2. When sending a request for information to a person, an undertaking or an association of undertakings, the Commission shall at the same time send a copy of

[62] Article 9(10) replaced by Reg. 1310/97 Art. 1(8)(c) as from 1 March 1998.
[63] Words added by Reg. 1310/97 Art. 1(9)(a) as from 1 March 1998.
[64] Phrase replaced by Reg. 1310/97 Art. 1(9)(b) as from 1 March 1998.

the request to the competent authority of the Member State within the territory of which the residence of the person or the seat of the undertaking or association of undertakings is situated.

3. In its request the Commission shall state the legal basis and the purpose of the request and also the penalties provided for in Article 14(1)(c) for supplying incorrect information.

4. The information requested shall be provided, in the case of undertakings, by their owners or their representatives and, in the case of legal persons, companies or firms, or of associations having no legal personality, by the persons authorised to represent them by law or by their statutes.

5. Where a person, an undertaking or an association of undertakings does not provide the information requested within the period fixed by the Commission or provides incomplete information, the Commission shall by decision require the information to be provided. The decision shall specify what information is required, fix an appropriate period within which it is to be supplied and state the penalties provided for in Articles 14(1)(c) and 15(1)(a) and the right to have the decision reviewed by the Court of Justice.

6. The Commission shall at the same time send a copy of its decision to the competent authority of the Member State within the territory of which the residence of the person or the seat of the undertaking or association of undertakings is situated.

Article 12 Investigations by the authorities of the Member States

1. At the request of the Commission, the competent authorities of the Member **7–039**
States shall undertake the investigations which the Commission considers to be necessary under Article 13(1), or which it has ordered by decision pursuant to Article 13(3). The officials of the competent authorities of the Member States responsible for conducting those investigations shall exercise their powers upon production of an authorisation in writing issued by the competent authority of the Member State within the territory of which the investigation is to be carried out. Such authorisation shall specify the subject matter and purpose of the investigation.

2. If so requested by the Commission or by the competent authority of the Member State within the territory of which the investigation is to be carried out, officials of the Commission may assist the officials of that authority in carrying out their duties.

Article 13 Investigative powers of the Commission

1. In carrying out the duties assigned to it by this Regulation, the Commission may **7–040**
undertake all necessary investigations into undertakings and associations of undertakings.

To that end the officials authorised by the Commission shall be empowered:

(a) to examine the books and other business records;
(b) to take or demand copies of or extracts from the books and business records;
(c) to ask for oral explanations on the spot;
(d) to enter any premises, land and means of transport of undertakings.

2. The officials of the Commission authorised to carry out the investigations shall exercise their powers on production of an authorisation in writing specifying the subject matter and purpose of the investigation and the penalties provided for in Article 14(1)(d) in cases where production of the required books or other business records is incomplete. In good time before the investigation, the Commission shall inform, in writing, the competent authority of the Member State within the territory of which the investigation is to be carried out of the investigation and of the identities of the authorised officials.

3. Undertakings and associations of undertakings shall submit to investigations ordered by decision of the Commission. The decision shall specify the subject matter and purpose of the investigation, appoint the date on which it shall begin and state the penalties provided for in Articles 14(1)(d) and 15(1)(b) and the right to have the decision reviewed by the Court of Justice.

4. The Commission shall in good time and in writing inform the competent authority of the Member State within the territory of which the investigation is to be carried out of its intention of taking a decision pursuant to paragraph 3. It shall hear the competent authority before taking its decision.

5. Officials of the competent authority of the Member State within the territory of which the investigation is to be carried out may, at the request of that authority or of the Commission, assist the officials of the Commission in carrying out their duties.

6. Where an undertaking or association of undertakings opposes an investigation ordered pursuant to this Article, the Member State concerned shall afford the necessary assistance to the officials authorised by the Commission to enable them to carry out their investigation. To this end the Member States shall, after consulting the Commission, take the necessary measures within one year of the entry into force of this Regulation.

Article 14 Fines

7–041 1. The Commission may by decision impose on the persons referred to in Article 3(1)(b), undertakings or associations of undertakings fines of from [EUR][65] 1,000 to 50,000 where intentionally or negligently:
(a) they fail to notify a concentration in accordance with Article 4;
(b) they supply incorrect or misleading information in a notification pursuant to Article 4;
(c) they supply incorrect information in response to a request made pursuant to Article 11 or fail to supply information within the period fixed by a decision taken pursuant to Article 11;
(d) they produce the required books or other business records in incomplete form during investigations under Article 12 or 13, or refuse to submit to an investigation ordered by decision taken pursuant to Article 13.

2. The Commission may by decision impose fines not exceeding 10 per cent of the aggregate turnover of the undertakings concerned within the meaning of Article 5 on the persons or undertakings concerned where, either intentionally or negligently, they:
(a) fail to comply with an obligation imposed by decision pursuant to Article 7(4) or 8(2), second sub-paragraph;
(b) put into effect a concentration in breach of Article 7(1) or disregard a decision taken pursuant to Article 7(2);
(c) put into effect a concentration declared incompatible with the common market by decision pursuant to Article 8(3) or do not take the measures ordered by decision pursuant to Article 8(4).

3. In setting the amount of a fine, regard shall be had to the nature and gravity of the infringement.

4. Decisions taken pursuant to paragraphs 1 and 2 shall not be of criminal law nature.

[65] References to ECU replaced with references to euros (EUR) by Reg. 1103/97 Art. 2 ([1997] OJ L162/1) as from 1 January 1999.

Article 15 Periodic penalty payments

1. The Commission may by decision impose on the persons referred to in Article 3(1)(b), undertakings or associations of undertakings concerned periodic penalty payments of up to [EUR][66] 25,000 for each day of delay calculated from the date set in the decision, in order to compel them: **7–042**

(a) to supply complete and correct information which it has requested by decision pursuant to Article 11;

(b) to submit to an investigation which it has ordered by decision pursuant to Article 13.

2. The Commission may by decision impose on the persons referred to in Article 3(1)(b) or on undertakings periodic penalty payments of up to [EUR] 100,000 for each day of delay calculated from the date set in the decision, in order to compel them:

(a) to comply with an obligation imposed by decision pursuant to Article 7(4) or Article 8(2), second sub-paragraph, or

(b) to apply the measures ordered by decision pursuant to Article 8(4).

3. Where the persons referred to in Article 3(1)(b), undertakings or associations of undertakings have satisfied the obligation which it was the purpose of the periodic penalty payment to enforce, the Commission may set the total amount of the periodic penalty payments at a lower figure than that which would arise under the original decision.

Article 16 Review by the Court of Justice

The Court of Justice shall have unlimited jurisdiction within the meaning of Article [229] of the Treaty to review decisions whereby the Commission has fixed a fine or periodic penalty payments it may cancel, reduce or increase the fine or periodic penalty payments imposed. **7–043**

Article 17 Professional secrecy

1. Information acquired as a result of the application of Article 11, 12, 13 and 18 shall be used only for the purposes of the relevant request, investigation or hearing. **7–044**

2. Without prejudice to Articles 4(3), 18 and 20, the Commission and the competent authorities of the Member States, their officials and other servants shall not disclose information they have acquired through the application of this Regulation of the kind covered by the obligation of professional secrecy.

3. Paragraphs 1 and 2 shall not prevent publication of general information or of surveys which do not contain information relating to particular undertakings or associations of undertakings.

Article 18 Hearing of the parties and of third persons

1. Before taking any decision provided for in [Article 7(4)],[67] Article 8(2), second sub-paragraph, and (3) to (5) and Articles 14 and 15, the Commission shall give the persons, undertakings and associations of undertakings concerned the opportunity, at every stage of the procedure up to the consultation of the Advisory Committee, of making known their views on the objections against them. **7–045**

[2. By way of derogation from paragraph 1, a decision to grant a derogation from suspension as referred to in Article 7(4) may be taken provisionally, without the

---

[66] References to ECU replaced with references to euros (EUR) by Reg. 1103/97 Art. 2 ([1997] OJ L162/1) as from 1 January 1999.

[67] Words replaced by Reg. 1310/97 Art. 1(10)(a) as from 1 March 1998.

persons, undertakings or associations of undertakings concerned being given the opportunity to make known their views beforehand, provided that the Commission gives them that opportunity as soon as possible after having taken its decision.][68]

3. The Commission shall base its decision only on objections on which the parties have been able to submit their observations. The rights of the defence shall be fully respected in the proceedings. Access to the file shall be open at least to the parties directly involved, subject to the legitimate interest of undertakings in the protection of their business secrets.

4. In so far as the Commission or the competent authorities of the Member States deem it necessary, they may also hear other natural or legal persons. Natural or legal persons showing a sufficient interest and especially members of the administrative or management bodies of the undertakings concerned or the recognised representatives of their employees shall be entitled, upon application, to be heard.

Article 19 Liaison with the authorities of the Member States

7–046 1. The Commission shall transmit to the competent authorities of the Member States copies of notifications within three working days and, as soon as possible, copies of the most important documents lodged with or issued by the Commission pursuant to this Regulation. [Such documents shall include commitments which are intended by the parties to form the basis for a decision pursuant to Articles 6(1)(b) or 8(2).][69]

2. The Commission shall carry out the procedures set out in this Regulation in close and constant liaison with the competent authorities of the Member States, which may express their views upon those procedures. For the purposes of Article 9 it shall obtain information from the competent authority of the Member State as referred to in paragraph 2 of that Article and give it the opportunity to make known its views at every stage of the procedure up to the adoption of a decision pursuant to paragraph 3 of that Article to that end it shall give it access to the file.

3. An Advisory Committee on concentrations shall be consulted before any decision is taken pursuant to Article 8(2) to (5), 14 or 15, or any provisions are adopted pursuant to Article 23.

4. The Advisory Committee shall consist of representatives of the authorities of the Member States. Each Member State shall appoint one or two representatives if unable to attend, they may be replaced by other representatives. At least one of the representatives of a Member State shall be competent in matters of restrictive practices and dominant positions.

5. Consultation shall take place at a joint meeting convened at the invitation of and chaired by the Commission. A summary of the case, together with an indication of the most important documents and a preliminary draft of the decision to be taken for each case considered, shall be sent with the invitation. The meeting shall take place not less than 14 days after the invitation has been sent. The Commission may in exceptional cases shorten that period as appropriate in order to avoid serious harm to one or more of the undertakings concerned by a concentration.

6. The Advisory Committee shall deliver an opinion on the Commission's draft decision, if necessary by taking a vote. The Advisory Committee may deliver an

[68] Article 18(2) replaced by Reg. 1310/97 Art. 1(10)(b) as from 1 March 1998.
[69] Words added by Reg. 1310/97 Art. 1(11) as from 1 March 1998.

opinion even if some members are absent and unrepresented. The opinion shall be delivered in writing and appended to the draft decision. The Commission shall take the utmost account of the opinion delivered by the Committee. It shall inform the Committee of the manner in which its opinion has been taken into account.

7. The Advisory Committee may recommend publication of the opinion. The Commission may carry out such publication. The decision to publish shall take due account of the legitimate interest of undertakings in the protection of their business secrets and of the interest of the undertakings concerned in such publication's taking place.

Article 20 Publication of decisions

1. The Commission shall publish the decisions which it takes pursuant to Article 8(2) to (5) in the *Official Journal of the European Communities*. **7–047**

2. The publication shall state the names of the parties and the main content of the decision it shall have regard to the legitimate interest of undertakings in the protection of their business secrets.

Article 21 Jurisdiction

1. Subject to review by the Court of Justice, the Commission shall have sole jurisdiction to take the decisions provided for in this Regulation. **7–048**

2. No Member State shall apply its national legislation on competition to any concentration that has a Community dimension.

The first sub-paragraph shall be without prejudice to any Member State's power to carry out any enquiries necessary for the application of Article 9(2) or after referral, pursuant to Article 9(3), first sub-paragraph, indent (b), or (5), to take the measures strictly necessary for the application of Article 9(8).

3. Notwithstanding paragraphs 1 and 2, Member States may take appropriate measures to protect legitimate interests other than those taken into consideration by this Regulation and compatible with the general principles and other provisions of Community law.

Public security, plurality of the media and prudential rules shall be regarded as legitimate interests within the meaning of the first sub-paragraph.

Any other public interest must be communicated to the Commission by the Member State concerned and shall be recognised by the Commission after an assessment of its compatibility with the general principles and other provisions of Community law before the measures referred to above may be taken. The Commission shall inform the Member State concerned of its decision within one month of that communication.

Article 22 Application of the Regulation

[1. This Regulation alone shall apply to concentrations as defined in Article 3, and Regulations 17,[70] 1017/68,[71] 4056/86[72] and 3975/87[73] shall not apply, except in relation to joint ventures that do not have a Community dimension and which have their object or effect the coordination of the competitive behaviour of undertakings that remain independent. **7–049**

2. . . .][74]

[70] [1959–1962] OJ, Eng. Spec. Ed., p.87: first regulation implementing Arts 81 and 82 of the Treaty (see above).

[71] [1968(I)] OJ, Eng. Spec. Ed., p.302: application of rules of competition to transport by rail, road and inland waterway.

[72] [1986] OJ L378/4: application of Arts 81 and 82 of the Treaty to maritime transport.

[73] [1987] OJ L374/1: application of the rules on competition to air transport.

[74] Article 22(1) and (2) replaced by Reg. 1310/97 Art. 1(12)(a) ([1997] OJ L180/1) as from 1 March 1998.

[3. If the Commission finds, at the request of a Member State or at the joint request of two or more Member States, that a concentration as defined in Article 3 that has no Community dimension within the meaning of Article 1 creates or strengthens a dominant position as a result of which effective competition would be significantly impeded within the territory of the Member State or States making the joint request, it may, insofar as that concentration affects trade between Member States, adopt the decisions provided for in Article 8(2), second sub-paragraph, (3) and (4).][75]

[4. Articles 2(1)(a) and (b), 5, 6, 8 and 10 to 20 shall apply to a request made pursuant to paragraph 3. Article 7 shall apply to the extent that the concentration has not been put into effect on the date on which the Commission informs the parties that a request has been made.

The period within which proceedings may be initiated pursuant to Article 10(1) shall begin on the day following that of the receipt of the request from the Member State or States concerned. The request must be made within one month at most of the date on which the concentration was made known to the Member State or to all Member States making a joint request or effected. This period shall begin on the date of the first of those events.][76]

5. Pursuant to paragraph 3 the Commission shall take only the measures strictly necessary to maintain or restore effective competition within the territory of the Member State [or States][77] at the request of which it intervenes.

6. [. . .][78]

Article 23 Implementing provisions

7–050 The Commission shall have the power to adopt implementing provisions concerning the form, content and other details of notifications pursuant to Article 4, [time-limits pursuant to Articles 7, 9, 10 and 22],[79] and hearings pursuant to Article 18.

[The Commission shall have the power to lay down the procedure and time-limits for the submission of commitments pursuant to Articles 6(2) and 8(2).][80, 81]

Article 24 Relations with non-member countries

7–051 1. The Member States shall inform the Commission of the general difficulties encountered by their undertakings with concentrations as defined in Article 3 in a non-member country.

2. Initially not more than one year after the entry into force of this Regulation and thereafter periodically the Commission shall draw up a report examining the treatment accorded to Community undertakings, in the terms referred to in paragraphs 3 and 4, as regards concentrations in non-member countries. The Commission shall submit those reports to the Council, together with any recommendations.

3. Whenever it appears to the Commission, either on the basis of the reports referred to in paragraph 2 or on the basis of other information, that a non-member country does not grant Community undertakings treatment comparable to that

[75] Article 22(3) replaced by Reg. 1310/97 Art. 1(12)(b) as from 1 March 1998.
[76] Article 22(4) replaced by Reg. 1310/97 Art. 1(12)(c) as from 1 March 1998.
[77] Words added by Reg. 1310/97 Art. 1(12)(d) as from 1 March 1998.
[78] Article 22(6) deleted by Reg. 1310/97 Art. 1(12)(e) as from 1 March 1998.
[79] Words replaced by Reg. 1310/97 Art. 1(13)(a) as from 1 March 1998.
[80] Sub-paragraph added by Reg. 1310/97 Art. 1(13)(a) as from 1 March 1998.
[81] Current implementing regulation: Reg. 447/98 on the notifications, time-limits and hearings provided for in Regulation 4064/89 ([1998] OJ L61/1).

granted by the Community to undertakings from that non-member country, the Commission may submit proposals to the Council for an appropriate mandate for negotiation with a view to obtaining comparable treatment for Community undertakings.

4. Measures taken under this Article shall comply with the obligations of the Community or of the Member States, without prejudice to Article 307 of the Treaty, under international agreements, whether bilateral of multilateral.

Article 25 Entry into force

1. This Regulation shall enter into force on 21 September 1990. **7–052**

2. This Regulation shall not apply to any concentration which was the subject of an agreement or announcement or where control was acquired within the meaning of Article 4(1) before the date of this Regulation's entry into force and it shall not in any circumstances apply to any concentration in respect of which proceedings were initiated before that date by a Member State's authority with responsibility for competition.

This Regulation shall be binding in its entirety and directly applicable in all Member States.

Commission Regulation 240/96 of 31 January 1996, on the application of Article [81(3)] of the Treaty to certain categories of technology transfer agreements

([1996] OJ L31/2; Doc. Ref. 31996R0240)

The Commission of the European Communities, **7–053**

Having regard to the Treaty establishing the European Community,

Having regard to Council Regulation 19/65 of 2 March 1965, on the application of Article [81(3)] of the Treaty to certain categories of agreements and concerted practices,[82] as last amended by the Act of Accession of Austria, Finland and Sweden, and in particular Article 1 thereof,

Having published a draft of this Regulation,[83]

After consulting the Advisory Committee on Restrictive Practices and Dominant Positions,

Whereas:

(1) Regulation 19/65 empowers the Commission to apply Article [81(3)] of the Treaty by regulation to certain categories of agreements and concerted practices falling within the scope of Article [81(1)] which include restrictions imposed in relation to the acquisition or use of industrial property rights—in particular of patents, utility models, designs or trademarks—or to the rights arising out of contracts for assignment of, or the right to use, a method of manufacture of knowledge relating to use or to the application of industrial processes.

(2) The Commission has made use of this power by adopting Regulation 2349/84 of 23 July 1984, on the application of Article [81(3)] of the Treaty to certain categories of patent licensing agreements,[84] as last amended by Regulation 2131/95,[85] and Regulation 556/89 of 30 November 1988, on the application of Article [81(3)] of the Treaty to certain categories of know-how licensing agreements,[86] as last amended by the Act of Accession of Austria, Finland and Sweden.

(3) These two block exemptions ought to be combined into a single regulation covering technology transfer agreements, and the rules governing patent licensing

---

[82] OJ 1965–1966, Eng. Spec. Ed., p.35.

[83] [1994] OJ C178/3.

[84] [1984] OJ L219/15.

[85] [1995] OJ L214/6.

[86] [1989] OJ L61/1.

agreements and agreements for the licensing of know-how ought to be harmonized and simplified as far as possible, in order to encourage the dissemination of technical knowledge in the Community and to promote the manufacture of technically more sophisticated products. In those circumstances Regulation 556/89 should be repealed.

(4) This Regulation should apply to the licensing of Member States' own patents, Community patents[87] and European patents[88] ("pure" patent licensing agreements). It should also apply to agreements for the licensing of non-patented technical information such as descriptions of manufacturing processes, recipes, formulae, designs or drawings, commonly termed 'know-how' ('pure' know-how licensing agreements), and to combined patent and know-how licensing agreements ("mixed" agreements), which are playing an increasingly important role in the transfer of technology. For the purposes of this Regulation, a number of terms are defined in Article 10.

(5) Patent or know-how licensing agreements are agreements whereby one undertaking which holds a patent or know-how ("the licensor") permits another undertaking ("the licensee") to exploit the patent thereby licensed, or communicates the know-how to it, in particular for purposes of manufacture, use or putting on the market. In the light of experience acquired so far, it is possible to define a category of licensing agreements covering all or part of the common market which are capable of falling within the scope of Article [81(1)] but which can normally be regarded as satisfying the conditions laid down in Article [81(3)], where patents are necessary for the achievement of the objects of the licensed technology by a mixed agreement or where know-how—whether it is ancillary to patents or independent of them—is secret, substantial and identified in any appropriate form. These criteria are intended only to ensure that the licensing of the know-how or the grant of the patent licence justifies a block exemption of obligations restricting competition. This is without prejudice to the right of the parties to include in the contract provisions regarding other obligations, such as the obligation to pay royalties, even if the block exemption no longer applies.

(6) It is appropriate to extend the scope of this Regulation to pure or mixed agreements containing the licensing of intellectual property rights other than patents (in particular, trademarks, design rights and copyright, especially software protection), when such additional licensing contributes to the achievement of the objects of the licensed technology and contains only ancillary provisions.

(7) Where such pure or mixed licensing agreements contain not only obligations relating to territories within the common market but also obligations relating to non-member countries, the presence of the latter does not prevent this Regulation from applying to the obligations relating to territories within the common market. Where licensing agreements for non-member countries or for territories which extend beyond the frontiers of the Community have effects within the common market which may fall within the scope of Article [81(1)], such agreements should be covered by this Regulation to the same extent as would agreements for territories within the common market.

(8) The objective being to facilitate the dissemination of technology and the improvement of manufacturing processes, this Regulation should apply only where the licensee himself manufactures the licensed products or has them manufactured for his account, or where the licensed product is a service, provides the service himself or has the service provided for his account, irrespective of whether or not the licensee is also entitled to use confidential information provided by the licensor for the promotion and sale of the licensed product. The scope of this Regulation should therefore exclude agreements solely for the purpose of sale. Also to be excluded from the scope of this Regulation are agreements relating to marketing know-how communicated in the context of

[87] Convention for the European patent for the common market (Community Patent Convention) of 15 December 1975, [1976] OJ L17/1.

[88] Convention on the grant of European patents (European Patent Convention) of 5 October 1973.

franchising arrangements and certain licensing agreements entered into in connection with arrangements such as joint ventures or patent pools and other arrangements in which a licence is granted in exchange for other licences not related to improvements to or new applications of the licensed technology. Such agreements pose different problems which cannot at present be dealt with in a single regulation (Article 5).

(9) Given the similarity between sale and exclusive licensing, and the danger that the requirements of this Regulation might be evaded by presenting as assignments what are in fact exclusive licenses restrictive of competition, this Regulation should apply to agreements concerning the assignment and acquisition of patents or know-how where the risk associated with exploitation remains with the assignor. It should also apply to licensing agreements in which the licensor is not the holder of the patent or know-how but is authorised by the holder to grant the licence (as in the case of sub-licences) and to licensing agreements in which the parties' rights or obligations are assumed by connected undertakings (Article 6).

(10) Exclusive licensing agreements, *i.e.* agreements in which the licensor undertakes not to exploit the licensed technology in the licensed territory himself or to grant further licences there, may not be in themselves incompatible with Article [81(1)] where they are concerned with the introduction and protection of a new technology in the licensed territory, by reason of the scale of the research which has been undertaken, of the increase in the level of competition, in particular inter-brand competition, and of the competitiveness of the undertakings concerned resulting from the dissemination of innovation within the Community. In so far as agreements of this kind fall, in other circumstances, within the scope of Article [81(1)], it is appropriate to include them in Article 1 in order that they may also benefit from the exemption.

(11) The exemption of export bans on the licensor and on the licensees does not prejudice any developments in the case law of the Court of Justice in relation to such agreements, notably with respect to Articles [28] to [30] and Article [81(1)]. This is also the case, in particular, regarding the prohibition on the licensee from selling the licensed product in territories granted to other licensees (passive competition).

(12) The obligations listed in Article 1 generally contribute to improving the production of goods and to promoting technical progress. They make the holders of patents or know-how more willing to grant licences and licensees more inclined to undertake the investment required to manufacture, use and put on the market a new product or to use a new process. Such obligations may be permitted under this Regulation in respect of territories where the licensed product is protected by patents as long as these remain in force.

(13) Since the point at which the know-how ceases to be secret can be difficult to determine, it is appropriate, in respect of territories where the licensed technology comprises know-how only, to limit such obligations to a fixed number of years. Moreover, in order to provide sufficient periods of protection, it is appropriate to take as the starting-point for such periods the date on which the product is first put on the market in the Community by a licensee.

(14) Exemption under Article [81(3)] of longer periods of territorial protection for know-how agreements, in particular in order to protect expensive and risky investment or where the parties were not competitors at the date of the grant of the licence, can be granted only by individual decision. On the other hand, parties are free to extend the term of their agreements in order to exploit any subsequent improvement and to provide for the payment of additional royalties. However, in such cases, further periods of territorial protection may be allowed only starting from the date of licensing of the secret improvements in the Community, and by individual decision. Where the research for improvements results in innovations which are distinct from the licensed technology the parties may conclude a new agreement benefiting from an exemption under this Regulation.

7–054 (15) Provision should also be made for exemption of an obligation on the licensee not to put the product on the market in the territories of other licensees, the permitted period for such an obligation (this obligation would ban not just active competition but passive competition too) should, however, be limited to a few years from the date on which the licensed product is first put on the market in the Community by a licensee, irrespective of whether the licensed technology comprises know-how, patents or both in the territories concerned.

(16) The exemption of territorial protection should apply for the whole duration of the periods thus permitted, as long as the patents remain in force or the know-how remains secret and substantial. The parties to a mixed patent and know-how licensing agreement must be able to take advantage in a particular territory of the period of protection conferred by a patent or by the know-how, whichever is the longer.

(17) The obligations listed in Article 1 also generally fulfil the other conditions for the application of Article [81(3)]. Consumers will, as a rule, be allowed a fair share of the benefit resulting from the improvement in the supply of goods on the market. To safeguard this effect, however, it is right to exclude from the application of Article 1 cases where the parties agree to refuse to meet demand from users or resellers within their respective territories who would resell for export, or to take other steps to impede parallel imports. The obligations referred to above thus only impose restrictions which are indispensable to the attainment of their objectives.

(18) It is desirable to list in this Regulation a number of obligations that are commonly found in licensing agreements but are normally not restrictive of competition, and to provide that in the event that because of the particular economic or legal circumstances they should fall within Article [85(1)], they too will be covered by the exemption. This list, in Article 2, is not exhaustive.

(19) This Regulation must also specify what restrictions or provisions may not be included in licensing agreements if these are to benefit from the block exemption. The restrictions listed in Article 3 may fall under the prohibition of Article [81(1)], but in their case there can be no general presumption that, although they relate to the transfer of technology, they will lead to the positive effects required by Article [81(3)], as would be necessary for the granting of a block exemption. Such restrictions can be declared exempt only by an individual decision, taking account of the market position of the undertakings concerned and the degree of concentration on the relevant market.

(20) The obligations on the licensee to cease using the licensed technology after the termination of the agreement (Article 2(1)(3)) and to make improvements available to the licensor (Article 2(1)(4)) do not generally restrict competition. The post-term use ban may be regarded as a normal feature of licensing, as otherwise the licensor would be forced to transfer his know-how or patents in perpetuity. Undertakings by the licensee to grant back to the licensor a licence for improvements to the licensed know-how and/or patents are generally not restrictive of competition if the licensee is entitled by the contract to share in future experience and inventions made by the licensor. On the other hand, a restrictive effect on competition arises where the agreement obliges the licensee to assign to the licensor rights to improvements of the originally licensed technology that he himself has brought about (Article 3(6)).

(21) The list of clauses which do not prevent exemption also includes an obligation on the licensee to keep paying royalties until the end of the agreement independently of whether or not the licensed know-how has entered into the public domain through the action of third parties or of the licensee himself (Article 2(1)(7)). Moreover, the parties must be free, in order to facilitate payment, to spread the royalty payments for the use of the licensed technology over a period extending beyond the duration of the licensed patents, in particular by setting lower royalty rates. As a rule, parties do not need to be protected against the foreseeable financial consequences of an agreement freely entered into, and

they should therefore be free to choose the appropriate means of financing the technology transfer and sharing between them the risks of such use. However, the setting of rates of royalty so as to achieve one of the restrictions listed in Article 3 renders the agreement ineligible for the block exemption.

(22) An obligation on the licensee to restrict his exploitation of the licensed technology to one or more technical fields of application ("fields of use") or to one or more product markets is not caught by Article [81(1)] either, since the licensor is entitled to transfer the technology only for a limited purpose (Article 2(1)(8)).

(23) Clauses whereby the parties allocate customers within the same technological field of use or the same product market, either by an actual prohibition on supplying certain classes of customer or through an obligation with an equivalent effect, would also render the agreement ineligible for the block exemption where the parties are competitors for the contract products (Article 3(4)). Such restrictions between undertakings which are not competitors remain subject to the opposition procedure. Article 3 does not apply to cases where the patent or know-how licence is granted in order to provide a single customer with a second source of supply. In such a case, a prohibition on the second licensee from supplying persons other than the customer concerned is an essential condition for the grant of a second licence, since the purpose of the transaction is not to create an independent supplier in the market. The same applies to limitations on the quantities the licensee may supply to the customer concerned (Article 2(1)(13)).

(24) Besides the clauses already mentioned, the list of restrictions which render the block exemption inapplicable also includes restrictions regarding the selling prices of the licensed product or the quantities to be manufactured or sold, since they seriously limit the extent to which the licensee can exploit the licensed technology and since quantity restrictions particularly may have the same effect as export bans (Article 3(1) and (5)). This does not apply where a licence is granted for use of the technology in specific production facilities and where both a specific technology is communicated for the setting-up, operation and maintenance of these facilities and the licensee is allowed to increase the capacity of the facilities or to set up further facilities for its own use on normal commercial terms. On the other hand, the licensee may lawfully be prevented from using the transferred technology to set up facilities for third parties, since the purpose of the agreement is not to permit the licensee to give other producers access to the licensor's technology while it remains secret or protected by patent (Article 2(1)(12)).

(25) Agreements which are not automatically covered by the exemption because they contain provisions that are not expressly exempted by this Regulation and not expressly excluded from exemption, including those listed in Article 4(2), may, in certain circumstances, nonetheless be presumed to be eligible for application of the block exemption. It will be possible for the Commission rapidly to establish whether this is the case on the basis of the information undertakings are obliged to provide under Commission Regulation 3385/94.[89] The Commission may waive the requirement to supply specific information required in form A/B but which it does not deem necessary. The Commission will generally be content with communication of the text of the agreement and with an estimate, based on directly available data, of the market structure and of the licensee's market share. Such agreements should therefore be deemed to be covered by the exemption provided for in this Regulation where they are notified to the Commission and the Commission does not oppose the application of the exemption within a specified period of time.

(26) Where agreements exempted under this Regulation nevertheless have effects incompatible with Article [81(3)], the Commission may withdraw the block exemption, in particular where the licensed products are not faced with real competition in the licensed territory (Article 7). This could also be the case where the licensee has a strong position on the market. In assessing the competition the

[89] [1994] OJ L377/28.

Commission will pay special attention to cases where the licensee has more than 40 per cent of the whole market for the licensed products and of all the products or services which customers consider interchangeable or substitutable on account of their characteristics, prices and intended use.

(27) Agreements which come within the terms of Articles 1 and 2 and which have neither the object nor the effect of restricting competition in any other way need no longer be notified. Nevertheless, undertakings will still have the right to apply in individual cases for negative clearance or for exemption under Article [81(3)] in accordance with Council Regulation 17,[90] as last amended by the Act of Accession of Austria, Finland and Sweden. They can in particular notify agreements obliging the licensor not to grant other licences in the territory, where the licensee's market share exceeds or is likely to exceed 40 per cent,

Has adopted this Regulation:

Article 1 [The exemption: permitted restrictions of competition]

7–055 1. Pursuant to Article [81(3)] of the Treaty and subject to the conditions set out below, it is hereby declared that Article [81(1)] of the Treaty shall not apply to pure patent licensing or know-how licensing agreements and to mixed patent and know-how licensing agreements, including those agreements containing ancillary provisions relating to intellectual property rights other than patents, to which only two undertakings are party and which include one or more of the following obligations:

(1) an obligation on the licensor not to license other undertakings to exploit the licensed technology in the licensed territory;
(2) an obligation on the licensor not to exploit the licensed technology in the licensed territory himself;
(3) an obligation on the licensee not to exploit the licensed technology in the territory of the licensor within the common market;
(4) an obligation on the licensee not to manufacture or use the licensed product, or use the licensed process, in territories within the common market which are licensed to other licensees;
(5) an obligation on the licensee not to pursue an active policy of putting the licensed product on the market in the territories within the common market which are licensed to other licensees, and in particular not to engage in advertising specifically aimed at those territories or to establish any branch or maintain an distribution depot there;
(6) an obligation on the licensee not to put the licensed product on the market in the territories licensed to other licensees within the common market in response to unsolicited orders;
(7) an obligation on the licensee to use only the licensor's trademark or get up to distinguish the licensed product during the term of the agreement, provided that the licensee is not prevented from identifying himself as the manufacturer of the licensed products;
(8) an obligation on the licensee to limit his production of the licensed product to the quantities he requires in manufacturing his own products and to sell the licensed product only as an integral part of or a replacement part for his own products or otherwise in connection with the sale of his own products, provided that such quantities are freely determined by the licensee.

2. Where the agreement is a pure patent licensing agreement, the exemption of the obligations referred to in paragraph 1 is granted only to the extent that and for as long as the licensed product is protected by parallel patents, in the territories

[90] First Reg. implementing Arts 81 and 82 of the Treaty, [1959–1962] OJ, Eng.Spec. Ed., p.87 (see above).

respectively of the licensee (points (1), (2), (7) and (8)), the licensor (point (3)) and other licensees (points (4) and (5). The exemption of the obligation referred to in point (6) of paragraph 1 is granted for a period not exceeding five years from the date when the licensed product is first put on the market within the common market by one of the licensees, to the extent that and for as long as, in these territories, this product is protected by parallel patents.

3. Where the agreement is a pure know-how licensing agreement, the period for which the exemption of the obligations referred to in points (1) to (5) of paragraph 1 is granted may not exceed ten years from the date when the licensed product is first put on the market within the common market by one of the licensees.

The exemption of the obligation referred to in point (6) of paragraph 1 is granted for a period not exceeding five years from the date when the licensed product is first put on the market within the common market by one of the licensees.

The obligations referred to in points (7) and (8) of paragraph 1 are exempted during the lifetime of the agreement for as long as the know-how remains secret and substantial.

However, the exemption in paragraph 1 shall apply only where the parties have identified in any appropriate form the initial know-how and any subsequent improvements to it which become available to one party and are communicated to the other party pursuant to the terms of the agreement and to the purpose thereof, and only for as long as the know-how remains secret and substantial.

4. Where the agreement is a mixed patent and know-how licensing agreement, the exemption of the obligations referred to in points (1) to (5) of paragraph 1 shall apply in Member States in which the licensed technology is protected by necessary patents for as long as the licensed product is protected in those Member States by such patents if the duration of such protection exceeds the periods specified in paragraph 3.

The duration of the exemption provided in point (6) of paragraph 1 may not exceed the five-year period provided for in paragraphs 2 and 3.

However, such agreements qualify for the exemption referred to in paragraph 1 only for as long as the patents remain in force or to the extent that the know-how is identified and for as long as it remains secret and substantial whichever period is the longer.

5. The exemption provided for in paragraph 1 shall also apply where in a particular agreement the parties undertake obligations of the types referred to in that paragraph but with a more limited scope than is permitted by that paragraph.

Article 2 [Generally non-restrictive obligations]

1. Article 1 shall apply notwithstanding the presence in particular of any of the following clauses, which are generally not restrictive of competition: **7–056**

(1) an obligation on the licensee not to divulge the know-how communicated by the licensor the licensee may be held to this obligation after the agreement has expired;

(2) an obligation on the licensee not to grant sublicences or assign the licence;

(3) an obligation on the licensee not to exploit the licensed know-how or patents after termination of the agreement in so far and as long as the know-how is still secret or the patents are still in force;

(4) an obligation on the licensee to grant to the licensor a licence in respect of his own improvements to or his new applications of the licensed technology, provided:

— that, in the case of severable improvements, such a licence is not exclusive, so that the licensee is free to use his own improvements or to license them to third parties, in so far as that does not involve disclosure of the know-how communicated by the licensor that is still secret,

— and that the licensor undertakes to grant an exclusive or non-exclusive licence of his own improvements to the licensee;

(5) an obligation on the licensee to observe minimum quality specifications, including technical specifications, for the licensed product or to procure goods or services from the licensor or from an undertaking designated by the licensor, in so far as these quality specifications, products or services are necessary for:

(a) a technically proper exploitation of the licensed technology; or

(b) ensuring that the product of the licensee conforms to the minimum quality specifications that are applicable to the licensor and other licensees;

and to allow the licensor to carry out related checks;

(6) obligations:

(a) to inform the licensor of misappropriation of the know-how or of infringements of the licensed patents; or

(b) to take or to assist the licensor in taking legal action against such misappropriation or infringements;

(7) an obligation on the licensee to continue paying the royalties:

(a) until the end of the agreement in the amounts, for the periods and according to the methods freely determined by the parties, in the event of the know-how becoming publicly known other than by action of the licensor, without prejudice to the payment of any additional damages in the event of the know-how becoming publicly known by the action of the licensee in breach of the agreement;

(b) over a period going beyond the duration of the licensed patents, in order to facilitate payment;

(8) an obligation on the licensee to restrict his exploitation of the licensed technology to one or more technical fields of application covered by the licensed technology or to one or more product markets;

(9) an obligation on the licensee to pay a minimum royalty or to produce a minimum quantity of the licensed product or to carry out a minimum number of operations exploiting the licensed technology;

(10) an obligation on the licensor to grant the licensee any more favourable terms that the licensor may grant to another undertaking after the agreement is entered into;

(11) an obligation on the licensee to mark the licensed product with an indication of the licensor's name or of the licensed patent;

(12) an obligation on the licensee not to use the licensor's technology to construct facilities for third parties this is without prejudice to the right of the licensee to increase the capacity of his facilities or to set up additional facilities for his own use on normal commercial terms, including the payment of additional royalties;

(13) an obligation on the licensee to supply only a limited quantity of the licensed product to a particular customer, where the licence was granted so that the customer might have a second source of supply inside the licensed territory this provision shall also apply where the customer is the licensee, and the licence which was granted in order to provide a second source of supply provides that the customer is himself to manufacture the licensed products or to have them manufactured by a subcontractor;

(14) a reservation by the licensor of the right to exercise the rights conferred by a patent to oppose the exploitation of the technology by the licensee outside the licensed territory;

(15) a reservation by the licensor of the right to terminate the agreement if the licensee contests the secret or substantial nature of the licensed know-how or challenges the validity of licensed patents within the common market belonging to the licensor or undertakings connected with him;

(16) a reservation by the licensor of the right to terminate the licence agreement of a patent if the licensee raises the claim that such a patent is not necessary;

(17) an obligation on the licensee to use his best endeavours to manufacture and market the licensed product;

(18) a reservation by the licensor of the right to terminate the exclusivity granted to the licensee and to stop licensing improvements to him when the licensee enters into competition within the common market with the licensor, with undertakings connected with the licensor or with other undertakings in respect of research and development, production, use or distribution of competing products, and to require the licensee to prove that the licensed know-how is not being used for the production of products and the provision of services other than those licensed.

2. In the event that, because of particular circumstances, the clauses referred to in paragraph 1 fall within the scope of Article [81(1)], they shall also be exempted even if they are not accompanied by any of the obligations exempted by Article 1.

3. The exemption in paragraph 2 shall also apply where an agreement contains clauses of the types referred to in paragraph 1 but with a more limited scope than is permitted by that paragraph.

Article 3 [Prohibited restrictions of competition]

Article 1 and Article 2(2) shall not apply where: **7–057**

(1) one party is restricted in the determination of prices, components of prices or discounts for the licensed products;

(2) one party is restricted from competing within the common market with the other party, with undertakings connected with the other party or with other undertakings in respect of research and development, production, use or distribution of competing products without prejudice to the provisions of Article 2(1)(17) and (18);

(3) one or both of the parties are required without any objectively justified reason:

  (a) to refuse to meet orders from users or resellers in their respective territories who would market products in other territories within the common market;

  (b) to make it difficult for users or resellers to obtain the products from other resellers within the common market, and in particular to exercise intellectual property rights or take measures so as to prevent users or resellers from obtaining outside, or from putting on the market in the licensed territory products which have been lawfully put on the market within the common market by the licensor or with his consent or do so as a result of a concerted practice between them;

(4) the parties were already competing manufacturers before the grant of the licence and one of them is restricted, within the same technical field of use or within the same product market, as to the customers he may serve, in particular by being prohibited from supplying certain classes of user, employing certain forms of distribution or, with the aim of sharing customers, using certain types of packaging for the products, save as provided in Article 1(1)(7) and Article 2(1)(13);

(5) the quantity of the licensed products one party may manufacture or sell or the number of operations exploiting the licensed technology he may carry out are subject to limitations, save as provided in Article(1)(8) and Article 2(1)(13);

(6) the licensee is obliged to assign in whole or in part to the licensor rights to improvements to or new applications of the licensed technology;

(7) the licensor is required, albeit in separate agreements or through automatic prolongation of the initial duration of the agreement by the inclusion of any new improvements, for a period exceeding that referred to in Article 1(2) and (3) not to license other undertakings to exploit the licensed technology in the licensed territory, or a party is required for a period exceeding that referred to in Article 1(2) and (3) or Article 1(4) not to exploit the licensed technology in the territory of the other party or of other licensees.

Article 4 [Opposition procedure]

7–058 1. The exemption provided for in Articles 1 and 2 shall also apply to agreements containing obligations restrictive of competition which are not covered by those Articles and do not fall within the scope of Article 3, on condition that the agreements in question are notified to the Commission in accordance with the provisions of Articles 1, 2 and 3 of Regulation 3385/94 and that the Commission does not oppose such exemption within a period of four months.

2. Paragraph 1 shall apply, in particular, where:

(a) the licensee is obliged at the time the agreement is entered into to accept quality specifications or further licences or to procure goods or services which are not necessary for a technically satisfactory exploitation of the licensed technology or for ensuring that the production of the licensee conforms to the quality standards that are respected by the licensor and other licensees;

(b) the licensee is prohibited from contesting the secrecy or the substantiality of the licensed know-how or from challenging the validity of patents licensed within the common market belonging to the licensor or undertakings connected with him.

3. The period of four months referred to in paragraph 1 shall run from the date on which the notification takes effect in accordance with Article 4 of Regulation 3385/94.

4. The benefit of paragraphs 1 and 2 may be claimed for agreements notified before the entry into force of this Regulation by submitting a communication to the Commission referring expressly to this Article and to the notification. Paragraph 3 shall apply *mutatis mutandis.*

5. The Commission may oppose the exemption within a period of four months. It shall oppose exemption if it receives a request to do so from a Member State within two months of the transmission to the Member State of the notification referred to in paragraph 1 or of the communication referred to in paragraph 4. This request must be justified on the basis of considerations relating to the competition rules of the Treaty.

6. The Commission may withdraw the opposition to the exemption at any time. However, where the opposition was raised at the request of a Member State and this request is maintained, it may be withdrawn only after consultation of the Advisory Committee on Restrictive Practices and Dominant Positions.

7. If the opposition is withdrawn because the undertakings concerned have shown that the conditions of Article [81(3)] are satisfied, the exemption shall apply from the date of notification.

8. If the opposition is withdrawn because the undertakings concerned have amended the agreement so that the conditions of Article [81(3)] are satisfied, the exemption shall apply from the date on which the amendments take effect.

9. If the Commission opposes exemption and the opposition is not withdrawn, the effects of the notification shall be governed by the provisions of Regulation 17.

Article 5 [Excluded types of agreement]

7–059 1. This Regulation shall not apply to:

(1) agreements between members of a patent or know-how pool which relate to the pooled technologies;

(2) licensing agreements between competing undertakings which hold interests in a joint venture, or between one of them and the joint venture, if the licensing agreements relate to the activities of the joint venture;

(3) agreements under which one party grants the other a patent and/or know-how licence and in exchange the other party, albeit in separate agreements or through connected undertakings, grants the first party a

patent, trademark or know-how licence or exclusive sales rights, where the parties are competitors in relation to the products covered by those agreements;

(4) licensing agreements containing provisions relating to intellectual property rights other than patents which are not ancillary;

(5) agreements entered into solely for the purpose of sale.

2. This Regulation shall nevertheless apply:

(4) to agreements to which paragraph 1(2) applies, under which a parent undertaking grants the joint venture a patent or know-how licence, provided that the licensed products and the other goods and services of the participating undertakings which are considered by users to be interchangeable or substitutable in view of their characteristics, price and intended use represent:
- in case of a licence limited to production, not more than 20 per cent, and
- in case of a licence covering production and distribution, not more than 10 per cent;

of the market for the licensed products and all interchangeable or substitutable goods and services;

(5) to agreements to which paragraph 1(1) applies and to reciprocal licences within the meaning of paragraph 1(3), provided the parties are not subject to any territorial restriction within the common market with regard to the manufacture, use or putting on the market of the licensed products or to the use of the licensed or pooled technologies.

3. This Regulation shall continue to apply where, for two consecutive financial years, the market shares in paragraph 2(1) are not exceeded by more than one-tenth where that limit is exceeded, this Regulation shall continue to apply for a period of six months from the end of the year in which the limit was exceeded.

Article 6 [Particular types of agreement included]

This Regulation shall also apply to: **7–060**

(1) agreements where the licensor is not the holder of the know-how or the patentee, but is authorised by the holder or the patentee to grant a licence;

(2) assignments of know-how, patents or both where the risk associated with exploitation remains with the assignor, in particular where the sum payable in consideration of the assignment is dependent on the turnover obtained by the assignee in respect of products made using the know-how or the patents, the quantity of such products manufactured or the number of operations carried out employing the know-how or the patents;

(3) licensing agreements in which the rights or obligations of the licensor or the licensee are assumed by undertakings connected with them.

Article 7 [Withdrawal of exemption]

The Commission may withdraw the benefit of this Regulation, pursuant to Article **7–061** 7 of Regulation 19/65, where it finds in a particular case that an agreement exempted by this Regulation nevertheless has certain effects which are incompatible with the conditions laid down in Article [81(3)] of the Treaty, and in particular where:

(1) the effect of the agreement is to prevent the licensed products from being exposed to effective competition in the licensed territory from identical goods or services or from goods or services considered by users as interchangeable or substitutable in view of their characteristics, price and

intended use, which may in particular occur where the licensee's market share exceeds 40 per cent;

(2) without prejudice to Article 1(1)(6), the licensee refuses, without any objectively justified reason, to meet unsolicited orders from users or resellers in the territory of other licensees,

(3) the parties:

(a) without any objectively justified reason, refuse to meet orders from users or resellers in their respective territories who would market the products in other territories within the common market, or

(b) make it difficult for users or resellers to obtain the products from other resellers within the common market, and in particular where they exercise intellectual property rights or take measures so as to prevent resellers or users from obtaining outside, or from putting on the market in the licensed territory products which have been lawfully put on the market within the common market by the licensor or with his consent,

(4) the parties were competing manufacturers at the date of the grant of the licence and obligations on the licensee to produce a minimum quantity or to use his best endeavours as referred to in Article 2(1), (9) and (17) respectively have the effect of preventing the licensee from using competing technologies.

Article 8 [Rights deemed to be patents]

7–062 1. For purposes of this Regulation:

(a) patent applications

(b) utility models

(c) applications for registration of utility models

(d) topographies of semiconductor products

(e) *certificats d'utilité* and *certificats d'addition* under French law

(f) applications for *certificats d'utilité* and *certificats d'addition* under French law

(g) supplementary protection certificates for medicinal products or other products for which such supplementary protection certificates may be obtained

(h) plant breeder's certificates,

shall be deemed to be patents.

2. This Regulation shall also apply to agreements relating to the exploitation of an invention if an application within the meaning of paragraph 1 is made in respect of the invention for a licensed territory after the date when the agreements were entered into but within the time-limits set by the national law or the international convention to be applied.

3. This Regulation shall furthermore apply to pure patent or know-how licensing agreements or to mixed agreements whose initial duration is automatically prolonged by the inclusion of any new improvements, whether patented or not, communicated by the licensor, provided that the licensee has the right to refuse such improvements or each party has the right to terminate the agreement at the expiry of the initial term of an agreement and at least every three years thereafter.

Article 9 [Professional secrecy]

7–063 1. Information acquired pursuant to Article 4 shall be used only for the purposes of this Regulation.

2. The Commission and the authorities of the Member States, their officials and other servants shall not disclose information acquired by them pursuant to this Regulation of the kind covered by the obligation of professional secrecy.

3. The provisions of paragraphs 1 and 2 shall not prevent publication of general information or surveys which do not contain information relating to particular undertakings or associations of undertakings.

Article 10 [Definitions]

For purposes of this Regulation: **7–064**

(1) "know-how" means a body of technical information that is secret, substantial and identified in any appropriate form;

(2) "secret" means that the know-how package as a body or in the precise configuration and assembly of its components is not generally known or easily accessible, so that part of its value consists in the lead which the licensee gains when it is communicated to him it is not limited to the narrow sense that each individual component of the know-how should be totally unknown or unobtainable outside the licensor's business;

(3) "substantial" means that the know-how includes information which must be useful, *i.e.* can reasonably be expected at the date of conclusion of the agreement to be capable of improving the competitive position of the licensee, for example by helping him to enter a new market or giving him an advantage in competition with other manufacturers or providers of services who do not have access to the licensed secret know-how or other comparable secret know-how;

(4) "identified" means that the know-how is described or recorded in such a manner as to make it possible to verify that it satisfies the criteria of secrecy and substantiality and to ensure that the licensee is not unduly restricted in his exploitation of his own technology, to be identified the know-how can either be set out in the licence agreement or in a separate document or recorded in any other appropriate form at the latest when the know-how is transferred or shortly thereafter, provided that the separate document or other record can be made available if the need arises;

(5) "necessary patents" are patents where a licence under the patent is necessary for the putting into effect of the licensed technology in so far as, in the absence of such a licence, the realization of the licensed technology would not be possible or would by possible only to a lesser extent or in more difficult or costly conditions. Such patents must therefore be of technical, legal or economic interest to the licensee;

(6) "licensing agreement" means pure patent licensing agreements and pure know-how licensing agreements as well as mixed patent and know-how licensing agreements;

(7) "licensed technology" means the initial manufacturing know-how or the necessary product and process patents, or both, existing at the time the first licensing agreement is concluded, and improvements subsequently made to the know-how or patents, irrespective of whether and to what extent they are exploited by the parties or by other licensees;

(8) "the licensed products" are goods or services the production or provision of which requires the use of the licensed technology;

(9) "the licensee's market share" means the proportion which the licensed products and other goods or services provided by the licensee, which are considered by users to be interchangeable or substitutable for the licensed products in view of their characteristics, price and intended use, represent the entire market for the licensed products and all other interchangeable or substitutable goods and services in the common market or a substantial part of it;

(10) "exploitation" refers to any use of the licensed technology in particular in the production, active or passive sales in a territory even if not coupled with manufacture in that territory, or leasing of the licensed products;

(11) "the licensed territory" is the territory covering all or at least part of the common market where the licensee is entitled to exploit the licensed technology;

(12) "territory of the licensor" means territories in which the licensor has not granted any licences for patents and/or know-how covered by the licensing agreement;

(13) "parallel patents" means patents which, in spite of the divergences which remain in the absence of any unification of national rules concerning industrial property, protect the same invention in various Member States;

(14) "connected undertakings" means:

(a) undertakings in which a party to the agreement, directly or indirectly:

— owns more than half the capital or business assets, or

— has the power to exercise more than half the voting rights, or

— has the power to appoint more than half the members of the supervisory board, board of directors or bodies legally representing the undertaking, or

— has the right to manage the affairs of the undertaking;

(b) undertakings which, directly or indirectly, have in or over a party to the agreement the rights or powers listed in (a);

(c) undertakings in which an undertaking referred to in (b), directly or indirectly, has the rights or powers listed in (a);

(d) undertakings in which the parties to the agreement or undertakings connected with them jointly have the rights or powers listed in (a): such jointly controlled undertakings are considered to be connected with each of the parties to the agreement;

(15) "ancillary provisions" are provisions relating to the exploitation of intellectual property rights other than patents, which contain no obligations restrictive of competition other than those also attached to the licensed know-how or patents and exempted under this Regulation;

(16) "obligation" means both contractual obligation and a concerted practice;

(17) "competing manufacturers" or manufacturers of "competing products" means manufacturers who sell products which, in view of their characteristics, price and intended use, are considered by users to be interchangeable or substitutable for the licensed products.

Article 11 [Repeal; transitional provisions]

7–065 1. Regulation 556/89 is hereby repealed with effect from 1 April 1996.

2. Regulation 2349/84 shall continue to apply until 31 March 1996.

3. The prohibition in Article [81(1)] of the Treaty shall not apply to agreements in force on 31 March 1996 which fulfil the exemption requirements laid down by Regulation 2349/84 or 556/89.

Article 12 [Assessments and reports]

7–066 1. The Commission shall undertake regular assessments of the application of this Regulation, and in particular of the opposition procedure provided for in Article 4.

2. The Commission shall draw up a report on the operation of this Regulation before the end of the fourth year following its entry into force and shall, on that basis, assess whether any adaptation of the Regulation is desirable.

Article 13 [Entry into force; expiry]

7–067 This Regulation shall enter into force on 1 April 1996.

It shall apply until 31 March 2006.

Article 11(2) of this Regulation shall, however, enter into force on 1 January 1996.

This Regulation shall be binding in its entirety and directly applicable in all Member States.

Commission Notice on the definition of the relevant market for the ourposes of Community competition law

([1997] OJ C372/5, Doc. Ref. 397Y1209(01))

I—Introduction

1. The purpose of this notice is to provide guidance as to how the Commission applies the concept of relevant product and geographic market in its ongoing enforcement of Community competition law, in particular the application of Regulations No. 17 and 4064/89, their equivalents in other sectoral applications such as transport, coal and steel, and agriculture, and the relevant provisions of the EEA agreement.[91] Throughout this notice, references to Articles [81] and [82] of the Treaty and to merger control are to be understood as referring to the equivalent provisions in the EEA Agreement and the ECSC Treaty. 7–068

2. Market definition is a tool to identify and define the boundaries of competition between firms. It serves to establish the framework within which competition policy is applied by the Commission. The main purpose of market definition is to identify in a systematic way the competitive constraints that the undertakings involved[92] face. The objective of defining a market in both its product and geographic dimension is to identify those actual competitors of the undertakings involved that are capable of constraining their behaviour and of preventing them from behaving independently of an effective competitive pressure. It is from this perspective, that the market definition makes it possible, *inter alia*, to calculate market shares that would convey meaningful information regarding market power for the purposes of assessing dominance or for the purposes of applying Article [81].

3. It follows from the above, that the concept of "relevant market" is different from other concepts of market often used in other contexts. For instance, companies often use the term "market" to refer to the area where it sells its products or to refer broadly to the industry or sector where it belongs.

4. The definition of the relevant market in both its product and geographic dimensions often has a decisive influence on the assessment of a competition case. By rendering public the procedures the Commission follows when considering market definition and by indicating the criteria and evidence on which it relies to reach a decision, the Commission expects to increase the transparency of its policy and decision making in the area of competition policy.

5. Increased transparency will also result in companies and their advisors being able to better anticipate the possibility that the Commission would raise competition concerns in an individual case. Companies could, therefore, take such a possibility into account in their own internal decision-making when contemplating, for instance, acquisitions, the creation of joint ventures or the establishment of certain agreements. It is also intended that companies should be in a better position to understand what sort of information the Commission considers relevant for the purposes of market definition.

---

[91] The focus of assessment in State aid cases is the aid recipient and the industry/sector concerned rather than identification of competitive constraints faced by the aid recipient. When consideration of market power and therefore of the relevant market are raised in any particular case, elements of the approach outlined here might serve as a basis for the assessment of State aid cases.

[92] For the purposes of this notice, the undertakings involved will be, in the case of a concentration, the parties to the concentration; in investigations within the meaning of Article [82] of the Treaty, the undertaking being investigated or the complainants; for investigations within the meaning of Article[81], the parties to the agreement.

6. The Commission's interpretation of the notion of relevant market is without prejudice to the interpretation which may be given by the Court of Justice or the Court of First Instance of the European Communities.

II—Definition of Relevant Market

Definition of relevant product and relevant geographic market

7–069 7. The Regulations based on Articles [81] and [82] of the Treaty, in particular in section 6 of Form A/B with respect to Regulation 17, as well as in section 6 of Form CO with respect to Regulation 4064/89 on the control of concentrations having a Community dimension have laid down the following definitions. "Relevant product markets" are defined as follows:

> "A relevant product market comprises all those products and/or services which are regarded as interchangeable or substitutable by the consumer, by reason of the products' characteristics, their prices and their intended use."

8. "Relevant geographic markets" are defined as follows:

> "The relevant geographic market comprises the area in which the undertakings concerned are involved in the supply and demand of products or services, in which the conditions of competition are sufficiently homogeneous and which can be distinguished from neighbouring areas because the conditions of competition are appreciably different in those areas".

9. The relevant market within which to assess a given competition issue is therefore established by the combination of the product and geographic markets. The Commission interprets the definitions at paragraphs 7 and 8 (which reflect the jurisprudence of the Court of Justice and the Court of First Instance as well as its own decisional practice) according to the orientations defined in this Notice.

Concept of relevant market and objectives of Community competition policy

7–070 10. The concept of relevant market is closely related to the objectives pursued under Community competition policy. For example under the Community's merger control, the objective in controlling structural changes in the supply of a product/service is to prevent the creation or reinforcement of a dominant position as a result of which effective competition would be significantly impeded in a substantial part of the common market. Under the Community's competition policy, a dominant position is such that a firm or group of firms would be in a position to behave to an appreciable extent independently of its competitors, customers and ultimately of its consumers.[93] Such a position would usually arise when a firm or group of firms would account for a large share of the supply in any given market, provided that other factors analysed in the assessment (such as entry barriers, capacity of reaction of customers, etc.) point in the same direction.

11. The same approach is followed by the Commission in its application of Article [82] of the Treaty to firms that enjoy a single or collective dominant position. Under Regulation 17 the Commission has the power to investigate and bring to an end abuses of such a dominant position, which must also be defined by reference

[93] Definition given by the Court of Justice in its judgment of 13 February 1979 in *Hoffmann-La Roche* (Case 85/76) [1979] ECR 461, and confirmed in subsequent judgments.

to the relevant market. Markets may also need to be defined in the application of Article [81] of the Treaty, in particular, in determining whether an appreciable restriction of competition exists or in establishing if the condition under Article [81(3)(b)] for an exemption from the application of Article [81(1)] is met.

12. The criteria to define the relevant market are applied generally for the analysis of certain behaviours in the market and for the analysis of structural changes in the supply of products. This methodology, though, might lead to different results depending on the nature of the competition issue being examined. For instance, the scope of the geographic market might be different when analysing a concentration, where the analysis is essentially prospective, than when analysing past behaviour. The different time horizon considered in each case might lead to the result that different geographic markets are defined for the same products depending on whether the Commission is examining a change in the structure of supply, such as a concentration or a co-operative joint venture, or issues relating to certain past behaviour.

Basic principles for market definition

Competitive constraints

13. Firms are subject to three main sources of competitive constraints: demand substitutability, supply substitutability and potential competition. From an economic point of view, for the definition of the relevant market, demand substitution constitutes the most immediate and effective disciplinary force on the suppliers of a given product, in particular in relation to their pricing decisions. A firm or a group of firms cannot have a significant impact on the prevailing conditions of sale, such as prices, if its customers are in a position to switch easily to available substitute products or to suppliers located elsewhere. Basically, the exercise of market definition consists in identifying the effective alternative sources of supply for the customers of the undertakings involved, both in terms of products/services and geographic location of suppliers. **7–071**

14. The competitive constraints arising from supply side substitutability other then those described in paragraphs 20–23 and from potential competition are in general less immediate and in any case require an analysis of additional factors. As a result such constraints are taken into account at the assessment stage of competition analysis.

Demand substitution

15. The assessment of demand substitution entails a determination of the range of products which are viewed as substitutes by the consumer. One way of making this determination can be viewed, as a speculative experiment, postulating a hypothetical small, non-transitory change in relative prices and evaluating the likely reactions of customers to that increase. The exercise of market definition focuses on prices for operational and practical purposes, and more precisely on demand substitution arising from small, permanent changes in relative prices. This concept can provide clear indications as to the evidence that is relevant in defining markets. **7–072**

16. Conceptually, this approach means that, starting from the type of products that the undertakings involved sell and the area in which they sell them, additional products and areas will be included in, or excluded from, the market definition depending on whether competition from these other products and areas affect or restrain sufficiently the pricing of the parties' products in the short term.

17. The question to be answered is whether the parties' customers would switch to readily available substitutes or to suppliers located elsewhere in response to a hypothetical small (in the range 5% to 10%) but permanent relative price increase in the products and areas being considered. If substitution were enough to make the price increase unprofitable because of the resulting loss of sales, additional substitutes and areas are included in the relevant market. This would be done until the set of products and geographical areas is such that small, permanent increases in relative prices would be profitable. The equivalent analysis is applicable in cases concerning the concentration of buying power, where the starting point would then be the supplier and the price test serves to identify the alternative distribution channels or outlets for the supplier's products. In the application of these principles, careful account should be taken of certain particular situations as described within paragraphs 56 and 58.

18. A practical example of this test can be provided by its application to a merger of, for instance, soft-drink bottlers. An issue to examine in such a case would be to decide whether different flavours of soft drinks belong to the same market. In practice, the question to address would be whether consumers of flavour A would switch to other flavours when confronted with a permanent price increase of 5% to 10% for flavour A. If a sufficient number of consumers would switch to, say, flavour B, to such an extent that the price increase for flavour A would not be profitable owing to the resulting loss of sales, then the market would comprise at least flavours A and B. The process would have to be extended in addition to other available flavours until a set of products is identified for which a price rise would not induce a sufficient substitution in demand.

19. Generally, and in particular for the analysis of merger cases, the price to take into account will be the prevailing market price. This may not be the case where the prevailing price has been determined in the absence of sufficient competition. In particular for the investigation of abuses of dominant positions, the fact that the prevailing price might already have been substantially increased will be taken into account.

Supply substitution

7–073 20. Supply-side substitutability may also be taken into account when defining markets in those situations in which its effects are equivalent to those of demand substitution in terms of effectiveness and immediacy. This means that suppliers are able to switch production to the relevant products and market them in the short term[94] without incurring significant additional costs or risks in response to small and permanent changes in relative prices. When these conditions are met, the additional production that is put on the market will have a disciplinary effect on the competitive behaviour of the companies involved. Such an impact in terms of effectiveness and immediacy is equivalent to the demand substitution effect.

21. These situations typically arise when companies market a wide range of qualities or grades of one product; even if, for a given final customer or group of consumers, the different qualities are not substitutable, the different qualities will be grouped into one product market, provided that most of the suppliers are able to offer and sell the various qualities immediately and without the significant increases in costs described above. In such cases, the relevant product market will

[94] That is such a period that does not entail a significant adjustment of existing tangible and intangible assets (see paragraph 23).

encompass all products that are substitutable in demand and supply, and the current sales of those products will be aggregated so as to give the total value or volume of the market. The same reasoning may lead to group different geographic areas.

22. A practical example of the approach to supply-side substitutability when defining product markets is to be found in the case of paper. Paper is usually supplied in a range of different qualities, from standard writing paper to high quality papers to be used, for instance, to publish art books. From a demand point of view, different qualities of paper cannot be used for any given use, *i.e.* an art book or a high quality publication cannot be based on lower quality papers. However, paper plants are prepared to manufacture the different qualities, and production can be adjusted with negligible costs and in a short time-frame. In the absence of particular difficulties in distribution, paper manufacturers are able therefore, to compete for orders of the various qualities, in particular if orders are placed with sufficient lead time to allow for modification of production plans. Under such circumstances, the Commission would not define a separate market for each quality of paper and its respective use. The various qualities of paper are included in the relevant market, and their sales added up to estimate total market value and volume.

23. When supply-side substitutability would entail the need to adjust significantly existing tangible and intangible assets, additional investments, strategic decisions or time delays, it will not be considered at the stage of market definition. Examples where supply-side substitution did not induce the Commission to enlarge the market aré offered in the area of consumer products, in particular for branded beverages. Although bottling plants may in principle bottle different beverages, there are costs and lead times involved (in terms of advertising, product testing and distribution) before the products can actually be sold. In these cases, the effects of supply-side substitutability and other forms of potential competition would then be examined at a later stage.

Potential competition

24. The third source of competitive constraint, potential competition, is not taken into account when defining markets, since the conditions under which potential competition will actually represent an effective competitive constraint depend on the analysis of specific factors and circumstances related to the conditions of entry. If required, this analysis is only carried out at a subsequent stage, in general once the position of the companies involved in the relevant market has already been ascertained, and when such position gives rise to concerns from a competition point of view. **7–074**

III—Evidence Relied on to Define Relevant Markets

The process of defining the relevant market in practice

Product dimension

25. There is a range of evidence permitting an assessment of the extent to which substitution would take place. In individual cases, certain types of evidence will be determinant, depending very much on the characteristics and specificity of the industry and products or services that are being examined. The same type of evidence may be of no importance in other cases. In most cases, a decision will have to be based on the consideration of a number of criteria and different items of evidence. The Commission follows an open approach to empirical evidence, **7–075**

aimed at making an effective use of all available information which may be relevant in individual cases. The Commission does not follow a rigid hierarchy of different sources of information or types of evidence.

26. The process of defining relevant markets may be summarised as follows: on the basis of the preliminary information available or information submitted by the undertakings involved, the Commission will usually be in a position to broadly establish the possible relevant markets within which, for instance, a concentration or a restriction of competition has to be assessed. In general, and for all practical purposes when handling individual cases, the question will usually be to decide on a few alternative possible relevant markets. For instance, with respect to the product market, the issue will often be to establish whether product A and product B belong or do not belong to the same product market. It is often the case that the inclusion of product B would be enough to remove any competition concerns.

27. In such situations it is not necessary to consider whether the market includes additional products, or to reach a definitive conclusion on the precise product market. If under the conceivable alternative market definitions the operation in question does not raise competition concerns, the question of market definition will be left open, reducing thereby the burden on companies to supply information.

Geographic dimension

7–076 28. The Commission's approach to geographic market definition might be summarised as follows: it will take a preliminary view of the scope of the geographic market on the basis of broad indications as to the distribution of market shares between the parties and their competitors, as well as a preliminary analysis of pricing and price differences at national and Community or EEA level. This initial view is used basically as a working hypothesis to focus the Commission's enquiries for the purposes of arriving at a precise geographic market definition.

29. The reasons behind any particular configuration of prices and market shares need to be explored. Companies might enjoy high market shares in their domestic markets just because of the weight of the past, and conversely, a homogeneous presence of companies throughout the EEA might be consistent with national or regional geographic markets. The initial working hypothesis will therefore be checked against an analysis of demand characteristics (importance of national or local preferences, current patterns of purchases of customers, product differentiation/brands, other) in order to establish whether companies in different areas do indeed constitute a real alternative source of supply for consumers. The theoretical experiment is again based on substitution arising from changes in relative prices, and the question to answer is again whether the customers of the parties would switch their orders to companies located elsewhere in the short term and at a negligible cost.

30. If necessary, a further check on supply factors will be carried out to ensure that those companies located in differing areas do not face impediments in developing their sales on competitive terms throughout the whole geographic market. This analysis will include an examination of requirements for a local presence in order to sell in that area, the conditions of access to distribution channels, costs associated with setting up a distribution network, and the presence or absence of regulatory barriers arising from public procurement, price regulations, quotas

and tariffs limiting trade or production, technical standards, monopolies, freedom of establishment, requirements for administrative authorisations, packaging regulations, etc. In short, the Commission will identify possible obstacles and barriers isolating companies located in a given area from the competitive pressure of companies located outside that area, so as to determine the precise degree of market interpenetration at national, European or global level.

31. The actual pattern and evolution of trade flows offers useful supplementary indications as to the economic importance of each demand or supply factor mentioned above, and the extent to which they may or may not constitute actual barriers creating different geographic markets. The analysis of trade flows will generally address the question of transport costs and the extent to which these may hinder trade between different areas, having regard to plant location, costs of production and relative price levels.

Market integration in the Community

32. Finally, the Commission also takes into account the continuing process of market integration, in particular in the Community, when defining geographic markets, especially in the area of concentrations and structural joint ventures. The measures adopted and implemented in the internal market programme to remove barriers to trade and further integrate the Community markets cannot be ignored when assessing the effects on competition of a concentration or a structural joint venture. A situation where national markets have been artificially isolated from each other because of the existence of legislative barriers that have now been removed will generally lead to a cautious assessment of past evidence regarding prices, market shares or trade patterns. A process of market integration that would, in the short term, lead to wider geographic markets may therefore be taken into consideration when defining the geographic market for the purposes of assessing concentrations and joint ventures. **7–077**

The process of gathering evidence

33. When a precise market definition is deemed necessary, the Commission will often contact the main customers and the main companies in the industry to enquire into their views about the boundaries of product and geographic markets and to obtain the necessary factual evidence to reach a conclusion. The Commission might also contact the relevant professional associations, and companies active in upstream markets, so as to be able to define, in so far as necessary, separate product and geographic markets, for different levels of production or distribution of the products/services in question. It might also request additional information to the undertakings involved. **7–078**

34. Where appropriate, the Commission will address written requests for information to the market players mentioned above. These requests will usually include questions relating to the perceptions of companies about reactions to hypothetical price increases and their views of the boundaries of the relevant market. They will also ask for provision of the factual information the Commission deems necessary to reach a conclusion on the extent of the relevant market. The Commission might also discuss with marketing directors or other officers of those companies to gain a better understanding on how negotiations between suppliers and customers take place and better understand issues relating to the definition of the relevant market. Where appropriate, they might also carry out visits or inspections to the premises of the parties, their customers and/or their competitors, in order to better understand how products are manufactured and sold.

35. The type of evidence relevant to reach a conclusion as to the product market can be categorised as follows:

Evidence to define markets—product dimension

7–079 36. An analysis of the product characteristics and its intended use allows the Commission, as a first step, to limit the field of investigation of possible substitutes. However, product characteristics and intended use are insufficient to show whether two products are demand substitutes. Functional interchangeability or similarity in characteristics may not, in themselves, provide sufficient criteria, because the responsiveness of customers to relative price changes may be determined by other considerations as well. For example, there may be different competitive constraints in the original equipment market for car components and in spare parts, thereby leading to a separate delineation of two relevant markets. Conversely, differences in product characteristics are not in themselves sufficient to exclude demand substitutability, since this will depend to a large extent on how customers value different characteristics.

37. The type of evidence the Commission considers relevant to assess whether two products are demand substitutes can be categorised as follows:

38. *Evidence of substitution in the recent past.* In certain cases, it is possible to analyse evidence relating to recent past events or shocks in the market that offer actual examples of substitution between two products. When available, this sort of information will normally be fundamental for market definition. If there have been changes in relative prices in the past (all else being equal), the reactions in terms of quantities demanded will be determinant in establishing substitutability. Launches of new products in the past can also offer useful information, when it is possible to precisely analyse which products have lost sales to the new product.

39. There are a number of *quantitative tests* that have specifically been designed for the purpose of delineating markets. These tests consist of various econometric and statistical approaches estimates of elasticities and cross-price elasticities[95] for the demand of a product, tests based on similarity of price movements over time, the analysis of causality between price series and similarity of price levels and/or their convergence. The Commission takes into account the available quantitative evidence capable of withstanding rigorous scrutiny for the purposes of establishing patterns of substitution in the past.

40. *Views of customers and competitors.* The Commission often contacts the main customers and competitors of the companies involved in its enquiries, to gather their views on the boundaries of the product market as well as most of the factual information it requires to reach a conclusion on the scope of the market. Reasoned answers of customers and competitors as to what would happen if relative prices for the candidate products were to increase in the candidate geographic area by a small amount (for instance of 5% to 10%) are taken into account when they are sufficiently backed by factual evidence.

41. *Consumer preferences.* In the case of consumer goods, it may be difficult for the Commission to gather the direct views of end consumers about substitute products. Marketing studies that companies have commissioned in the past and that are used by companies in their own decision-making as to pricing of their products and/or marketing actions may provide useful information for the Commission's delineation of the relevant market. Consumer surveys on usage patterns and attitudes, data from consumer's purchasing patterns, the views expressed by retailers and more generally, market research studies submitted by the parties and their competitors are taken into account to establish whether an

[95] Own-price elasticity of demand for product X is a measure of the responsiveness of demand for X to percentage change in its own price. Cross-price elasticity between products X and Y is the responsiveness of demand for product X to percentage change in the price of product Y.

economically significant proportion of consumers consider two products as substitutable, also taking into account the importance of brands for the products in question. The methodology followed in consumer surveys carried out ad hoc by the undertakings involved or their competitors for the purposes of a merger procedure or a procedure pursuant to Regulation 17 will usually be scrutinised with utmost care. Unlike pre-existing studies, they have not been prepared in the normal course of business for the adoption of business decisions.

42. *Barriers and costs associated with switching demand to potential substitutes.* There are a number of barriers and costs that might prevent the Commission from considering two prima facie demand substitutes as belonging to one single product market. It is not possible to provide an exhaustive list of all the possible barriers to substitution and of switching costs. These barriers or obstacles might have a wide range of origins, and in its decisions, the Commission has been confronted with regulatory barriers or other forms of State intervention, constraints arising in downstream markets, need to incur specific capital investment or loss in current output in order to switch to alternative inputs, the location of customers, specific investment in production process, learning and human capital investment, retooling costs or other investments, uncertainty about quality and reputation of unknown suppliers, and others.

43. *Different categories of customers and price discrimination.* The extent of the product market might be narrowed in the presence of distinct groups of customers. A distinct group of customers for the relevant product may constitute a narrower, distinct market when such a group could be subject to price discrimination. This will usually be the case when two conditions are met: (a) it is possible to identify clearly which group an individual customer belongs to at the moment of selling the relevant products to him, and (b) trade among customers or arbitrage by third parties should not be feasible.

Evidence for defining markets—geographic dimension

44. The type of evidence the Commission considers relevant to reach a conclusion **7–080**
as to the geographic market can be categorised as follows:

45. *Past evidence of diversion of orders to other areas.* In certain cases, evidence on changes in prices between different areas and consequent reactions by customers might be available. Generally, the same quantitative tests used for product market definition might as well be used in geographic market definition, bearing in mind that international comparisons of prices might be more complex due to a number of factors such as exchange rate movements, taxation and product differentiation.

46. *Basic demand characteristics.* The nature of demand for the relevant product may in itself determine the scope of the geographical market. Factors such as national preferences or preferences for national brands, language, culture and life style, and the need for a local presence have a strong potential to limit the geographic scope of competition.

47. *Views of customers and competitors.* Where appropriate, the Commission will contact the main customers and competitors of the parties in its enquiries, to gather their views on the boundaries of the geographic market as well as most of the factual information it requires to reach a conclusion on the scope of the market when they are sufficiently backed by factual evidence.

48. *Current geographic pattern of purchases.* An examination of the customers' current geographic pattern of purchases provides useful evidence as to the possible scope of the geographic market. When customers purchase from companies located anywhere in the Community or the EEA on similar terms, or they procure their supplies through effective tendering procedures in which companies from anywhere in the Community or the EEA submit bids, usually the geographic market will be considered to be Community-wide.

49. *Trade flows/pattern of shipments.* When the number of customers is so large that it is not possible to obtain through them a clear picture of geographic purchasing patterns, information on trade flows might be used alternatively, provided that the trade statistics are available with a sufficient degree of detail for the relevant products. Trade flows, and above all, the rationale behind trade flows provide useful insights and information for the purpose of establishing the scope of the geographic market but are not in themselves conclusive.

50. *Barriers and switching costs associated to divert orders to companies located in other areas.* The absence of trans-border purchases or trade flows, for instance, does not necessarily mean that the market is at most national in scope. Still, barriers isolating the national market have to be identified before it is concluded that the relevant geographic market in such a case is national. Perhaps the clearest obstacle for a customer to divert its orders to other areas is the impact of transport costs and transport restrictions arising from legislation or from the nature of the relevant products. The impact of transport costs will usually limit the scope of the geographic market for bulky, low-value products, bearing in mind that a transport disadvantage might also be compensated by a comparative advantage in other costs (labour costs or raw materials). Access to distribution in a given area, regulatory barriers still existing in certain sectors, quotas and custom tariffs might also constitute barriers isolating a geographic area from the competitive pressure of companies located outside that area. Significant switching costs in procuring supplies from companies located in other countries constitute additional sources of such barriers.

51. On the basis of the evidence gathered, the Commission will then define a geographic market that could range from a local dimension to a global one, and there are examples of both local and global markets in past decisions of the Commission.

52. The paragraphs above describe the different factors which might be relevant to define markets. This does not imply that in each individual case it will be necessary to obtain evidence and assess each of these factors. Often in practice the evidence provided by a subset of these factors will be sufficient to reach a conclusion, as shown in the past decisional practice of the Commission.

IV—Calculation of Market Share

7–081 53. The definition of the relevant market in both its product and geographic dimensions allows the identification of the suppliers and the customers/consumers active on that market. On that basis, a total market size and market shares for each supplier can be calculated on the basis of their sales of the relevant products in the relevant area. In practice, the total market size and market shares are often available from market sources, *i.e.* companies' estimates, studies commissioned from industry consultants and/or trade associations. When this is not the case, or when available estimates are not reliable, the Commission will usually ask each supplier in the relevant market to provide its own sales in order to calculate total market size and market shares.

54. If sales are usually the reference to calculate market shares, there are nevertheless other indications that, depending on the specific products or industry in question, can offer useful information such as, in particular, capacity, the number of players in bidding markets, units of fleet as in aerospace, or the reserves held in the case of sectors such as mining.

55. As a rule of thumb, both volume sales and value sales provide useful information. In cases of differentiated products, sales in value and their associated market share will usually be considered to better reflect the relative position and strength of each supplier.

V—Additional Considerations

56. There are certain areas where the application of the principles above has to be undertaken with care. This is the case when considering primary and secondary markets, in particular, when the behaviour of undertakings at a point in time has to be analysed pursuant to Article [82]. The method of defining markets in these cases is the same, *i.e.* assessing the responses of customers based on their purchasing decisions to relative price changes, but taking into account as well, constraints on substitution imposed by conditions in the connected markets. A narrow definition of market for secondary products, for instance, spare parts, may result when compatibility with the primary product is important. Problems of finding compatible secondary products together with the existence of high prices and a long lifetime of the primary products may render relative price increases of secondary products profitable. A different market definition may result if significant substitution between secondary products is possible or if the characteristics of the primary products make quick and direct consumer responses to relative price increases of the secondary products feasible. **7–082**

57. In certain cases, the existence of chains of substitution might lead to the definition of a relevant market where products or areas at the extreme of the market are not directly substitutable. An example might be provided by the geographic dimension of a product with significant transport costs. In such cases, deliveries from a given plant are limited to a certain area around each plant by the impact of transport costs. In principle, such an area could constitute the relevant geographic market. However, if the distribution of plants is such that there are considerable overlaps between the areas around different plants, it is possible that the pricing of those products will be constrained by a chain substitution effect, and lead to the definition of a broader geographic market. The same reasoning may apply if product B is a demand substitute for products A and C. Even if products A and C are not direct demand substitutes, they might be found to be in the same relevant product market since their respective pricing might be constrained by substitution to B.

58. From a practical perspective, the concept of chains of substitution has to be corroborated by actual evidence, for instance related to price interdependence at the extremes of the chains of substitution, in order to lead to an extension of the relevant market in an individual case. Price levels at the extremes of the chains would have to be of the same magnitude as well.

Commission Regulation 2842/98 of 22 December 1998, on the hearing of parties in certain proceedings under Articles [81] and [82] of the EC Treaty

([1998] OJ L354/18; Doc. Ref. 31998R2842)

The Commission of the European Communities, **7–083**

Having regard to the Treaty establishing the European Community,

Having regard to the Agreement on the European Economic Area,

Having regard to Council Regulation 17 of 6 February 1962, First Regulation implementing Articles [81] and [82] of the Treaty,[96] as last amended by the Act of Accession of Austria, Finland and Sweden, and in particular Article 24 thereof,

Having regard to Council Regulation 1017/68 of 19 July 1968, applying rules of competition to transport by rail, road and inland waterway,[97] as last amended by the Act of Accession of Austria, Finland and Sweden, and in particular Article 29 thereof,

Having regard to Council Regulation 4056/86 of 22 December 1986, laying down detailed rules for the application of Articles [81] and [82] of the Treaty to

[96] [1959–1962] OJ, Eng. Spec. Ed., p.87 (see above).
[97] [1968(I)] OJ, Eng. Spec. Ed., p.302.

maritime transport,[98] as last amended by the Act of Accession of Austria, Finland and Sweden, and in particular Article 26 thereof,

Having regard to Council Regulation 3975/87 of 14 December 1987, laying down the procedure for the application of the rules on competition to undertakings in the air transport sector,[99] as last amended by Regulation 2410/92,[1] and in particular Article 19 thereof,

Having consulted the appropriate Advisory Committees on Restrictive Practices and Dominant Positions,

(1) Whereas a great deal of experience has been acquired in the application of Commission Regulation 99/63 of 25 July 1963, on the hearings provided for in Article 19(1) and (2) of Regulation 17,[2] Commission Regulation 1630/69 of 8 August 1969, on the hearings provided for in Article 26(1) and (2) of Council Regulation 1017/68 of 19 July 1968,[3] Section II of Commission Regulation 4260/88 of 16 December 1988, on the communications, complaints and applications and the hearings provided for in Council Regulation 4056/86 laying down detailed rules for the application of Articles [81] and [82] of the Treaty to maritime transport,[4] as last amended by the Act of Accession of Austria, Finland and Sweden, and Section II of Commission Regulation 4261/88 of 16 December 1988, on the complaints, applications and hearings provided for in Council Regulation 3975/87 laying down the procedure for the application of the rules on competition to undertakings in the air transport sector[5];

(2) Whereas that experience has revealed the need to improve certain procedural aspects of those Regulations whereas it is appropriate for the sake of clarity to adopt a single Regulation on the various hearing procedures laid down by Regulation 17, Regulation 1017/68, Regulation 4056/86 and Regulation 3975/87 whereas, accordingly, Regulations 99/63 and 1630/69 should be replaced, and Sections II of Regulations 4260/88 and 4261/88 should be deleted and replaced;

(3) Whereas the provisions relating to the Commission's procedure under Decision 94/810 of 12 December 1994, on the terms of reference of hearing officers in competition procedures before the Commission[6] should be framed in such a way as to safeguard fully the right to be heard and the rights of defence whereas for these purposes, the Commission should distinguish between the respective rights to be heard of the parties to which the Commission has addressed objections, of the applicants and complainants, and of other third parties;

(4) Whereas in accordance with the principle of the rights of defence, the parties to which the Commission has addressed objections should be given the opportunity to submit their comments on all the objections which the Commission proposes to take into account in its decisions;

(5) Whereas the applicants and complainants should be granted the opportunity of expressing their views, if the Commission considers that there are insufficient grounds for granting the application or acting on the complaint whereas the applicant or complainant should be provided with a copy of the non-confidential version of the objections and should be permitted to make known its views in writing where the Commission raises objections;

(6) Whereas other third parties having sufficient interest should also be given the opportunity of expressing their views in writing where they make a written application to do so;

---

[98] [1986] OJ L378/4.
[99] [1987] OJ L374/1.
[1] [1992] OJ L240/18.
[2] [1963] OJ 127/2268.
[3] [1969] OJ L209/11.
[4] [1988] OJ L376/1.
[5] [1988] OJ L376/10.
[6] [1994] OJ L330/67. Decision 94/810 has been repealed and replaced by Decision 2001/462 on the terms of reference of hearing officers in certain competition proceedings ([2001] OJ L162/21) (see below).

(7) Whereas the various parties entitled to submit comments should do so in writing, both in their own interest and in the interests of sound administration, without prejudice to the possibility of an oral hearing where appropriate to supplement the written procedure;

(8) Whereas it is necessary to define the rights of persons who are to be heard and on what conditions they may be represented or assisted;

(9) Whereas the Commission should continue to respect the legitimate interest of undertakings in the protection of their business secrets and other confidential information;

(10) Whereas compatibility should be ensured between the Commission's current administrative practices and the case law of the Court of Justice and the Court of First Instance of the European Communities in accordance with the Commission notice on the internal rules of procedure for processing requests for access to the file in cases pursuant to Articles [81] and [82] of the Treaty, Articles 65 and 66 of the ECSC Treaty and Council Regulation 4064/89[7];

(11) Whereas to facilitate the proper conduct of the hearing it is appropriate to allow statements made by each person at a hearing to be recorded;

(12) Whereas in the interest of legal certainty, it is appropriate to set the time-limit for the submissions by the various persons pursuant to this Regulation by defining the date by which the submission must reach the Commission;

(13) Whereas the appropriate Advisory Committee under Article 10(3) of Regulation 17, Article 16(3) of Regulation 1017/68, Article 15(3) of Regulation 4056/86 or Article 8(3) of Regulation 3975/87 must deliver its opinion on the basis of a preliminary draft decision whereas it should therefore be consulted on a case after the inquiry in that case has been completed whereas such consultation should not prevent the Commission from reopening an inquiry if need be,

Has adopted this Regulation:

Chapter I—Scope

Article 1 [Application of the Regulation]

This Regulation shall apply to the hearing of parties under Article 19(1) and (2) of Regulation 17, Article 26(1) and (2) of Regulation 1017/68, Article 23(1) and (2) of Regulation 4056/86 and Article 16(1) and (2) of Regulation 3975/87. **7–084**

Chapter II—Hearing of Parties to Which the Commission has Addressed Objections

Article 2 [Right to be heard]

1. The Commission shall hear the parties to which it has addressed objections before consulting the appropriate Advisory Committee under Article 10(3) of Regulation 17, Article 16(3) of Regulation 1017/68, Article 15(3) of Regulation 4056/86 or Article 8(3) of Regulation 3975/87. **7–085**

2. The Commission shall in its decisions deal only with objections in respect of which the parties have been afforded the opportunity of making their views known.

Article 3 [Statements of objections]

1. The Commission shall inform the parties in writing of the objections raised against them. The objections shall be notified to each of them or to a duly appointed agent. **7–086**

2. The Commission may inform the parties by giving notice in the *Official Journal of the European Communities*, if from the circumstances of the case this appears

[7] [1997] OJ C23/3.

appropriate, in particular where notice is to be given to a number of undertakings but no joint agent has been appointed. The notice shall have regard to the legitimate interests of the undertakings in the protection of their business secrets and other confidential information.

3. A fine or a periodic penalty payment may be imposed on a party only if the objections have been notified in the manner provided for in paragraph 1.

4. The Commission shall, when giving notice of objections, set a date by which the parties may inform it in writing of their views.

5. The Commission shall set a date by which the parties may indicate any parts of the objections which in their view contain business secrets or other confidential material. If they do not do so by that date, the Commission may assume that the objections do not contain such information.

Article 4 [Right to reply]

7–087 1. Parties which wish to make known their views on the objections raised against them shall do so in writing and by the date referred to in Article 3(4). The Commission shall not be obliged to take into account written comments received after that date.

2. The parties may in their written comments set out all matters relevant to their defence. They may attach any relevant documents as proof of the facts set out and may also propose that the Commission hear persons who may corroborate those facts.

Article 5

7–088 The Commission shall afford to parties against which objections have been raised the opportunity to develop their arguments at an oral hearing, if they so request in their written comments.

Chapter III—Hearing of Applicants and Complainants

Article 6 [Insufficient grounds for action]

7–089 Where the Commission, having received an application made under Article 3(2) of Regulation 17 or a complaint made under Article 10 of Regulation 1017/68, Article 10 of Regulation 4056/86 or Article 3(1) of Regulation 3975/87, considers that on the basis of the information in its possession there are insufficient grounds for granting the application or acting on the complaint, it shall inform the applicant or complainant of its reasons and set a date by which the applicant or complainant may make known its views in writing.

Article 7 [Opportunity to scrutinise objections]

7–090 Where the Commission raises objections relating to an issue in respect of which it has received an application on a complaint as referred to in Article 6, it shall provide an applicant or complainant with a copy of the non-confidential version of the objections and set a date by which the applicant or complainant may make known its views in writing.

Article 8 [Opportunity for oral argument]

The Commission may, where appropriate, afford to applicants and complainants the opportunity of orally expressing their views, if they so request in their written comments. **7–091**

Chapter IV—Hearing of Other Third Parties

Article 9 [Hearing of other parties with sufficient interest]

1. If parties other than those referred to in Chapters II and III apply to be heard and show a sufficient interest, the Commission shall inform them in writing of the nature and subject matter of the procedure and shall set a date by which they may make known their views in writing. **7–092**

2. The Commission may, where appropriate, invite parties referred to in paragraph 1 to develop their arguments at the oral hearing of the parties against which objections have been raised, if they so request in their written comments.

3. The Commission may afford to any other third parties the opportunity of orally expressing their views.

Chapter V—General Provisions

Article 10 [Role of Hearing Officer]

Hearings shall be conducted by the Hearing Officer.[8] **7–093**

Article 11 [Invitation to attend hearing]

1. The Commission shall invite the persons to be heard to attend the oral hearing on such date as it shall appoint. **7–094**

2. The Commission shall invite the competent authorities of the Member States to take part in the oral hearing.

Article 12 [Representation at hearings; conduct of hearings]

1. Persons invited to attend shall either appear in person or be represented by legal representatives or by representatives authorised by their constitution as appropriate. Undertakings and associations of undertakings may be represented by a duly authorised agent appointed from among their permanent staff. **7–095**

2. Persons heard by the Commission may be assisted by their legal advisers or other qualified persons admitted by the Hearing Officer.

3. Oral hearings shall not be public. Each person shall be heard separately or in the presence of other persons invited to attend. In the latter case, regard shall be had to the legitimate interest of the undertakings in the protection of their business secrets and other confidential information.

4. The statements made by each person heard shall be recorded on tape. The recording shall be made available to such persons on request, by means of a copy from which business secrets and other confidential information shall be deleted.

Article 13 [Confidentiality]

1. Information, including documents, shall not be communicated or made accessible in so far as it contains business secrets of any party, including the parties to which the Commission has addressed objections, applicants and complainants **7–096**

[8] See Decision 2001/462 on the terms of reference of hearing officers in certain competition proceedings ([2001] OJ L162/21).

and other third parties, or other confidential information or where internal documents of the authorities are concerned. The Commission shall make appropriate arrangements for allowing access to the file, taking due account of the need to protect business secrets, internal Commission documents and other confidential information.

2. Any party which makes known its views under the provisions of this Regulation shall clearly identify any material which it considers to be confidential, giving reasons, and provide a separate non-confidential version by the date set by the Commission. If it does not do so by the set date, the Commission may assume that the submission does not contain such material.

Article 14 [Setting of dates]

7–097 In setting the dates provided for in Articles 3(4), 6, 7 and 9(1), the Commission shall have regard both to the time required for preparation of the submission and to the urgency of the case. The time allowed in each case shall be at least two weeks it may be extended.

Chapter VI—Final Provisions

Article 15 [Repeals and deletions]

7–098 1. Regulations 99/63 and 1630/69 are repealed.

2. Sections II of Regulations 4260/88 and 4261/88 are deleted.

Article 16 [Entry into force]

7–099 This Regulation shall enter into force on 1 February 1999.

This Regulation shall be binding in its entirety and directly applicable in all Member States.

Commission Regulation 2790/1999 of 22 December 1999, on the application of Article 81(3) of the Treaty to categories of vertical agreements and concerted practices

([1999] OJ L336/21; Doc. Ref. 31999R2790)

7–100 *The Commission of the European Communities*,
Having regard to the Treaty establishing the European Community,

Having regard to Council Regulation 19/65 of 2 March 1965, on the application of Article [81(3)] of the Treaty to certain categories of agreements and concerted practices,[9] as last amended by Regulation 1215/1999,[10] and in particular Article 1 thereof,

Having published a draft of this Regulation,[11]

Having consulted the Advisory Committee on Restrictive Practices and Dominant Positions,

Whereas:

(1) Regulation 19/65 empowers the Commission to apply Article 81(3) of the Treaty (formerly Article 85(3)) by regulation to certain categories of vertical agreements and corresponding concerted practices falling within Article 81(1).

(2) Experience acquired to date makes it possible to define a category of vertical agreements which can be regarded as normally satisfying the conditions laid down in Article 81(3).

[9] [1965–1966] OJ, Eng. Spec. Ed., p.35.
[10] [1999] OJ L148/1.
[11] [1999] OJ C270/7.

(3) This category includes vertical agreements for the purchase or sale of goods or services where these agreements are concluded between non-competing undertakings, between certain competitors or by certain associations of retailers of goods; it also includes vertical agreements containing ancillary provisions on the assignment or use of intellectual property rights; for the purposes of this Regulation, the term "vertical agreements" includes the corresponding concerted practices.

(4) For the application of Article 81(3) by regulation, it is not necessary to define those vertical agreements which are capable of falling within Article 81(1); in the individual assessment of agreements under Article 81(1), account has to be taken of several factors, and in particular the market structure on the supply and purchase side.

(5) The benefit of the block exemption should be limited to vertical agreements for which it can be assumed with sufficient certainty that they satisfy the conditions of Article 81(3).

(6) Vertical agreements of the category defined in this Regulation can improve economic efficiency within a chain of production or distribution by facilitating better coordination between the participating undertakings; in particular, they can lead to a reduction in the transaction and distribution costs of the parties and to an optimisation of their sales and investment levels.

(7) The likelihood that such efficiency-enhancing effects will outweigh any anti-competitive effects due to restrictions contained in vertical agreements depends on the degree of market power of the undertakings concerned and, therefore, on the extent to which those undertakings face competition from other suppliers of goods or services regarded by the buyer as interchangeable or substitutable for one another, by reason of the products' characteristics, their prices and their intended use.

(8) It can be presumed that, where the share of the relevant market accounted for by the supplier does not exceed 30 per cent, vertical agreements which do not contain certain types of severely anti-competitive restraints generally lead to an improvement in production or distribution and allow consumers a fair share of the resulting benefits; in the case of vertical agreements containing exclusive supply obligations, it is the market share of the buyer which is relevant in determining the overall effects of such vertical agreements on the market.

(9) Above the market share threshold of 30 per cent, there can be no presumption that vertical agreements falling within the scope of Article 81(1) will usually give rise to objective advantages of such a character and size as to compensate for the disadvantages which they create for competition.

(10) This Regulation should not exempt vertical agreements containing restrictions which are not indispensable to the attainment of the positive effects mentioned above; in particular, vertical agreements containing certain types of severely anti-competitive restraints such as minimum and fixed resale-prices, as well as certain types of territorial protection, should be excluded from the benefit of the block exemption established by this Regulation irrespective of the market share of the undertakings concerned.

(11) In order to ensure access to or to prevent collusion on the relevant market, certain conditions are to be attached to the block exemption; to this end, the exemption of non-compete obligations should be limited to obligations which do not exceed a definite duration; for the same reasons, any direct or indirect obligation causing the members of a selective distribution system not to sell the brands of particular competing suppliers should be excluded from the benefit of this Regulation.

(12) The market-share limitation, the non-exemption of certain vertical agreements and the conditions provided for in this Regulation normally ensure that the agreements to which the block exemption applies do not enable the participating undertakings to eliminate competition in respect of a substantial part of the products in question.

(13) In particular cases in which the agreements falling under this Regulation nevertheless have effects incompatible with Article 81(3), the Commission may withdraw the benefit of the block exemption; this may occur in particular where the buyer has significant market power in the relevant market in which it resells the goods or provides the services or where parallel networks of vertical agreements have similar effects which significantly restrict access to a relevant market or competition therein; such cumulative effects may for example arise in the case of selective distribution or non-compete obligations.

(14) Regulation 19/65 empowers the competent authorities of Member States to withdraw the benefit of the block exemption in respect of vertical agreements having effects incompatible with the conditions laid down in Article 81(3), where such effects are felt in their respective territory, or in a part thereof, and where such territory has the characteristics of a distinct geographic market;

Member States should ensure that the exercise of this power of withdrawal does not prejudice the uniform application throughout the common market of the Community competition rules or the full effect of the measures adopted in implementation of those rules.

(15) In order to strengthen supervision of parallel networks of vertical agreements which have similar restrictive effects and which cover more than 50 per cent of a given market, the Commission may declare this Regulation inapplicable to vertical agreements containing specific restraints relating to the market concerned, thereby restoring the full application of Article 81 to such agreements.

(16) This Regulation is without prejudice to the application of Article 82.

(17) In accordance with the principle of the primacy of Community law, no measure taken pursuant to national laws on competition should prejudice the uniform application throughout the common market of the Community competition rules or the full effect of any measures adopted in implementation of those rules, including this Regulation,

Has adopted this Regulation:

Article 1 [Definitions]

7–101 For the purposes of this Regulation:

(a) "competing undertakings" means actual or potential suppliers in the same product market; the, product market includes goods or services which are regarded by the buyer as interchangeable with or substitutable for the contract goods or services, by reason of the products' characteristics, their prices and their intended use;

(b) "non-compete obligation" means any direct or indirect obligation causing the buyer not to manufacture, purchase, sell or resell goods or services which compete with the contract goods or services, or any direct or indirect obligation on the buyer to purchase from the supplier or from another undertaking designated by the supplier more than 80 per cent of the buyer's total purchases of the contract goods or services and their substitutes on the relevant market, calculated on the basis of the value of its purchases in the preceding calendar year;

(c) "exclusive supply obligation" means any direct or indirect obligation causing the supplier to sell the goods or services specified in the agreement only to one buyer inside the Community for the purposes of a specific use or for resale;

(d) "selective distribution system" means a distribution system where the supplier undertakes to sell the contract goods or services, either directly or indirectly, only to distributors selected on the basis of specified criteria and where these distributors undertake not to sell such goods or services to unauthorised distributors;

(e) "intellectual property rights" includes industrial property rights, copyright and neighbouring rights;

(f) "know-how" means a package of non-patented practical information, resulting from experience and testing by the supplier, which is secret, substantial and identified: in this context, "secret" means that the know-how, as a body or in the precise configuration and assembly of its components, is not generally known or easily accessible;

"substantial" means that the know-how includes information which is indispensable to the buyer for the use, sale or resale of the contract goods or services;

"identified" means that the know-how must be described in a sufficiently comprehensive manner so as to make it possible to verify that it fulfils the criteria of secrecy and substantiality;

(g) "buyer" includes an undertaking which, under an agreement falling within Article 81(1) of the Treaty, sells goods or services on behalf of another undertaking.

Article 2 [Exemption]

1. Pursuant to Article 81(3) of the Treaty and subject to the provisions of this Regulation, it is hereby declared that Article 81(1) shall not apply to agreements or concerted practices entered into between two or more undertakings each of which operates, for the purposes of the agreement, at a different level of the production or distribution chain, and relating to the conditions under which the parties may purchase, sell or resell certain goods or services ("vertical agreements"). **7–102**

This exemption shall apply to the extent that such agreements contain restrictions of competition falling within the scope of Article 81(1) ("vertical restraints").[12]

2. The exemption provided for in paragraph 1 shall apply to vertical agreements entered into between an association of undertakings and its members, or between such an association and its suppliers, only if all its members are retailers of goods and if no individual member of the association, together with its connected undertakings, has a total annual turnover exceeding EUR 50 million; vertical agreements entered into by such associations shall be covered by this Regulation without prejudice to the application of Article 81 to horizontal agreements concluded between the members of the association or decisions adopted by the association.

3. The exemption provided for in paragraph 1 shall apply to vertical agreements containing provisions which relate to the assignment to the buyer or use by the buyer of intellectual property rights, provided that those provisions do not constitute the primary object of such agreements and are directly related to the use, sale or resale of goods or services by the buyer or its customers. The exemption applies on condition that, in relation to the contract goods or services, those provisions do not contain restrictions of competition having the same object or effect as vertical restraints which are not exempted under this Regulation.

4. The exemption provided for in paragraph 1 shall not apply to vertical agreements entered into between competing undertakings; however, it shall apply where competing undertakings enter into a non-reciprocal vertical agreement and:

(a) the buyer has a total annual turnover not exceeding EUR 100 million, or

(b) the supplier is a manufacturer and a distributor of goods, while the buyer is a distributor not manufacturing goods competing with the contract goods, or

[12] For analysis of whether a vertical agreement contains restrictions falling within the scope of Art. 81(1), see the Guidelines on vertical restraints ([2000] OJ C291/1).

(c) the supplier is a provider of services at several levels of trade, while the buyer does not provide competing services at the level of trade where it purchases the contract services.

5. This Regulation shall not apply to vertical agreements the subject matter of which falls within the scope of any other block exemption regulation.

Article 3 [Market share threshold]

7–103 1. Subject to paragraph 2 of this Article, the exemption provided for in Article 2 shall apply on condition that the market share held by the supplier does not exceed 30 per cent of the relevant market on which it sells the contract goods or services.

2. In the case of vertical agreements containing exclusive supply obligations, the exemption provided for in Article 2 shall apply on condition that the market share held by the buyer does not exceed 30 per cent of the relevant market on which it purchases the contract goods or services.

Article 4 [Agreements not covered by the exemption]

7–104 The exemption provided for in Article 2 shall not apply to vertical agreements which, directly or indirectly, in isolation or in combination with other factors under the control of the parties, have as their object:

(a) the restriction of the buyer's ability to determine its sale price, without prejudice to the possibility of the supplier's imposing a maximum sale price or recommending a sale price, provided that they do not amount to a fixed or minimum sale price as a result of pressure from, or incentives offered by, any of the parties;

(b) the restriction of the territory into which, or of the customers to whom, the buyer may sell the contract goods or services, except:

— the restriction of active sales into the exclusive territory or to an exclusive customer group reserved to the supplier or allocated by the supplier to another buyer, where such a restriction does not limit sales by the customers of the buyer,

— the restriction of sales to end users by a buyer operating at the wholesale level of trade,

— the restriction of sales to unauthorised distributors by the members of a selective distribution system, and

— the restriction of the buyer's ability to sell components, supplied for the purposes of incorporation, to customers who would use them to manufacture the same type of goods as those produced by the supplier;

(c) the restriction of active or passive sales to end users by members of a selective distribution system operating at the retail level of trade, without prejudice to the possibility of prohibiting a member of the system from operating out of an unauthorised place of establishment;

(d) the restriction of cross-supplies between distributors within a selective distribution system, including between distributors operating at different level of trade;

(e) the restriction agreed between a supplier of components and a buyer who incorporates those components, which limits the supplier to selling the components as spare parts to end-users or to repairers or other service providers not entrusted by the buyer with the repair or servicing of its goods.

Article 5 [Prohibited ("hard-core") restrictions]

7–105 The exemption provided for in Article 2 shall not apply to any of the following obligations contained in vertical agreements:

(a) any direct or indirect non-compete obligation, the duration of which is indefinite or exceeds five years. A non-compete obligation which is tacitly renewable beyond a period of five years is to be deemed to have been concluded for an indefinite duration. However, the time limitation of five years shall not apply where the contract goods or services are sold by the buyer from premises and land owned by the supplier or leased by the supplier from third parties not connected with the buyer, provided that the duration of the non-compete obligation does not exceed the period of occupancy of the premises and land by the buyer;

(b) any direct or indirect obligation causing the buyer, after termination of the agreement, not to manufacture, purchase, sell or resell goods or services, unless such obligation:
- relates to goods or services which compete with the contract goods or services, and
- is limited to the premises and land from which the buyer has operated during the contract period, and
- is indispensable to protect know-how transferred by the supplier to the buyer, and provided that the duration of such non-compete obligation is limited to a period of one year after termination of the agreement; this obligation is without prejudice to the possibility of imposing a restriction which is unlimited in time on the use and disclosure of know-how which has not entered the public domain;

(c) any direct or indirect obligation causing the members of a selective distribution system not to sell the brands of particular competing suppliers.

Article 6 [Withdrawal of exemption by the Commission]

The Commission may withdraw the benefit of this Regulation, pursuant to Article 7(1) of Regulation 19/65, where it finds in any particular case that vertical agreements to which this Regulation applies nevertheless have effects which are incompatible with the conditions laid down in Article 81(3) of the Treaty, and in particular where access to the relevant market or competition therein is significantly restricted by the cumulative effect of parallel networks of similar vertical restraints implemented by competing suppliers or buyers. **7–106**

Article 7 [Withdrawal of exemption by Member State authorities]

Where in any particular case vertical agreements to which the exemption provided for in Article 2 applies have effects incompatible with the conditions laid down in Article 81(3) of the Treaty in the territory of a Member State, or in a part thereof, which has all the characteristics of a distinct geographic market, the competent authority of that Member State may withdraw the benefit of application of this Regulation in respect of that territory, under the same conditions as provided in Article 6. **7–107**

Article 8 [Withdrawal in respect of parallel networks]

1. Pursuant to Article 1a of Regulation 19/65, the Commission may by regulation declare that, where parallel networks of similar vertical restraints cover more than 50 per cent of a relevant market, this Regulation shall not apply to vertical agreements containing specific restraints relating to that market. **7–108**

2. A regulation pursuant to paragraph 1 shall not become applicable earlier than six months following its adoption.

Article 9 [Application of market share threshold]

1. The market share of 30 per cent provided for in Article 3(1) shall be calculated on the basis of the market sales value of the contract goods or services and other goods or services sold by the supplier, which are regarded as interchangeable or substitutable by the buyer, by reason of the products' characteristics, their prices **7–109**

and their intended use; if market sales value data are not available, estimates based on other reliable market information, including market sales volumes, may be used to establish the market share of the undertaking concerned. For the purposes of Article 3(2), it is either the market purchase value or estimates thereof which shall be used to calculate the market share.

2. For the purposes of applying the market share, threshold provided for in Article 3 the following rules shall apply:
(a) the market share shall be calculated on the basis of data relating to the preceding calendar year;
(b) the market share shall include any goods or services supplied to integrated distributors for the purposes of sale;
(c) if the market share is initially not more than 30 per cent but subsequently rises above that level without exceeding 35 per cent, the exemption provided for in Article 2 shall continue to apply for a period of two consecutive calendar years following the year in which the 30 per cent market share threshold was first exceeded;
(d) if the market share is initially not more than 30 per cent but subsequently rises above 35 per cent, the exemption provided for in Article 2 shall continue to apply for one calendar year following the year in which the level of 35 per cent was first exceeded;
(e) the benefit of points (c) and (d) may not be combined so as to exceed a period of two calendar years.

Article 10 [Calculation of total annual turnover]

7–110 1. For the purpose of calculating total annual turnover within the meaning of Article 2(2) and (4), the turnover achieved during the previous financial year by the relevant party to the vertical agreement and the turnover achieved by its connected undertakings in respect of all goods and services, excluding all taxes and other duties, shall be added together. For this purpose, no account shall be taken of dealings between the party to the vertical agreement and its connected undertakings or between its connected undertakings.

2. The exemption provided for in Article 2 shall remain applicable where, for any period of two consecutive financial years, the total annual turnover threshold is exceeded by no more than 10 per cent.

Article 11 [Connected undertakings]

7–111 1. For the purposes of this Regulation, the terms "undertaking", "supplier" and "buyer" shall include their respective connected undertakings.

2. "Connected undertakings" are:
(a) undertakings in which a party to the agreement, directly or indirectly:
— has the power to exercise more than half the voting rights, or
— has the power to appoint more than half the members of the supervisory board, board of management or bodies legally representing the undertaking, or
— has the right to manage the undertaking's affairs;
(b) undertakings which directly or indirectly have, over a party to the agreement, the rights or powers listed in (a);
(c) undertakings in which an undertaking referred to in (b) has, directly or indirectly, the rights or powers listed in (a);

(d) undertakings in which a party to the agreement together with one or more of the undertakings referred to in (a), (b) or (c), or in which two or more of the latter undertakings, jointly have the rights or powers listed in (a);

(e) undertakings in which the rights or the powers listed in (a) are jointly held by:

— parties to the agreement or their respective connected undertakings referred to in (a) to (d), or

— one or more of the parties to the agreement or one or more of their connected undertakings referred to in (a) to (d) and one or more third parties.

3. For the purposes of Article 3, the market share held by the undertakings referred to in paragraph 2(e) of this Article shall be apportioned equally to each undertaking having the rights or the powers listed in paragraph 2(a).

Article 12 [Transitional provisions]

1. The exemptions provided for in Commission Regulations 1983/83,[13] 1984/83[14] **7–112**
and 4087/88[15] shall continue to apply until 31 May 2000.

2. The prohibition laid down in Article 81(1) of the EC Treaty shall not apply during the period from 1 June 2000 to 31 December 2001, in respect of agreements already in force on 31 May 2000 which do not satisfy the conditions for exemption provided for in this Regulation but which satisfy the conditions for exemption provided for in Regulations 1983/83, 1984/83 or 4087/88.

Article 13 [Effective dates; expiry]

This Regulation shall enter into force on 1 January 2000. **7–113**

It shall apply from 1 June 2000, except for Article 12(1) which shall apply from 1 January 2000.

This Regulation shall expire on 31 May 2010.

This Regulation shall be binding in its entirety and directly applicable in all Member States.

Commission Regulation 2658/2000 of 29 November 2000, on the application of Article 81(3) of the Treaty to categories of specialisation agreements

([2000] OJ L304/3; Doc. Ref. 32000R2658)

The Commission of the European Communities, **7–114**

Having regard to the Treaty establishing the European Community,

Having regard to Council Regulation 2821/71 of 20 December 1971, on the application of Article [81(3)] of the Treaty to categories of agreements, decisions and concerted practices,[16] as last amended by the Act of Accession of Austria, Finland and Sweden, and in particular Article 1(1)(c) thereof,

Having published a draft of this Regulation,[17]

Having consulted the Advisory Committee on Restrictive Practices and Dominant Positions,

Whereas:

(1) Regulation 2821/71 empowers the Commission to apply Article 81(3) (formerly Article 85(3)) of the Treaty by regulation to certain categories of agreements, decisions and concerted practices falling within the scope of Article 81(1) which have as their object specialisation, including agreements necessary for achieving it.

---

[13] [1983] OJ L173/1: block exemption in respect of exclusive distribution agreements.

[14] [1983] OJ L173/5: block exemption in respect of exclusive purchasing agreements.

[15] [1988] OJ L359/46: block exemption in respect of franchise agreements.

[16] [1971(III)] OJ, Eng. Spec. Ed., p.1032.

[17] [2000] OJ C118/3.

(2) Pursuant to Regulation 2821/71, in particular, the Commission has adopted Regulation 417/85 of 19 December 1984, on the application of Article [81(3)] of the Treaty to categories of specialisation agreements,[18] as last amended by Regulation 2236/97.[19] Regulation 417/85 expires on 31 December 2000.

(3) A new regulation should meet the two requirements of ensuring effective protection of competition and providing adequate legal security for undertakings. The pursuit of these objectives should take account of the need to simplify administrative supervision and the legislative framework to as great an extent as possible. Below a certain level of market power it can, for the application of Article 81(3), in general be presumed that the positive effects of specialisation agreements will outweigh any negative effects on competition.

(4) Regulation 2821/71 requires the exempting regulation of the Commission to define the categories of agreements, decisions and concerted practices to which it applies, to specify the restrictions or clauses which may, or may not, appear in the agreements, decisions and concerted practices, and to specify the clauses which must be contained in the agreements, decisions and concerted practices or the other conditions which must be satisfied.

(5) It is appropriate to move away from the approach of listing exempted clauses and to place greater emphasis on defining the categories of agreements which are exempted up to a certain level of market power and on specifying the restrictions or clauses which are not to be contained in such agreements. This is consistent with an economics-based approach which assesses the impact of agreements on the relevant market.

(6) For the application of Article 81(3) by regulation, it is not necessary to define those agreements which are capable of falling within Article 81(1). In the individual assessment of agreements under Article 81(1), account has to be taken of several factors, and in particular the market structure on the relevant market.

(7) The benefit of the block exemption should be limited to those agreements for which it can be assumed with sufficient certainty that they satisfy the conditions of Article 81(3).

(8) Agreements on specialisation in production generally contribute to improving the production or distribution of goods, because the undertakings concerned can concentrate on the manufacture of certain products and thus operate more efficiently and supply the products more cheaply. Agreements on specialisation in the provision of services can also be said to generally give rise to similar improvements. It is likely that, given effective competition, consumers will receive a fair share of the resulting benefit.

(9) Such advantages can arise equally from agreements whereby one participant gives up the manufacture of certain products or provision of certain services in favour of another participant ("unilateral specialisation"), from agreements whereby each participant gives up the manufacture of certain products or provision of certain services in favour of another participant ("reciprocal specialisation") and from agreements whereby the participants undertake to jointly manufacture certain products or provide certain services ("joint production").

(10) As unilateral specialisation agreements between non-competitors may benefit from the block exemption provided by Commission Regulation 2790/1999 of 22 December 1999, on the application of Article 81(3) of the Treaty to categories of vertical agreements and concerted practices,[20] the application of the present Regulation to unilateral specialisation agreements should be limited to agreements between competitors.

(11) All other agreements entered into between undertakings relating to the conditions under which they specialise in the production of goods and/or services

[18] [1985] OJ L53/1.
[19] [1997] OJ L306/12.
[20] [1999] OJ L336/21 (see above).

should fall within the scope of this Regulation. The block exemption should also apply to provisions contained in specialisation agreements which do not constitute the primary object of such agreements, but are directly related to and necessary for their implementation, and to certain related purchasing and marketing arrangements.

(12) To ensure that the benefits of specialisation will materialise without one party leaving the market downstream of production, unilateral and reciprocal specialisation agreements should only be covered by this Regulation where they provide for supply and purchase obligations. These obligations may, but do not have to, be of an exclusive nature.

(13) It can be presumed that, where the participating undertakings' share of the relevant market does not exceed 20 per cent, specialisation agreements as defined in this Regulation will, as a general rule, give rise to economic benefits in the form of economies of scale or scope or better production technologies, while allowing consumers a fair share of the resulting benefits.

(14) This Regulation should not exempt agreements containing restrictions which are not indispensable to attain the positive effects mentioned above. In principle certain severe anti-competitive restraints relating to the fixing of prices charged to third parties, limitation of output or sales, and allocation of markets or customers should be excluded from the benefit of the block exemption established by this Regulation irrespective of the market share of the undertakings concerned.

(15) The market share limitation, the non-exemption of certain agreements and the conditions provided for in this Regulation normally ensure that the agreements to which the block exemption applies do not enable the participating undertakings to eliminate competition in respect of a substantial part of the products or services in question.

(16) In particular cases in which the agreements falling under this Regulation nevertheless have effects incompatible with Article 81(3) of the Treaty, the Commission may withdraw the benefit of the block exemption.

(17) In order to facilitate the conclusion of specialisation agreements, which can have a bearing on the structure of the participating undertakings, the period of validity of this Regulation should be fixed at 10 years.

(18) This Regulation is without prejudice to the application of Article 82 of the Treaty.

(19) In accordance with the principle of the primacy of Community law, no measure taken pursuant to national laws on competition should prejudice the uniform application throughout the common market of the Community competition rules or the full effect of any measures adopted in implementation of those rules, including this Regulation,

Has adopted this Regulation:

Article 1 Exemption

1. Pursuant to Article 81(3) of the Treaty and subject to the provisions of this Regulation, it is hereby declared that Article 81(1) shall not apply to the following agreements entered into between two or more undertakings (hereinafter referred to as "the parties") which relate to the conditions under which those undertakings specialise in the production of products (hereinafter referred to as "specialisation agreements"): **7–115**

(a) unilateral specialisation agreements, by virtue of which one party agrees to cease production of certain products or to refrain from producing those products and to purchase them from a competing undertaking, while the competing undertaking agrees to produce and supply those products; or

(b) reciprocal specialisation agreements, by virtue of which two or more parties on a reciprocal basis agree to cease or refrain from producing certain but different products and to purchase these products from the other parties, who agree to supply them; or

(c) joint production agreements, by virtue of which two or more parties agree to produce certain products jointly.
This exemption shall apply to the extent that such specialisation agreements contain restrictions of competition falling within the scope of Article 81(1) of the Treaty.[21]

2. The exemption provided for in paragraph 1 shall also apply to provisions contained in specialisation agreements, which do not constitute the primary object of such agreements, but are directly related to and necessary for their implementation, such as those concerning the assignment or use of intellectual property rights.

The first sub-paragraph does, however, not apply to provisions which have the same object as the restrictions of competition enumerated in Article 5(1).

Article 2 Definitions

7–116 For the purposes of this Regulation:

1. "Agreement" means an agreement, a decision of an association of undertakings or a concerted practice.

2. "Participating undertakings" means undertakings party to the agreement and their respective connected undertakings.

3. "Connected undertakings" means:
(a) undertakings in which a party to the agreement, directly or indirectly:
  (i) has the power to exercise more than half the voting rights, or
  (ii) has the power to appoint more than half the members of the supervisory board, board of management or bodies legally representing the undertaking, or
  (iii) has the right to manage the undertaking's affairs;
(b) undertakings which directly or indirectly have, over a party to the agreement, the rights or powers listed in (a);
(c) undertakings in which an undertaking referred to in (b) has, directly or indirectly, the rights or powers listed in (a);
(d) undertakings in which a party to the agreement together with one or more of the undertakings referred to in (a), (b) or (c), or in which two or more of the latter undertakings, jointly have the rights or powers listed in (a);
(e) undertakings in which the rights or the powers listed in (a) are jointly held by:
  (i) parties to the agreement or their respective connected undertakings referred to in (a) to (d), or
  (ii) one or more of the parties to the agreement or one or more of their connected undertakings referred to in (a) to (d) and one or more third parties.

4. "Product" means a good and/or a service, including both intermediary goods and/or services and final goods and/or services, with the exception of distribution and rental services.

5. "Production" means the manufacture of goods or the provision of services and includes production by way of subcontracting.

6. "Relevant market" means the relevant product and geographic market(s) to which the products, which are the subject matter of a specialisation agreement, belong.

7. "Competing undertaking" means an undertaking that is active on the relevant market (an actual competitor) or an undertaking that would, on realistic grounds,

[21] For analysis of whether a specialisation agreement contains restrictions falling within the scope of Art. 81(1), see the Guidelines on the applicability of Art. 81 of the EC Treaty to horizontal co-operation agreements ([2001] OJ C3/2).

undertake the necessary additional investments or other necessary switching costs so that it could enter the relevant market in response to a small and permanent increase in relative prices (a potential competitor).

8. "Exclusive supply obligation" means an obligation not to supply a competing undertaking other than a party to the agreement with the product to which the specialisation agreement relates.

9. "Exclusive purchase obligation" means an obligation to purchase the product to which the specialisation agreement relates only from the party which agrees to supply it.

Article 3 Purchasing and marketing arrangements

The exemption provided for in Article 1 shall also apply where: **7–117**
(a) the parties accept an exclusive purchase and/or exclusive supply obligation in the context of a unilateral or reciprocal specialisation agreement or a joint production agreement, or
(b) the parties do not sell the products which are the object of the specialisation agreement independently but provide for joint distribution or agree to appoint a third party distributor on an exclusive or non-exclusive basis in the context of a joint production agreement provided that the third party is not a competing undertaking.

Article 4 Market share threshold

The exemption provided for in Article 1 shall apply on condition that the combined market share of the participating undertakings does not exceed 20 per cent of the relevant market. **7–118**

Article 5 Agreements not covered by the exemption

1. The exemption provided for in Article 1 shall not apply to agreements which, directly or indirectly, in isolation or in combination with other factors under the control of the parties, have as their object: **7–119**
(a) the fixing of prices when selling the products to third parties;
(b) the limitation of output or sales; or
(c) the allocation of markets or customers.

2. Paragraph 1 shall not apply to:
(a) provisions on the agreed amount of products in the context of unilateral or reciprocal specialisation agreements or the setting of the capacity and production volume of a production joint venture in the context of a joint production agreement;
(b) the setting of sales targets and the fixing of prices that a production joint venture charges to its immediate customers in the context of point (b) of Article 3.

Article 6 Application of the market share threshold

1. For the purposes of applying the market share threshold provided for in Article 4 the following rules shall apply: **7–120**

(a) the market share shall be calculated on the basis of the market sales value; if market sales value data are not available, estimates based on other reliable market information, including market sales volumes, may be used to establish the market share of the undertaking concerned;
(b) the market share shall be calculated on the basis of data relating to the preceding calendar year;
(c) the market share held by the undertakings referred to in point 3(e) of Article 2 shall be apportioned equally to each undertaking having the rights or the powers listed in point 3(a) of Article 2.

2. If the market share referred to in Article 4 is initially not more than 20 per cent but subsequently rises above this level without exceeding 25 per cent, the exemption provided for in Article 1 shall continue to apply for a period of two consecutive calendar years following the year in which the 20 per cent threshold was first exceeded.

3. If the market share referred to in Article 4 is initially not more than 20 per cent but subsequently rises above 25 per cent, the exemption provided for in Article 1 shall continue to apply for one calendar year following the year in which the level of 25 per cent was first exceeded.

4. The benefit of paragraphs 2 and 3 may not be combined so as to exceed a period of two calendar years.

Article 7 Withdrawal

7–121 The Commission may withdraw the benefit of this Regulation, pursuant to Article 7 of Regulation 2821/71, where, either on its own initiative or at the request of a Member State or of a natural or legal person claiming a legitimate interest, it finds in a particular case that an agreement to which the exemption provided for in Article 1 applies nevertheless has effects which are incompatible with the conditions laid down in Article 81(3) of the Treaty, and in particular where:
(a) the agreement is not yielding significant results in terms of rationalisation or consumers are not receiving a fair share of the resulting benefit, or
(b) the products which are the subject of the specialisation are not subject in the common market or a substantial part thereof to effective competition from identical products or products considered by users to be equivalent in view of their characteristics, price and intended use.

Article 8 Transitional period

7–122 The prohibition laid down in Article 81(1) of the Treaty shall not apply during the period from 1 January 2001, to 30 June 2002, in respect of agreements already in force on 31 December 2000, which do not satisfy the conditions for exemption provided for in this Regulation but which satisfy the conditions for exemption provided for in Regulation 417/85.

Article 9 Period of validity

7–123 This Regulation shall enter into force on 1 January 2001.
It shall expire on 31 December 2010.

This Regulation shall be binding in its entirety and directly applicable in all Member States.

Commission Regulation 2659/2000 of 29 November 2000, on the application of Article 81(3) of the Treaty to categories of research and development agreements

([2000] OJ L304/7; Doc. Ref. 32000R2659)

The Commission of the European Communities, **7–124**
Having regard to the Treaty establishing the European Community,

Having regard to Council Regulation 2821/71 of 20 December 1971, on application of Article [81(3)] of the Treaty to categories of agreements, decisions and concerted practices,[22] as last amended by the Act of Accession of Austria, Finland and Sweden, and in particular Article 1(1)(b) thereof,

Having published a draft of this Regulation,[23]

Having consulted the Advisory Committee on Restrictive Practices and Dominant Positions,

Whereas:

(1) Regulation 2821/71 empowers the Commission to apply Article 81(3) (formerly Article 85(3)) of the Treaty by regulation to certain categories of agreements, decisions and concerted practices falling within the scope of Article 81(1) which have as their object the research and development of products or processes up to the stage of industrial application, and exploitation of the results, including provisions regarding intellectual property rights.

(2) Article 163(2) of the Treaty calls upon the Community to encourage undertakings, including small and medium-sized undertakings, in their research and technological development activities of high quality, and to support their efforts to cooperate with one another. Pursuant to Council Decision 1999/65 of 22 December 1998, concerning the rules for the participation of undertakings, research centres and universities and for the dissemination of research results for the implementation of the fifth framework programme of the European Community (1998–2002)[24] and Commission Regulation 996/1999[25] on the implementation of Decision 1999/65, indirect research and technological development (RTD) actions supported under the fifth framework programme of the Community are required to be carried out cooperatively.

(3) Agreements on the joint execution of research work or the joint development of the results of the research, up to but not including the stage of industrial application, generally do not fall within the scope of Article 81(1) of the Treaty. In certain circumstances, however, such as where the parties agree not to carry out other research and development in the same field, thereby forgoing the opportunity of gaining competitive advantages over the other parties, such agreements may fall within Article 81(1) and should therefore be included within the scope of this Regulation.

(4) Pursuant to Regulation 2821/71, the Commission has, in particular, adopted Regulation 418/85 of 19 December 1984, on the application of Article [81(3)] of the Treaty to categories of research and development agreements,[26] as last amended by Regulation 2236/97.[27] Regulation 418/85 expires on 31 December 2000.

(5) A new regulation should meet the two requirements of ensuring effective protection of competition and providing adequate legal security for undertakings. The pursuit of these objectives should take account of the need to simplify administrative supervision and the legislative framework to as great an extent

[22] [1971(III)] OJ, Eng. Spec. Ed., p.1032.
[23] [2000] OJ C118/3.
[24] [1999] OJ L26/46.
[25] [1999] OJ L122/9.
[26] [1985] OJ L53/5.
[27] [1997] OJ L306/12.

possible. Below a certain level of market power it can, for the application of Article 81(3), in general be presumed that the positive effects of research and development agreements will outweigh any negative effects on competition.

(6) Regulation 2821/71 requires the exempting regulation of the Commission to define the categories of agreements, decisions and concerted practices to which it applies, to specify the restrictions or clauses which may, or may not, appear in the agreements, decisions and concerted practices, and to specify the clauses which must be contained in the agreements, decisions and concerted practices or the other conditions which must be satisfied.

(7) It is appropriate to move away from the approach of listing exempted clauses and to place greater emphasis on defining the categories of agreements which are exempted up to a certain level of market power and on specifying the restrictions or clauses which are not to be contained in such agreements. This is consistent with an economics based approach which assesses the impact of agreements on the relevant market.

(8) For the application of Article 81(3) by regulation, it is not necessary to define those agreements which are capable of falling within Article 81(1). In the individual assessment of agreements under Article 81(1), account has to be taken of several factors, and in particular the market structure on the relevant market.

(9) The benefit of the block exemption should be limited to those agreements for which it can be assumed with sufficient certainty that they satisfy the conditions of Article 81(3).

(10) Cooperation in research and development and in the exploitation of the results generally promotes technical and economic progress by increasing the dissemination of know-how between the parties and avoiding duplication of research and development work, by stimulating new advances through the exchange of complementary know-how, and by rationalising the manufacture of the products or application of the processes arising out of the research and development.

(11) The joint exploitation of results can be considered as the natural consequence of joint research and development. It can take different forms such as manufacture, the exploitation of intellectual property rights that substantially contribute to technical or economic progress, or the marketing of new products.

(12) Consumers can generally be expected to benefit from the increased volume and effectiveness of research and development through the introduction of new or improved products or services or the reduction of prices brought about by new or improved processes.

(13) In order to attain the benefits and objectives of joint research and development the benefit of this Regulation should also apply to provisions contained in research and development agreements which do not constitute the primary object of such agreements, but are directly related to and necessary for their implementation.

(14) In order to justify the exemption, the joint exploitation should relate to products or processes for which the use of the results of the research and development is decisive, and each of the parties is given the opportunity of exploiting any results that interest it. However, where academic bodies, research institutes or undertakings which supply research and development as a commercial service without normally being active in the exploitation of results participate in research and development, they may agree to use the results of research and development solely for the purpose of further research. Similarly, non-competitors may agree to limit their right to exploitation to one or more technical fields of application to facilitate cooperation between parties with complementary skills.

(15) The exemption granted under this Regulation should be limited to research and development agreements which do not afford the undertakings the possibility of eliminating competition in respect of a substantial part of the products or services in question. It is necessary to exclude from the block exemption agreements between competitors whose combined share of the market

for products or services capable of being improved or replaced by the results of the research and development exceeds a certain level at the time the agreement is entered into.

(16) In order to guarantee the maintenance of effective competition during joint exploitation of the results, provision should be made for the block exemption to cease to apply if the parties' combined share of the market for the products arising out of the joint research and development becomes too great. The exemption should continue to apply, irrespective of the parties' market shares, for a certain period after the commencement of joint exploitation, so as to await stabilisation of their market shares, particularly after the introduction of an entirely new product, and to guarantee a minimum period of return on the investments involved.

(17) This Regulation should not exempt agreements containing restrictions which are not indispensable to attain the positive effects mentioned above. In principle certain severe anti-competitive restraints such as limitations on the freedom of parties to carry out research and development in a field unconnected to the agreement, the fixing of prices charged to third parties, limitations on output or sales, allocation of markets or customers, and limitations on effecting passive sales for the contract products in territories reserved for other parties should be excluded from the benefit of the block exemption established by this Regulation irrespective of the market share of the undertakings concerned.

(18) The market share limitation, the non-exemption of certain agreements, and the conditions provided for in this Regulation normally ensure that the agreements to which the block exemption applies do not enable the participating undertakings to eliminate competition in respect of a substantial part of the products or services in question.

(19) In particular cases in which the agreements falling under this Regulation nevertheless have effects incompatible with Article 81(3) of the Treaty, the Commission may withdraw the benefit of the block exemption.

(20) Agreements between undertakings which are not competing manufacturers of products capable of being improved or replaced by the results of the research and development will only eliminate effective competition in research and development in exceptional circumstances. It is therefore appropriate to enable such agreements to benefit from the block exemption irrespective of market share and to address such exceptional cases by way of withdrawal of its benefit.

(21) As research and development agreements are often of a long-term nature, especially where the cooperation extends to the exploitation of the results, the period of validity of this Regulation should be fixed at 10 years.

(22) This Regulation is without prejudice to the application of Article 82 of the Treaty.

(23) In accordance with the principle of the primacy of Community law, no measure taken pursuant to national laws on competition should prejudice the uniform application throughout the common market of the Community competition rules or the full effect of any measures adopted in implementation of those rules, including this Regulation,

Has adopted this Regulation:

Article 1 Exemption

1. Pursuant to Article 81(3) of the Treaty and subject to the provisions of this Regulation, it is hereby declared that Article 81(1) shall not apply to agreements entered into between two or more undertakings (hereinafter referred to as "the parties") which relate to the conditions under which those undertakings pursue: **7–125**

(a) joint research and development of products or processes and joint exploitation of the results of that research and development;

(b) joint exploitation of the results of research and development of products or processes jointly carried out pursuant to a prior agreement between the same parties; or
(c) joint research and development of products or processes excluding joint exploitation of the results.

This exemption shall apply to the extent that such agreements (hereinafter referred to as "research and development agreements") contain restrictions of competition falling within the scope of Article 81(1).[28]

2. The exemption provided for in paragraph 1 shall also apply to provisions contained in research and development agreements which do not constitute the primary object of such agreements, but are directly related to and necessary for their implementation, such as an obligation not to carry out, independently or together with third parties, research and development in the field to which the agreement relates or in a closely connected field during the execution of the agreement.

The first sub-paragraph does, however, not apply to provisions which have the same object as the restrictions of competition enumerated in Article 5(1).

Article 2 Definitions

7–126 For the purposes of this Regulation:

1. "agreement" means an agreement, a decision of an association of undertakings or a concerted practice;

2. "participating undertakings" means undertakings party to the research and development agreement and their respective connected undertakings;

3. "connected undertakings" means:
(a) undertakings in which a party to the research and development agreement, directly or indirectly:
  (i) has the power to exercise more than half the voting rights,
  (ii) has the power to appoint more than half the members of the supervisory board, board of management or bodies legally representing the undertaking, or
  (iii) has the right to manage the undertaking's affairs;
(b) undertakings which directly or indirectly have, over a party to the research and development agreement, the rights or powers listed in (a);
(c) undertakings in which an undertaking referred to in (b) has, directly or indirectly, the rights or powers listed in (a);
(d) undertakings in which a party to the research and development agreement together with one or more of the undertakings referred to in (a), (b) or (c), or in which two or more of the latter undertakings, jointly have the rights or powers listed in (a);
(e) undertakings in which the rights or the powers listed in (a) are jointly held by:
  (i) parties to the research and development agreement or their respective connected undertakings referred to in (a) to (d), or
  (ii) one or more of the parties to the research and development agreement or one or more of their connected undertakings referred to in (a) to (d) and one or more third parties;

4. "research and development" means the acquisition of know-how relating to products or processes and the carrying out of theoretical analysis, systematic study or experimentation, including experimental production, technical testing of products or processes, the establishment of the necessary facilities and the obtaining of intellectual property rights for the results;

[28] For analysis of whether an R&D agreement contains restrictions falling within the scope of Art. 81(1), see the Guidelines on the applicability of Art. 81 of the EC Treaty to horizontal co-operation agreements ([2001] OJ C3/2).

5. "product" means a good and/or a service, including both intermediary goods and/or services and final goods and/or services;

6. "contract process" means a technology or process arising out of the joint research and development;

7. "contract product" means a product arising out of the joint research and development or manufactured or provided applying the contract processes;

8. "exploitation of the results" means the production or distribution of the contract products or the application of the contract processes or the assignment or licensing of intellectual property rights or the communication of know-how required for such manufacture or application;

9. "intellectual property rights" includes industrial property-rights, copyright and neighbouring rights;

10. "know-how" means a package of non-patented practical information, resulting from experience and testing, which is secret, substantial and identified: in this context, "secret" means that the know-how is not generally known or easily accessible; "substantial" means that the know-how includes information which is indispensable for the manufacture of the contract products or the application of the contract processes; "identified" means that the know-how is described in a sufficiently comprehensive manner so as to make it possible to verify that it fulfils the criteria of secrecy and substantiality;

11. research and development, or exploitation of the results, are carried out "jointly" where the work involved is:
(a) carried out by a joint team, organisation or undertaking,
(b) jointly entrusted to a third party, or
(c) allocated between the parties by way of specialisation in research, development, production or distribution;

12. "competing undertaking" means an undertaking that is supplying a product capable of being improved or replaced by the contract product (an actual competitor) or an undertaking that would, on realistic grounds, undertake the necessary additional investments or other necessary switching costs so that it could supply such a product in response to a small and permanent increase in relative prices (a potential competitor);

13. "relevant market for the contract products" means the relevant product and geographic market(s) to which the contract products belong.

Article 3 Conditions for exemption

1. The exemption provided for in Article 1 shall apply subject to the conditions set out in paragraphs 2 to 5. **7–127**

2. All the parties must have access to the results of the joint research and development for the purposes of further research or exploitation. However, research institutes, academic bodies, or undertakings which supply research and development as a commercial service without normally being active in the exploitation of results may agree to confine their use of the results for the purposes of further research.

3. Without prejudice to paragraph 2, where the research and development agreement provides only for joint research and development, each party must be free independently to exploit the results of the joint research and development

and any pre-existing know-how necessary for the purposes of such exploitation. Such right to exploitation may be limited to one or more technical fields of application, where the parties are not competing undertakings at the time the research and development agreement is entered into.

4. Any joint exploitation must relate to results which are protected by intellectual property rights or constitute know-how, which substantially contribute to technical or economic progress and the results must be decisive for the manufacture of the contract products or the application of the contract processes.

5. Undertakings charged with manufacture by way of specialisation in production must be required to fulfil orders for supplies from all the parties, except where the research and development agreement also provides for joint distribution.

Article 4 Market share threshold and duration of exemption

7–128 1. Where the participating undertakings are not competing undertakings, the exemption provided for in Article 1 shall apply for the duration of the research and development. Where the results are jointly exploited, the exemption shall continue to apply for seven years from the time the contract products are first put on the market within the common market.

2. Where two or more of the participating undertakings are competing undertakings, the exemption provided for in Article 1 shall apply for the period referred to in paragraph 1 only if, at the time the research and development agreement is entered into, the combined market share of the participating undertakings does not exceed 25 per cent of the relevant market for the products capable of being improved or replaced by the contract products.

3. After the end of the period referred to in paragraph 1, the exemption shall continue to apply as long as the combined market share of the participating undertakings does not exceed 25 per cent of the relevant market for the contract products.

Article 5 Agreements not covered by the exemption

7–129 1. The exemption provided for in Article 1 shall not apply to research and development agreements which, directly or indirectly, in isolation or in combination with other factors under the control of the parties, have as their object:

(a) the restriction of the freedom of the participating undertakings to carry out research and development independently or in cooperation with third parties in a field unconnected with that to which the research and development relates or, after its completion, in the field to which it relates or in a connected field;

(b) the prohibition to challenge after completion of the research and development the validity of intellectual property rights which the parties hold in the common market and which are relevant to the research and development or, after the expiry of the research and development agreement, the validity of intellectual property rights which the parties hold in the common market and which protect the results of the research and development, without prejudice to the possibility to provide for termination of the research and development agreement in the event of one of the parties challenging the validity of such intellectual property rights;

(c) the limitation of output or sales;

(d) the fixing of prices when selling the contract product to third parties;

(e) the restriction of the customers that the participating undertakings may serve, after the end of seven years from the time the contract products are first put on the market within the common market;

(f) the prohibition to make passive sales of the contract products in territories reserved for other parties;

(g) the prohibition to put the contract products on the market or to pursue an active sales policy for them in territories within the common market that are reserved for other parties after the end of seven years from the time the contract products are first put on the market within the common market;
(h) the requirement not to grant licences to third parties to manufacture the contract products or to apply the contract processes where the exploitation by at least one of the parties of the results of the joint research and development is not provided for or does not take place;
(i) the requirement to refuse to meet demand from users or resellers in their respective territories who would market the contract products in other territories within the common market; or
(j) the requirement to make it difficult for users or resellers to obtain the contract products from other resellers within the common market, and in particular to exercise intellectual property rights or take measures so as to prevent users or resellers from obtaining, or from putting on the market within the common market, products which have been lawfully put on the market within the Community by another party or with its consent.

2. Paragraph 1 shall not apply to:
(a) the setting of production targets where the exploitation of the results includes the joint production of the contract products;
(b) the setting of sales targets and the fixing of prices charged to immediate customers where the exploitation of the results includes the joint distribution of the contract products.

Article 6 Application of the market share threshold

1. For the purposes of applying the market share threshold provided for in Article 4 the following rules shall apply: **7–130**
(a) the market share shall be calculated on the basis of the market sales value; if market sales value data are not available, estimates based on other reliable market information, including market sales volumes, may be used to establish the market share of the undertaking concerned;
(b) the market share shall be calculated on the basis of data relating to the preceding calendar year;
(c) the market share held by the undertakings referred to in point 3(e) of Article 2 shall be apportioned equally to each undertaking having the rights or the powers listed in point 3(a) of Article 2.

2. If the market share referred to in Article 4(3) is initially not more than 25 per cent but subsequently rises above this level without exceeding 30 per cent, the exemption provided for in Article 1 shall continue to apply for a period of two consecutive calendar years following the year in which the 25 per cent threshold was first exceeded.

3. If the market share referred to in Article 4(3) is initially not more than 25 per cent but subsequently rises above 30 per cent, the exemption provided for in Article 1 shall continue to apply for one calendar year following the year in which the level of 30 per cent was first exceeded.

4. The benefit of paragraphs 2 and 3 may not be combined so as to exceed a period of two calendar years.

Article 7 Withdrawal

The Commission may withdraw the benefit of this Regulation, pursuant to Article 7 of Regulation 2821/71, where, either on its own initiative or at the request of a **7–131**

Member State or of a natural or legal person claiming a legitimate interest, it finds in a particular case that a research and development agreement to which the exemption provided for in Article 1 applies nevertheless has effects which are incompatible with the conditions laid down in Article 81(3) of the Treaty, and in particular where:

(a) the existence of the research and development agreement substantially restricts the scope for third parties to carry-out research and development in the relevant field because of the limited research capacity available elsewhere;
(b) because of the particular structure of supply, the existence of the research and development agreement substantially restricts the access of third parties to the market for the contract products;
(c) without any objectively valid reason, the parties do not exploit the results of the joint research and development;
(d) the contract products are not subject in the whole or a substantial part of the common market to effective competition from identical products or products considered by users as equivalent in view of their characteristics, price and intended use;
(e) the existence of the research and development agreement would eliminate effective competition in research and development on a particular market.

Article 8 Transitional period

7–132 The prohibition laid down in Article 81(1) of the Treaty shall not apply during the period from 1 January 2001, to 30 June 2002, in respect of agreements already in force on 31 December 2000, which do not satisfy the conditions for exemption provided for in this Regulation but which satisfy the conditions for exemption provided for in Regulation 418/85.

Article 9 Period of validity

7–133 This Regulation shall enter into force on 1 January 2001.
It shall expire on 31 December 2010.

This Regulation shall be binding in its entirety and directly applicable in all Member States.

Commission Notice on agreements of minor importance which do not appreciably restrict competition under Article 81(1) of the Treaty establishing the European Community (*de minimis*)[29]

([2001] OJ C368/13, Doc. Ref. 52001XC1222(03))

I [—Introduction]

7–134 1. Article 81(1) prohibits agreements between undertakings which may affect trade between Member States and which have as their object or effect the prevention, restriction or distortion of competition within the common market. The Court of Justice of the European Communities has clarified that this provision is not applicable where the impact of the agreement on intra-Community trade or on competition is not appreciable.

2. In this notice the Commission quantifies, with the help of market share thresholds, what is not an appreciable restriction of competition under Article 81 of the EC Treaty. This negative definition of appreciability does not imply that agreements between undertakings which exceed the thresholds set out in this

[29] This notice replaces the notice on agreements of minor importance published in [1997] OJ C372/13.

notice appreciably restrict competition. Such agreements may still have only a negligible effect on competition and may therefore not be prohibited by Article 81(1).[30]

3. Agreements may in addition not fall under Article 81(1) because they are not capable of appreciably affecting trade between Member States. This notice does not deal with this issue. It does not quantify what does not constitute an appreciable effect on trade. It is however acknowledged that agreements between small and medium-sized undertakings, as defined in the Annex to Commission Recommendation 96/280,[31] are rarely capable of appreciably affecting trade between Member States. Small and medium-sized undertakings are currently defined in that recommendation as undertakings which have fewer than 250 employees and have either an annual turnover not exceeding EUR 40 million or an annual balance-sheet total not exceeding EUR 27 million.

4. In cases covered by this notice the Commission will not institute proceedings either upon application or on its own initiative. Where undertakings assume in good faith that an agreement is covered by this notice, the Commission will not impose fines. Although not binding on them, this notice also intends to give guidance to the courts and authorities of the Member States in their application of Article 81.

5. This notice also applies to decisions by associations of undertakings and to concerted practices.

6. This notice is without prejudice to any interpretation of Article 81 which may be given by the Court of Justice or the Court of First Instance of the European Communities.

II [—Criteria For Determining Minor Agreements]

7. The Commission holds the view that agreements between undertakings which affect trade between Member States do not appreciably restrict competition within the meaning of Article 81(1): **7–135**

(a) if the aggregate market share held by the parties to the agreement does not exceed 10 per cent on any of the relevant markets affected by the agreement, where the agreement is made between undertakings which are actual or potential competitors on any of these markets (agreements between competitors);[32] or

[30] See, for instance, the judgment of the Court of Justice in *Bagnasco (Carlos) v. Banca Popolare di Novara and Casa di Risparmio di Genova e Imperia* (Joined Cases C–215/96 and C–216/96) [1999] ECR. I–135, points 34–35. This notice is also without prejudice to the principles for assessment under Art. 81(1) as expressed in the Commission notice "Guidelines on the applicability of Article 81 of the EC Treaty to horizontal co-operation agreements" ([2001] OJ C3/2), in particular points 17–31 inclusive, and in the Commission notice "Guidelines on vertical restraints", [2000] OJ C291/1, in particular points 5–20 inclusive.

[31] [1996] OJ L107/4. This recommendation will be revised. It is envisaged to increase the annual turnover threshold from EUR 40 million to EUR 50 million and the annual balance-sheet total threshold from EUR 27 million to EUR 43 million.

[32] On what are actual or potential competitors, see the Commission notice "Guidelines on the applicability of Article 81 of the EC Treaty to horizontal co-operation agreements", [2001] OJ C3/2, para. 9. A firm is treated as an actual competitor if it is either active on the same relevant market or if, in the absence of the agreement, it is able to switch production to the relevant products and market them in the short term without incurring significant additional costs or risks in response to a small and permanent increase in relative prices (immediate supply-side substitutability). A firm is treated as a potential competitor if there is evidence that, absent the agreement, this firm could and would be likely to undertake the necessary additional investments or other necessary switching costs so that it could enter the relevant market in response to a small and permanent increase in relative prices.

(b) if the market share held by each of the parties to the agreement does not exceed 15 per cent on any of the relevant markets affected by the agreement, where the agreement is made between undertakings which are not actual or potential competitors on any of these markets (agreements between non-competitors).

In cases where it is difficult to classify the agreement as either an agreement between competitors or an agreement between non-competitors the 10 per cent threshold is applicable.

8. Where in a relevant market competition is restricted by the cumulative effect of agreements for the sale of goods or services entered into by different suppliers or distributors (cumulative foreclosure effect of parallel networks of agreements having similar effects on the market), the market share thresholds under point 7 are reduced to 5 per cent, both for agreements between competitors and for agreements between non-competitors. Individual suppliers or distributors with a market share not exceeding 5 per cent are in general not considered to contribute significantly to a cumulative foreclosure effect.[33] A cumulative foreclosure effect is unlikely to exist if less than 30 per cent of the relevant market is covered by parallel (networks of) agreements having similar effects.

9. The Commission also holds the view that agreements are not restrictive of competition if the market shares do not exceed the thresholds of respectively 10 per cent, 15 per cent and 5 per cent set out in point 7 and 8 during two successive calendar years by more than 2 percentage points.

10. In order to calculate the market share, it is necessary to determine the relevant market. This consists of the relevant product market and the relevant geographic market. When defining the relevant market, reference should be had to the notice on the definition of the relevant market for the purposes of Community competition law.[34] The market shares are to be calculated on the basis of sales value data or, where appropriate, purchase value data. If value data are not available, estimates based on other reliable market information, including volume data, may be used.

11. Points 7, 8 and 9 do not apply to agreements containing any of the following hardcore restrictions:

(1) as regards agreements between competitors as defined in point 7, restrictions which, directly or indirectly, in isolation or in combination with other factors under the control of the parties, have as their object[35]:
   (a) the fixing of prices when selling the products to third parties;
   (b) the limitation of output or sales;
   (c) the allocation of markets or customers;
(2) as regards agreements between non-competitors as defined in point 7, restrictions which, directly or indirectly, in isolation or in combination with other factors under the control of the parties, have as their object:
   (a) the restriction of the buyer's ability to determine its sale price, without prejudice to the possibility of the supplier imposing a maximum sale price or recommending a sale price, provided that they do not amount to a fixed or minimum sale price as a result of pressure from, or incentives offered by, any of the parties;

[33] See also the Commission notice "Guidelines on vertical restraints", [2000] OJ C291/1, in particular paras 73, 142, 143 and 189. While in the guidelines on vertical restraints in relation to certain restrictions reference is made not only to the total but also to the tied market share of a particular supplier or buyer, in this notice all market share thresholds refer to total market shares.

[34] [1997] OJ C372/5.

[35] Without prejudice to situations of joint production with or without joint distribution as defined in Art. 5, para. 2, of Commission Reg. 2658/2000 and Art. 5, para. 2, of Commission Reg. 2659/2000, [2000] OJ L304/3 and 7 respectively (see above).

(b) the restriction of the territory into which, or of the customers to whom, the buyer may sell the contract goods or services, except the following restrictions which are not hardcore:
- the restriction of active sales into the exclusive territory or to an exclusive customer group
- reserved to the supplier or allocated by the supplier to another buyer, where such a restriction does not limit sales by the customers of the buyer,
- the restriction of sales to end users by a buyer operating at the wholesale level of trade,
- the restriction of sales to unauthorised distributors by the members of a selective distribution system, and
- the restriction of the buyer's ability to sell components, supplied for the purposes of incorporation, to customers who would use them to manufacture the same type of goods as those produced by the supplier;

(c) the restriction of active or passive sales to end users by members of a selective distribution system operating at the retail level of trade, without prejudice to the possibility of prohibiting a member of the system from operating out of an unauthorised place of establishment;

(d) the restriction of cross-supplies between distributors within a selective distribution system, including between distributors operating at different levels of trade;

(e) the restriction agreed between a supplier of components and a buyer who incorporates those components, which limits the supplier's ability to sell the components as spare parts to end users or to repairers or other service providers not entrusted by the buyer with the repair or servicing of its goods;

(3) as regards agreements between competitors as defined in point 7, where the competitors operate, for the purposes of the agreement, at a different level of the production or distribution chain, any of the hardcore restrictions listed in paragraph (1) and (2) above.

12. (1) For the purposes of this notice, the terms "undertaking", "party to the agreement", "distributor", "supplier" and "buyer" shall include their respective connected undertakings.

(2) "Connected undertakings" are:

(a) undertakings in which a party to the agreement, directly or indirectly:
- has the power to exercise more than half the voting rights, or
- has the power to appoint more than half the members of the supervisory board, board of management or bodies legally representing the undertaking, or
- has the right to manage the undertaking's affairs;

(b) undertakings which directly or indirectly have, over a party to the agreement, the rights or powers listed in (a);

(c) undertakings in which an undertaking referred to in (b) has, directly or indirectly, the rights or powers listed in (a);

(d) undertakings in which a party to the agreement together with one or more of the undertakings referred to in (a), (b) or (c), or in which two or more of the latter undertakings, jointly have the rights or powers listed in (a);

(e) undertakings in which the rights or the powers listed in (a) are jointly held by:
- parties to the agreement or their respective connected undertakings referred to in (a) to (d), or
- one or more of the parties to the agreement or one or more of their connected undertakings referred to in (a) to (d) and one or more third parties.

(3) For the purposes of paragraph 2(e), the market share held by these jointly held undertakings shall be apportioned equally to each undertaking having the rights or the powers listed in paragraph 2(a).

Council Regulation 1/2003 of 16 December 2002, on the implementation of the rules on competition laid down in Articles 81 and 82 of the Treaty

([2003] OJ L1/1; Doc. Ref. 32003R0001)

7–136 *The Council of the European Union*,
Having regard to the Treaty establishing the European Community, and in particular Article 83 thereof,

Having regard to the proposal from the Commission[36],

Having regard to the opinion of the European Parliament[37],

Having regard to the opinion of the European Economic and Social Committee[38],

Whereas:

(1) In order to establish a system which ensures that competition in the common market is not distorted, Articles 81 and 82 of the Treaty must be applied effectively and uniformly in the Community. Council Regulation 17 of 6 February 1962, first Regulation implementing Articles [81] and [82] of the Treaty[39], has allowed a Community competition policy to develop that has helped to disseminate a competition culture within the Community. In the light of experience, however, that Regulation should now be replaced by legislation designed to meet the challenges of an integrated market and a future enlargement of the Community.

(2) In particular, there is a need to rethink the arrangements for applying the exception from the prohibition on agreements, which restrict competition, laid down in Article 81(3) of the Treaty. Under Article 83(2)(b) of the Treaty, account must be taken in this regard of the need to ensure effective supervision, on the one hand, and to simplify administration to the greatest possible extent, on the other.

(3) The centralised scheme set up by Regulation 17 no longer secures a balance between those two objectives. It hampers application of the Community competition rules by the courts and competition authorities of the Member States, and the system of notification it involves prevents the Commission from concentrating its resources on curbing the most serious infringements. It also imposes considerable costs on undertakings.

(4) The present system should therefore be replaced by a directly applicable exception system in which the competition authorities and courts of the Member States have the power to apply not only Article 81(1) and Article 82 of the Treaty, which have direct applicability by virtue of the case-law of the Court of Justice of the European Communities, but also Article 81(3) of the Treaty.

(5) In order to ensure an effective enforcement of the Community competition rules and at the same time the respect of fundamental rights of defence, this Regulation should regulate the burden of proof under Articles 81 and 82 of the Treaty. It should be for the party or the authority alleging an infringement of Article 81(1) and Article 82 of the Treaty to prove the existence thereof to the required legal standard. It should be for the undertaking or association of undertakings invoking the benefit of a defence against a finding of an infringement to demonstrate to the required legal standard that the conditions for applying such defence are satisfied. This Regulation affects neither national rules on the standard of proof nor obligations of competition authorities and courts of the

---

[36] [2000] OJ C365E/284.

[37] [2002] C72E/305.

[38] [2001] OJ C155/73.

[39] [1959–1962] OJ Eng. Spec. Ed., p.87. Regulation as last amended by Regulation 1216/1999 ([1999] OJ L148/5). The titles of the Regulations referred to in this Regulation have been adjusted to take account of the renumbering of the Articles of the EC Treaty, in accordance with Art.12 of the Treaty of Amsterdam.

Member States to ascertain the relevant facts of a case, provided that such rules and obligations are compatible with general principles of Community law.

(6) In order to ensure that the Community competition rules are applied effectively, the competition authorities of the Member States should be associated more closely with their application. To this end, they should be empowered to apply Community law.

(7) National courts have an essential part to play in applying the Community competition rules. When deciding disputes between private individuals, they protect the subjective rights under Community law, for example by awarding damages to the victims of infringements. The role of the national courts here complements that of the competition authorities of the Member States. They should therefore be allowed to apply Articles 81 and 82 of the Treaty in full.

(8) In order to ensure the effective enforcement of the Community competition rules and the proper functioning of the cooperation mechanisms contained in this Regulation, it is necessary to oblige the competition authorities and courts of the Member States to also apply Articles 81 and 82 of the Treaty where they apply national competition law to agreements and practices which may affect trade between Member States. In order to create a level playing field for agreements, decisions by associations of undertakings and concerted practices within the internal market, it is also necessary to determine pursuant to Article 83(2)(e) of the Treaty the relationship between national laws and Community competition law. To that effect it is necessary to provide that the application of national competition laws to agreements, decisions or concerted practices within the meaning of Article 81(1) of the Treaty may not lead to the prohibition of such agreements, decisions and concerted practices if they are not also prohibited under Community competition law. The notions of agreements, decisions and concerted practices are autonomous concepts of Community competition law covering the coordination of behaviour of undertakings on the market as interpreted by the Community courts. Member States should not under this Regulation be precluded from adopting and applying on their territory stricter national competition laws which prohibit or impose sanctions on unilateral conduct engaged in by undertakings. These stricter national laws may include provisions which prohibit or impose sanctions on abusive behaviour toward economically dependent undertakings. Furthermore, this Regulation does not apply to national laws which impose criminal sanctions on natural persons except to the extent that such sanctions are the means whereby competition rules applying to undertakings are enforced.

(9) Articles 81 and 82 of the Treaty have as their objective the protection of competition on the market. This Regulation, which is adopted for the implementation of these Treaty provisions, does not preclude Member States from implementing on their territory national legislation, which protects other legitimate interests provided that such legislation is compatible with general principles and other provisions of Community law. In so far as such national legislation pursues predominantly an objective different from that of protecting competition on the market, the competition authorities and courts of the Member States may apply such legislation on their territory. Accordingly, Member States may under this Regulation implement on their territory national legislation that prohibits or imposes sanctions on acts of unfair trading practice, be they unilateral or contractual. Such legislation pursues a specific objective, irrespective of the actual or presumed effects of such acts on competition on the market. This is particularly the case of legislation which prohibits undertakings from imposing on their trading partners, obtaining or attempting to obtain from them terms and conditions that are unjustified, disproportionate or without consideration.

(10) Regulations such as 19/65[40], 2821/71[41], 3976/87[42], 1534/91[43], or 479/92[44] empower the Commission to apply Article 81(3) of the Treaty by Regulation to certain categories of agreements, decisions by associations of undertakings and concerted practices. In the areas defined by such Regulations, the Commission has adopted and may continue to adopt so called "block" exemption Regulations by which it declares Article 81(1) of the Treaty inapplicable to categories of agreements, decisions and concerted practices. Where agreements, decisions and concerted practices to which such Regulations apply nonetheless have effects that are incompatible with Article 81(3) of the Treaty, the Commission and the competition authorities of the Member States should have the power to withdraw in a particular case the benefit of the block exemption Regulation.

(11) For it to ensure that the provisions of the Treaty are applied, the Commission should be able to address decisions to undertakings or associations of undertakings for the purpose of bringing to an end infringements of Articles 81 and 82 of the Treaty. Provided there is a legitimate interest in doing so, the Commission should also be able to adopt decisions which find that an infringement has been committed in the past even if it does not impose a fine. This Regulation should also make explicit provision for the Commission's power to adopt decisions ordering interim measures, which has been acknowledged by the Court of Justice.

(12) This Regulation should make explicit provision for the Commission's power to impose any remedy, whether behavioural or structural, which is necessary to bring the infringement effectively to an end, having regard to the principle of proportionality. Structural remedies should only be imposed either where there is no equally effective behavioural remedy or where any equally effective behavioural remedy would be more burdensome for the undertaking concerned than the structural remedy. Changes to the structure of an undertaking as it existed before the infringement was committed would only be proportionate where there is a substantial risk of a lasting or repeated infringement that derives from the very structure of the undertaking.

(13) Where, in the course of proceedings which might lead to an agreement or practice being prohibited, undertakings offer the Commission commitments such as to meet its concerns, the Commission should be able to adopt decisions which make those commitments binding on the undertakings concerned. Commitment decisions should find that there are no longer grounds for action by the Commission without concluding whether or not there has been or still is an infringement. Commitment decisions are without prejudice to the powers of competition authorities and courts of the Member States to make such a finding and decide upon the case. Commitment decisions are not appropriate in cases where the Commission intends to impose a fine.

(14) In exceptional cases where the public interest of the Community so requires, it may also be expedient for the Commission to adopt a decision of a declaratory nature finding that the prohibition in Article 81 or Article 82 of the

---

[40] Council Regulation 19/65 of 2 March 1965 on the application of Article [81(3)] of the Treaty to certain categories of agreements and concerted practices ([1965–1966] OJ Eng. Spec. Ed., p. 35). Regulation as last amended by Regulation 1215/1999 ([1999] OJ L148/1).

[41] Council Regulation 2821/71 of 20 December 1971 on the application of Article [81(3)] of the Treaty to categories of agreements, decisions and concerted practices ([1971 (III)] OJ Eng. Spec. Ed., p. 1032]). Regulation as last amended by the Act of Accession of 1994.

[42] Council Regulation 3976/87 of 14 December 1987 on the application of Article [81(3)] of the Treaty to certain categories of agreements and concerted practices in the air transport sector ([1987] OJ L374/9). Regulation as last amended by the Act of Accession of 1994.

[43] Council Regulation 1534/91 of 31 May 1991 on the application of Article [81(3)] of the Treaty to certain categories of agreements, decisions and concerted practices in the insurance sector ([1991] OJ L143/1).

[44] Council Regulation 479/92 of 25 February 1992 on the application of Article [81(3)] of the Treaty to certain categories of agreements, decisions and concerted practices between liner shipping companies (consortia) ([1992] OJ L55/3). Regulation amended by the Act of Accession of 1994.

Treaty does not apply, with a view to clarifying the law and ensuring its consistent application throughout the Community, in particular with regard to new types of agreements or practices that have not been settled in the existing case-law and administrative practice.

(15) The Commission and the competition authorities of the member sates should form together a network of public authorities applying the Community competition rules in close cooperation. For that purpose it is necessary to set up arrangements for information and consultation. Further modalities for the cooperation within the network will be laid down and revised by the Commission, in close cooperation with the Member States.

(16) Notwithstanding any national provision to the contrary, the exchange of information and the use of such information in evidence should be allowed between the members of the network even where the information is confidential. This information may be used for the application of Articles 81 and 82 of the Treaty as well as for the parallel application of national competition law, provided that the latter application relates to the same case and does not lead to a different outcome. When the information exchanged is used by the receiving authority to impose sanctions on undertakings, there should be no other limit to the use of the information than the obligation to use it for the purpose for which it was collected given the fact that the sanctions imposed on undertakings are of the same type in all systems. The rights of defence enjoyed by undertakings in the various systems can be considered as sufficiently equivalent. However, as regards natural persons, they may be subject to substantially different types of sanctions across the various systems. Where that is the case, it is necessary to ensure that information can only be used if it has been collected in a way which respects the same level of protection of the rights of defence of natural persons as provided for under the national rules of the receiving authority.

(17) If the competition rules are to be applied consistently and, at the same time, the network is to be managed in the best possible way, it is essential to retain the rule that the competition authorities of the Member States are automatically relieved of their competence if the Commission initiates its own proceedings. Where a competition authority of a Member State is already acting on a case and the Commission intends to initiate proceedings, it should endeavour to do so as soon as possible. Before initiating proceedings, the Commission should consult the national authority concerned.

(18) To ensure that cases are dealt with by the most appropriate authorities within the network, a general provision should be laid down allowing a competition authority to suspend or close a case on the ground that another authority is dealing with it or has already dealt with it, the objective being that each case should be handled by a single authority. This provision should not prevent the Commission from rejecting a complaint for lack of Community interest, as the case-law of the Court of Justice has acknowledged it may do, even if no other competition authority has indicated its intention of dealing with the case.

(19) The Advisory Committee on Restrictive Practices and Dominant Positions set up by Regulation 17 has functioned in a very satisfactory manner. It will fit well into the new system of decentralised application. It is necessary, therefore, to build upon the rules laid down by Regulation 17, while improving the effectiveness of the organisational arrangements. To this end, it would be expedient to allow opinions to be delivered by written procedure. The Advisory Committee should also be able to act as a forum for discussing cases that are being handled by the competition authorities of the Member States, so as to help safeguard the consistent application of the Community competition rules.

(20) The Advisory Committee should be composed of representatives of the competition authorities of the Member States. For meetings in which general issues are being discussed, Member States should be able to appoint an additional representative. This is without prejudice to members of the committee being assisted by other experts from the Member States.

(21) Consistency in the application of the competition rules also requires that arrangements be established for cooperation between the courts of the Member States and the Commission. This is relevant for all courts of the Member States that apply Articles 81 and 82 of the Treaty, whether applying these rules in lawsuits between private parties, acting as public enforcers or as review courts. In particular, national courts should be able to ask the Commission for information or for its opinion on points concerning the application of Community competition law. The Commission and the competition authorities of the Member States should also be able to submit written or oral observations to courts called upon to apply Article 81 or Article 82 of the Treaty. These observations should be submitted within the framework of national procedural rules and practices including those safeguarding the rights of the parties. Steps should therefore be taken to ensure that the Commission and the competition authorities of the Member States are kept sufficiently well informed of proceedings before national courts.

(22) In order to ensure compliance with the principles of legal certainty and the uniform application of the Community competition rules in a system of parallel powers, conflicting decisions must be avoided. It is therefore necessary to clarify, in accordance with the case-law of the Court of Justice, the effects of Commission decisions and proceedings on courts and competition authorities of the Member States. Commitment decisions adopted by the Commission do not affect the power of the courts and the competition authorities of the Member States to apply Articles 81 and 82 of the Treaty.

(23) The Commission should be empowered throughout the Community to require such information to be supplied as is necessary to detect any agreement, decision or concerted practice prohibited by Article 81 of the Treaty or any abuse of a dominant position prohibited by Article 82 of the Treaty. When complying with a decision of the Commission, undertakings cannot be forced to admit that they have committed an infringement, but they are in any event obliged to answer factual questions and to provide documents, even if this information may be used to establish against them or against another undertaking the existence of an infringement.

(24) The Commission should also be empowered to undertake such inspections as are necessary to detect any agreement, decision or concerted practice prohibited by Article 81 of the Treaty or any abuse of a dominant position prohibited by Article 82 of the Treaty. The competition authorities of the Member States should cooperate actively in the exercise of these powers.

(25) The detection of infringements of the competition rules is growing ever more difficult, and, in order to protect competition effectively, the Commission's powers of investigation need to be supplemented. The Commission should in particular be empowered to interview any persons who may be in possession of useful information and to record the statements made. In the course of an inspection, officials authorised by the Commission should be empowered to affix seals for the period of time necessary for the inspection. Seals should normally not be affixed for more than 72 hours. Officials authorised by the Commission should also be empowered to ask for any information relevant to the subject matter and purpose of the inspection.

(26) Experience has shown that there are cases where business records are kept in the homes of directors or other people working for an undertaking. In order to safeguard the effectiveness of inspections, therefore, officials and other persons authorised by the Commission should be empowered to enter any premises where business records may be kept, including private homes. However, the exercise of this latter power should be subject to the authorisation of the judicial authority.

(27) Without prejudice to the case-law of the Court of Justice, it is useful to set out the scope of the control that the national judicial authority may carry out when it authorises, as foreseen by national law including as a precautionary measure, assistance from law enforcement authorities in order to overcome possible

opposition on the part of the undertaking or the execution of the decision to carry out inspections in non-business premises. It results from the case-law that the national judicial authority may in particular ask the Commission for further information which it needs to carry out its control and in the absence of which it could refuse the authorisation. The case-law also confirms the competence of the national courts to control the application of national rules governing the implementation of coercive measures.

(28) In order to help the competition authorities of the Member States to apply Articles 81 and 82 of the Treaty effectively, it is expedient to enable them to assist one another by carrying out inspections and other fact-finding measures.

(29) Compliance with Articles 81 and 82 of the Treaty and the fulfilment of the obligations imposed on undertakings and associations of undertakings under this Regulation should be enforceable by means of fines and periodic penalty payments. To that end, appropriate levels of fine should also be laid down for infringements of the procedural rules.

(30) In order to ensure effective recovery of fines imposed on associations of undertakings for infringements that they have committed, it is necessary to lay down the conditions on which the Commission may require payment of the fine from the members of the association where the association is not solvent. In doing so, the Commission should have regard to the relative size of the undertakings belonging to the association and in particular to the situation of small and medium-sized enterprises. Payment of the fine by one or several members of an association is without prejudice to rules of national law that provide for recovery of the amount paid from other members of the association.

(31) The rules on periods of limitation for the imposition of fines and periodic penalty payments were laid down in Council Regulation 2988/74[45], which also concerns penalties in the field of transport. In a system of parallel powers, the acts, which may interrupt a limitation period, should include procedural steps taken independently by the competition authority of a Member State. To clarify the legal framework, Regulation 2988/74 should therefore be amended to prevent it applying to matters covered by this Regulation, and this Regulation should include provisions on periods of limitation.

(32) The undertakings concerned should be accorded the right to be heard by the Commission, third parties whose interests may be affected by a decision should be given the opportunity of submitting their observations beforehand, and the decisions taken should be widely publicised. While ensuring the rights of defence of the undertakings concerned, in particular, the right of access to the file, it is essential that business secrets be protected. The confidentiality of information exchanged in the network should likewise be safeguarded.

(33) Since all decisions taken by the Commission under this Regulation are subject to review by the Court of Justice in accordance with the Treaty, the Court of Justice should, in accordance with Article 229 thereof be given unlimited jurisdiction in respect of decisions by which the Commission imposes fines or periodic penalty payments.

(34) The principles laid down in Articles 81 and 82 of the Treaty, as they have been applied by Regulation 17, have given a central role to the Community bodies. This central role should be retained, whilst associating the Member States more closely with the application of the Community competition rules. In accordance with the principles of subsidiarity and proportionality as set out in Article 5 of the Treaty, this Regulation does not go beyond what is necessary in order to achieve its objective, which is to allow the Community competition rules to be applied effectively.

(35) In order to attain a proper enforcement of Community competition law, Member States should designate and empower authorities to apply Articles 81

[45] Council Regulation 2988/74 of 26 November 1974 concerning limitation periods in proceedings and the enforcement of sanctions under the rules of the [European Community] relating to transport and competition ([1974] OJ L319/1).

and 82 of the Treaty as public enforcers. They should be able to designate administrative as well as judicial authorities to carry out the various functions conferred upon competition authorities in this Regulation. This Regulation recognises the wide variation which exists in the public enforcement systems of Member States. The effects of Article 11(6) of this Regulation should apply to all competition authorities. As an exception to this general rule, where a prosecuting authority brings a case before a separate judicial authority, Article 11(6) should apply to the prosecuting authority subject to the conditions in Article 35(4) of this Regulation. Where these conditions are not fulfilled, the general rule should apply. In any case, Article 11(6) should not apply to courts insofar as they are acting as review courts.

(36) As the case-law has made it clear that the competition rules apply to transport, that sector should be made subject to the procedural provisions of this Regulation. Council Regulation No. 141 of 26 November 1962 exempting transport from the application of Regulation 17[46] should therefore be repealed and Regulations 1017/68[47], 4056/86[48] and 3975/87[49] should be amended in order to delete the specific procedural provisions they contain.

(37) This Regulation respects the fundamental rights and observes the principles recognised in particular by the Charter of Fundamental Rights of the European Union. Accordingly, this Regulation should be interpreted and applied with respect to those rights and principles.

(38) Legal certainty for undertakings operating under the Community competition rules contributes to the promotion of innovation and investment. Where cases give rise to genuine uncertainty because they present novel or unresolved questions for the application of these rules, individual undertakings may wish to seek informal guidance from the Commission. This Regulation is without prejudice to the ability of the Commission to issue such informal guidance,

Has adopted this Regulation:

Chapter I—Principles

Article 1 Application of Articles 81 and 82 of the Treaty

7–137 1. Agreements, decisions and concerted practices caught by Article 81(1) of the Treaty which do not satisfy the conditions of Article 81(3) of the Treaty shall be prohibited, no prior decision to that effect being required.

2. Agreements, decisions and concerted practices caught by Article 81(1) of the Treaty which satisfy the conditions of Article 81(3) of the Treaty shall not be prohibited, no prior decision to that effect being required.

3. The abuse of a dominant position referred to in Article 82 of the Treaty shall be prohibited, no prior decision to that effect being required.

Article 2 Burden of proof

7–138 In any national or Community proceedings for the application of Articles 81 and 82 of the Treaty, the burden of proving an infringement of Article 81(1) or of

---

[46] [1959–1962] OJ Eng. Spec. Ed., p. 291; Regulation as last amended by Regulation 1002/67 ([1967] JO 306/1).

[47] Council Regulation 1017/68 of 19 July 1968 applying rules of competition to transport by rail, road and inland waterway ([1968 (I)] OJ Eng. Spec. Ed., p. 302). Regulation as last amended by the Act of Accession of 1994.

[48] Council Regulation 4056/86 of 22 December 1986 laying down detailed rules for the application of Articles [81] and [82] of the Treaty to maritime transport ([1986] OJ L378/4). Regulation as last amended by the Act of Accession of 1994.

[49] Council Regulation 3975/87 of 14 December 1987 laying down the procedure for the application of the rules on competition to undertakings in the air transport sector ([1987] OJ L374/1). Regulation as last amended by Regulation 2410/92 ([1992] OJ L240/18).

Article 82 of the Treaty shall rest on the party or the authority alleging the infringement. The undertaking or association of undertakings claiming the benefit of Article 81(3) of the Treaty shall bear the burden of proving that the conditions of that paragraph are fulfilled.

Article 3 Relationship between Articles 81 and 82 of the Treaty and national competition laws

1. Where the competition authorities of the Member States or national courts apply national competition law to agreements, decisions by associations of undertakings or concerted practices within the meaning of Article 81(1) of the Treaty which may affect trade between Member States within the meaning of that provision, they shall also apply Article 81 of the Treaty to such agreements, decisions or concerted practices. Where the competition authorities of the Member States or national courts apply national competition law to any abuse prohibited by Article 82 of the Treaty, they shall also apply Article 82 of the Treaty. **7–139**

2. The application of national competition law may not lead to the prohibition of agreements, decisions by associations of undertakings or concerted practices which may affect trade between Member States but which do not restrict competition within the meaning of Article 81(1) of the Treaty, or which fulfil the conditions of Article 81(3) of the Treaty or which are covered by a Regulation for the application of Article 81(3) of the Treaty. Member States shall not under this Regulation be precluded from adopting and applying on their territory stricter national laws which prohibit or sanction unilateral conduct engaged in by undertakings.

3. Without prejudice to general principles and other provisions of Community law, paragraphs 1 and 2 do not apply when the competition authorities and the courts of the Member States apply national merger control laws nor do they preclude the application of provisions of national law that predominantly pursue an objective different from that pursued by Articles 81 and 82 of the Treaty.

Chapter II—Powers

Article 4 Powers of the Commission

For the purpose of applying Articles 81 and 82 of the Treaty, the Commission shall have the powers provided for by this Regulation. **7–140**

Article 5 Powers of the competition authorities of the Member States

The competition authorities of the Member States shall have the power to apply Articles 81 and 82 of the Treaty in individual cases. For this purpose, acting on their own initiative or on a complaint, they may take the following decisions: **7–141**

— requiring that an infringement be brought to an end,
— ordering interim measures,
— accepting commitments,
— imposing fines, periodic penalty payments or any other penalty provided for in their national law.

Where on the basis of the information in their possession the conditions for prohibition are not met they may likewise decide that there are no grounds for action on their part.

Article 6 Powers of the national courts

7–142 National courts shall have the power to apply Articles 81 and 82 of the Treaty.

Chapter III—Commission Decisions

Article 7 Finding and termination of infringement

7–143 1. Where the Commission, acting on a complaint or on its own initiative, finds that there is an infringement of Article 81 or of Article 82 of the Treaty, it may by decision require the undertakings and associations of undertakings concerned to bring such infringement to an end. For this purpose, it may impose on them any behavioural or structural remedies which are proportionate to the infringement committed and necessary to bring the infringement effectively to an end. Structural remedies can only be imposed either where there is no equally effective behavioural remedy or where any equally effective behavioural remedy would be more burdensome for the undertaking concerned than the structural remedy. If the Commission has a legitimate interest in doing so, it may also find that an infringement has been committed in the past.

2. Those entitled to lodge a complaint for the purposes of paragraph 1 are natural or legal persons who can show a legitimate interest and Member States.

Article 8 Interim measures

7–144 1. In cases of urgency due to the risk of serious and irreparable damage to competition, the Commission, acting on its own initiative may by decision, on the basis of a *prima facie* finding of infringement, order interim measures.

2. A decision under paragraph 1 shall apply for a specified period of time and may be renewed in so far this is necessary and appropriate.

Article 9 Commitments

7–145 1. Where the Commission intends to adopt a decision requiring that an infringement be brought to an end and the undertakings concerned offer commitments to meet the concerns expressed to them by the Commission in its preliminary assessment, the Commission may by decision make those commitments binding on the undertakings. Such a decision may be adopted for a specified period and shall conclude that there are no longer grounds for action by the Commission.

2. The Commission may, upon request or on its own initiative, re-open the proceedings:
(a) where there has been a material change in any of the facts on which the decision was based;
(b) where the undertakings concerned act contrary to their commitments; or
(c) where the decision was based on incomplete, incorrect or misleading information provided by the parties.

Article 10 Finding of inapplicability

7–146 Where the Community public interest relating to the application of Articles 81 and 82 of the Treaty so requires, the Commission, acting on its own initiative, may by decision find that Article 81 of the Treaty is not applicable to an agreement, a decision by an association of undertakings or a concerted practice, either because the conditions of Article 81(1) of the Treaty are not fulfilled, or because the conditions of Article 81(3) of the Treaty are satisfied.

The Commission may likewise make such a finding with reference to Article 82 of the Treaty.

Chapter IV—Cooperation

Article 11 Cooperation between the Commission and the competition authorities of the Member States

1. The Commission and the competition authorities of the Member States shall apply the Community competition rules in close cooperation. **7–147**

2. The Commission shall transmit to the competition authorities of the Member States copies of the most important documents it has collected with a view to applying Articles 7, 8, 9, 10 and Article 29(1). At the request of the competition authority of a Member State, the Commission shall provide it with a copy of other existing documents necessary for the assessment of the case.

3. The competition authorities of the Member States shall, when acting under Article 81 or Article 82 of the Treaty, inform the Commission in writing before or without delay after commencing the first formal investigative measure. This information may also be made available to the competition authorities of the other Member States.

4. No later than 30 days before the adoption of a decision requiring that an infringement be brought to an end, accepting commitments or withdrawing the benefit of a block exemption Regulation, the competition authorities of the Member States shall inform the Commission. To that effect, they shall provide the Commission with a summary of the case, the envisaged decision or, in the absence thereof, any other document indicating the proposed course of action. This information may also be made available to the competition authorities of the other Member States. At the request of the Commission, the acting competition authority shall make available to the Commission other documents it holds which are necessary for the assessment of the case. The information supplied to the Commission may be made available to the competition authorities of the other Member States. National competition authorities may also exchange between themselves information necessary for the assessment of a case that they are dealing with under Article 81 or Article 82 of the Treaty.

5. The competition authorities of the Member States may consult the Commission on any case involving the application of Community law.

6. The initiation by the Commission of proceedings for the adoption of a decision under Chapter III shall relieve the competition authorities of the Member States of their competence to apply Articles 81 and 82 of the Treaty. If a competition authority of a Member State is already acting on a case, the Commission shall only initiate proceedings after consulting with that national competition authority.

Article 12 Exchange of information

1. For the purpose of applying Articles 81 and 82 of the Treaty the Commission and the competition authorities of the Member States shall have the power to provide one another with and use in evidence any matter of fact or of law, including confidential information. **7–148**

2. Information exchanged shall only be used in evidence for the purpose of applying Article 81 or Article 82 of the Treaty and in respect of the subject-matter for which it was collected by the transmitting authority. However, where national competition law is applied in the same case and in parallel to Community

competition law and does not lead to a different outcome, information exchanged under this Article may also be used for the application of national competition law.

3. Information exchanged pursuant to paragraph 1 can only be used in evidence to impose sanctions on natural persons where:

— the law of the transmitting authority foresees sanctions of a similar kind in relation to an infringement of Article 81 or Article 82 of the Treaty or, in the absence thereof,
— the information has been collected in a way which respects the same level of protection of the rights of defence of natural persons as provided for under the national rules of the receiving authority. However, in this case, the information exchanged cannot be used by the receiving authority to impose custodial sanctions.

Article 13 Suspension or termination of proceedings

7–149 1. Where competition authorities of two or more Member States have received a complaint or are acting on their own initiative under Article 81 or Article 82 of the Treaty against the same agreement, decision of an association or practice, the fact that one authority is dealing with the case shall be sufficient grounds for the others to suspend the proceedings before them or to reject the complaint. The Commission may likewise reject a complaint on the ground that a competition authority of a Member State is dealing with the case.

2. Where a competition authority of a Member State or the Commission has received a complaint against an agreement, decision of an association or practice which has already been dealt with by another competition authority, it may reject it.

Article 14 Advisory Committee

7–150 1. The Commission shall consult an Advisory Committee on Restrictive Practices and Dominant Positions prior to the taking of any decision under Articles 7, 8, 9, 10, 23, Article 24(2) and Article 29(1).

2. For the discussion of individual cases, the Advisory Committee shall be composed of representatives of the competition authorities of the Member States. For meetings in which issues other than individual cases are being discussed, an additional Member State representative competent in competition matters may be appointed. Representatives may, if unable to attend, be replaced by other representatives.

3. The consultation may take place at a meeting convened and chaired by the Commission, held not earlier than 14 days after dispatch of the notice convening it, together with a summary of the case, an indication of the most important documents and a preliminary draft decision. In respect of decisions pursuant to Article 8, the meeting may be held seven days after the dispatch of the operative part of a draft decision. Where the Commission dispatches a notice convening the meeting which gives a shorter period of notice than those specified above, the meeting may take place on the proposed date in the absence of an objection by any Member State. The Advisory Committee shall deliver a written opinion on the Commission's preliminary draft decision. It may deliver an opinion even if some members are absent and are not represented. At the request of one or several members, the positions stated in the opinion shall be reasoned.

4. Consultation may also take place by written procedure. However, if any Member State so requests, the Commission shall convene a meeting. In case of written procedure, the Commission shall determine a time-limit of not less than 14 days within which the Member States are to put forward their observations for

circulation to all other Member States. In case of decisions to be taken pursuant to Article 8, the time-limit of 14 days is replaced by seven days. Where the Commission determines a time-limit for the written procedure which is shorter than those specified above, the proposed time-limit shall be applicable in the absence of an objection by any Member State.

5. The Commission shall take the utmost account of the opinion delivered by the Advisory Committee. It shall inform the Committee of the manner in which its opinion has been taken into account.

6. Where the Advisory Committee delivers a written opinion, this opinion shall be appended to the draft decision. If the Advisory Committee recommends publication of the opinion, the Commission shall carry out such publication taking into account the legitimate interest of undertakings in the protection of their business secrets.

7. At the request of a competition authority of a Member State, the Commission shall include on the agenda of the Advisory Committee cases that are being dealt with by a competition authority of a Member State under Article 81 or Article 82 of the Treaty. The Commission may also do so on its own initiative. In either case, the Commission shall inform the competition authority concerned.

A request may in particular be made by a competition authority of a Member State in respect of a case where the Commission intends to initiate proceedings with the effect of Article 11(6).

The Advisory Committee shall not issue opinions on cases dealt with by competition authorities of the Member States. The Advisory Committee may also discuss general issues of Community competition law.

Article 15 Cooperation with national courts

1. In proceedings for the application of Article 81 or Article 82 of the Treaty, courts of the Member States may ask the Commission to transmit to them information in its possession or its opinion on questions concerning the application of the Community competition rules. **7–151**

2. Member States shall forward to the Commission a copy of any written judgment of national courts deciding on the application of Article 81 or Article 82 of the Treaty. Such copy shall be forwarded without delay after the full written judgment is notified to the parties.

3. Competition authorities of the Member States, acting on their own initiative, may submit written observations to the national courts of their Member State on issues relating to the application of Article 81 or Article 82 of the Treaty. With the permission of the court in question, they may also submit oral observations to the national courts of their Member State. Where the coherent application of Article 81 or Article 82 of the Treaty so requires, the Commission, acting on its own initiative, may submit written observations to courts of the Member States. With the permission of the court in question, it may also make oral observations.

For the purpose of the preparation of their observations only, the competition authorities of the Member States and the Commission may request the relevant court of the Member State to transmit or ensure the transmission to them of any documents necessary for the assessment of the case.

4. This Article is without prejudice to wider powers to make observations before courts conferred on competition authorities of the Member States under the law of their Member State.

Article 16 Uniform application of Community competition law

1. When national courts rule on agreements, decisions or practices under Article **7–152**
81 or Article 82 of the Treaty which are already the subject of a Commission

decision, they cannot take decisions running counter to the decision adopted by the Commission. They must also avoid giving decisions which would conflict with a decision contemplated by the Commission in proceedings it has initiated. To that effect, the national court may assess whether it is necessary to stay its proceedings. his obligation is without prejudice to the rights and obligations under Article 234 of the Treaty.

2. When competition authorities of the Member States rule on agreements, decisions or practices under Article 81 or Article 82 of the Treaty which are already the subject of a Commission decision, they cannot take decisions which would run counter to the decision adopted by the Commission.

Chapter V—Powers of Investigation

Article 17 Investigations into sectors of the economy and into types of agreements

7–153 1. Where the trend of trade between Member States, the rigidity of prices or other circumstances suggest that competition may be restricted or distorted within the common market, the Commission may conduct its inquiry into a particular sector of the economy or into a particular type of agreements across various sectors. In the course of that inquiry, the Commission may request the undertakings or associations of undertakings concerned to supply the information necessary for giving effect to Articles 81 and 82 of the Treaty and may carry out any inspections necessary for that purpose.

The Commission may in particular request the undertakings or associations of undertakings concerned to communicate to it all agreements, decisions and concerted practices.

The Commission may publish a report on the results of its inquiry into particular sectors of the economy or particular types of agreements across various sectors and invite comments from interested parties.

2. Articles 14, 18, 19, 20, 22, 23 and 24 shall apply *mutatis mutandis*.

Article 18 Requests for information

7–154 1. In order to carry out the duties assigned to it by this Regulation, the Commission may, by simple request or by decision, require undertakings and associations of undertakings to provide all necessary information.

2. When sending a simple request for information to an undertaking or association of undertakings, the Commission shall state the legal basis and the purpose of the request, specify what information is required and fix the time-limit within which the information is to be provided, and the penalties provided for in Article 23 for supplying incorrect or misleading information.

3. Where the Commission requires undertakings and associations of undertakings to supply information by decision, it shall state the legal basis and the purpose of the request, specify what information is required and fix the time-limit within which it is to be provided. It shall also indicate the penalties provided for in Article 23 and indicate or impose the penalties provided for in Article 24. It shall further indicate the right to have the decision reviewed by the Court of Justice.

4. The owners of the undertakings or their representatives and, in the case of legal persons, companies or firms, or associations having no legal personality, the persons authorised to represent them by law or by their constitution shall supply the information requested on behalf of the undertaking or the association of undertakings concerned. Lawyers duly authorised to act may supply the information on behalf of their clients. The latter shall remain fully responsible if the information supplied is incomplete, incorrect or misleading.

5. The Commission shall without delay forward a copy of the simple request or of the decision to the competition authority of the Member State in whose

territory the seat of the undertaking or association of undertakings is situated and the competition authority of the Member State whose territory is affected.

6. At the request of the Commission the governments and competition authorities of the Member States shall provide the Commission with all necessary information to carry out the duties assigned to it by this Regulation.

Article 19 Power to take statements

1. In order to carry out the duties assigned to it by this Regulation, the Commission may interview any natural or legal person who consents to be interviewed for the purpose of collecting information relating to the subject-matter of an investigation. **7–155**

2. Where an interview pursuant to paragraph 1 is conducted in the premises of an undertaking, the Commission shall inform the competition authority of the Member State in whose territory the interview takes place. If so requested by the competition authority of that Member State, its officials may assist the officials and other accompanying persons authorised by the Commission to conduct the interview.

Article 20 The Commission's powers of inspection

1. In order to carry out the duties assigned to it by this Regulation, the Commission may conduct all necessary inspections of undertakings and associations of undertakings. **7–156**

2. The officials and other accompanying persons authorised by the Commission to conduct an inspection are empowered:

(a) to enter any premises, land and means of transport of undertakings and associations of undertakings;
(b) to examine the books and other records related to the business, irrespective of the medium on which they are stored;
(c) to take or obtain in any form copies of or extracts from such books or records;
(d) to seal any business premises and books or records for the period and to the extent necessary for the inspection;
(e) to ask any representative or member of staff of the undertaking or association of undertakings for explanations on facts or documents relating to the subject-matter and purpose of the inspection and to record the answers.

3. The officials and other accompanying persons authorised by the Commission to conduct an inspection shall exercise their powers upon production of a written authorisation specifying the subject matter and purpose of the inspection and the penalties provided for in Article 23 in case the production of the required books or other records related to the business is incomplete or where the answers to questions asked under paragraph 2 of the present Article are incorrect or misleading. In good time before the inspection, the Commission shall give notice of the inspection to the competition authority of the Member State in whose territory it is to be conducted.

4. Undertakings and associations of undertakings are required to submit to inspections ordered by decision of the Commission. The decision shall specify the subject matter and purpose of the inspection, appoint the date on which it is to begin and indicate the penalties provided for in Articles 23 and 24 and the right to have the decision reviewed by the Court of Justice. The Commission shall take such decisions after consulting the competition authority of the Member State in whose territory the inspection is to be conducted.

5. Officials of as well as those authorised or appointed by the competition authority of the Member State in whose territory the inspection is to be conducted shall, at the request of that authority or of the Commission, actively assist the

officials and other accompanying persons authorised by the Commission. To this end, they shall enjoy the powers specified in paragraph 2.

6. Where the officials and other accompanying persons authorised by the Commission find that an undertaking opposes an inspection ordered pursuant to this Article, the Member State concerned shall afford them the necessary assistance, requesting where appropriate the assistance of the police or of an equivalent enforcement authority, so as to enable them to conduct their inspection.

7. If the assistance provided for in paragraph 6 requires authorisation from a judicial authority according to national rules, such authorisation shall be applied for. Such authorisation may also be applied for as a precautionary measure.

8. Where authorisation as referred to in paragraph 7 is applied for, the national judicial authority shall control that the Commission decision is authentic and that the coercive measures envisaged are neither arbitrary nor excessive having regard to the subject matter of the inspection. In its control of the proportionality of the coercive measures, the national judicial authority may ask the Commission, directly or through the Member State competition authority, for detailed explanations in particular on the grounds the Commission has for suspecting infringement of Articles 81 and 82 of the Treaty, as well as on the seriousness of the suspected infringement and on the nature of the involvement of the undertaking concerned. However, the national judicial authority may not call into question the necessity for the inspection nor demand that it be provided with the information in the Commission's file. The lawfulness of the Commission decision shall be subject to review only by the Court of Justice.

Article 21 Inspection of other premises

7–157 1. If a reasonable suspicion exists that books or other records related to the business and to the subject matter of the inspection, which may be relevant to prove a serious violation of Article 81 or Article 82 of the Treaty, are being kept in any other premises, land and means of transport, including the homes of directors, managers and other members of staff of the undertakings and associations of undertakings concerned, the Commission can by decision order an inspection to be conducted in such other premises, land and means of transport.

2. The decision shall specify the subject matter and purpose of the inspection, appoint the date on which it is to begin and indicate the right to have the decision reviewed by the Court of Justice. It shall in particular state the reasons that have led the Commission to conclude that a suspicion in the sense of paragraph 1 exists. The Commission shall take such decisions after consulting the competition authority of the Member State in whose territory the inspection is to be conducted.

3. A decision adopted pursuant to paragraph 1 cannot be executed without prior authorisation from the national judicial authority of the Member State concerned. The national judicial authority shall control that the Commission decision is authentic and that the coercive measures envisaged are neither arbitrary nor excessive having regard in particular to the seriousness of the suspected infringement, to the importance of the evidence sought, to the involvement of the undertaking concerned and to the reasonable likelihood that business books and records relating to the subject matter of the inspection are kept in the premises for which the authorisation is requested. The national judicial authority may ask the Commission, directly or through the Member State competition authority, for detailed explanations on those elements which are necessary to allow its control of the proportionality of the coercive measures envisaged.

However, the national judicial authority may not call into question the necessity for the inspection nor demand that it be provided with information in the

Commission's file. The lawfulness of the Commission decision shall be subject to review only by the Court of Justice.

4. The officials and other accompanying persons authorised by the Commission to conduct an inspection ordered in accordance with paragraph 1 of this Article shall have the powers set out in Article 20(2)(a), (b) and (c). Article 20(5) and (6) shall apply *mutatis mutandis*.

Article 22 Investigations by competition authorities of Member States

1. The competition authority of a Member State may in its own territory carry out any inspection or other fact-finding measure under its national law on behalf and for the account of the competition authority of another Member State in order to establish whether there has been an infringement of Article 81 or Article 82 of the Treaty. Any exchange and use of the information collected shall be carried out in accordance with Article 12. **7–158**

2. At the request of the Commission, the competition authorities of the Member States shall undertake the inspections which the Commission considers to be necessary under Article 20(1) or which it has ordered by decision pursuant to Article 20(4). The officials of the competition authorities of the Member States who are responsible for conducting these inspections as well as those authorised or appointed by them shall exercise their powers in accordance with their national law.

If so requested by the Commission or by the competition authority of the Member State in whose territory the inspection is to be conducted, officials and other accompanying persons authorised by the Commission may assist the officials of the authority concerned.

Chapter VI—Penalties

Article 23 Fines

1. The Commission may by decision impose on undertakings and associations of undertakings fines not exceeding 1% of the total turnover in the preceding business year where, intentionally or negligently: **7–159**

(a) they supply incorrect or misleading information in response to a request made pursuant to Article 17 or Article 18(2);
(b) in response to a request made by decision adopted pursuant to Article 17 or Article 18(3), they supply incorrect, incomplete or misleading information or do not supply information within the required time-limit;
(c) they produce the required books or other records related to the business in incomplete form during inspections under Article 20 or refuse to submit to inspections ordered by a decision adopted pursuant to Article 20(4);
(d) in response to a question asked in accordance with Article 20(2)(e),
   — they give an incorrect or misleading answer,
   — they fail to rectify within a time-limit set by the Commission an incorrect, incomplete or misleading answer given by a member of staff, or
   — they fail or refuse to provide a complete answer on facts relating to the subject-matter and purpose of an inspection ordered by a decision adopted pursuant to Article 20(4);
(e) seals affixed in accordance with Article 20(2)(d) by officials or other accompanying persons authorised by the Commission have been broken.

2. The Commission may by decision impose fines on undertakings and associations of undertakings where, either intentionally or negligently:

(a) they infringe Article 81 or Article 82 of the Treaty; or
(b) they contravene a decision ordering interim measures under Article 8; or
(c) they fail to comply with a commitment made binding by a decision pursuant to Article 9.

For each undertaking and association of undertakings participating in the infringement, the fine shall not exceed 10% of its total turnover in the preceding business year.

Where the infringement of an association relates to the activities of its members, the fine shall not exceed 10% of the sum of the total turnover of each member active on the market affected by the infringement of the association.

3. In fixing the amount of the fine, regard shall be had both to the gravity and to the duration of the infringement.

4. When a fine is imposed on an association of undertakings taking account of the turnover of its members and the association is not solvent, the association is obliged to call for contributions from its members to cover the amount of the fine.

Where such contributions have not been made to the association within a time-limit fixed by the Commission, the Commission may require payment of the fine directly by any of the undertakings whose representatives were members of the decision-making bodies concerned of the association.

After the Commission has required payment under the second subparagraph, where necessary to ensure full payment of the fine, the Commission may require payment of the balance by any of the members of the association which were active on the market on which the infringement occurred.

However, the Commission shall not require payment under the second or the third subparagraph from undertakings which show that they have not implemented the infringing decision of the association and either were not aware of its existence or have actively distanced themselves from it before the Commission started investigating the case.

The financial liability of each undertaking in respect of the payment of the fine shall not exceed 10% of its total turnover in the preceding business year.

5. Decisions taken pursuant to paragraphs 1 and 2 shall not be of a criminal law nature.

Article 24 Periodic penalty payments

7–160 1. The Commission may, by decision, impose on undertakings or associations of undertakings periodic penalty payments not exceeding 5% of the average daily turnover in the preceding business year per day and calculated from the date appointed by the decision, in order to compel them:

(a) to put an end to an infringement of Article 81 or Article 82 of the Treaty, in accordance with a decision taken pursuant to Article 7;
(b) to comply with a decision ordering interim measures taken pursuant to Article 8;
(c) to comply with a commitment made binding by a decision pursuant to Article 9;
(d) to supply complete and correct information which it has requested by decision taken pursuant to Article 17 or Article 18(3);
(e) to submit to an inspection which it has ordered by decision taken pursuant to Article 20(4).

2. Where the undertakings or associations of undertakings have satisfied the obligation which the periodic penalty payment was intended to enforce, the Commission may fix the definitive amount of the periodic penalty payment at a figure lower than that which would arise under the original decision. Article 23(4) shall apply correspondingly.

CHAPTER VII—LIMITATION PERIODS

Article 25 Limitation periods for the imposition of penalties

7–161 1. The powers conferred on the Commission by Articles 23 and 24 shall be subject to the following limitation periods:

(a) three years in the case of infringements of provisions concerning requests for information or the conduct of inspections;
(b) five years in the case of all other infringements.

2. Time shall begin to run on the day on which the infringement is committed. However, in the case of continuing or repeated infringements, time shall begin to run on the day on which the infringement ceases.

3. Any action taken by the Commission or by the competition authority of a Member State for the purpose of the investigation or proceedings in respect of an infringement shall interrupt the limitation period for the imposition of fines or periodic penalty payments. The limitation period shall be interrupted with effect from the date on which the action is notified to at least one undertaking or association of undertakings which has participated in the infringement. Actions which interrupt the running of the period shall include in particular the following:
(a) written requests for information by the Commission or by the competition authority of a Member State;
(b) written authorisations to conduct inspections issued to its officials by the Commission or by the competition authority of a Member State;
(c) the initiation of proceedings by the Commission or by the competition authority of a Member State;
(d) notification of the statement of objections of the Commission or of the competition authority of a Member State.

4. The interruption of the limitation period shall apply for all the undertakings or associations of undertakings which have participated in the infringement.

5. Each interruption shall start time running afresh. However, the limitation period shall expire at the latest on the day on which a period equal to twice the limitation period has elapsed without the Commission having imposed a fine or a periodic penalty payment. That period shall be extended by the time during which limitation is suspended pursuant to paragraph 6.

6. The limitation period for the imposition of fines or periodic penalty payments shall be suspended for as long as the decision of the Commission is the subject of proceedings pending before the Court of Justice.

Article 26 Limitation period for the enforcement of penalties

1. The power of the Commission to enforce decisions taken pursuant to Articles 23 and 24 shall be subject to a limitation period of five years. **7–162**

2. Time shall begin to run on the day on which the decision becomes final.

3. The limitation period for the enforcement of penalties shall be interrupted:
(a) by notification of a decision varying the original amount of the fine or periodic penalty payment or refusing an application for variation;
(b) by any action of the Commission or of a Member State, acting at the request of the Commission, designed to enforce payment of the fine or periodic penalty payment.

4. Each interruption shall start time running afresh.

5. The limitation period for the enforcement of penalties shall be suspended for so long as:
(a) time to pay is allowed;
(b) enforcement of payment is suspended pursuant to a decision of the Court of Justice.

Chapter VIII—Hearings and Professional Secrecy

Article 27 Hearing of the parties, complainants and others

7–163 1. Before taking decisions as provided for in Articles 7, 8, 23 and Article 24(2), the Commission shall give the undertakings or associations of undertakings which are the subject of the proceedings conducted by the Commission the opportunity of being heard on the matters to which the Commission has taken objection. The Commission shall base its decisions only on objections on which the parties concerned have been able to comment. Complainants shall be associated closely with the proceedings.

2. The rights of defence of the parties concerned shall be fully respected in the proceedings. They shall be entitled to have access to the Commission's file, subject to the legitimate interest of undertakings in the protection of their business secrets. The right of access to the file shall not extend to confidential information and internal documents of the Commission or the competition authorities of the Member States. In particular, the right of access shall not extend to correspondence between the Commission and the competition authorities of the Member States, or between the latter, including documents drawn up pursuant to Articles 11 and 14. Nothing in this paragraph shall prevent the Commission from disclosing and using information necessary to prove an infringement.

3. If the Commission considers it necessary, it may also hear other natural or legal persons. Applications to be heard on the part of such persons shall, where they show a sufficient interest, be granted. The competition authorities of the Member States may also ask the Commission to hear other natural or legal persons.

4. Where the Commission intends to adopt a decision pursuant to Article 9 or Article 10, it shall publish a concise summary of the case and the main content of the commitments or of the proposed course of action. Interested third parties may submit their observations within a time-limit which is fixed by the Commission in its publication and which may not be less than one month. Publication shall have regard to the legitimate interest of undertakings in the protection of their business secrets.

Article 28 Professional secrecy

7–164 1. Without prejudice to Articles 12 and 15, information collected pursuant to Articles 17 to 22 shall be used only for the purpose for which it was acquired.

2. Without prejudice to the exchange and to the use of information foreseen in Articles 11, 12, 14, 15 and 27, the Commission and the competition authorities of the Member States, their officials, servants and other persons working under the supervision of these authorities as well as officials and civil servants of other authorities of the Member States shall not disclose information acquired or exchanged by them pursuant to this Regulation and of the kind covered by the obligation of professional secrecy. This obligation also applies to all representatives and experts of Member States attending meetings of the Advisory Committee pursuant to Article 14.

Chapter IX—Exemption Regulations

Article 29 Withdrawal in individual cases

7–165 1. Where the Commission, empowered by a Council Regulation, such as Regulations 19/65, 2821/71, 3976/87, 1534/91 or 479/92, to apply Article 81(3) of the Treaty by Regulation, has declared Article 81(1) of the Treaty inapplicable to certain categories of agreements, decisions by associations of undertakings or concerted practices, it may, acting on its own initiative or on a complaint, withdraw the benefit of such an exemption Regulation when it finds that in any particular case an agreement, decision or concerted practice to which the exemption Regulation applies has certain effects which are incompatible with Article 81(3) of the Treaty.

2. Where, in any particular case, agreements, decisions by associations of undertakings or concerted practices to which a Commission Regulation referred to in paragraph 1 applies have effects which are incompatible with Article 81(3) of the Treaty in the territory of a Member State, or in a part thereof, which has all the characteristics of a distinct geographic market, the competition authority of that Member State may withdraw the benefit of the Regulation in question in respect of that territory.

Chapter X—General Provisions

Article 30 Publication of decisions

1. The Commission shall publish the decisions, which it takes pursuant to Articles 7 to 10, 23 and 24. **7–166**

2. The publication shall state the names of the parties and the main content of the decision, including any penalties imposed. It shall have regard to the legitimate interest of undertakings in the protection of their business secrets.

Article 31 Review by the Court of Justice

The Court of Justice shall have unlimited jurisdiction to review decisions whereby the Commission has fixed a fine or periodic penalty payment. It may cancel, reduce or increase the fine or periodic penalty payment imposed. **7–167**

Article 32 Exclusions

This Regulation shall not apply to: **7–168**
(a) international tramp vessel services as defined in Article 1(3)(a) of Regulation 4056/86;
(b) a maritime transport service that takes place exclusively between ports in one and the same Member State as foreseen in Article 1(2) of Regulation 4056/86;
(c) air transport between Community airports and third countries.

Article 33 Implementing provisions

1. The Commission shall be authorised to take such measures as may be appropriate in order to apply this Regulation. The measures may concern, *inter alia*: **7–169**
(a) the form, content and other details of complaints lodged pursuant to Article 7 and the procedure for rejecting complaints;
(b) the practical arrangements for the exchange of information and consultations provided for in Article 11;
(c) the practical arrangements for the hearings provided for in Article 27.

2. Before the adoption of any measures pursuant to paragraph 1, the Commission shall publish a draft thereof and invite all interested parties to submit their

comments within the time-limit it lays down, which may not be less than one month. Before publishing a draft measure and before adopting it, the Commission shall consult the Advisory Committee on Restrictive Practices and Dominant Positions.

Chapter XI—Transitional, Amending and Final Provisions

Article 34 Transitional provisions

7–170 1. Applications made to the Commission under Article 2 of Regulation 17, notifications made under Articles 4 and 5 of that Regulation and the corresponding applications and notifications made under Regulations 1017/68, 4056/86 and 3975/87 shall lapse as from the date of application of this Regulation.

2. Procedural steps taken under Regulation 17 and Regulations 1017/68, 4056/86 and 3975/87 shall continue to have effect for the purposes of applying this Regulation.

Article 35 Designation of competition authorities of Member States

7–171 1. The Member States shall designate the competition authority or authorities responsible for the application of Articles 81 and 82 of the Treaty in such a way that the provisions of this Regulation are effectively complied with. The measures necessary to empower those authorities to apply those Articles shall be taken before 1 May 2004. The authorities designated may include courts.

2. When enforcement of Community competition law is entrusted to national administrative and judicial authorities, the Member States may allocate different powers and functions to those different national authorities, whether administrative or judicial.

3. The effects of Article 11(6) apply to the authorities designated by the Member States including courts that exercise functions regarding the preparation and the adoption of the types of decisions foreseen in Article 5. The effects of Article 11(6) do not extend to courts insofar as they act as review courts in respect of the types of decisions foreseen in Article 5.

4. Notwithstanding paragraph 3, in the Member States where, for the adoption of certain types of decisions foreseen in Article 5, an authority brings an action before a judicial authority that is separate and different from the prosecuting authority and provided that the terms of this paragraph are complied with, the effects of Article 11(6) shall be limited to the authority prosecuting the case which shall withdraw its claim before the judicial authority when the Commission opens proceedings and this withdrawal shall bring the national proceedings effectively to an end.

Article 36 Amendment of Regulation 1017/68

7–172 [Not reproduced here.]

Article 37 Amendment of Regulation 2988/74

7–173 [Not reproduced here.]

Article 38 Amendment of Regulation 4056/86

7–174 [Not reproduced here.]

Article 39 Amendment of Regulation 3975/87

7–175 [Not reproduced here.]

Article 40 Amendment of Regulations 19/65, 2821/71 and 1534/91

[Not reproduced here.] **7–176**

Article 41 Amendment of Regulation 3976/87

[Not reproduced here.] **7–177**

Article 42 Amendment of Regulation 479/92

[Not reproduced here.] **7–178**

Article 43 Repeal of Regulations 17 and 141/62

1. Regulation 17 is repealed with the exception of Article 8(3) which continues to apply to decisions adopted pursuant to Article 81(3) of the Treaty prior to the date of application of this Regulation until the date of expiration of those decisions. **7–179**

2. Regulation 141/62 is repealed.

3. References to the repealed Regulations shall be construed as references to this Regulation.

Article 44 Report on the application of the present Regulation

Five years from the date of application of this Regulation, the Commission shall report to the European Parliament and the Council on the functioning of this Regulation, in particular on the application of Article 11(6) and Article 17. **7–180**

On the basis of this report, the Commission shall assess whether it is appropriate to propose to the Council a revision of this Regulation.

Article 45 Entry into force

This Regulation shall enter into force on the 20th day following that of its publication in the *Official Journal of the European Communities*[50]. **7–181**

It shall apply from 1 May 2004.

This Regulation shall be binding in its entirety and directly applicable in all Member States.

[50] Regulation 1/2003 was published in the *Official Journal* on 4 January 2003.

Article 40 Amendment of Regulations 19/65, 2821/71 and 1534/91

[Not reproduced here] 7-126

Article 41 Amendment of Regulation 3976/87

[Not reproduced here] 7-127

Article 42 Amendment of Regulation 479/92

[Not reproduced here] 7-128

Article 43 Repeal of Regulations 17 and 141/62

1. Regulation 17 is repealed with the exception of Article 8(3) which continues to apply to decisions adopted pursuant to Article 81(3) of the Treaty prior to the date of application of this Regulation until the date of expiration of those decisions. 7-129

2. Regulation 141/62 is repealed.

3. References to the repealed Regulations shall be construed as references to this Regulation.

Article 44 Report on the application of the present Regulation

Five years from the date of application of this Regulation, the Commission shall report to the European Parliament and the Council on the functioning of this Regulation, in particular on the application of Article 11(6) and Article 17. 7-130

On the basis of this report, the Commission shall assess whether it is appropriate to propose to the Council a revision of this Regulation.

Article 45 Entry into force

This Regulation shall enter into force on the 20th day following that of its publication in the *Official Journal of the European Communities*. 7-131

It shall apply from 1 May 2004.

This Regulation shall be binding in its entirety and directly applicable in all Member States.

CHAPTER 8

SOCIAL POLICY: EQUAL PAY AND TREATMENT

Council Directive 75/117 of 10 February 1975, on the approximation of the laws of the Member States relating to the application of the principle of equal pay for men and women

([1975] OJ L45/19; Doc. Ref. 31975L0117)

The Council of the European Communities, **8–001**
Having regard to the Treaty establishing the [European Community], and in particular Article [94] thereof,

Having regard to the proposal from the Commission,

Having regard to the Opinion of the European Parliament,[1]

Having regard to the Opinion of the Economic and Social Committee,[2]

[1] Whereas implementation of the principle that men and women should receive equal pay contained in Article [141] of the Treaty is an integral part of the establishment and functioning of the common market,

[2] Whereas it is primarily the responsibility of the Member States to ensure the application of this principle by means of appropriate laws, regulations and administrative provisions,

[3] Whereas the Council resolution of 21 January 1974,[3] concerning a social action programme, aimed at making it possible to harmonize living and working conditions while the improvement is being maintained and at achieving a balanced social and economic development of the Community, recognized that priority should be given to action taken on behalf of women as regards access to employment and vocational training and advancement, and as regards working conditions, including pay,

[4] Whereas it is desirable to reinforce the basic laws by standards aimed at facilitating the practical application of the principle of equality in such a way that all employees in the Community can be protected in these matters,

[5] Whereas differences continue to exist in the various Member States despite the efforts made to apply the resolution of the conference of the Member States of 30 December 1961, on equal pay for men and women and whereas, therefore, the national provisions should be approximated as regards application of the principle of equal pay,

Has adopted this Directive:

Article 1 [Principle of equal pay]

The principle of equal pay for men and women outlined in Article [141] of the Treaty, hereinafter called "principle of equal pay", means, for the same work or for work to which equal value is attributed, the elimination of all discrimination on grounds of sex with regard to all aspects and conditions of remuneration. **8–002**

In particular, where a job classification system is used for determining pay, it must be based on the same criteria for both men and women and so drawn up as to exclude any discrimination on grounds of sex.

---

[1] [1974] OJ C55/43.

[2] [1974] OJ C88/7.

[3] [1974] OJ C13/1.

Article 2 [Defence of rights]

8–003 Member States shall introduce into their national legal systems such measures as are necessary to enable all employees who consider themselves wronged by failure to apply the principle of equal pay to pursue their claims by judicial process after possible recourse to other competent authorities.

Article 3 [Abolition of discrimination]

8–004 Member States shall abolish all discrimination between men and women arising from laws, regulations or administrative provisions which is contrary to the principle of equal pay.

Article 4 [Compliance]

8–005 Member States shall take the necessary measures to ensure that provisions appearing in collective agreements, wage scales, wage agreements or individual contracts of employment which are contrary to the principle of equal pay shall be, or may be declared, null and void or may be amended.

Article 5 [Protection against dismissal]

8–006 Member States shall take the necessary measures to protect employees against dismissal by the employer as a reaction to a complaint within the undertaking or to any legal proceedings aimed at enforcing compliance with the principle of equal pay.

Article 6 [Application of principle of equal pay]

8–007 Member States shall, in accordance with their national circumstances and legal systems, take the measures necessary to ensure that the principle of equal pay is applied. They shall see that effective means are available to take care that this principle is observed.

Article 7 [Dissemination of information]

8–008 Member States shall take care that the provisions adopted pursuant to this Directive, together with the relevant provisions already in force, are brought to the attention of employees by all appropriate means, for example at their place of employment.

Article 8 [Implementation]

8–009 1. Member States shall put into force the laws, regulations and administrative provisions necessary in order to comply with this Directive within one year of its notification and shall immediately inform the Commission thereof.

2. Member States shall communicate to the Commission the texts of the laws, regulations and administrative provisions which they adopt in the field covered by this Directive.

Article 9 [Report on application]

8–010 Within two years of the expiry of the one-year period referred to in Article 8, Member States shall forward all necessary information to the Commission to enable it to draw up a report on the application of this Directive for submission to the Council.

Article 10 [Addressees]

This Directive is addressed to the Member States. **8–011**

Council Directive 76/207 of 9 February 1976, on the implementation of the principle of equal treatment for men and women as regards access to employment, vocational training and promotion, and working conditions

([1976] OJ L39/40; Doc. Ref. 31976L0207)

The Council of the European Communities, **8–012**
Having regard to the Treaty establishing the [European Community], and in particular Article [308] thereof,

Having regard to the proposal from the Commission,

Having regard to the opinion of the European Parliament,[4]

Having regard to the opinion of the Economic and Social Committee,[5]

[1] Whereas the Council, in its resolution of 21 January 1974, concerning a social action programme,[6] included among the priorities action for the purpose of achieving equality between men and women as regards access to employment and vocational training and promotion and as regards working conditions, including pay,

[2] Whereas, with regard to pay, the Council adopted on 10 February 1975, Directive 75/117 on the approximation of the laws of the Member States relating to the application of the principle of equal pay for men and women,[7]

[3] Whereas Community action to achieve the principle of equal treatment for men and women in respect of access to employment and vocational training and promotion and in respect of other working conditions also appears to be necessary whereas, equal treatment for male and female workers constitutes one of the objectives of the Community, in so far as the harmonisation of living and working conditions while maintaining their improvement are *inter alia* to be furthered whereas the Treaty does not confer the necessary specific powers for this purpose,

[4] Whereas the definition and progressive implementation of the principle of equal treatment in matters of social security should be ensured by means of subsequent instruments,

Has adopted this Directive:

Article 1 [Purpose]

1. The purpose of this Directive is to put into effect in the Member States the **8–013** principle of equal treatment for men and women as regards access to employment, including promotion, and to vocational training and as regards working conditions and, on the conditions referred to in paragraph 2, social security. This principle is hereinafter referred to as "the principle of equal treatment".

[1a. Member States shall actively take into account the objective of equality between men and women when formulating and implementing laws, regulations, administrative provisions, policies and activities in the areas referred to in paragraph 1.][8]

2. With a view to ensuring the progressive implementation of the principle of equal treatment in matters of social security, the Council, acting on a proposal

[4] [1975] OJ C111/14.
[5] [1975] OJ C286/8.
[6] [1974] OJ C13/1.
[7] [1975] OJ L45/19 (see above).
[8] Article 1(1a) inserted by Directive 2002/73 ([2002] OJ L269/15), Art. 1(1) with effect from 5 October 2002. Member States are to comply by 5 October 2005.

from the Commission, will adopt provisions defining its substance, its scope and the arrangements for its application.[9]

[Article 2 [Principle of equal treatment]

8–014 1. For the purposes of the following provisions, the principle of equal treatment shall mean that there shall be no discrimination whatsoever on grounds of sex either directly or indirectly by reference in particular to marital or family status.

2. For the purposes of this Directive, the following definitions shall apply:

— direct discrimination: where one person is treated less favourably on grounds of sex than another is, has been or would be treated in a comparable situation,
— indirect discrimination: where an apparently neutral provision, criterion or practice would put persons of one sex at a particular disadvantage compared with persons of the other sex, unless that provision, criterion or practice is objectively justified by a legitimate aim, and the means of achieving that aim are appropriate and necessary,
— harassment: where an unwanted conduct related to the sex of a person occurs with the purpose or effect of violating the dignity of a person, and of creating an intimidating, hostile, degrading, humiliating or offensive environment,
— sexual harassment: where any form of unwanted verbal, non-verbal or physical conduct of a sexual nature occurs, with the purpose or effect of violating the dignity of a person, in particular when creating an intimidating, hostile, degrading, humiliating or offensive environment.

3. Harassment and sexual harassment within the meaning of this Directive shall be deemed to be discrimination on the grounds of sex and therefore prohibited.

A person's rejection of, or submission to, such conduct may not be used as a basis for a decision affecting that person.

4. An instruction to discriminate against persons on grounds of sex shall be deemed to be discrimination within the meaning of this Directive.

5. Member States shall encourage, in accordance with national law, collective agreements or practice, employers and those responsible for access to vocational training to take measures to prevent all forms of discrimination on grounds of sex, in particular harassment and sexual harassment at the workplace.

6. Member States may provide, as regards access to employment including the training leading thereto, that a difference of treatment which is based on a characteristic related to sex shall not constitute discrimination where, by reason of the nature of the particular occupational activities concerned or of the context in which they are carried out, such a characteristic constitutes a genuine and determining occupational requirement, provided that the objective is legitimate and the requirement is proportionate.

7. This Directive shall be without prejudice to provisions concerning the protection of women, particularly as regards pregnancy and maternity.

A woman on maternity leave shall be entitled, after the end of her period of maternity leave, to return to her job or to an equivalent post on terms and conditions which are no less favourable to her and to benefit from any improvement in working conditions to which she would be entitled during her absence.

Less favourable treatment of a woman related to pregnancy or maternity leave within the meaning of Directive 92/85[10] shall constitute discrimination within the meaning of this Directive.

[9] See now Directive 79/7, [1979] OJ L6/24 (below).

[10] Directive 92/85 of 19 October 1992 on the introduction of measures to encourage improvements in the safety and health at work of pregnant workers and workers who have recently given birth or are breastfeeding [1992] OJ L348/1 (see Chapter 10, below).

This Directive shall also be without prejudice to the provisions of Council Directive 96/34 of 3 June 1996 on the framework agreement on parental leave concluded by UNICE, CEEP and the ETUC[11] and of Council Directive 92/85 of 19 October 1992 on the introduction of measures to encourage improvements in the safety and health at work of pregnant workers and workers who have recently given birth or are breastfeeding (tenth individual Directive within the meaning of Article 16(1) of Directive 89/391). It is also without prejudice to the right of Member States to recognise distinct rights to paternity and/or adoption leave. Those Member States which recognise such rights shall take the necessary measures to protect working men and women against dismissal due to exercising those rights and ensure that, at the end of such leave, they shall be entitled to return to their jobs or to equivalent posts on terms and conditions which are no less favourable to them, and to benefit from any improvement in working conditions to which they would have been entitled during their absence.

8. Member States may maintain or adopt measures within the meaning of Article 141(4) of the Treaty with a view to ensuring full equality in practice between men and women.][12]

[Article 3 [Application of the principle]

1. Application of the principle of equal treatment means that there shall be no direct or indirect discrimination on the grounds of sex in the public or private sectors, including public bodies, in relation to: **8–015**

(a) conditions for access to employment, to self-employment or to occupation, including selection criteria and recruitment conditions, whatever the branch of activity and at all levels of the professional hierarchy, including promotion;
(b) access to all types and to all levels of vocational guidance, vocational training, advanced vocational training and retraining, including practical work experience;
(c) employment and working conditions, including dismissals, as well as pay as provided for in Directive 75/117[13];
(d) membership of, and involvement in, an organisation of workers or employers, or any organisation whose members carry on a particular profession, including the benefits provided for by such organisations.

2. To that end, Member States shall take the necessary measures to ensure that:

(a) any laws, regulations and administrative provisions contrary to the principle of equal treatment are abolished;
(b) any provisions contrary to the principle of equal treatment which are included in contracts or collective agreements, internal rules of undertakings or rules governing the independent occupations and professions and workers' and employers' organisations shall be, or may be declared, null and void or are amended.][14]

Article 4 [Application of the principle to vocational training]

[. . .][15] **8–016**

Article 5 [Application of the principle to working conditions]

[. . .][16] **8–017**

[11] [1996] OJ L145/4 (see below).

[12] Article 2 replaced by Directive 2002/73, Art. 1(2) with effect from 5 October 2002. Member States are to comply by 5 October 2005.

[13] See above.

[14] Article 3 replaced by Directive 2002/73, Art. 1(3) with effect from 5 October 2002. Member States are to comply by 5 October 2005.

[15] Article 4 deleted by Directive 2002/73, Art. 1(4) with effect from 5 October 2002.

[16] Article 5 deleted by Directive 2002/73, Art. 1(4) with effect from 5 October 2002.

[Article 6 [Defence of rights]

8–018 1. Member States shall ensure that judicial and/or administrative procedures, including where they deem it appropriate conciliation procedures, for the enforcement of obligations under this Directive are available to all persons who consider themselves wronged by failure to apply the principle of equal treatment to them, even after the relationship in which the discrimination is alleged to have occurred has ended.

2. Member States shall introduce into their national legal systems such measures as are necessary to ensure real and effective compensation or reparation as the Member States so determine for the loss and damage sustained by a person injured as a result of discrimination contrary to Article 3, in a way which is dissuasive and proportionate to the damage suffered; such compensation or reparation may not be restricted by the fixing of a prior upper limit, except in cases where the employer can prove that the only damage suffered by an applicant as a result of discrimination within the meaning of this Directive is the refusal to take his/her job application into consideration.

3. Member States shall ensure that associations, organisations or other legal entities which have, in accordance with the criteria laid down by their national law, a legitimate interest in ensuring that the provisions of this Directive are complied with, may engage, either on behalf or in support of the complainants, with his or her approval, in any judicial and/or administrative procedure provided for the enforcement of obligations under this Directive.

4. Paragraphs 1 and 3 are without prejudice to national rules relating to time-limits for bringing actions as regards the principle of equal treatment.][17]

[Article 7 [Protection against dismissal]

8–019 Member States shall introduce into their national legal systems such measures as are necessary to protect employees, including those who are employees' representatives provided for by national laws and/or practices, against dismissal or other adverse treatment by the employer as a reaction to a complaint within the undertaking or to any legal proceedings aimed at enforcing compliance with the principle of equal treatment.][18]

Article 8 [Dissemination of information]

8–020 Member States shall take care that the provisions adopted pursuant to this Directive, together with the relevant provisions already in force, are brought to the attention of employees by all appropriate means, for example at their place of employment.

[Article 8a [Supervisory bodies]

8–021 1. Member States shall designate and make the necessary arrangements for a body or bodies for the promotion, analysis, monitoring and support of equal treatment

[17] Article 6 replaced by Directive 2002/73, Art. 1(5) with effect from 5 October 2002. Member States are to comply by 5 October 2005.

[18] Article 7 replaced by Directive 2002/73, Art. 1(6) with effect from 5 October 2002. Member States are to comply by 5 October 2005.

of all persons without discrimination on the grounds of sex. These bodies may form part of agencies charged at national level with the defence of human rights or the safeguard of individuals' rights.

2. Member States shall ensure that the competences of these bodies include:
(a) without prejudice to the right of victims and of associations, organisations or other legal entities referred to in Article 6(3), providing independent assistance to victims of discrimination in pursuing their complaints about discrimination;
(b) conducting independent surveys concerning discrimination;
(c) publishing independent reports and making recommendations on any issue relating to such discrimination.][19]

[Article 8b [Promotion of equal treatment]

1. Member States shall, in accordance with national traditions and practice, take adequate measures to promote social dialogue between the social partners with a view to fostering equal treatment, including through the monitoring of workplace practices, collective agreements, codes of conduct, research or exchange of experiences and good practices. **8–022**

2. Where consistent with national traditions and practice, Member States shall encourage the social partners, without prejudice to their autonomy, to promote equality between women and men and to conclude, at the appropriate level, agreements laying down anti-discrimination rules in the fields referred to in Article 1 which fall within the scope of collective bargaining. These agreements shall respect the minimum requirements laid down by this Directive and the relevant national implementing measures.

3. Member States shall, in accordance with national law, collective agreements or practice, encourage employers to promote equal treatment for men and women in the workplace in a planned and systematic way.

4. To this end, employers should be encouraged to provide at appropriate regular intervals employees and/or their representatives with appropriate information on equal treatment for men and women in the undertaking.

Such information may include statistics on proportions of men and women at different levels of the organisation and possible measures to improve the situation in co-operation with employees' representatives.][20]

[Article 8c [Dialogue with NGOs]

Member States shall encourage dialogue with appropriate non-governmental organisations which have, in accordance with their national law and practice, a legitimate interest in contributing to the fight against discrimination on grounds of sex with a view to promoting the principle of equal treatment.][21] **8–023**

[Article 8d [Sanctions]

Member States shall lay down the rules on sanctions applicable to infringements of the national provisions adopted pursuant to this Directive, and shall take all measures necessary to ensure that they are applied. **8–024**

The sanctions, which may comprise the payment of compensation to the victim, must be effective, proportionate and dissuasive. The Member States shall notify

[19] Article 8a inserted by Directive 2002/73, Art. 1(7) with effect from 5 October 2002. Member States are to comply by 5 October 2005.

[20] Article 8b inserted by Directive 2002/73, Art. 1(7) with effect from 5 October 2002. Member States are to comply by 5 October 2005.

[21] Article 8c inserted by Directive 2002/73, Art. 1(7) with effect from 5 October 2002. Member States are to comply by 5 October 2005.

those provisions to the Commission by 5 October 2005 at the latest and shall notify it without delay of any subsequent amendment affecting them.][22]

[Article 8e [More favourable national laws]

8–025 1. Member States may introduce or maintain provisions which are more favourable to the protection of the principle of equal treatment than those laid down in this Directive.

2. The implementation of this Directive shall under no circumstances constitute grounds for a reduction in the level of protection against discrimination already afforded by Member States in the fields covered by this Directive.][23]

Article 9 [Implementation]

8–026 1. Member States shall put into force the laws, regulations and administrative provisions necessary in order to comply with this Directive within 30 months of its notification and shall immediately inform the Commission thereof.

However, as regards the first part of Article 3(2)(c) and the first part of Article 5(2)(c), Member States shall carry out a first examination and if necessary a first revision of the laws, regulations and administrative provisions referred to therein within four years of notification of this Directive.

2. Member States shall periodically assess the occupational activities referred to in Article 2(2) in order to decide, in the light of social developments, whether there is justification for maintaining the exclusions concerned. They shall notify the Commission of the results of this assessment.

3. Member States shall also communicate to the Commission the texts of laws, regulations and administrative provisions which they adopt in the field covered by this Directive.

Article 10 [Report on application]

8–027 Within two years following expiry of the 30-month period laid down in the first sub-paragraph of Article 9(1), Member States shall forward all necessary information to the Commission to enable it to draw up a report on the application of this Directive for submission to the Council.

Article 11 [Addressees]

8–028 This Directive is addressed to the Member States.

Council Directive 79/7 of 19 December 1978, on the progressive implementation of the principle of equal treatment for men and women in matters of social security

([1979] OJ L6/24; Doc. Ref. 31979L0007)

8–029 *The Council of the European Communities*,

Having regard to the Treaty establishing the [European Community], and in particular Article [308] thereof,

Having regard to the proposal from the Commission,[24]

Having regard to the opinion of the European Parliament,[25]

[22] Article 8d inserted by Directive 2002/73, Art. 1(7) with effect from 5 October 2002. Member States are to comply by 5 October 2005.

[23] Article 8e inserted by Directive 2002/73, Art. 1(7) with effect from 5 October 2002. Member States are to comply by 5 October 2005.

[24] [1977] OJ C34/3.

[25] [1977] OJ C299/13.

Having regard to the opinion of the Economic and Social Committee,[26]

[1] Whereas Article 1(2) of Council Directive 76/207 of 9 February 1976, on the implementation of the principle of equal treatment for men and women as regards access to employment, vocational training and promotion, and working conditions[27] provides that, with a view to ensuring the progressive implementation of the principle of equal treatment in matters of social security, the Council, acting on a proposal from the Commission, will adopt provisions defining its substance its scope and the arrangements for its application whereas the Treaty does not confer the specific powers required for this purpose,

[2] Whereas the principle of equal treatment in matters of social security should be implemented in the first place in the statutory schemes which provide protection against the risks of sickness, invalidity, old age, accidents at work, occupational diseases and unemployment, and in social assistance in so far as it is intended to supplement or replace the abovementioned schemes,

[3] Whereas the implementation of the principle of equal treatment in matters of social security does not prejudice the provisions relating to the protection of women on the ground of maternity whereas, in this respect, Member States may adopt specific provisions for women to remove existing instances of unequal treatment,

Has adopted this Directive:

Article 1 [Purpose]

The purpose of this Directive is the progressive implementation, in the field of social security and other elements of social protection provided for in Article 3, of the principle of equal treatment for men and women in matters of social security, hereinafter referred to as "the principle of equal treatment". **8–030**

Article 2 [Scope: persons]

This Directive shall apply to the working population—including self-employed persons, workers and self-employed persons whose activity is interrupted by illness, accident or involuntary unemployment and persons seeking employment—and to retired or invalidated workers and self-employed persons. **8–031**

Article 3 [Scope: social security schemes]

1. This Directive shall apply to: **8–032**

(a) statutory schemes which provide protection against the following risks:
- — sickness,
- — invalidity,
- — old age,
- — accidents at work and occupational diseases,
- — unemployment

(b) social assistance, in so far as it is intended to supplement or replace the schemes referred to in (a).

2. This Directive shall not apply to the provisions concerning survivors' benefits nor to those concerning family benefits, except in the case of family benefits granted by way of increases of benefits due in respect of the risks referred to in paragraph 1(a).

3. With a view to ensuring implementation of the principle of equal treatment in occupational schemes, the Council, acting on a proposal from the Commission, will adopt provisions defining its substance, its scope and the arrangements for its application.[28]

---

[26] [1977] OJ C180/36.

[27] [1976] OJ L39/40 (see above).

[28] See Directive 86/378, [1986] OJ L225/40 (below).

Article 4 [The principle of equal treatment]

8–033 1. The principle of equal treatment means that there shall be no discrimination whatsoever on ground of sex either directly, or indirectly by reference in particular to marital or family status, in particular as concerns:
— the scope of the schemes and the conditions of access thereto,
— the obligation to contribute and the calculation of contributions,
— the calculation of benefits including increases due in respect of a spouse and for dependants and the conditions governing the duration and retention of entitlement to benefits.

2. The principle of equal treatment shall be without prejudice to the provisions relating to the protection of women on the grounds of maternity.

Article 5 [Compliance]

8–034 Member States shall take the measures necessary to ensure that any laws, regulations and administrative provisions contrary to the principle of equal treatment are abolished.

Article 6 [Defence of rights]

8–035 Member States shall introduce into their national legal systems such measures as art necessary to enable all persons who consider themselves wronged by failure to apply the principle of equal treatment to pursue their claims by judicial process, possibly after recourse to other competent authorities.

Article 7 [Exclusions]

8–036 1. This Directive shall be without prejudice to the right of Member States to exclude from its scope:
(a) the determination of personable age for the purposes of granting old-age and retirement pensions and the possible consequences thereof for other benefits;
(b) advantages in respect of old-age pension schemes granted to persons who have brought up children the acquisition of benefit entitlements following periods of interruption of employment due to the bringing up of children;
(c) the granting of old-age or invalidity benefit entitlements by virtue of the derived entitlements of a wife;
(d) the granting of increases of long-term invalidity, old-age, accidents at work and occupational disease benefits for a dependent wife;
(e) the consequences of the exercise, before the adoption of this Directive, of a right of option not to acquire rights or incur obligations under a statutory scheme.

2. Member States shall periodically examine matters excluded under paragraph 1 in order to ascertain, in the light of social developments in the matter concerned, whether there is justification for maintaining the exclusions concerned.

Article 8 [Implementation]

8–037 1. Member States shall bring into force the laws, regulations and administrative provisions necessary to comply with this Directive within six years of its notification. They shall immediately inform the Commission thereof.

2. Member States shall communicate to the Commission the text of laws, regulations and administrative provisions which they adopt in the field covered by this Directive, including measures adopted pursuant to Article 7(2).

They shall inform the Commission of their reasons for maintaining any existing provisions on the matters referred to in Article 7(1) and of the possibilities for reviewing them at a later date.

Article 9 [Report on application]

Within seven years of notification of this Directive, Member States shall forward all information necessary to the Commission to enable it to draw up a report on the application of this Directive for submission to the Council and to propose such further measures as may be required for the implementation of the principle of equal treatment. **8–038**

Article 10 [Addressees]

This Directive is addressed to the Member States. **8–039**

Council Directive 86/378 of 24 July 1986, on the implementation of the principle of equal treatment for men and women in occupational social security schemes

([1986] OJ L225/40, corrigenda [1986] OJ L283/27, [1997] OJ L241/8; Doc. Ref. 31986L0378)

The Council of the European Communities, **8–040**

Having regard to the Treaty establishing the [European Community], and in particular Articles [94] and [308] thereof,

Having regard to the proposal from the Commission,[29]

Having regard to the opinion of the European Parliament,[30]

Having regard to the opinion of the Economic and Social Committee,[31]

[1] Whereas the Treaty provides that each Member State shall ensure the application of the principle that men and women should receive equal pay for equal work whereas "pay" should be taken to mean the ordinary basic or minimum wage or salary and any other consideration, whether in cash or in kind, which the worker receives, directly of indirectly, from his employer in respect of his employment,

[2] Whereas, although the principle of equal pay does indeed apply directly in cases where discrimination can be determined solely on the basis of the criteria of equal treatment and equal pay, there are also situations in which implementation of this principle implies the adoption of additional measures which more clearly define its scope,

[3] Whereas Article 1(2) of Council Directive 76/207 of 9 February 1976, on the implementation of the principle of equal treatment for men and women as regards access to employment, vocational training and promotion, and working conditions[32] provides that, with a view to ensuring the progressive implementation of the principle of equal treatment in matters of social security, the Council, acting on a proposal from the Commission, will adopt provisions defining its substance, its scope and the arrangements for its application whereas the Council adopted to this end Directive 79/7 of December 19, 1978, on the progressive implementation of the principle of equal treatment for men and women in matters of social security,[33]

[4] Whereas Article 3(3) of Directive 79/7 provides that, with a view to ensuring implementation of the principle of equal treatment in occupational schemes, the Council, acting on a proposal from the Commission, will adopt provisions defining its substance, its scope and the arrangements for its application,

[5] Whereas the principle of equal treatment should be implemented in occupational social security schemes which provide protection against the risks specified in Article 3(1) of Directive 79/7 as well as those which provide employees with any other consideration in cash or in kind within the meaning of the Treaty,

---

[29] [1983] OJ C134/7.

[30] [1984] OJ C117/169.

[31] [1984] OJ C35/7.

[32] [1976] OJ L39/40 (see above).

[33] [1979] OJ L6/24 (see above).

[6] Whereas implementation of the principle of equal treatment does not prejudice the provisions relating to the protection of women by reason of maternity,

Has adopted this Directive:

Article 1 [Object]

8–041 The object of this Directive is to implement, in occupational social security schemes, the principle of equal treatment for men and women, hereinafter referred to as "the principle of equal treatment".

Article 2 [Scope: occupational security schemes]

8–042 1. "Occupational social security schemes" means schemes not governed by Directive 79/7 whose purpose is to provide workers, whether employees or self-employed, in an undertaking or group of undertakings, area of economic activity, occupational sector or group of sectors with benefits intended to supplement the benefits provided by statutory social security schemes or to replace them, whether membership of such schemes is compulsory or optional.

2. This Directive does not apply to:

(a) individual contracts for self-employed workers;
(b) schemes for self-employed workers having only one member;
(c) insurance contracts to which the employer is not a party, in the case of salaried workers;
(d) optional provisions of occupational schemes offered to participants individually to guarantee them:
— either additional benefits, or
— a choice of date on which the normal benefits for self-employed workers will start, or a choice between several benefits;
(e) occupational schemes in so far as benefits are financed by contributions paid by workers on a voluntary basis.

3. This Directive does not preclude an employer granting to persons who have already reached the retirement age for the purposes of granting a pension by virtue of an occupational scheme, but who have not yet reached the retirement age for the purposes of granting a statutory retirement pension, a pension supplement, the aim of which is to make equal or more nearly equal the overall amount of benefit paid to these persons in relation to the amount paid to persons of the other sex in the same situation who have already reached the statutory retirement age, until the persons benefiting from the supplement reach the statutory retirement age.][34]

---

[34] Article 2 substituted by Directive 96/97 ([1997] OJ L46/20, corrigendum [1999] OJ L151/39), Art. 1(1) as from 9 March 1997, applying as required by Directive 96/97, Art. 2:

"1. Any measure implementing this Directive, as regards paid workers, must cover all benefits derived from periods of employment subsequent to 17 May 1990 and shall apply retroactively to that date, without prejudice to workers or those claiming under them who have, before that date, initiated legal proceedings or raised an equivalent claim under national law. In that event, the implementation measures must apply retroactively to 8 April 1976 and must cover all the benefits derived from periods of employment after that date. For Member States which acceded to the Community after 8 April 1976, and before 17 May 1990, that date shall be replaced by the date on which Article [141] of the Treaty became applicable on their territory.

2. The second sentence of paragraph 1 shall not prevent national rules relating to time limits for bringing actions under national law from being relied on against workers or those claiming under them who initiated legal proceedings or raise an equivalent claim under national law before 17 May 1990, provided that they are not less favourable for that type of action than for similar actions of a domestic nature and that they do not render the exercise of Community law impossible in practice.

3. For Member States whose accession took place after 17 May 1990 and who were on 1 January 1994 Contracting Parties to the Agreement on the European Economic Area, the date of 17 May 1990 in the first sentence of paragraph 1 of this Directive is replaced by 1 January 1994."

[Article 3 [Scope: persons]

This Directive shall apply to members of the working population, including self-employed persons, persons whose activity is interrupted by illness, maternity, accident or involuntary unemployment and persons seeking employment, to retired and disabled workers and to those claiming under them, in accordance with national law and/or practice.][35] **8–043**

Article 4 [Scope of the Directive: risks]

This Directive shall apply to: **8–044**

(a) occupational schemes which provide protection against the following risks:
  — sickness,
  — invalidity,
  — old age, including early retirement,
  — industrial accidents and occupational diseases,
  — unemployment

(b) occupational schemes which provide for other social benefits, in cash or in kind, and in particular survivors' benefits and family allowances, if such benefits are accorded to employed persons and thus constitute a consideration paid by the employer to the worker by reason of the latter's employment.

Article 5 [Principle of equal treatment]

1. Under the conditions laid down in the following provisions, the principle of equal treatment implies that there shall be no discrimination on the basis of sex, either directly or indirectly, by reference in particular to marital or family status, especially as regards: **8–045**

— the scope of the schemes and the conditions of access to them
— the obligation to contribute and the calculation of contributions
— the calculation of benefits, including supplementary benefits due in respect of a spouse or dependants, and the conditions governing the duration and retention of entitlement to benefits.

2. The principle of equal treatment shall not prejudice the provisions relating to the protection of women by reason of maternity.

[Article 6 [Specific provisions covered]

1. Provisions contrary to the principle of equal treatment shall include those based on sex, either directly or indirectly, in particular by reference to marital or family status, for: **8–046**

(a) determining the persons who may participate in an occupational scheme;
(b) fixing the compulsory or optional nature of participation in an occupational scheme;
(c) laying down different rules as regards the age of entry into the scheme or the minimum period of employment or membership of the scheme required to obtain the benefits thereof;
(d) laying down different rules, except as provided for in points (h) and (i), for the reimbursement of contributions when a worker leaves a scheme without having fulfilled the conditions guaranteeing a deferred right to long-term benefits;

[35] Article 3 substituted by Directive 96/97 Art. 1(2) as from 9 March 1997 (for application see footnote 34 above).

(e) setting different conditions for the granting of benefits or restricting such benefits to workers of one or other of the sexes;
(f) fixing different retirement ages;
(g) suspending the retention or acquisition of rights during periods of maternity leave or leave for family reasons which are granted by law or agreement and are paid by the employer;
(h) setting different levels of benefit, except in so far as may be necessary to take account of actuarial calculation factors which differ according to sex in the case of defined-contribution schemes.
In the case of funded defined-benefit schemes, certain elements (examples of which are annexed) may be unequal where the inequality of the amounts results from the effects of the use of actuarial factors differing according to sex at the time when the scheme's funding is implemented;
(i) setting different levels for workers' contributions;
setting different levels for employers' contributions, except:
— in the case of defined-contribution schemes if the aim is to equalize the amount of the final benefits or to make them more nearly equal for both sexes,
— in the case of funded defined-benefit schemes where the employer's contributions are intended to ensure the adequacy of the funds necessary to cover the cost of the benefits defined,
(j) laying down different standards or standards applicable only to workers of a specified sex, except as provided for in points (h) and (i), as regards the guarantee or retention of entitlement to deferred benefits when a worker leaves a scheme.

2. Where the granting of benefits within the scope of this Directive is left to the discretion of the scheme's management bodies, the latter must comply with the principle of equal treatment.][36]

Article 7 [Compliance]

8–047 Member States shall take all necessary steps to ensure that:
(a) provisions contrary to the principle of equal treatment in legally compulsory collective agreements, staff rules of undertakings or any other arrangements relating to occupational schemes are null and void, or may be declared null and void or amended
(b) schemes containing such provisions may not be approved or extended by administrative measures.

[Article 8 [Implementation for self-employed workers]

8–048 1. Member States shall take the necessary steps to ensure that the provisions of occupational schemes for self-employed workers contrary to the principle of equal treatment are revised with effect from 1 January 1993, at the latest.

2. This Directive shall not preclude rights and obligations relating to a period of membership of an occupational scheme for self-employed workers prior to revision of that scheme from remaining subject to the provisions of the scheme in force during that period.][37]

[Article 9 [Deferred implementation for self-employed workers]

8–049 As regards schemes for self-employed workers, Member States may defer compulsory application of the principle of equal treatment with regard to:

[36] Article 6 substituted by Directive 96/97 Art. 1(3) as from 9 March 1997 (for application see footnote 34 above).
[37] Article 8 substituted by Directive 96/97 Art. 1(4) as from 9 March 1997 (for application see footnote 34 above).

(a) determination of pensionable age for the granting of old-age or retirement pensions, and the possible implications for other benefits:
— either until the date on which such equality is achieved in statutory schemes,
— or, at the latest, until such equality is prescribed by a directive;
(b) survivors' pensions until Community law establishes the principle of equal treatment in statutory social security schemes in that regard;
(c) the application of the first sub-paragraph of point (i) of Article 6(1) to take account of the different actuarial calculation factors, at the latest until 1 January 1999.][38]

[Article 9a [Flexible pensionable ages]

Where men and women may claim a flexible pensionable age under the same conditions, this shall not be deemed to be incompatible with this Directive.][39] **8–050**

Article 10 [Defence of rights]

Member States shall introduce into their national legal systems such measures as are necessary to enable all persons who consider themselves injured by failure to apply the principle of equal treatment to pursue their claims before the courts, possibly after bringing the matters before other competent authorities. **8–051**

Article 11 [Protection against dismissal]

Member States shall take all the necessary steps to protect worker against dismissal where this constitutes a response on the part of the employer to a complaint made at undertaking level or to the institution of legal proceedings aimed at enforcing compliance with the principle of equal treatment. **8–052**

Article 12 [Implementation]

1. Member States shall bring into force such laws, regulations and administrative provisions as are necessary in order to comply with this Directive at the latest three years after notification thereof.[40] They shall immediately inform the Commission thereof. **8–053**

2. Member States shall communicate to the Commission at the latest five years after notification of this Directive all information necessary to enable the Commission to draw up a report on the application of this Directive for submission to the Council.

Article 13 [Addressees]

This Directive is addressed to the Member States. **8–054**

[Annex

Examples of elements which may be unequal, in respect of funded defined-benefit schemes, as referred to in Article 6(h): **8–055**
— conversion into a capital sum of part of a periodic pension,
— transfer of pension rights,

[38] Article 9 substituted by Directive 96/97 Art. 1(5) as from 9 March 1997 (for application see footnote 34 above).
[39] Article 9a inserted by Directive 96/97 Art. 1(6) as from 9 March 1997 (for application see footnote 34 above).
[40] This Directive was notified to the Member States on 30 July 1986.

— a reversionary pension payable to a dependant in return for the surrender of part of a pension,
— a reduced pension where the worker opts to take early retirement.][41]

Council Directive 86/613 of 11 December 1986, on the application of the principle of equal treatment between men and women engaged in an activity, including agriculture, in a self-employed capacity, and on the protection of self-employed women during pregnancy and motherhood

([1986] OJ L359/56; Doc. Ref. 31986L0613)

8–056 *The Council of the European Communities,*

Having regard to the Treaty establishing the [European Community], and in particular Articles [94] and [308] thereof,

Having regard to the proposal from the Commission,[42]

Having regard to the opinion of the European Parliament,[43]

Having regard to the opinion of the Economic and Social Committee,[44]

[1] Whereas, in its resolution of 12 July 1982, on the promotion of equal opportunities for women,[45] the Council approved the general objectives of the Commission communication concerning a new Community action programme on the promotion of equal opportunities for women (1982 to 1985) and expressed the will to implement appropriate measures to achieve them,

[2] Whereas action 5 of the programme referred to above concerns the application of the principle of equal treatment to self-employed women and to women in agriculture,

[3] Whereas the implementation of the principle of equal pay for men and women workers, as laid down in Article [141] of the Treaty, forms an integral part of the establishment and functioning of the common market,

[4] Whereas on 10 February 1975, the Council adopted Directive 75/117 on the approximation of the laws of the Member States relating to the application of the principle of equal pay for men and women,[46]

[5] Whereas, as regards other aspects of equality of treatment between men and women, on 9 February 1976, the Council adopted Directive 76/207 on the implementation of the principle of equal treatment for men and women as regards access to employment, vocational training and promotion, and working conditions[47] and on 19 December 1978 Directive 79/7 on the progressive implementation of the principle of equal treatment for men and women in matters of social security,[48]

[6] Whereas, as regards persons engaged in a self-employed capacity, in an activity in which their spouses are also engaged, the implementation of the principle of equal treatment should be pursued through the adoption of detailed provisions designed to cover the specific situation of these persons,

[7] Whereas differences persist between the Member States in this field, whereas, therefore it is necessary to approximate national provisions with regard to the application of the principle of equal treatment,

[8] Whereas in certain respects the Treaty does not confer the powers necessary for the specific actions required,

[41] Annex inserted by Directive 96/97 Art. 1(7) as from 9 March 1997 (for application see footnote 34 above).
[42] [1984] OJ C113/4.
[43] [1984] OJ C172/90.
[44] [1984] OJ C343/1.
[45] [1982] OJ C186/3.
[46] [1975] OJ L45/19 (see above).
[47] [1975] OJ L39/40 (see above).
[48] [1979] OJ L6/24 (see above).

[9] Whereas the implementation of the principle of equal treatment is without prejudice to measures concerning the protection of women during pregnancy and motherhood,
Has adopted this Directive:

Section I—Aims and Scope

Article 1 [Purpose]

The purpose of this Directive is to ensure, in accordance with the following provisions, application in the Member States of the principle of equal treatment as between men and women engaged in an activity in a self-employed capacity, or contributing to the pursuit of such an activity, as regards those aspects not covered by Directives 76/207 and 79/7. **8–057**

Article 2 [Scope]

This Directive covers: **8–058**
(a) self-employed workers, *i.e.* all persons pursuing a gainful activity for their own account, under the conditions laid down by national law, including farmers and members of the liberal professions
(b) their spouses, not being employees or partners, where they habitually, under the conditions laid down by national law, participate in the activities of the self-employed worker and perform the same tasks or ancillary tasks.

Article 3 [Principle of equal treatment]

For the purposes of this Directive the principle of equal treatment implies the absence of all discrimination on grounds of sex, either directly or indirectly, by reference in particular to marital or family status. **8–059**

Section II—Equal Treatment Between Self-employed Male and Female Workers—Position of the Spouses Without Professional Status of Self-employed Workers—Protection of Self-employed Workers or Wives of Self-employed Workers During Pregnancy and Motherhood

Article 4 [Elimination of contrary provisions]

As regards self-employed persons, Member States shall take the measures necessary to ensure the elimination of all provisions which are contrary to the principle of equal treatment as defined in Directive 76/207, especially in respect of the establishment, equipment or extension of a business or the launching or extension of any other form of self-employed activity including financial facilities. **8–060**

Article 5 [Formation of company between spouses]

Without prejudice to the specific conditions for access to certain activities which apply equally to both sexes, Member States shall take the measures necessary to ensure that the conditions for the formation of a company between spouses are not more restrictive than the conditions for the formation of a company between unmarried persons. **8–061**

Article 6 [Voluntary membership of contributory scheme]

Where a contributory social security system for self-employed workers exists in a Member State, that Member State shall take the necessary measures to enable the spouses referred to in Article 2(b) who are not protected under the self-employed worker's social security scheme to join a contributory social security scheme voluntarily. **8–062**

Article 7 **[Recognition of the work of spouses]**

8–063 Member States shall undertake to examine under what conditions recognition of the work of the spouses referred to in Article 2(b) may be encouraged and, in the light of such examination, consider any appropriate steps for encouraging such recognition.

Article 8 **[Pregnancy and motherhood]**

8–064 Member States shall undertake to examine whether, and under what conditions, female self-employed workers and the wives of self-employed workers may, during interruptions in their occupational activity owing to pregnancy or motherhood,
— have access to services supplying temporary replacements or existing national social services, or
— be entitled to cash benefits under a social security scheme or under any other public social protection system.

Section III—General and Final Provisions

Article 9 **[Defence of right]**

8–065 Member States shall introduce into their national legal systems such measures as are necessary to enable all persons who consider themselves wronged by failure to apply the principle of equal treatment in self-employed activities to pursue their claims by judicial process, possibly after recourse to other competent authorities.

Article 10 **[Dissemination of information]**

8–066 Member States shall ensure that the measures adopted pursuant to this Directive, together with the relevant provisions already in force, are brought to the attention of bodies representing self-employed workers and vocational training centres.

Article 11 **[Review]**

8–067 The Council shall review this Directive, on a proposal from the Commission, before 1 July 1993.

Article 12 **[Implementation]**

8–068 1. Member States shall bring into force the laws, regulations and administrative provisions necessary to comply with this Directive not later than 30 June 1989.

However, if a Member State which, in order to comply with Article 5 of this Directive, has to amend its legislation on matrimonial rights and obligations, the date on which such Member State must comply with Article 5 shall be 30 June 1991.

2. Member States shall immediately inform the Commission of the measures taken to comply with this Directive.

Article 13 [Report on application]

Member States shall forward to the Commission, not later than 30 June 1991, all the information necessary to enable it to draw up a report on the application of this Directive for submission to the Council. **8–069**

Article 14 [Addressees]

This Directive is addressed to the Member States. **8–070**

Council Directive 96/34 of 3 June 1996, on the framework agreement on parental leave concluded by UNICE, CEEP and the ETUC

([1996] OJ L145/4; Doc. Ref. 31996L0034)

The Council of the European Union, **8–071**

Having regard to the Agreement on social policy, annexed to the Protocol (No. 14) on social policy, annexed to the Treaty establishing the European Community, and in particular Article 4(2) thereof,[49]

Having regard to the proposal from the Commission,

(1) Whereas on the basis of the Protocol on social policy, the Member States, with the exception of the United Kingdom of Great Britain and Northern Ireland,[50] (hereinafter referred to as "the Member States"), wishing to pursue the course mapped out by the 1989 Social Charter have concluded an Agreement on social policy amongst themselves;

(2) Whereas management and labour may, in accordance with Article 4(2) of the Agreement on social policy, request jointly that agreements at Community level be implemented by a Council decision on a proposal from the Commission;

(3) Whereas paragraph 16 of the Community Charter of the Fundamental Social Rights of Workers on equal treatment for men and women provides, *inter alia*, that "measures should also be developed enabling men and women to reconcile their occupational and family obligations";

(4) Whereas the Council, despite the existence of a broad consensus, has not been able to act on the proposal for a Directive on parental leave for family reasons,[51] as amended[52] on 15 November 1984;

(5) Whereas the Commission, in accordance with Article 3(2) of the Agreement on social policy,[53] consulted management and labour on the possible direction of Community action with regard to reconciling working and family life;

(6) Whereas the Commission, considering after such consultation that Community action was desirable, once again consulted management and labour on the substance of the envisaged proposal in accordance with Article 3(3) of the said Agreement;

(7) Whereas the general cross-industry organisations (Unice, CEEP and the ETUC) informed the Commission in their joint letter of 5 July 1995, of their desire to initiate the procedure provided for by Article 4 of the said Agreement[54]:

(8) Whereas the said cross-industry organisations concluded, on 14 December 1995, a framework agreement on parental leave whereas they have forwarded to the Commission their joint request to implement this framework agreement by a Council Decision on a proposal from the Commission in accordance with Article 4(2) of the said Agreement;

(9) Whereas the Council, in its Resolution of 6 December 1994, on certain aspects for a European Union social policy a contribution to economic and social

---

[49] Now incorporated in Art. 139 of the EC Treaty.

[50] But see Directive 97/75 ([1998] OJ L10/24) extending this Directive to the UK following incorporation of the Agreement on Social Policy into the Treaty.

[51] [1983] OJ C333/6.

[52] [1984] OJ C316/7.

[53] Now incorporated in Art. 138 of the EC Treaty.

[54] Now incorporated in Art. 139 of the EC Treaty.

convergence in the Union,[55] asked the two sides of industry to make use of the possibilities for concluding agreements, since they are as a rule closer to social reality and to social problems whereas in Madrid, the members of the European Council from those States which have signed the Agreement on social policy welcomed the conclusion of this framework agreement;

(10) Whereas the signatory parties wanted to conclude a framework agreement setting out minimum requirements on parental leave and time off from work on grounds of *force majeure* and referring back to the Member States and/or management and labour for the definition of the conditions under which parental leave would be implemented, in order to take account of the situation, including the situation with regard to family policy, existing in each Member State, particularly as regards the conditions for granting parental leave and exercise of the right to parental leave;

(11) Whereas the proper instrument for implementing this framework agreement is a Directive within the meaning of Article [249] of the Treaty whereas it is therefore binding on the Member States as to the result to be achieved, but leaves them the choice of form and methods;

(12) Whereas, in keeping with the principle of subsidiarity and the principle of proportionality as set out in Article [5] of the Treaty, the objectives of this Directive cannot be sufficiently achieved by the Member States and can therefore be better achieved by the Community whereas this Directive is confined to the minimum required to achieve these objectives and does not go beyond what is necessary to achieve that purpose;

(13) Whereas the Commission has drafted its proposal for a Directive, taking into account the representative status of the signatory parties, their mandate and the legality of the clauses of the framework agreement and compliance with the relevant provisions concerning small and medium-sized undertakings;

(14) Whereas the Commission, in accordance with its Communication of 14 December 1993, concerning the implementation of the Protocol on social policy, informed the European Parliament by sending it the text of the framework agreement, accompanied by its proposal for a Directive and the explanatory memorandum;

(15) Whereas the Commission also informed the Economic and Social Committee by sending it the text of the framework agreement, accompanied by its proposal for a Directive and the explanatory memorandum;

(16) Whereas clause 4 point 2 of the framework agreement states that the implementation of the provisions of this agreement does not constitute valid grounds for reducing the general level of protection afforded to workers in the field of this agreement. This does not prejudice the right of Member States and/or management and labour to develop different legislative, regulatory or contractual provisions, in the light of changing circumstances (including the introduction of non-transferability), as long as the minimum requirements provided for in the present agreement are complied with;

(17) Whereas the Community Charter of the Fundamental Social Rights of Workers recognizes the importance of the fight against all forms of discrimination, especially based on sex, colour, race, opinions and creeds;

(18) Whereas Article [6(2)] of the Treaty on European Union provides that "the Union shall respect fundamental rights, as guaranteed by the European Convention for the Protection of Human Rights and Fundamental Freedoms signed in Rome on 4 November 1950, and as they result from the constitutional traditions common to the Member States, as general principles of Community law";

(19) Whereas the Member States can entrust management and labour, at their joint request, with the implementation of this Directive, as long as they take all the

[55] [1994] OJ C368/6.

necessary steps to ensure that they can at all times guarantee the results imposed by this Directive;

(20) Whereas the implementation of the framework agreement contributes to achieving the objectives under Article 1 of the Agreement on social policy,[56]

Has adopted this Directive:

Article 1 Implementation of the framework agreement

The purpose of this Directive is to put into effect the annexed framework agreement on parental leave concluded on 14 December 1995, between the general cross-industry organizations (Unice, CEEP and the ETUC). **8–072**

Article 2 Final provisions

1. The Member States shall bring into force the laws, regulations and administrative provisions necessary to comply with this Directive by 3 June 1998 at the latest or shall ensure by that date at the latest that management and labour have introduced the necessary measures by agreement, the Member States being required to take any necessary measure enabling them at any time to be in a position to guarantee the results imposed by this Directive. They shall forthwith inform the Commission thereof. **8–073**

[1a. As regards the United Kingdom of Great Britain and Northern Ireland, the date of 3 June 1998 in paragraph 1 shall be replaced by 15 December 1999.][57]

2. The Member States may have a maximum additional period of one year, if this is necessary to take account of special difficulties or implementation by a collective agreement.

They must forthwith inform the Commission of such circumstances.

3. When Member States adopt the measures referred to in paragraph 1, they shall contain a reference to this Directive or be accompanied by such reference on the occasion of their official publication. The methods of making such reference shall be laid down by Member States.

Article 3 [Addressees]

This Directive is addressed to the Member States. **8–074**

Annex—Framework Agreement on Parental Leave

PREAMBLE

The enclosed framework agreement represents an undertaking by Unice, CEEP and the ETUC to set out minimum requirements on parental leave and time off from work on grounds of *force majeure*, as an important means of reconciling work and family life and promoting equal opportunities and treatment between men and women. **8–075**

ETUC, Unice and CEEP request the Commission to submit this framework agreement to the Council for a Council Decision making these minimum requirements binding in the Member States of the European Community, with the exception of the United Kingdom of Great Britain and Northern Ireland.

I—GENERAL CONSIDERATIONS

(1) Having regard to the Agreement on social policy annexed to the Protocol on social policy, annexed to the Treaty establishing the European Community, and in particular Articles 3(4) and 4(2) thereof,[58] **8–076**

[56] Now incorporated in Art. 136 of the EC Treaty.

[57] Article 2(1a) inserted by Directive 97/75 ([1998] OJ L10/24) Art. 2 as from 5 February 1998.

[58] Now incorporated in Art. 138 and 139 of the EC Treaty.

(2) Whereas Article 4(2) of the Agreement on social policy provides that agreements concluded at Community level shall be implemented, at the joint request of the signatory parties, by a Council decision on a proposal from the Commission,

(3) Whereas the Commission has announced its intention to propose a Community measure on the reconciliation of work and family life,

(4) Whereas the Community Charter of Fundamental Social Rights stipulates at point 16 dealing with equal treatment that measures should be developed to enable men and women to reconcile their occupational and family obligations,

(5) Whereas the Council Resolution of 6 December 1994, recognises that an effective policy of equal opportunities presupposes an integrated overall strategy allowing for better organization of working hours and greater flexibility, and for an easier return to working life, and notes the important role of the two sides of industry in this area and in offering both men and women an opportunity to reconcile their work responsibilities with family obligations,

(6) Whereas measures to reconcile work and family life should encourage the introduction of new flexible ways of organising work and time which are better suited to the changing needs of society and which should take the needs of both undertakings and workers into account,

(7) Whereas family policy should be looked at in the context of demographic changes, the effects of the ageing population, closing the generation gap and promoting women's participation in the labour force,

(8) Whereas men should be encouraged to assume an equal share of family responsibilities, for example they should be encouraged to take parental leave by means such as awareness programmes,

(9) Whereas the present agreement is a framework agreement setting out minimum requirements and provisions for parental leave, distinct from maternity leave, and for time off from work on grounds of *force majeure*, and refers back to Member States and social partners for the establishment of the conditions of access and detailed rules of application in order to take account of the situation in each Member State,

(10) Whereas Member States should provide for the maintenance of entitlements to benefits in kind under sickness insurance during the minimum period of parental leave,

(11) Whereas Member States should also, where appropriate under national conditions and taking into account the budgetary situation, consider the maintenance of entitlements to relevant social security benefits as they stand during the minimum period of parental leave,

(12) Whereas this agreement takes into consideration the need to improve social policy requirements, to enhance the competitiveness of the Community economy and to avoid imposing administrative, financial and legal constraints in a way which would impede the creation and development of small and medium-sized undertakings,

(13) Whereas management and labour are best placed to find solutions that correspond to the needs of both employers and workers and must therefore have conferred on them a special role in the implementation and application of the present agreement,

The Signatory Parties have agreed the following:

II—CONTENT

Clause 1: Purpose and scope

8–077 1. This agreement lays down minimum requirements designed to facilitate the reconciliation of parental and professional responsibilities for working parents.

2. This agreement applies to all workers, men and women, who have an employment contract or employment relationship as defined by the law, collective agreements or practices in force in each Member State.

Clause 2: Parental leave

1. This agreement grants, subject to clause 2.2, men and women workers an individual right to parental leave on the grounds of the birth or adoption of a child to enable them to take care of that child, for at least three months, until a given age up to eight years to be defined by Member States and/or management and labour. **8–078**

2. To promote equal opportunities and equal treatment between men and women, the parties to this agreement consider that the right to parental leave provided for under clause 2.1 should, in principle, be granted on a non-transferable basis.

3. The conditions of access and detailed rules for applying parental leave shall be defined by law and/or collective agreement in the Member States, as long as the minimum requirements of this agreement are respected. Member States and/or management and labour may, in particular:
(a) decide whether parental leave is granted on a full-time or part-time basis, in a piecemeal way or in the form of a time-credit system;
(b) make entitlement to parental leave subject to a period of work qualification and/or a length of service qualification which shall not exceed one year;
(c) adjust conditions of access and detailed rules for applying parental leave to the special circumstances of adoption;
(d) establish notice periods to be given by the worker to the employer when exercising the right to parental leave, specifying the beginning and the end of the period of leave;
(e) define the circumstances in which an employer, following consultation in accordance with national law, collective agreements and practices, is allowed to postpone the granting of parental leave for justifiable reasons related to the operation of the undertaking (*e.g.* where work is of a seasonal nature, where a replacement cannot be found within the notice period, where a significant proportion of the workforce applies for parental leave at the same time, where a specific function is of strategic importance). Any problem arising from the application of this provision should be dealt with in accordance with national law, collective agreements and practices;
(f) in addition to (e), authorise special arrangements to meet the operational and organisational requirements of small undertakings.

4. In order to ensure that workers can exercise their right to parental leave, Member States and/or management and labour shall take the necessary measures to protect workers against dismissal on the grounds of an application for, or the taking of, parental leave in accordance with national law, collective agreements or practices.

5. At the end of parental leave, workers shall have the right to return to the same job or, if that is not possible, to an equivalent or similar job consistent with their employment contract or employment relationship.

6. Rights acquired or in the process of being acquired by the worker on the date on which parental leave starts shall be maintained as they stand until the end of parental leave. At the end of parental leave, these rights, including any changes arising from national law, collective agreements or practice, shall apply.

7. Member States and/or management and labour shall define the status of the employment contract or employment relationship for the period of parental leave.

8. All matters relating to social security in relation to this agreement are for consideration and determination by Member States according to national law, taking into account the importance of the continuity of the entitlements to social security cover under the different schemes, in particular health care.

Clause 3: Time off from work on grounds of *force majeure*

8–079 1. Member States and/or management and labour shall take the necessary measures to entitle workers to time off from work, in accordance with national legislation, collective agreements and/or practice, on grounds of *force majeure* for urgent family reasons in cases of sickness or accident making the immediate presence of the worker indispensable.

2. Member States and/or management and labour may specify the conditions of access and detailed rules for applying clause 3.1 and limit this entitlement to a certain amount of time per year and/or per case.

Clause 4: Final provisions

8–080 1. Member States may apply or introduce more favourable provisions that those set out in this agreement.

2. Implementation of the provisions of this agreement shall not constitute valid grounds for reducing the general level of protection afforded to workers in the field covered by this agreement. This shall not prejudice the right of Member States and/or management and labour to develop different legislative, regulatory or contractual provisions, in the light of changing circumstances (including the introduction of non-transferability), as long as the minimum requirements provided for in the present agreement are complied with.

3. The present agreement shall not prejudice the right of management and labour to conclude, at the appropriate level including European level, agreements adapting and/or complementing the provisions of this agreement in order to take into account particular circumstances.

4. Member States shall adopt the laws, regulations and administrative provisions necessary to comply with the Council decision within a period of two years from its adoption or shall ensure that management and labour introduce the necessary measures by way of agreement by the end of this period. Member States may, if necessary to take account of particular difficulties or implementation by collective agreement, have up to a maximum of one additional year to comply with this decision.

5. The prevention and settlement of disputes and grievances arising from the application of this agreement shall be dealt with in accordance with national law, collective agreements and practices.

6. Without prejudice to the respective role of the Commission, national courts and the Court of Justice, any matter relating to the interpretation of this agreement at European level should, in the first instance, be referred by the Commission to the signatory parties who will give an opinion.

7. The signatory parties shall review the application of this agreement five years after the date of the Council decision if requested by one of the parties to this agreement.

Council Directive 97/80 of 15 December 1997 on the burden of proof in cases of discrimination based on sex

([1998] OJ L14/6; Doc. Ref. 31997L0080)

8–081 *The Council of the European Union*,
Having regard to the Agreement on social policy annexed to the Protocol (No. 14) on social policy annexed to the Treaty establishing the European Community, and in particular Article 2(2) thereof,[59]

[59] Now incorporated in Art. 137 of the EC Treaty.

Having regard to the proposal from the Commission,[60]
Having regard to the opinion of the Economic and Social Committee,[61]
Acting, in accordance with the procedure laid down in Article [252] of the Treaty, in cooperation with the European Parliament,[62]

(1) Whereas, on the basis of the Protocol on social policy annexed to the Treaty, the Member States, with the exception of the United Kingdom of Great Britain and Northern Ireland[63] (hereinafter called "the Member States"), wishing to implement the 1989 Social Charter, have concluded an Agreement on social policy[64];

(2) Whereas the Community Charter of the Fundamental Social Rights of Workers recognizes the importance of combating every form of discrimination, including discrimination on grounds of sex, colour, race, opinions and beliefs;

(3) Whereas paragraph 16 of the Community Charter of the Fundamental Social Rights of Workers on equal treatment for men and women, provides, *inter alia*, that "action should be intensified to ensure the implementation of the principle of equality for men and women as regards, in particular, access to employment, remuneration, working conditions, social protection, education, vocational training and career development";

(4) Whereas, in accordance with Article 3(2) of the Agreement on social policy,[65] the Commission has consulted management and labour at Community level on the possible direction of Community action on the burden of proof in cases of discrimination based on sex;

(5) Whereas the Commission, considering Community action advisable after such consultation, once again consulted management and labour on the content of the proposal contemplated in accordance with Article 3(3) of the same Agreement[66] whereas the latter have sent their opinions to the Commission;

(6) Whereas, after the second round of consultation, neither management nor labour have informed the Commission of their wish to initiate the process—possibly leading to an agreement—provided for in Article 4 of the same Agreement[67];

(7) Whereas, in accordance with Article 1 of the Agreement,[68] the Community and the Member States have set themselves the objective, *inter alia*, of improving living and working conditions whereas effective implementation of the principle of equal treatment for men and women would contribute to the achievement of that aim;

(8) Whereas the principle of equal treatment was stated in Article [141] of the Treaty, in Council Directive 75/117 of 10 February 1975, on the approximation of the laws of the Member States relating to the application of the principle of equal pay for men and women[69] and in Council Directive 76/207 of 9 February 1976 on the implementation of the principle of equal treatment for men and women as regards access to employment, vocational training and promotion and working conditions[70];

(9) Whereas Council Directive 92/85 of 19 October 1992, on the introduction of measures to encourage improvements in the safety and health at work of pregnant

[60] [1996] OJ C332/11 and [1997] OJ C185/21.

[61] [1997] OJ C133/34.

[62] Opinion of the European Parliament of 10 April 1997 ([1997] OJ C132/215), Common Position of the Council of 24 July 1997 ([1997] OJ C307/6) and Decision of the European Parliament of 6 November 1997 ([1997] OJ C358).

[63] But see Directive 98/52 ([1998] OJ L205/66) extending this Directive to the UK following incorporation of the Agreement on Social Policy into the Treaty.

[64] Now incorporated in Arts 136–140 of the EC Treaty.

[65] Now incorporated in Art. 138 of the EC Treaty.

[66] *ibid.*

[67] Now incorporated in Art. 139 of the EC Treaty.

[68] Now incorporated in Art. 136 of the EC Treaty.

[69] [1975] OJ L45/19 (see above).

[70] [1976] OJ L39/40 (see above).

workers and workers who have recently given birth or are breast-feeding[71] also contributes to the effective implementation of the principle of equal treatment for men and women whereas that Directive should not work to the detriment of the aforementioned Directives on equal treatment whereas, therefore, female workers covered by that Directive should likewise benefit from the adaptation of the rules on the burden of proof;

(10) Whereas Council Directive 96/34 of 3 June 1996, on the framework agreement on parental leave concluded by UNICE, CEEP and the ETUC,[72] is also based on the principle of equal treatment for men and women;

(11) Whereas the references to "judicial process" and "court" cover mechanisms by means of which disputes may be submitted for examination and decision to independent bodies which may hand down decisions that are binding on the parties to those disputes;

(12) Whereas the expression "out-of-court procedures" means in particular procedures such as conciliation and mediation;

(13) Whereas the appreciation of the facts from which it may be presumed that there has been direct or indirect discrimination is a matter for national judicial or other competent bodies, in accordance with national law or practice;

(14) Whereas it is for the Member States to introduce, at any appropriate stage of the proceedings, rules of evidence which are more favourable to plaintiffs;

(15) Whereas it is necessary to take account of the specific features of certain Member States' legal systems, *inter alia* where an inference of discrimination is drawn if the respondent fails to produce evidence that satisfies the court or other competent authority that there has been no breach of the principle of equal treatment;

(16) Whereas Member States need not apply the rules on the burden of proof to proceedings in which it is for the court or other competent body to investigate the facts of the case whereas the procedures thus referred to are those in which the plaintiff is not required to prove the facts, which it is for the court or competent body to investigate;

(17) Whereas plaintiffs could be deprived of any effective means of enforcing the principle of equal treatment before the national courts if the effect of introducing evidence of an apparent discrimination were not to impose upon the respondent the burden of proving that his practice is not in fact discriminatory;

(18) Whereas the Court of Justice of the European Communities has therefore held that the rules on the burden of proof must be adapted when there is a prima facie case of discrimination and that, for the principle of equal treatment to be applied effectively, the burden of proof must shift back to the respondent when evidence of such discrimination is brought;

(19) Whereas it is all the more difficult to prove discrimination when it is indirect whereas it is therefore important to define indirect discrimination;

(20) Whereas the aim of adequately adapting the rules on the burden of proof has not been achieved satisfactorily in all Member States and, in accordance with the principle of subsidiarity stated in Article [5] of the Treaty and with that of proportionality, that aim must be attained at Community level whereas this Directive confines itself to the minimum action required and does not go beyond what is necessary for that purpose,

Has adopted this Directive:

Article 1 Aim

8–082 The aim of this Directive shall be to ensure that the measures taken by the Member States to implement the principle of equal treatment are made more

[71] [1992] OJ L348/1.
[72] [1996] OJ L145/4 (see above).

effective, in order to enable all persons who consider themselves wronged because the principle of equal treatment has not been applied to them to have their rights asserted by judicial process after possible recourse to other competent bodies.

Article 2 Definitions

1. For the purposes of this Directive, the principle of equal treatment shall mean that there shall be no discrimination whatsoever based on sex, either directly or indirectly. **8–083**

2. For purposes of the principle of equal treatment referred to in paragraph 1, indirect discrimination shall exist where an apparently neutral provision, criterion or practice disadvantages a substantially higher proportion of the members of one sex unless that provision, criterion or practice is appropriate and necessary and can be justified by objective factors unrelated to sex.

Article 3 Scope

1. This Directive shall apply to: **8–084**

(a) the situations covered by Article [141] of the Treaty and by Directives 75/117, 76/207 and, in so far as discrimination based on sex is concerned, 92/85 and 96/34;
(b) any civil or administrative procedure concerning the public or private sector which provides for means of redress under national law pursuant to the measures referred to in (a) with the exception of out-of-court procedures of a voluntary nature or provided for in national law.

2. This Directive shall not apply to criminal procedures, unless otherwise provided by the Member States.

Article 4 Burden of proof

1. Member States shall take such measures as are necessary, in accordance with their national judicial systems, to ensure that, when persons who consider themselves wronged because the principle of equal treatment has not been applied to them establish, before a court or other competent authority, facts from which it may be presumed that there has been direct or indirect discrimination, it shall be for the respondent to prove that there has been no breach of the principle of equal treatment. **8–085**

2. This Directive shall not prevent Member States from introducing rules of evidence which are more favourable to plaintiffs.

3. Member States need not apply paragraph 1 to proceedings in which it is for the court or competent body to investigate the facts of the case.

Article 5 Information

Member States shall ensure that measures taken pursuant to this Directive, together with the provisions already in force, are brought to the attention of all the persons concerned by all appropriate means. **8–086**

Article 6 Non-regression

Implementation of this Directive shall under no circumstances be sufficient grounds for a reduction in the general level of protection of workers in the areas to which it applies, without prejudice to the Member States' right to respond to changes in the situation by introducing laws, regulations and administrative provisions which differ from those in force on the notification of this Directive, provided that the minimum requirements of this Directive are complied with. **8–087**

Article 7 Implementation

8–088 The Member States shall bring into force the laws, regulations and administrative provisions necessary for them to comply with this Directive by 1 January 2001. They shall immediately inform the Commission thereof.

[As regards the United Kingdom of Great Britain and Northern Ireland, the date of 1 January 2001 in paragraph 1 shall be replaced by 22 July 2001.][73]

When the Member States adopt those measures they shall contain a reference to this Directive or shall be accompanied by such a reference on the occasion of their official publication. The methods of making such references shall be laid down by the Member States.

The Member States shall communicate to the Commission, within two years of the entry into force of this Directive, all the information necessary for the Commission to draw up a report to the European Parliament and the Council on the application of this Directive.

Article 8 [Addressees]

8–089 This Directive is addressed to the Member States.

Council Directive 2000/43 of 29 June 2000, implementing the principle of equal treatment between persons irrespective of racial or ethnic origin

([2000] OJ L180/22; Doc. Ref. 32000L0043)

The Council of the European Union,

8–090 Having regard to the Treaty establishing the European Community and in particular Article 13 thereof,

Having regard to the proposal from the Commission,

Having regard to the opinion of the European Parliament,[74]

Having regard to the opinion of the Economic and Social Committee,[75]

Having regard to the opinion of the Committee of the Regions,[76]

Whereas:

(1) The Treaty on European Union marks a new stage in the process of creating an ever closer union among the peoples of Europe.

(2) In accordance with Article 6 of the Treaty on European Union, the European Union is founded on the principles of liberty, democracy, respect for human rights and fundamental freedoms, and the rule of law, principles which are common to the Member States, and should respect fundamental rights as guaranteed by the European Convention for the protection of Human Rights and Fundamental Freedoms and as they result from the constitutional traditions common to the Member States, as general principles of Community Law.

(3) The right to equality before the law and protection against discrimination for all persons constitutes a universal right recognised by the Universal Declaration of Human Rights, the United Nations Convention on the Elimination of all forms of Discrimination Against Women, the International Convention on the Elimination of all forms of Racial Discrimination and the United Nations Covenants on Civil and Political Rights and on Economic, Social and Cultural Rights and by the European Convention for the Protection of Human Rights and Fundamental Freedoms, to which all Member States are signatories.

(4) It is important to respect such fundamental rights and freedoms, including the right to freedom of association. It is also important, in the context of the access to and provision of goods and services, to respect the protection of private and family life and transactions carried out in this context.

[73] Words inserted by Directive 98/52 Art. 2 as from 22 July 1998.

[74] Opinion delivered on 18 May 2000.

[75] Opinion delivered on 12 April 2000.

[76] Opinion delivered on 31 May 2000.

(5) The European Parliament has adopted a number of Resolutions on the fight against racism in the European Union.

(6) The European Union rejects theories which attempt to determine the existence of separate human races. The use of the term "racial origin" in this Directive does not imply an acceptance of such theories.

(7) The European Council in Tampere, on 15 and 16 October 1999, invited the Commission to come forward as soon as possible with proposals implementing Article 13 of the EC Treaty as regards the fight against racism and xenophobia.

(8) The Employment Guidelines 2000 agreed by the European Council in Helsinki, on 10 and 11 December 1999, stress the need to foster conditions for a socially inclusive labour market by formulating a coherent set of policies aimed at combating discrimination against groups such as ethnic minorities.

(9) Discrimination based on racial or ethnic origin may undermine the achievement of the objectives of the EC Treaty, in particular the attainment of a high level of employment and of social protection, the raising of the standard of living and quality of life, economic and social cohesion and solidarity. It may also undermine the objective of developing the European Union as an area of freedom, security and justice.

(10) The Commission presented a communication on racism, xenophobia and anti-Semitism in December 1995.

(11) The Council adopted on 15 July 1996, Joint Action (96/443/JHA) concerning action to combat racism and xenophobia[77] under which the Member States undertake to ensure effective judicial co-operation in respect of offences based on racist or xenophobic behaviour.

(12) To ensure the development of democratic and tolerant societies which allow the participation of all persons irrespective of racial or ethnic origin, specific action in the field of discrimination based on racial or ethnic origin should go beyond access to employed and self-employed activities and cover areas such as education, social protection including social security and health-care, social advantages and access to and supply of goods and services.

(13) To this end, any direct or indirect discrimination based on racial or ethnic origin as regards the areas covered by this Directive should be prohibited throughout the Community. This prohibition of discrimination should also apply to nationals of third countries, but does not cover differences of treatment based on nationality and is without prejudice to provisions governing the entry and residence of third-country nationals and their access to employment and to occupation.

(14) In implementing the principle of equal treatment irrespective of racial or ethnic origin, the Community should, in accordance with Article 3(2) of the EC Treaty, aim to eliminate inequalities, and to promote equality between men and women, especially since women are often the victims of multiple discrimination.

(15) The appreciation of the facts from which it may be inferred that there has been direct or indirect discrimination is a matter for national judicial or other competent bodies, in accordance with rules of national law or practice. Such rules may provide in particular for indirect discrimination to be established by any means including on the basis of statistical evidence.

(16) It is important to protect all natural persons against discrimination on grounds of racial or ethnic origin. Member States should also provide, where appropriate and in accordance with their national traditions and practice, protection for legal persons where they suffer discrimination on grounds of the racial or ethnic origin of their members.

(17) The prohibition of discrimination should be without prejudice to the maintenance or adoption of measures intended to prevent or compensate for disadvantages suffered by a group of persons of a particular racial or ethnic origin, and such measures may permit organisations of persons of a particular racial or

---

[77] [1996] OJ L185/5.

ethnic origin where their main object is the promotion of the special needs of those persons.

(18) In very limited circumstances, a difference of treatment may be justified where a characteristic related to racial or ethnic origin constitutes a genuine and determining occupational requirement, when the objective is legitimate and the requirement is proportionate. Such circumstances should be included in the information provided by the Member States to the Commission.

(19) Persons who have been subject to discrimination based on racial and ethnic origin should have adequate means of legal protection. To provide a more effective level of protection, associations or legal entities should also be empowered to engage, as the Member States so determine, either on behalf or in support of any victim, in proceedings, without prejudice to national rules of procedure concerning representation and defence before the courts.

(20) The effective implementation of the principle of equality requires adequate judicial protection against victimisation.

(21) The rules on the burden of proof must be adapted when there is a prima facie case of discrimination and, for the principle of equal treatment to be applied effectively, the burden of proof must shift back to the respondent when evidence of such discrimination is brought.

(22) Member States need not apply the rules on the burden of proof to proceedings in which it is for the court or other competent body to investigate the facts of the case. The procedures thus referred to are those in which the plaintiff is not required to prove the facts, which it is for the court or competent body to investigate.

(23) Member States should promote dialogue between the social partners and with non-governmental organisations to address different forms of discrimination and to combat them.

(24) Protection against discrimination based on racial or ethnic origin would itself be strengthened by the existence of a body or bodies in each Member State, with competence to analyse the problems involved, to study possible solutions and to provide concrete assistance for the victims.

(25) This Directive lays down minimum requirements, thus giving the Member States the option of introducing or maintaining more favourable provisions. The implementation of this Directive should not serve to justify any regression in relation to the situation which already prevails in each Member State.

(26) Member States should provide for effective, proportionate and dissuasive sanctions in case of breaches of the obligations under this Directive.

(27) The Member States may entrust management and labour, at their joint request, with the implementation of this Directive as regards provisions falling within the scope of collective agreements, provided that the Member States take all the necessary steps to ensure that they can at all times guarantee the results imposed by this Directive.

(28) In accordance with the principles of subsidiarity and proportionality as set out in Article 5 of the EC Treaty, the objective of this Directive, namely ensuring a common high level of protection against discrimination in all the Member States, cannot be sufficiently achieved by the Member States and can therefore, by reason of the scale and impact of the proposed action, be better achieved by the Community. This Directive does not go beyond what is necessary in order to achieve those objectives,

Has adopted this Directive:

Chapter I—General Provisions

Article 1 Purpose

8–091 The purpose of this Directive is to lay down a framework for combating discrimination on the grounds of racial or ethnic origin, with a view to putting into effect in the Member States the principle of equal treatment.

Article 2 Concept of discrimination

1. For the purposes of this Directive, the principle of equal treatment shall mean that there shall be no direct or indirect discrimination based on racial or ethnic origin. **8–092**

2. For the purposes of paragraph 1:
(a) direct discrimination shall be taken to occur where one person is treated less favourably than another is, has been or would be treated in a comparable situation on grounds of racial or ethnic origin;
(b) indirect discrimination shall be taken to occur where an apparently neutral provision, criterion or practice would put persons of a racial or ethnic origin at a particular disadvantage compared with other persons, unless that provision, criterion or practice is objectively justified by a legitimate aim and the means of achieving that aim are appropriate and necessary.

3. Harassment shall be deemed to be discrimination within the meaning of paragraph 1, when an unwanted conduct related to racial or ethnic origin takes place with the purpose or effect of violating the dignity of a person and of creating an intimidating, hostile, degrading, humiliating or offensive environment. In this context, the concept of harassment may be defined in accordance with the national laws and practice of the Member States.

4. An instruction to discriminate against persons on grounds of racial or ethnic origin shall be deemed to be discrimination within the meaning of paragraph 1.

Article 3 Scope

1. Within the limits of the powers conferred upon the Community, this Directive shall apply to all persons, as regards both the public and private sectors, including public bodies, in relation to: **8–093**
(a) conditions for access to employment, to self-employment and to occupation, including selection criteria and recruitment conditions, whatever the branch of activity and at all levels of the professional hierarchy, including promotion;
(b) access to all types and to all levels of vocational guidance, vocational training, advanced vocational training and retraining, including practical work experience;
(c) employment and working conditions, including dismissals and pay;
(d) membership of and involvement in an organisation of workers or employers, or any organisation whose members carry on a particular profession, including the benefits provided for by such organisations;
(e) social protection, including social security and healthcare;
(f) social advantages;
(g) education;
(h) access to and supply of goods and services which are available to the public, including housing.

2. This Directive does not cover difference of treatment based on nationality and is without prejudice to provisions and conditions relating to the entry into and residence of third-country nationals and stateless persons on the territory of Member States, and to any treatment which arises from the legal status of the third-country nationals and stateless persons concerned.

Article 4 Genuine and determining occupational requirements

Notwithstanding Article 2(1) and (2), Member States may provide that a difference of treatment which is based on a characteristic related to racial or ethnic origin shall not constitute discrimination where, by reason of the nature of the particular occupational activities concerned or of the context in which they are carried out, such a characteristic constitutes a genuine and determining **8–094** occupational requirement, provided that the objective is legitimate and the requirement is proportionate.

Article 5 Positive action

8–095 With a view to ensuring full equality in practice, the principle of equal treatment shall not prevent any Member State from maintaining or adopting specific measures to prevent or compensate for disadvantages linked to racial or ethnic origin.

Article 6 Minimum requirements

8–096 1. Member States may introduce or maintain provisions which are more favourable to the protection of the principle of equal treatment than those laid down in this Directive.

2. The implementation of this Directive shall under no circumstances constitute grounds for a reduction in the level of protection against discrimination already afforded by Member States in the fields covered by this Directive.

Chapter II—Remedies and Enforcement

Article 7 Defence of rights

8–097 1. Member States shall ensure that judicial and/or administrative procedures, including where they deem it appropriate conciliation procedures, for the enforcement of obligations under this Directive are available to all persons who consider themselves wronged by failure to apply the principle of equal treatment to them, even after the relationship in which the discrimination is alleged to have occurred has ended.

2. Member States shall ensure that associations, organisations or other legal entities, which have, in accordance with the criteria laid down by their national law, a legitimate interest in ensuring that the provisions of this Directive are complied with, may engage, either on behalf or in support of the complainant, with his or her approval, in any judicial and/or administrative procedure provided for the enforcement of obligations under this Directive.

3. Paragraphs 1 and 2 are without prejudice to national rules relating to time limits for bringing actions as regards the principle of equality of treatment.

Article 8 Burden of proof

8–098 1. Member States shall take such measures as are necessary, in accordance with their national judicial systems, to ensure that, when persons who consider themselves wronged because the principle of equal treatment has not been applied to them establish, before a court or other competent authority, facts from which it may be presumed that there has been direct or indirect discrimination, it shall be for the respondent to prove that there has been no breach of the principle of equal treatment.

2. Paragraph 1 shall not prevent Member States from introducing rules of evidence which are more favourable to plaintiffs.

3. Paragraph 1 shall not apply to criminal procedures.

4. Paragraphs 1, 2 and 3 shall also apply to any proceedings brought in accordance with Article 7(2).

5. Member States need not apply paragraph 1 to proceedings in which it is for the court or competent body to investigate the facts of the case.

Article 9 Victimisation

Member States shall introduce into their national legal systems such measures as are necessary to protect individuals from any adverse treatment or adverse consequence as a reaction to a complaint or to proceedings aimed at enforcing compliance with the principle of equal treatment. **8–099**

Article 10 Dissemination of information

Member States shall take care that the provisions adopted pursuant to this Directive, together with the relevant provisions already in force, are brought to the attention of the persons concerned by all appropriate means throughout their territory. **8–100**

Article 11 Social dialogue

1. Member States shall, in accordance with national traditions and practice, take adequate measures to promote the social dialogue between the two sides of industry with a view to fostering equal treatment, including through the monitoring of workplace practices, collective agreements, codes of conduct, research or exchange of experiences and good practices. **8–101**

2. Where consistent with national traditions and practice, Member States shall encourage the two sides of the industry without prejudice to their autonomy to conclude, at the appropriate level, agreements laying down anti-discrimination rules in the fields referred to in Article 3 which fall within the scope of collective bargaining. These agreements shall respect the minimum requirements laid down by this Directive and the relevant national implementing measures.

Article 12 Dialogue with non-governmental organisations

Member States shall encourage dialogue with appropriate non-governmental organisations which have, in accordance with their national law and practice, a legitimate interest in contributing to the fight against discrimination on grounds of racial and ethnic origin with a view to promoting the principle of equal treatment. **8–102**

Chapter III—Bodies for the Promotion of Equal Treatment

Article 13 [Designation; competences]

1. Member States shall designate a body or bodies for the promotion of equal treatment of all persons without discrimination on the grounds of racial or ethnic origin. These bodies may form part of agencies charged at national level with the defence of human rights or the safeguard of individuals' rights. **8–103**

2. Member States shall ensure that the competences of these bodies include:
— without prejudice to the right of victims and of associations, organisations or other legal entities referred to in Article 7(2), providing independent assistance to victims of discrimination in pursuing their complaints about discrimination,
— conducting independent surveys concerning discrimination,
— publishing independent reports and making recommendations on any issue relating to such discrimination.

Chapter IV—Final Provisions

Article 14 Compliance

8–104 Member States shall take the necessary measures to ensure that:

(a) any laws, regulations and administrative provisions contrary to the principle of equal treatment are abolished;

(b) any provisions contrary to the principle of equal treatment which are included in individual or collective contracts or agreements, internal rules of undertakings, rules governing profit-making or non-profit-making associations, and rules governing the independent professions and workers' and employers' organisations, are or may be declared, null and void or are amended.

Article 15 Sanctions

8–105 Member States shall lay down the rules on sanctions applicable to infringements of the national provisions adopted pursuant to this Directive and shall take all measures necessary to ensure that they are applied. The sanctions, which may comprise the payment of compensation to the victim, must be effective, proportionate and dissuasive. The Member States shall notify those provisions to the Commission by 19 July 2003, at the latest and shall notify it without delay of any subsequent amendment affecting them.

Article 16 Implementation

8–106 Member States shall adopt the laws, regulations and administrative provisions necessary to comply with this Directive by 19 July 2003, or may entrust management and labour, at their joint request, with the implementation of this Directive as regards provisions falling within the scope of collective agreements. In such cases, Member States shall ensure that by 19 July 2003, management and labour introduce the necessary measures by agreement, Member States being required to take any necessary measures to enable them at any time to be in a position to guarantee the results imposed by this Directive. They shall forthwith inform the Commission thereof.

When Member States adopt these measures, they shall contain a reference to this Directive or be accompanied by such a reference on the occasion of their official publication. The methods of making such a reference shall be laid down by the Member States.

Article 17 Report

8–107 1. Member States shall communicate to the Commission by 19 July 2005, and every five years thereafter, all the information necessary for the Commission to draw up a report to the European Parliament and the Council on the application of this Directive.

2. The Commission's report shall take into account, as appropriate, the views of the European Monitoring Centre on Racism and Xenophobia, as well as the viewpoints of the social partners and relevant non-governmental organisations. In accordance with the principle of gender mainstreaming, this report shall, *inter alia*, provide an assessment of the impact of the measures taken on women and men. In the light of the information received, this report shall include, if necessary, proposals to revise and update this Directive.

Article 18 Entry into force

8–108 This Directive shall enter into force on the day of its publication in the *Official Journal of the European Communities*.[78]

[78] The Directive was published on 19 July 2000.

Article 19 Addressees

This Directive is addressed to the Member States. **8–109**

Council Directive 2000/78 of 27 November 2000, establishing a general framework for equal treatment in employment and occupation

([2000] OJ L303/16; Doc. Ref. 32000L0078)

The Council of the European Union, **8–110**

Having regard to the Treaty establishing the European Community, and in particular Article 13 thereof,

Having regard to the proposal from the Commission,[79]

Having regard to the Opinion of the European Parliament,[80]

Having regard to the Opinion of the Economic and Social Committee,[81]

Having regard to the Opinion of the Committee of the Regions,[82]

Whereas:

(1) In accordance with Article 6 of the Treaty on European Union, the European Union is founded on the principles of liberty, democracy, respect for human rights and fundamental freedoms, and the rule of law, principles which are common to all Member States and it respects fundamental rights, as guaranteed by the European Convention for the Protection of Human Rights and Fundamental Freedoms and as they result from the constitutional traditions common to the Member States, as general principles of Community law.

(2) The principle of equal treatment between women and men is well established by an important body of Community law, in particular in Council Directive 76/207 of 9 February 1976, on the implementation of the principle of equal treatment for men and women as regards access to employment, vocational training and promotion, and working conditions.[83]

(3) In implementing the principle of equal treatment, the Community should, in accordance with Article 3(2) of the EC Treaty, aim to eliminate inequalities, and to promote equality between men and women, especially since women are often the victims of multiple discrimination.

(4) The right of all persons to equality before the law and protection against discrimination constitutes a universal right recognised by the Universal Declaration of Human Rights, the United Nations Convention on the Elimination of All Forms of Discrimination against Women, United Nations Covenants on Civil and Political Rights and on Economic, Social and Cultural Rights and by the European Convention for the Protection of Human Rights and Fundamental Freedoms, to which all Member States are signatories. Convention No. 111 of the International Labour Organisation (ILO) prohibits discrimination in the field of employment and occupation.

(5) It is important to respect such fundamental rights and freedoms. This Directive does not prejudice freedom of association, including the right to establish unions with others and to join unions to defend one's interests.

(5) It is important to respect such fundamental rights and freedoms. This Directive does not prejudice freedom of association, including the right to establish unions with others and to join unions to defend one's interests.

(6) The Community Charter of the Fundamental Social Rights of Workers recognises the importance of combating every form of discrimination, including the need to take appropriate action for the social and economic integration of elderly and disabled people.

---

[79] [2000] OJ C177/42.

[80] Opinion delivered on 12 October 2000.

[81] [2000] OJ C204/82.

[82] [2000] OJ C226/1.

[83] [1976] OJ L39/40 (see above).

(7) The EC Treaty includes among its objectives the promotion of co-ordination between employment policies of the Member States. To this end, a new employment chapter was incorporated in the EC Treaty as a means of developing a co-ordinated European strategy for employment to promote a skilled, trained and adaptable workforce.

(8) The Employment Guidelines for 2000 agreed by the European Council at Helsinki on 10 and 11 December 1999, stress the need to foster a labour market favourable to social integration by formulating a coherent set of policies aimed at combating discrimination against groups such as persons with disability. They also emphasise the need to pay particular attention to supporting older workers, in order to increase their participation in the labour force.

(9) Employment and occupation are key elements in guaranteeing equal opportunities for all and contribute strongly to the full participation of citizens in economic, cultural and social life and to realising their potential.

(10) On 29 June 2000, the Council adopted Directive 2000/43[84] implementing the principle of equal treatment between persons irrespective of racial or ethnic origin. That Directive already provides protection against such discrimination in the field of employment and occupation.

(11) Discrimination based on religion or belief, disability, age or sexual orientation may undermine the achievement of the objectives of the EC Treaty, in particular the attainment of a high level of employment and social protection, raising the standard of living and the quality of life, economic and social cohesion and solidarity, and the free movement of persons.

(12) To this end, any direct or indirect discrimination based on religion or belief, disability, age or sexual orientation as regards the areas covered by this Directive should be prohibited throughout the Community. This prohibition of discrimination should also apply to nationals of third countries but does not cover differences of treatment based on nationality and is without prejudice to provisions governing the entry and residence of third-country nationals and their access to employment and occupation.

(13) This Directive does not apply to social security and social protection schemes whose benefits are not treated as income within the meaning given to that term for the purpose of applying Article 141 of the EC Treaty, nor to any kind of payment by the State aimed at providing access to employment or maintaining employment.

(14) This Directive shall be without prejudice to national provisions laying down retirement ages.

8–111 (15) The appreciation of the facts from which it may be inferred that there has been direct or indirect discrimination is a matter for national judicial or other competent bodies, in accordance with rules of national law or practice. Such rules may provide, in particular, for indirect discrimination to be established by any means including on the basis of statistical evidence.

(16) The provision of measures to accommodate the needs of disabled people at the workplace plays an important role in combating discrimination on grounds of disability.

(17) This Directive does not require the recruitment, promotion, maintenance in employment or training of an individual who is not competent, capable and available to perform the essential functions of the post concerned or to undergo the relevant training, without prejudice to the obligation to provide reasonable accommodation for people with disabilities.

(18) This Directive does not require, in particular, the armed forces and the police, prison or emergency services to recruit or maintain in employment persons who do not have the required capacity to carry out the range of functions that they may be called upon to perform with regard to the legitimate objective of preserving the operational capacity of those services.

[84] [2000] OJ L180/22 (see above).

(19) Moreover, in order that the Member States may continue to safeguard the combat effectiveness of their armed forces, they may choose not to apply the provisions of this Directive concerning disability and age to all or part of their armed forces. The Member States which make that choice must define the scope of that derogation.

(20) Appropriate measures should be provided, *i.e.* effective and practical measures to adapt the workplace to the disability, for example adapting premises and equipment, patterns of working time, the distribution of tasks or the provision of training or integration resources.

(21) To determine whether the measures in question give rise to a disproportionate burden, account should be taken in particular of the financial and other costs entailed, the scale and financial resources of the organisation or undertaking and the possibility of obtaining public funding or any other assistance.

(22) This Directive is without prejudice to national laws on marital status and the benefits dependent thereon.

(23) In very limited circumstances, a difference of treatment may be justified where a characteristic related to religion or belief, disability, age or sexual orientation constitutes a genuine and determining occupational requirement, when the objective is legitimate and the requirement is proportionate. Such circumstances should be included in the information provided by the Member States to the Commission.

(24) The European Union in its Declaration No. 11 on the status of churches and non-confessional organisations, annexed to the Final Act of the Amsterdam Treaty, has explicitly recognised that it respects and does not prejudice the status under national law of churches and religious associations or communities in the Member States and that it equally respects the status of philosophical and non-confessional organisations. With this in view, Member States may maintain or lay down specific provisions on genuine, legitimate and justified occupational requirements which might be required for carrying out an occupational activity.

(25) The prohibition of age discrimination is an essential part of meeting the aims set out in the Employment Guidelines and encouraging diversity in the workforce. However, differences in treatment in connection with age may be justified under certain circumstances and therefore require specific provisions which may vary in accordance with the situation in Member States. It is therefore essential to distinguish between differences in treatment which are justified, in particular by legitimate employment policy, labour market and vocational training objectives, and discrimination which must be prohibited.

(26) The prohibition of discrimination should be without prejudice to the maintenance or adoption of measures intended to prevent or compensate for disadvantages suffered by a group of persons of a particular religion or belief, disability, age or sexual orientation, and such measures may permit organisations of persons of a particular religion or belief, disability, age or sexual orientation where their main object is the promotion of the special needs of those persons.

(27) In its Recommendation 86/379 of 24 July 1986, on the employment of disabled people in the Community,[85] the Council established a guideline framework setting out examples of positive action to promote the employment and training of disabled people, and in its Resolution of 17 June 1999, on equal employment opportunities for people with disabilities,[86] affirmed the importance of giving specific attention inter alia to recruitment, retention, training and lifelong learning with regard to disabled persons.

(28) This Directive lays down minimum requirements, thus giving the Member States the option of introducing or maintaining more favourable provisions. The

[85] [1986] OJ L225/43.
[86] [1999] OJ C186/3.

implementation of this Directive should not serve to justify any regression in relation to the situation which already prevails in each Member State.

(29) Persons who have been subject to discrimination based on religion or belief, disability, age or sexual orientation should have adequate means of legal protection. To provide a more effective level of protection, associations or legal entities should also be empowered to engage in proceedings, as the Member States so determine, either on behalf or in support of any victim, without prejudice to national rules of procedure concerning representation and defence before the courts.

(30) The effective implementation of the principle of equality requires adequate judicial protection against victimisation.

(31) The rules on the burden of proof must be adapted when there is a prima facie case of discrimination and, for the principle of equal treatment to be applied effectively, the burden of proof must shift back to the respondent when evidence of such discrimination is brought. However, it is not for the respondent to prove that the plaintiff adheres to a particular religion or belief, has a particular disability, is of a particular age or has a particular sexual orientation.

(32) Member States need not apply the rules on the burden of proof to proceedings in which it is for the court or other competent body to investigate the facts of the case. The procedures thus referred to are those in which the plaintiff is not required to prove the facts, which it is for the court or competent body to investigate.

(33) Member States should promote dialogue between the social partners and, within the framework of national practice, with non-governmental organisations to address different forms of discrimination at the workplace and to combat them.

(34) The need to promote peace and reconciliation between the major communities in Northern Ireland necessitates the incorporation of particular provisions into this Directive.

(35) Member States should provide for effective, proportionate and dissuasive sanctions in case of breaches of the obligations under this Directive.

(36) Member States may entrust the social partners, at their joint request, with the implementation of this Directive, as regards the provisions concerning collective agreements, provided they take any necessary steps to ensure that they are at all times able to guarantee the results required by this Directive.

(37) In accordance with the principle of subsidiarity set out in Article 5 of the EC Treaty, the objective of this Directive, namely the creation within the Community of a level playing-field as regards equality in employment and occupation, cannot be sufficiently achieved by the Member States and can therefore, by reason of the scale and impact of the action, be better achieved at Community level. In accordance with the principle of proportionality, as set out in that Article, this Directive does not go beyond what is necessary in order to achieve that objective,

Has adopted this Directive:

Chapter I—General Provisions

Article 1 Purpose

8–112 The purpose of this Directive is to lay down a general framework for combating discrimination on the grounds of religion or belief, disability, age or sexual orientation as regards employment and occupation, with a view to putting into effect in the Member States the principle of equal treatment.

Article 2 Concept of discrimination

8–113 1. For the purposes of this Directive, the "principle of equal treatment" shall mean that there shall be no direct or indirect discrimination whatsoever on any of the grounds referred to in Article 1.

2. For the purposes of paragraph 1:
(a) direct discrimination shall be taken to occur where one person is treated less favourably than another is, has been or would be treated in a comparable situation, on any of the grounds referred to in Article 1;
(b) indirect discrimination shall be taken to occur where an apparently neutral provision, criterion or practice would put persons having a particular religion or belief, a particular disability, a particular age, or a particular sexual orientation at a particular disadvantage compared with other persons unless:
 (i) that provision, criterion or practice is objectively justified by a legitimate aim and the means of achieving that aim are appropriate and necessary, or
 (ii) as regards persons with a particular disability, the employer or any person or organisation to whom this Directive applies, is obliged, under national legislation, to take appropriate measures in line with the principles contained in Article 5 in order to eliminate disadvantages entailed by such provision, criterion or practice.

3. Harassment shall be deemed to be a form of discrimination within the meaning of paragraph 1, when unwanted conduct related to any of the grounds referred to in Article 1 takes place with the purpose or effect of violating the dignity of a person and of creating an intimidating, hostile, degrading, humiliating or offensive environment. In this context, the concept of harassment may be defined in accordance with the national laws and practice of the Member States.

4. An instruction to discriminate against persons on any of the grounds referred to in Article 1 shall be deemed to be discrimination within the meaning of paragraph 1.

5. This Directive shall be without prejudice to measures laid down by national law which, in a democratic society, are necessary for public security, for the maintenance of public order and the prevention of criminal offences, for the protection of health and for the protection of the rights and freedoms of others.

Article 3 Scope

1. Within the limits of the areas of competence conferred on the Community, this Directive shall apply to all persons, as regards both the public and private sectors, including public bodies, in relation to: **8–114**
(a) conditions for access to employment, to self-employment or to occupation, including selection criteria and recruitment conditions, whatever the branch of activity and at all levels of the professional hierarchy, including promotion;
(b) access to all types and to all levels of vocational guidance, vocational training, advanced vocational training and retraining, including practical work experience;
(c) employment and working conditions, including dismissals and pay;
(d) membership of, and involvement in, an organisation of workers or employers, or any organisation whose members carry on a particular profession, including the benefits provided for by such organisations.

2. This Directive does not cover differences of treatment based on nationality and is without prejudice to provisions and conditions relating to the entry into and residence of third-country nationals and stateless persons in the territory of Member States, and to any treatment which arises from the legal status of the third-country nationals and stateless persons concerned.

3. This Directive does not apply to payments of any kind made by state schemes or similar, including state social security or social protection schemes.

4. Member States may provide that this Directive, in so far as it relates to discrimination on the grounds of disability and age, shall not apply to the armed forces.

Article 4 Occupational requirements

8–115 1. Notwithstanding Article 2(1) and (2), Member States may provide that a difference of treatment which is based on a characteristic related to any of the grounds referred to in Article 1 shall not constitute discrimination where, by reason of the nature of the particular occupational activities concerned or of the context in which they are carried out, such a characteristic constitutes a genuine and determining occupational requirement, provided that the objective is legitimate and the requirement is proportionate.

2. Member States may maintain national legislation in force at the date of adoption of this Directive or provide for future legislation incorporating national practices existing at the date of adoption of this Directive pursuant to which, in the case of occupational activities within churches and other public or private organisations the ethos of which is based on religion or belief, a difference of treatment based on a person's religion or belief shall not constitute discrimination where, by reason of the nature of these activities or of the context in which they are carried out, a person's religion or belief constitute a genuine, legitimate and justified occupational requirement, having regard to the organisation's ethos. This difference of treatment shall be implemented taking account of Member States' constitutional provisions and principles, as well as the general principles of Community law, and should not justify discrimination on another ground.

Provided that its provisions are otherwise complied with, this Directive shall thus not prejudice the right of churches and other public or private organisations, the ethos of which is based on religion or belief, acting in conformity with national constitutions and laws, to require individuals working for them to act in good faith and with loyalty to the organisation's ethos.

Article 5 Reasonable accommodation for disabled persons

8–116 In order to guarantee compliance with the principle of equal treatment in relation to persons with disabilities, reasonable accommodation shall be provided. This means that employers shall take appropriate measures, where needed in a particular case, to enable a person with a disability to have access to, participate in, or advance in employment, or to undergo training, unless such measures would impose a disproportionate burden on the employer. This burden shall not be disproportionate when it is sufficiently remedied by measures existing within the framework of the disability policy of the Member State concerned.

Article 6 Justification of differences of treatment on grounds of age

8–117 1. Notwithstanding Article 2(2), Member States may provide that differences of treatment on grounds of age shall not constitute discrimination, if, within the context of national law, they are objectively and reasonably justified by a legitimate aim, including legitimate employment policy, labour market and vocational training objectives, and if the means of achieving that aim are appropriate and necessary.

Such differences of treatment may include, among others:

(a) the setting of special conditions on access to employment and vocational training, employment and occupation, including dismissal and remuneration conditions, for young people, older workers and persons with caring responsibilities in order to promote their vocational integration or ensure their protection;

(b) the fixing of minimum conditions of age, professional experience or seniority in service for access to employment or to certain advantages linked to employment;

(c) the fixing of a maximum age for recruitment which is based on the training requirements of the post in question or the need for a reasonable period of employment before retirement.

2. Notwithstanding Article 2(2), Member States may provide that the fixing for occupational social security schemes of ages for admission or entitlement to retirement or invalidity benefits, including the fixing under those schemes of different ages for employees or groups or categories of employees, and the use, in the context of such schemes, of age criteria in actuarial calculations, does not constitute discrimination on the grounds of age, provided this does not result in discrimination on the grounds of sex.

Article 7 Positive action

1. With a view to ensuring full equality in practice, the principle of equal treatment shall not prevent any Member State from maintaining or adopting specific measures to prevent or compensate for disadvantages linked to any of the grounds referred to in Article 1. **8–118**

2. With regard to disabled persons, the principle of equal treatment shall be without prejudice to the right of Member States to maintain or adopt provisions on the protection of health and safety at work or to measures aimed at creating or maintaining provisions or facilities for safeguarding or promoting their integration into the working environment.

Article 8 Minimum requirements

1. Member States may introduce or maintain provisions which are more favourable to the protection of the principle of equal treatment than those laid down in this Directive. **8–119**

2. The implementation of this Directive shall under no circumstances constitute grounds for a reduction in the level of protection against discrimination already afforded by Member States in the fields covered by this Directive.

Chapter II—Remedies and Enforcement

Article 9 Defence of rights

1. Member States shall ensure that judicial and/or administrative procedures, including where they deem it appropriate conciliation procedures, for the enforcement of obligations under this Directive are available to all persons who consider themselves wronged by failure to apply the principle of equal treatment to them, even after the relationship in which the discrimination is alleged to have occurred has ended. **8–120**

2. Member States shall ensure that associations, organisations or other legal entities which have, in accordance with the criteria laid down by their national law, a legitimate interest in ensuring that the provisions of this Directive are complied with, may engage, either on behalf or in support of the complainant, with his or her approval, in any judicial and/or administrative procedure provided for the enforcement of obligations under this Directive.

3. Paragraphs 1 and 2 are without prejudice to national rules relating to time-limits for bringing actions as regards the principle of equality of treatment.

Article 10 Burden of proof

1. Member States shall take such measures as are necessary, in accordance with their national judicial systems, to ensure that, when persons who consider themselves wronged because the principle of equal treatment has not been applied to them establish, before a court or other competent authority, facts from which it may be presumed that there has been direct or indirect discrimination, it shall be for the respondent to prove that there has been no breach of the principle of equal treatment. **8–121**

2. Paragraph 1 shall not prevent Member States from introducing rules of evidence which are more favourable to plaintiffs.

3. Paragraph 1 shall not apply to criminal procedures.

4. Paragraphs 1, 2 and 3 shall also apply to any legal proceedings commenced in accordance with Article 9(2).

5. Member States need not apply paragraph 1 to proceedings in which it is for the court or competent body to investigate the facts of the case.

Article 11 Victimisation

8–122 Member States shall introduce into their national legal systems such measures as are necessary to protect employees against dismissal or other adverse treatment by the employer as a reaction to a complaint within the undertaking or to any legal proceedings aimed at enforcing compliance with the principle of equal treatment.

Article 12 Dissemination of information

8–123 Member States shall take care that the provisions adopted pursuant to this Directive, together with the relevant provisions already in force in this field, are brought to the attention of the persons concerned by all appropriate means, for example at the workplace, throughout their territory.

Article 13 Social dialogue

8–124 1. Member States shall, in accordance with their national traditions and practice, take adequate measures to promote dialogue between the social partners with a view to fostering equal treatment, including through the monitoring of workplace practices, collective agreements, codes of conduct and through research or exchange of experiences and good practices.

2. Where consistent with their national traditions and practice, Member States shall encourage the social partners, without prejudice to their autonomy, to conclude at the appropriate level agreements laying down anti-discrimination rules in the fields referred to in Article 3 which fall within the scope of collective bargaining. These agreements shall respect the minimum requirements laid down by this Directive and by the relevant national implementing measures.

Article 14 Dialogue with non-governmental organisations

8–125 Member States shall encourage dialogue with appropriate non-governmental organisations which have, in accordance with their national law and practice, a legitimate interest in contributing to the fight against discrimination on any of the grounds referred to in Article 1 with a view to promoting the principle of equal treatment.

Chapter III—Particular Provisions

Article 15 Northern Ireland

8–126 1. In order to tackle the under-representation of one of the major religious communities in the police service of Northern Ireland, differences in treatment regarding recruitment into that service, including its support staff, shall not constitute discrimination insofar as those differences in treatment are expressly authorised by national legislation.

2. In order to maintain a balance of opportunity in employment for teachers in Northern Ireland while furthering the reconciliation of historical divisions between the major religious communities there, the provisions on religion or

belief in this Directive shall not apply to the recruitment of teachers in schools in Northern Ireland in so far as this is expressly authorised by national legislation.

CHAPTER IV—FINAL PROVISIONS

Article 16 Compliance

Member States shall take the necessary measures to ensure that: **8–127**

(a) any laws, regulations and administrative provisions contrary to the principle of equal treatment are abolished;

(b) any provisions contrary to the principle of equal treatment which are included in contracts or collective agreements, internal rules of undertakings or rules governing the independent occupations and professions and workers' and employers' organisations are, or may be, declared null and void or are amended.

Article 17 Sanctions

Member States shall lay down the rules on sanctions applicable to infringements **8–128** of the national provisions adopted pursuant to this Directive and shall take all measures necessary to ensure that they are applied. The sanctions, which may comprise the payment of compensation to the victim, must be effective, proportionate and dissuasive. Member States shall notify those provisions to the Commission by 2 December 2003, at the latest and shall notify it without delay of any subsequent amendment affecting them.

Article 18 Implementation

Member States shall adopt the laws, regulations and administrative provisions **8–129** necessary to comply with this Directive by 2 December 2003, at the latest or may entrust the social partners, at their joint request, with the implementation of this Directive as regards provisions concerning collective agreements. In such cases, Member States shall ensure that, no later than 2 December 2003, the social partners introduce the necessary measures by agreement, the Member States concerned being required to take any necessary measures to enable them at any time to be in a position to guarantee the results imposed by this Directive. They shall forthwith inform the Commission thereof.

In order to take account of particular conditions, Member States may, if necessary, have an additional period of 3 years from 2 December 2003, that is to say a total of six years, to implement the provisions of this Directive on age and disability discrimination. In that event they shall inform the Commission forthwith. Any Member State which chooses to use this additional period shall report annually to the Commission on the steps it is taking to tackle age and disability discrimination and on the progress it is making towards implementation. The Commission shall report annually to the Council.

When Member States adopt these measures, they shall contain a reference to this Directive or be accompanied by such reference on the occasion of their official publication. The methods of making such reference shall be laid down by Member States.

Article 19 Report

1. Member States shall communicate to the Commission, by 2 December 2005, at **8–130** the latest and every five years thereafter, all the information necessary for the Commission to draw up a report to the European Parliament and the Council on the application of this Directive.

2. The Commission's report shall take into account, as appropriate, the viewpoints of the social partners and relevant non-governmental organisations. In

accordance with the principle of gender mainstreaming, this report shall, *inter alia*, provide an assessment of the impact of the measures taken on women and men. In the light of the information received, this report shall include, if necessary, proposals to revise and update this Directive.

Article 20 Entry into force

8–131 This Directive shall enter into force on the day of its publication in the *Official Journal of the European Communities*.[87]

Article 21 Addressees

8–132 This Directive is addressed to the Member States.

[87] The Directive was published on 2 December 2000.

CHAPTER 9

SOCIAL POLICY: WORKER PROTECTION

Council Directive 80/987 of 20 October 1980, on the protection of employees in the event of the insolvency of their employer[1]

([1980] OJ L283/23; Doc. Ref. 31980L0987)

The Council of the European Communities, 9–001

Having regard to the Treaty establishing the [European Community], and in particular Article [94] thereof,

Having regard to the proposal from the Commission,[2]

Having regard to the opinion of the European Parliament,[3]

Having regard to the opinion of the Economic and Social Committee,[4]

[1] Whereas it is necessary to provide for the protection of employees in the event of the insolvency of their employer, in particular in order to guarantee payment of their outstanding claims, while taking account of the need for balanced economic and social development in the Community;

[2] Whereas differences still remain between the Member States as regards the extent of the protection of employees in this respect whereas efforts should be directed towards reducing these differences, which can have a direct effect on the functioning of the common market;

[3] Whereas the approximation of laws in this field should, therefore, be promoted while the improvement within the meaning of Article [136] of the Treaty is maintained;

Whereas as a result of the geographical situation and the present job structures in that area, the labour market in Greenland is fundamentally different from that of the other areas of the Community;

[4] Whereas to the extent that the Hellenic Republic is to become a member of the European Economic Community on January 1, 1981, in accordance with the Act concerning the Conditions of Accession of the Hellenic Republic and the Adjustments to the Treaties, it is appropriate to stipulate in the Annex to the Directive under the heading "Greece", those categories of employees whose claims may be excluded in accordance with Article 1(2) of the Directive,

Has adopted this Directive:

[SECTION I—SCOPE AND DEFINITIONS

Article 1 [Scope]

1. This Directive shall apply to employees' claims arising from contracts of employment or employment relationships and existing against employers who are in a state of insolvency within the meaning of Article 2(1). 9–002

2. Member States may, by way of exception, exclude claims by certain categories of employee from the scope of this Directive, by virtue of the existence of other forms of guarantee if it is established that these offer the persons concerned a degree of protection equivalent to that resulting from this Directive.

3. Where such provision already applies in their national legislation, Member States may continue to exclude from the scope of this Directive:

---

[1] Title of the Directive replaced by Directive 2002/74 ([2002] OJ L270/10) Art. 1(1) with effect from 8 October 2002.

[2] [1978] OJ C135/2.

[3] [1979] OJ C39/26.

[4] [1979] OJ C105/15.

(a) domestic servants employed by a natural person;
(b) share-fishermen.

Article 2 [Definitions]

9–003 1. For the purposes of this Directive, an employer shall be deemed to be in a state of insolvency where a request has been made for the opening of collective proceedings based on insolvency of the employer, as provided for under the laws, regulations and administrative provisions of a Member State, and involving the partial or total divestment of the employer's assets and the appointment of a liquidator or a person performing a similar task, and the authority which is competent pursuant to the said provisions has:
(a) either decided to open the proceedings, or
(b) established that the employer's undertaking or business has been definitively closed down and that the available assets are insufficient to warrant the opening of the proceedings.

2. This Directive is without prejudice to national law as regards the definition of the terms "employee", "employer", "pay", "right conferring immediate entitlement" and "right conferring prospective entitlement".

However, the Member States may not exclude from the scope of this Directive:
(a) part-time employees within the meaning of Directive 97/81;[5]
(b) workers with a fixed-term contract within the meaning of Directive 1999/70[6];
(c) workers with a temporary employment relationship within the meaning of Article 1(2) of Directive 91/383.[7]

3. Member States may not set a minimum duration for the contract of employment or the employment relationship in order for workers to qualify for claims under this Directive.

4. This Directive does not prevent Member States from extending workers' protection to other situations of insolvency, for example where payments have been de facto stopped on a permanent basis, established by proceedings different from those mentioned in paragraph 1 as provided for under national law.

Such procedures shall not however create a guarantee obligation for the institutions of the other Member States in the cases referred to in Section IIIa.][8]

Section II—Provisions Concerning Guarantee Institutions

[Article 3 [Guarantee of outstanding claims]

9–004 1. Member States shall take the measures necessary to ensure that guarantee institutions guarantee, subject to Article 4, payment of employees' outstanding claims resulting from contracts of employment or employment relationships, including, where provided for by national law, severance pay on termination of employment relationships.

The claims taken over by the guarantee institution shall be the outstanding pay claims relating to a period prior to and/or, as applicable, after a given date determined by the Member States.][9]

---

[5] Directive 97/81concerning the Framework Agreement on part-time work concluded by UNICE, CEEP and the ETUC [1998] OJ L14/9 (see below).

[6] Directive 1999/70 concerning the framework agreement on fixed-term work concluded by ETUC, UNICE and CEEP [1999] OJ L175/43.

[7] Directive 91/383 supplementing the measures to encourage improvements in the safety and health at work of workers with a fixed-duration employment relationship or a temporary employment relationship [1991] OJ L206/19.

[8] Section I replaced by Directive 2002/74 ([2002] OJ L270/10), Art. 1(2) with effect from 8 October 2002. Member States are to comply by 8 October 2005.

[9] Art. 3 replaced by Directive 2002/74, Art. 1(3) with effect from 8 October 2002. Member States are to comply by 8 October 2005.

[Article 4 [Limit to liability of guarantee institutions]

1. Member States shall have the option to limit the liability of the guarantee institutions referred to in Article 3. **9–005**

2. When Member States exercise the option referred to in paragraph 1, they shall specify the length of the period for which outstanding claims are to be met by the guarantee institution. However, this may not be shorter than a period covering the remuneration of the last three months of the employment relationship prior to and/or after the date referred to in Article 3. Member States may include this minimum period of three months in a reference period with a duration of not less than six months.

Member States having a reference period of not less than 18 months may limit the period for which outstanding claims are met by the guarantee institution to eight weeks. In this case, those periods which are most favourable to the employee are used for the calculation of the minimum period.

3. Furthermore, Member States may set ceilings on the payments made by the guarantee institution. These ceilings must not fall below a level which is socially compatible with the social objective of this Directive.

When Member States exercise this option, they shall inform the Commission of the methods used to set the ceiling.][10]

Article 5 [Organisation of guarantee institutions]

Member States shall lay down detailed rules for the organisation, financing and operation of the guarantee institutions, complying with the following principles in particular: **9–006**

(a) the assets of the institutions shall be independent of the employers' operating capital and be inaccessible to proceedings for insolvency;

(b) employers shall contribute to financing, unless it is fully covered by the public authorities;

(c) the institutions' liabilities shall not depend on whether or not obligations to contribute to financing have been fulfilled.

Section III—Provisions Concerning Social Security

Article 6 [Guarantee does not cover social security contributions]

Member States may stipulate that Articles 3, 4 and 5 shall not apply to contributions due under national statutory social security schemes or under supplementary company or inter-company pension schemes outside the national statutory social security schemes. **9–007**

Article 7 [Protection of benefits]

Member States shall take the measures necessary to ensure that non-payment of compulsory contributions due from the employer, before the onset of his insolvency, to their insurance institutions under national statutory social security schemes does not adversely affect employees' benefit entitlement in respect of these insurance institutions inasmuch as the employees' contributions were deducted at source from the remuneration paid. **9–008**

Article 8 [Protection of pension rights]

Member States shall ensure that the necessary measures are taken to protect the interests of employees and of persons having already left the employer's **9–009**

[10] Art. 4 replaced by Directive 2002/74, Art. 1(3) with effect from 8 October 2002. Member States are to comply by 8 October 2005.

undertaking or business at the date of the onset of the employer's insolvency in respect of rights conferring on them immediate or prospective entitlement to old-age benefits, including survivors' benefits, under supplementary company or inter-company pension schemes outside the national statutory social security schemes.

[SECTION IIIA—PROVISIONS CONCERNING TRANSNATIONAL SITUATIONS

Article 8a [Undertakings operating in two or more Member States]

9–010 1. When an undertaking with activities in the territories of at least two Member States is in a state of insolvency within the meaning of Article 2(1), the institution responsible for meeting employees' outstanding claims shall be that in the Member State in whose territory they work or habitually work.

2. The extent of employees' rights shall be determined by the law governing the competent guarantee institution.

3. Member States shall take the measures necessary to ensure that, in the cases referred to in paragraph 1, decisions taken in the context of insolvency proceedings referred to in Article 2(1), which have been requested in another Member State, are taken into account when determining the employer's state of insolvency within the meaning of this Directive.

Article 8b [Exchange of information]

9–011 1. For the purposes of implementing Article 8a, Member States shall make provision for the sharing of relevant information between their competent administrative authorities and/or the guarantee institutions mentioned in Article 3, making it possible in particular to inform the guarantee institution responsible for meeting the employees' outstanding claims.

2. Member States shall notify the Commission and the other Member States of the contact details of their competent administrative authorities and/or guarantee institutions. The Commission shall make these communications publicly accessible.][11]

SECTION IV—GENERAL AND FINAL PROVISIONS

Article 9 [More favourable laws]

9–012 This Directive shall not affect the option of Member States to apply or introduce laws, regulations or administrative provisions which are more favourable to employees.

[Implementation of this Directive shall not under any circumstances be sufficient grounds for a regression in relation to the current situation in the Member States and in relation to the general level of protection of workers in the area covered by it.][12]

Article 10 [Avoidance of abuse]

9–013 This Directive shall not affect the option of Member States:
(a) to take the measures necessary to avoid abuses
(b) to refuse or reduce the liability referred to in Article 3 or the guarantee obligation referred to in Article 7 if it appears that fulfilment of the obligation is unjustifiable because of the existence of special links between the employee

[11] Section IIIa inserted by Directive 2002/74, Art. 1(4) with effect from 8 October 2002. Member States are to comply by 8 October 2005.

[12] In Art. 9, second paragraph inserted by Directive 2002/74, Art. 1(5) with effect from 8 October 2002. Member States are to comply by 8 October 2005.

and the employer and of common interests resulting in collusion between them.

(c) to refuse or reduce the liability referred to in Article 3 or the guarantee obligation referred to in Article 7 in cases where the employee, on his or her own or together with his or her close relatives, was the owner of an essential part of the employer's undertaking or business and had a considerable influence on its activities.][13]

Article 10a [Notification of national insolvency proceedings]

1. Member States shall notify the Commission and the other Member States of the types of national insolvency proceedings falling within the scope of this Directive, and of any amendments relating thereto. The Commission shall publish these communications in the *Official Journal of the European Communities*.][14] **9–014**

Article 11 [Implementation]

1. Member States shall bring into force the laws, regulations and administrative provisions necessary to comply with this Directive within 36 months of its notification. They shall forthwith inform the Commission thereof. **9–015**

2. Member States shall communicate to the Commission the texts of the laws, regulations and administrative provisions which they adopt in the field governed by this Directive.

Article 12 [Report]

Within 18 months of the expiry of the period of 36 months laid down in Article 11(1), Member States shall forward all relevant information to the Commission in order to enable it to draw up a report on the application of this Directive for submission to the Council. **9–016**

Article 13 [Addressees]

This Directive is addressed to the Member States. **9–017**

ANNEX—[...][15]

Council Directive 89/391 of 12 June 1989, on the introduction of measures to encourage improvements in the safety and health of workers at work

([1989] OJ L183/1, corrigendum [1990] OJ L275/42; Doc. Ref. 31989L0391)

The Council of the European Communities, **9–018**

Having regard to the Treaty establishing the [European Community], and in particular Article [138] thereof,

Having regard to the proposal from the Commission,[16] drawn up after consultation with the Advisory Committee on Safety, Hygiene and Health Protection at Work,

In co-operation with the European Parliament,[17]

Having regard to the opinion of the Economic and Social Committee,[18]

---

[13] In Art. 10, point (c) inserted by Directive 2002/74, Art. 1(6) with effect from 8 October 2002. Member States are to comply by 8 October 2005.

[14] Art. 10a inserted by Directive 2002/74, Art. 1(7) with effect from 8 October 2002. Member States are to comply by 8 October 2005.

[15] Annex deleted by Directive 2002/74, Art. 1(8) with effect from 8 October 2002.

[16] [1988] OJ C141/1.

[17] [1988] OJ C326/102, and [1989] OJ C158.

[18] [1988] OJ C175/22.

[1] Whereas Article [138] of the Treaty provides that the Council shall adopt, by means of Directives, minimum requirements for encouraging improvements, especially in the working environment, to guarantee a better level of protection of the safety and health of workers;

[2] Whereas this Directive does not justify any reduction in levels of protection already achieved in individual Member States, the Member State being committed, under the Treaty to encouraging improvements in conditions in this area and to harmonising conditions while maintaining the improvements made;

[3] Whereas it is known that workers can be exposed to the effects of dangerous environmental factors at the work place during the course of their working life;

[4] Whereas, pursuant to Article [138] of the Treaty, such Directives must avoid imposing administrative, financial and legal constraints which would hold back the creation and development of small and medium-sized undertakings;

[5] Whereas the communication from the Commission on its programme concerning safety, hygiene and health at work[19] provides for the adoption of Directives designed to guarantee the safety and health of workers;

[6] Whereas the Council, in its resolution of 12 December 1987, on safety, hygiene and health at work,[20] took note of the Commission's intention to submit to the Council in the near future a Directive on the organisation of the safety and health of workers at the work place;

[7] Whereas in February 1988 the European Parliament adopted four resolutions following the debate on the internal market and worker protection; whereas these resolutions specifically invited the Commission to draw up a framework Directive to serve as a basis for more specific Directives covering all the risks connected with safety and health at the work place;

[8] Whereas Member States have a responsibility to encourage improvements in the safety and health of workers on their territory; whereas taking measures to protect the health and safety of workers at work also helps, in certain cases, to preserve the health and possibly the safety of persons residing with them;

[9] Whereas Member States' legislative systems covering safety and health at the work place differ widely and need to be improved; whereas national provisions on the subject, which often include technical specifications and/or self-regulatory standards, may result in different levels of safety and health protection and allow competition at the expense of safety and health;

[10] Whereas the incidence of accidents at work and occupational diseases is still too high; whereas preventive measures must be introduced or improved without delay in order to safeguard the safety and health of workers and ensure a higher degree of protection;

[11] Whereas, in order to ensure an improved degree of protection, workers and/or their representatives must be informed of the risks to their safety and health and of the measures required to reduce or eliminate these risks; whereas they must also be in a position to contribute, by means of balanced participation in accordance with national laws and/or practices, to seeing that the necessary protective measures are taken;

[12] Whereas information, dialogue and balanced participation on safety and health at work must be developed between employers and workers and/or their representatives by means of appropriate procedures and instruments, in accordance with national laws and/or practices;

[13] Whereas the improvement of workers' safety, hygiene and health at work is an objective which should not be subordinated to purely economic considerations;

[14] Whereas employers shall be obliged to keep themselves informed of the latest advances in technology and scientific findings concerning work-place design, account being taken of the inherent dangers in their undertaking, and to inform accordingly the workers' representatives exercising participation rights

---

[19] [1988] OJ C28/3.
[20] [1988] OJ C28/1.

under this Directive, so as to be able to guarantee a better level of protection of workers' health and safety;

[15] Whereas the provisions of this Directive apply, without prejudice to more stringent present or future Community provisions, to all risks, and in particular to those arising from the use at work of chemical, physical and biological agents covered by Directive 80/1107,[21] as last amended by Directive 88/642[22];

[16] Whereas, pursuant to Decision 74/325,[23] the Advisory Committee on Safety, Hygiene and Health Protection at Work is consulted by the Commission on the drafting of proposals in this field;

[17] Whereas a Committee composed of members nominated by the Member States needs to be set up to assist the Commission in making the technical adaptations to the individual Directives provided for in this Directive,

Has adopted this Directive:

SECTION I—GENERAL PROVISIONS

Article 1 Object

1. The object of this Directive is to introduce measures to encourage improvements in the safety and health of workers at work. **9–019**

2. To that end it contains general principles concerning the prevention of occupational risks, the protection of safety and health, the elimination of risk and accident factors, the informing, consultation, balanced participation in accordance with national laws and/or practices and training of workers and their representatives, as well as general guidelines for the implementation of the said principles.

3. This Directive shall be without prejudice to existing or future national and Community provisions which are more favourable to protection of the safety and health of workers at work.

Article 2 Scope

1. This Directive shall apply to all sectors of activity, both public and private (industrial, agricultural, commercial, administrative, service, educational, cultural, leisure, etc.). **9–020**

2. This Directive shall not be applicable where characteristics peculiar to certain specific public service activities, such as the armed forces or the police, or to certain specific activities in the civil protection services inevitably conflict with it. In that event, the safety and health of workers must be ensured as far as possible in the light of the objectives of this Directive.

Article 3 Definitions

For the purposes of this Directive, the following terms shall have the following meanings: **9–021**

(a) worker: any person employed by an employer, including trainees and apprentices but excluding domestic servants;

(b) employer: any natural or legal person who has an employment relationship with the worker and has responsibility for the undertaking and/or establishment;

(c) workers' representative with specific responsibility for the safety and health of workers: any person elected, chosen or designated in accordance with national laws and/or practices to represent workers where problems arise relating to the safety and health protection of workers at work;

---

[21] [1980] OJ L327/8.

[22] [1988] OJ L356/74.

[23] [1974] OJ L185/15.

(d) prevention: all the steps or measures taken or planned at all stages of work in the undertaking to prevent or reduce occupational risks.

Article 4 [Enforcement]

9–022 1. Member States shall take the necessary steps to ensure that employers, workers and workers' representatives are subject to the legal provisions necessary for the implementation of this Directive.

2. In particular, Member States shall ensure adequate controls and supervision.

Section II—Employers' Obligations

Article 5 General provision

9–023 1. The employer shall have a duty to ensure the safety and health of workers in every aspect related to the work.

2. Where, pursuant to Article 7(3), an employer enlists competent external services or persons, this shall not discharge him from his responsibilities in this area.

3. The workers' obligations in the field of safety and health at work shall not affect the principle of the responsibility of the employer.

4. This Directive shall not restrict the option of Member States to provide for the exclusion or the limitation of employers' responsibility where occurrences are due to unusual and unforeseeable circumstances, beyond the employers' control, or to exceptional events, the consequences of which could not have been avoided despite the exercise of all due care.

Member States need not exercise the option referred to in the first sub-paragraph.

Article 6 General obligations on employers

9–024 1. Within the context of his responsibilities, the employer shall take the measures necessary for the safety and health protection of workers, including prevention of occupational risks and provision of information and training, as well as provision of the necessary organisation and means.

The employer shall be alert to the need to adjust these measures to take account of changing circumstances and aim to improve existing situations.

2. The employer shall implement the measures referred to in the first sub-paragraph of paragraph 1 on the basis of the following general principles of prevention:

(a) avoiding risks;
(b) evaluating the risks which cannot be avoided;
(c) combating the risks at source;
(d) adapting the work to the individual, especially as regards the design of work places, the choice of work equipment and the choice of working and production methods, with a view, in particular, to alleviating monotonous work and work at a predetermined work-rate and to reducing their effect on health;
(e) adapting to technical progress;
(f) replacing the dangerous by the non-dangerous or the less dangerous;
(g) developing a coherent overall prevention policy which covers technology, organisation of work, working conditions, social relationships and the influence of factors related to the working environment;
(h) giving collective protective measures priority over individual protective measures;
(i) giving appropriate instructions to the workers.

3. Without prejudice to the other provisions of this Directive, the employer shall, taking into account the nature of the activities of the enterprise and/or establishment:

(a) evaluate the risks to the safety and health of workers, *inter alia* in the choice of work equipment, the chemical substances or preparations used, and the fitting-out of work places.
Subsequent to this evaluation and as necessary, the preventive measures and the working and production methods implemented by the employer must:
- assure an improvement in the level of protection afforded to workers with regard to safety and health,
- be integrated into all the activities of the undertaking and/or establishment and at all hierarchical levels;

(b) where he entrusts tasks to a worker, take into consideration the worker's capabilities as regards health and safety;

(c) ensure that the planning and introduction of new technologies are the subject of consultation with the workers and/or their representatives, as regards the consequences of the choice of equipment, the working conditions and the working environment for the safety and health of workers;

(d) take appropriate steps to ensure that only workers who have received adequate instructions may have access to areas where there is serious and specific danger.

4. Without prejudice to the other provisions of this Directive, where several undertakings share a work place, the employers shall co-operate in implementing the safety, health and occupational hygiene provisions and, taking into account the nature of the activities, shall co-ordinate their actions in matters of the protection and prevention of occupational risks, and shall inform one another and their respective workers and/or workers' representatives of these risks.

5. Measures related to safety, hygiene and health at work may in no circumstances involve the workers in financial cost.

Article 7 Protective and preventive services

1. Without prejudice to the obligations referred to in Articles 5 and 6, the employer shall designate one or more workers to carry out activities related to the protection and prevention of occupational risks for the undertaking and/or establishment. **9–025**

2. Designated workers may not be placed at any disadvantage because of their activities related to the protection and prevention of occupational risks.
Designated workers shall be allowed adequate time to enable them to fulfil their obligations arising from this Directive.

3. If such protective and preventive measures cannot be organised for lack of competent personnel in the undertaking and/or establishment, the employer shall enlist competent external services or persons.

4. Where the employer enlists such services or persons, he shall inform them of the factors known to affect, or suspected of affecting, the safety and health of the workers and they must have access to the information referred to in Article 10(2).

5. In all cases:
- the workers designated must have the necessary capabilities and the necessary means,
- the external services or persons consulted must have the necessary aptitudes and the necessary personal and professional means, and
- the workers designated and the external services or persons consulted must be sufficient in number to deal with the organisation of protective and preventive measures, taking into account the size of the undertaking and/or

establishment and/or the hazards to which the workers are exposed and their distribution throughout the entire undertaking and/or establishment.

6. The protection from, and prevention of, the health and safety risks which form the subject of this Article shall be the responsibility of one or more workers, of one service or of separate services whether from inside or outside the undertaking and/or establishment.

The worker(s) and/or agency(ies) must work together whenever necessary.

7. Member States may define, in the light of the nature of the activities and size of the undertakings, the categories of undertakings in which the employer, provided he is competent, may himself take responsibility for the measures referred to in paragraph 1.

8. Member States shall define the necessary capabilities and aptitudes referred to in paragraph 5.
They may determine the sufficient number referred to in paragraph 5.

Article 8 First aid, fire-fighting and evacuation of workers, serious and imminent danger

9–026 1. The employer shall:
— take the necessary measures for first aid, fire-fighting and evacuation of workers, adapted to the nature of the activities and the size of the undertaking and/or establishment and taking into account other persons present,
— arrange any necessary contacts with external services, particularly as regards first aid, emergency medical care, rescue work and fire-fighting.

2. Pursuant to paragraph 1, the employer shall, *inter alia*, for first aid, fire-fighting and the evacuation of workers, designate the workers required to implement such measures.
The number of such workers, their training and the equipment available to them shall be adequate, taking account of the size and/or specific hazards of the undertaking and/or establishment.

3. The employer shall:
(a) as soon as possible, inform all workers who are, or may be, exposed to serious and imminent danger of the risk involved and of the steps taken or to be taken as regards protection;
(b) take action and give instructions to enable workers in the event of serious, imminent and unavoidable danger to stop work and/or immediately to leave the work place and proceed to a place of safety;
(c) save in exceptional cases for reasons duly substantiated, refrain from asking workers to resume work in a working situation where there is still a serious and imminent danger.

4. Workers who, in the event of serious, imminent and unavoidable danger, leave their workstation and/or a dangerous area may not be placed at any disadvantage because of their action and must be protected against any harmful and unjustified consequences, in accordance with national laws and/or practices.

5. The employer shall ensure that all workers are able, in the event of serious and imminent danger to their own safety and/or that of other persons, and where the immediate superior responsible cannot be contacted, to take the appropriate steps in the light of their knowledge and the technical means at their disposal, to avoid the consequences of such danger.

Their actions shall not place them at any disadvantage, unless they acted carelessly or there was negligence on their part.

Article 9 Various obligations on employers

1. The employer shall: 9–027
(a) be in possession of an assessment of the risks to safety and health at work, including those facing groups of workers exposed to particular risks;
(b) decide on the protective measures to be taken and, if necessary, the protective equipment to be used;
(c) keep a list of occupational accidents resulting in a worker being unfit for work for more than three working days;
(d) draw up, for the responsible authorities and in accordance with national laws and/or practices, reports on occupational accidents suffered by his workers.

2. Member States shall define, in the light of the nature of the activities and size of the undertakings, the obligations to be met by the different categories of undertakings in respect of the drawing-up of the documents provided for in paragraph 1(a) and (b) and when preparing the documents provided for in paragraph 1(c) and (d).

Article 10 Worker information

1. The employer shall take appropriate measures so that workers and/or their representatives in the undertaking and/or establishment receive, in accordance with national laws and/or practices which may take account, *inter alia*, of the size of the undertaking and/or establishment, all the necessary information concerning: 9–028
(a) the safety and health risks and protective and preventive measures and activities in respect of both the undertaking and/or establishment in general and each type of workstation and/or job;
(b) the measures taken pursuant to Article 8(2).

2. The employer shall take appropriate measures so that employers of workers from any outside undertakings and/or establishments engaged in work in his undertaking and/or establishment receive, in accordance with national laws and/or practices, adequate information concerning the points referred to in paragraph 1(a) and (b) which is to be provided to the workers in question.

3. The employer shall take appropriate measures so that workers with specific functions in protecting the safety and health of workers, or workers' representatives with specific responsibility for the safety and health of workers shall have access, to carry out their functions and in accordance with national laws and/or practices, to:
(a) the risk assessment and protective measures referred to in Article 9(1)(a) and (b);
(b) the list and reports referred to in Article 9(1)(c) and (d);
(c) the information yielded by protective and preventive measures, inspection agencies and bodies responsible for safety and health.

Article 11 Consultation and participation of workers

1. Employers shall consult workers and/or their representatives and allow them to take part in discussions on all questions relating to safety and health at work. 9–029

This presupposes:
— the consultation of workers,
— the right of workers and/or their representatives to make proposals,
— balanced participation in accordance with national laws and/or practices.

2. Workers or workers' representatives with specific responsibility for the safety and health of workers shall take part in a balanced way, in accordance with

national laws and/or practices, or shall be consulted in advance and in good time by the employer with regard to:

(a) any measure which may substantially affect safety and health;
(b) the designation of workers referred to in Articles 7(1) and 8 (2) and the activities referred to in Article 7(1);
(c) the information referred to in Articles 9(1) and 10;
(d) the enlistment, where appropriate, of the competent services or persons outside the undertaking and/or establishment, as referred to in Article 7(3);
(e) the planning and organisation of the training referred to in Article 12.

3. Workers' representatives with specific responsibility for the safety and health of workers shall have the right to ask the employer to take appropriate measures and to submit proposals to him to that end to mitigate hazards for workers and/or to remove sources of danger.

4. The workers referred to in paragraph 2 and the workers' representatives referred to in paragraphs 2 and 3 may not be placed at a disadvantage because of their respective activities referred to in paragraphs 2 and 3.

5. Employers must allow workers' representatives with specific responsibility for the safety and health of workers adequate time off work, without loss of pay, and provide them with the necessary means to enable such representatives to exercise their rights and functions deriving from this Directive.

6. Workers and/or their representatives are entitled to appeal, in accordance with national law and/or practice, to the authority responsible for safety and health protection at work if they consider that the measures taken and the means employed by the employer are inadequate for the purposes of ensuring safety and health at work.

Workers' representatives must be given the opportunity to submit their observations during inspection visits by the competent authority.

Article 12 Training of workers

9–030 1. The employer shall ensure that each worker receives adequate safety and health training, in particular in the form of information and instructions specific to his workstation or job:

— on recruitment,
— in the event of a transfer or a change of job,
— in the event of the introduction of new work equipment or a change in equipment,
— in the event of the introduction of any new technology.

The training shall be:

— adapted to take account of new or changed risks, and
— repeated periodically if necessary.

2. The employer shall ensure that workers from outside undertakings and/or establishments engaged in work in his undertaking and/or establishment have in fact received appropriate instructions regarding health and safety risks during their activities in his undertaking and/or establishment.

3. Workers' representatives with a specific role in protecting the safety and health of workers shall be entitled to appropriate training.

4. The training referred to in paragraphs 1 and 3 may not be at the workers' expense or at that of the workers' representatives.

The training referred to in paragraph 1 must take place during working hours.

The training referred to in paragraph 3 must take place during working hours or in accordance with national practice either within or outside the undertaking and/or the establishment.

SECTION III—WORKERS' OBLIGATIONS

Article 13 [Workers' responsibilities]

1. It shall be the responsibility of each worker to take care as far as possible of his own safety and health and that of other persons affected by his acts or Commissions at work in accordance with his training and the instructions given by his employer. **9–031**

2. To this end, workers must in particular, in accordance with their training and the instructions given by their employer:

(a) make correct use of machinery, apparatus, tools, dangerous substances, transport equipment and other means of production;

(b) make correct use of the personal protective equipment supplied to them and, after use, return it to its proper place;

(c) refrain from disconnecting, changing or removing arbitrarily safety devices fitted, *e.g.* to machinery, apparatus, tools, plant and buildings, and use such safety devices correctly;

(d) immediately inform the employer and/or the workers with specific responsibility for the safety and health of workers of any work situation they have reasonable grounds for considering represents a serious and immediate danger to safety and health and of any shortcomings in the protection arrangements;

(e) co-operate, in accordance with national practice, with the employer and/or workers with specific responsibility for the safety and health of workers, for as long as may be necessary to enable any tasks or requirements imposed by the competent authority to protect the safety and health of workers at work to be carried out;

(f) co-operate, in accordance with national practice, with the employer and/or workers with specific responsibility for the safety and health of workers, for as long as may be necessary to enable the employer to ensure that the working environment and working conditions are safe and pose no risk to safety and health within their field of activity.

SECTION IV—MISCELLANEOUS PROVISIONS

Article 14 Health surveillance

1. To ensure that workers receive health surveillance appropriate to the health and safety risks they incur at work, measures shall be introduced in accordance with national law and/or practices. **9–032**

2. The measures referred to in paragraph 1 shall be such that each worker, if he so wishes, may receive health surveillance at regular intervals.

3. Health surveillance may be provided as part of a national health system.

Article 15 Risk groups

Particularly sensitive risk groups must be protected against the dangers which specifically affect them. **9–033**

Article 16 Individual Directives—Amendments—General scope of this Directive

9–034 1. The Council, acting on a proposal from the Commission based on Article [138] of the Treaty, shall adopt individual Directives, *inter alia*, in the areas listed in the Annex.[24]

2. This Directive and, without prejudice to the procedure referred to in Article 17 concerning technical adjustments, the individual Directives may be amended in accordance with the procedure provided for in Article [138] of the Treaty.

3. The provisions of this Directive shall apply in full to all the areas covered by the individual Directives, without prejudice to more stringent and/or specific provisions contained in these individual Directives.

Article 17 Committee

9–035 1. For the purely technical adjustments to the individual Directives provided for in Article 16(1) to take account of:

---

[24] Individual directives adopted under Art. 16(1) currently in force:

- Directive 89/654 concerning the minimum safety and health requirements for the workplace (first individual Directive) ([1989] OJ L393/1);
- Directive 89/655 concerning the minimum safety and health requirements for the use of work equipment by workers at work (second individual Directive) ([1989] OJ L393/13);
- Directive 89/656 on the minimum health and safety requirements for the use by workers of personal protective equipment at the workplace (third individual Directive) ([1989] OJ L393/18);
- Directive 90/269 on the minimum health and safety requirements for the manual handling of loads where there is a risk particularly of back injury to workers (fourth individual Directive) ([1990] OJ L156/9);
- Directive 90/270 on the minimum safety and health requirements for work with display screen equipment (fifth individual Directive) ([1990] OJ L156/14);
- Directive 90/394 on the protection of workers from the risks related to exposure to carcinogens at work (sixth individual Directive) ([1990] OJ L196/1);
- Directive 92/57 on the implementation of minimum safety and health requirements at temporary or mobile construction sites (eighth individual Directive) ([1992] OJ L245/6);
- Directive 92/58 on the minimum requirements for the provision of safety and/or health signs at work (ninth individual Directive) ([1992] OJ L245/23);
- Directive 92/85 on the introduction of measures to encourage improvements in the safety and health at work of pregnant workers and workers who have recently given birth or are breastfeeding (10th individual Directive) ([1992] OJ L348/1) (see below);
- Directive 92/91 concerning the minimum requirements for improving the safety and health protection of workers in the mineral-extracting industries through drilling (11th individual Directive) ([1992] OJ L348/9);
- Directive 92/104 on the minimum requirements for improving the safety and health protection of workers in surface and underground mineral-extracting industries (12th individual Directive) ([1992] OJ L404/10);
- Directive 93/103 concerning the minimum safety and health requirements for work on board fishing vessels (13th individual Directive) ([1993] OJ L307/1);
- Directive 98/24 on the protection of the health and safety of workers from the risks related to chemical agents at work (14th individual Directive) ([1998] OJ L131/11);
- Directive 1999/92 on minimum requirements for improving the safety and health protection of workers potentially at risk from explosive atmospheres (15th individual Directive) ([1999] OJ L23/57);
- Directive 2000/54 on the protection of workers from risks related to exposure to biological agents at work (seventh individual Directive) ([2000] OJ L262/21);
- Directive 2002/44 on the minimum health and safety requirements regarding the exposure of workers to the risks arising from physical agents (vibration) (16th individual Directive) ([2002] OJ L177/13);
- Directive 2003/10 on the minimum health and safety requirements regarding the exposure of workers to the risks arising from physical agents (noise) (17th individual Directive) ([2003] OJ L42/38).

— the adoption of Directives in the field of technical harmonisation and standardisation, and/or
— technical progress, changes in international regulations or specifications, and new findings.

The Commission shall be assisted by a committee composed of the representatives of the Member States and chaired by the representative of the Commission.

2. The representative of the Commission shall submit to the committee a draft of the measures to be taken.

The committee shall deliver its opinion on the draft within a time-limit which the chairman may lay down according to the urgency of the matter.

The opinion shall be delivered by the majority laid down in Article [205(2)] of the Treaty in the case of decisions which the Council is required to adopt on a proposal from the Commission.

The votes of the representatives of the Member States within the committee shall be weighted in the manner set out in that Article. The chairman shall not vote.

3. The Commission shall adopt the measures envisaged if they are in accordance with the opinion of the committee.

If the measures envisaged are not in accordance with the opinion of the committee, or if no opinion is delivered, the Commission shall, without delay, submit to the Council a proposal relating to the measures to be taken. The Council shall act by a qualified majority.

If, on the expiry of three months from the date of the referral to the Council, the Council has not acted, the proposed measures shall be adopted by the Commission.

Article 18 Final provisions

1. Member States shall bring into force the laws, regulations and administrative provisions necessary to comply with this Directive by 31 December 1992. **9–036**

They shall forthwith inform the Commission thereof.

2. Member States shall communicate to the Commission the texts of the provisions of national law which they have already adopted or adopt in the field covered by this Directive.

3. Member States shall report to the Commission every five years on the practical implementation of the provisions of this Directive, indicating the points of view of employers and workers.

The Commission shall inform the European Parliament, the Council, the Economic and Social Committee and the Advisory Committee on Safety, Hygiene and Health Protection at Work.

4. The Commission shall submit periodically to the European Parliament, the Council and the Economic and Social Committee a report on the implementation of this Directive, taking into account paragraphs 1 to 3.

Article 19 [Addressees]

This Directive is addressed to the Member States. **9–037**

Annex—List of Areas Referred to in Article 16(1)

— Work places **9–038**
— Work equipment
— Personal protective equipment
— Work with visual display units

— Handling of heavy loads involving risk of back injury
— Temporary or mobile work sites
— Fisheries and agriculture

Council Directive 91/533 of 14 October 1991 on an employer's obligation to inform employees of the conditions applicable to the contract or employment relationship

([1991] OJ L288/32; Doc. Ref. 31991L0533)

9–039 *The Council of the European Communities*,

Having regard to the Treaty establishing the European Economic Community, and in particular Article [94] thereof,

Having regard to the proposal from the Commission,[25]

Having regard to the opinion of the European Parliament,[26]

Having regard to the opinion of the Economic and Social Committee,[27]

[1] Whereas the development, in the Member States, of new forms of work has led to an increase in the number of types of employment relationship;

[2] Whereas, faced with this development, certain Member States have considered it necessary to subject employment relationships to formal requirements whereas these provisions are designed to provide employees with improved protection against possible infringements of their rights and to create greater transparency on the labour market;

[3] Whereas the relevant legislation of the Member States differs considerably on such fundamental points as the requirement to inform employees in writing of the main terms of the contract or employment relationship;

[4] Whereas differences in the legislation of Member States may have a direct effect on the operation of the common market;

[5] Whereas Article [136] of the Treaty provides for the Member States to agree upon the need to promote improved working conditions and an improved standard of living for workers, so as to make possible their harmonisation while the improvement is being maintained;

[6] Whereas point 9 of the Community Charter of Fundamental Social Rights for Workers, adopted at the Strasbourg European Council on 9 December 1989, by the Heads of State and Government of 11 Member States, states: "The conditions of employment of every worker of the European Community shall be stipulated in laws, a collective agreement or a contract of employment, according to arrangements applying in each country.";

[7] Whereas it is necessary to establish at Community level the general requirement that every employee must be provided with a document containing information on the essential elements of his contract or employment relationship;

[8] Whereas, in view of the need to maintain a certain degree of flexibility in employment relationships, Member States should be able to exclude certain limited cases of employment relationship from this Directive's scope of application;

[9] Whereas the obligation to provide information may be met by means of a written contract, a letter of appointment or one or more other documents or, if they are lacking, a written statement signed by the employer;

[10] Whereas, in the case of expatriation of the employee, the latter must, in addition to the main terms of his contract or employment relationship, be supplied with relevant information connected with his secondment;

[11] Whereas, in order to protect the interests of employees with regard to obtaining a document, any change in the main terms of the contract or employment relationship must be communicated to them in writing;

[25] [1991] OJ C24/3.
[26] [1991] OJ C240/21.
[27] [1991] OJ C159/32.

[12] Whereas it is necessary for Member States to guarantee that employees can claim the rights conferred on them by this Directive;

[13] Whereas Member States are to adopt the laws, regulations and legislative provisions necessary to comply with this Directive or are to ensure that both sides of industry set up the necessary provisions by agreement, with Member States being obliged to take the necessary steps enabling them at all times to guarantee the results imposed by this Directive,

Has adopted this Directive:

Article 1 Scope

1. This Directive shall apply to every paid employee having a contract or employment relationship defined by the law in force in a Member State and/or governed by the law in force in a Member State. **9–040**

2. Member States may provide that this Directive shall not apply to employees having a contract or employment relationship:

(a) — with a total duration not exceeding one month, and/or
— with a working week not exceeding eight hours or

(b) of a casual and/or specific nature provided, in these cases, that its non-application is justified by objective considerations.

Article 2 Obligation to provide information

1. An employer shall be obliged to notify an employee to whom this Directive applies, hereinafter referred to as "the employee", of the essential aspects of the contract or employment relationship. **9–041**

2. The information referred to in paragraph 1 shall cover at least the following:

(a) the identities of the parties;

(b) the place of work where there is no fixed or main place of work, the principle that the employee is employed at various places and the registered place of business or, where appropriate, the domicile of the employer;

(c)(i) the title, grade, nature or category of the work for which the employee is employed; or

(ii) a brief specification or description of the work;

(d) the date of commencement of the contract or employment relationship;

(e) in the case of a temporary contract or employment relationship, the expected duration thereof;

(f) the amount of paid leave to which the employee is entitled or, where this cannot be indicated when the information is given, the procedures for allocating and determining such leave;

(g) the length of the periods of notice to be observed by the employer and the employee should their contract or employment relationship be terminated or, where this cannot be indicated when the information is given, the method for determining such periods of notice;

(h) the initial basic amount, the other component elements and the frequency of payment of the remuneration to which the employee is entitled;

(i) the length of the employee's normal working day or week;

(j) where appropriate;

(i) the collective agreements governing the employee's conditions of work; or

(ii) in the case of collective agreements concluded outside the business by special joint bodies or institutions, the name of the competent body or joint institution within which the agreements were concluded.

3. The information referred to in paragraph 2(f), (g), (h) and (i) may, where appropriate, be given in the form of a reference to the laws, regulations and administrative or statutory provisions or collective agreements governing those particular points.

Article 3 Means of information

9–042 1. The information referred to in Article 2(2) may be given to the employee, not later than two months after the commencement of employment, in the form of:
(a) a written contract of employment; and/or
(b) a letter of engagement; and/or
(c) one or more other written documents, where one of these documents contains at least all the information referred to in Article 2(2) (a), (b), (c), (d), (h) and (i).

2. Where none of the documents referred to in paragraph 1 is handed over to the employee within the prescribed period, the employer shall be obliged to give the employee, not later than two months after the commencement of employment, a written declaration signed by the employer and containing at least the information referred to in Article 2(2).

Where the document(s) referred to in paragraph 1 contain only part of the information required, the written declaration provided for in the first sub-paragraph of this paragraph shall cover the remaining information.

3. Where the contract or employment relationship comes to an end before expiry of a period of two months as from the date of the start of work, the information provided for in Article 2 and in this Article must be made available to the employee by the end of this period at the latest.

Article 4 Expatriate employees

9–043 1. Where an employee is required to work in a country or countries other than the Member State whose law and/or practice governs the contract or employment relationship, the document(s) referred to in Article 3 must be in his/her possession before his/her departure and must include at least the following additional information:
(a) the duration of the employment abroad;
(b) the currency to be used for the payment of remuneration;
(c) where appropriate, the benefits in cash or kind attendant on the employment abroad;
(d) where appropriate, the conditions governing the employee's repatriation.

2. The information referred to in paragraph 1(b) and (c) may, where appropriate, be given in the form of a reference to the laws, regulations and administrative or statutory provisions or collective agreements governing those particular points.

3. Paragraphs 1 and 2 shall not apply if the duration of the employment outside the country whose law and/or practice governs the contract or employment relationship is one month or less.

Article 5 Modification of aspects of the contract or employment relationship

9–044 1. Any change in the details referred to in Articles 2(2) and 4(1) must be the subject of a written document to be given by the employer to the employee at the earliest opportunity and not later than one month after the date of entry into effect of the change in question.

2. The written document referred to in paragraph 1 shall not be compulsory in the event of a change in the laws, regulations and administrative or statutory provisions or collective agreements cited in the documents referred to in Article 3, supplemented, where appropriate, pursuant to Article 4(1).

Article 6 **Form and proof of the existence of a contract or employment relationship and procedural rules**

This Directive shall be without prejudice to national law and practice concerning: **9–045**
- the form of the contract or employment relationship,
- proof as regards the existence and content of a contract or employment relationship,
- the relevant procedural rules.

Article 7 **More favourable provisions**

This Directive shall not affect Member States' prerogative to apply or to introduce **9–046** laws, regulations or administrative provisions which are more favourable to employees or to encourage or permit the application of agreements which are more favourable to employees.

Article 8 **Defence of rights**

1. Member States shall introduce into their national legal systems such measures **9–047** as are necessary to enable all employees who consider themselves wronged by failure to comply with the obligations arising from this Directive to pursue their claims by judicial process after possible recourse to other competent authorities.

2. Member States may provide that access to the means of redress referred to in paragraph 1 are subject to the notification of the employer by the employee and the failure by the employer to reply within 15 days of notification.

However, the formality of prior notification may in no case be required in the cases referred to in Article 4, neither for workers with a temporary contract or employment relationship, nor for employees not covered by a collective agreement or by collective agreements relating to the employment relationship.

Article 9 **Final provisions**

1. Member States shall adopt the laws, regulations and administrative provisions **9–048** necessary to comply with this Directive no later than June 30, 1993, or shall ensure by that date that the employers' and workers' representatives introduce the required provisions by way of agreement, the Member States being obliged to take the necessary steps enabling them at all times to guarantee the results imposed by this Directive.

They shall forthwith inform the Commission thereof.

2. Member States shall take the necessary measures to ensure that, in the case of employment relationships in existence upon entry into force of the provisions that they adopt, the employer gives the employee, on request, within two months of receiving that request any of the documents referred to in Article 3, supplemented, where appropriate, pursuant to Article 4(1).

3. When Member States adopt the measures referred to in paragraph 1, such measures shall contain a reference to this Directive or shall be accompanied by such reference on the occasion of their official publication. The methods of making such a reference shall be laid down by the Member States.

4. Member States shall forthwith inform the Commission of the measures they take to implement this Directive.

Article 10 [Addressees]

9–049 This Directive is addressed to the Member States

Council Directive 92/85 of 19 October 1992, on the introduction of measures to encourage improvements in the safety and health at work of pregnant workers and workers who have recently given birth or are breast-feeding (tenth individual Directive within the meaning of Article 16 (1) of Directive 89/391)

([1992] OJ L348/1; Doc. Ref. 31992L0085)

9–050 *The Council of the European Communities,*

Having regard to the Treaty establishing the European Economic Community, and in particular Article [138] thereof,

Having regard to the proposal from the Commission, drawn up after consultation with the Advisory Committee on Safety, Hygiene and Health Protection at work,[28]

In co-operation with the European Parliament,[29]

Having regard to the opinion of the Economic and Social Committee,[30]

[1] Whereas Article [138] of the Treaty provides that the Council shall adopt, by means of directives, minimum requirements for encouraging improvements, especially in the working environment, to protect the safety and health of workers;

[2] Whereas this Directive does not justify any reduction in levels of protection already achieved in individual Member States, the Member States being committed, under the Treaty, to encouraging improvements in conditions in this area and to harmonising conditions while maintaining the improvements made;

[3] Whereas, under the terms of Article [138] of the Treaty, the said directives are to avoid imposing administrative, financial and legal constraints in a way which would hold back the creation and development of small and medium-sized undertakings;

[4] Whereas, pursuant to Decision 74/325,[31] as last amended by the 1985 Act of Accession, the Advisory Committee on Safety, Hygiene and Health protection at Work is consulted by the Commission on the drafting of proposals in this field;

[5] Whereas the Community Charter of the fundamental social rights of workers, adopted at the Strasbourg European Council on 9 December 1989, by the Heads of State or Government of 11 Member States, lays down, in paragraph 19 in particular, that: "Every worker must enjoy satisfactory health and safety conditions in his working environment. Appropriate measures must be taken in order to achieve further harmonisation of conditions in this area while maintaining the improvements made";

[6] Whereas the Commission, in its action programme for the implementation of the Community Charter of the fundamental social rights of workers, has included among its aims the adoption by the Council of a Directive on the protection of pregnant women at work;

[7] Whereas Article 15 of Council Directive 89/391 of 12 June 1989, on the introduction of measures to encourage improvements in the safety and health of workers at work[32] provides that particularly sensitive risk groups must be protected against the dangers which specifically affect them;

[8] Whereas pregnant workers, workers who have recently given birth or who are breast-feeding must be considered a specific risk group in many respects, and measures must be taken with regard to their safety and health;

[9] Whereas the protection of the safety and health of pregnant workers, workers who have recently given birth or workers who are breast-feeding should

---

28 [1990] OJ C281/3 and [1991] OJ C25/9.

29 [1991] OJ C19/177 and [1992] OJ C150/99.

30 [1991] OJ C41/29.

31 [1974] OJ L185/15.

32 [1989] OJ L183/1 (see above).

not treat women on the labour market unfavourably nor work to the detriment of directives concerning equal treatment for men and women;

[10] Whereas some types of activities may pose a specific risk, for pregnant workers, workers who have recently given birth or workers who are breast-feeding, of exposure to dangerous agents, processes or working conditions whereas such risks must therefore be assessed and the result of such assessment communicated to female workers and/or their representatives;

[11] Whereas, further, should the result of this assessment reveal the existence of a risk to the safety or health of the female worker, provision must be made for such worker to be protected;

[12] Whereas pregnant workers and workers who are breast-feeding must not engage in activities which have been assessed as revealing a risk of exposure, jeopardising safety and health, to certain particularly dangerous agents or working conditions;

[13] Whereas provision should be made for pregnant workers, workers who have recently given birth or workers who are breast-feeding not to be required to work at night where such provision is necessary from the point of view of their safety and health;

[14] Whereas the vulnerability of pregnant workers, workers who have recently given birth or who are breast-feeding makes it necessary for them to be granted the right to maternity leave of at least 14 continuous weeks, allocated before and/or after confinement, and renders necessary the compulsory nature of maternity leave of at least two weeks, allocated before and/or after confinement;

[15] Whereas the risk of dismissal for reasons associated with their condition may have harmful effects on the physical and mental state of pregnant workers, workers who have recently given birth or who are breast-feeding whereas provision should be made for such dismissal to be prohibited;

[16] Whereas measures for the organisation of work concerning the protection of the health of pregnant workers, workers who have recently given birth or workers who are breast-feeding would serve no purpose unless accompanied by the maintenance of rights linked to the employment contract, including maintenance of payment and/or entitlement to an adequate allowance;

[17] Whereas, moreover, provision concerning maternity leave would also serve no purpose unless accompanied by the maintenance of rights linked to the employment contract and or entitlement to an adequate allowance;

[18] Whereas the concept of an adequate allowance in the case of maternity leave must be regarded as a technical point of reference with a view to fixing the minimum level of protection and should in no circumstances be interpreted as suggesting an analogy between pregnancy and illness,

Has adopted this Directive:

SECTION I—PURPOSE AND DEFINITIONS

Article 1 Purpose

1. The purpose of this Directive, which is the tenth individual Directive within the meaning of Article 16(1) of Directive 89/391, is to implement measures to encourage improvements in the safety and health at work of pregnant workers and workers who have recently given birth or who are breast-feeding. **9–051**

2. The provisions of Directive 89/391, except for Article 2(2) thereof, shall apply in full to the whole area covered by paragraph 1, without prejudice to any more stringent and/or specific provisions contained in this Directive.

3. This Directive may not have the effect of reducing the level of protection afforded to pregnant workers, workers who have recently given birth or who are breast-feeding as compared with the situation which exists in each Member State on the date on which this Directive is adopted.

Article 2 Definitions

9–052 For the purposes of this Directive:

(a) pregnant worker shall mean a pregnant worker who informs her employer of her condition, in accordance with national legislation and/or national practice;

(b) worker who has recently given birth shall mean a worker who has recently given birth within the meaning of national legislation and/or national practice and who informs her employer of her condition, in accordance with that legislation and/or practice;

(c) worker who is breast-feeding shall mean a worker who is breast-feeding within the meaning of national legislation and/or national practice and who informs her employer of her condition, in accordance with that legislation and/or practice.

SECTION II—GENERAL PROVISIONS

Article 3 Guidelines

9–053 1. In consultation with the Member States and assisted by the Advisory Committee on Safety, Hygiene and Health Protection at Work, the Commission shall draw up guidelines on the assessment of the chemical, physical and biological agents and industrial processes considered hazardous for the safety or health of workers within the meaning of Article.

The guidelines referred to in the first subparagraph shall also cover movements and postures, mental and physical fatigue and other types of physical and mental stress connected with the work done by workers within the meaning of Article 2.

2. The purpose of the guidelines referred to in paragraph 1 is to serve as a basis for the assessment referred to in Article 4(1).

To this end, Member States shall bring these guidelines to the attention of all employers and all female workers and/or their representatives in the respective Member State.

Article 4 Assessment and information

9–054 1. For all activities liable to involve a specific risk of exposure to the agents, processes or working conditions of which a non-exhaustive list is given in Annex I, the employer shall assess the nature, degree and duration of exposure, in the undertaking and/or establishment concerned, of workers within the meaning of Article 2, either directly or by way of the protective and preventive services referred to in Article 7 of Directive 89/391, in order to:

— assess any risks to the safety or health and any possible effect on the pregnancy or breast-feeding of workers within the meaning of Article 2,

— decide what measures should be taken.

2. Without prejudice to Article 10 of Directive 89/391, workers within the meaning of Article 2 and workers likely to be in one of the situations referred to in Article 2 in the undertaking and/or establishment concerned and/or their representatives shall be informed of the results of the assessment referred to in paragraph 1 and of all measures to be taken concerning health and safety at work.

Article 5 Action further to the results of the assessment

9–055 1. Without prejudice to Article 6 of Directive 89/391, if the results of the assessment referred to in Article 4(1) reveal a risk to the safety or health or an effect on the pregnancy or breast-feeding of a worker within the meaning of Article 2, the employer shall take the necessary measures to ensure that, by temporarily adjusting the working conditions and/or the working hours of the worker concerned, the exposure of that worker to such risks is avoided.

2. If the adjustment of her working conditions and/or working hours is not technically and/or objectively feasible, or cannot reasonably be required on duly substantiated grounds, the employer shall take the necessary measures to move the worker concerned to another job.

3. If moving her to another job is not technically and/or objectively feasible or cannot reasonably be required on duly substantiated grounds, the worker concerned shall be granted leave in accordance with national legislation and/or national practice for the whole of the period necessary to protect her safety or health.

4. The provisions of this Article shall apply *mutatis mutandis* to the case where a worker pursuing an activity which is forbidden pursuant to Article 6 becomes pregnant or starts breast-feeding and informs her employer thereof.

Article 6 Cases in which exposure is prohibited

In addition to the general provisions concerning the protection of workers, in particular those relating to the limit values for occupational exposure: **9–056**

1. pregnant workers within the meaning of Article 2(a) may under no circumstances be obliged to perform duties for which the assessment has revealed a risk of exposure, which would jeopardise safety or health, to the agents and working conditions listed in Annex II, Section A;
2. workers who are breast-feeding, within the meaning of Article 2(c), may under no circumstances be obliged to perform duties for which the assessment has revealed a risk of exposure, which would jeopardise safety or health, to the agents and working conditions listed in Annex II, Section B.

Article 7 Night work

1. Member States shall take the necessary measures to ensure that workers referred to in Article 2 are not obliged to perform night work during their pregnancy and for a period following childbirth which shall be determined by the national authority competent for safety and health, subject to submission, in accordance with the procedures laid down by the Member States, of a medical certificate stating that this is necessary for the safety or health of the worker concerned. **9–057**

2. The measures referred to in paragraph 1 must entail the possibility, in accordance with national legislation and/or national practice, of:

(a) transfer to daytime work; or
(b) leave from work or extension of maternity leave where such a transfer is not technically and/or objectively feasible or cannot reasonably by required on duly substantiated grounds.

Article 8 Maternity leave

1. Member States shall take the necessary measures to ensure that workers within the meaning of Article 2 are entitled to a continuous period of maternity leave of a least 14 weeks allocated before and/or after confinement in accordance with national legislation and/or practice. **9–058**

2. The maternity leave stipulated in paragraph 1 must include compulsory maternity leave of at least two weeks allocated before and/or after confinement in accordance with national legislation and/or practice.

Article 9 Time off for ante-natal examinations

Member States shall take the necessary measures to ensure that pregnant workers within the meaning of Article 2(a) are entitled to, in accordance with national **9–059** legislation and/or practice, time off, without loss of pay, in order to attend ante-natal examinations, if such examinations have to take place during working hours.

Article 10 Prohibition of dismissal

9–060 In order to guarantee workers, within the meaning of Article 2, the exercise of their health and safety protection rights as recognised under this Article, it shall be provided that:

1. Member States shall take the necessary measures to prohibit the dismissal of workers, within the meaning of Article 2, during the period from the beginning of their pregnancy to the end of the maternity leave referred to in Article 8(1), save in exceptional cases not connected with their condition which are permitted under national legislation and/or practice and, where applicable, provided that the competent authority has given its consent;
2. if a worker, within the meaning of Article 2, is dismissed during the period referred to in point 1, the employer must cite duly substantiated grounds for her dismissal in writing;
3. Member States shall take the necessary measures to protect workers, within the meaning of Article 2, from consequences of dismissal which is unlawful by virtue of point 1.

Article 11 Employment rights

9–061 In order to guarantee workers within the meaning of Article 2 the exercise of their health and safety protection rights as recognised in this Article, it shall be provided that:

1. in the cases referred to in Articles 5, 6 and 7, the employment rights relating to the employment contract, including the maintenance of a payment to, and/or entitlement to an adequate allowance for, workers within the meaning of Article 2, must be ensured in accordance with national legislation and/or national practice;
2. in the case referred to in Article 8, the following must be ensured:
   (a) the rights connected with the employment contract of workers within the meaning of Article 2, other than those referred to in point (b) below;
   (b) maintenance of a payment to, and/or entitlement to an adequate allowance for, workers within the meaning of Article 2;
3. the allowance referred to in point 2(b) shall be deemed adequate if it guarantees income at least equivalent to that which the worker concerned would receive in the event of a break in her activities on grounds connected with her state of health, subject to any ceiling laid down under national legislation[33];

[33] Statement of the Council and the Commission concerning Article 11(3) of Directive 92/85, entered in the minutes of the 1608th meeting of the Council (Luxembourg, 19 October 1992): *The Council and the Commission* stated that: "In determining the level of the allowances referred to in Article 11(2)(b) and (3), reference shall be made, for purely technical reasons, to the allowance which a worker would receive in the event of a break in her activities on grounds connected with her state of health. Such a reference is not intended in any way to imply that pregnancy and childbirth be equated with sickness. The national social security legislation of all Member States provides for an allowance to be paid during an absence from work due to sickness. The link with such allowance in the chosen formulation is simply intended to serve as a concrete, fixed reference amount in all Member States for the determination of the minimum amount of maternity allowance payable. In so far as allowances are paid in individual Member States which exceed those provided for in the Directive, such allowances are, of course, retained. This is clear from Article 1(3) of the Directive."

4. Member States may make entitlement to pay or the allowance referred to in points 1 and 2(b) conditional upon the worker concerned fulfilling the conditions of eligibility for such benefits laid down under national legislation.

These conditions may under no circumstances provide for periods of previous employment in excess of 12 months immediately prior to the presumed date of confinement.

Article 12 Defence of rights

Member States shall introduce into their national legal systems such measures as are necessary to enable all workers who should themselves wronged by failure to comply with the obligations arising from this Directive to pursue their claims by judicial process (and/or, in accordance with national laws and/or practices) by recourse to other competent authorities. **9–062**

Article 13 Amendments to the Annexes

1. Strictly technical adjustments to Annex I as a result of technical progress, changes in international regulations or specifications and new findings in the area covered by this Directive shall be adopted in accordance with the procedure laid down in Article 17 of Directive 89/391. **9–063**

2. Annex II may be amended only in accordance with the procedure laid down in Article [138] of the Treaty.

Article 14 Final provisions

1. Member States shall bring into force the laws, regulations and administrative provisions necessary to comply with this Directive not later than two years after the adoption thereof or ensure, at the latest two years after adoption of this Directive, that the two sides of industry introduce the requisite provisions by means of collective agreements, with Member States being required to make all the necessary provisions to enable them at all times to guarantee the results laid down by this Directive. They shall forthwith inform the Commission thereof. **9–064**

2. When Member States adopt the measures referred to in paragraph 1, they shall contain a reference of this Directive or shall be accompanied by such reference on the occasion of their official publication. The methods of making such a reference shall be laid down by the Member States.

3. Member States shall communicate to the Commission the texts of the essential provisions of national law which they have already adopted or adopt in the field governed by this Directive.

4. Member States shall report to the Commission every five years on the practical implementation of the provisions of this Directive, indicating the points of view of the two sides of industry.

However, Member States shall report for the first time to the Commission on the practical implementation of the provisions of this Directive, indicating the points of view of the two sides of industry, four years after its adoption.

The Commission shall inform the European Parliament, the Council, the Economic and Social Committee and the Advisory Committee on Safety, Hygiene and Health Protection at Work.

5. The Commission shall periodically submit to the European Parliament, the Council and the Economic and Social Committee a report on the implementation of this Directive, taking into account paragraphs 1, 2 and 3.

6. The Council will re-examine this Directive, on the basis of an assessment carried out on the basis of the reports referred to in the second subparagraph of paragraph 4 and, should the need arise, of a proposal, to be submitted by the Commission at the latest five years after adoption of the Directive.

Article 15 [Addressees]

9–065 This Directive is addressed to the Member States.

ANNEX I—NON-EXHAUSTIVE LIST OF AGENTS, PROCESSES AND WORKING CONDITIONS REFERRED TO IN ARTICLE 4(1)

A. Agents

9–066 1. Physical agents where these are regarded as agents causing foetal lesions and/or likely to disrupt placental attachment, and in particular:

(a) shocks, vibration or movement;
(b) handling of loads entailing risks, particularly of a dorsolumbar nature;
(c) noise;
(d) ionizing radiation;[34]
(e) non-ionizing radiation;
(f) extremes of cold or heat;
(g) movements and postures, travelling—either inside or outside the establishment—mental and physical fatigue and other physical burdens connected with the activity of the worker within the meaning of Article 2 of the Directive.

2. Biological agents

Biological agents of risk groups 2, 3 and 3 within the meaning of Article 2(d) numbers 2, 3 and 4 of Directive 90/679,[35] in so far as it is known that these agents or the therapeutic measures necessitated by such agents endanger the health of pregnant women and the unborn child and in so far as they do not yet appear in Annex II.

3. Chemical agents

The following chemical agents in so far as it is known that they endanger the health of pregnant women and the unborn child and in so far as they do not yet appear in Annex II:

(a) substances labelled R 40, R 45, R 46, and R 47 under Directive 67/548 [36] in so far as they do not yet appear in Annex II;
(b) chemical agents in Annex I to Directive 90/394 [37];
(c) mercury and mercury derivatives;
(d) antimitotic drugs;
(e) carbon monoxide;
(f) chemical agents of known and dangerous percutaneous absorption.

B. Processes

9–067 Industrial processes listed in Annex I to Directive 90/394.

C. Working conditions

9–068 Underground mining work.

[34] See Directive 80/836/Euratom ([1980] OJ L246/1).

[35] [1990] OJ L374/1 [on the protection of workers from risks related to exposure to biological agents at work].

[36] [1967] OJ L196/1 [on the approximation of laws, regulations and administrative provisions relating to the classification, packaging and labelling of dangerous substances]. Directive as last amended by Directive 90/517 ([1990] OJ L287/37).

[37] [1990] OJ L196/1 [on the protection of workers from the risks related to exposure to carcinogens at work].

Annex II—Non-Exhaustive List of Agents and Working Conditions Referred to in Article 6

A. Pregnant workers within the meaning of Article 2(a)

1. Agents 9–069

(a) Physical agents

Work in hyperbaric atmosphere, *e.g.* pressurised enclosures and underwater diving.

(b) Biological agents

The following biological agents:

— toxoplasma,

— rubella virus,

unless the pregnant workers are proved to be adequately protected against such agents by immunisation.

(c) Chemical agents

Lead and lead derivatives in so far as these agents are capable of being absorbed by the human organism.

2. Working conditions

Underground mining work.

B. Workers who are breast-feeding within the meaning of Article 2(c)

1. Agents 9–070

(a) Chemical agents

Lead and lead derivatives in so far as these agents are capable of being absorbed by the human organism.

2. Working conditions

Underground mining work.

Council Directive 93/104 of 23 November 1993, concerning certain aspects of the organisation of working time

([1993] OJ L307/18; Doc. Ref. 31993L0104)

The Council of the European Union, 9–071

Having regard to the Treaty establishing the European Community, and in particular Article [138] thereof,

Having regard to the proposal from the Commission,[38]

In co-operation with the European Parliament,[39]

Having regard to the opinion of the Economic and Social Committee,[40]

[1] Whereas Article [138] of the Treaty provides that the Council shall adopt, by means of directives, minimum requirements for encouraging improvements, especially in the working environment, to ensure a better level of protection of the safety and health of workers;

[2] Whereas, under the terms of that Article, those directives are to avoid imposing administrative, financial and legal constraints in a way which would hold back the creation and development of small and medium-sized undertakings;

[3] Whereas the provisions of Council Directive 89/391 of 12 June 1989, on the introduction of measures to encourage improvements in the safety and health of workers at work[41] are fully applicable to the areas covered by this Directive without prejudice to more stringent and/or specific provisions contained therein;

---

[38] [1990] OJ C254/4.

[39] [1991] OJ C72/95 and Decision of 27 October 1993.

[40] [1991] OJ C60/26.

[41] [1989] OJ L183/1 (see above).

[4] Whereas the Community Charter of the Fundamental Social Rights of Workers, adopted at the meeting of the European Council held at Strasbourg on 9 December 1989, by the Heads of State or of Government of 11 Member States, and in particular points 7, first sub-paragraph, 8 and 19, first sub-paragraph, thereof, declared that:

"7. The completion of the internal market must lead to an improvement in the living and working conditions of workers in the European Community. This process must result from an approximation of these conditions while the improvement is being maintained, as regards in particular the duration and organisation of working time and forms of employment other than open-ended contracts, such as fixed-term contracts, part-time working, temporary work and seasonal work.

8. Every worker in the European Community shall have a right to a weekly rest period and to annual paid leave, the duration of which must be progressively harmonized in accordance with national practices.

19. Every worker must enjoy satisfactory health and safety conditions in his working environment. Appropriate measures must be taken in order to achieve further harmonisation of conditions in this area while maintaining the improvements made";

[5] Whereas the improvement of workers' safety, hygiene and health at work is an objective which should not be subordinated to purely economic considerations;

[6] Whereas this Directive is a practical contribution towards creating the social dimension of the internal market;

[7] Whereas laying down minimum requirements with regard to the organisation of working time is likely to improve the working conditions of workers in the Community;

[8] Whereas, in order to ensure the safety and health of Community workers, the latter must be granted minimum daily, weekly and annual periods of rest and adequate breaks whereas it is also necessary in this context to place a maximum limit on weekly working hours;

[9] Whereas account should be taken of the principles of the International Labour Organisation with regard to the organisation of working time, including those relating to night work;

[10] Whereas, with respect to the weekly rest period, due account should be taken of the diversity of cultural, ethnic, religious and other factors in the Member States; whereas, in particular, it is ultimately for each Member State to decide whether Sunday should be included in the weekly rest period, and if so to what extent;

[11] Whereas research has shown that the human body is more sensitive at night to environmental disturbances and also to certain burdensome forms of work organisation and that long periods of night work can be detrimental to the health of workers and can endanger safety at the workplace;

[12] Whereas there is a need to limit the duration of periods of night work, including overtime, and to provide for employers who regularly use night workers to bring this information to the attention of the competent authorities if they so request;

[13] Whereas it is important that night workers should be entitled to a free health assessment prior to their assignment and thereafter at regular intervals and that whenever possible they should be transferred to day work for which they are suited if they suffer from health problems;

[14] Whereas the situation of night and shift workers requires that the level of safety and health protection should be adapted to the nature of their work and that the organisation and functioning of protection and prevention services and resources should be efficient;

[15] Whereas specific working conditions may have detrimental effects on the safety and health of workers; whereas the organisation of work according to a

certain pattern must take account of the general principle of adapting work to the worker;

[16] Whereas, given the specific nature of the work concerned, it may be necessary to adopt separate measures with regard to the organisation of working time in certain sectors or activities which are excluded from the scope of this Directive[42];

[17] Whereas, in view of the question likely to be raised by the organisation of working time within an undertaking, it appears desirable to provide for flexibility in the application of certain provisions of this Directive, whilst ensuring compliance with the principles of protecting the safety and health of workers;

[18] Whereas it is necessary to provide that certain provisions may be subject to derogations implemented, according to the case, by the Member States or the two sides of industry whereas, as a general rule, in the event of a derogation, the workers concerned must be given equivalent compensatory rest periods,

Has adopted this Directive:

Section I—Scope and Definitions

Article 1 Purpose and scope

1. This Directive lays down minimum safety and health requirements for the organisation of working time. **9–072**

2. This Directive applies to:
(a) minimum periods of daily rest, weekly rest and annual leave, to breaks and maximum weekly working time; and
(b) certain aspects of night work, shift work and patterns of work.

[3. This Directive shall apply to all sectors of activity, both public and private, within the meaning of Article 2 of Directive 89/391, without prejudice to Articles 14 and 17 of this Directive.

This Directive shall not apply to seafarers, as defined in Council Directive 1999/63 of 21 June 1999, concerning the Agreement on the organisation of working time of seafarers, concluded by the European Community Shipowners' Association (ECSA) and the Federation of Transport Workers' Unions in the European Union (FST)[43] without prejudice to Article 2(8) of this Directive.][44]

4. The provisions of Directive 89/391 are fully applicable to the matters referred to in paragraph 2, without prejudice to more stringent and/or specific provisions contained in this Directive.

Article 2 Definitions

For the purposes of this Directive, the following definitions shall apply: **9–073**
1. "working time" shall mean any period during which the worker is working, at the employer's disposal and carrying out his activity or duties, in accordance with national laws and/or practice;
2. "rest period" shall mean any period which is not working time;
3. "night time" shall mean any period of not less than seven hours, as defined by national law, and which must include in any case the period between midnight and 5 a.m.;

[42] See Directive 2000/34 amending Directive 93/104 to cover sectors and activities excluded from that Directive [2000] OJ L195/41, and Directive 2002/15 on the organisation of working time of persons performing mobile and road transport activities [2002] OJ L80/35.

[43] [1999] OJ L167/33.

[44] Article 1(3) substituted by Directive 2000/34 Art. 1(1) as from 1 August 2000.

4. "night worker" shall mean:
   (a) on the one hand, any worker, who, during night time, works at least three hours of his daily working time as a normal course; and
   (b) on the other hand, any worker who is likely during night time to work a certain proportion of his annual working time, as defined at the choice of the Member State concerned:
      (i) by national legislation, following consultation with the two sides of industry; or
      (ii) by collective agreements or agreements concluded between the two sides of industry at national or regional level
5. "shift work" shall mean any method of organising work in shifts whereby workers succeed each other at the same work stations according to a certain pattern, including a rotating pattern, and which may be continuous or discontinuous, entailing the need for workers to work at different times over a given period of days or weeks;
6. "shift worker" shall mean any worker whose work schedule is part of shift work.
7. "mobile worker" shall mean any worker employed as a member of travelling or flying personnel by an undertaking which operates transport services for passengers or goods by road, air or inland waterway.
8. "offshore work" shall mean work performed mainly on or from offshore installations (including drilling rigs), directly or indirectly in connection with the exploration, extraction or exploitation of mineral resources, including hydrocarbons, and diving in connection with such activities, whether performed from an offshore installation or a vessel.
9. "adequate rest" shall mean that workers have regular rest periods, the duration of which is expressed in units of time and which are sufficiently long and-continuous to ensure that, as a result of fatigue or other irregular working patterns, they do not cause injury to themselves, to fellow workers or to others and that they do not damage their health, either in the short term or in the longer term.][45]

Section II—Minimum Rest Periods—Other Aspects of the Organisation of Working Time

Article 3 Daily rest

9–074 Member States shall take the measures necessary to ensure that every worker is entitled to a minimum daily rest period of 11 consecutive hours per 24-hour period.

Article 4 Breaks

9–075 Member States shall take the measures necessary to ensure that, where the working day is longer than six hours, every worker is entitled to a rest break, the details of which, including duration and the terms on which it is granted, shall be laid down in collective agreements or agreements between the two sides of industry or, failing that, by national legislation.

Article 5 Weekly rest period

9–076 Member States shall take the measures necessary to ensure that, per each seven-day period, every worker is entitled to a minimum uninterrupted rest period of 24 hours plus the 11 hours' daily rest referred to in Article 3.
[. . .][46]

If objective, technical or work organisation conditions so justify, a minimum rest period of 24 hours may be applied.

---

[45] Article 2(7)–(9) inserted by Directive 2000/34 Art. 1(2) as from 1 August 2000.
[46] Words repealed by Directive 2000/34 Art. 1(3) as from 1 August 2000.

Article 6 **Maximum weekly working time**

Member States shall take the measures necessary to ensure that, in keeping with the need to protect the safety and health of workers: **9–077**

1. the period of weekly working time is limited by means of laws, regulations or administrative provisions or by collective agreements or agreements between the two sides of industry;
2. the average working time for each seven-day period, including overtime, does not exceed 48 hours.

Article 7 **Annual leave**

1. Member States shall take the measures necessary to ensure that every worker is entitled to paid annual leave of at least four weeks in accordance with the conditions for entitlement to, and granting of, such leave laid down by national legislation and/or practice. **9–078**

2. The minimum period of paid annual leave may not be replaced by an allowance in lieu, except where the employment relationship is terminated.

Section III—Night Work—Shift Work—Patterns of Work

Article 8 **Length of night work**

Member States shall take the measures necessary to ensure that: **9–079**

1. normal hours of work for night workers do not exceed an average of eight hours in any 24-hour period;
2. night workers whose work involves special hazards or heavy physical or mental strain do not work more than eight hours in any period of 24 hours during which they perform night work.

For the purposes of the aforementioned, work involving special hazards or heavy physical or mental strain shall be defined by national legislation and/or practice or by collective agreements or agreements concluded between the two sides of industry, taking account of the specific effects and hazards of night work.

Article 9 **Health assessment and transfer of night workers to day work**

1. Member States shall take the measures necessary to ensure that: **9–080**

(a) night workers are entitled to a free health assessment before their assignment and thereafter at regular intervals;

(b) night workers suffering from health problems recognised as being connected with the fact that they perform night work are transferred whenever possible to day work to which they are suited.

2. The free health assessment referred to in paragraph 1(a) must comply with medical confidentiality.

3. The free health assessment referred to in paragraph 1(a) may be conducted within the national health system.

Article 10 **Guarantees for night-time working**

Member States may make the work of certain categories of night workers subject to certain guarantees, under conditions laid down by national legislation and/or practice, in the case of workers who incur risks to their safety or health linked to night-time working. **9–081**

Article 11 **Notification of regular use of night workers**

Member States shall take the measures necessary to ensure that an employer who regularly uses night workers brings this information to the attention of the competent authorities if they so request. **9–082**

Article 12 Safety and health protection

9–083 Member States shall take the measures necessary to ensure that:

1. night workers and shift workers have safety and health protection appropriate to the nature of their work;
2. appropriate protection and prevention services or facilities with regard to the safety and health of night workers and shift workers are equivalent to those applicable to other workers and are available at all times.

Article 13 Pattern of work

9–084 Member States shall take the measures necessary to ensure that an employer who intends to organise work according to a certain pattern takes account of the general principle of adapting work to the worker, with a view, in particular, to alleviating monotonous work and work at a predetermined work-rate, depending on the type of activity, and of safety and health requirements, especially as regards breaks during working time.

SECTION IV—MISCELLANEOUS PROVISIONS

[Article 14 More specific Community provisions

9–085 This Directive shall not apply where other Community instruments contain more specific requirements relating to the organisation of working time for certain occupations or occupational activities.][47]

Article 15 More favourable provisions

9–086 This Directive shall not affect Member States' right to apply or introduce laws, regulations or administrative provisions more favourable to the protection of the safety and health of workers or to facilitate or permit the application of collective agreements or agreements concluded between the two sides of industry which are more favourable to the protection of the safety and health of workers.

Article 16 Reference periods

9–087 Member States may lay down:

1. for the application of Article 5 (weekly rest period), a reference period not exceeding 14 days;
2. for the application of Article 6 (maximum weekly working time), a reference period not exceeding four months.

   The periods of paid annual leave, granted in accordance with Article 7, and the periods of sick leave shall not be included or shall be neutral in the calculation of the average;
3. for the application of Article 8 (length of night work), a reference period defined after consultation of the two sides of industry or by collective agreements or agreements concluded between the two sides of industry at national or regional level.

   If the minimum weekly rest period of 24 hours required by Article 5 falls within that reference period, it shall not be included in the calculation of the average.

Article 17 Derogations

9–088 1. With due regard for the general principles of the protection of the safety and health of workers, Member States may derogate from Article 3, 4, 5, 6, 8 or 16 when, on account of the specific characteristics of the activity concerned, the

[47] Article 14 substituted by Directive 2000/34 Art. 1(4) as from 1 August 2000.

duration of the working time is not measured and/or predetermined or can be determined by the workers themselves, and particularly in the case of:
(a) managing executives or other persons with autonomous decision-taking powers;
(b) family workers or;
(c) workers officiating at religious ceremonies in churches and religious communities.

2. Derogations may be adopted by means of laws, regulations or administrative provisions or by means of collective agreements or agreements between the two sides of industry provided that the workers concerned are afforded equivalent periods of compensatory rest or that, in exceptional cases in which it is not possible, for objective reasons, to grant such equivalent periods of compensatory rest, the workers concerned are afforded appropriate protection:
[2.1. from Articles 3, 4, 5, 8 and 16:
(a) in the case of activities where the worker's place of work and his place of residence are distant from one another, including offshore work, or where the worker's different places of work are distant from one another;
(b) in the case of security and surveillance activities requiring a permanent presence in order to protect property and persons, particularly security guards and caretakers or security firms;
(c) in the case of activities involving the need for continuity of service or production, particularly:
(i) services relating to the reception, treatment and/or care provided by hospitals or similar establishments, including the activities of doctors in training, residential institutions and prisons;
(ii) dock or airport workers;
(iii) press, radio, television, cinematographic production, postal and telecommunications services, ambulance, fire and civil protection services;
(iv) gas, water and electricity production, transmission and distribution, household refuse collection and incineration plants;
(v) industries in which work cannot be interrupted on technical grounds;
(vi) research and development activities;
(vii) agriculture;
(viii) workers concerned with the carriage of passengers on regular urban transport services;
(d) where there is a foreseeable surge of activity, particularly in:
(i) agriculture;
(ii) tourism;
(iii) postal services;
(e) in the case of persons working in railway transport:
(i) whose activities are intermittent;
(ii) who spend their working time on board-trains; or
(iii) whose activities are linked to transport timetables and to ensuring the continuity and regularity of traffic.][48]
2.2. from Articles 3, 4, 5, 8 and 16:
(a) in the circumstances described in Article 5(4) of Directive 89/391;
(b) in cases of accident or imminent risk of accident;
2.3. from Articles 3 and 5:
(a) in the case of shift work activities, each time the worker changes shift and cannot take daily and/or weekly rest periods between the end of one shift and the start of the next one;
(b) in the case of activities involving periods of work split up over the day, particularly those of cleaning staff.
[2.4. from Articles 6 and 16(2) in the case of doctors in training:

[48] Article 17(2.1) substituted by Directive 2000/34 Art. 1(5) as from 1 August 2000.

(a) with respect to Article 6, for a transitional period of five years from 1 August 2004.

(i) Member States may have up to two more years, if necessary, to take account of difficulties in meeting the working time provisions with respect to their responsibilities for the organisation and delivery of health services and medical care. At least six months before the end of the transitional period, the Member State concerned shall inform the Commission giving its reasons, so that the Commission can give an opinion, after appropriate consultations, within the three months following receipt of such information. If the Member State does not follow the opinion of the Commission, it will justify its decision. The notification and justification of the Member State and the opinion of the Commission shall be published in the Official Journal of the European Communities and forwarded to the European Parliament.

(ii) Member States may have an additional period of up to one year, if necessary, to take account of special difficulties in meeting the above-mentioned responsibilities. They shall follow the procedure set out in paragraph (i).

Within the context of the transitional period:

(iii) Member States shall ensure that in no case will the number of weekly working hours exceed an average of 58 during the first three years of the transitional period, an average of 56 for the following two years and an average of 52 for any remaining period.

(iv) The employer shall consult the representatives of the employees in good time with a view to reaching an agreement, wherever possible, on the arrangements applying to the transitional period. Within the limits set out in point (iii), such an agreement may cover:

— the average number of weekly hours of work during the transitional period; and

— the measures to be adopted to reduce weekly working hours to an average of 48 by the end of the transitional period;

(b) with respect to Article 16(2), provided that the reference period does not exceed 12 months, during the first part of the transitional period-specified in paragraph (a)(iii), and six months thereafter.][49]

3. Derogations may be made from Articles 3, 4, 5, 8 and 16 by means of collective agreements or agreements concluded between the two sides of industry at national or regional level or, in conformity with the rules laid down by them, by means of collective agreements or agreements concluded between the two sides of industry at a lower level.

Member States in which there is no statutory system ensuring the conclusion of collective agreements or agreements concluded between the two sides of industry at national or regional level, on the matters covered by this Directive, or those Member States in which there is a specific legislative framework for this purpose and within the limits thereof, may, in accordance with national legislation and/or practice, allow derogations from Articles 3, 4, 5, 8 and 16 by way of collective agreements or agreements concluded between the two sides of industry at the appropriate collective level.

The derogations provided for in the first and second sub-paragraphs shall be allowed on condition that equivalent compensating rest periods are granted to the workers concerned or, in exceptional cases where it is not possible for objective reasons to grant such periods, the workers concerned are afforded appropriate protection.

Member States may lay down rules:

— for the application of this paragraph by the two sides of industry, and

---

[49] Article 17(2.4) inserted by Directive 2000/34 Art. 1(6) as from 1 August 2000.

— for the extension of the provisions of collective agreements or agreements concluded in conformity with this paragraph to other workers in accordance with national legislation and/or practice.

4. The option to derogate from point 2 of Article 16, provided in paragraph 2, points 2.1. and 2.2. and in paragraph 3 of this Article, may not result in the establishment of a reference period exceeding six months.

However, Member States shall have the option, subject to compliance with the general principles relating to the protection of the safety and health of workers, of allowing, for objective or technical reasons or reasons concerning the organisation of work, collective agreements or agreements concluded between the two sides of industry to set reference periods in no event exceeding 12 months.

Before the expiry of a period of seven years from the date referred to in Article 18(1)(a), the Council shall, on the basis of a Commission proposal accompanied by an appraisal report, re-examine the provisions of this paragraph and decide what action to take.

[Article 17a Mobile workers and offshore work

1. Articles 3, 4, 5 and 8 shall not apply to mobile workers.[50] **9–089**

2. Member States shall, however, take the necessary measures to ensure that such mobile workers are entitled to adequate rest, except in the circumstances laid down in Article 17(2.2).

3. Subject to compliance with the general principles relating to the protection of the safety and health of workers, and provided that there is consultation of representatives of the employer and employees concerned and efforts to encourage all relevant forms of social dialogue, including negotiation if the parties so wish, Member States may, for objective or technical reasons or reasons concerning the organisation of work, extend the reference period referred to in Article 16(2) to twelve months in respect of workers who mainly perform offshore work.

4. On 1 August 2005 the Commission shall, after consulting the Member States and management and labour at European level, review the operation of the provisions with regard to offshore workers from a health and safety perspective with a view to presenting, if need be, the appropriate modifications.

Article 17b Workers on board sea-going fishing vessels

1. Articles 3, 4, 5, 6 and 8 shall not apply to any worker on board a sea-going fishing vessel flying the flag of a Member State. **9–090**

2. Member States shall, however, take the necessary measures to ensure that any worker on board a sea-going fishing vessel flying the flag of a Member State is entitled to adequate rest and to limit the number of hours of work to 48 hours a week on average calculated over a reference period not exceeding 12 months.

3. Within the limits set out in paragraphs 2, 4 and 5 Member States shall take the necessary measures to ensure that, in keeping with the need to protect the safety and health of such workers,

---

[50] However, see now Directive 2002/15 of the European Parliament and of the Council of 11 March 2002 on the organisation of the working time of persons performing mobile road transport activities ([2002] OJ L80/35) (see below).

(a) the working hours are limited to a maximum number of hours which shall not be exceeded in a given period of time, or
(b) a minimum number of hours of rest are provided-within a given period of time.

The maximum number of hours of work or minimum number of hours of rest shall be specified by law, regulations, administrative provisions or by collective agreements or agreements between the two sides of the industry.

4. The limits on hours of work or rest shall be either:
(a) maximum hours of work which shall not exceed:
  (i) 14 hours in any 24-hour period, and
  (ii) 72 hours in any seven-day period; or
(b) minimum hours of rest which shall not be less than:
  (i) 10 hours in any 24-hour period, and
  (ii) 77 hours in any seven-day period.

5. Hours of rest may be divided into no more than two periods, one of which shall be at least six hours in length, and the interval between consecutive periods of rest shall not exceed 14 hours.

6. In accordance with the general principles of the protection of the health and safety of workers, and for objective or technical reasons or reasons concerning the organisation of work, Member States may allow exceptions, including the establishment of reference periods, to the limits laid down in paragraphs 2, 4 and 5. Such exceptions shall, as far as possible, comply with the standards laid down but may take account of more frequent or longer leave periods or the granting of compensatory leave for the workers. These exceptions may be laid down by means of:
  (i) laws, regulations or administrative provisions provided there is consultation, where possible, of the representatives of the employers and workers concerned and efforts are made to encourage all relevant forms of social dialogue, or
  (ii) collective agreements or agreements between the two sides of industry.

7. The master of a sea-going fishing vessel shall have the right to require workers on board to perform any hours of work necessary for the immediate safety of the; vessel, persons on board or cargo, or for the purpose of giving assistance to other vessels or persons in distress at sea.

8. Member States may provide that workers on board sea-going fishing vessels for which national legislation or practice determines that these vessels are not allowed to operate in a specific period of the calendar year exceeding one month, shall take annual leave in accordance with Article 7 within the abovementioned period.][51]

Article 18 Final provisions

9–091 1. (a) Member States shall adopt the laws, regulations and administrative provisions necessary to comply with this Directive by 23 November 1996, or shall ensure by that date that the two sides of industry establish the necessary measures by agreement, with Member States being obliged to take any necessary steps to enable them to guarantee at all times that the provisions laid down by this Directive are fulfilled.
(b) (i) However, a Member State shall have the option not to apply Article 6, while respecting the general principles of the protection of the safety and health of workers, and provided it takes the necessary measures to ensure that:

[51] Articles 7a–7b inserted by Directive 2000/34 Art. 1(7) as from 1 August 2000.

— no employer requires a worker to work more than 48 hours over a seven-day period, calculated as an average for the reference period referred to in point 2 of Article 16, unless he has first obtained the worker's agreement to perform such work,
— no worker is subjected to any detriment by his employer because he is not willing to give his agreement to perform such work,
— the employer keeps up-to-date records of all workers who carry out such work,
— the records are placed at the disposal of the competent authorities, which may, for reasons connected with the safety and/or health of workers, prohibit or restrict the possibility of exceeding the maximum weekly working hours,
— the employer provides the competent authorities at their request with information on cases in which agreement has been given by workers to perform work exceeding 48 hours over a period of seven days, calculated as an average for the reference period referred to in point 2 of Article 16.

Before the expiry of a period of seven years from the date referred to in (a), the Council shall, on the basis of a Commission proposal accompanied by an appraisal report, re-examine the provisions of this point (i) and decide on what action to take.

(ii) Similarly, Member States shall have the option, as regards the application of Article 7, of making use of a transitional period of not more than three years from the date referred to in (a), provided that during that transitional period:
— every worker receives three weeks' paid annual leave in accordance with the conditions for the entitlement to, and granting of, such leave laid down by national legislation and/or practice, and
— the three-week period of paid annual leave may not be replaced by an allowance in lieu, except where the employment relationship is terminated.

(c) Member States shall forthwith inform the Commission thereof.

2. When Member States adopt the measures referred to in paragraph 1, they shall contain a reference to this Directive or shall be accompanied by such reference on the occasion of their official publication. The methods of making such a reference shall be laid down by the Member States.

3. Without prejudice to the right of Member States to develop, in the light of changing circumstances, different legislative, regulatory or contractual provisions in the field of working time, as long as the minimum requirements provided for in this Directive are complied with, implementation of this Directive shall not constitute valid grounds for reducing the general level of protection afforded to workers.

4. Member States shall communicate to the Commission the texts of the provisions of national law already adopted or being adopted in the field governed by this Directive.

5. Member States shall report to the Commission every five years on the practical implementation of the provisions of this Directive, indicating the viewpoints of the two sides of industry.

The Commission shall inform the European Parliament, the Council, the Economic and Social Committee and the Advisory Committee on Safety, Hygiene and Health Protection at Work thereof.

6. Every five years the Commission shall submit to the European Parliament, the Council and the Economic and Social Committee a report on the application of this Directive taking into account paragraphs 1, 2, 3, 4 and 5.

Article 19 [Addressees]

9–092 This Directive is addressed to the Member States.

Council Directive 94/33 of 22 June 1994, on the protection of young people at work

([1994] OJ L216/12; Doc. Ref. 31994L0033)

9–093 *The Council of the European Union,*

Having regard to the Treaty establishing the European Community, and in particular Article [138] thereof,

Having regard to the proposal from the Commission,[52]

Having regard to the opinion of the Economic and Social Committee,[53]

Acting in accordance with the procedure referred to in Article [252] of the Treaty,[54]

[1] Whereas Article [138] of the Treaty provides that the Council shall adopt, by means of directives, minimum requirements to encourage improvements, especially in the working environment, as regards the health and safety of workers;

[2] Whereas, under that Article, such directives must avoid imposing administrative, financial and legal constraints in a way which would hold back the creation and development of small and medium-sized undertakings;

[3] Whereas points 20 and 22 of the Community Charter of the Fundamental Social Rights of Workers, adopted by the European Council in Strasbourg on 9 December 1989, state that:

> "20. Without prejudice to such rules as may be more favourable to young people, in particular those ensuring their preparation for work through vocational training, and subject to derogations limited to certain light work, the minimum employment age must not be lower than the minimum school-leaving age and, in any case, not lower than 15 years;
>
> 22. Appropriate measures must be taken to adjust labour regulations applicable to young workers so that their specific development and vocational training and access to employment needs are met.
>
> The duration of work must, in particular, be limited—without it being possible to circumvent this limitation through recourse to overtime—and night work prohibited in the case of workers of under eighteen years of age, save in the case of certain jobs laid down in national legislation or regulations.";

[4] Whereas account should be taken of the principles of the International Labour Organisation regarding the protection of young people at work, including those relating to the minimum age for access to employment or work;

[5] Whereas, in this Resolution on child labour[55], the European Parliament summarised the various aspects of work by young people and stressed its effects on their health, safety and physical and intellectual development, and pointed to the need to adopt a Directive harmonising national legislation in the field;

[6] Whereas Article 15 of Council Directive 89/391 of 12 June 1989, on the introduction of measures to encourage improvements in the safety and health of workers at work[56] provides that particularly sensitive risk groups must be protected against the dangers which specifically affect them;

---

[52] [1992] OJ C84/7.

[53] [1992] OJ C313/70.

[54] Opinion of the European Parliament of 17 December 1992 ([1993] OJ C21/167). Council Common Position of 23 November 1993 and Decision of the European Parliament of 9 March 1994 ([1994] OJ C91/89).

[55] [1987] OJ C190/44.

[56] [1989] OJ L183/1 (see above).

[7] Whereas children and adolescents must be considered specific risk groups, and measures must be taken with regard to their safety and health;

[8] Whereas the vulnerability of children calls for Member States to prohibit their employment and ensure that the minimum working or employment age is not lower than the minimum age at which compulsory schooling as imposed by national law ends or 15 years in any event; whereas derogations from the prohibition on child labour may be admitted only in special cases and under the conditions stipulated in this Directive; whereas, under no circumstances, may such derogations be detrimental to regular school attendance or prevent children benefiting fully from their education;

[9] Whereas, in view of the nature of the transition from childhood to adult life, work by adolescents should be strictly regulated and protected;

[10] Whereas every employer should guarantee young people working conditions appropriate to their age;

[11] Whereas employers should implement the measures necessary to protect the safety and health of young people on the basis on an assessment of work-related hazards to the young;

[12] Whereas Member States should protect young people against any specific risks arising from their lack of experience, absence of awareness of existing or potential risks, or from their immaturity;

[13] Whereas Member States should therefore prohibit the employment of young people for the work specified by this Directive;

[14] Whereas the adoption of specific minimal requirements in respect of the organization of working time is likely to improve working conditions for young people;

[15] Whereas the maximum working time of young people should be strictly limited and night work by young people should be prohibited, with the exception of certain jobs specified by national legislation or rules;

[16] Whereas Member States should take the appropriate measures to ensure that the working time of adolescents receiving school education does not adversely affect their ability to benefit from that education;

[17] Whereas time spent on training by young persons working under a theoretical and/or practical combined work/training scheme or an in-plant work-experience should be counted as working time;

[18] Whereas, in order to ensure the safety and health of young people, the latter should be granted minimum daily, weekly and annual periods of rest and adequate breaks;

[19] Whereas, with respect to the weekly rest period, due account should be taken of the diversity of cultural, ethnic, religious and other factors prevailing in the Member States; whereas in particular, it is ultimately for each Member State to decide whether Sunday should be included in the weekly rest period, and if so to what extent;

[20] Whereas appropriate work experience may contribute to the aim of preparing young people for adult working and social life, provided it is ensured that any harm to their safety, health and development is avoided;

[21] Whereas, although derogations from the bans and limitations imposed by this Directive would appear indispensable for certain activities or particular situations, applications thereof must not prejudice the principles underlying the established protection system;

[22] Whereas this Directive constitutes a tangible step towards developing the social dimension of the internal market;

[23] Whereas the application in practice of the system of protection laid down by this Directive will require that Member States implement a system of effective and proportionate measures;

[24] Whereas the implementation of some provisions of this Directive poses particular problems for one Member State with regard to its system of protection for young people at work; whereas that Member State should therefore be

allowed to refrain from implementing the relevant provisions for a suitable period,
Has adopted this Directive:

SECTION I

Article 1 Purpose

9–094 1. Member States shall take the necessary measures to prohibit work by children.
They shall ensure, under the conditions laid down by this Directive, that the minimum working or employment age is not lower than the minimum age at which compulsory full-time schooling as imposed by national law ends or 15 years in any event.

2. Member States ensure that work by adolescents is strictly regulated and protected under the conditions laid down in this Directive.

3. Member States shall ensure in general that employers guarantee that young people have working conditions which suit their age.
They shall ensure that young people are protected against economic exploitation and against any work likely to harm their safety, health or physical, mental, moral or social development or to jeopardise their education.

Article 2 Scope

9–095 1. This Directive shall apply to any person under 18 years of age having an employment contract or an employment relationship defined by the law in force in a Member State and/or governed by the law in force in a Member State.

2. Member States may make legislative or regulatory provision for this Directive not to apply, within the limits and under the conditions which they set by legislative or regulatory provision, to occasional work or short-term work involving:
(a) domestic service in a private household, or
(b) work regarded as not being harmful, damaging or dangerous to young people in a family undertaking.

Article 3 Definitions

9–096 For the purposes of this Directive:
(a) "young person" shall mean any person under 18 years of age referred to in Article 2(1);
(b) "child" shall mean any young person of less than 15 years of age or who is still subject to compulsory full-time schooling under national law;
(c) "adolescent" shall mean any young person of at least 15 years of age but less than 18 years of age who is no longer subject to compulsory full-time schooling under national law;
(d) "light work" shall mean all work which, on account of the inherent nature of the tasks which it involves and the particular conditions under which they are performed:
(i) is not likely to be harmful to the safety, health or development of children, and
(ii) is not such as to be harmful to their attendance at school, their participation in vocational guidance or training programmes approved by the competent authority or their capacity to benefit from the instruction received;

(e) "working time" shall mean any period during which the young person is at work, at the employer's disposal and carrying out his activity or duties in accordance with national legislation and/or practice;
(f) "rest period" shall mean any period which is not working time.

Article 4 Prohibition of work by children

1. Member States shall adopt the measures necessary to prohibit work by children. **9–097**

2. Taking into account the objectives set out in Article 1, Member States may make legislative or regulatory provision for the prohibition of work by children not to apply to:
(a) children pursuing the activities set out in Article 5;
(b) children of at least 14 years of age working under a combined work/training scheme or an in-plant work-experience scheme, provided that such work is done in accordance with the conditions laid down by the competent authority;
(c) children of at least 14 years of age performing light work other than that covered by Article 5; light work other than that covered by Article 5 may, however, be performed by children of 13 years of age for a limited number of hours per week in the case of categories of work determined by national legislation.

3. Member States that make use of the opinion referred to in paragraph 2(c) shall determine, subject to the provisions of this Directive, the working conditions relating to the light work in question.

Article 5 Cultural or similar activities

1. The employment of children for the purposes of performance in cultural, artistic, sports or advertising activities shall be subject to prior authorisation to be given by the competent authority in individual cases. **9–098**

2. Member States shall by legislative or regulatory provision lay down the working conditions for children in the cases referred to in paragraph 1 and the details of the prior authorisation procedure, on condition that the activities:
(i) are not likely to be harmful to the safety, health or development of children, and
(ii) are not such as to be harmful to their attendance at school, their participation in vocational guidance or training programmes approved by the competent authority or their capacity to benefit from the instruction received.

3. By way of derogation from the procedure laid down in paragraph 1, in the case of children of at least 13 years of age, Member States may authorise, by legislative or regulatory provision, in accordance with conditions which they shall determine, the employment of children for the purposes of performance in cultural, artistic, sports or advertising activities.

4. The Member States which have a specific authorisation system for modelling agencies with regard to the activities of children may retain that system.

SECTION II

Article 6 General obligations on employers

1. Without prejudice to Article 4(1), the employer shall adopt the measures necessary to protect the safety and health of young people, taking particular account of the specific risks referred to in Article 7(1). **9–099**

2. The employer shall implement the measures provided for in paragraph 1 on the basis of an assessment of the hazards to young people in connection with their work.

The assessment must be made before young people begin work and when there is any major change in working conditions and must pay particular attention to the following points:
(a) the fitting-out and layout of the workplace and the workstation;
(b) the nature, degree and duration of exposure to physical, biological and chemical agents;
(c) the form, range and use of work equipment, in particular agents, machines, apparatus and devices, and the way in which they are handled;
(d) the arrangement of work processes and operations and the way in which these are combined (organisation of work);
(e) the level of training and instruction given to young people.
Where this assessment shows that there is a risk to the safety, the physical or mental health or development of young people, an appropriate free assessment and monitoring of their health shall be provided at regular intervals without prejudice to Directive 89/391.

The free health assessment and monitoring may form part of a national health system.

3. The employer shall inform young people of possible risks and of all measures adopted concerning their safety and health.

Furthermore, he shall inform the legal representatives of children of possible risks and of all measures adopted concerning children's safety and health.

4. The employer shall involve the protective and preventive services referred to in Article 7 of Directive 89/391 in the planning, implementation and monitoring of the safety and health conditions applicable to young people.

Article 7 Vulnerability of young people—Prohibition of work

9–100 1. Member States shall ensure that young people are protected from any specific risks to their safety, health and development which are a consequence of their lack of experience, of absence of awareness of existing or potential risks or of the fact that young people have not yet fully matured.

2. Without prejudice to Article 4(1), Member States shall to this end prohibit the employment of young people for:
(a) work which is objectively beyond their physical or psychological capacity;
(b) work involving harmful exposure to agents which are toxic, carcinogenic, cause heritable genetic damage, or harm to the unborn child or which in any other way chronically affect human health;
(c) work involving harmful exposure to radiation;
(d) work involving the risk of accidents which it may be assumed cannot be recognised or avoided by young persons owing to their insufficient attention to safety or lack of experience or training; or
(e) work in which there is a risk to health from extreme cold or heat, or from noise or vibration.

Work which is likely to entail specific risks for young people within the meaning of paragraph 1 includes:
— work involving harmful exposure to the physical, biological and chemical agents referred to in point I of the Annex, and
— processes and work referred to in point II of the Annex.

3. Member States may, by legislative or regulatory provision, authorise derogations from paragraph 2 in the case of adolescents where such derogations are indispensable for their vocational training, provided that protection of their safety and health is ensured by the fact that the work is performed under the supervision of a competent person within the meaning of Article 7 of Directive 89/391 and provided that the protection afforded by that Directive is guaranteed.

Section III

Article 8 Working time

1. Member States which make use of the option in Article 4(2)(b) or (c) shall adopt the measures necessary to limit the working time of children to: **9–101**
(a) eight hours a day and 40 hours a week for work performed under a combined work/training scheme or an in-plant work-experience scheme;
(b) two hours on a school day and 12 hours a week for work performed in term-time outside the hours fixed for school attendance, provided that this is not prohibited by national legislation and/or practice in no circumstances may the daily working time exceed seven hours this limit may be raised to eight hours in the case of children who have reached the age of 15;
(c) seven hours a day and 35 hours a week for work performed during a period of at least a week when school is not operating these limits may be raised to eight hours a day and 40 hours a week in the case of children who have reached the age of 15;
(d) seven hours a day and 35 hours a week for light work performed by children no longer subject to compulsory full-time schooling under national law.

2. Member States shall adopt the measures necessary to limit the working time of adolescents to eight hours a day and 40 hours a week.

3. The time spent on training by a young person working under a theoretical and/or practical combined work/training scheme or an in-plant work-experience scheme shall be counted as working time.

4. Where a young person is employed by more than one employer, working days and working time shall be cumulative.

5. Member States may, by legislative or regulatory provision, authorise derogations from paragraph 1(a) and paragraph 2 either by way of exception or where there are objective grounds for so doing.

Member States shall, by legislative or regulatory provision, determine the conditions, limits and procedure for implementing such derogations.

Article 9 Night work

1. (a) Member States which make use of the option in Article 4(2)(b) or (c) shall adopt the measures necessary to prohibit work by children between 8 p.m. and 6 a.m. **9–102**
(b) Member States shall adopt the measures necessary to prohibit work by adolescents either between 10 p.m. and 6 a.m. or between 11 p.m. and 7 a.m.
2. (a) Member States may, by legislative or regulatory provision, authorise work by adolescents in specific areas of activity during the period in which night work is prohibited as referred to in paragraph 1(b).

In that event, Member States shall take appropriate measures to ensure that the adolescent is supervised by an adult where such supervision is necessary for the adolescent's protection.
(b) If point (a) is applied, work shall continue to be prohibited between midnight and 4 a.m.

However, Member States may, by legislative or regulatory provision, authorise work by adolescents during the period in which night work is prohibited in the following cases, where there are objective grounds for so doing and provided that adolescents are allowed suitable compensatory rest time and that the objectives set out in Article 1 are not called into question:
— work performed in the shipping or fisheries sectors

— work performed in the context of the armed forces or the police
— work performed in hospitals or similar establishments
— cultural, artistic, sports or advertising activities.

3. Prior to any assignment to night work and at regular intervals thereafter, adolescents shall be entitled to a free assessment of their health and capacities, unless the work they do during the period during which work is prohibited is of an exceptional nature.

Article 10 Rest period

9–103 1. (a) Member States which make use of the option in Article 4(2)(b) or (c) shall adopt the measures necessary to ensure that, for each 24-hour period, children are entitled to a minimum rest period of 14 consecutive hours.
(b) Member States shall adopt the measures necessary to ensure that, for each 24-hour period, adolescents are entitled to a minimum rest period of 12 consecutive hours.

2. Member States shall adopt the measures necessary to ensure that, for each seven-day period:
— children in respect of whom they have made use of the option in Article 4(2)(b) or (c), and
— adolescents are entitled to a minimum rest period of two days, which shall be consecutive if possible.

Where justified by technical or organisation reasons, the minimum rest period may be reduced, but may in no circumstances be less than 36 consecutive hours.

The minimum rest period referred to in the first and second sub-paragraphs shall in principle include Sunday.

3. Member States may, by legislative or regulatory provision, provide for the minimum rest periods referred to in paragraphs 1 and 2 to be interrupted in the case of activities involving periods of work that are split up over the day or are of short duration.

4. Member States may make legislative or regulatory provision for derogations from paragraph 1(b) and paragraph 2 in respect of adolescents in the following cases, where there are objective grounds for so doing and provided that they are granted appropriate compensatory rest time and that the objectives set out in Article 1 are not called into question:
(a) work performed in the shipping or fisheries sectors;
(b) work performed in the context of the armed forces or the police;
(c) work performed in hospitals or similar establishments;
(d) work performed in agriculture;
(e) work performed in the tourism industry or in the hotel, restaurant and café sector;
(f) activities involving periods of work split up over the day.

Article 11 Annual rest

9–104 Member States which make use of the option referred to in Article 4(2)(b) or (c) shall see to it that a period free of any work is included, as far as possible, in the school holidays of children subject to compulsory full-time schooling under national law.

Article 12 Breaks

9–105 Member States shall adopt the measures necessary to ensure that, where daily working time is more than four and a half hours, young people are entitled to a break of at least 30 minutes, which shall be consecutive if possible.

Article 13 Work by adolescents in the event of *force majeure*

Member States may, by legislative or regulatory provision, authorise derogations from Article 8(2), Article 9(1)(b), Article 10(1)(b) and, in the case of adolescents, Article 12, for work in the circumstances referred to in Article 5(4) of Directive 89/391, provided that such work is of a temporary nature and must be performed immediately, that adult workers are not available and that the adolescents are allowed equivalent compensatory rest time within the following three weeks. **9–106**

SECTION IV

Article 14 Measures

Each Member State shall lay down any necessary measures to be applied in the event of failure to comply with the provisions adopted in order to implement this Directive such measures must be effective and proportionate. **9–107**

Article 15 Adaptation of the Annex

Adaptations of a strictly technical nature to the Annex in the light of technical progress, changes in international rules or specifications and advances in knowledge in the field covered by this Directive shall be adopted in accordance with the procedure provided for in Article 17 of Directive 89/391. **9–108**

Article 16 Non-reducing clause

Without prejudice to the right of Member States to develop, in the light of changing circumstances, different provisions on the protection of young people, as long as the minimum requirements provided for by this Directive are complied with, the implementation of this Directive shall not constitute valid grounds for reducing the general level of protection afforded to young people. **9–109**

Article 17 Final provisions

1. (a) Member States shall bring into force the laws, regulations and administrative provisions necessary to comply with this Directive not later than 22 June 1996 or ensure, by that date at the latest, that the two sides of industry introduce the requisite provisions by means of collective agreements, with Member States being required to make all the necessary provisions to enable them at all times to guarantee the results laid down by this Directive. **9–110**

(b) The United Kingdom may refrain from implementing the first sub-paragraph of Article 8(1)(b) with regard to the provision relating to the maximum weekly working time, and also Article 8(2) and Article 9(1)(b) and (2) for a period of four years from the date specified in sub-paragraph (a).

The Commission shall submit a report on the effects of this provision.

The Council, acting in accordance with the conditions laid down by the Treaty, shall decide whether this period should be extended.

(c) Member States shall forthwith inform the Commission thereof.

2. When Member States adopt the measures referred to in paragraph 1, such measures shall contain a reference to this Directive or shall be accompanied by

such reference on the occasion of their official publication. The methods of making such reference shall be laid down by Member States.

3. Member States shall communicate to the Commission the texts of the main provisions of national law which they have already adopted or adopt in the field governed by this Directive.

4. Member States shall report to the Commission every five years on the practical implementation of the provisions of this Directive, indicating the viewpoints of the two sides of industry.

The Commission shall inform the European Parliament, the Council and the Economic and Social Committee thereof.

5. The Commission shall periodically submit to the European Parliament, the Council and the Economic and Social Committee a report on the application of this Directive taking into account paragraphs 1, 2, 3 and 4.

Article 18 [Addressees]

9–111 This Directive is addressed to the Member States.

Annex—Non-exhaustive List of Agents, Processes and Work (Article 7(2), second sub-paragraph)

I. Agents

9–112 1. Physical agents
(a) Ionising radiation;
(b) Work in a high-pressure atmosphere, *e.g.* in pressurised containers, diving.

2. Biological agents
(a) Biological agents belonging to groups 3 and 4 within the meaning of Article 2(d) of Council Directive 90/679 of 26 November 1990, on the protection of workers from risks related to exposure to biological agents at work (Seventh individual Directive within the meaning of Article 16(1) of Directive 89/391).[57]

3. Chemical agents
(a) Substances and preparations classified according to Council Directive 67/548 of 27 June 1967, on the approximation of laws, regulations and administrative provisions relating to the classification, packaging and labelling of dangerous substances[58] with amendments and Council Directive 88/379 of 7 June 1988, on the approximation of the laws, regulations and administrative provisions of the Member States relating to the classification, packaging and labelling of dangerous preparations[59]as toxic (T), very toxic (Tx), corrosive (C) or explosive (E);
(b) Substances and preparations classified according to Directives 67/548 and 88/379 as harmful (Xn) and with one or more of the following risk phrases:
— danger of very serious irreversible effects (R39),
— possible risk of irreversible effects (R40),
— may cause sensitisation by inhalation (R42),
— may cause sensitisation by skin contact (R43),

[57] [1990] OJ L374/1.
[58] [1967] OJ 196/1. Directive as last amended by Directive 93/679 ([1993 OJ L268/71).
[59] [1988] OJ L187/14. Directive as last amended by Directive 93/18 ([1993] OJ L104/46).

— may cause cancer (R45),
— may cause heritable genetic damage (R46),
— danger of serious damage to health by prolonged exposure (R48),
— may impair fertility (R60),
— may cause harm to the unborn child (R61);

(c) Substances and preparations classified according to Directives 67/548 and 88/379 as irritant (Xi) and with one or more of the following risk phrases:
— highly flammable (R12),
— may cause sensitisation by inhalation (R42),
— may cause sensitisation by skin contact (R43);

(d) Substances and preparations referred to Article 2(c) of Council Directive 90/394 of 28 June 1990, on the protection of workers from the risks related to exposure to carcinogens at work (Sixth individual Directive within the meaning of Article 16(1) of Directive 89/391[60];

(e) Lead and compounds thereof, inasmuch as the agents in question are absorbable by the human organism;

(f) Asbestos.

II. Processes and work

1. Processes at work referred to in Annex I to Directive 90/394. **9–113**
2. Manufacture and handling of devices, fireworks or other objects containing explosives.
3. Work with fierce of poisonous animals.
4. Animal slaughtering on an industrial scale.
5. Work involving the handling of equipment for the production, storage or application of compressed, liquified or dissolved gases.
6. Work with vats, tanks, reservoirs or carboys containing chemical agents referred to in 1.3.
7. Work involving a risk of structural collapse.
8. Work involving high-voltage electrical hazards.
9. Work the pace of which is determined by machinery and involving payment by results.

Council Directive 94/45 of 22 September 1994, on the establishment of a European Works Council or a procedure in Community-scale undertakings and Community-scale groups of undertakings for the purposes of informing and consulting employees

([1994] OJ L254/64; Doc. Ref. 31994L0045)

The Council of the European Union, **9–114**

Having regard to the Agreement on social policy annexed to Protocol 14 on social policy annexed to the Treaty establishing the European Community, and in particular Article 2(2) thereof,[61]

Having regard to the proposal from the Commission,[62]

Having regard to the opinion of the Economic and Social Committee,[63]

Acting in accordance with the procedure referred to in Article [252] of the Treaty,[64]

[1] Whereas, on the basis of the Protocol on Social Policy annexed to the Treaty establishing the European Community, the Kingdom of Belgium, the Kingdom of Denmark, the Federal Republic of Germany, the Hellenic Republic, the Kingdom

[60] [1990] OJ L196/1.
[61] Now incorporated in Art. 137(2) of the EC Treaty.
[62] [1994] OJ C135/8 and [1994] OJ C199/10.
[63] Opinion delivered on 1 June 1994.
[64] Opinion of the European Parliament of 4 May 1994 ([1994] OJ C205) and Council common position of 18 July 1994 ([1994] OJ C244/37).

of Spain, the French Republic, Ireland, the Italian Republic, the Grand Duchy of Luxembourg, the Kingdom of the Netherlands and the Portuguese Republic (hereinafter referred to as "the Member States"),[65] desirous of implementing the Social Charter of 1989, have adopted an Agreement on Social Policy;

[2] Whereas Article 2(2) of the said Agreement authorises the Council to adopt minimum requirements by means of directives;

[3] Whereas, pursuant to Article 1 of the Agreement,[66] one particular objective of the Community and the Member States is to promote dialogue between management and labour;

[4] Whereas point 17 of the Community Charter of Fundamental Social Rights of Workers provides, *inter alia*, that information, consultation and participation for workers must be developed along appropriate lines, taking account of the practices in force in different Member States whereas the Charter states that "this shall apply especially in companies or groups of companies having establishments or companies in two or more Member States";

[5] Whereas the Council, despite the existence of a broad consensus among the majority of Member States, was unable to act on the proposal for a Council Directive on the establishment of a European Works Council in Community-scale undertakings or groups of undertakings for the purposes of informing and consulting employees,[67] as amended on 3 December 1991[68];

[6] Whereas the Commission, pursuant to Article 3(2) of the Agreement on Social Policy,[69] has consulted management and labour at Community level on the possible direction of Community action on the information and consultation of workers in Community-scale undertakings and Community-scale groups of undertakings;

[7] Whereas the Commission, considering after this consultation that Community action was advisable, has again consulted management and labour on the content of the planned proposal, pursuant to Article 3(3) of the said Agreement,[70] and management and labour have presented their opinions to the Commission;

[8] Whereas, following this second phase of consultation, management and labour have not informed the Commission of their wish to initiate the process which might lead to the conclusion of an agreement, as provided for in Article 4 of the Agreement;

[9] Whereas the functioning of the internal market involves a process of concentrations of undertakings, cross-border mergers, take-overs, joint ventures and, consequently, a transnationalisation of undertakings and groups of undertakings; whereas, if economic activities are to develop in a harmonious fashion, undertakings and groups of undertakings operating in two or more Member States must inform and consult the representatives of those of their employees that are affected by their decisions;

[10] Whereas procedures for informing and consulting employees as embodied in legislation or practice in the Member States are often not geared to the transnational structure of the entity which takes the decisions affecting those employees; whereas this may lead to the unequal treatment of employees affected by decisions within one and the same undertaking or group of undertakings;

[11] Whereas appropriate provisions must be adopted to ensure that the employees of Community-scale undertakings are properly informed and consulted when decisions which affect them are taken in a Member State other than that in which they are employed;

---

[65] See Directive 97/74 ([1998] OJ L10/22) extending this Directive to the UK following incorporation of the Agreement on Social Policy into the Treaty.

[66] Now incorporated in Art. 136 of the EC Treaty.

[67] [1991] OJ C39/10.

[68] [1991] OJ C336/11.

[69] Now incorporated in Art. 138(2) of the EC Treaty.

[70] Now incorporated in Art. 138(3) of the EC Treaty.

[12] Whereas, in order to guarantee that the employees of undertakings or groups of undertakings operating in two or more Member States are properly informed and consulted, it is necessary to set up European Works Councils or to create other suitable procedures for the transnational information and consultation of employees;

[13] Whereas it is accordingly necessary to have a definition of the concept of controlling undertaking relating solely to this Directive and not prejudging definitions of the concepts of group or control which might be adopted in texts to be drafted in the future;

[14] Whereas the mechanisms for informing and consulting employees in such undertakings or groups must encompass all of the establishments or, as the case may be, the group's undertakings located within the Member States, regardless of whether the undertaking or the group's controlling undertaking has its central management inside or outside the territory of the Member States;

[15] Whereas, in accordance with the principle of autonomy of the parties, it is for the representatives of employees and the management of the undertaking or the group's controlling undertaking to determine by agreement the nature, composition, the function, mode of operation, procedures and financial resources of European Works Councils or other information and consultation procedures so as to suit their own particular circumstances;

[16] Whereas, in accordance with the principle of subsidiarity, it is for the Member States to determine who the employees' representatives are and in particular to provide, if they consider appropriate, for a balanced representation of different categories of employees;

[17] Whereas, however, provision should be made for certain subsidiary requirements to apply should the parties so decide or in the event of the central management refusing to initiate negotiations or in the absence of agreement subsequent to such negotiations;

[18] Whereas, moreover, employees' representatives may decide not to seek the setting-up of a European Works Council or the parties concerned may decide on other procedures for the transnational information and consultation of employees;

[19] Whereas, without prejudice to the possibility of the parties deciding otherwise, the European Works Council set up in the absence of agreement between the parties must, in order to fulfil the objective of this Directive, be kept informed and consulted on the activities of the undertaking or group of undertakings so that it may assess the possible impact on employees' interests in at least two different Member States; whereas, to that end, the undertaking or controlling undertaking must be required to communicate to the employees' appointed representatives general information concerning the interests of employees and information relating more specifically to those aspects of the activities of the undertaking or group of undertakings which affect employees' interests; whereas the European Works Council must be able to deliver an opinion at the end of that meeting;

[20] Whereas certain decisions having a significant effect on the interests of employees must be the subject of information and consultation of the employees' appointed representatives as soon as possible;

[21] Whereas provision should be made for the employees' representatives acting within the framework of the Directive to enjoy, when exercising their functions, the same protection and guarantees similar to those provided to employees' representatives by the legislation and/or practice of the country of employment; whereas they must not be subject to any discrimination as a result of the lawful exercise of their activities and must enjoy adequate protection as regards dismissal and other sanctions;

[22] Whereas the information and consultation provisions laid down in this Directive must be implemented in the case of an undertaking or a group's controlling undertaking which has its central management outside the territory of

the Member States by its representative agent, to be designated if necessary, in one of the Member States or, in the absence of such an agent, by the establishment or controlled undertaking employing the greatest number of employees in the Member States;

[23] Whereas special treatment should be accorded to Community-scale undertakings and groups of undertakings in which there exists, at the time when this Directive is brought into effect, an agreement, covering the entire workforce, providing for the transnational information and consultation of employees;

[24] Whereas the Member States must take appropriate measures in the event of failure to comply with the obligations laid down in this Directive,

Has adopted this Directive:

Section I—General

Article 1 Objective

9–115 1. The purpose of this Directive is to improve the right to information and to consultation of employees in Community-scale undertakings and Community-scale groups of undertakings.

2. To that end, a European Works Council or a procedure for informing and consulting employees shall be established in every Community-scale undertaking and every Community-scale group of undertakings, where requested in the manner laid down in Article 5(1), with the purpose of informing and consulting employees under the terms, in the manner and with the effects laid down in this Directive.

3. Notwithstanding paragraph 2, where a Community-scale group of undertakings within the meaning of Article 2(1)(c) comprises one or more undertakings or groups of undertakings which are Community-scale undertakings or Community-scale groups of undertakings within the meaning of Article 2(1)(a) or (c), a European Works Council shall be established at the level of the group unless the agreements referred to in Article 6 provide otherwise.

4. Unless a wider scope is provided for in the agreements referred to in Article 6, the powers and competence of European Works Councils and the scope of information and consultation procedures established to achieve the purpose specified in paragraph 1 shall, in the case of a Community-scale undertaking, cover all the establishments located within the Member States and, in the case of a Community-scale group of undertakings, all group undertakings located within the Member States.

5. Member States may provide that this Directive shall not apply to merchant navy crews.

Article 2 Definitions

9–116 1. For the purposes of this Directive:

(a) "Community-scale undertaking" means any undertaking with at least 1000 employees within the Member States and at least 150 employees in each of at least two Member States;

(b) "group of undertakings" means a controlling undertaking and its controlled undertakings;

(c) "Community-scale group of undertakings" means a group of undertakings with the following characteristics:

— at least 1000 employees within the Member States,

— at least two group undertakings in different Member States, and
— at least one group undertaking with at least 150 employees in one Member State and at least one other group undertaking with at least 150 employees in another Member State;

(d) "employees representatives" means the employees' representatives provided for by national law and/or practice;
(e) "central management" means the central management of the Community-scale undertaking or, in the case of a Community-scale group of undertakings, of the controlling undertaking;
(f) "consultation" means the exchange of views and establishment of dialogue between employees' representatives and central management or any more appropriate level of management;
(g) "European Works Council" means the council established in accordance with Article 1(2) or the provisions of the Annex, with the purpose of informing and consulting employees;
(h) "special negotiating body" means the body established in accordance with Article 5(2) to negotiate with the central management regarding the establishment of a European Works Council or a procedure for informing and consulting employees in accordance with Article 1(2).

2. For the purposes of this Directive, the prescribed thresholds for the size of the workforce shall be based on the average number of employees, including part-time employees, employed during the previous two years calculated according to national legislation and/or practice.

Article 3 Definition of "controlling undertaking"

1. For the purposes of this Directive, "controlling undertaking" means an undertaking which can exercise a dominant influence over another undertaking ("the controlled undertaking") by virtue, for example, of ownership, financial participation or the rules which govern it. **9–117**

2. The ability to exercise a dominant influence shall be presumed, without prejudice to proof to the contrary, when, in relation to another undertaking directly or indirectly:

(a) holds a majority of that undertaking's subscribed capital; or
(b) controls a majority of the votes attached to that undertaking's issued share capital; or
(c) can appoint more than half of the members of that undertaking's administrative, management or supervisory body.

3. For the purposes of paragraph 2, a controlling undertaking's rights as regards voting and appointment shall include the rights of any other controlled undertaking and those of any person or body acting in his or its own name but on behalf of the controlling undertaking or of any other controlled undertaking.

4. Notwithstanding paragraphs 1 and 2, an undertaking shall not be deemed to be a "controlling undertaking" with respect to another undertaking in which it has holdings where the former undertaking is a company referred to in Article 3(5)(a) or (c) of Council Regulation 4064/89 of 21 December 1989, on the control of concentrations between undertakings.[71]

5. A dominant influence shall not be presumed to be exercised solely by virtue of the fact that an office holder is exercising his functions, according to the law of a Member State relating to liquidation, winding up, insolvency, cessation of payments, compositions or analogous proceedings.

6. The law applicable in order to determine whether an undertaking is a "controlling undertaking" shall be the law of the Member State which governs

[71] [1989] OJ L395/1 (see Chapter 8 "Competition").

that undertaking. Where the law governing that undertaking is not that of a Member State, the law applicable shall be the law of the Member State within whose territory the representative of the undertaking or, in the absence of such a representative, the central management of the group undertaking which employs the greatest number of employees is situated.

7. Where, in the case of a conflict of laws in the application of paragraph 2, two or more undertakings from a group satisfy one or more of the criteria laid down in that paragraph, the undertaking which satisfies the criterion laid down in point (c) thereof shall be regarded as the controlling undertaking, without prejudice to proof that another undertaking is able to exercise a dominant influence.

Section II—Establishment of a European Works Council or an Employee Information and Consultation Procedure

Article 4 Responsibility for the establishment of a European Works Council or an employee information and consultation procedure

9–118 1. The central management shall be responsible for creating the conditions and means necessary for the setting up of a European Works Council or an information and consultation procedure, as provided for in Article 1(2), in a Community-scale undertaking and a Community-scale group of undertakings.

2. Where the central management is not situated in a Member State, the central management's representative agent in a Member State, to be designated if necessary, shall take on the responsibility referred to in paragraph 1.

In the absence of such a representative, the management of the establishment or group undertaking employing the greatest number of employees in any one Member State shall take on the responsibility referred to in paragraph 1.

3. For the purposes of this Directive, the representative or representatives or, in the absence of any such representatives, the management referred to in the second sub-paragraph of paragraph 2, shall be regarded as the central management.

Article 5 Special negotiating body

9–119 1. In order to achieve the objective in Article 1(1), the central management shall initiate negotiations for the establishment of a European Works Council or an information and consultation procedure on its own initiative or at the written request of at least 100 employees or their representatives in at least two undertakings or establishments in at least two different Member States.

2. For this purpose, a special negotiating body shall be established in accordance with the following guidelines:

(a) The Member States shall determine the method to be used for the election or appointment of the members of the special negotiating body who are to be elected or appointed in their territories.

Member States shall provide that employees in undertakings and/or establishments in which there are no employees' representatives through no fault of their own, have the right to elect or appoint members of the special negotiating body.

The second sub-paragraph shall be without prejudice to national legislation and/or practice laying down thresholds for the establishment of employee representation bodies.

(b) The special negotiating body shall have a minimum of three and a maximum of [18][72] members.

---

[72] Number substituted by Directive 97/74 ([1998] OJ L10/22) Art. 2 as from 5 February 1998.

(c) In these elections or appointments, it must be ensured:
- — firstly, that each Member State in which the Community-scale undertaking has one or more establishments or in which the Community-scale group of undertakings has the controlling undertaking or one or more controlled undertakings is represented by one member,
- — secondly, that there are supplementary members in proportion to the number of employees working in the establishments, the controlling undertaking or the controlled undertakings as laid down by the legislation of the Member State within the territory of which the central management is situated.

(d) The central management and local management shall be informed of the composition of the special negotiating body.

3. The special negotiating body shall have the task of determining, with the central management, by written agreement, the scope, composition, functions, and term of office of the European Works Council(s) or the arrangements for implementing a procedure for the information and consultation of employees.

4. With a view to the conclusion of an agreement in accordance with Article 6, the central management shall convene a meeting with the special negotiating body. It shall inform the local managements accordingly.

For the purpose of the negotiations, the special negotiating body may be assisted by experts of its choice.

5. The special negotiating body may decide, by at least two-thirds of the votes, not to open negotiations in accordance with paragraph 4, or to terminate the negotiations already opened.

Such a decision shall stop the procedure to conclude the agreement referred to in Article 6. Where such a decision has been taken, the provisions in the Annex shall not apply.

A new request to convene the special negotiating body may be made at the earliest two years after the abovementioned decision unless the parties concerned lay down a shorter period.

6. Any expenses relating to the negotiations referred to in paragraphs 3 and 4 shall be borne by the central management so as to enable the special negotiating body to carry out its task in an appropriate manner.

In compliance with this principle, Member States may lay down budgetary rules regarding the operation of the special negotiating body. They may in particular limit the funding to cover one expert only.

Article 6 Content of the agreement

1. The central management and the special negotiating body must negotiate in a spirit of cooperation with a view to reaching an agreement on the detailed arrangements for implementing the information and consultation of employees provided for in Article 1(1). **9–120**

2. Without prejudice to the autonomy of the parties, the agreement referred to in paragraph 1 between the central management and the special negotiating body shall determine:

(a) the undertakings of the Community-scale group of undertakings or the establishments of the Community-scale undertaking which are covered by the agreement;

(b) the composition of the European Works Council, the number of members, the allocation of seats and the term of office;

(c) the functions and the procedure for information and consultation of the European Works Council;

(d) the venue, frequency and duration of meetings of the European Works Council;

(e) the financial and material resources to be allocated to the European Works Council;
(f) the duration of the agreement and the procedure for its renegotiation.

3. The central management and the special negotiating body may decide, in writing, to establish one or more information and consultation procedures instead of a European Works Council.

The agreement must stipulate by what method the employees' representatives shall have the right to meet to discuss the information conveyed to them.

This information shall relate in particular to transnational questions which significantly affect workers' interests.

4. The agreements referred to in paragraphs 2 and 3 shall not, unless provision is made otherwise therein, be subject to the subsidiary requirements of the Annex.

5. For the purposes of concluding the agreements referred to in paragraphs 2 and 3, the special negotiating body shall act by a majority of its members.

Article 7 Subsidiary requirements

9–121 1. In order to achieve the objective in Article 1(1), the subsidiary requirements laid down by the legislation of the Member State in which the central management is situated shall apply:

— where the central management and the special negotiating body so decide, or
— where the central management refuses to commence negotiations within six months of the request referred to in Article 5(1), or
— where, after three years from the date of this request, they are unable to conclude an agreement as laid down in Article 6 and the special negotiating body has not taken the decision provided for in Article 5(5).

2. The subsidiary requirements referred to in paragraph 1 as adopted in the legislation of the Member States must satisfy the provisions set out in the Annex.

Section III—Miscellaneous Provisions

Article 8 Confidential information

9–122 1. Member States shall provide that members of special negotiating bodies or of European Works Councils and any experts who assist them are not authorised to reveal any information which has expressly been provided to them in confidence.

The same shall apply to employees' representatives in the framework of an information and consultation procedure.

This obligation shall continue to apply, wherever the persons referred to in the first and second sub-paragraphs are, even after the expiry of their terms of office.

2. Each Member State shall provide, in specific cases and under the conditions and limits laid down by national legislation, that the central management situated in its territory is not obliged to transmit information when its nature is such that, according to objective criteria, it would seriously harm the functioning of the undertakings concerned or would be prejudicial to them.

A Member State may make such dispensation subject to prior administrative or judicial authorisation.

3. Each Member State may lay down particular provisions for the central management of undertakings in its territory which pursue directly and essentially the aim of ideological guidance with respect to information and the expression of

opinions, on condition that, at the date of adoption of this Directive such particular provisions already exist in the national legislation.

Article 9 Operation of European Works Council and information and consultation procedure for workers

The central management and the European Works Council shall work in a spirit of co-operation with due regard to their reciprocal rights and obligations. **9–123**

The same shall apply to co-operation between the central management and employees' representatives in the framework of an information and consultation procedure for workers.

Article 10 Protection of employees' representatives

Members of special negotiating bodies, members of European Works Councils and employees' representatives exercising their functions under the procedure referred to in Article 6(3) shall, in the exercise of their functions, enjoy the same protection and guarantees provided for employees' representatives by the national legislation and/or practice in force in their country of employment. **9–124**

This shall apply in particular to attendance at meetings of special negotiating bodies or European Works Councils or any other meetings within the framework of the agreement referred to in Article 6(3), and the payment of wages for members who are on the staff of the Community-scale undertaking or the Community-scale group of undertakings for the period of absence necessary for the performance of their duties.

Article 11 Compliance with this Directive

1. Each Member State shall ensure that the management of establishments of a Community-scale undertaking and the management of undertakings which form part of a Community-scale group of undertakings which are situated within its territory and their employees' representatives or, as the case may be, employees abide by the obligations laid down by this Directive, regardless of whether or not the central management is situated within its territory. **9–125**

2. Member States shall ensure that the information on the number of employees referred to in Article 2(1)(a) and (c) is made available by undertakings at the request of the parties concerned by the application of this Directive.

3. Member States shall provide for appropriate measures in the event of failure to comply with this Directive in particular, they shall ensure that adequate administrative or judicial procedures are available to enable the obligations deriving from this Directive to be enforced.

4. Where Member States apply Article 8, they shall make provision for administrative or judicial appeal procedures which the employees' representatives may initiate when the central management requires confidentiality or does not give information in accordance with that Article.

Such procedures may include procedures designed to protect the confidentiality of the information in question.

Article 12 Link between this Directive and other provisions

1. This Directive shall apply without prejudice to measures taken pursuant to Council Directive 75/129 of 17 February 1975, on the approximation of the laws of the Member States relating to collective redundancies,[73] and to Council Directive 77/187 of 14 February 1977, on the approximation of the laws of the Member **9–126**

[73] [1975] OJ L48/29. Directive as last amended by Directive 92/56 ([1992] OJ L245/3). [Directive 75/129 has since been replaced by Directive 98/59, see below.]

States relating to the safeguarding of employees' rights in the event of transfers of undertakings, businesses or parts of businesses.[74]

2. This Directive shall be without prejudice to employees' existing rights to information and consultation under national law.

Article 13 Agreements in force

9–127 1. Without prejudice to paragraph 2, the obligations arising from this Directive shall not apply to Community-scale undertakings or Community-scale groups of undertakings in which, on the date laid down in Article 14(1) for the implementation of this Directive or the date of its transposition in the Member State in question, where this is earlier than the abovementioned date, there is already an agreement, covering the entire workforce, providing for the transnational information and consultation of employees.

2. When the agreements referred to in paragraph 1 expire, the parties to those agreements may decide jointly to renew them.

Where this is not the case, the provisions of this Directive shall apply.

Article 14 Final provisions

9–128 1. Member States shall bring into force the laws, regulations and administrative provisions necessary to comply with this Directive no later than 22 September 1996, or shall ensure by that date at the latest that management and labour introduce the required provisions by way of agreement, the Member States being obliged to take all necessary steps enabling them at all times to guarantee the results imposed by this Directive. They shall forthwith inform the Commission thereof.

2. When Member States adopt these measures, they shall contain a reference to this Directive or shall be accompanied by such reference on the occasion of their official publication. The methods of making such reference shall be laid down by Member States.

Article 15 Review by the Commission

9–129 Not later than 22 September 1999, the Commission shall, in consultation with the Member States and with management and labour at European level, review its operation and, in particular examine whether the workforce size thresholds are appropriate with a view to proposing suitable amendments to the Council, where necessary.

Article 16 [Addressees]

9–130 This Directive is addressed to the Member States.

Annex—Subsidiary Requirements Referred to in Article 7 of the Directive

9–131 1. In order to achieve the objective in Article 1(1) of the Directive and in the cases provided for in Article 7(1) of the Directive, the establishment, composition and competence of a European Works Council shall be governed by the following rules:

[74] [1977] OJ L61/26. [Directive 77/187 has since been replaced by Directive 2001/23, see below.]

(a) The competence of the European Works Council shall be limited to information and consultation on the matters which concern the Community-scale undertaking or Community-scale group of undertakings as a whole or at least two of its establishments or group undertakings situated in different Member States.

In the case of undertakings or groups of undertakings referred to in Article 4(2), the competence of the European Works Council shall be limited to those matters concerning all their establishments or group undertakings situated within the Member States or concerning at least two of their establishments or group undertakings situated in different Member States.

(b) The European Works Council shall be composed of employees of the Community-scale undertaking or Community-scale group of undertakings elected or appointed from their number by the employees' representatives or, in the absence thereof, by the entire body of employees.

The election or appointment of members of the European Works Council shall be carried out in accordance with national legislation and/or practice.

(c) The European Works Council shall have a minimum of three members and a maximum of 30.

Where its size so warrants, it shall elect a select committee from among its members, comprising at most three members.

It shall adopt its own rules of procedure.

(d) In the election or appointment of members of the European Works Council, it must be ensured:

— firstly, that each Member State in which the Community-scale undertaking has one or more establishments or in which the Community-scale group of undertakings has the controlling undertaking or one or more controlled undertakings is represented by one member,

— secondly, that there are supplementary members in proportion to the number of employees working in the establishments, the controlling undertaking or the controlled undertakings as laid down by the legislation of the Member State within the territory of which the central management is situated.

(e) The central management and any other more appropriate level of management shall be informed of the composition of the European Works Council.

(f) Four years after the European Works Council is established it shall examine whether to open negotiations for the conclusion of the agreement referred to in Article 6 of the Directive or to continue to apply the subsidiary requirements adopted in accordance with this Annex.

Articles 6 and 7 of the Directive shall apply, *mutatis mutandis*, if a decision has been taken to negotiate an agreement according to Article 6 of the Directive, in which case "special negotiating body" shall be replaced by "European Works Council".

2. The European Works Council shall have the right to meet with the central management once a year, to be informed and consulted, on the basis of a report drawn up by the central management, on the progress of the business of the Community-scale undertaking or Community-scale group of undertakings and its prospects. The local managements shall be informed accordingly.

The meeting shall relate in particular to the structure, economic and financial situation, the probable development of the business and of production and sales, the situation and probable trend of employment, investments, and substantial changes concerning organisation, introduction of new working methods or production processes, transfers of production, mergers, cut-backs or closures of undertakings, establishments or important parts thereof, and collective redundancies.

3. Where there are exceptional circumstances affecting the employees' interests to a considerable extent, particularly in the event of relocations, the closure of

establishments or undertakings or collective redundancies, the select committee or, where no such committee exists, the European Works Council shall have the right to be informed. It shall have the right to meet, at its request, the central management, or any other more appropriate level of management within the Community-scale undertaking or group of undertakings having its own powers of decision, so as to be informed and consulted on measures significantly affecting employees' interests.

Those members of the European Works Council who have been elected or appointed by the establishments and/or undertakings which are directly concerned by the measures in question shall also have the right to participate in the meeting organized with the select committee.

This information and consultation meeting shall take place as soon as possible on the basis of a report drawn up by the central management or any other appropriate level of management of the Community-scale undertaking or group of undertakings, on which an opinion may be delivered at the end of the meeting or within a reasonable time.

This meeting shall not affect the prerogatives of the central management.

4. The Member States may lay down rules on the chairing of information and consultation meetings.

Before any meeting with the central management, the European Works Council or the select committee, where necessary enlarged in accordance with the second paragraph of point 3, shall be entitled to meet without the management concerned being present.

5. Without prejudice to Article 8 of the Directive, the members of the European Works Council shall inform the representatives of the employees of the establishments or of the undertakings of a Community-scale group of undertakings or, in the absence of representatives, the workforce as a whole, of the content and outcome of the information and consultation procedure carried out in accordance with this Annex.

6. The European Works Council or the select committee may be assisted by experts of its choice, in so far as this is necessary for it to carry out its tasks.

7. The operating expenses of the European Works Council shall be borne by the central management.

The central management concerned shall provide the members of the European Works Council with such financial and material resources as enable them to perform their duties in an appropriate manner.

In particular, the cost of organising meetings and arranging for interpretation facilities and the accommodation and travelling expenses of members of the European Works Council and its select committee shall be met by the central management unless otherwise agreed.

In compliance with these principles, the Member States may lay down budgetary rules regarding the operation of the European Works Council. They may in particular limit funding to cover one expert only.

Council Directive 97/81 of 15 December 1997, concerning the Framework Agreement on part-time work concluded by UNICE, CEEP and the ETUC

([1998] OJ L14/9; Doc. Ref. 31997L0081)

9–132 *The Council of the European Union,*

Having regard to the Agreement on social policy annexed to the Protocol (No. 14) on social policy, annexed to the Treaty establishing the European Community, and in particular Article 4(2) thereof,[75]

Having regard to the proposal from the Commission,

[75] Now incorporated in Art. 139(2) of the EC Treaty.

(1) Whereas on the basis of the Protocol on social policy annexed to the Treaty establishing the European Community, the Member States, with the exception of the United Kingdom of Great Britain and Northern Ireland (hereinafter referred to as "the Member States"),[76] wishing to continue along the path laid down in the 1989 Social Charter, have concluded an agreement on social policy;

(2) Whereas management and labour (the social partners) may, in accordance with Article 4(2) of the Agreement on social policy, request jointly that agreements at Community level be implemented by a Council decision on a proposal from the Commission;

(3) Whereas point 7 of the Community Charter of the Fundamental Social Rights of Workers provides, *inter alia*, that "the completion of the internal market must lead to an improvement in the living and working conditions of workers in the European Community. This process must result from an approximation of these conditions while the improvement is being maintained, as regards in particular (...) forms of employment other than open-ended contracts, such as fixed-term contracts, part-time working, temporary work and seasonal work";

(4) Whereas the Council has not reached a decision on the proposal for a Directive on certain employment relationships with regard to distortions of competition,[77] as amended,[78] nor on the proposal for a Directive on certain employment relationships with regard to working conditions[79];

(5) Whereas the conclusions of the Essen European Council stressed the need to take measures to promote employment and equal opportunities for women and men, and called for measures with a view to increasing the employment-intensiveness of growth, in particular by a more flexible organisation of work in a way which fulfils both the wishes of employees and the requirements of competition;

(6) Whereas the Commission, in accordance with Article 3(2) of the Agreement on social policy,[80] has consulted management and labour on the possible direction of Community action with regard to flexible working time and job security;

(7) Whereas the Commission, considering after such consultation that Community action was desirable, once again consulted management and labour at Community level on the substance of the envisaged proposal in accordance with Article 3(3) of the said Agreement[81];

(8) Whereas the general cross-industry organisations, the Union of Industrial and Employer's Confederations of Europe (UNICE), the European Centre of Enterprises with Public Participation (CEEP) and the European Trade Union Confederation (ETUC) informed the Commission in their joint letter of 19 June 1996, of their desire to initiate the procedure provided for in Article 4 of the Agreement on social policy; whereas they asked the Commission, in a joint letter dated 12 March 1997, for a further three months; whereas the Commission complied with this request;

(9) Whereas the said cross-industry organisations concluded, on 6 June 1997, a Framework Agreement on part-time work whereas they forwarded to the Commission their joint request to implement this Framework Agreement by a Council decision on a proposal from the Commission, in accordance with Article 4(2) of the said Agreement;

(10) Whereas the Council, in its Resolution of 6 December 1994, on prospects for a European Union social policy: contribution to economic and social convergence in the Union,[82] asked management and labour to make use of the

[76] But see Directive 98/23 ([1998] OJ L131/10) extending this Directive to the UK following incorporation of the Agreement on Social Policy into the Treaty.

[77] [1990] OJ C224/6.

[78] [1990] OJ C305/8.

[79] [1990] OJ C224/4.

[80] Now incorporated in Art. 138(2) of the EC Treaty.

[81] Now incorporated in Art. 138(3) of the EC Treaty.

[82] [1994] OJ C368/6.

opportunities for concluding agreements, since they are as a rule closer to social reality and to social problems;

(11) Whereas the signatory parties wished to conclude a framework agreement on part-time work setting out the general principles and minimum requirements for part-time working; whereas they have demonstrated their desire to establish a general framework for eliminating discrimination against part-time workers and to contribute to developing the potential for part-time work on a basis which is acceptable for employers and workers alike;

(12) Whereas the social partners wished to give particular attention to part-time work, while at the same time indicating that it was their intention to consider the need for similar agreements for other flexible forms of work;

(13) Whereas, in the conclusions of the Amsterdam European Council, the Heads of State and Government of the European Union strongly welcomed the agreement concluded by the social partners on part-time work;

(14) Whereas the proper instrument for implementing the Framework Agreement is a Directive within the meaning of Article [249] of the Treaty; whereas it therefore binds the Member States as to the result to be achieved, whilst leaving national authorities the choice of form and methods;

(15) Whereas, in accordance with the principles of subsidiarity and proportionality as set out in Article [5] of the Treaty, the objectives of this Directive cannot be sufficiently achieved by the Member States and can therefore be better achieved by the Community; whereas this Directive does not go beyond what is necessary for the attainment of those objectives;

(16) Whereas, with regard to terms used in the Framework Agreement which are not specifically defined therein, this Directive leaves Member States free to define those terms in accordance with national law and practice, as is the case for other social policy Directives using similar terms, providing that the said definitions respect the content of the Framework Agreement;

(17) Whereas the Commission has drafted its proposal for a Directive, in accordance with its Communication of 14 December 1993, concerning the application of the Protocol (No. 14) on social policy and its Communication of 18 September 1996, concerning the development of the social dialogue at Community level, taking into account the representative status of the signatory parties and the legality of each clause of the Framework Agreement;

(18) Whereas the Commission has drafted its proposal for a Directive in compliance with Article 2(2) of the Agreement on social policy[83] which provides that Directives in the social policy domain "shall avoid imposing administrative, financial and legal constraints in a way which would hold back the creation and development of small and medium-sized undertakings";

(19) Whereas the Commission, in accordance with its Communication of 14 December 1993, concerning the application of the Protocol (No. 14) on social policy, informed the European Parliament by sending it the text of its proposal for a Directive containing the Framework Agreement;

(20) Whereas the Commission also informed the Economic and Social Committee;

(21) Whereas Clause 6.1 of the Framework Agreement provides that Member States and/or the social partners may maintain or introduce more favourable provisions;

(22) Whereas Clause 6.2 of the Framework Agreement provides that implementation of this Directive may not serve to justify any regression in relation to the situation which already exists in each Member State;

(23) Whereas the Community Charter of the Fundamental Social Rights of Workers recognises the importance of the fight against all forms of discrimination, especially based on sex, colour, race, opinion and creed;

[83] Now incorporated in Art. 137(2) of the EC Treaty.

(24) Whereas Article [6(2)] of the Treaty on European Union states that the Union shall respect fundamental rights, as guaranteed by the European Convention for the Protection of Human Rights and Fundamental Freedoms and as they result from the constitutional traditions common to the Member States, as general principles of Community law;

(25) Whereas the Member States may entrust the social partners, at their joint request, with the implementation of this Directive, provided that the Member States take all the necessary steps to ensure that they can at all times guarantee the results imposed by this Directive;

(26) Whereas the implementation of the Framework Agreement contributes to achieving the objectives under Article 1 of the Agreement on social policy,[84]

Has adopted this Directive:

Article 1 [Purpose]

The purpose of this Directive is to implement the Framework Agreement on part-time work concluded on 6 June 1997, between the general cross-industry organisations (UNICE, CEEP and the ETUC) annexed hereto. **9–133**

Article 2 [Implementation]

1. Member States shall bring into force the laws, regulations and administrative provisions necessary to comply with this Directive not later than 20 January 2000, or shall ensure that, by that date at the latest, the social partners have introduced the necessary measures by agreement, the Member States being required to take any necessary measures to enable them at any time to be in a position to guarantee the results imposed by this Directive. They shall forthwith inform the Commission thereof. **9–134**

Member States may have a maximum of one more year, if necessary, to take account of special difficulties or implementation by a collective agreement.

They shall inform the Commission forthwith in such circumstances.

When Member States adopt the measures referred to in the first sub-paragraph, they shall contain a reference to this Directive or shall be accompanied by such reference on the occasion of their official publication. The methods of making such a reference shall be laid down by the Member States.

[1a. As regards the United Kingdom of Great Britain and Northern Ireland, the date of 20 January 2000 in paragraph 1 shall be replaced by the date of 7 April 2000.][85]

2. Member States shall communicate to the Commission the text of the main provisions of domestic law which they have adopted or which they adopt in the field governed by this Directive.

Article 3 [Entry into force]

This Directive shall enter into force on the day of its publication in the *Official Journal of the European Communities*.[86] **9–135**

---

[84] Now incorporated in Art. 136 of the EC Treaty.

[85] Article 2(1a) inserted by Directive 98/23 Art. 2 as from 25 May 1998.

[86] The Directive was published on 20 January 1998.

Article 4 [Addressees]

9–136 This Directive is addressed to the Member States.

Annex—Union of Industrial and Employers' Confederations of Europe, European Trade Union Confederation, European Centre of Enterprises with Public Participation—Framework Agreement on Part-time Work

PREAMBLE

9–137 This Framework Agreement is a contribution to the overall European strategy on employment. Part-time work has had an important impact on employment in recent years. For this reason, the parties to this agreement have given priority attention to this form of work. It is the intention of the parties to consider the need for similar agreements relating to other forms of flexible work.

Recognising the diversity of situations in Member States and acknowledging that part-time work is a feature of employment in certain sectors and activities, this Agreement sets out the general principles and minimum requirements relating to part-time work. It illustrates the willingness of the social partners to establish a general framework for the elimination of discrimination against part-time workers and to assist the development of opportunities for part-time working on a basis acceptable to employers and workers.

This Agreement relates to employment conditions of part-time workers recognising that matters concerning statutory social security are for decision by the Member States. In the context of the principle of non-discrimination, the parties to this Agreement have noted the Employment Declaration of the Dublin European Council of December 1996, wherein the Council *inter alia* emphasised the need to make social security systems more employment-friendly by "developing social protection systems capable of adapting to new patterns of work and of providing appropriate protection to people engaged in such work". The parties to this Agreement consider that effect should be given to this Declaration.

ETUC, UNICE and CEEP request the Commission to submit this Framework Agreement to the Council for a decision making these requirements binding in the Member States which are party to the Agreement on social policy annexed to the Protocol (No. 14) on social policy annexed to the Treaty establishing the European Community.

The parties to this Agreement ask the Commission, in its proposal to implement this Agreement, to request that Member States adopt the laws, regulations and administrative provisions necessary to comply with the Council decision within a period of two years from its adoption or ensure[87] that the social partners establish the necessary measures by way of agreement by the end of this period. Member States may, if necessary to take account of particular difficulties or implementation by collective agreement, have up to a maximum of one additional year to comply with this provision.

Without prejudice to the role of national courts and the Court of Justice, the parties to this agreement request that any matter relating to the interpretation of this agreement at European level should, in the first instance, be referred by the Commission to them for an opinion.

GENERAL CONSIDERATIONS

9–138 1. Having regard to the Agreement on social policy annexed to the Protocol (No. 14) on social policy annexed to the Treaty establishing the European Community, and in particular Articles 3(4) and 4(2) thereof,[88]

[87] Within the meaning of Article 2(4) of the Agreement on social policy of the Treaty establishing the European Community. [Now incorporated in Art. 137(4) of the EC Treaty.]

[88] Now incorporated in Art. 138(4) and 139(2) of the EC Treaty.

2. Whereas Article 4(2) of the Agreement on social policy provides that agreements concluded at Community level may be implemented, at the joint request of the signatory parties, by a Council decision on a proposal from the Commission;

3. Whereas, in its second consultation document on flexibility of working time and security for workers, the Commission announced its intention to propose a legally binding Community measure;

4. Whereas the conclusions of the European Council meeting in Essen emphasised the need for measures to promote both employment and equal opportunities for women and men, and called for measures aimed at "increasing the employment intensiveness of growth, in particular by more flexible organisation of work in a way which fulfils both the wishes of employees and the requirements of competition";

5. Whereas the parties to this agreement attach importance to measures which would facilitate access to part-time work for men and women in order to prepare for retirement, reconcile professional and family life, and take up education and training opportunities to improve their skills and career opportunities for the mutual benefit of employers and workers and in a manner which would assist the development of enterprises;

6. Whereas this Agreement refers back to Member States and social partners for the arrangements for the application of these general principles, minimum requirements and provisions, in order to take account of the situation in each Member State;

7. Whereas this Agreement takes into consideration the need to improve social policy requirements, to enhance the competitiveness of the Community economy and to avoid imposing administrative, financial and legal constraints in a way which would hold back the creation and development of small and medium-sized undertakings;

8. Whereas the social partners are best placed to find solutions that correspond to the needs of both employers and workers and must therefore be given a special role in the implementation and application of this Agreement.

The signatory parties have agreed the following:

Clause 1: Purpose

The purpose of this Framework Agreement is: **9–139**

(a) to provide for the removal of discrimination against part-time workers and to improve the quality of part-time work;
(b) to facilitate the development of part-time work on a voluntary basis and to contribute to the flexible organisation of working time in a manner which takes into account the needs of employers and workers.

Clause 2: Scope

1. This Agreement applies to part-time workers who have an employment contract or employment relationship as defined by the law, collective agreement or practice in force in each Member State. **9–140**

2. Member States, after consultation with the social partners in accordance with national law, collective agreements or practice, and/or the social partners at the appropriate level in conformity with national industrial relations practice may, for objective reasons, exclude wholly or partly from the terms of this Agreement part-time workers who work on a casual basis. Such exclusions should be reviewed periodically to establish if the objective reasons for making them remain valid.

Clause 3: Definitions

9–141 For the purpose of this agreement:

1. The term "part-time worker" refers to an employee whose normal hours of work, calculated on a weekly basis or on average over a period of employment of up to one year, are less than the normal hours of work of a comparable full-time worker.
2. The term "comparable full-time worker" means a full-time worker in the same establishment having the same type of employment contract or relationship, who is engaged in the same or a similar work/occupation, due regard being given to other considerations which may include seniority and qualification/skills.

   Where there is no comparable full-time worker in the same establishment, the comparison shall be made by reference to the applicable collective agreement or, where there is no applicable collective agreement, in accordance with national law, collective agreements or practice.

Clause 4: Principle of non-discrimination

9–142 1. In respect of employment conditions, part-time workers shall not be treated in a less favourable manner than comparable full-time workers solely because they work part time unless different treatment is justified on objective grounds.

2. Where appropriate, the principle of *pro rata temporis* shall apply.

3. The arrangements for the application of this clause shall be defined by the Member States and/or social partners, having regard to European legislation, national law, collective agreements and practice.

4. Where justified by objective reasons, Member States after consultation of the social partners in accordance with national law, collective agreements or practice and/or social partners may, where appropriate, make access to particular conditions of employment subject to a period of service, time worked or earnings qualification. Qualifications relating to access by part-time workers to particular conditions of employment should be reviewed periodically having regard to the principle of non-discrimination as expressed in Clause 4.1.

Clause 5: Opportunities for part-time work

9–143 1. In the context of Clause 1 of this Agreement and of the principle of non-discrimination between part-time and full-time workers:

(a) Member States, following consultations with the social partners in accordance with national law or practice, should identify and review obstacles of a legal or administrative nature which may limit the opportunities for part-time work and, where appropriate, eliminate them;

(b) the social partners, acting within their sphere of competence and through the procedures set out in collective agreements, should identify and review obstacles which may limit opportunities for part-time work and, where appropriate, eliminate them.

2. A worker's refusal to transfer from full-time to part-time work or vice-versa should not in itself constitute a valid reason for termination of employment, without prejudice to termination in accordance with national law, collective agreements and practice, for other reasons such as may arise from the operational requirements of the establishment concerned.

3. As far as possible, employers should give consideration to:

(a) requests by workers to transfer from full-time to part-time work that becomes available in the establishment;

(b) requests by workers to transfer from part-time to full-time work or to increase their working time should the opportunity arise;

(c) the provision of timely information on the availability of part-time and full-time positions in the establishment in order to facilitate transfers from full-time to part-time or vice versa;
(d) measures to facilitate access to part-time work at all levels of the enterprise, including skilled and managerial positions, and where appropriate, to facilitate access by part-time workers to vocational training to enhance career opportunities and occupational mobility;
(e) the provision of appropriate information to existing bodies representing workers about part-time working in the enterprise.

Clause 6: Provisions on implementation

1. Member States and/or social partners may maintain or introduce more favourable provisions than set out in this agreement. **9–144**

2. Implementation of the provisions of this Agreement shall not constitute valid grounds for reducing the general level of protection afforded to workers in the field of this agreement. This does not prejudice the right of Member States and/or social partners to develop different legislative, regulatory or contractual provisions, in the light of changing circumstances, and does not prejudice the application of Clause 5.1 as long as the principle of non-discrimination as expressed in Clause 4.1 is complied with.

3. This Agreement does not prejudice the right of the social partners to conclude, at the appropriate level, including European level, agreements adapting and/or complementing the provisions of this Agreement in a manner which will take account of the specific needs of the social partners concerned.

4. This Agreement shall be without prejudice to any more specific Community provisions, and in particular Community provisions concerning equal treatment or opportunities for men and women.

5. The prevention and settlement of disputes and grievances arising from the application of this Agreement shall be dealt with in accordance with national law, collective agreements and practice.

6. The signatory parties shall review this Agreement, five years after the date of the Council decision, if requested by one of the parties to this Agreement.

Council Directive 98/59 of 20 July 1998, on the approximation of the laws of the Member States relating to collective redundancies

([1998] OJ L225/16; Doc. Ref. 31998L0059)

The Council of the European Union, **9–145**

Having regard to the Treaty establishing the European Community, and in particular Article [94] thereof,

Having regard to the proposal from the Commission,

Having regard to the opinion of the European Parliament,[89]

Having regard to the opinion of the Economic and Social Committee,[90]

(1) Whereas for reasons of clarity and rationality Council Directive 75/129 of 17 February 1975, on the approximation of the laws of the Member States relating to collective redundancies[91] should be consolidated;

---

[89] [1998] OJ C210.
[90] [1997] OJ C158/11.
[91] [1975] OJ L48/29. Directive as amended by Directive 92/56 ([1992] OJ L245/3).

(2) Whereas it is important that greater protection should be afforded to workers in the event of collective redundancies while taking into account the need for balanced economic and social development within the Community;

(3) Whereas, despite increasing convergence, differences still remain between the provisions in force in the Member States concerning the practical arrangements and procedures for such redundancies and the measures designed to alleviate the consequences of redundancy for workers;

(4) Whereas these differences can have a direct effect on the functioning of the internal market;

(5) Whereas the Council resolution of 21 January 1974, concerning a social action programme[92] made provision for a directive on the approximation of Member States' legislation on collective redundancies;

(6) Whereas the Community Charter of the fundamental social rights of workers, adopted at the European Council meeting held in Strasbourg on 9 December 1989, by the Heads of State or Government of 11 Member States, states, *inter alia*, in point 7, first paragraph, first sentence, and second paragraph in point 17, first paragraph and in point 18, third indent:

> "7. The completion of the internal market must lead to an improvement in the living and working conditions of workers in the European Community (. . .) The improvement must cover, where necessary, the development of certain aspects of employment regulations such as procedures for collective redundancies and those regarding bankruptcies.
>
> (. . .)
>
> 17. Information, consultation and participation for workers must be developed along appropriate lines, taking account of the practices in force in the various Member States.
>
> (. . .)
>
> 18. Such information, consultation and participation must be implemented in due time, particularly in the following cases:
>
> (— . . .)
>
> (— . . .)
>
> —in cases of collective redundancy procedures
>
> (— . . .)",

(7) Whereas this approximation must therefore be promoted while the improvement is being maintained within the meaning of Article [136] of the Treaty;

(8) Whereas, in order to calculate the number of redundancies provided for in the definition of collective redundancies within the meaning of this Directive, other forms of termination of employment contracts on the initiative of the employer should be equated to redundancies, provided that there are at least five redundancies;

(9) Whereas it should be stipulated that this Directive applies in principle also to collective redundancies resulting where the establishment's activities are terminated as a result of a judicial decision;

(10) Whereas the Member States should be given the option of stipulating that workers' representatives may call on experts on grounds of the technical complexity of the matters which are likely to be the subject of the informing and consulting;

(11) Whereas it is necessary to ensure that employers' obligations as regards information, consultation and notification apply independently of whether the decision on collective redundancies emanates from the employer or from an undertaking which controls that employer;

(12) Whereas Member States should ensure that workers' representatives and/or workers have at their disposal administrative and/or judicial procedures in order to ensure that the obligations laid down in this Directive are fulfilled;

---

[92] [1974] OJ C13/1.

(13) Whereas this Directive must not affect the obligations of the Member States concerning the deadlines for transposition of the Directives set out in Annex I, Part B,
Has adopted this Directive:

Section I—Definitions And Scope

Article 1 [Definitions; exceptions]

1. For the purposes of this Directive: **9–146**
(a) "collective redundancies" means dismissals effected by an employer for one or more reasons not related to the individual workers concerned where, according to the choice of the Member States, the number of redundancies is:
  (i) either, over a period of 30 days:
  — at least 10 in establishments normally employing more than 20 and less than 100 workers,
  — at least 10 per cent of the number of workers in establishments normally employing at least 100 but less than 300 workers,
  — at least 30 in establishments normally employing 300 workers or more,
  (ii) or, over a period of 90 days, at least 20, whatever the number of workers normally employed in the establishments in question;
(b) "workers' representatives" means the workers' representatives provided for by the laws or practices of the Member States.

For the purpose of calculating the number of redundancies provided for in the first sub-paragraph of point (a), terminations of an employment contract which occur on the employer's initiative for one or more reasons not related to the individual workers concerned shall be assimilated to redundancies, provided that there are at least five redundancies.

2. This Directive shall not apply to:
(a) collective redundancies effected under contracts of employment concluded for limited periods of time or for specific tasks except where such redundancies take place prior to the date of expiry or the completion of such contracts;
(b) workers employed by public administrative bodies or by establishments governed by public law (or, in Member States where this concept is unknown, by equivalent bodies);
(c) the crews of seagoing vessels.

Section II—Information and Consultation

Article 2 [Consultations with workers' representatives]

1. Where an employer is contemplating collective redundancies, he shall begin consultations with the workers' representatives in good time with a view to reaching an agreement. **9–147**

2. These consultations shall, at least, cover ways and means of avoiding collective redundancies or reducing the number of workers affected, and of mitigating the consequences by recourse to accompanying social measures aimed, *inter alia*, at aid for redeploying or retraining workers made redundant.

Member States may provide that the workers' representatives may call on the services of experts in accordance with national legislation and/or practice.

3. To enable workers' representatives to make constructive proposals, the employers shall in good time during the course of the consultations:
(a) supply them with all relevant information and
(b) in any event notify them in writing of:
  (i) the reasons for the projected redundancies;
  (ii) the number of categories of workers to be made redundant;

(iii) the number and categories of workers normally employed;
(iv) the period over which the projected redundancies are to be effected;
(v) the criteria proposed for the selection of the workers to be made redundant in so far as national legislation and/or practice confers the power therefor upon the employer;
(vi) the method for calculating any redundancy payments other than those arising out of national legislation and/or practice.
The employer shall forward to the competent public authority a copy of, at least, the elements of the written communication which are provided for in the first sub-paragraph, point (b), sub-points (i) to (v).

4. The obligations laid down in paragraphs 1, 2 and 3 shall apply irrespective of whether the decision regarding collective redundancies is being taken by the employer or by an undertaking controlling the employer.
In considering alleged breaches of the information, consultation and notification requirements laid down by this Directive, account shall not be taken of any defence on the part of the employer on the ground that the necessary information has not been provided to the employer by the undertaking which took the decision leading to collective redundancies.

SECTION III—PROCEDURE FOR COLLECTIVE REDUNDANCIES

Article 3 [Notification]

9–148 1. Employers shall notify the competent public authority in writing of any projected collective redundancies.
However, Member States may provide that in the case of planned collective redundancies arising from termination of the establishment's activities as a result of a judicial decision, the employer shall be obliged to notify the competent public authority in writing only if the latter so requests.
This notification shall contain all relevant information concerning the projected collective redundancies and the consultations with workers' representatives provided for in Article 2, and particularly the reasons for the redundancies, the number of workers to be made redundant, the number of workers normally employed and the period over which the redundancies are to be effected.

2. Employers shall forward to the workers' representatives a copy of the notification provided for in paragraph 1.
The workers' representatives may send any comments they may have to the competent public authority.

Article 4 [Time-limit]

9–149 1. Projected collective redundancies notified to the competent public authority shall take effect not earlier than 30 days after the notification referred to in Article 3(1) without prejudice to any provisions governing individual rights with regard to notice of dismissal.
Member States may grant the competent public authority the power to reduce the period provided for in the preceding sub-paragraph.

2. The period provided for in paragraph 1 shall be used by the competent public authority to seek solutions to the problems raised by the projected collective redundancies.

3. Where the initial period provided for in paragraph 1 is shorter than 60 days, Member States may grant the competent public authority the power to extend the initial period to 60 days following notification where the problems raised by the projected collective redundancies are not likely to be solved within the initial period.

Member States may grant the competent public authority wider powers of extension.

The employer must be informed of the extension and the grounds for it before expiry of the initial period provided for in paragraph 1.

4. Member States need not apply this Article to collective redundancies arising from termination of the establishment's activities where this is the result of a judicial decision.

Section IV—Final Provisions

Article 5 [More favourable provisions]

This Directive shall not affect the right of Member States to apply or to introduce laws, regulations or administrative provisions which are more favourable to workers or to promote or to allow the application of collective agreements more favourable to workers. **9–150**

Article 6 [Enforcement]

Member States shall ensure that judicial and/or administrative procedures for the enforcement of obligations under this Directive are available to the workers' representatives and/or workers. **9–151**

Article 7 [Communication of national measures]

Member States shall forward to the Commission the text of any fundamental provisions of national law already adopted or being adopted in the area governed by this Directive. **9–152**

Article 8 [Repeals]

1. The Directives listed in Annex I, Part A, are hereby repealed without prejudice to the obligations of the Member States concerning the deadlines for transposition of the said Directive set out in Annex I, Part B. **9–153**

2. References to the repealed Directives shall be construed as references to this Directive and shall be read in accordance with the correlation table in Annex II.

Article 9 [Entry into force]

This Directive shall enter into force on the 20th day following its publication in the *Official Journal of the European Communities*.[93] **9–154**

Article 10 [Addressees]

This Directive is addressed to the Member States. **9–155**

Annex I

PART A—REPEALED DIRECTIVES (REFERRED TO BY ARTICLE 8)

Council Directive 75/129 and its following amendment: **9–156**
Council Directive 92/56.

[93] The Directive was published on 12 August 1998.

PART B—DEADLINES FOR TRANSPOSITION INTO NATIONAL LAW (REFERRED TO BY ARTICLE 8)

9–157

Directive	Deadline for transposition
75/129 ([1975] OJ L48/29)	19 February 1977
92/56 ([1992] OJ L245/3)	24 June 1994

Annex II—Correlation Table

[Table not reproduced.]

Council Directive 2001/23 of 12 March 2001, on the approximation of the laws of the Member States relating to the safeguarding of employees' rights in the event of transfers of undertakings, businesses or parts of undertakings or businesses

([2001] OJ L82/16; Doc. Ref. 32001L0023)

9–158 *The Council of the European Union,*

Having regard to the Treaty establishing the European Community, and in particular Article 94 thereof,

Having regard to the proposal from the Commission,

Having regard to the opinion of the European Parliament,[94]

Having regard to the opinion of the Economic and Social Committee,[95]

Whereas:

(1) Council Directive 77/187 of 14 February 1977, on the approximation of the laws of the Member States relating to the safeguarding of employees' rights in the event of transfers of undertakings, businesses or parts of undertakings or businesses[96] has been substantially amended.[97] In the interests of clarity and rationality, it should therefore be codified.

(2) Economic trends are bringing in their wake, at both national and Community level, changes in the structure of undertakings, through transfers of undertakings, businesses or parts of undertakings or businesses to other employers as a result of legal transfers or mergers.

(3) It is necessary to provide for the protection of employees in the event of a change of employer, in particular, to ensure that their rights are safeguarded.

(4) Differences still remain in the Member States as regards the extent of the protection of employees in this respect and these differences should be reduced.

(5) The Community Charter of the Fundamental Social Rights of Workers adopted on 9 December 1989 ("Social Charter") states, in points 7, 17 and 18 in particular that: "The completion of the internal market must lead to an improvement in the living and working conditions of workers in the European Community. The improvement must cover, where necessary, the development of certain aspects of employment regulations such as procedures for collective redundancies and those regarding bankruptcies. Information, consultation and participation for workers must be developed along appropriate lines, taking account of the practice in force in the various Member States. Such information, consultation and participation must be implemented in due time, particularly in connection with restructuring operations in undertakings or in cases of mergers having an impact on the employment of workers".

(6) In 1977 the Council adopted Directive 77/187 to promote the harmonisation of the relevant national laws ensuring the safeguarding of the rights of employees

[94] Opinion delivered on 25 October 2000.

[95] [2000] OJ C367/21.

[96] [1977] OJ L61/26.

[97] See Annex I, Part A.

and requiring transferors and transferees to inform and consult employees' representatives in good time.

(7) That Directive was subsequently amended in the light of the impact of the internal market, the legislative tendencies of the Member States with regard to the rescue of undertakings in economic difficulties, the case law of the Court of Justice of the European Communities, Council Directive 75/129 of 17 February 1975, on the approximation of the laws of the Member States relating to collective redundancies[98] and the legislation already in force in most Member States.

(8) Considerations of legal security and transparency required that the legal concept of transfer be clarified in the light of the case law of the Court of Justice. Such clarification has not altered the scope of Directive 77/187 as interpreted by the Court of Justice.

(9) The Social Charter recognises the importance of the fight against all forms of discrimination, especially based on sex, colour, race, opinion and creed.

(10) This Directive should be without prejudice to the time-limits set out in Annex I Part B within which the Member States are to comply with Directive 77/187, and the act amending it,

Has adopted this Directive:

Chapter I—Scope and Definitions

Article 1 [Scope]

1. (a) This Directive shall apply to any transfer of an undertaking, business, or part of an undertaking or business to another employer as a result of a legal transfer or merger. **9–159**

(b) Subject to sub-paragraph (a) and the following provisions of this Article, there is a transfer within the meaning of this Directive where there is a transfer of an economic entity which retains its identity, meaning an organised grouping of resources which has the objective of pursuing an economic activity, whether or not that activity is central or ancillary.

(c) This Directive shall apply to public and private undertakings engaged in economic activities whether or not they are operating for gain. An administrative reorganisation of public administrative authorities, or the transfer of administrative functions between public administrative authorities, is not a transfer within the meaning of this Directive.

2. This Directive shall apply where and in so far as the undertaking, business or part of the undertaking or business to be transferred is situated within the territorial scope of the Treaty.

3. This Directive shall not apply to seagoing vessels.

Article 2 [Definitions]

1. For the purposes of this Directive: **9–160**

(a) "transferor" shall mean any natural or legal person who, by reason of a transfer within the meaning of Article 1(1), ceases to be the employer in respect of the undertaking, business or part of the undertaking or business;

(b) "transferee" shall mean any natural or legal person who, by reason of a transfer within the meaning of Article 1(1), becomes the employer in respect of the undertaking, business or part of the undertaking or business;

(c) "representatives of employees" and related expressions shall mean the representatives of the employees provided for by the laws or practices of the Member States;

[98] [1975] OJ L48/29. Directive replaced by Directive 98/59 ([1998] OJ L225/16) (see above).

(d) "employee" shall mean any person who, in the Member State concerned, is protected as an employee under national employment law.

2. This Directive shall be without prejudice to national law as regards the definition of contract of employment or employment relationship.

However, Member States shall not exclude from the scope of this Directive contracts of employment or employment relationships solely because:

(a) of the number of working hours performed or to be performed,

(b) they are employment relationships governed by a fixed-duration contract of employment within the meaning of Article 1(1) of Council Directive 91/383 of 25 June 1991 supplementing the measures to encourage improvements in the safety and health at work of workers with a fixed-duration employment relationship or a temporary employment relationship,[99] or

(c) they are temporary employment relationships within the meaning of Article 1(2) of Directive 91/383, and the undertaking, business or part of the undertaking or business transferred is, or is part of, the temporary employment business which is the employer.

Chapter II—Safeguarding of Employees' Rights

Article 3 **[Transfer of rights and obligations]**

9–161 1. The transferor's rights and obligations arising from a contract of employment or from an employment relationship existing on the date of a transfer shall, by reason of such transfer, be transferred to the transferee.

Member States may provide that, after the date of transfer, the transferor and the transferee shall be jointly and severally liable in respect of obligations which arose before the date of transfer from a contract of employment or an employment relationship existing on the date of the transfer.

2. Member States may adopt appropriate measures to ensure that the transferor notifies the transferee of all the rights and obligations which will be transferred to the transferee under this Article, so far as those rights and obligations are or ought to have been known to the transferor at the time of the transfer. A failure by the transferor to notify the transferee of any such right or obligation shall not affect the transfer of that right or obligation and the rights of any employees against the transferee and/or transferor in respect of that right or obligation.

3. Following the transfer, the transferee shall continue to observe the terms and conditions agreed in any collective agreement on the same terms applicable to the transferor under that agreement, until the date of termination or expiry of the collective agreement or the entry into force or application of another collective agreement.

Member States may limit the period for observing such terms and conditions with the proviso that it shall not be less than one year.

4. (a) Unless Member States provide otherwise, paragraphs 1 and 3 shall not apply in relation to employees' rights to old-age, invalidity or survivors' benefits under supplementary company or intercompany pension schemes outside the statutory social security schemes in Member States.

(b) Even where they do not provide in accordance with sub-paragraph (a) that paragraphs 1 and 3 apply in relation to such rights, Member States shall adopt the measures necessary to protect the interests of employees and of persons no longer employed in the transferor's business at the time of the transfer in respect of rights conferring on them immediate or prospective

[99] [1991] OJ L206/19.

entitlement to old age benefits, including survivors' benefits, under supplementary schemes referred to in sub-paragraph (a).

Article 4 [Dismissals]

1. The transfer of the undertaking, business or part of the undertaking or business shall not in itself constitute grounds for dismissal by the transferor or the transferee. This provision shall not stand in the way of dismissals that may take place for economic, technical or organisational reasons entailing changes in the workforce. **9–162**

Member States may provide that the first sub-paragraph shall not apply to certain specific categories of employees who are not covered by the laws or practice of the Member States in respect of protection against dismissal.

2. If the contract of employment or the employment relationship is terminated because the transfer involves a substantial change in working conditions to the detriment of the employee, the employer shall be regarded as having been responsible for termination of the contract of employment or of the employment relationship.

Article 5 [Insolvency]

1. Unless Member States provide otherwise, Articles 3 and 4 shall not apply to any transfer of an undertaking, business or part of an undertaking or business where the transferor is the subject of bankruptcy proceedings or any analogous insolvency proceedings which have been instituted with a view to the liquidation of the assets of the transferor and are under the supervision of a competent public authority (which may be an insolvency practitioner authorised by a competent public authority). **9–163**

2. Where Articles 3 and 4 apply to a transfer during insolvency proceedings which have been opened in relation to a transferor (whether or not those proceedings have been instituted with a view to the liquidation of the assets of the transferor) and provided that such proceedings are under the supervision of a competent public authority (which may be an insolvency practitioner determined by national law) a Member State may provide that:

(a) notwithstanding Article 3(1), the transferor's debts arising from any contracts of employment or employment relationships and payable before the transfer or before the opening of the insolvency proceedings shall not be transferred to the transferee, provided that such proceedings give rise, under the law of that Member State, to protection at least equivalent to that provided for in situations covered by Council Directive 80/987 of 20 October 1980, on the approximation of the laws of the Member States relating to the protection of employees in the event of the insolvency of their employer,[1] and, or alternatively, that,

(b) the transferee, transferor or person or persons exercising the transferor's functions, on the one hand, and the representatives of the employees on the other hand may agree alterations, in so far as current law or practice permits, to the employees' terms and conditions of employment designed to safeguard employment opportunities by ensuring the survival of the undertaking, business or part of the undertaking or business.

3. A Member State may apply paragraph 20(b) to any transfers where the transferor is in a situation of serious economic crisis, as defined by national law, provided that the situation is declared by a competent public authority and open to judicial supervision, on condition that such provisions already existed in national law on 17 July 1998.

[1] [1980] OJ L283/23 (see above). Directive as last amended by the 1994 Act of Accession.

The Commission shall present a report on the effects of this provision before 17 July 2003, and shall submit any appropriate proposals to the Council.

4. Member States shall take appropriate measures with a view to preventing misuse of insolvency proceedings in such a way as to deprive employees of the rights provided for in this Directive.

Article 6 [Employees' representatives]

9–164 1. If the undertaking, business or part of an undertaking or business preserves its autonomy, the status and function of the representatives or of the representation of the employees affected by the transfer shall be preserved on the same terms and subject to the same conditions as existed before the date of the transfer by virtue of law, regulation, administrative provision or agreement, provided that the conditions necessary for the constitution of the employee's representation are fulfilled.

The first sub-paragraph shall not supply if, under the laws, regulations, administrative provisions or practice in the Member States, or by agreement with the representatives of the employees, the conditions necessary for the reappointment of the representatives of the employees or for the reconstitution of the representation of the employees are fulfilled.

Where the transferor is the subject of bankruptcy proceedings or any analogous insolvency proceedings which have been instituted with a view to the liquidation of the assets of the transferor and are under the supervision of a competent public authority (which may be an insolvency practitioner authorised by a competent public authority), Member States may take the necessary measures to ensure that the transferred employees are properly represented until the new election or designation of representatives of the employees.

If the undertaking, business or part of an undertaking or business does not preserve its autonomy, the Member States shall take the necessary measures to ensure that the employees transferred who were represented before the transfer continue to be properly represented during the period necessary for the reconstitution or reappointment of the representation of employees in accordance with national law or practice.

2. If the term of office of the representatives of the employees affected by the transfer expires as a result of the transfer, the representatives shall continue to enjoy the protection provided by the laws, regulations, administrative provisions or practice of the Member States.

Chapter III—Information and Consultation

Article 7 [Information for employees' representatives]

9–165 1. The transferor and transferee shall be required to inform the representatives of their respective employees affected by the transfer of the following:

— the date or proposed date of the transfer,
— the reasons for the transfer,
— the legal, economic and social implications of the transfer for the employees,
— any measures envisaged in relation to the employees.

The transferor must give such information to the representatives of his employees in good time, before the transfer is carried out.

The transferee must give such information to the representatives of his employees in good time, and in any event before his employees are directly affected by the transfer as regards their conditions of work and employment.

2. Where the transferor or the transferee envisages measures in relation to his employees, he shall consult the representatives of this employees in good time on such measures with a view to reaching an agreement.

3. Member States whose laws, regulations or administrative provisions provide that representatives of the employees may have recourse to an arbitration board to obtain a decision on the measures to be taken in relation to employees may limit the obligations laid down in paragraphs 1 and 2 to cases where the transfer carried out gives rise to a change in the business likely to entail serious disadvantages for a considerable number of the employees.

The information and consultations shall cover at least the measures envisaged in relation to the employees.

The information must be provided and consultations take place in good time before the change in the business as referred to in the first sub-paragraph is effected.

4. The obligations laid down in this Article shall apply irrespective of whether the decision resulting in the transfer is taken by the employer or an undertaking controlling the employer.

In considering alleged breaches of the information and consultation requirements laid down by this Directive, the argument that such a breach occurred because the information was not provided by an undertaking controlling the employer shall not be accepted as an excuse.

5. Member States may limit the obligations laid down in paragraphs 1, 2 and 3 to undertakings or businesses which, in terms of the number of employees, meet the conditions for the election or nomination of a collegiate body representing the employees.

6. Member States shall provide that, where there are no representatives of the employees in an undertaking or business through no fault of their own, the employees concerned must be informed in advance of:
— the date or proposed date of the transfer,
— the reason for the transfer,
— the legal, economic and social implications of the transfer for the employees,
— any measures envisaged in relation to the employees.

Chapter IV—Final Provisions

Article 8 [More favourable provisions]

This Directive shall not affect the right of Member States to apply or introduce laws, regulations or administrative provisions which are more favourable to employees or to promote or permit collective agreements or agreements between social partners more favourable to employees. **9–166**

Article 9 [Defence of rights]

Member States shall introduce into their national legal systems such measures as are necessary to enable all employees and representatives of employees who consider themselves wronged by failure to comply with the obligations arising from this Directive to pursue their claims by judicial process after possible recourse to other competent authorities. **9–167**

Article 10 [Report]

The Commission shall submit to the Council an analysis of the effect of the provisions of this Directive before 17 July 2006. It shall propose any amendment which may seem necessary. **9–168**

Article 11 [Communication of national measures]

Member States shall communicate to the Commission the texts of the laws, regulations and administrative provisions which they adopt in the field covered by this Directive. **9–169**

Article 12 [Repeal]

9–170 Directive 77/187, as amended by the Directive referred to in Annex I, Part A, is repealed, without prejudice to the obligations of the Member States concerning the time limits for implementation set out in Annex I, Part B.

References to the repealed Directive shall be construed as references to this Directive and shall be read in accordance with the correlation table in Annex II.

Article 13 [Entry into force]

9–171 This Directive shall enter into force on the 20th day following its publication in the *Official Journal of the European Communities*.[2]

Article 14 [Addressees]

9–172 This Directive is addressed to the Member States.

Annex I

PART A—REPEALED DIRECTIVE AND ITS AMENDING DIRECTIVE (REFERRED TO IN ARTICLE 12)

9–173 Council Directive 77/187 (OJ 1977 L61/26)
Council Directive 98/50 (OJ 1998 L201/88)

PART B—DEADLINES FOR TRANSPOSITION INTO NATIONAL LAW (REFERRED TO IN ARTICLE 12)

9–174

Directive	Deadline for transposition
77/187	16 February 1979
98/50	17 July 2001

Annex II—Correlation Table

9–175 [Table not reproduced.]

Directive 2002/14 of the European Parliament and of the Council of 11 March 2002, establishing a general framework for informing and consulting employees in the European Community

([2002] OJ L80/29; Doc. Ref. 32002l0014)

9–176 *The European Parliament and the Council of the European Union,*
Having regard to the Treaty establishing the European Community, and in particular Article 137(2) thereof,

Having regard to the proposal from the Commission,[3]

Having regard to the opinion of the Economic and Social Committee,[4]

Having regard to the opinion of the Committee of the Regions,[5]

Acting in accordance with the procedure referred to in Article 251(4), and in the light of the joint text approved by the Conciliation Committee on 23 January 2002,[6]

[2] The Directive was published on 22 March 2001.

[3] [1999] OJ C2/3.

[4] [1999] OJ C258/24.

[5] [2001] OJ C144/58.

[6] Opinion of the European Parliament of 14 April 1999 ([1999] OJ C219/223), confirmed on 16 September 1999 ([2000] OJ C54/55), Council Common Position of 27 July 2001 ([2001] OJ C307/16) and Decision of the European Parliament of 23 October 2001. Decision of the European Parliament of 5 February 2002 and Decision of the Council of 18 February 2002.

Whereas:

(1) Pursuant to Article 136 of the Treaty, a particular objective of the Community and the Member States is to promote social dialogue between management and labour.

(2) Point 17 of the Community Charter of Fundamental Social Rights of Workers provides, *inter alia*, that information, consultation and participation for workers must be developed along appropriate lines, taking account of the practices in force in different Member States.

(3) The Commission consulted management and labour at Community level on the possible direction of Community action on the information and consultation of employees in undertakings within the Community.

(4) Following this consultation, the Commission considered that Community action was advisable and again consulted management and labour on the contents of the planned proposal; management and labour have presented their opinions to the Commission.

(5) Having completed this second stage of consultation, management and labour have not informed the Commission of their wish to initiate the process potentially leading to the conclusion of an agreement.

(6) The existence of legal frameworks at national and Community level intended to ensure that employees are involved in the affairs of the undertaking employing them and in decisions which affect them has not always prevented serious decisions affecting employees from being taken and made public without adequate procedures having been implemented beforehand to inform and consult them.

(7) There is a need to strengthen dialogue and promote mutual trust within undertakings in order to improve risk anticipation, make work organisation more flexible and facilitate employee access to training within the undertaking while maintaining security, make employees aware of adaptation needs, increase employees' availability to undertake measures and activities to increase their employability, promote employee involvement in the operation and future of the undertaking and increase its competitiveness.

(8) There is a need, in particular, to promote and enhance information and consultation on the situation and likely development of employment within the undertaking and, where the employer's evaluation suggests that employment within the undertaking may be under threat, the possible anticipatory measures envisaged, in particular in terms of employee training and skill development, with a view to offsetting the negative developments or their consequences and increasing the employability and adaptability of the employees likely to be affected.

(9) Timely information and consultation is a prerequisite for the success of the restructuring and adaptation of undertakings to the new conditions created by globalisation of the economy, particularly through the development of new forms of organisation of work.

(10) The Community has drawn up and implemented an employment strategy based on the concepts of "anticipation", "prevention" and "employability", which are to be incorporated as key elements into all public policies likely to benefit employment, including the policies of individual undertakings, by strengthening the social dialogue with a view to promoting change compatible with preserving the priority objective of employment.

(11) Further development of the internal market must be properly balanced, maintaining the essential values on which our societies are based and ensuring that all citizens benefit from economic development.

(12) Entry into the third stage of economic and monetary union has extended and accelerated the competitive pressures at European level. This means that more supportive measures are needed at national level.

(13) The existing legal frameworks for employee information and consultation at Community and national level tend to adopt an excessively *a posteriori*

approach to the process of change, neglect the economic aspects of decisions taken and do not contribute either to genuine anticipation of employment developments within the undertaking or to risk prevention.

(14) All of these political, economic, social and legal developments call for changes to the existing legal framework providing for the legal and practical instruments enabling the right to be informed and consulted to be exercised.

(15) This Directive is without prejudice to national systems regarding the exercise of this right in practice where those entitled to exercise it are required to indicate their wishes collectively.

(16) This Directive is without prejudice to those systems which provide for the direct involvement of employees, as long as they are always free to exercise the right to be informed and consulted through their representatives.

(17) Since the objectives of the proposed action, as outlined above, cannot be adequately achieved by the Member States, in that the object is to establish a framework for employee information and consultation appropriate for the new European context described above, and can therefore, in view of the scale and impact of the proposed action, be better achieved at Community level, the Community may adopt measures in accordance with the principle of subsidiarity as set out in Article 5 of the Treaty. In accordance with the principle of proportionality, as set out in that Article, this Directive does not go beyond what is necessary in order to achieve these objectives.

(18) The purpose of this general framework is to establish minimum requirements applicable throughout the Community while not preventing Member States from laying down provisions more favourable to employees.

(19) The purpose of this general framework is also to avoid any administrative, financial or legal constraints which would hinder the creation and development of small and medium-sized undertakings. To this end, the scope of this Directive should be restricted, according to the choice made by Member States, to undertakings with at least 50 employees or establishments employing at least 20 employees.

(20) This takes into account and is without prejudice to other national measures and practices aimed at fostering social dialogue within companies not covered by this Directive and within public administrations.

(21) However, on a transitional basis, Member States in which there is no established statutory system of information and consultation of employees or employee representation should have the possibility of further restricting the scope of the Directive as regards the numbers of employees.

(22) A Community framework for informing and consulting employees should keep to a minimum the burden on undertakings or establishments while ensuring the effective exercise of the rights granted.

(23) The objective of this Directive is to be achieved through the establishment of a general framework comprising the principles, definitions and arrangements for information and consultation, which it will be for the Member States to comply with and adapt to their own national situation, ensuring, where appropriate, that management and labour have a leading role by allowing them to define freely, by agreement, the arrangements for informing and consulting employees which they consider to be best suited to their needs and wishes.

(24) Care should be taken to avoid affecting some specific rules in the field of employee information and consultation existing in some national laws, addressed to undertakings or establishments which pursue political, professional, organisational, religious, charitable, educational, scientific or artistic aims, as well as aims involving information and the expression of opinions.

(25) Undertakings and establishments should be protected against disclosure of certain particularly sensitive information.

(26) The employer should be allowed not to inform and consult where this would seriously damage the undertaking or the establishment or where he has to

comply immediately with an order issued to him by a regulatory or supervisory body.

(27) Information and consultation imply both rights and obligations for management and labour at undertaking or establishment level.

(28) Administrative or judicial procedures, as well as sanctions that are effective, dissuasive and proportionate in relation to the seriousness of the offence, should be applicable in cases of infringement of the obligations based on this Directive.

(29) This Directive should not affect the provisions, where these are more specific, of Council Directive 98/59 of 20 July 1998 on the approximation of the laws of the Member States relating to collective redundancies[7] and of Council Directive 2001/23 of 12 March 2001 on the approximation of the laws of the Member States relating to the safeguarding of employees' rights in the event of transfers of undertakings, businesses or parts of undertakings or businesses.[8]

(30) Other rights of information and consultation, including those arising from Council Directive 94/45 of 22 September 1994 on the establishment of a European Works Council or a procedure in Community-scale undertakings and Community-scale groups of undertakings for the purposes of informing and consulting employees,[9] should not be affected by this Directive.

(31) Implementation of this Directive should not be sufficient grounds for a reduction in the general level of protection of workers in the areas to which it applies,

Have adopted this Directive:

Article 1 Object and principles

1. The purpose of this Directive is to establish a general framework setting out minimum requirements for the right to information and consultation of employees in undertakings or establishments within the Community. **9–177**

2. The practical arrangements for information and consultation shall be defined and implemented in accordance with national law and industrial relations practices in individual Member States in such a way as to ensure their effectiveness.

3. When defining or implementing practical arrangements for information and consultation, the employer and the employees' representatives shall work in a spirit of cooperation and with due regard for their reciprocal rights and obligations, taking into account the interests both of the undertaking or establishment and of the employees.

Article 2 Definitions

For the purposes of this Directive: **9–178**

(a) "undertaking" means a public or private undertaking carrying out an economic activity, whether or not operating for gain, which is located within the territory of the Member States;

(b) "establishment" means a unit of business defined in accordance with national law and practice, and located within the territory of a Member State, where an economic activity is carried out on an ongoing basis with human and material resources;

---

[7] [1998] OJ L225/16 (see above).

[8] [2001] OJ L82/16 (see above).

[9] [1994] OJ L254/64 (see above). Directive as amended by Directive 97/74 ([1998] OJ L10/22).

(c) "employer" means the natural or legal person party to employment contracts or employment relationships with employees, in accordance with national law and practice;
(d) "employee" means any person who, in the Member State concerned, is protected as an employee under national employment law and in accordance with national practice;
(e) "employees' representatives" means the employees' representatives provided for by national laws and/or practices;
(f) "information" means transmission by the employer to the employees' representatives of data in order to enable them to acquaint themselves with the subject matter and to examine it;
(g) "consultation" means the exchange of views and establishment of dialogue between the employees' representatives and the employer.

Article 3 Scope

9–179 1. This Directive shall apply, according to the choice made by Member States, to:
(a) undertakings employing at least 50 employees in any one Member State, or
(b) establishments employing at least 20 employees in any one Member State.
Member States shall determine the method for calculating the thresholds of employees employed.

2. In conformity with the principles and objectives of this Directive, Member States may lay down particular provisions applicable to undertakings or establishments which pursue directly and essentially political, professional organisational, religious, charitable, educational, scientific or artistic aims, as well as aims involving information and the expression of opinions, on condition that, at the date of entry into force of this Directive, provisions of that nature already exist in national legislation.

3. Member States may derogate from this Directive through particular provisions applicable to the crews of vessels plying the high seas.

Article 4 Practical arrangements for information and consultation

9–180 1. In accordance with the principles set out in Article 1 and without prejudice to any provisions and/or practices in force more favourable to employees, the Member States shall determine the practical arrangements for exercising the right to information and consultation at the appropriate level in accordance with this Article.

2. Information and consultation shall cover:
(a) information on the recent and probable development of the undertaking's or the establishment's activities and economic situation;
(b) information and consultation on the situation, structure and probable development of employment within the undertaking or establishment and on any anticipatory measures envisaged, in particular where there is a threat to employment;
(c) information and consultation on decisions likely to lead to substantial changes in work organisation or in contractual relations, including those covered by the Community provisions referred to in Article 9(1).

3. Information shall be given at such time, in such fashion and with such content as are appropriate to enable, in particular, employees' representatives to conduct an adequate study and, where necessary, prepare for consultation.

4. Consultation shall take place:
(a) while ensuring that the timing, method and content thereof are appropriate;
(b) at the relevant level of management and representation, depending on the subject under discussion;

(c) on the basis of information supplied by the employer in accordance with Article 2(f) and of the opinion which the employees' representatives are entitled to formulate;
(d) in such a way as to enable employees' representatives to meet the employer and obtain a response, and the reasons for that response, to any opinion they might formulate;
(e) with a view to reaching an agreement on decisions within the scope of the employer's powers referred to in paragraph 2(c).

Article 5 Information and consultation deriving from an agreement

Member States may entrust management and labour at the appropriate level, including at undertaking or establishment level, with defining freely and at any time through negotiated agreement the practical arrangements for informing and consulting employees. These agreements, and agreements existing on the date laid down in Article 11, as well as any subsequent renewals of such agreements, may establish, while respecting the principles set out in Article 1 and subject to conditions and limitations laid down by the Member States, provisions which are different from those referred to in Article 4. **9–181**

Article 6 Confidential information

1. Member States shall provide that, within the conditions and limits laid down by national legislation, the employees' representatives, and any experts who assist them, are not authorised to reveal to employees or to third parties, any information which, in the legitimate interest of the undertaking or establishment, has expressly been provided to them in confidence. This obligation shall continue to apply, wherever the said representatives or experts are, even after expiry of their terms of office. However, a Member State may authorise the employees' representatives and anyone assisting them to pass on confidential information to employees and to third parties bound by an obligation of confidentiality. **9–182**

2. Member States shall provide, in specific cases and within the conditions and limits laid down by national legislation, that the employer is not obliged to communicate information or undertake consultation when the nature of that information or consultation is such that, according to objective criteria, it would seriously harm the functioning of the undertaking or establishment or would be prejudicial to it.

3. Without prejudice to existing national procedures, Member States shall provide for administrative or judicial review procedures for the case where the employer requires confidentiality or does not provide the information in accordance with paragraphs 1 and 2. They may also provide for procedures intended to safeguard the confidentiality of the information in question.

Article 7 Protection of employees' representatives

Member States shall ensure that employees' representatives, when carrying out their functions, enjoy adequate protection and guarantees to enable them to perform properly the duties which have been assigned to them. **9–183**

Article 8 Protection of rights

1. Member States shall provide for appropriate measures in the event of non-compliance with this Directive by the employer or the employees' representatives. In particular, they shall ensure that adequate administrative or judicial procedures are available to enable the obligations deriving from this Directive to be enforced. **9–184**

2. Member States shall provide for adequate sanctions to be applicable in the

event of infringement of this Directive by the employer or the employees' representatives.

These sanctions must be effective, proportionate and dissuasive.

Article 9 Link between this Directive and other Community and national provisions

9–185 1. This Directive shall be without prejudice to the specific information and consultation procedures set out in Article 2 of Directive 98/59 and Article 7 of Directive 2001/23.

2. This Directive shall be without prejudice to provisions adopted in accordance with Directives 94/45 and 97/74.

3. This Directive shall be without prejudice to other rights to information, consultation and participation under national law.

4. Implementation of this Directive shall not be sufficient grounds for any regression in relation to the situation which already prevails in each Member State and in relation to the general level of protection of workers in the areas to which it applies.

Article 10 Transitional provisions

9–186 Notwithstanding Article 3, a Member State in which there is, at the date of entry into force of this Directive, no general, permanent and statutory system of information and consultation of employees, nor a general, permanent and statutory system of employee representation at the workplace allowing employees to be represented for that purpose, may limit the application of the national provisions implementing this Directive to:

(a) undertakings employing at least 150 employees or establishments employing at least 100 employees until 23 March 2007, and

(b) undertakings employing at least 100 employees or establishments employing at least 50 employees during the year following the date in point (a).

Article 11 Transposition

9–187 1. Member States shall adopt the laws, regulations and administrative provisions necessary to comply with this Directive not later than March 23, 2005, or shall ensure that management and labour introduce by that date the required provisions by way of agreement, the Member States being obliged to take all necessary steps enabling them to guarantee the results imposed by this Directive at all times. They shall forthwith inform the Commission thereof.

2. Where Member States adopt these measures, they shall contain a reference to this Directive or shall be accompanied by such reference on the occasion of their official publication. The methods of making such reference shall be laid down by the Member States.

Article 12 Review by the Commission

9–188 Not later than 23 March 2007, the Commission shall, in consultation with the Member States and the social partners at Community level, review the application of this Directive with a view to proposing any necessary amendments.

Article 13 Entry into force

9–189 This Directive shall enter into force on the day of its publication in the *Official Journal of the European Communities*.[10]

[10] The Directive was published on 23 March 2002.

Article 14 Addresses

This Directive is addressed to the Member States. **9–190**

Council Recommendation 2003/134 of 18 February 2003 concerning the improvement of the protection of the health and safety at work of self-employed workers

([2003] OJ L53/45; Doc. Ref. 32003H0134)

The Council of the European Union, **9–191**

Having regard to the Treaty establishing the European Community, and in particular Article 308 thereof,

Having regard to the proposal for a recommendation from the Commission,

Having regard to the opinion of the European Parliament,[11]

Having regard to the opinion of the European Economic and Social Committee,[12]

Whereas:

(1) The Communication from the Commission on a Community programme concerning safety, hygiene and health at work (1996 to 2000)[13] provided for examining the need for a proposal for a Council recommendation concerning the health and safety of self-employed workers, given the ever-increasing number of such workers.

(2) The European Parliament in its Resolution[14] on the General framework for action by the Commission in the field of safety, hygiene and health protection at work (1994 to 2000) proposes that it include measures to extend the framework Directive to self-employed workers. The European Parliament in its Resolution[15] on the mid-term report on the implementation of this programme again draws attention to the category of self-employed workers, who are largely outside the scope of the legislation, and stresses that the growth in subcontracting has led to an increase in the number of accidents at work.

(3) The Commission Communication of 11 March 2002 – "Adapting to change in work and society: a new Community strategy on health and safety at work 2002 to 2006" – and Council Resolution of 3 June 2002 on a new Community strategy on health and safety at work (2002 to 2006), which aim at instilling a culture of prevention and influencing behaviour, should, wherever possible, be taken into account by both employed and self-employed workers.

(4) The social partners attach particular importance to the protection of the health and safety of both self-employed workers and of other persons working at the same workplace, and almost all are in favour of a Community action in the form of a Council recommendation focusing on high-risk sectors and notably on information and awareness-raising measures on risk prevention, appropriate training and medical surveillance.

(5) As a general rule, workers who exercise their occupational activity in a manner which does not involve an employment relationship with an employer or, more generally, does not make them subordinate to a third person are not covered by the Community Directives on health and safety at work, in particular framework Council Directive 89/391 of 12 June 1989 on the introduction of measures to encourage improvements in the safety and health of workers at work.[16] Moreover, these workers are not covered in certain Member States by the legislation applicable in the field of health and safety at work.

---

[11] Opinion of 23 October 2002.

[12] [2002] OJ C241/139.

[13] [1995] OJ C262/18.

[14] [1994] OJ C205/478.

[15] Resolution of the EP of 25 February 1999 (A4–0050/1999).

[16] [1989] OJ L183/1 (see above).

(6) Self-employed workers, irrespective of whether they work alone or with employees, may be subject to health and safety risks similar to those experienced by employees.

(7) Through their activities self-employed workers may jeopardise the safety and health of other persons working at the same workplace.

(8) There are also certain "high-risk" sectors in the Community in which the number of self-employed workers is very high (agriculture, fishing, construction, transport).

(9) The recent recommendation by the ILO accompanying the Convention concerning health and safety in agriculture[17] stipulates that Member States must progressively extend to self-employed farmers the protection applicable to workers, taking account of the views of representative organisations of self-employed farmers if necessary.

(10) Work accidents and occupational diseases to which self-employed workers are particularly exposed result in high costs in both social and human terms.

(11) For these reasons, it is appropriate to take account of the category of self-employed workers and in this recommendation to focus on preventing the risks of occupational accidents and diseases to which self-employed workers are exposed.

(12) The need to take account of the specific situation of the self-employed has already been recognised in relation to work carried out at temporary or mobile construction sites, as Directive 92/57[18] provides for the extension to the self-employed of certain relevant provisions on the use of work equipment and protective equipment.

(13) Improving the standards of safety and health of self-employed workers can improve the conditions of competition and competitiveness on a European level.

(14) It is also necessary to improve access of self-employed workers to training and information with a view both to improving their own health and safety and that of the persons working at the same workplace.

(15) Member States should choose the means they deem to be most appropriate to meet the objectives.

(16) This recommendation does not affect existing or future national provisions providing for a higher degree of protection.

(17) In the current situation, the Member States are in the best position to take appropriate measures, whereby the Community should also contribute towards achieving the objectives of this recommendation.

(18) The proposal was drawn up following consultation with the social partners, in accordance with Article 138(2) and (3) of the EC Treaty, and with the Advisory Committee on Safety, Hygiene and Health Protection at Work,

Hereby recommends that Member States:

1. promote, in the context of their policies on preventing occupational accidents and diseases, the safety and health of self-employed workers, while taking account of the special risks existing in specific sectors and the specific nature of the relationship between contracting undertakings and self-employed workers;
2. when promoting health and safety for self-employed workers, choose the measures they deem to be most appropriate, such as one or more of the following: legislation, incentives, information campaigns and encouragement of relevant stakeholders;

---

[17] ILO, Convention 184/2001 of 21 June 2001.

[18] Council Directive 92/57 of 24 June 1992 on the implementation of minimum safety and health requirements at temporary or mobile construction sites (eighth individual Directive within the meaning of Article 16 (1) of Directive 89/391) [1992] OJ L245/6.

3. take the necessary measures, including awareness-raising campaigns, so that self-employed workers can obtain from the competent services and/or bodies, as well as from their own representative organisations, useful information and advice on the prevention of occupational accidents and diseases;
4. take the measures necessary so that self-employed workers can have access to sufficient training to acquire appropriate safety and health skills;
5. facilitate easy access to this information and training without involving excessive expense for self-employed workers;
6. in accordance with national law and/or practice, allow self-employed workers who so wish to have access to health surveillance appropriate to the risks to which they are exposed;
7. in the context of their policies on preventing occupational accidents and diseases, take account of available information on experience in other Member States;
8. examine, at the end of a four-year period starting with the adoption of this recommendation, the effectiveness of existing national measures or measures taken subsequent to the adoption of this recommendation and inform the Commission of their findings.

CHAPTER 10

FUNDAMENTAL RIGHTS

Charter of fundamental rights of the European Union of 7 December 2000

([2000] OJ C364/1; Doc. Ref. 32000Y1218(01))

The European Parliament, the Council and the Commission solemnly proclaim the text below as the Charter of fundamental rights of the European Union. **10–001**

PREAMBLE

The peoples of Europe, in creating an ever closer union among them, are resolved to share a peaceful future based on common values.

Conscious of its spiritual and moral heritage, the Union is founded on the indivisible, universal values of human dignity, freedom, equality and solidarity; it is based on the principles of democracy and the rule of law. It places the individual at the heart of its activities, by establishing the citizenship of the Union and by creating an area of freedom, security and justice.

The Union contributes to the preservation and to the development of these common values while respecting the diversity of the cultures and traditions of the peoples of Europe as well as the national identities of the Member States and the organisation of their public authorities at national, regional and local levels; it seeks to promote balanced and sustainable development and ensures free movement of persons, goods, services and capital, and the freedom of establishment.

To this end, it is necessary to strengthen the protection of fundamental rights in the light of changes in society, social progress and scientific and technological developments by making those rights more visible in a Charter.

This Charter reaffirms, with due regard for the powers and tasks of the Community and the Union and the principle of subsidiarity, the rights as they result, in particular, from the constitutional traditions and international obligations common to the Member States, the Treaty on European Union, the Community Treaties, the European Convention for the Protection of Human Rights and Fundamental Freedoms, the Social Charters adopted by the Community and by the Council of Europe and the case-law of the Court of Justice of the European Communities and of the European Court of Human Rights.

Enjoyment of these rights entails responsibilities and duties with regard to other persons, to the human community and to future generations.

The Union therefore recognises the rights, freedoms and principles set out hereafter.

CHAPTER I—DIGNITY

Article 1 Human dignity

Human dignity is inviolable. It must be respected and protected. **10–002**

Article 2 Right to life

1. Everyone has the right to life. **10–003**

2. No-one shall be condemned to the death penalty, or executed.

Article 3 **Right to the integrity of the person**

10–004 1. Everyone has the right to respect for his or her physical and mental integrity.

2. In the fields of medicine and biology, the following must be respected in particular:
— the free and informed consent of the person concerned, according to the procedures laid down by law,
— the prohibition of eugenic practices, in particular those aiming at the selection of persons,
— the prohibition on making the human body and its parts as such a source of financial gain,
— the prohibition of the reproductive cloning of human beings.

Article 4 **Prohibition of torture and inhuman or degrading treatment or punishment**

10–005 No one shall be subjected to torture or to inhuman or degrading treatment or punishment.

Article 5 **Prohibition of slavery and forced labour**

10–006 1. No one shall be held in slavery or servitude.

2. No one shall be required to perform forced or compulsory labour.

3. Trafficking in human beings is prohibited.

CHAPTER II—FREEDOMS

Article 6 **Right to liberty and security**

Everyone has the right to liberty and security of person.

Article 7 **Respect for private and family life**

10–007 Everyone has the right to respect for his or her private and family life, home and communications.

Article 8 **Protection of personal data**

10–008 1. Everyone has the right to the protection of personal data concerning him or her.

2. Such data must be processed fairly for specified purposes and on the basis of the consent of the person concerned or some other legitimate basis laid down by law. Everyone has the right of access to data which has been collected concerning him or her, and the right to have it rectified.

3. Compliance with these rules shall be subject to control by an independent authority.

Article 9 **Right to marry and right to found a family**

10–009 The right to marry and the right to found a family shall be guaranteed in accordance with the national laws governing the exercise of these rights.

Article 10 **Freedom of thought, conscience and religion**

10–010 1. Everyone has the right to freedom of thought, conscience and religion. This right includes freedom to change religion or belief and freedom, either alone or in community with others and in public or in private, to manifest religion or belief, in worship, teaching, practice and observance.

2. The right to conscientious objection is recognised, in accordance with the national laws governing the exercise of this right.

Article 11 Freedom of expression and information

1. Everyone has the right to freedom of expression. This right shall include freedom to hold opinions and to receive and impart information and ideas without interference by public authority and regardless of frontiers. **10–012**

2. The freedom and pluralism of the media shall be respected.

Article 12 Freedom of assembly and of association

1. Everyone has the right to freedom of peaceful assembly and to freedom of association at all levels, in particular in political, trade union and civic matters, which implies the right of everyone to form and to join trade unions for the protection of his or her interests. **10–013**

2. Political parties at Union level contribute to expressing the political will of the citizens of the Union.

Article 13 Freedom of the arts and sciences

The arts and scientific research shall be free of constraint. Academic freedom shall be respected. **10–014**

Article 14 Right to education

1. Everyone has the right to education and to have access to vocational and continuing training. **10–015**

2. This right includes the possibility to receive free compulsory education.

3. The freedom to found educational establishments with due respect for democratic principles and the right of parents to ensure the education and teaching of their children in conformity with their religious, philosophical and pedagogical convictions shall be respected, in accordance with the national laws governing the exercise of such freedom and right.

Article 15 Freedom to choose an occupation and right to engage in work

1. Everyone has the right to engage in work and to pursue a freely chosen or accepted occupation. **10–016**

2. Every citizen of the Union has the freedom to seek employment, to work, to exercise the right of establishment and to provide services in any Member State.

3. Nationals of third countries who are authorised to work in the territories of the Member States are entitled to working conditions equivalent to those of citizens of the Union.

Article 16 Freedom to conduct a business

The freedom to conduct a business in accordance with Community law and national laws and practices is recognised. **10–017**

Article 17 Right to property

1. Everyone has the right to own, use, dispose of and bequeath his or her lawfully acquired possessions. No one may be deprived of his or her possessions, except in **10–018**

the public interest and in the cases and under the conditions provided for by law, subject to fair compensation being paid in good time for their loss. The use of property may be regulated by law in so far as is necessary for the general interest.

2. Intellectual property shall be protected.

Article 18 Right to asylum

10–019 The right to asylum shall be guaranteed with due respect for the rules of the Geneva Convention of 28 July 1951 and the Protocol of 31 January 1967 relating to the status of refugees and in accordance with the Treaty establishing the European Community.

Article 19 Protection in the event of removal, expulsion or extradition

10–020 1. Collective expulsions are prohibited.

2. No one may be removed, expelled or extradited to a State where there is a serious risk that he or she would be subjected to the death penalty, torture or other inhuman or degrading treatment or punishment.

CHAPTER III—EQUALITY

Article 20 Equality before the law

10–021 Everyone is equal before the law.

Article 21 Non-discrimination

10–022 1. Any discrimination based on any ground such as sex, race, colour, ethnic or social origin, genetic features, language, religion or belief, political or any other opinion, membership of a national minority, property, birth, disability, age or sexual orientation shall be prohibited.

2. Within the scope of application of the Treaty establishing the European Community and of the Treaty on European Union, and without prejudice to the special provisions of those Treaties, any discrimination on grounds of nationality shall be prohibited.

Article 22 Cultural, religious and linguistic diversity

10–023 The Union shall respect cultural, religious and linguistic diversity.

Article 23 Equality between men and women

10–024 Equality between men and women must be ensured in all areas, including employment, work and pay.

The principle of equality shall not prevent the maintenance or adoption of measures providing for specific advantages in favour of the under-represented sex.

Article 24 The rights of the child

10–025 1. Children shall have the right to such protection and care as is necessary for their well-being. They may express their views freely. Such views shall be taken into consideration on matters which concern them in accordance with their age and maturity.

2. In all actions relating to children, whether taken by public authorities or private institutions, the child's best interests must be a primary consideration.

3. Every child shall have the right to maintain on a regular basis a personal relationship and direct contact with both his or her parents, unless that is contrary to his or her interests.

Article 25 The rights of the elderly

The Union recognises and respects the rights of the elderly to lead a life of dignity and independence and to participate in social and cultural life. **10–026**

Article 26 Integration of persons with disabilities

The Union recognises and respects the right of persons with disabilities to benefit from measures designed to ensure their independence, social and occupational integration and participation in the life of the community. **10–027**

CHAPTER IV—SOLIDARITY

Article 27 Workers' right to information and consultation within the undertaking

Workers or their representatives must, at the appropriate levels, be guaranteed information and consultation in good time in the cases and under the conditions provided for by Community law and national laws and practices. **10–028**

Article 28 Right of collective bargaining and action

Workers and employers, or their respective organisations, have, in accordance with Community law and national laws and practices, the right to negotiate and conclude collective agreements at the appropriate levels and, in cases of conflicts of interest, to take collective action to defend their interests, including strike action. **10–029**

Article 29 Right of access to placement services

Everyone has the right of access to a free placement service. **10–030**

Article 30 Protection in the event of unjustified dismissal

Every worker has the right to protection against unjustified dismissal, in accordance with Community law and national laws and practices. **10–031**

Article 31 Fair and just working conditions

1. Every worker has the right to working conditions which respect his or her health, safety and dignity. **10–032**

2. Every worker has the right to limitation of maximum working hours, to daily and weekly rest periods and to an annual period of paid leave.

Article 32 Prohibition of child labour and protection of young people at work

The employment of children is prohibited. The minimum age of admission to employment may not be lower than the minimum school-leaving age, without prejudice to such rules as may be more favourable to young people and except for limited derogations. Young people admitted to work must have working conditions appropriate to their age and be protected against economic exploitation and any work likely to harm their safety, health or physical, mental, moral or social development or to interfere with their education. **10–033**

Article 33 Family and professional life

1. The family shall enjoy legal, economic and social protection. **10–034**

2. To reconcile family and professional life, everyone shall have the right to

protection from dismissal for a reason connected with maternity and the right to paid maternity leave and to parental leave following the birth or adoption of a child.

Article 34 Social security and social assistance

10–035 1. The Union recognises and respects the entitlement to social security benefits and social services providing protection in cases such as maternity, illness, industrial accidents, dependency or old age, and in the case of loss of employment, in accordance with the rules laid down by Community law and national laws and practices.

2. Everyone residing and moving legally within the European Union is entitled to social security benefits and social advantages in accordance with Community law and national laws and practices.

3. In order to combat social exclusion and poverty, the Union recognises and respects the right to social and housing assistance so as to ensure a decent existence for all those who lack sufficient resources, in accordance with the rules laid down by Community law and national laws and practices.

Article 35 Health care

10–036 Everyone has the right of access to preventive health care and the right to benefit from medical treatment under the conditions established by national laws and practices. A high level of human health protection shall be ensured in the definition and implementation of all Union policies and activities.

Article 36 Access to services of general economic interest

10–037 The Union recognises and respects access to services of general economic interest as provided for in national laws and practices, in accordance with the Treaty establishing the European Community, in order to promote the social and territorial cohesion of the Union.

Article 37 Environmental protection

10–038 A high level of environmental protection and the improvement of the quality of the environment must be integrated into the policies of the Union and ensured in accordance with the principle of sustainable development.

Article 38 Consumer protection

10–039 Union policies shall ensure a high level of consumer protection.

CHAPTER V—CITIZENS' RIGHTS

Article 39 Right to vote and to stand as a candidate at elections to the European Parliament

10–040 1. Every citizen of the Union has the right to vote and to stand as a candidate at elections to the European Parliament in the Member State in which he or she resides, under the same conditions as nationals of that State.

2. Members of the European Parliament shall be elected by direct universal suffrage in a free and secret ballot.

Article 40 Right to vote and to stand as a candidate at municipal elections

Every citizen of the Union has the right to vote and to stand as a candidate at municipal elections in the Member State in which he or she resides under the same conditions as nationals of that State. **10–041**

Article 41 Right to good administration

1. Every person has the right to have his or her affairs handled impartially, fairly and within a reasonable time by the institutions and bodies of the Union. **10–042**

2. This right includes:
— the right of every person to be heard, before any individual measure which would affect him or her adversely is taken;
— the right of every person to have access to his or her file, while respecting the legitimate interests of confidentiality and of professional and business secrecy;
— the obligation of the administration to give reasons for its decisions.

3. Every person has the right to have the Community make good any damage caused by its institutions or by its servants in the performance of their duties, in accordance with the general principles common to the laws of the Member States.

4. Every person may write to the institutions of the Union in one of the languages of the Treaties and must have an answer in the same language.

Article 42 Right of access to documents

Any citizen of the Union, and any natural or legal person residing or having its registered office in a Member State, has a right of access to European Parliament, Council and Commission documents. **10–043**

Article 43 Ombudsman

Any citizen of the Union and any natural or legal person residing or having its registered office in a Member State has the right to refer to the Ombudsman of the Union cases of maladministration in the activities of the Community institutions or bodies, with the exception of the Court of Justice and the Court of First Instance acting in their judicial role. **10–044**

Article 44 Right to petition

Any citizen of the Union and any natural or legal person residing or having its registered office in a Member State has the right to petition the European Parliament. **10–045**

Article 45 Freedom of movement and of residence

1. Every citizen of the Union has the right to move and reside freely within the territory of the Member States. **10–046**

2. Freedom of movement and residence may be granted, in accordance with the Treaty establishing the European Community, to nationals of third countries legally resident in the territory of a Member State.

Article 46 Diplomatic and consular protection

10–047 Every citizen of the Union shall, in the territory of a third country in which the Member State of which he or she is a national is not represented, be entitled to protection by the diplomatic or consular authorities of any Member State, on the same conditions as the nationals of that Member State.

CHAPTER VI—JUSTICE

Article 47 Right to an effective remedy and to a fair trial

10–048 Everyone whose rights and freedoms guaranteed by the law of the Union are violated has the right to an effective remedy before a tribunal in compliance with the conditions laid down in this Article.

Everyone is entitled to a fair and public hearing within a reasonable time by an independent and impartial tribunal previously established by law.

Everyone shall have the possibility of being advised, defended and represented.

Legal aid shall be made available to those who lack sufficient resources in so far as such aid is necessary to ensure effective access to justice.

Article 48 Presumption of innocence and right of defence

10–049 1. Everyone who has been charged shall be presumed innocent until proved guilty according to law.

2. Respect for the rights of the defence of anyone who has been charged shall be guaranteed.

Article 49 Principles of legality and proportionality of criminal offences and penalties

10–050 1. No one shall be held guilty of any criminal offence on account of any act or omission which did not constitute a criminal offence under national law or international law at the time when it was committed. Nor shall a heavier penalty be imposed than that which was applicable at the time the criminal offence was committed. If, subsequent to the commission of a criminal offence, the law provides for a lighter penalty, that penalty shall be applicable.

2. This Article shall not prejudice the trial and punishment of any person for any act or omission which, at the time when it was committed, was criminal according to the general principles recognised by the community of nations.

3. The severity of penalties must not be disproportionate to the criminal offence.

Article 50 Right not to be tried or punished twice in criminal proceedings for the same criminal offence

10–051 No one shall be liable to be tried or punished again in criminal proceedings for an offence for which he or she has already been finally acquitted or convicted within the Union in accordance with the law.

CHAPTER VII—GENERAL PROVISIONS

Article 51 Scope

10–052 1. The provisions of this Charter are addressed to the institutions and bodies of the Union with due regard for the principle of subsidiarity and to the Member States

only when they are implementing Union law. They shall therefore respect the rights, observe the principles and promote the application thereof in accordance with their respective powers.
2. This Charter does not establish any new power or task for the Community or the Union, or modify powers and tasks defined by the Treaties.

Article 52 Scope of guaranteed rights

1. Any limitation on the exercise of the rights and freedoms recognised by this Charter must be provided for by law and respect the essence of those rights and freedoms. Subject to the principle of proportionality, limitations may be made only if they are necessary and genuinely meet objectives of general interest recognised by the Union or the need to protect the rights and freedoms of others. **10–053**

2. Rights recognised by this Charter which are based on the Community Treaties or the Treaty on European Union shall be exercised under the conditions and within the limits defined by those Treaties.

3. In so far as this Charter contains rights which correspond to rights guaranteed by the Convention for the Protection of Human Rights and Fundamental Freedoms, the meaning and scope of those rights shall be the same as those laid down by the said Convention. This provision shall not prevent Union law providing more extensive protection.

Article 53 Level of protection

Nothing in this Charter shall be interpreted as restricting or adversely affecting human rights and fundamental freedoms as recognised, in their respective fields of application, by Union law and international law and by international agreements to which the Union, the Community or all the Member States are party, including the European Convention for the Protection of Human Rights and Fundamental Freedoms, and by the Member States' constitutions. **10–054**

Article 54 Prohibition of abuse of rights

Nothing in this Charter shall be interpreted as implying any right to engage in any activity or to perform any act aimed at the destruction of any of the rights and freedoms recognised in this Charter or at their limitation to a greater extent than is provided for herein. **10–055**

INDEX